Politics, Society, and the Klan in Alabama, 1915–1949

Politics, Society, and the Klan in Alabama, 1915–1949

Glenn Feldman

THE UNIVERSITY OF ALABAMA PRESS

Tuscaloosa and London

1   2   3   4   5   6   7   8   9   •   07   06   05   04   03   02   01   00   99

Publication of this volume has been supported in part by a
subvention from the Center for Labor Education and Research
and the School of Business, The University of Alabama at Birmingham.

The photograph on the front cover of the paperback edition is
courtesy of Birmingham Public Library Archives.

∞

The paper on which this book is printed meets the minimum requirements of American
National Standard for Information Science-Permanence of Paper for Printed Library
Materials, ANSI Z39.48-1984.

Library of Congress Cataloging-in-Publication Data

Feldman, Glenn.
    Politics, society, and the Klan in Alabama, 1915–1949 / Glenn
Feldman.
       p. cm.
    Includes bibliographical references (p.) and index.
    ISBN 0-8173-0983-7 (alk. paper)
    ISBN 0-8173-0984-5 (pbk. : alk. paper)
    1. Ku Klux Klan (1915–)—Alabama—History.   2. Alabama—Race
relations— History—20th century.   3. Alabama—Social
conditions—20th century.   4. Alabama—Politics and
government— 1865–1950.   I. Title.
    HS2330.K63 F44 1999
    322.4′2′09761′0904—dc21
                              99-6123

British Library Cataloguing-in-Publication Data available

For Hallie, "my sweetheart." With all my love . . .

Contents

Illustrations

Acknowledgments

So many individuals have helped with this project in so many ways that some must necessarily go unnamed, but they do not go unappreciated. My wife, Jeannie, has been a constant source of support, encouragement, faith, confidence, understanding, and love. In my darkest moments of despair that this book would never see the light of day, she was there for me. I am blessed to have her; she is truly a dream come true. Our two sweet little daughters—Hallie Elizabeth, three and a half, and Rebecca Margaret, seven months—have inspired me to work to make them proud and by their very existence remind me of what is most important in life. For as long as Hallie's been alive she's been my sunshine, in her own way, with my work. This book is my gift to her. My parents, Julia Gárate Burgos Feldman and Brian Feldman, have literally, emotionally, morally, financially, and spiritually sustained me. I hope they know how great my love and esteem for them is and how great my appreciation for their countless sacrifices and acts of love, large and small. My siblings, Richard, Vicky, and Danny, as well as lifelong friends John Sherman, Jak and Judy Karn, have been steady beacons of support and aid. Thanks to these special people for their love, friendship, and constancy.

Gratitude is also due those who read parts or all of this work at its various stages. Their efforts have surely helped me to produce a stronger book. Special thanks go to Wayne Flynt for his herculean efforts, discerning eye, unfailing encouragement, and consistent wisdom in this endeavor as in so many others. Allen W. Jones got me involved in, and inspired by, this type of research as a graduate student in History, and I am deeply grateful to him. Robin Fabel, Larry Gerber, and Gerry Gryski at Auburn University also read and commented on the manuscript. I am grateful for the comments made on individual chapters by readers at the *Journal of Southern History* and the *Historical Journal*. I also thank the University of Alabama Press's external readers for providing insightful and valuable suggestions that clearly made this a better book.

For their personal support, I thank Susan Youngblood Ashmore, Steve McFarland, Junius Rodriguez, James Wood Sims, and Carol Ann Vaughn. I must thank, in an army of archivists and librarians, Jim Baggett, Ed Bridges, Dixie Dysart, Janet Frederick, Gene Geiger, Joyce Hicks, Jeff Jakeman, Norwood Kerr, Mark Palmer, Debbie Pendleton, Buddy Sledge, Jerry Stephens, Harmon Straiton, Carolyn Walden, Liz Wells, and Marvin Whiting. I received research assistance from the Friends of the Alabama Department of Archives and History, Auburn University, and especially from the Center for Labor Education and Research (CLEAR) and the School of Business, both at the University of Alabama at Birmingham. I also thank my dean, W. Jack Duncan, for providing an atmosphere conducive to the pursuit of excellence in research. I am grateful to my colleagues at CLEAR for their many kinds of support, especially Ralph Johnson, the director of the center, who believed in this project; faculty members Judi King and Ed Brown; and program coordinators Melanie Hightower and Alison Schmied; and secretary Charmagne Sturgis. My thanks also to the staff of the University of Alabama Press, Mindy Wilson, assistant acquisitions editor, and Marcia Brubeck, my copy editor. Finally, I want to express heartfelt gratitude to Nicole Mitchell, the Press's director and editor-in-chief. I will always remember fondly her encouragement, advice, and aid throughout the publishing process.

Politics, Society, and the Klan in Alabama, 1915–1949

Introduction

The words "Ku Klux Klan" bring a host of images to mind. Most of these have been seared into the recesses of our collective consciousness by television, motion pictures, books, and other media. The Klan, for most of us, summons images that are eerie, macabre, mysterious, and at times even morbid. We think of shadowy figures in ghostly raiment, of giant wooden crosses burning in remote fields surrounded by hundreds of ghoulish figures, of ritual chanting by troupes of men gone mad at least temporarily, of shrieks in the night, gunshots, screams, and poltergeists on horseback, of mutilated black corpses hanging from trees, of blood, of riotous clashes on bridges and highways, of a sniper's lone bullet suddenly piercing the cover of night.

The Klan, while certainly all of these things, was a lot more. It was many things that most of us would rather forget. The KKK was, at various times throughout its long history, a powerful political organization and a fraternal and civic group that was tolerated by many people and even applauded by some.

This book focuses on the Klan phenomenon in Alabama, one of the nation's most important and infamous states. The example of Alabama will, I hope, afford insight into the most visible, resilient, and terrible version of fascism that America has ever produced.

Alabama, it must be said, is a special state. In virtually every period of American history it has made a name for itself, often for the worst reasons. During the 1890s, Alabamians lynched more people than any other state in the Union. In the 1920s, and even before, Birmingham earned a reputation as "bad, bad Birmingham," the "murder capital of the world." During the Great Depression, when the South enjoyed the dubious distinction of being the nation's number one economic problem, Birmingham gained notoriety as the hardest-hit town in America, a place that, in the 1960s, Martin Luther King called the "most segregated city in America." During that strife-filled decade, Anniston, Birmingham, Montgomery, Selma, Lowndes and Macon Counties, and the University of Alabama all became the sites of epic events in the civil rights struggle, further securing Alabama's niche in our shared consciousness.[1]

Of course Alabama is not so very distinctive that its own patterns cannot illuminate experience in the rest of the South. Alabama is generally representative of the states of the Deep South, and its experience, while often more intense, has usually reflected events elsewhere. The same relationship can often be seen between the experience of Dixie and that of the nation at large.

The revised Ku Klux Klan exploded onto the American cultural scene in the early 1920s like a shooting star. It burned brightly for a while and then just as suddenly seemed to fade from view. Since that time scholars have pondered the meaning, methods, motivations, and secrets of the hooded order. While this study does not deal with the Klan exclusively in the 1920s, the interpretive works dealing with that era are the most relevant to us.

HISTORICAL THEORY AND WRITINGS ON THE KLAN

Traditional writing on the Klan in the 1920s took the work of John Moffat Mecklin, a Dartmouth sociologist, as its point of departure. In 1924, Mecklin put forward a thesis that remained the conventional wisdom for over four decades—almost an eternity in historiographical terms. The "second Klan," Mecklin thought, was, like its Reconstruction counterpart, primarily a rural phenomenon. It consisted of unsophisticated country folk who, deprived of the cultural advantages of the city, fell prey to those impulses that ignorance breeds: fundamentalism, antiintellectualism, antimodernism, and bigotry. The second Klan, so the stereotype went, was southern, violent, white supremacist, and rural.[2]

Subsequent works on the Klan in the 1920s, in line with this reasoning, portrayed the movement as the violent reaction of rural fundamentalist "losers" on the economic periphery of the South and Midwest who felt alienated by the decade's modernism, prosperity, and new values. Those who followed the traditional thesis were many and were often not as careful as they should have been. Mecklin himself spoke of the KKK in almost explicitly sexual terms: the "petty impotence of the small-town mind" allegedly led to enforced conformity and an "affinity for the 'crude ejaculations' of Mr. [William Jennings] Bryan and the Fundamentalists."[3]

A host of noted historians produced works that essentially adhered to Mecklin's thesis. Frank Tannenbaum emphasized the rural and small-town aspects of the second Klan in his 1924 classic, *Darker Phases of the South*. Robert and Helen Lynd explored the model of urban-rural conflict in *Middletown*, their seminal study of Muncie, Indiana. Henry Peck Fry's work was also part of the first wave of traditional scholarship. Stanley Frost can be grouped with its exponents, although he identified an excess of patriotism accompanying World War I as contributing to the emergence of the modern Klan.[4]

A second wave of the traditional school described the KKK as flourishing in a benighted, southern, rural, violent, and economically marginal culture. The passing years conferred a respectability on this view, so that scholars with the stature of Richard Hofstadter, William Leuchtenburg, and John D. Hicks could be found toeing the traditional line on the issue. In his classic 1955 work, *The Age of Reform,* Hofstadter mused on the "shabbiness of the evangelical mind" as an attribute intrinsic to the 1920s Klan. Later, in an equally famous essay, he argued that the second Klan reflected a long-standing "paranoid style" in American politics that encompassed movements such as Know-Nothingism, Antimasonry, and, in more recent years, McCarthyism and the John Birch Society. The paranoid politician, Hofstadter argued, was a "true believer" of the type described by Eric Hoffer, a person who secularized a "religiously derived view of the world to deal with political issues in Christian imagery" and saw it as his patriotic duty to intercept an intricate conspiracy that imperiled millions of unknowing citizens.[5]

Other influential works took the same tack. David Brion Davis's work offered parallels in examining right-wing movements in antebellum America. According to Davis, the absence of institutional controls in Jacksonian America had created a cultural vacuum that prompted a rootless people to unite in targeting allegedly antidemocratic churches and secret societies such as the Mormons, the Masons, and the Catholics. W. J. Cash's noted study *The Mind of the South* also substantially followed Mecklin's thesis.[6]

Some recent works have relied on the traditional thesis as well. During the turbulent 1960s, studies by William Randel and Arnold Rice generally followed the conventional mode of thinking. In *The Politics of Unreason* (1970), Seymour Martin Lipset and Earl Raab, like David B. Davis, located the roots of Ku Kluxism and McCarthyism in intolerant antebellum movements such as Antimasonry. Following Hofstadter's lead, these scholars noted that groups like the Klan tended to imitate their victims, for example, by appropriating the ritual, mystery, and vestments of the Roman Catholic Church. A number of recent works have described the second KKK in harsh terms similar to those of John Mecklin. David Shannon called the Klan a "hate organization" that accommodated regional prejudices against blacks, Jews, Catholics, immigrants, and others, while John George and Laird Wilcox termed it the largest extremist group in the twentieth-century United States and "probably the most intolerant and violence-prone overall." Robert Moats Miller emphasized its resilient racism and argued that the "good men" who joined the KKK "simply failed to discern" the order's true nature.[7]

The earliest revision of the dominant thesis can be found in Norman Weaver's 1954 Ph.D. dissertation on the second Klan in Wisconsin, Indiana, Ohio, and Michigan. Weaver argued that the revitalized KKK was not inherently violent or xenophobic. Rather, midwestern Knights concentrated on defending Protestant values and temperance. David Chalmers's magisterial *Hooded Americanism,* published in 1965, meticulously examined the Klan throughout the nation. Chalmers's work discovered a strong Klan presence in many urban centers and regions previously thought to have been unreceptive to the order. Charles Alexander's 1965 study of the Invisible Empire in the Southwest admitted that the order was violent but stipulated that its terrorism was directed at moral offenders rather than at those previously thought to have held a monopoly on the Klan lash: blacks, Catholics, Jews, and immigrants. Alexander also identified postwar patriotism as responsible for the society's revival rather than relying, as the traditional explanation had done, on urban-rural conflict, fundamentalism, economic instability, and bigotry. Philanthropy, social work, and civic activity dominated KKK activity, Alexander suggested, not violence. In most of the communities in which the Klan appeared, local residents not only tolerated it but actually welcomed it.[8]

Kenneth T. Jackson's *The Ku Klux Klan in the City* (1967) dramatically challenged the traditional view by arguing that the second Klan flourished just as strongly in urban areas as in rural ones. Cities gave the Klan its leadership, largest membership, newspaper support, and most impressive political successes. The metropolis, and not the rural hinterland, was the ideal breeding ground for the Klan germ after World War I. According to Jackson's profile, the typical 1920s Klansman was a lower-middle-class white Anglo-Saxon Protestant who felt threatened by the change in postwar America. The Klansman lived in urban districts sandwiched between black, immigrant, or non-Protestant ghettoes and more insulated affluent neighborhoods.[9]

Jackson and Chalmers together dealt a stunning blow to the edifice of traditional historiography on the Klan. By the middle 1960s the second Klan, like the race problem in general, had acquired a complexion that was distinctly national and urban as well as southern and rural.[10]

This strain of revisionism has not faded entirely from view. For example, Stanley Coben deemphasized violence, fundamentalism, and the small town in understanding the second KKK as defending Victorian values rather than reflecting an urban-rural split. Ellis Hawley also specifically avoided the urban-rural thesis when he described the second Klan as "the most prominent manifestation of the traditionalist counterattack against modern ways." A more recent examination of Memphis's 1923 elections portrayed the city's Knights as mainstream moral reformers rather than the purveyors of "exotic or extreme attitudes," and recent work has confirmed the revisionists' notion that Catholics were more often the victims of the second KKK than African Americans.[11]

Recently, postrevisionists have offered a third interpretation of the 1920s Klan. These revisionists, who call themselves the Populist-Civic School, have challenged both traditional and revised interpretations by stressing the complex and heterogeneous quality of the secret order. Focusing less on ideology than on census data and (when possible) rare membership rolls, this school has made a number of valuable contributions. According to populist scholars, the second Klan possessed urban as well as rural strength. Its members were not aberrant extremists in their nativism and racism but rather held attitudes that were relatively typical for their time periods and locales. Rare acts of violence were usually the handiwork of an unrepresentative splinter rather than the larger body of Klansmen. Mainstream Protestant churches offered more support for the Klan than fringe evangelical sects, and local concerns exercised a far greater influence on klaverns than a uniform national program or ideology. Perhaps most important, populist scholars discovered that the revised KKK provided a political mouthpiece for the middle-class masses whose political interests were habitually ignored by entrenched elites.[12]

Shawn Lay, one of the foremost spokesmen for the Populist School, argued persuasively that civic and political action was the most consuming pastime of these Knights, that political success often brought intramural struggle in its wake, and that a dichotomous view of the KKK as "conservative" and its opponents as "liberal" is simplistic.[13]

Populist scholars, like the wave of revisionist historians before them, have shown clearly that the second Klan was far more ensconced in American life than many of us would like to admit. Work done by the revisionist and populist school after the heyday of the traditional school has revealed that in the 1920s Ohio had 400,000 Klansmen, Pennsylvania 100,000, and Chicago 50,000. Indiana's Klan had more political clout in its state than any other Klan. The KKK elected not only an Indiana governor and a U.S. senator but eleven other governors and a host of U.S. congressmen and state and local officials. The 1920s Klan pushed a historic bill dealing with public schools through Oregon's state legislature and also enjoyed remarkable popularity in Wisconsin, Michigan, New Jersey, and New York. Klan agitation led to the impeachment of one governor, and on one memorable occasion, 40,000 Knights paraded down Pennsylvania Avenue. Liberals Harry Truman and Hugo L. Black, later a U.S. senator and a Supreme Court justice, were members. President Warren G. Harding joined the secret order in the Green Room of the White House. Woodrow Wilson, a historian, political scientist, and university administrator in addition to being a U.S. president, was a sympathizer. The Klan even had a chapter at Harvard University.[14]

Recently, historian Nancy MacLean has finessed some of the tenets of the Populist School in an impressive study of a klavern in Clarke County, Georgia. MacLean described the 1920s Knights as "reactionary populists" and shunned "false polarities" like urban-versus-rural and civic-versus-violent. She stressed that the Klan in the 1920s was many different things all at once.[15]

THE PLACE OF THIS BOOK ON THE KLAN

Studies of the twentieth-century revised Klan have traditionally confined themselves to the 1920s and have usually paid special attention to the period between 1915 and 1930. As instructive as such histories have been, they often mislead readers in two ways: they suggest (1) that the 1920s version of the Klan was absolutely separate, distinct, and different from what came before and has since come after and (2) that the Klan phenomenon in fact died out after 1929 only to be recreated out of whole cloth during the civil rights struggles of the 1950s and 1960s.

By spanning the years 1915 to 1949, this book seeks to dispel these two misconceptions. The example of Alabama's Klan, considered from its twentieth-century revival in 1915 through the 1940s, shows that, while the 1920s version of the Klan was distinct, it shared many features with both its Reconstruction progenitor and the various phases of the KKK that came after 1929. Many parallels are particularly apparent throughout the 1930s and 1940s. By the same token, the Alabama example teaches us that the KKK did not die off completely after 1929—far from it. While the Klan did lose considerable membership strength and popularity after 1929, it persisted at a significant level for the next two decades. It simply cannot be said that there was no Klan during the depression of the 1930s or that the "third Klan," begun during the 1950s, was a wholly independent reaction to the fledgling civil rights movement. These points become very clear—at least in the case of Alabama—once we examine the period after 1929. When we extend our scrutiny to the 1940s, furthermore, a number of important parallels are evident between the Klan of the 1920s and the post–World War II order. There are problems, though, with inclusion of the Klan as it existed after 1949. While the Klan of the 1950s owed much to its antecedents in the 1920s, 1930s, and 1940s, it also reflected white backlash to the modern civil rights movement to an unprecedented extent.

The present book demonstrates that the story of even the 1920s Klan in Alabama actually encompassed two Klan phases. During the first, from 1916 until about 1925, the Klan enjoyed wide popular support. During the second, the Klan encountered brief but virulent opposition and weakened considerably until its virtual demise in 1929. During the first phase the Klan garnered strong support from Alabama's planters and industrialists, who, initially at least, compared it favorably to the Reconstruction Klan of their fathers. During the latter phase, the Klan encountered strong opposition from this Big Mule/Black Belt alliance. Alabama's first Klan of the 1920s was a mass movement. It comprised 115,000 men by the end of 1924. Its grand dragon claimed 150,000 members in 1925. The second phase was characterized by a dwindling membership that reached fewer than 6,000 members by the end of the decade.[16]

The findings of this book corroborate much of the Populist-Civic School's theses. The case of Alabama clearly suggests that the 1920s Klan represented a political mouthpiece for plain folk in their struggle against entrenched elites. Although we have no significant membership list for Alabama, members in Alabama seem to have been members of the middle class, people with ordinary social backgrounds, as suggested by the Populist-Civic School.

Notably, Alabama's experience, and perhaps that of the South as a whole, may have differed from that of the rest of the nation with respect to violence. The frequency, intensity, and general acceptance of Klan violence in Alabama seems to have been significantly greater than in other states and regions that have been studied. Many Alabamians, confronted by overwhelming evidence of Klan involvement in violent activity, simply concluded that most of the order's victims—"uppity" blacks, moral nonconformists, and religious or ethnic minorities—somehow had it "coming to them" anyway.[17] The righteous in Alabama habitually used violence to pun-

fronted the Klan in more recent years. As the Populist-Civic School has shown, the biases of 1920s Klansmen were often the biases of their 1920s adversaries and were shared by almost everyone else in white society, especially on matters of race.[19] Seldom did the Klan's elite opponents challenge the order's racism, prejudices, or kaleidoscope of intolerance. Adversaries were slow to condemn its violence. While some Alabamians during the 1920s opposed the Klan on principle, many others waged a more "pragmatic opposition."

It is easy to form the impression that the Klan died completely at the end of the 1920s only to reemerge in 1954 as a full-blown entity in response to the South's looming crisis over segregation. This statement undeniably has some truth. Nevertheless, a small core of determined right-wing Klan members remained active from 1930 to 1954 and has been largely overlooked by historians. These Knights, stripped of substantial political influence, waged a rearguard action that was more extreme and less representative of white society than that mounted by the 1920s order had been. Their targets were Alabama's Communists, liberals, unionists, and blacks who sought political and racial equality. The activities of this "hidden" or "lost Klan" during the New Deal and World War II exhibited striking similarities to those of the 1920s Klan and arguably bridged the gap between the diverse and inclusive 1920s Klan and the smaller anti–civil rights Klan of the 1960s.

The resistance of some Alabamians to the KKK continued into the 1930s and 1940s but shifted its focus. Most opponents of the KKK during the depression and war years criticized the Klan not because of its political power, as had the opposition during the 1920s, but because it presented an obstacle to the courting of outside capital and federal relief or because its excesses threatened to prompt federal intrusion into the race issue. Such intrusion was understood as a threat to more traditional forms of racial and social control. Often the Klan's most ardent critics in Alabama were whites who were wedded to these traditional forms of control. Other opponents were decent men and women who, while not yet ready to abandon segregation, deplored the violence associated with the order. Still other critics were New South businessmen who were concerned about negative national publicity and the adverse effects that Klan violence might have on the importation of northern capital. Such opposition was vigorous, genuine, effective, and, yet again, generally "pragmatic."

The Klan presence during the 1930s and 1940s was considerably smaller than the Klan of the 1920s and the hard-core racial Klan of the 1950s and 1960s. During the depression, Klan infatuation with radicals reached unprecedented levels, and Knights largely ceased to regard Roman Catholicism and moral nonconformity as the menaces they had once been thought to be. Blacks and Jews remained targets, in part because they made up the bulk of Alabama's small radical cadre. Labor union activists, though, were repressed—a marked change from the early 1920s, when unions, women, farmers, and temperance groups briefly united with the Klan in political coalition against the planters and industrialists.[20] Among the small number of Klansmen who persisted into 1940s Alabama, race concerns became increasingly dominant—a single-mindedness that contrasted dramatically with the group's wide range of concerns during the 1920s. Post–World War II Klansmen were also of more modest social origin than the members of the widespread second Klan.

The bridge Klan of the 1930s and 1940s, in short, neither exhibited absolute continuity nor represented a complete departure from its predecessors. It seems more meaningful to speak of "qualified continuity." Several "career Klansmen" were members of the order from the 1920s to the 1960s in Alabama. The preservation of white supremacy continued to be a goal of primary importance to the group; violence retained its allure and its prevalence. During the 1930s Jews felt Klan persecution, as they had during the 1920s, largely because of their leadership role in Alabama's small Communist movement. During the late 1940s, Alabama Klansmen rediscovered one of their favorite 1920s victims, the moral nonconformist, and went on a spree of moral authoritarianism and morally inspired violence strikingly reminiscent of Klan activities two decades earlier. From the 1920s until the end of the 1940s, KKK victims continued to be outsiders at odds with Alabama's dominant culture, whether racially, religiously, politically, economically, or morally.

Origins of the Revised Klan

In 1920 Americans grappled with a bewildering array of changes. The U.S. Census Bureau announced that for the first time in the nation's history a majority of Americans lived in urban settings. Women won the right to vote. Many observers hoped that the "weaker sex" would exert a healing effect on politics, but some believed that exposure to political disease entailed the risk of contamination. The Great War, with its unparalleled waste of human life, shocked a generation. The nation found little solace in the aftermath of war. Domestic violence racked the country as the "red Summer" redefined the meaning and the regional character of racial turmoil. During the world war, Russia's Bolshevik Revolution raised the terrifying specter of "Reds" and anarchists plotting from within. In the postwar period, worry turned to fear, then paranoia, as American authorities brutally stamped out a largely illusory menace in the Red Scare of 1919–1920. Labor and management clashed in a record number of strikes in 1919. Disillusionment set in as people began to realize that the unspeakable violence of World War I had not made the world safe for democracy. America's failure to join the League of Nations only underscored the stinging reality that countries were still at odds after the Peace of Versailles.[1]

Meanwhile, foreigners continued to pour in from southern and eastern Europe. For many old-stock Americans this new immigration was unwelcome. It contrasted sharply with the earlier, acceptable nineteenth-century immigration of Anglo-Saxons, a movement in which many older-stock Americans had taken part. The new Jewish and Catholic immigrants were strange peoples with strange ways. They huddled together by choice and necessity, often in urban ghettoes. They spoke their own languages, retained their own style of dress and customs, published newspapers in their mother tongues, and seemed to have an unsettling predilection for joining labor unions. With them, they brought little or no experience with democratic regimes; many native whites exposed their prejudices by assuming that all immigrants were anarchists and Reds. The unwelcome ways of the new-comers included a taste for alcohol and political bosses that shocked and dismayed average Americans. Catholics, in particular, were suspected of har-boring a dangerous allegiance to a foreign prince who dictated their every move from Rome.[2]

Race relations offered little comfort. During the exigencies of World War I, hundreds of thousands of blacks had fled southern repression, served in the army, or worked jobs formerly reserved for whites. Postwar competition for jobs and housing led to increased tensions. In 1919, racial strains boiled over as major race riots erupted in twenty-five cities. The race issue would never again be considered entirely a southern problem.[3]

After the war, cultural values seemed as vulnerable to assault as white supremacy and ethnic integrity. The automobile, with its inherent anonym-ity, was called a "motel on four wheels" by some. Teens enjoyed unprece-dented freedom from parental supervision as they engaged in sexual experi-mentation in backseats across America. The image of the liberated flapper, although it applied to only a small minority, threatened citizens who felt more comfortable when women hewed to the more traditional roles of mother, sister, daughter, or wife. Freudian psychology, modernism, material values, and the intellectual alienation of a "Lost Generation" seemed to be eroding traditional American culture at an alarming rate.[4]

Many Americans found these changes, taken together, to be dizzying, even overwhelming. Society seemed to have shaken loose from its tradi-tional moorings and was drifting without purpose or direction. Frightened, politically powerless, economically challenged, and desperate for some mea-sure of control over their lives, millions of men and women turned to the Ku Klux Klan for salvation. Millions more hoped they would be successful.

ORIGINS AND WORLD WAR I

The second Klan was founded on Thanksgiving night 1915 atop Stone Mountain, Georgia, just outside Atlanta, the marquee city of the New South. William Joseph Simmons, an Alabama native, led a group of twenty-odd shivering men to the top of the mountain, where they lit a cross and sum-moned the Invisible Empire back into existence after a forty-year hiatus. The ceremony followed the Atlanta premier of D. W. Griffith's classic silent movie, *Birth of a Nation,* based on the Reverend Thomas Dixon's romantic account of the Reconstruction KKK.[5]

Simmons stressed the ties between the original Klan and his revised version. He repeatedly referred to the Reconstruction order during the Stone Mountain ceremony, which was held on land borrowed from the Venables of Atlanta, a leading family in the original Klan. Simmons also arranged to have three Reconstruction Klansmen present to lend an aura of authenticity and continuity to the inaugural proceedings.[6]

Joseph Simmons himself claimed a close link with the original order. Born in Harpersville, Alabama, in 1880, the son of a Reconstruction Klansman, he had tried his hand at medical school and the Methodist ministry but had failed at both. By 1912 he had become a professional fraternalist boasting membership in a staggering array of organizations.[7]

Despite Simmons's efforts to tie the new order to its precursor, the 1920s Klan departed from its Reconstruction counterpart in its spiritual, ideological, and sometimes physical kinship with the many preparedness and patriotic societies that had been spawned by American involvement in World War I. The Reconstruction Klan had no counterpart in this regard.

Prior to the First World War, a series of preparedness societies took root, thanks largely to the efforts of General Leonard Wood and Theodore Roosevelt, president during the Progressive Era. The preparedness societies—notably the American Defense Society (ADS), the National Security League (NSL), and the Navy League—emphasized the need to build and maintain a larger army and navy, to require universal military training, and to silence internal dissent. These groups waged a relentless ideological battle to guarantee conformity and support for the war through a barrage of speakers, books, pamphlets, articles, movies, political lobbying, and gigantic parades. Their efforts often went beyond patriotism, preparedness, and propaganda into outright nativism.[8]

In 1916, progressive President Woodrow Wilson espoused the cause of preparedness when he voiced the nativist and antiradical concern with "one-hundred percent Americanism," an issue indelibly associated both with the societies and with the newly founded Ku Klux Klan. Wilson echoed the fears and anxieties of many in prewar America by expounding the "dangers of 'hyphenated Americanism.'" "There are citizens of the United States, I blush to admit," Wilson said, "born under other flags but welcomed under our generous naturalization laws . . . who have poured the poison of disloyalty into the very arteries of our national life. . . . Such creatures of passion, disloyalty, and anarchy must be crushed out." "The melting pot has not melted," the educational director of the NSL agreed. "In the bottom . . . there lie heaps of unfused metal."[9]

During World War I, anxiety turned to paranoia. States banned the German language in their churches and schools. People renamed sauerkraut "liberty cabbage." The German measles became "liberty measles." In the spring of 1918, Congress passed the Espionage and Sedition Act. In this climate, a number of patriotic societies sprang up to help Americans win the war at home by assuring that the country's citizens supported the war and its aims and rejected anything that could possibly be construed as a foreign threat, including labor unions and immigrants. These patriotic societies combined their efforts with antiimmigrant preparedness groups such as the ADS and the NSL. They also worked in conjunction with official agencies like George Creel's Committee on Public Information (CPI), the Justice Department, and state councils of defense, and they often advocated disregard for civil liberties and engaged in extralegal activity to advance the war effort. Violence did not lag far behind. The 250,000-man American Protective League (APL) was, in the words of historian William Pencak, a "privately-organized red squad" and, according to historian David Kennedy, "a quasi-vigilante organization . . . , a band of amateur sleuths and loyalty enforcers . . . , [and an] unruly *posse comitatus* on an unprecedented national scale." The APL, in conjunction with local police and Justice Department agents—and a number of lesser-known but picaresque organizations such as the Terrible Threateners, the Sedition Slammers, the Boy Spies, and the Liberty League—tracked down suspected German spies and conducted numerous "slacker" raids designed to net immigrant draft-dodgers.[10]

After the war, unspent patriotic zeal found an outlet in a number of organizations (figure 1), the most prominent of which was the newly organized American Legion. Anxious about a radical threat made visceral by the Bolshevik Revolution, the Legion emphasized "one-hundred percent Americanism," military strength, isolationism, a denial of the right of revolution, an aversion to organized labor, and a decidedly anticorporation element. During the Red Scare, the Legion and wartime patriotic societies such as the ADS and the NSL joined with the newly revised KKK to crack down on suspected radicals and anarchists. Groups like the Allied Liberty League, the Sentinels of the Republic, the Crusaders, and the American Vigilant Intelligence Federation were also quite active.[11]

The Klan of the 1920s had much in common with the preparedness and patriotic societies: nativism, vigilantism, an anticorporation bent, a love of conformity, "one-hundred percent Americanism," a distaste for immigrants, radicals, and labor unions, and a desire to coordinate their activities with constituted authority. Klan Wizard Joseph Simmons was connected to the Atlanta APL as well as to a lesser-known group modeled on the League and called the Citizens' Bureau of Investigation. In wartime Alabama, conservative allies of U.S. senator Oscar W. Underwood such as Forney Johnston, Lloyd Hooper, and Victor Hanson dominated the state's council of defense. After the war, though, KKK membership overlapped strongly with the leadership of Alabama's American Legion.[12]

1. 1921 Klansman Kneeling Before the Cross and Flag. The patriotism accompanying World War I boosted membership in the second Klan, but membership did not really begin to take off until the early 1920s. Courtesy Birmingham Public Library Archives, Cat. No. 25.36.

Simmons envisaged his empire to be a fraternal, patriotic, native white Protestant order based on the firm foundation of the original KKK. Building on a solid core of white separatist tenets borrowed from the first Klan, Simmons extended the mission of the modern order. The new Klan would look beyond the exalted but worn duty of keeping the black man in his place. Foremost among the assorted perceived new dangers was the threat that Protestant America would be swallowed up by hordes of eastern and southern European immigrants. To their African American, Catholic, Jewish, and immigrant enemies Klansmen soon added liberals, unionists, women suffragists, "wets," and anyone who deviated from what they called "one-hundred percent Americanism."

JOSEPH SIMMONS, RECONSTRUCTION, AND PATRICIAN SUPPORT

In actuality, the revised Klan organization both followed and departed from the Reconstruction model. Simmons's empire sported new divisions—

"realms," "dominions," and local chapters termed "klaverns." His Klan also inherited the Reconstruction tendency to emphasize the mysterious, the macabre, and the ghoulish in order to attract persons captivated by the mystique as well as to intimidate those likely to be frightened by such vivid imagery.[13]

Despite the slow and mostly urban beginning of Simmons's Klan, a remarkable series of events in 1921 combined to transform the KKK into a thriving national concern.[14] Opposition from the National Association for the Advancement of Colored People (NAACP) and a series of exposés in the *New York World* had the ironic effect of boosting public interest in the group. Simmons hired E. Y. Clarke and Elizabeth Tyler, two professional publicity agents, who used state-of-the-art marketing techniques to bring in thousands of new memberships at ten dollars each. An investigation by the U.S. Congress also provided exposure that resulted in increased membership.[15]

A natural showman, the Reverend Simmons was primarily responsible for the Klan's dramatic success at the 1921 hearings of the House Rules Committee. Simmons gave a moving performance in which he portrayed his Klan, despite abundant evidence to the contrary, as far removed from the antiblack, anti-Catholic, and anti-Semitic organization many congressmen believed it to be. The former preacher told story after story about his childhood in rural Alabama. He spoke of playing, fishing, and hunting with blacks, of teaching them the alphabet, and of writing love letters for illiterate men of color. "If this organization is unworthy," Simmons vowed, "then let me know and I will destroy it, but if it is not, let it stand." He called upon God to forgive those who persecuted the KKK. At one especially poignant moment, he fainted. Years later Simmons admitted: "Congress made us."[16]

The hearings, the articles, and the marketing campaign had a phenomenal effect. By the end of 1924, the KKK claimed 115,000 members in 148 Alabama klaverns and 4 to 6 million members nationwide. Branches even opened in England, France, Germany, Wales, Canada, Mexico, New Zealand, China, and the Panama Canal Zone.[17]

The second Klan also tapped into a pool of ready-made fears and insecurities that expressly derived from World War I.[18] The upshot of these shocks and traumas was the acceleration of a recent trend toward conservatism—in both political and economic affairs. The conservatism that had accompanied America's involvement in world war, and had ended much of its turn-of-the-century experiment with progressive reform,[19] became unnaturally accelerated by peace and its convulsive aftershocks. The result was an enhanced predisposition toward conservatism, even reactionaryism, with a return to traditional values and an intensification of the Progressive Era's darker tendencies, such as nativism, racism, and moral intolerance. For many, the Ku Klux Klan was an important part of the answer.

Joseph Simmons's Klan was clearly quite different from the 1860s order, but, in Alabama, revival entailed conscious attempts to link the new society to its Reconstruction progenitor. Newspapers in Birmingham and Montgomery hailed the return of the KKK as "awe-inspiring" and reminisced fondly about the original order. Enthusiastic editors revived Dunning School depictions of Reconstruction and the KKK, romanticizing the original order as having saved southern civilization from a reign of terror induced by impudent blacks, scoundrelly carpetbaggers, and treasonous scalawags.[20]

Soon after the inaugural ceremony atop Stone Mountain, Colonel Simmons tried to exploit ties between the Reconstruction Klan and his new order by sending racist editor Jonathan Frost to recruit Confederate veterans in Alabama. The choice was unfortunate. In 1916, Frost made an aborted attempt to seize control of the fledgling Alabama Klan, embezzled several thousand dollars, and vanished.[21]

Despite the initial setback, the young Alabama Klan was buoyed by the attitude of Birmingham's Big Mule industrialists and their Black Belt political allies. Although the alliance bitterly opposed the Klan later in the decade, initially at least it greeted news of the hooded revival with undisguised enthusiasm. The KKK, for men like Victor Hanson—publisher of the *Birmingham News,* the *Birmingham Ledger,* and the *Montgomery Advertiser*—was, in 1921, a welcome addition. Hanson, Oscar Underwood, and other Big Mules initially equated Simmons's Klan with the Klan of their fathers and with the political redemption of the white South from the "hell" of federally imposed Reconstruction.[22]

Planter/industrialist approbation of the revised Klan was most evident in the large city newspapers in which the tandem exercised influence. Attempts to link the second KKK with its Reconstruction ancestor were an important reason for the order's initial positive reception. The *Montgomery Advertiser,* long the chief organ of Black Belt political interests, observed in 1918 that Simmons's new Klan "bore all the ear-marks of the ancient and honorable order that [had] placed white supremacy back in the saddle after a reign of terror for several years at the hands of negroes and scalawags." A massive Klan initiation in Birmingham in January 1921 provided a perfect forum for similar praise from the Big Mule/Black Belt press. Victor Hanson's *Birmingham News,* the principal mouthpiece of the state's industrial interests, lauded the event as evidence of justifiable white outrage at "Negro uppitiness" following World War I that recalled black insolence after the Civil War. Hanson's paper also glorified both the original and revised versions of the sheeted order. Frederick I. Thompson's *Birmingham Age-Herald,* another major industrialist organ, was hardly less congratulatory. Thompson, like Hanson, was a charter member of the Big Mule/Black Belt coalition and owned several large daily newspapers in Mobile, Montgomery, and Birmingham. The patrician organ extolled the work done by the original Klan in safeguarding the South during Reconstruction, described members of the new order as the cream of southern society, and jointly praised both incarnations of the group.[23]

In assisting with the revival, Alabama's Big Mules took pains to praise the new order as an extension of the noble Reconstruction Klan. Major Willis Julian Milner—one of Birmingham's founding fathers, a leading industrialist, and a Confederate veteran—praised original Klansmen as the saviors of white civilization during the hellish days of Reconstruction. He railed against carpetbaggers and scalawags as "a flock of Vultures" who sought to "insert their felonious talons into the hearts of unborn babes." Milner toasted the courage, manhood, and integrity of the Reconstruction KKK and spoke of the immutably low "character . . . [of the] Negro."[24]

The favorable reception given to the revised KKK in Alabama was in large part the fruit of Joseph Simmons's painstaking efforts to establish his order as the legitimate successor to the original Klan (see figure 2). "The present Klan is . . . the reincarnation . . . of the spirit and mission of the Anglo-Saxon," he wrote. "The name of the old Klan has been taken by the new as a heritage . . . , a mantle one worthy generation might gall upon the shoulders of its successor . . . to maintain Anglo-Saxon civilization . . . from . . . [the] invasion of alien people of whatever clime or color."[25] Accordingly, Simmons buttressed the rhetoric with symbolic displays. The new KKK awarded "hero medals" to any 1920s Knight who had been a member of the Reconstruction order. One Scottsboro den singled out fourteen men to receive hero crosses for being part of the "valiant and noble host of the Original Klan of the [Eighteen-] Sixties." Birmingham dens named themselves after Confederate war heroes Robert E. Lee, Thomas "Stonewall" Jackson, and Nathan Bedford Forrest.[26]

Symbolism and rhetoric also found echoes at the popular level. A Talladegan later remembered that "everybody knew that when [the] Carpetbaggers and Northern capitalists took control of the South after the Civil War and helped bring poverty and misery to its citizens. . . . it was the Ku Klux Klan that saved the South. . . . To accept the [1920s KKK] was much like an expression of appreciation for what their grandfathers had done."[27]

The constitution of the revised KKK also emphasized continuity with the original order "for the same spiritual purposes as it originally had." The revised Klan claimed the "object, ritual, regalias, and emblems" of the origi-

2. 1920s Klansman on Horseback. During the 1920s, Knights in Alabama and throughout the South sought to evoke nostalgic memories of the Reconstruction Klan. Courtesy Birmingham Public Library Archives, Cat. No. 816.13.79.

nal KKK as "a precious heritage we shall jealously keep, forever maintain and valiantly protect."[28]

While Big Mule/Black Belt newspapers glorified the original Klan and welcomed its revival, connections between the two Klans were also painfully evident to black editors. Chicago's *Defender* announced the Klan's rebirth by describing the original society in less than flattering terms: "The name Ku Klux implies disorder, bloodshed, rapine, and everything [aimed at the] destruction of government." A black editor in New York concurred that the Klan was "a 'league with Satan and a covenant with hell. . . . ' The groans of the negroes done to death without judge or jury still ring in our ears. . . . the stench from burning flesh still offends the nostrils of Almighty God." [29]

Nevertheless, the Klan of the 1920s was separate and distinct from the old Klan in a number of important ways. New marketing techniques led to gigantic galas designed to increase membership, and the new Knights displayed a novel concern with civic affairs, religion, and community morality. Perhaps more important, though, the revised Klan was a child of the Progressive Era—albeit a child traumatized in its infancy by the external and internal threats that America had endured in connection with World War I. While it lacked much of progressivism's undeniable liberalism, it did share a passion for political change and reform, an extension of democracy, a vehicle for the concerns of white middle-class Protestants, and, like the Progressive Era, a diversity of purpose and membership that still defies simple explanation. Moreover, World War I acted as the forge that heated the Progressive Era's less attractive features to a white-hot intensity and imprinted them upon the new Ku Klux Klan: racism, nativism, xenophobia, and even a willingness to use violence to maintain conformity, compel patriotism, and secure traditional values such as prohibition.

In Alabama, the revised Klan eventually enjoyed success by almost any standard. Although membership was slipping nationally, Grand Dragon James Esdale claimed 150,000 members in 1926.[30] The figure is somewhat suspect because, during Esdale's long tenure as the state's leading Klansman, his capacity for self-promotion was exceeded only by his ability to alienate friend and foe alike. A Klan slate won a majority in Birmingham's bitterly contested 1925 city elections and with it control over city government. In 1926, the KKK swept Alabama's state elections, placing members of the order in the governor's mansion, the attorney general's office, and the U.S. Senate. Politicians who owed their allegiance to the Klan came to control counties virtually in their entirety. Judges, solicitors, sheriffs, police chiefs, county clerks, and a host of other city, county, and state officials belonged to the hooded order.

2

The Civic, Educational, and Progressive Klan

Today it seems contradictory, even awkward, to write of a civic or progressive Klan, given the blood-stained history of the order in American life. During the 1920s, though, the Klan not only was concerned with civic affairs and progressive matters but pursued these concerns actively and vigorously in Alabama and in most other states where it became active.

Civic and educational activity was largely the function of the revised order's vast heterogeneity and diversity. Because it encompassed virtually every aspect of middle-class life, a significant portion of its raison d'être was the perpetuation of old-stock middle-class American values—among them, hard work, patriotism, public education, temperance, and traditional forms of morality. The Klan spent much time, money, and energy in Alabama and elsewhere on patriotic, educational, and civic guidance and even made charitable contributions to the communities in which it flourished.

To say that the 1920s Klan had a strong civic, educational, and progressive component, however, does not for one moment discount its more insidious manifestations. It does not deny, lessen, or mitigate the fact that one of the Klan's components, especially in Alabama, was intensely violent and morally intolerant. When we speak of the civic Klan, we acknowledge that the 1920s order was complex in its composition and varied in its personality.

"100 PERCENT AMERICANISM"

One of the second Klan's central missions was the advocacy, propagation, and preservation of patriotism, a derivative of its slogan "100 percent Americanism." Alabama Knights spent a great deal of time promulgating the patriotic creed with which most of them had been raised. They dis-

3. Automobile Parade in Montgomery, 1925. The 1920s Klan often promoted itself using automobile parades that featured crosses and American flags as well as the mysterious-looking hoods and robes. Courtesy Alabama State Department of Archives and History.

tributed flags, sponsored contests, and preached loyalty to country and nation—both among the impressionable young and among the suspect immigrants. World War I engendered this type of civic activity and, once present,
kept it fueled. In October 1918, for example, the Klan's arrival in Troy was
heralded by an automobile parade (see figure 3) featuring circulars warning immigrant "slackers" to join the army and civilians to buy Liberty
Bonds. In Montgomery, a nocturnal caravan of eighteen cars wound its way
through the city's business district. A few weeks later, a hundred uniformed
Klansmen carrying American flags marched from the state capitol to the
city square. On both occasions large crowds witnessed the spectacles and
were admonished by the robed Klansmen to do their best for the war effort.
Klaverns in Mobile, Anniston, Birmingham, Tuscaloosa, and other areas
around the state celebrated Flag Day, supported the American Boy Scouts,
and made patriotic gestures that sometimes spilled over into antiforeign behavior.[1]

Talladega County's klavern was particularly active in civic and patriotic
affairs. Its members consistently took part in a host of civic, patriotic, and
educational projects not unlike those of other fraternal groups of the time.
Klansmen bought and donated large American flags to every public school

in Sylacauga and staged elaborate ceremonies at the schools. Women members of the Klan auxiliary played prominent roles in these activities. In Talladega, the Klanswomen bought and donated smaller flags to ensure that every single classroom in the county had an American flag prominently dislayed. Klansmen and women auxiliaries in Anniston, Brundige, York, and Etowah took part in similar activities and often coordinated their campaigns and donations with speeches, fireworks, parades, barbecues, and other patriotic demonstrations.[2]

Other members of the revised Klan were less genteel in the matter of inculcating patriotism and civic virtue. Birmingham's klaverns, especially, adopted a more forceful approach than their brethren around the state. Perhaps this was not surprising, given the notoriously violent history of the young city. Vigilantism on the part of the Birmingham Klan found its counterpart in the activities of some of the preparedness and patriotic societies associated with World War I. In the middle-class suburb of Woodlawn, three robed Klansmen kidnapped a soft-drink stand operator and flogged him for not holding a steady job during the war. Knights tarred, feathered, and beat another Birmingham man for not working. Birmingham's Kluxers bought war bonds, supported "work or fight" laws, and sometimes took the Protestant work ethic to an extreme. In 1918, Birmingham Knights countered an Italian neighborhood parade with an impromptu demonstration of their own. They seized an immigrant "slacker," compelled him to confess that he had dodged military service because he had a "yellow streak up his back," and, together with a cheering throng that included many who were not members of the order, ran him out of town on a rail.[3]

In Alabama, the organization had its early centers in cities such as Birmingham. Klaverns in Birmingham, Mobile, and Montgomery were especially strong. Mobile alone was home to 3,500 Klansmen, Montgomery's Klan No. 3 was the lodge of several prominent Alabama politicians, and Birmingham's Robert E. Lee Klavern No. 1 was the largest den in the South and the oldest functioning klavern in America. Organized in 1916, the Lee Klavern was the quintessential civic-minded klavern. It boasted a membership of 10,000, published a weekly newspaper, and sponsored a drum and band corps. It even ran an orphanage dubbed "Klan Haven." Birmingham's police chief was a member together with at least half of the city's police force and a number of judges and other city and county officials. The city itself boasted between 15,000 and 18,000 Klansmen, over half the number of the city's registered voters. In addition to the Lee Klavern, Birmingham was home to the large Nathan Bedford Forrest Klavern No. 60 in Woodlawn as well as three Klan buildings, the state headquarters, and strong units in Bessemer, Ensley, Avondale, North Birmingham, and Tarrant City.[4]

In 1925, the Lee Klan sold its headquarters, ironically, to three Jewish businessmen. Almost immediately it purchased for $180,000 the Birmingham Athletic Club, which had ample space for meetings and recreational and bathing facilities for Klansmen and their families. Less than a year later, Lee's leadership sold the Athletic Club for a tidy profit of $20,000 and opted to rent space.[5]

During the 1920s, with television a thing of the future, the Klan supplied many people with opportunities for recreation and entertainment that were otherwise lacking, especially in Alabama's small towns and rural areas. Klan functions and celebrations played somewhat the same role that politics had played in earlier decades. Rallies, barbecues, festivals, and speeches afforded occasions for many in the community—Klan members and others as well, including those who were just plain curious or bored—to get together. Sometimes the point was to celebrate shared values but at other times it was simply to "do something."

Galas and open air celebrations varied from small events to sensational affairs. Modest celebrations took place in Ashland, Wilsonville, Phenix City, Woodstock, Sheffield, Eufaula, and Union Springs, while huge galas occurred elsewhere. Clanton Kluxers initiated 300 men; Huntsville and Sylacauga dens initiated 500 apiece. Talladega hosted a parade of 200 Knights with a concert and minstrel show. Galas in 1924 at Calera and Anniston featured parades, floats, fireworks, a light show, a barbecue, a march by the women's Klan auxiliary, fiery crosses, speeches, and baseball games. Luverne, Florence, Scottsboro, and DeKalb also sponsored massive open air celebrations, but none topped the Lee Klavern's 1923 initiation at Edgewood Park, which included air stunts, barbecue, dancing, swimming, concerts, and five members of the imperial kloncium in attendance as 1,500 new members joined. During this monster event the future U.S. senator and Supreme Court justice Hugo Black joined the KKK.[6]

Klan leaders also sponsored elaborate parades to highlight the regalia, ceremony, tradition, and mystery of the order. Parades came in all sizes. Goodwater and Sylacauga Knights staged a joint parade in 1921 that consisted of only 44 men; at Notasulga only 17 marched. A Eufaula parade, though, consisted of 300 Klansmen, and a march to Talladega involved over 800 robed members. Other parades during the 1920s took place in Avondale, Demopolis, and Huntsville. Close ties between the Birmingham police and the KKK meant that some parades included police escorts.[7]

Initiations gave the Klan ideal opportunities to overawe communities. In 1922 Anniston's Klan held festivities on a large sandbar in Oxford Lake, featuring a barbecue beneath a huge electric cross, parades, and fireworks as 400 men joined the order. A thousand robed Klansmen came to the events on special trains from all around the state.[8] Birmingham initiations were massive affairs. Leaders of the Nathan Bedford Forrest Klavern (figure 4) invited the press and public from around the country to a spectacle at the state fairgrounds as twenty-one mounted Klansmen kept curious spectators at bay. Over 500 "aliens" took their oaths on a cold and muddy field with Joseph Simmons presiding. Big Mule/Black Belt newspapers responded with lavish praise for the secret order. Another 700 men joined the KKK at the Dixie Flying Field. In 1923 the Lee and Forrest lodges sponsored monster initiations that featured Klan bands, barbecues, fireworks, a car giveaway, 3,800 initiates, and an estimated 100,000 spectators from around the South. A year later, five Birmingham klaverns joined at East Lake Park to sponsor the largest single initiation in the Southeast, 4,107 new members, and over 50,000 spectators. The celebration featured a parade through downtown Birmingham of 5,000 Klansmen in full regalia and over a thousand automobiles. Special trains brought Knights from towns around Alabama and from as far away as Indiana.[9]

Throughout the decade, initiations and Klan parades occurred virtually all over the state: in Birmingham, Greensboro, Brundige, Evergreen, and Tuscumbia, in Winston, Franklin, Autauga, and Bibb Counties, and in many other spots.[10] Few rural demonstrations, though, could compare with Lee County's October 1925 "Klan Day" at the East Alabama Fair. Ten thousand spectators, including 2,000 Klansmen, witnessed the "naturalization" of 200 aliens into the society. The gala featured fireworks, two Klan bands, a carnival, races, a 1,500-man parade, martial music, fiery crosses, robed horses, and a bevy of American flags. Alabama grand dragon James Esdale put in an appearance, as did the state's foremost Klan lecturer, W. Earl Hotalen, a Methodist minister. Special trains carried Knights to Opelika from Montgomery, Tuskegee, Notasulga, Sylacauga, Alexander City, Goodwater, Camp Hill, and Dadeville. The following year, Lee County replicated Klan Day, complete with a speech by Earl Hotalen, fifty robed horses, and forty-two additional inductees. Opelika itself, as one awed resident observed, was literally filled with men, women, and children in white robes.[11]

Of course, like other fraternal organizations of the time, the Klan put on galas and parades in order to boost membership. As a result, recruitment speeches were often part of the festivities. In 1921 an Atlanta Klansman espoused white supremacy, immigration restrictions, and a curb on the number of foreign-language newspapers and told crowds in Demopolis and Montgomery that only Protestants really belonged in the United States: "Everyone else is an invited guest." He scored the most points with his listeners, though, when he paid tribute to the original KKK.[12] Speeches were often tailored to local concerns. A Knight speaking in south Alabama de-

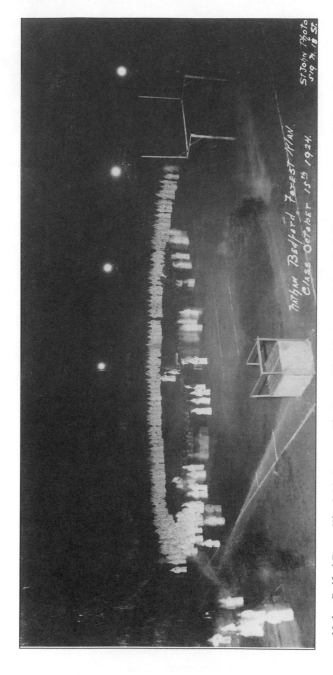

Nathan Bedford Forrest Klan.
Class October 15th 1924.
St John Photo
Jug 7th 18 St.

4. Nathan Bedford Forrest Klan Initiation, 1924. The Forrest Klan No. 60, named for a Civil War general, was one of Birmingham's most powerful and controversial klaverns and was based in the suburb of Woodlawn. Courtesy Birmingham Public Library Archives, Cat. No. 46.32+.

clared that the order was the friend of "good blacks" who knew their place. In Selma, a hooded speaker geared much of his address to the many women present.[13]

CHARITY, EDUCATION, AND LAW ENFORCEMENT

Like other fraternal organizations of the time, the 1920s Klan engaged in charitable activities as a part of its civic program. Most of the charity was aimed at supporting the causes in which many Klan members and their families believed: public education, Protestant Christianity, and patriotic organizations for adults and youth. Blount County's klavern was an especially active leader in providing charity to the people in and around Oneonta. Throughout the 1920s, Knights donated money to hospitals, visited sick children, gave food and clothing to widows, and provided Christmas toys for the needy. Talladega County Knights did the same for Sylacauga and the surrounding area. Clay County and Scottsboro Knights sponsored funerals, the Jack Jolly Klan of Tuscaloosa gave a local den of Boy Scouts $640 to help purchase new campgrounds, and a Huntsville klavern donated $200 for a memorial room at the city hospital.[14]

Private charity was another vehicle through which the Klan demonstrated its vitality and civic-mindedness during the 1920s. Ironically, through its relief efforts, Alabama's KKK functioned somewhat like the political machines of the Northeast that it often railed against. By supplementing meager governmental programs, the secret order provided valuable services while it cultivated significant community support. Sylacauga Klansmen, for example, provided food and money to the family of one local man who had been disabled by acute arthritis. When a Clay County widow and her children took refuge in a storm pit, Klansmen built her a small house. Blount County Knights also helped support widows and their families. In early 1926, Woodlawn's klavern staged a play at the Jefferson Theatre in Birmingham and donated the profits to charity. The purpose of the play, which had a cast of 500 persons, was to "revive . . . [the] Klan spirit" in the community.[15]

The wide variation in Klan activities most likely reflected the diversity of its members, many of whom also belonged to other fraternal and civic lodges. Official Klan sources and at least one Talladega partisan claimed that only "the best people" made up the Alabama Klan in the 1920s—judges, lawyers, doctors, bankers, and ministers. Attorney Ira Thompson saw his role as Crenshaw County's Klan cyclops in the same light as he did his other civic memberships. In addition to being the local Klan leader, Thompson served as the treasurer for a Masonic hall, sat on the board of the Methodist church, and was the captain of the local artillery unit of the state militia. He described his membership, at least until the mid-1920s, as mostly middle-class individuals, with some professionals—doctors, lawyers, teachers, bankers—as well as small merchants and artisans.[16]

Other observers, mainly noted liberals, took a different view of the local Klan. Irving Engel, a Jewish attorney, described the Birmingham Klansmen he saw as members of the lower and working class. Liberal activist Palmer Weber remembered rural Klansmen as mostly poor dirt farmers. Montgomery's Virginia Durr called the KKK "poor country fellows" looked down on as "a bunch of trash, common, low-down people." In truth, the 1920s Klan was as widespread as it was diverse, so that its character depended on where an inquirer looked. Still, the 1920s Klan was certainly more middle class in social origin than later manifestations of the order.[17]

In keeping with its middle-class notions of civic duty, many in Alabama's second Klan placed particular emphasis on the support of public education. At the national level, the KKK tried to purchase two universities and turn them into bastions of Klan education, but both attempts eventually fell through. Oregon Klansmen played a major role in securing passage of a law mandating public school attendance. In Alabama, 1920s Knights advocated merit pay for teachers and manifested a genuine concern for the future of state-sponsored education—a decidedly reform-minded proposition then and now in states of the Deep South such as Alabama. Klansmen also worked constantly for improvements—both in terms of quality and financial support—for schools and especially those in Alabama's poorer and rural areas. The concern for rural white education had, as its important antecedent, traditional average white concerns with being caught in the web of disfranchisement, largely spun by privileged Redeemers at Alabama's 1901 constitutional convention, a web that included literacy, property, and educational requirements for voters. In Alabama as in Oregon, Klansmen were in the vanguard of the movement for a mandatory school attendance law for children between seven and sixteen.[18]

In 1925, Birmingham officials decided to close the city's schools five weeks early because of a shortage in revenue. The crisis furnished a fine opportunity for civic Ku Kluxism. Great Titan Bert E. Thomas, perhaps the most civic-minded Knight in the state, coordinated a series of Klan fund raisers to pay teacher salaries and keep the schools open. The successful fund-raising efforts included concerts by a Blount County fiddler and a traveling quartet. The KKK raised $3,500 from one downtown concert alone.[19]

As admirable as these projects undoubtedly were, some education-minded Klansmen were motivated by more than just a love of learning.

Some Knights supported public education partly because they feared paro-chial education and opposed the "un-American" and "un-democratic" in-doctrination that they associated with Catholic schools.[20] While civic and educational efforts appealed to some Klansmen whose motives were beyond reproach, these activities also struck a common chord among nativists and religious bigots. Support for public education was another way of combat-ing Catholic education, just as efforts at "Americanization" were often im-bued with a dread of immigration, alcohol, political machines, and religions other than Protestant Christianity. Many Protestants harbored a profound fear of a church that they saw as evil, foreign, and menacing to the "Ameri-can" way of life. Klan publications in Alabama betrayed an obsession with so-called aliens. The most intense anti-Catholics forgot that Catholicism was also a Christian religion, in fact, that it was the very mother church from which the Protestant sects had sprung. Many also interpreted "Ameri-canism" in a narrow fashion to include only white Anglo-Protestant cul-ture.[21]

Perhaps one of the greatest ironies of the 1920s Klan was that the same organization that produced some of the worst vigilante violence and may-hem ever seen in Alabama also had a strong element within it that earned a living enforcing the law while another component regarded law enforce-ment as a central part of its civic mission. Many in the revised order saw themselves as the civilian arm of local law enforcement. Indeed, Birming-ham's Klan rolls and official law enforcement membership overlapped sig-nificantly. Police Chief T. J. Shirley (figure 5) was such a satisfied member of Birmingham's Robert E. Lee Klavern that he advised his opposite num-ber in Nashville to organize his own klavern to assist police in enforcing the law. During the Christmas season of 1921, Jefferson County Klan lead-ers volunteered to supply Birmingham with a thousand hooded deputies in order to maintain order. Klan members served as pallbearers at the funerals of several deputies in 1922, and more than one city policeman was impli-cated in Klan floggings. At Brandon, a hundred robed Knights paraded in support of law enforcement and pledged to help officers execute the law. Anniston Klansmen promised to assist local police in an antivice campaign and responded to death threats against their police chief and Governor Thomas E. Kilby by offering to shed blood in their defense. In Talladega, some townspeople welcomed KKK aid to city police during the 1920s.[22]

The line between hooded vigilantism and official law enforcement was sometimes a fine one. The Klan involved itself in law enforcement despite the public condemnation by Imperial Wizard Hiram Evans of "meddling in other people's business" as a "super-government." Evans enjoyed clear authority after 1923 although he was a native Alabama dentist whose elec-

5. T. J. Shirley, ca. 1925. A severe-looking customer, Shirley served as Birmingham police chief during the 1920s and was a member of the local Klan. Courtesy Birmingham Public Library Archives, Portraits.

tion as imperial wizard had been somewhat slyly arranged. Yet in his home state, the KKK often took the law into its own hands. One Klan scholar has noted that most of Birmingham's police officers, "if not all of them," were members of the masked society during the 1920s.[23] Still, despite the ironies, much of the assistance that Alabama's hooded order rendered to constituted authority—both in official law enforcement activities and in extralegal and vigilante campaigns—was consistent with the Klan's conception of its civic duty.

Moreover, most average Alabamians accepted the 1920s Klan in its various roles. It is difficult to exaggerate the extent to which the KKK was an accepted part of community life during the decade. In Atlanta, the KKK purchased a large mansion in an affluent neighborhood to serve as the residence of its imperial wizard. Sylacauga sported a two-story Klan structure downtown, the Gadsden klavern owned a hall on one of its town's most valuable lots, and Birmingham had at least two large buildings that were owned by the Klan.[24] Merchants throughout the state placed Trade with a Klansman (TWK) placards in the windows of their businesses, and the Alabama leadership published a *TWK Monthly* featuring Klan news, editorials, and advertisements. In 1919, the KKK even appeared in an Alabama state college yearbook in the section on student organizations.[25]

Press support for the secret order was also substantial. Until the mid-1920s, Big Mule publishers and editors heartily endorsed the revised Klan. Throughout the decade, Klan advertisements regularly appeared in the *Oneonta Southern Democrat,* the *Selma Journal,* and other Alabama newspapers.[26] Some papers, like the *Prattville Progress,* praised Klan gatherings as "beautiful and interesting," distinguished by "perfect order and good feeling." Klansmen also drew on favorable press when they could, even if it did not originate at home. Bessemer Knights elicited community support by feeding locals a steady diet of right-wing propaganda. They paid for and handed out 500 free copies of the Masons' Washington (D.C.) *Fellowship Forum* each week.[27]

Despite its many civic and educational activities during the 1920s, the KKK was racked by internal dissension from time to time. Like other fraternal organizations, klavern leaders relied on *Robert's Rules of Order* to help maintain decorum, order, and procedure at their local meetings.[28]

GRAND DRAGON ESDALE

As the 1920s progressed, the cloud cover of civic routine gradually parted to reveal a squall of stunning proportions. Initial rumblings appeared in the form of a series of challenges to Alabama grand dragon James Esdale. Many of them sprang from his autocratic style. "There [is] no democracy in the Klan," he was fond of saying, and many in the order agreed with him—at least with respect to life in the Klan under his leadership.[29] Esdale's first important test came in Woodlawn, a typically middle-class suburb of Birmingham. In a series of lightning moves, Esdale shut down the local Klan, deposed its leaders, and handpicked a new slate of officers. The trouble began when Esdale and Woodlawn's exalted cyclops had a political difference of opinion. M. E. Reaves wanted to mobilize the Klan vote in 1926 for Montgomery cyclops Bibb Graves, but the grand dragon favored the more subtle course of just publicizing the colonel's membership in the Klan. Graves was a Montgomery politico who had earlier opposed the Big Mule/ Black Belt coalition and would eventually, as a two-term governor, constitute a progressive alternative to the stagnant conservatism of planters and industrialists. Money was important to the often testy Esdale. Reaves, although popular with his men, was a poor bookkeeper. Only 400 of his 2,700 men had paid their most recent dues, much of which was supposed to go directly into Esdale's pocket. The den had spent $23,000 on a hooded extravaganza—$16,000 more than Esdale had authorized. Finally, the Forrest klavern had failed to pay the rent on its huge new meeting hall.[30]

Esdale moved quickly to discipline the contumacious local. He suspended Reaves, locked up the hall, and seized the unit's charter. Esdale then sent Bert Thomas to the Wahouma den to represent him at a raucous meeting in January 1927. The great titan deposed Woodlawn's officers and temporarily replaced them with a slate chosen by Esdale. Horace C. Wilkinson—Klan politico extraordinaire, former cyclops of the Woodlawn Klan, and an intimate of Esdale's—presented a plan to pay off the local's $21,000 debt with a 7 percent loan. As Thomas and Wilkinson spoke, a phalanx of plainclothes Klan guards flanked them. Despite the show of force, the meeting bordered on open riot, and the crowd repeatedly booed and hissed Thomas's faint praise for their embattled cyclops.[31]

In the interest of democratic decorum, Esdale's envoys allowed the impeached cyclops to speak. Reaves denied allegations of misconduct and mismanagement, expressed pride in his close friendship with the governor-elect, and declared that his upcoming trial before state Klan leaders had been rigged. The Reverend Earl Hotalen gave the meeting some semblance of order by reminding everyone present that the Klan was not the personal property of James Esdale, M. E. Reaves, or anyone else except Jesus Christ.[32]

Soon afterward, the battle ended when Thomas held a second meeting to elect new officers. Just 141 members showed up, but they elected a Birmingham police sergeant as cyclops and named two plumbers, two carpenters, four small merchants, a lumberman, an electrician, a former schoolteacher, and a railroad engineer as their new officers. As Reaves had foretold, a Klan tribunal in Birmingham upheld his suspension, and an imperial kloncium in Atlanta expelled him.[33] The seeds of future discontent, though, were sown by the formation of a second Woodlawn klavern. The unaffiliated splinter, made up of some of Reeves's old lodge, was more militant than most. The rogue den especially disliked attorney Hugo Black because members felt that he was "too soft on nigras and Jews."[34]

Esdale's next headache revolved around plans for Bibb Graves's inauguration as governor. Montgomery's city council had passed an ordinance expressly forbidding the parading of masked Kluxers. Not wanting to parade sans their identity-concealing garb, Montgomery Klansmen faced a tough choice. Attorney general–elect Charlie McCall led the forces within Montgomery's Klan No. 3 who wanted to parade on the capitol grounds, an area under state control. McCall held six degrees, mostly in law, from Georgetown and American Universities in Washington, D.C. The son of a state politician, he had left Alabama for about a decade, first serving in World War I, then attending three law schools simultaneously while holding down a job in the office of the judge advocate general of the U.S. Army. Upon his return to Alabama, McCall joined Montgomery's Klavern No. 3, cultivated a friendship with Bibb Graves, its cyclops, and began to ride the crest of Klan popularity into the attorney general's office.[35]

Cyclops Graves presided over a rowdy meeting to discuss McCall's proposal. Graves's opposition to McCall's idea killed the plan and sparked what would, by year's end, become a conflagration of epic proportions between the two men. Eventually, a compromise was worked out whereby Esdale and Hiram Evans sat with Graves on the inaugural platform.[36]

The security of Klan meetings was an additional problem for Esdale and other Klan leaders. The *Birmingham Age-Herald,* owned and operated by Frederick I. Thompson, a confirmed probusiness conservative, infiltrated several Birmingham klaverns and began publishing details of their meetings. Matters reached a boiling point when Esdale filed suit over a newspaper report that he had personally advocated violence at a Klan meeting and that he had guaranteed immunity for floggers, actions that had reportedly elicited the unqualified sympathy of public officials. Robert E. Lee's cyclops had allegedly echoed Esdale's call for violence.[37]

In the ensuing furor, Esdale filed a lawsuit for $300,000, which Thompson viewed as a compliment. The publisher also leaked plans for a clever defense that entailed summoning every member of the Lee Klavern and thereby making their identities public knowledge. When an inferior court judge ruled that a mass subpoena was permissible, Esdale balked and settled out of court. Thompson sold the *Age-Herald* to Victor Hanson, giving the Big Mule control of four of the state's largest newspapers, but the sale still left him with three large dailies of his own—the *Register* and *News-Item,* both based in Mobile, and the *Montgomery Journal*—as well as his seat on the Associated Press's board of national directors.[38]

An intriguing feature of the Esdale-Thompson fracas was the participation of Charlie McCall. The new attorney general had caused something of a minor scandal himself when, as one of his first official acts, he tried to make James Esdale an assistant on his staff. The grand dragon relieved what promised to be a hot controversy, though, when he removed his name from active consideration. Still, McCall lent the prestige of his office to the KKK as he joined Esdale's libel suit against the *Age-Herald*.[39]

Before abandoning the matter, Jim Esdale fired a few parting shots at the Big Mules and their press allies. In a broadsheet sent to every Klansman in Alabama, Esdale denounced Frederick Thompson and Victor Hanson as "leeches . . . , parasites . . . , [and] crooks" who catered to a readership of "suckers." "Let 'em write and let 'em howl," Esdale advised his faithful associates. "Nobody believes the wild yarns they are flaunting. . . . They don't believe the tales themselves but they think [they] . . . should make an easy seller for the newspaper. . . . [The Klan] furnishes a means for a lot of hicks to make a living running a newspaper who would otherwise have to go out and toil for a . . . living like all honest people do."[40]

If Esdale was given to hyperbole, he was at least correct about one thing. The *Age-Herald* had indeed infiltrated the city's lodges and was regularly reporting Klan proceedings to a curious public. Klan leaders eventually banished at least three informants from their ranks, but by that time considerable damage had been done.[41] Details about Klan procedures concerning violence were made public by the informants as well as by other Knights who had left the order. The picture that emerges does much to dispel the common notion that violence was practiced by only "a few bad apples," aberrant extremists who were stimulated by sadism and addicted to the power inherent in dealing the lash to hapless victims. Only a few 1920s Klansmen personally participated in the violence, but much evidence suggests that many others in the order condoned, tolerated, and encouraged these acts. Most disturbing, perhaps, is evidence that Klan leaders commonly authorized vigilante terror.[42]

Other problems loomed for the Alabama Klan by the middle of the 1920s. Rumors circulated that a rupture had developed between James Esdale and the state's most visible Klansman, Governor Bibb Graves. The two clashed first over the admission of A. G. Patterson, president of the Public Service Commission, into the secret society. Graves had vehemently resisted Patterson's induction largely because Patterson, like Graves, aspired to be governor, but Esdale had bulldozed Patterson's initiation anyway. Graves reportedly responded by withholding state patronage to any close Esdale client. He was also allegedly unhappy with Esdale's expulsion of M. E. Reaves as cyclops of the Woodlawn klavern. After the ouster, Graves salved his friend's wounded pride by appointing him a county license inspector. Esdale also managed to irritate the more affluent members of Birmingham's Lee Klavern by scolding them for their lack of economy. Comparing the klavern's performance with that of a frugal lodge in Tuscaloosa, Esdale rebuked the Lee membership for their expensive luncheons and recommended that they bring brown bags to their meetings like their plain Tuscaloosa brethren.[43]

A Big Mule press, joined at the hip with the Black Belt oligarchy, exploited these rifts whenever it could. Pouncing on the Esdale-Graves feud, Grover C. Hall, the editor of the *Montgomery Advertiser,* claimed that the more sophisticated members of Alabama's KKK, repelled by Klan lawlessness and sickened by its violence, wanted to remove Esdale as grand dragon. "Good Klansmen," according to Hall, were disenchanted by Esdale's promotion of vigilantism and his general "lack of political acumen, savvy, and sophistication." "They do not think Jim is quite big enough for his responsibilities," Hall wrote. "His public statements usually make judicious Klansmen grieve and injudicious non-Klansmen roar with laughter."[44]

Still, Esdale managed to weather these storms because of his order's success in civic, patriotic, and educational endeavors and its generally good relationship with Alabama's public. Patronage was a valuable ally in Esdale's struggle for survival. Like many other fraternal groups, the Klan functioned as a job clearinghouse for Knights, their families, and their friends. Small merchants sometimes joined in pursuit of increased business; others merely sought a paying position. As the Alabama Klan increased its political power during the 1920s, the possibilities for government jobs broadened. The search for patronage became an important part of Klan life within many Alabama klaverns.

The patronage over which Graves and Esdale squabbled was the engine that drove the Klan political machine. Judges, solicitors, county prosecutors, sheriffs, deputies, local and state police, jury commissioners, the members of personnel boards, and the vast majority of town, city, county, and state officials were either outright Klan members or came under the order's thumb through fear, sympathy, political expedience, or some combination of these. Organizations such as the state police—founded with extensive powers in 1919 during a period of postwar anxiety over immigrants, blacks, and unionists—provided ideal sources of patronage, since they were supervised solely, and directly by the governor. The Klan's masterful control of jobs and patronage led the *New York World* to describe Alabama as absolutely "Klan-ridden." Charles Feidelson of the *Nation* named Alabama "the most completely Klan-controlled state in the Union . . . , a veritable Eden to the Knights." South Carolina's *Columbia Record* declared Klan control in Alabama so extensive as to make America ripe for a fascist dictatorship.[45]

During the 1920s, Kluxers all over the state inundated the governor's office with patronage requests. A state Klan notable later estimated that 95 percent of Bibb Graves's official appointments went to Klansmen. Klaverns routinely asked for, and received, hiring preference when Graves was governor. Springville's Klan No. 30 not only asked that its members get state offices but expressly listed St. Clair County rivals who were to be passed over. An Autauga den did the same. Barbour County Knights asked that one of their own be made superintendent of highways in their county. A Birmingham Klan judge recommended a Walker County Knight for state policeman, while Graves gave many Jefferson County appointments to Klan supporters.[46]

Conversely, patronage could be withheld to demonstrate the organization's power. J. A. Thornhill, a Decatur Klansman, found himself passed over for appointments as probate judge and county license inspector and finally demanded that Graves refund his investment. "Frankly governor, this is getting serious with me," Thornhill wrote. "No man would have done all that I did for you [in 1926] without an understanding. . . . you made me promises and . . . confirmed [them]. . . . Now that you are through with me, why not pay me?"[47]

Klan friendship and influence was clearly evident in the case of C. C. McClurkin, a Birmingham police sergeant and M. E. Reaves's successor as Woodlawn cyclops. In May 1927, city officials suspended McClurkin when they learned that he had been convicted of a statutory offense in another county twenty years before. A Klan-controlled civil service board, though, rescinded the suspension and reinstated McClurkin without even looking into the case.[48]

The civic, educational, and progressive aspects of life within the klaverns of the revised Klan were important elements of the order in Alabama but were only part of the story. Some civic-minded and educationally inclined Klansmen also turned their thoughts to ideas of patronage, and some became interested in political reform. The price of reform in Alabama, though, was rampant violence. Bibb Graves eventually posed a progressive alternative to the inert conservatism of the planters and industrialists. Hugo Black later became one of the leading liberals in the U.S. Senate. Yet some of Alabama's rank-and-file Klansmen were more concerned with the violent regulation of community morals and mores than with political reform. The price—a high one for Alabama—was something to which men like Graves and Black needed to reconcile themselves if they wanted to promote their progressive agendas.

3

The Moral and Religious Klan

It is difficult to determine exactly where religion left off and morality began for the 1920s Klan. The order was an exclusively Protestant organization and, accordingly, religion played an intrinsic role in revised Ku Kluxism—more so in the more religious southern states such as Alabama than in the strong Klans of the Northeast, Midwest, or Far West. Yet most Klan conceptions of conventional morality also derived from the group's understanding of evangelical Protestantism and its dictates on the subject. Like the morality-minded reform wing of the Progressives, which concerned itself with temperance and the movement for prohibition, many in Alabama's second Klan regarded alcohol as an immutable evil that jeopardized home, hearth, community, even personal salvation.[1] Such a peril, for some 1920s Knights, had to be eradicated. As with other religion-based crusades, the severity of the perceived threat decreed that virtually no means to combat it was off limits.

The line between civic activity and the sometimes violent policing of Alabama's community morality was similarly indistinct. Concern over community morals sprang from the culture of evangelical Christianity. Anxiety about the moral state of a believer's neighbors had long figured in doctrines and practices, especially those of Calvinism.[2] Many in the second Ku Klux Klan saw their civic duty as encompassing the policing of morals in a very basic way. A number of Alabama Knights sincerely believed that they had the right, indeed the duty, to uphold community standards on ethical issues just as they had the civic duty to help enforce secular laws. Moral principles, moreover, had as their source a higher basis than mere man-made laws and statutes. Again, for believers with such a mindset, violence was not out of bounds. It is perhaps just as important to remember, though, that the conduct of the moral watchdogs was essentially consistent with the activities of many of the civic-minded Knights who donated flags, conducted patriotic celebrations, and "encouraged" immigrants to find work to help the war effort. Both types of activity, at an elemental level, were concerned with active, hands-on citizenship that would remedy the shortcomings and preserve the virtues of the respective communities in which Klan members lived.

MAINLINE PROTESTANTISM

The Klan was perhaps most self-conscious when members attempted to curry support from Alabama's Protestant community. As the self-appointed guardians of Protestantism against the evils of Roman popery, alien Judaism, and internal moral decay, Alabama Kluxers enlisted the aid of pastors and Protestant congregations in their mission. One preferred way of doing so was to deliver donations to local churches in conspicuous ways. Typically, thirty or forty Klansmen in full regalia would enter a church in the midst of Sunday proceedings, march down a center aisle, and hand the pastor a note of support and an envelope stuffed with an undisclosed amount of cash. The Kluxers would then turn and exit as silently as they had come.[3]

Knights replicated this feat at Protestant churches—most of them mainline denominations—throughout the state during the early 1920s. In 1922 and 1923, Montgomery's active and civic-minded Klavern No. 3, led by politicos Bibb Graves and Charlie McCall, made a number of these visits. Klavern No. 3 delivered devotions to the Southside Baptist Church, the Second Baptist Church, the Protestant Church Council, and the Alabama Bible Society. In each of these cases, the presiding minister gratefully accepted the money and expressed his church's support and appreciation for the work and existence of the sheeted society. Similar scenes took place in Huntsville, Lineville, Wilsonville, Troy, and throughout Jefferson and Shelby Counties. On several occasions, grateful pastors even led Klansmen in singing.[4]

During the mid-1920s, these activities continued (figure 6). Clay County Klansmen made public donations to Baptist, Methodist, and Southern Methodist churches. The Andalusia den bestowed almost $1,600 on fundamentalist minister Bob Jones, a reactionary Klan sympathizer from Montgomery, when he visited Covington County. A Tuscaloosa preacher earned a $50 devotion for his 1925 sermon praising the Klan's stand on law enforcement, and Gadsden Kluxers gave one local minister an envelope stuffed with money. He was so moved by the act that, then and there, he publicly acknowledged his own membership in the secret order. A 1925 Klan parade

6. 1920s Klansmen with the Cross and Flag. 1920s Klansmen often prominently displayed their two favorite symbols, the cross of Christianity and the American flag. Courtesy Birmingham Public Library Archives, Cat. No. 25.39.

through Huffman, Trussville, and East Lake culminated in worship services at the Alton Methodist Church. Klansmen descended en masse on the South Avondale Baptist church to show support for a beleaguered pastor there. In Sylacauga, Knights sponsored a long series of religious tent revivals spanning eleven different meetings. The Klan's state newsletter also served as an employment service that matched pro-Klan preachers with like-minded congregations.[5]

Klan support for Protestant congregations was successful to the point of reciprocity. A recent biographer of Hugo Black claimed that nearly every Protestant minister in Alabama belonged to the KKK during the 1920s—almost certainly an overstatement. Yet many did belong. A Black Belt newspaper echoed the praise of one Birmingham preacher who lauded the 1920s Klan and claimed that his father had been a member of the Reconstruction order. Baptist pastor Hugh Tully of Wylam added that he had joined the 1920s order because "everyone of importance was a Klan member." On one rare occasion, Attalla Klansmen crossed the color line to donate money to black Baptists attending a conference. The gift left the delegates, by all accounts, "popeyed."[6]

Still, Protestant support for the Klan and tolerance of diversity seldom went hand in hand. At his many public lectures, Montgomery's Bob Jones spewed prejudice along with biblical quotations and pro-Klan rhetoric. Earl Hotalen, Alabama's foremost Klan preacher, sometimes regaled receptive crowds with his proclamations about the essential issues of the 1920s cultural wars: "Klancraft versus Roman priestcraft and Niggercraft."[7]

THE MONITORING OF MORALITY

In addition to buttressing community Protestantism, many klaverns in Alabama posed as the preservers of community morality in their local communities. They accomplished this task largely by preying on the insecurities of average Alabamians who felt threatened by the myriad of postwar challenges to traditional values. A Klan warning posted throughout Mobile today serves as an effective index of the breadth of postwar fears about the assault on conventional morality. Mobile residents awoke one morning in the summer of 1921 to find the following Klan notice tacked to trees, telephone poles, and billboards throughout the old port city: "Law violators! This is the first and last time that we will warn you! You . . . had better leave at once . . . taxi drivers, gamblers, thieves, loafers and any street mashers, bad women, shinny dealers and all violators of the law. . . . This is no negro whipping organization, but should an occasion arise, be ye well assured that we will not hesitate. . . . Mobile County must be clean."[8]

Some Klansmen punished their fellow Alabamians for deviating from norms relative to marriage and the family. For example, a Birmingham mob beat one man because he refused to remarry his former wife. Another band handcuffed, blindfolded, and beat a Bessemer miner because he had legally separated from his wife. In June 1922, robed nightriders attacked a married Lewisburg couple for sharing a physician's home with him. Klansmen assaulted the husband with a blunt instrument as he slept, leaving him unconscious in a pool of blood, and choked his wife until she also blacked out. A year later, Klansmen whipped a Pratt City barber who had remarried and was refusing to support his first wife. In 1924, masked men lashed a Phenix City man who was having domestic problems and a Walker County farmer who had made "improper advances" to a series of local women.[9]

Such activities proliferated throughout the decade. In 1925, Anniston Kluxers kidnapped a man because he and his wife had separated. In nearby Gadsden, a mob lashed a black man for his domestic troubles. Shelby County Knights were not as lenient; it took far less to provoke their ire. Twelve noose-carrying men chased a Shelby County farmhand fourteen miles in the dead of night because he had earlier cursed in front of a woman. The would-be victim, a young man, eventually outdistanced his older pursuers, perhaps saving his own life.[10]

Prostitution constituted another major moral concern for many Alabama Knights and their supporters throughout Alabama's local communities. Morality enforcement, particularly the policing of vices such as liquor and prostitution, consumed the energies of more than a few Kluxers. Talladega County Knights flogged one elderly farmer for allegedly housing prostitutes, making moonshine, and hosting dances. Three automobiles filled with sheeted Kluxers pulled up to the home of a Birmingham woman, charged her with adultery, and forcibly carried away her male visitor—presumably for a beating. Frequent cross-burnings and floggings also put the Klan message on vice across in Sylacauga, Anniston, Gadsden, Lincoln, Childersburg, and in Bibb and Shelby Counties.[11]

In January 1925, Klan chapters around the state launched a campaign to close suspected houses of ill repute. Within one week, masked Kluxers had burned crosses in front of ten Birmingham homes thought to be houses of prostitution. A raid on a black Birmingham brothel resulted in a special prize when nightriders discovered a former policeman enjoying the sexual favors of the black women within. Robed raiders equipped with a truck and several curtained cars brandished pistols and shotguns and fired volleys into the night air. In Birmingham, particularly brazen Kluxers issued a general invitation to the press to accompany them on their antiprostitution crusade; a reporter for the *Birmingham Age-Herald* accepted the invitation. Within a short time, seven reputed cathouses had closed their doors and a host of madams had left the city for more congenial climes. W. B. Cloe, Birmingham's public safety commissioner and a well-known ally of the Klan, informed the press that he welcomed hooded aid in the police battle against sexual immorality.[12] Knights replicated Birmingham's antivice campaign in Sylacauga, Bessemer, Montgomery, and other towns throughout Alabama.[13]

In their eagerness to control morality, Klansmen got so carried away at times that they censured a variety of other "wrong-doers." During one spree that had originally taken a house of prostitution as its target, Knights burned a cross at a neighbor's home because he had hired a black maid. Other masked Kluxers raised a flaming cross in the yard of B. B. Dorrough, a paragon of service to the Irondale Baptist Church, because he had publicly opposed a Klan-inspired teenage curfew. The disconsolate Dorrough, an avid admirer of the KKK, comforted himself by refusing to believe that the cross-burners were really representative of the order.[14]

While prostitution occasionally seized center stage in the Klan's morality play, alcohol was readily seen as the number one culprit and threat to traditional values. Temperance and Ku Kluxism overlapped in Alabama, as elsewhere, and prohibition groups were generally among the order's most visible and vocal supporters. Liquor consumption was particularly a problem for many members of the Klan because it not only threatened traditional morals and community values but also smacked of Catholicism, southern European immigrants, and comparable foreign threats to the fabric of traditional old-stock America.

In Alabama, violation of prohibition probably engendered more Klan violence in the name of morality than any other offense. In 1924 hooded mobs closed down twelve roadhouses in Jefferson and Shelby Counties in a stunning campaign, and Eastlake Kluxers nearly beat the operator of a barbecue stand to death for being considered "a menace to the community." Knights also flogged a Lawrence County planter and the managers of Thompson's Restaurant on Birmingham's southside, most probably for liquor violations.[15]

During the middle 1920s, Klan strength continued to manifest itself in convulsive bursts of intolerance designed to regulate societal morality. Many of the morality campaigns derived from a twisted perception of the traditional Protestant mandate to propagate the faith, and they sometimes required the acquiescence or even the active participation of law enforcement officers. For example, in 1925, Ku Klux bands closed down a number of taverns along Montgomery Highway in Jefferson and Shelby Counties through a series of threats, cross-burnings, and other sensational acts of intimidation (figure 7). The brazen conduct of disguised Kluxers suggested that they felt they had little to fear from constituted authority as punishment for their extralegal activities—and they were right. Local authorities,

7. Meeting of Robert E. Klan No. 1 and Cross-burning, 1920s. Birmingham's Lee Klavern was the oldest and most powerful klavern in the country and at one time boasted 10,000 members. Courtesy Birmingham Public Library Archives, Cat. No. 816.13-79.

who said they had wanted to "clean up the places anyhow," publicly endorsed the raids.[16]

Such encouragement likely fueled additional campaigns. In 1925, a hundred Klansmen raided a Brookside dance hall just south of Birmingham in order to end the "immorality." On this occasion, several sheriff's deputies actually accompanied the Klansmen and arrested four persons for violating prohibition. The only noticeable protest came from the pen of E. T. Leech, editor of the *Birmingham Post,* who presumed "of course . . . that all of this raiding is done by those who have never tasted a drink, never carried a gun and never broken a law." In Etowah County, Knights contributed to the moral policing by lashing two whites for bootlegging; Lee County Kluxers destroyed a number of stills.[17]

Klansmen patrolling vice eventually broadened their sights to include related offenses against notions of evangelical Protestant morality—variations on a theme. Hooded Klansmen burned crosses at an exclusive lodge on Shades Mountain, as well as at a private Birmingham residence, because dances were being held inside. Throughout the decade, Klansmen raided teenage couples in parked cars and provided license tags to police and parents in Troy, Gadsden, and along Birmingham's scenic Red Mountain, a popular "lovers' lane."[18]

THE CHINESE CAFÉ RAIDS

The most dramatic morality raids of the 1920s, though, were aimed at Birmingham's Chinese restaurants for their violation of the liquor law—although nativism played a part as well. The Chinese café raids, which began in January 1926, provide an intriguing example of Klan activity because they illuminate not only morality regulation and nativism but also internal schisms between politically oriented Knights and more zealous Ku Kluxers.

W. J. Worthington, a real estate tycoon and exalted cyclops of the Avondale KKK, masterminded the Chinese raids. Shortly after New Year's Day 1926, a dozen armed Klansmen invaded three downtown restaurants, declaring that they had arrived to search for liquor. An off-duty deputy sheriff, holding an arrest warrant, accompanied the masked party, which was led by Worthington. Gun-toting Kluxers bullied patrons, frisked men and women alike, and even forced patrons to submit to breath tests. At the end of the evening they took six "prisoners" to the county jail. The escapade came to an abrupt halt, though, when Chief Deputy Henry S. Hill tore up the warrants, released the prisoners, and declared the whole thing to be a huge mistake.[19]

While the raids rapidly became a cause célèbre in Birmingham, they also showed that the Alabama Klan, despite its religious and ethnic homogeneity, was far from being of one mind. The first noticeable rift formed between Sheriff T. J. Shirley and his chief deputy, Klansmen both. While Deputy Hill disowned the raids and called for the badge of the officer who had taken part, Shirley responded by publicly praising the raiding Klansmen.[20]

The Chinese proprietors helped create the next Klan fissure by hiring the Lee Klavern's top two legal guns, law partners Hugo Black and Crampton Harris. Two skilled Klan attorneys (George Frey and circuit judge Hugh A. Locke) opposed Black and Harris in court. Locke, a future gubernatorial candidate and a notorious segregationist, was particularly outspoken. The legal split reflected a rapidly growing rivalry between the powerful Lee Klavern and other units within Birmingham.[21]

A third rupture developed between Klansmen in the city government and the rogue Knights from Avondale. While James Marion "Jimmie" Jones, Jr., Klansman and president of the city commission, righteously condemned the Chinese cafés, he also encouraged his police chief to arrest the self-appointed moral police squad, including the county officer. Jones not only resented the county's and Worthington's encroachment into what he felt was his proper jurisdiction, he was also embarrassed by the Avondale interloper, who seemed to relish his newfound notoriety. When questioned about the cases, Worthington refused to talk, saying he could not betray Klan secrets. Later, Worthington tried to make Fred McDuff, Birmingham's police chief, drop the cases and urged defendants to keep mum. Worthington boasted that he carried a list of Methodist stewards who regularly met women other than their wives in private booths at the Chinese cafés. The "booths" were actually small rooms closed off by heavy curtains that afforded a good deal of privacy.[22]

While the *Birmingham Post* criticized the KKK, and the Avondale klavern's secretary publicly denounced the raids, the trials of W. J. Worthington and his accomplices went forward, making choice theater in Birmingham's prevailing prejudices. Attorney George Frey objected to the swearing in of one Chinese manager because he was not Christian; he declared that the swearing "meant nothing at all to him." Frey suggested that "Chinamen" had to swear by a white rooster or a totem pole before their oath would have the same force as that of "an ordinary person." Judge Hugh Locke, also engaged in defending the Klan, portrayed the café raiders as courageous citizens who had merely helped enforce the prohibition law. In the end four Klansmen were found guilty of disturbing the peace. Worthington and W. W. Israel were sentenced to ninety days in jail and $100 fines, the off-duty deputy to thirty days and a $100 fine, and the youngest raider to a suspended sentence. Locke vowed to appeal, though, and three months later, in an unusual case in which he did not utter a single word of defense, gained Worthington's acquittal. Cases against the other three defendants were soon dropped.[23]

Alabama's KKK usually got what it wanted in court eventually, even if it occasionally lost the early rounds of legal battles. Its success showed how hard it was to fight the order in court when much of the public's heart was obviously not in the fight.

WOMEN, MORALITY, AND THE KLAN

During the Chinese café raids, women were handled as roughly as men once they were suspected of breaking the community's moral code. In fact, much of the decade's concern with moral issues was tied to questions regarding the changing role of women in society. The stance taken on women by Alabama's 1920s Klan was curious and complex. In general, Alabama Klansmen felt that it was more important to maintain women's traditional roles than to heed traditional southern notions about chivalrous behavior. In other words, a number of Alabama Klansmen found it acceptable to violate the most sacred tenets of southern chivalry—that is, they beat women—in order to preserve traditional morality and gender roles for women. In this respect, the Klansmen who physically disciplined women had far more support and cooperation from other, Klan-sympathizing women than their male class "betters" did. The beating of women to compel submission galled the Klan's patrician political foes beyond endurance, for it brutalized their own most basic understanding of gender and societal roles. Women, whether or not they were formally affiliated with the Klan, seemed far more likely to indict the fallen of their own sex than the traditional, patrician males who offered the KKK its principal political opposition.

Ample rhetoric and lofty platitudes about the sanctity of white womanhood, in other words, did not prevent Klan terrorists from applying the lash to women. In fact, many Alabamians, male and female alike, demanded traditional behavior from women. Women who failed to comply placed themselves at serious risk. Separate sheeted mobs nearly beat Jefferson County and Walker County women to death for being too friendly to blacks. In 1918, Klan notices appeared in Alabama warning "loose women" not to tempt billeted soldiers into sin. Lewisburg Kluxers almost choked a woman to death for violating local mores.[24]

The concern with female morality crossed the color line: black women and white women were equally subject to regulation by a whip. Many of the assaults had sexual overtones. On a number of occasions, mobs of howling men stripped female victims naked before flogging them. In Bessemer, five masked Klansmen, later joined by others, disrobed and whipped a black woman for reasons that she "knew well enough." Walker County Knights undressed and flogged two sisters and their dates at the Stanford Mines near Parrish in 1926. Hooded Klansmen later burned one of the victims' homes because she had again taken up dating after being legally separated from her husband. The Walker mob's members were not wholly without chivalry, though: they whipped the weaker sex with switches and their male escorts with heavy wooden clubs.[25]

Still, Alabama's early KKK actively tried to recruit women as well as keep them "in their place." In 1923, a Louisiana Klan representative and his wife traveled to Montgomery to recruit members for the Ladies of the Invisible Empire. Bert E. Thomas, grand titan of the Alabama Klan, also traveled the state in 1923, trying to organize a Klan auxiliary for women. Atlanta's Joseph Simmons organized Birmingham women into a branch of the Kamelias, while Hiram Evans sponsored the rival Alabama Women of the KKK, a group that included the Ladies of the Invisible Empire, the League of Protestant Women, the American Women, and the Puritan Daughters.[26]

Male members of the Alabama Klan often worked closely with WKKK members, Kamelias, and other female supporters of the Klan—some of them the wives of Klansmen—as they sought to keep tabs on community morals. Klan women (figure 8) acted as the "eyes and ears" of local klaverns in targeting persons who later suffered the fiery cross or lash as punishment for their moral transgressions. Two Birmingham women, both of them Klan wives during the 1920s, later recalled that everyone in their circle knew who was and was not a member of the order. The KKK, a force for good in the community according to both women, punished people for drinking, adultery, and nonsupport.[27]

EARLY FORMS OF OPPOSITION

Eventually, violence, intimidation, and morality regulation led to various forms of opposition during these years. One Confederate veteran quit the Clay County Klan soon after joining because he despised its hypocrisy. Upon resigning, he noted with disgust that local Klansmen "were worse than the people they were whipping."[28]

Although armed opposition was rare, it did occur—sometimes with startling effectiveness. When a party of thirty-eight nightriders lit flaming crosses and tried to batter down the door of a Winston County farmer in 1925, he shot through it, killing a member of the masked mob. A Decatur

8. Klanswomen Attending a Rally, 1924. In some Alabama communities the Klan relied on women to watch for and report on local violations of traditional morality. Courtesy W. Stanley Hoole Department of Special Collections, The University of Alabama.

madam drove one Klan mob away by brandishing a shotgun as she shouted the names of several of the sheeted men who had been her customers. A black farmer in Cherokee County shot and killed a sheeted Kluxer who broke into his home; the farmer later surrendered himself to authorities at Centre. In Walker County, a coal miner dispersed twenty robed Knights by shooting two of their party but was himself seriously wounded. In 1926 a masked mob attacked a sleeping black woman in Blount County who had been accused of adultery. Her husband fended off the Klansmen and shot one in the hand, but his wife was killed in the ensuing hailstorm of gunfire.[29]

Several other incidents occurred. A twelve-year-old boy in the little town of Girard shot two Klansmen, killing one, as they beat his grandfather. Because the area had been the site of frequent Klan outrages, newsmen suggested giving the boy a medal for his heroics. The wife of the slain Kluxer and his mother both admitted that their loved one had been a member of the secret order, but the new widow consoled herself by reasoning that her husband had "died for his country" and "a good cause." In Pike County, an accused wife-beater turned the tables on visiting Klansmen by offering to "beat [the] hell out of the biggest man" in the group. Seeing no takers, he grabbed a porch chair and wrapped it around the head of the largest Kluxer he saw. Hooded men bolted in all directions. As soon as he came to, the unlucky Knight tendered his resignation. Nevertheless, such episodes were few and far between. Most victims simply endured their punishment and kept quiet.[30]

Perhaps more effective than physical opposition was the Klan's own ability to self-destruct. Several scandals during the period began to form small cracks in the moral foundation of the order. At the national level, a power struggle rocked the organization in 1923. Hiram Evans filed suit against Joseph Simmons, who countersued against Evans's election as imperial wizard. Simmons lost three staunch allies when Elizabeth Tyler left to remarry, Evans fired E. Y. Clarke, and Evans's publicity agent killed his personal attorney. By 1924, Evans had eased Simmons into retirement by offering him a $12,000 annual pension, a lump sum of $146,500, and the meaningless title of "emperor." The former wizard retired to Luverne, Alabama, where he died an invalid in 1945, but the feud laid bare a vulgar concern with profit at the highest levels of the organization.[31]

Other incidents also cast aspersions on the Klan's claims to moral purity. Simmons developed a fairly public drinking problem. Police arrested Bessie Tyler and E. Y. Clarke, drunk and half naked, in a hotel room. Clarke's wife sued for divorce, and authorities later convicted him of transporting whiskey and violating the Mann Act. The attempt by Alabama grand dragon

James Esdale to seize records from a Memphis klavern resulted in an intra-mural Klan shootout. Esdale, a proud and often irascible man, experienced a variety of problems, internal and external, during his long stewardship of the Alabama KKK.[32]

Perhaps the most disturbing aspect of the mania for morality regulation within the 1920s Klan was not its hypocrisy, its authoritarian nature, or even its violence but its deliberate and planned nature. After leaving the order, a number of former Kluxers reported that Klan leaders had regularly called for violent action against the order's enemies. F. M. Vann, exalted cyclops of the Roanoke den in Randolph County, resigned from the order because of his revulsion for the violence. Afterward he supplied information about Klan procedural policies on vigilantism to his brother, who was the county solicitor. According to the former cyclops, physical punishment usually be-gan with a neighborhood rumor of some perceived act of moral misconduct. Once a report had been made to the local klavern, the affected cyclops was expected to relate the charge to higher officers within the Klan. When the decision to use violence had been made, state officers relayed their de-cision back to the local cyclops. Local Knights would first "spot" the victim, locating him physically and making notes as to his habits. They would then import Kluxers from a neighboring den to carry out the actual flogging. The system provided built-in alibis for local Klansmen who might other-wise have become suspects in an ensuing investigation.[33] Vern M. Scott, a Talladegan who personally observed the 1920s Klan in action, described essentially the same process in that county.[34]

Procedures most likely varied from locality to locality, but in several re-spects the accounts are similar. The frequent violence of Alabama's Klan reflected planning and deliberation as opposed to spontaneity, as did its fo-cus on particular subjects at particular times and places: slackers, violators of prohibition, adulterers, prostitutes, and the like. Second, the Klan's success in blocking conviction of its members indicates that higher-ups knew how to cover up for their members—and knew what needed covering up—even if they had not known about the violence in advance and had not participated in planning it.

4

The Racist and Nativist Klan

The second Klan's attempt to regulate Alabama's societal morality derived much of its impetus from the order's exclusively Protestant orientation and a decidedly xenophobic impulse. It was a xenophobia broadly understood: a fear of things foreign that included people who were different racially, religiously, and ethnically as well as morally. The revised Klan thus shared something basic with its Reconstruction predecessor. Although World War I and 1919 clearly exacerbated xenophobic fears and thereby created a new situation and new imperatives for the second Klan, the basic urge to quash things foreign had roots at least as far back as the Reconstruction KKK and its campaign against freed blacks and Republicans of both colors. Much of the Reconstruction period in Alabama, and in the other southern states, involved efforts to recover political and social control from what were perceived as foreign and outside elements.

RACE

By the turn of the century, race relations had sunk to new lows throughout the country. Atlanta experienced a race riot in 1906; two years later one occurred in the northern town of Springfield, Illinois. After 1900, lynching was reserved almost exclusively for blacks (during the 1890s in Alabama, one in every three lynch victims had been white).[1] "Scientific racism" was generally accepted as wisdom. It acted as a positivist buttress that both reinforced and engendered racist attitudes and behaviors across the United States. Doctors, scientists, criminologists, statisticians, and psychologists north and south of the Mason-Dixon Line agreed that blacks were biologically "weaker," a burden to themselves and society because of their "simple minds," "primitive urges," and "lack of [sexual and moral] self-control." These attitudes found expression, not in the newsletters of racist groups on the lunatic fringe, but in respected and prestigious outlets such as the *American Journal of Psychiatry,* publications written by Cornell University faculty, and books sponsored by the American Economic Association.[2]

Given the national complexion of racism, it is not surprising that there was violence and prejudice against blacks and other biologically "inferior" groups considered by science to be something less than human. Nor should it be shocking that whites, in the region where most blacks lived, moved toward disenfranchisement and rigid segregation once it was clear that the federal government meant to offer no obstacle.[3] By the turn of the century, Henry Cabot Lodge's "force bill" had been defeated in the U.S. Senate. The U.S. Supreme Court, in a series of rulings, had declared that it intended to interpret the Fourteenth and Fifteenth Amendments in only the narrowest and least intrusive fashion.[4] Meanwhile, the Spanish-American War and the annexation of Cuba, the Philippines, and the Sandwich Islands had led the nation as a whole, for the first time, to sympathize with the southern position on the racial question. The *Brooklyn Eagle,* for example, advocated repeal of the Fifteenth Amendment and black suffrage because, it reasoned, "human nature is a higher constitution than the Federal compact. . . . [and] White control is a better preservative of government and civilization than Constitutional amendments, which threaten to ignore or cross it."[5] Disenfranchisement, the entrenchment of Jim Crow, and, indeed, the founding of the Ku Klux Klan, took place within the warm and nurturing climate of sympathetic national opinion.

Like its precursors in Alabama, the revised KKK spent much time and energy defining its enemies. Like its earlier and later counterparts, too, the second Klan made African Americans its foremost enemy. Joseph Simmons led the way by defining white supremacy as an immutable doctrine dictated by nature. From his imperial headquarters in Atlanta, he urged Alabama Knights to preserve racial integrity from the "foul touch of a lower stock" and to keep Caucasian blood and civilization pure.[6]

While southern Klansmen expressed considerable antipathy for Catholics, Jews, immigrants, and moral nonconformists, race was still central for most of them. In other sections of the country, Catholics received most of the Klan's attention, but in Alabama, and perhaps in much of the South, the race issue predominated. During the 1920s, southern blacks suffered—not to the extremes of Reconstruction—but still a great deal.

While Alabama Klansmen did attack whites—twelve in Birmingham alone in one four-month stretch—blacks were especially at risk. All kinds of behavior merited penalties. In Ensley, a mob flogged a black doctor for treating white female patients. Twelve Birmingham men beat a black porter for associating too closely with white women. Klansmen also made threats against the Alabama Power Company because blacks and whites were riding together on Montgomery's streetcars. City police denied that they had taken part in the masked beating of another Birmingham black despite evidence to the contrary.[7]

Economic motivations played an important role in Alabama racism. Poor and working-class whites had long feared economic leveling with blacks. In fact, some historians have cited this fear as the single greatest factor retarding the ability of white folk to sustain a challenge to entrenched white power in the Black Belt and industrial cities of Alabama.[8] During the 1920s, economic tensions persisted between average whites and blacks. In Selma, Klansmen who were most likely poor and working-class whites pressured blacks to give up their jobs in construction and farming. In 1924, Birmingham Klansmen lashed the white owner of a department store for hiring a black to head the carpet department.[9] Another Jefferson County mob flogged a black for doing his factory job too well.[10]

In a fundamental sense that superseded even class, racist Klan violence mirrored the state as a whole. Lynching had been a virtual cottage industry in Alabama during the 1880s and 1890s. During the early 1900s, the number of lynch victims fell, but blacks were targeted more exclusively than ever before. African Americans habitually succumbed to other forms of violence as well. Alabama prison guards flogged black inmates so viciously that they sometimes died.[11] Whites who associated too closely with blacks were also at risk. In 1921, a Birmingham mob mercilessly beat two men and a woman for being too friendly to blacks. City detectives dropped the case almost immediately—testimony to the closeness of the Klan's ties to the police.[12]

Postwar racial tensions fueled much of the violence. In one 1919 spree, Montgomery vigilantes lynched four separate blacks in twelve hours. A pro-Klan grand jury refused to return any indictments, though, prompting Judge Leon McCord, a patrician, to speak out against the evils of hooded violence. McCord declared that although there had been an obvious need for the KKK during Reconstruction, "there is no need now for the Ku Klux."[13]

During the first few years of the Klan's reincarnation, a trickle of such opposition to the order emanated from the business and legal communities, local governments, and civic associations; more came from Catholics, Jews, and northern critics.[14] Alabama blacks, though, resisted the modern Klan from the moment of its revival in 1915. Blacks had been the primary victims of the original Klan's atrocities, and for many, the painful memory of those days lingered. The revised Klan made it clear that blacks were still enemy number one. Imperial Wizard Hiram Evans repeatedly told hooded audiences that "all good things" throughout history had come from the white race. NAACP leaders realized that the new Klan wanted to curb black voting, preserve and control black labor at low wages, and violate constitutionally guaranteed civil rights. In Birmingham, black newspapers cautioned their readers against being taken in by the some of the more innocuous aspects of the new Klan. The main goal of the second Alabama Klan, they warned, as with its predecessor, was to ensure white supremacy at any cost.[15] One black kidnap victim did more than merely warn others; he shot two masked Klansmen before escaping during a struggle over a pistol in the backseat of a car.[16]

Alabama's revised KKK met virtually any gesture toward racial equality with violence and intimidation. In 1921, Mobile Knights warned black doctors that they had just three days to post the word "colored" on their shingles and stop treating white patients. Talladega mob members beat the president of the Alabama Negro Medical Association into senselessness, luring him from his home with a bogus emergency call. They left him to flounder in the woods for hours until an elderly white farmer helped him back to town.[17] Two black ministers received mail bombs in 1921. Nine Klansmen visited the editorial offices of the black *Baptist Leader* and warned newsmen to stop printing criticism of the Klan. The KKK took out a full-page advertisement in the *Birmingham News* to oppose spending taxes on black schools and, on the same night, staged a 300-car parade and burned an enormous cross on the top of Red Mountain.[18]

True crisis arrived in 1923 when federal officials announced that black physicians would begin working at Tuskegee's new veterans' hospital. Alabama Kluxers demonstrated their disapproval in a spectacular display that was backed by many others in the white community. Fifteen hundred Knights descended on Macon County to march, burn crosses, and intimidate the large black populace. Governor William "Plain Bill" Brandon asked the White House to help Alabamians keep the facility white. There was a thinly veiled threat of Klan violence against Robert R. Moton, the principal of the Tuskegee Institute, for siding with the black doctors, but he responded by threatening to lobby for a federal antilynching bill.[19] Faced with this prospect, the elites backed down.[20]

Flight, although the most common response by blacks, was itself dangerous. A Sheffield mob lynched two blacks in 1919 because they tried to flee north instead of staying to do farmwork for miserable wages in Shelby

County. Near Grimes, a Houston County mob shot a black man as he waited on a platform for a train to take him north. In 1920, 800 Klansmen marched through Calhoun and Talladega Counties to intimidate blacks into staying in Alabama. Still, 400,000 blacks left the South during World War I, many in response to just such Klan actions. Louis Leibold of the *New York Herald* interviewed fleeing Alabama blacks and estimated that 25,000 had left the state after the war, mostly to seek better pay and to escape epidemic violence by the Klan.[21]

From time to time, local authorities arrested Klansmen. Still, convictions were difficult to obtain in state courts because approval, support, and fear of the secret order were widespread.[22] Outright injustices occurred often. Klansmen flogged a sixteen-year-old black because he had fought with a white boy, and when the teen complained to Montgomery police, they arrested him for assault.[23]

African American leadership in Alabama was sometimes less than forceful in countering the hooded society. When a quiet Avondale minister received a Klan delegation warning him to leave town, Oscar Adams, the black publisher of the *Birmingham Reporter*, expressed doubt that the KKK had been involved and criticized the preacher. Adams, who can best be described as an accomodationist and at worst as the puppet of racist whites, did little to combat Klan depredations. He refused to speak out against the Alabama KKK, most likely in order to preserve a comfortable and profitable relationship with Birmingham's white power structure. When an Alabama mob lynched an interracial couple, Adams condoned the act by writing, "While the means of correction are unlawful, the spirit behind the act must be considered righteous and altogether pleasing."[24]

There were other apparent anomalies. In at least one instance, African Americans revealed just how thoroughly Klan violence had permeated both southern society and their own consciousness. Two Montgomery County blacks mimicked the Klan by whipping a black man who had separated from his wife and afterward warned their victim to leave the state unless he wanted to be castrated or killed.[25]

ETHNICITY, CREED, AND ORGANIZED LABOR

Obviously, blacks held no monopoly on Klan vengeance during the 1920s, but they continued to receive much attention, especially in the distinctive South. The South had long considered racial control the raison d'être of the Klan. The 1920s klaverns in other regions were freer to focus on Catholics, Jews, or immigrants because they did not carry the South's burden of racial conflict or its black population. In Alabama, Catholics, Jews, and immigrants were foreign elements and threatened the white-dominated culture in many of the same ways that blacks did.

Recent immigrants were readily identifiable as outsiders in Alabama, foreigners who were put at risk by the pronouncements of Klan leaders like Hiram Evans. The imperial wizard described immigration as "poison" and told his minions that the "time has come when the villains who have . . . led their countries to despoliation" should not be allowed to emigrate to America. He also nativistically attacked Catholics and Jews, "masses of ignorant, superstitious, religious devotees."[26]

Some Alabama Knights responded by terrorizing any immigrants they could find. Their activities in this regard overlapped with, and mimicked, those of a number of the patriotic societies associated with World War I. One masked Birmingham mob abducted the Rumanian owner of a confectionery and lashed him at gunpoint. Later, three hooded men flogged a German tailor and warned him to keep away from native women.[27] In 1923, seventy-five Kluxers took part in a march through "Dago Town," the West Blocton section of Bibb County. On another occasion, in order to protest bootlegging, Kluxers burned a cross in Bibb County's "Little Italy," a poor area occupied by immigrant coal miners. Every Italian head of household armed himself and mustered in the town square to await a Klan attack, but it never came.[28]

Alabama's religious, cultural, and ethnic homogeneity fueled such tendencies. In fact, 1920 Alabama was home to fewer than 18,000 immigrants, a mere 1.2 percent in a total population of 2.35 million. One-third of Alabama's sixty-seven counties, some with populations as large as 80,000, had fewer than 20 foreign-born residents.[29]

The revised KKK also targeted Jews. Initially, Joseph Simmons claimed that his order was not anti-Semitic, only "pro-Christian." In 1923, Hiram Evans dropped pretenses when he declared that the assimilation of foreign Jews had given America colic and that Jews were conspiring to "set up Jewland in America." Reams of Klan propaganda denounced Jews for instigating racial tension, plotting to overthrow all "Gentile" governments, colluding with Communists, and controlling every newspaper in New York.[30]

Anti-Semitism was quite prevalent among northern Knights, but Jews in Alabama also fell victim to the Klan in a number of ways. Irving Engel, a Birmingham attorney and later a Jewish leader of national repute, reluctantly moved to New York when he realized that Klan ascendance had made it almost impossible for him to win favorable verdicts in the city's courtrooms. Birmingham Knights burned crosses in front of Jewish homes, conspired to put Jewish-owned stores out of business, and had at least one Jewish comptroller fired. Talladega Kluxers boycotted Jewish-owned stores and ran one Jew out of town because he tried to marry a Protestant. Etowah County Klansmen terrorized a wealthy Jewish merchant until he surrendered the lease to his house and actually contributed money to the KKK.[31]

The situation in Montgomery was complicated by the fact that, in an older town, a powerful Klan presence shared physical space with Black Belt political power and a significant Jewish presence. Hooded Montgomery Knights burned five crosses in January 1925, one in a Jew's front yard. In response, Montgomery mayor William A. Gunter heatedly denounced the "disaster to the whole community" and declared that, regardless of race or creed, everyone in his city deserved to be treated fairly. Nevertheless, the KKK continued to organize boycotts of Jewish-owned businesses such as the Southern Dairies.[32]

The most celebrated example of anti-Semitic persecution during the 1920s came in the case of Chester Bandman, a Jewish high school principal in Birmingham. In early 1925 local Klansmen, afraid that Protestant children might fall under the spell of a Jew, lobbied to have Bandman fired from Woodlawn High School. When persuasion and threats failed, the Knights demanded that members of the city board of education dismiss Bandman. Finally, the Klan made life so miserable for Bandman that he resigned in 1926.[33]

Bandman seems to have been one of those rare educators who was universally loved by students, colleagues, and parents. The senior class bought him a watch and invited him back for commencement. Over 300 Woodlawn residents gathered at the local Presbyterian church to hold a rally on his behalf. The Woodlawn Parent-Teacher Association and the entire high school faculty backed him. Hugo Black called him "the best principal in the city" and said he would be pleased to have Bandman direct a school attended by his own children. The pastor of Woodlawn Presbyterian bitterly condemned the forced resignation: "All through my many years in public life, I have never met a whiter, cleaner, purer, and safer man than Chester A. Bandman—a man whose unswerving devotion has saved hundreds [of students] . . . from despair. . . . Professor Bandman may not be a Christian . . . but I dare say he is even better than 75 per cent of those [in] . . . our churches. . . . There are no charges, [against him, only] resentment on the ground that he is a Jew."[34]

Despite this vigorous show of support, in the end the Klan had its way, and Bandman left town. Maurine Slaughter, vice president of Woodlawn's senior class, recalled that area Kluxers ordered her not to invite Bandman to graduation. The KKK's reason was that Bandman had allegedly forbade the New Testament from being read during chapel period, but Slaughter, whose father was a Woodlawn Knight, explained that the excuse was a mere pretext.[35]

The *Memphis Commercial Appeal,* which received the 1923 Pulitzer Prize in journalism for its editorials criticizing the Klan, lectured Alabamians on the Woodlawn episode.

> Life was too short for Mr. Bandman and he went to Pittsburgh where he will continue teaching. . . . Funny about running Jews out of educational work. God Almighty directed the hands of Moses, a Jew, when he wrote some of the books of the Old Testament, which Christians profess to revere. David was a Jew, and so was Solomon, and they were scholars and prophets. . . . More of you might die of consumption and dyphtheria . . . except for the work of Koch and Metchnikoff. . . . Then there is Einstein. . . . People ought to be logical even in their hates. If people do not want Jews as educators they ought to refuse to accept any contributions that Jews have made toward education.[36]

Catholics also received attention from the revised KKK in Alabama during the 1920s, but in the state as a whole they were not persecuted more than other minorities. In Alabama, blacks remained the foremost Klan target. Still, during the 1920s anti-Catholicism was a strong new issue for the KKK. Joseph Simmons set the tone for his fellow Alabamians here, too, by denouncing Catholics as the explicit enemies of his new organization. As in his references to Jews, Simmons refused to admit that his order was "anti-Catholic," preferring the euphemism "pro-Protestant." The Alabamian Hiram Evans, who was his successor, and official Klan propaganda, were more blunt. They accused the Pope of making secret treaties to bring on World War I, of opposing republican forms of government, of controlling the press, and of stockpiling arms for an imminent Catholic takeover of Washington. Klaverns sponsored female lecturers posing as "escaped nuns" to relate ghastly tales about the carnal lust of priests and the evils of parochial education. The "nuns" displayed leather bags, which Catholics supposedly used to cremate the infant products of priest and nun sexual unions in the basement furnaces of their churches.[37]

Anti-Catholic rhetoric translated into specific acts of violence, intimidation, and bigotry at the local level. When Alabama Klansmen were able to lay their hands on Alabama's few Catholics, they often did so. In 1916, hooded Knights sent shock waves through Birmingham's small Catholic community by burning the Catholic church and school at Pratt City. Klansmen also encouraged people to boycott stores with Catholic owners or employees, pressured businesses to fire their Catholic employees, and protested the construction of at least one church simply because it was Catholic.[38]

Birmingham's 1917 city elections were particularly marred by anti-Catholic prejudice. Five city commissioners were elected with the strong support of the True Americans, a group prominent during World War I that repudiated Catholics, Jews, and other "foreign elements" in American society. In the race for the commission presidency, a physician in East Lake defeated the Episcopalian incumbent largely by accusing him of being a "tool of the Roman Catholic Church." In the midst of the campaign, Sidney J. Catts, a Baptist preacher and the governor of Florida, came to Birmingham to warn of the Catholic menace. A number of local Protestants swapped stories about the sexual immorality of Catholic clergy, stockpiled arms, and uttered prohibitions against lay reading of the Bible.[39]

In 1919 Thomas E. Kilby won the governorship largely by appealing to trenchant anti-Catholicism among his fellow Alabamians. Two years later, a Birmingham jury dominated by Klansmen acquitted a Knight who had confessed to killing a priest in broad daylight. In 1921, Governor Kilby fired his popular state police chief for conducting unauthorized liquor raids in Mobile. The underlying issue for many, however, was the Catholic faith and culture. One Mobile Protestant blamed the firing on the city's wet Catholic populace, "the people doing all they can to destroy our public schools and Protestantism from the world." "You have simply disgraced our Protestant Church," he informed the governor, "Never has there been such a frame-up of dirty Catholics and whiskey-heads before. I am tired of seeing my people treated by this horde of foreigners as if we were human dogs. . . . We are on the eve of a revolution in this country."[40]

The Klan fed on such narrow cultural and sectarian prejudice. On one occasion, twelve sheeted Mobile Knights raided a Catholic convent and playground, terrorizing a number of small children, who mistook them for ghosts. Soon after the raid, two brothers burned a Klan cross in front of a Catholic church at nearby Oakdale while services were under way inside. Kluxers burned five other crosses in Mobile on the same night in what smacked of an organized campaign of terror.[41]

In perhaps the most dramatic of these instances, twenty masked and robed Klansmen kidnapped Pearce DeBardeleben, a wealthy Sylacauga Catholic, took him to an isolated wood, and flogged him unmercifully. During the beating, they informed their victim that he was a threat to community morals for boasting that he could date any man's wife simply by offering her a box of candy. The Knights then gave the man ninety days to sell his drugstore and leave Talladega County. Initially, DeBardeleben refused to speak about the assault, but he eventually told how Klansmen had stripped him, tied him to a tree, and beat him with leather straps until they broke his jaw, turned his face into a bloody pulp, and knocked out most of his teeth. Talladega County's sheriff recognized that the Klan was responsible for the flogging, as did ambitious Birmingham attorney Horace C. Wilkinson. The Klan's real purpose, Wilkinson told a Justice Department official, "was to run all Catholics and Jews out of Sylacauga." Despite a spirited effort, Wilkinson lost a $250,000 lawsuit against the local Klan. Although it failed, the lawsuit was an innovative attempt to hit the hooded society in its pocketbook, a tactic that eventually succeeded in the 1980s. Ironically, Wilkinson later played a leading role in the KKK, charted its political strategy, and thrived as an anticorporation demagogue pitted against the state oligarchy.[42]

Anti–Catholic feeling was a function of Alabama's extreme homogeneity. Alabama was an exceedingly homogeneous place in virtually every respect except race. In 1920 the state was home to 2.35 million people, fewer than 62 percent of whom were white. Still, of these whites, the overwhelming majority were native-born, rural, and Protestant. Almost 99 percent of the state's population was native born, 78 percent lived in rural settings, and 96 percent were Protestant. Moreover, the majority of Alabama's half million urban residents could be found in just three cities: Birmingham, Mobile, and Montgomery. Almost 100,000 Alabamians lived in the state's medium-sized cities (those having populations between 10,000 and 25,000 people). A quarter of the Alabamians classified as "urban" by the 1920 census actually lived in small towns with between 2,500 and 10,000 residents. Catholics accounted for only 3.4 percent of the population. Jews were even scarcer, comprising fewer than 1 percent. Over 84 percent of the state's religious residents were either Baptists or Methodists. During the 1920s, out of almost 1,000 churches, Alabama had 119 Catholic churches and 21 Jewish synagogues.[43]

The second Klan's anti-Catholicism set it apart from its Reconstruction predecessor, but the issue is not clear-cut. Religious bigotry during the 1920s is arguably consistent with the original Klan's all-consuming racism. At its core the Reconstruction KKK opposed those who constituted an outside threat to the sanctity of regional solidarity—namely black and white Republicans. The 1920s Klan also opposed anyone perceived as disrupting status quo—not only blacks but also Catholics, Jews, immigrants, independent women, moral nonconformists, and unionists. At a fundamental level, the targets of both the Reconstruction and 1920s Klan were "outsiders" to most white Alabamians. They gravely threatened the ethnic stability of a region that had considered itself under siege since at least 1861.[44]

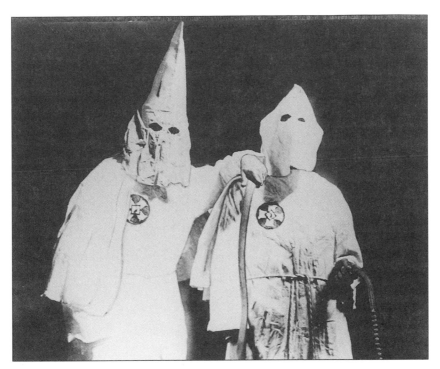

9. 1920s Klan Enforcers with the Tools of Their Trade. The weapons used by Alabama Klansmen included leather belts, rawhide whips, cat-o'-nine-tails, sticks, canes, clubs, baseball bats,
brass knuckles, and, on some occasions, even automobile fan belts and running boards. Courtesy Birmingham Public Library Archives, Cat. No. 816.13.79.

The relationship between the revised Klan and organized labor touched
on such exclusionary themes. Labor embraced far more recent immigrants
in its ranks than most other organizations in Alabama—and as such had a
greater percentage of Catholics and Jews than the rest of society.

Early on, some Klansmen and their leaders used violent means to combat
organized labor. Kluxers intervened in a June 1918 Mobile shipyard strike
to cane a union organizer, who later disappeared under mysterious circumstances. Also in 1918, Kluxers defused a Birmingham steel mill strike by
kidnapping a union leader. Three years later, hooded thugs abducted an AFL
labor organizer from a Mobile train and flogged him into unconsciousness.[45]
During a 1922 strike, Klansmen lashed two white railroad men in Tarrant
City, a Klan stronghold just north of Birmingham, and two black railroad-
ers in Montgomery. When the daughter of one elderly victim came to his
aid, his robed assailants beat her as well (figure 9).[46]

Elements of organized labor recognized the Klan hand behind such repression. Alabama's chief labor organ, the *Birmingham Labor Advocate,* blasted the KKK's "flaming cross and tar barrel" and sardonically advised the city to level its courthouse to make room for the KKK. In 1921, twenty-seven union locals denounced Klan parades collectively. The next year, in a move that showed just how fast local law enforcement could move when it felt obliged to, deputies arrested three black miners for sending a forged "Klan" threat to a promanagement deputy.[47]

Yet the Klan's relationship to labor during these years was complex. Klan leaders and union leaders often found themselves on the same side of the political fence when it came to combating the planters' and industrialists' stranglehold on state politics. During the 1920s, the Knights joined unionists, farmers, women, temperance groups, and churches to combat the Big Mule/Black Belt coalition—sometimes with a good deal of success.[48]

5

The Political Klan

In many ways, the political split that eventually manifested itself in Alabama—between pro- and anti-Klan factions—could trace its lineage to deep and abiding divisions within the state. For years a coalition of privileged Black Belt planters and their industrialist allies in Birmingham and Mobile had had an iron grip on state politics. Challenges from poor whites, sometimes with black allies, periodically threatened patrician control over state politics but never for very long. Black Belt whites, through a combination of force and fraud, exercised absolute control over the large black vote in their counties from Redemption in 1874 to the disenfranchisement constitution of 1901. Afterward, a malapportioned legislature helped perpetuate their disproportionate influence in state politics, especially legislative politics. The Big Mule and Little Mule allies of Birmingham and Mobile, respectively, accepted malapportionment largely because it guaranteed them, as coalition partners, a prominent place in state politics; accurate representation of their relatively heterogeneous ethnic, religious, and working-class populations would have been riskier. The coalition—variously known as the Bourbons, the Redeemers, the patricians, the oligarchy, the bosses, and so forth—favored the maintenance of a strict status quo that perpetuated its domination of politics, labor, race, and economics until the racial crises of the 1960s.[1]

Alabama's political split was largely sectional.[2] Oligarchical power rested in the fourteen Black Belt counties, which had large black populations and fertile black soil that formed a band from east to west across the southern half of the state. The planter-industrialist alliance of course also included the industrial and commercial counties of Jefferson and Mobile. Challengers to the alliance—whether in the form of Reconstruction Republicans, 1880s

Greenbackers, or the Populists of the 1890s—centered in the white hill counties of north Alabama and also the Wiregrass region of eleven counties in the southeastern corner of the state. These dissenting counties were the same regional areas that had opposed secession and had sided with the Union during the Civil War. The poor whites of north Alabama, although numerically superior to the patricians, repeatedly experienced electoral defeats because the oligarchy manipulated and controlled the black vote (the black vote was counted "in" and counted "out" as the need might arise) as well as the legislature. The Bourbons were also able to inflict defeat by skillfully using the race issue to persuade many poor whites to forsake their class interests (and a potential alliance with poor blacks) for the sake of white solidarity.[3]

In actual numbers, the Black Belt's 567,795 residents were badly outnumbered in 1920 by their north Alabama hill country and Wiregrass antagonists, whose counties, together, accounted for a million residents. Because of malapportionment, Jefferson, the most populous county in the state, had only one state senator; nevertheless, it did not push for reapportionment. Although Birmingham's industrialists ostensibly had little in common with the Black Belt, the two groups actually both opposed higher taxes, labor unions, and political change.[4]

OSCAR UNDERWOOD AND THE YOUNG HUGO BLACK

It quickly became apparent to many that the revised Klan's appetite for state and local politics was, perhaps, as consuming as its affinity for violence. Alabama's new KKK meant to continue the varied political activism that the order had practiced during Reconstruction. No longer the Democratic tormentors of Radical Republicans, the 1920s KKK had a new political agenda: to speak against the entrenched oligarchy on behalf of average Alabamians who had never been adequately represented by the planter/industrialist clique. In 1920, the KKK backed Lycurgus Breckinridge Musgrove—a millionaire coal operator, Klansman, and "fanatical prohibitionist" from Jasper—against a pillar of the oligarchy, incumbent U.S. senator Oscar W. Underwood (figure 10). Musgrove, who was reputed to be the richest man in Alabama, profited from a powerful but temporary coalition of women, organized labor, farmers, evangelicals, prohibitionists, and the KKK that showed best in north Alabama and the Wiregrass.[5] His campaign featured diatribes against "demon rum" and Catholics. With the support of figures such as American Legion colonel Harry M. Ayers, the Baptist editor of the *Anniston Star,* Musgrove ran a shockingly close race, losing 69,000 to

10. Senator Oscar W. Underwood, 1920s. Underwood served as Klan enemy number one in Alabama until his political retirement, an event for which the hooded machine took credit. Courtesy Alabama State Department of Archives and History.

61,000. In fact, Musgrove might have defeated Underwood had not a second prohibitionist candidate split the dry bloc by polling 26,000 votes.[6]

Four years later Musgrove again opposed Underwood, this time for presidential electors in Alabama. Bibbs Graves, a Klansman, army colonel, and American Legionnaire, ran Musgrove's campaign. William Jennings Bryan endorsed him, and reactionary Montgomery minister Bob Jones canvassed the state on his behalf. Graves, a veteran opponent of the oligarchy, himself later served two terms as Alabama governor, allied with labor, and ushered in a program of reform that threatened many of the most conservative values of the state's entrenched Democratic elite. Bob Jones, a well-known friend of the Klan, denounced Underwood's supporters as "the whiskey people, the Roman Catholics, and the lawless foreigners," but Musgrove was unable to run a close race. The KKK split its vote between Musgrove and a Jefferson County candidate, and the patricians retaliated with the lethal charge that forces "from outside of Alabama" were actually directing his campaign.[7]

At the local level, the KKK backed a 1923 measure to make Winston County's revenue board appointive rather than elective so that Republicans could not serve on it. Winston Kluxers even went so far as to threaten a local editor for opposing the bill. Florence Knights warned city commissioners to stop collecting street and school bonds despite the order's professed love for public education. Sheffield voters defeated a Klan-backed candidate for city commission, but in Birmingham, the KKK was so powerful that membership was a virtual prerequisite for employment as a policeman, a judge, or a local official.[8]

A legion of aspiring politicians such as Hugo Black, Horace Wilkinson, Bibb Graves, Charlie McCall, Hugh Locke, Ben Ray, George Frey, A. G. Patterson, Richard Rives, Walter Brower, and Cooper Green rushed to become members of the secret order. At the state level the KKK championed U.S. senator J. Thomas Heflin, a virulent racial and religious demagogue, part clown and part deadly serious segregationist, who had once enforced his own understanding of Jim Crow by gunning down a black passenger on a streetcar in Washington, D.C.[9]

In Alabama and elsewhere some worried that, as a result of its growing political power, the Klan was moving beyond the pale of law and order. Northern editors pressed Governor Thomas Kilby for a formal condemnation. Unlike Heflin, Kilby was not a Klansman, yet he still wished to avoid alienating the powerful organization. His reticence, while probably an astute move politically, did nothing to retard pro-Klan sentiment in Alabama and earned him the scorn of several observers. One disgusted Alabama native lambasted the governor as "pretty small fry" and "a jellyfish."[10]

Like Kilby, a number of politicians feared Klan retribution at the polls, but hooded politics hardly confined itself to the ballot box. "Politics," especially during these years, needs to be construed as more than voting or electoral maneuvering. Consider, for example, the October 1921 trial of E. R. Stephenson, a Birmingham preacher known as "the marrying parson." Stephenson shot and killed a Catholic priest in broad daylight, confessed to the crime, and nevertheless escaped conviction. A member of the local Klan, Stephenson was outraged when his daughter married a Puerto Rican paperhanger. Stephenson went to St. Paul's Cathedral and quarreled with the officiating priest. A fistfight ensued. Sometime during the dispute, the parson shot the priest three times, killing him instantly.[11]

The Stephenson trial quickly became a political and media circus. Local Klan groups hired Hugo Black, a brilliant young attorney who later became a Supreme Court justice. In 1921, though, Black, himself a Klansman, made the Puerto Rican's color, nationality, and religion prime issues in the murder trial. Black dimmed the courtroom lights to accentuate the groom's dark complexion, insinuated that he was partly black, and had jurors examine his skin coloring, fingernails, hair texture, and eyes. When the Puerto Rican protested that he was white and of Castilian descent, Black sardonically agreed that he had, indeed, "descended a long way."[12]

The trial quickly became entangled in city politics. Birmingham's incumbent commission president pandered to local prejudices by charging that his election opponent was "the candidate of the Roman Catholics." The exploitation of religious bias disgusted some national observers and gave Birmingham one of its many black eyes. A New York correspondent described the city as "a cesspool of religious bigotry, cultivated by ambitious ward politicians and coined into dollars by shrewd persons of the Simmons-Clarke-Tyler type."[13]

After deliberating for just four hours, the Stephenson jury reported a unanimous verdict of not guilty. Though few Alabamians voiced any complaint, former governor Emmett O'Neal spoke out. O'Neal, a representative of Birmingham's industrial interests and a longtime opponent of mob violence, condemned the city's "odious religious bigotry" and declared that Alabama was a barbarous place if murder could be excused whenever the victim was not a Protestant. In the trial's aftermath, it was learned that the KKK had raised a fund to defend Stephenson and that the jury's foreman and the city's police chief were also members of the secret order. Despite the tawdriness of the trial and the injustice of the verdict, opposition to the Klan remained at a marginal level in 1921 because the victim, a Catholic, had been an outsider well on the periphery of Alabama society.[14]

J. D. DOWLING AND THE 1924 NATIONAL DEMOCRATIC CONVENTION

Ironically, the most serious early blow that the Klan received, and one that certainly injured it politically, came in reaction to an incident in which Klansmen probably did not participate, namely the flogging of J. D. Dowling, the Jefferson County health inspector. On 17 May 1922, nine men abducted Dowling from his Birmingham home, lashed him at gunpoint, and stranded him, "barefoot, bleeding, and exhausted," in an isolated area.[15]

Reaction to the assault was unprecedented in Alabama. Although many Alabamians had been flogged by the Klan prior to the attack on Dowling, their cases had received scant attention from police, elites, and the media. During the year-long controversy following Dowling's attack, though, authorities arrested nine dairymen and plumbers who had been distressed by Dowling's strict enforcement of the health code. In the interim, most Alabama elites assumed that the Klan was behind the assault and directed the lion's share of their displeasure toward the secret society. Elites felt that the KKK had gone too far in flogging Dowling. He was not a black, a poor white, a Catholic, a Jew, or a recent immigrant; he was himself a member of the elite, a well-to-do Protestant physician who held a number of public offices. Dowling was well connected to Birmingham's business and civic leadership. Respectable Alabamians were repelled by the idea that Klan violence might extend to upper-class natives such as themselves.[16]

Birmingham's press, various civic associations, and elements of the political community rebelled against the Klan. Discontent gradually spread across the state. The *Birmingham News,* the quintessential Big Mule mouthpiece, called the Dowling incident "an unspeakable crime . . . , the most dastardly outrage in the history of the city," and offered a $250 reward. Another Big Mule organ and erstwhile supporter of the revised KKK, the *Birmingham Age-Herald,* declared its opposition to the order. The *Birmingham Reporter,* the city's main black newspaper and an instrument of white elites, deplored the assault and offered $3,000 in reward money. The Civitans followed with $500. Prominent citizens—including two judges, two former city commissioners, public health officers, and the president of the Birmingham Civic Association—condemned the attack. Some urged voters to reject Klan-backed candidates at the polls. Even Governor Kilby was moved to offer a reward. Victor Hanson's *Birmingham News* and *Montgomery Advertiser* noted that there was a fundamental distinction between the attack on Dowling and previous Klan attacks on "helpless Negroes and a few whites of no standing . . . , people of no special importance."[17]

Virtually every business and civic association in Birmingham spoke out against the assault: the Rotarians, Kiwanians, Chamber of Commerce, Junior Chamber of Commerce, American Legion, Exchange Club, Retail Credit Men, the League of Women Voters, and the Community Chest. Most placed the blame squarely on the Ku Klux Klan. A leading banker organized a Law and Order League to oppose the Klan. Former patrician governor William D. Jelks headed a Committee of Twenty-five to assist the city with law enforcement and recommended that Klansmen be flogged themselves if necessary. The pastors of the Southside Baptist and First Methodist churches also publicly opposed the secret society. Only the *Gadsden Journal* dampened the reaction by criticizing Birmingham's power structure for being "derelict and shameful" when a poor white or a black was victimized by the Klan.[18]

Legally, the Dowling episode turned out to be a disaster. After the dust had settled, two of the nine defendants won outright acquittals. A year later, authorities dropped the charges against the seven remaining defendants. The disappointing legal results should have been no surprise, though. Most Alabamians, even elite Alabamians, did not yet oppose the Klan's intrinsic ideas. For example, L. L. Gwaltney, the progressive editor of the *Alabama Baptist,* repeatedly stumbled on the Klan issue. He defended the KKK or suggested that the best way to rid Alabama of the Klan was first to abolish the Catholic Knights of Columbus. Congressman Samuel Hobbs, later a Dixiecrat and White Citizens' Council leader, opposed the 1920s KKK politically but insisted that it still had "good intentions." Overt press support from the *Centreville Press,* the *Selma Advance,* the *Abbeville Herald,* and other newspapers sustained the secret order.[19]

Yet despite its legal insignificance, uproar over the Dowling incident had serious political repercussions. The Birmingham Bar Association denounced the flogging and sent a questionnaire asking every prospective candidate for city office to declare any connection with the Klan. The bar also asked the city commission to pass an antimask law against the order and sent its questionnaire to the chief of police and the county sheriff to learn whether their officers were Klansmen. After early rumors that the commission would easily pass the mask ordinance, it unanimously rejected the measure and passed laws against flogging and kidnapping instead. Former Birmingham police commissioner Arlie Barber denounced the KKK and its candidates for city office. At one stormy three-hour commission meeting, hooded leaders imported a Baptist minister to plead their case. He defended the Klan, declared that it was "no nigger-whipping organization," and called it "the best friend" southern blacks had ever had.[20]

State legislator George P. Bondurant and former U.S. senator Frank White led the anti-Klan fight for the bar. Bondurant asked the 100 Klansmen who attended the commission meeting to unmask their order voluntarily. Himself no friend to the secret society, Bondurant had told Klan recruiters to go "to hell" when they asked him to join the order. White, a veteran member of the patrician coalition, took an even more aggressive tack by assuring Kluxers that Birmingham whites could "control the Negro without your help." White further threatened to make war on the hooded order. He also blamed the KKK for bringing flogging to a city that had allegedly never known such violence. Within days, the ambitious Horace C. Wilkinson spearheaded an effort to impeach the whole city commission for its failure to pass the antimask ordinance.[21]

Criticism of the Klan came from virtually every corner of elite white Alabama. Mobile and Huntsville passed antimask laws as their civic groups declared a crusade against the Klan. A Eufaula celebration featured warnings to the KKK from a Barbour County judge and the city's mayor; a Jasper newspaper compared Klan floggings to the misguided autos-da-fé of religious fanatics during the Reformation, and a Wilcox County editorial compared Klan sermons on law and order to "a skunk lecturing on sweet innocence." State legislators passed laws against lynching, whitecapping, and deputy sheriffs who surrendered their prisoners to vigilantes.[22]

Perhaps no two Alabama cities reacted to the Dowling episode more strongly than Montgomery and Selma, regional seats of Black Belt political power. Montgomerians organized a secret masked organization to combat the KKK called the Invisible Jungle, Knights of the Tiger's Eye, as city officials ripped down Klan warnings and passed their own antimask law. Montgomery's police commissioner ordered his men to arrest robed Knights on sight. Selma's chamber of commerce and American Legion denounced the Klan; Selma's city commission also passed an antimask ordinance. In criticizing the revised KKK, a Selma judge praised the original Klan for its ability to control and retain cheap black labor rather than force it to flee.[23]

While Reconstruction elites had winked at Klan excesses, in the New South 1920s businessmen, the firm political allies of patrician planters, shuddered at the thought of what Klan mayhem would cost them in dollars. While they no doubt appreciated the sentiment behind hooded action against organized labor, for instance, they realized that the spectacle of grown men parading around in sheets and whipping people was not likely to attract outside investment. The order was never definitely tied to the Dowling incident, but business and civic backlash targeted the KKK almost exclusively. Elites held the Klan accountable for breeding an atmosphere of vigilante violence and also feared that the order had crossed the line in punishing "one of them." By 1924, business elites and civic leaders joined to make up a strong anti-Klan faction in Alabama. Because of growing Klan aspirations and the predominance of big business, the fight for control of the state promised to be waged in the political arena between the oligarchy and the upstart KKK.

At the state and national level, Oscar Underwood, Alabama's senior U.S. senator, provided leadership for the planter/industrialist coalition. In Boston, Cleveland, Houston, and New York, and throughout Alabama, Underwood took pains to denounce the secret society. "I am not afraid either in a political or a personal sense of the Ku Klux Klan," he declared. "The organization is a national menace. [Both the Klan and] the United States of America cannot survive. Between the two, I choose my country."[24]

In June 1924 the quarrel between Underwood and the Klan reached a climax at the national Democratic convention in New York City. Forney Johnston—Birmingham attorney and son of an Alabama governor—nominated Underwood for president by dramatically attacking the KKK. Underwood and Johnston made Ku Kluxism the central issue of the convention when they proposed that the national party adopt an anti-Klan plank as part of its official platform. Kluxers responded by dubbing Underwood the "Jew, jug, and Jesuit" candidate. The convention deadlocked for a record 103 ballots, and fistfights erupted in the aisles. Tex Rickard, the famous boxing promoter, later remarked, "Of all the fights I ever pulled off in the old Garden, that was the best draw I ever saw."[25]

All twenty-four Alabama delegates—an index of the state's post-Dowling anti-Klan sentiment and patrician strength—voted to condemn the KKK, but the plank failed by a single vote, 542 to 541. More noteworthy, though, was Alabama's surprising stand. Prior to the vote, the Alabamians had impressed few. H. L. Mencken, editor of the *Baltimore Mercury* and an inveterate South-baiter, had called the Alabama delegates "such stupid fellows that a superficial observer might reasonably conclude that the State is only half-civilized." Yet the Klan vote allowed them to follow the brainchild of Forney Johnston. According to John W. Davis, the eventual Democratic candidate for president, Johnston "had the most beautiful brain of any man in this nation or anywhere else [I] . . . have ever known." While the ten other former Confederate states voted 211–12 *against* adoption of the plank, Alabama's vote to censure the KKK was unanimous.[26]

As measured by this vote, Alabama's patrician clique still controlled the state in 1924. Many lifelong oligarchs, handpicked by Underwood and former governor B. B. Comer, made up the Alabama delegation: men such as Donald Comer, Bill Brandon, Victor Hanson, Frederick Thompson, Joe Bonner, Thomas Kilby, John McDuffie, W. B. "Buck" Oliver, and, of course, Forney Johnston. Still, the 1924 convention was only a prelude. A decade-long fratricidal fight between the entrenched Democratic Party and the Klan's version of democracy promised to follow in the heart of Dixie. After the tumultuous national convention, the KKK swore political death to Oscar Underwood at its national conference and at a state meeting in Snowdoun. In November 1924, 7,000 Klansmen anticipated later events by elaborately burying Underwood in effigy at Birmingham's Rickwood Field.[27]

THE POLITICAL LIABILITY OF VIOLENCE

In its 1920s political war with the Redeemers, violence was definitely the Achilles heel of the Alabama Klan. Although Alabama Klansmen performed numerous works of charity and civic responsibility during the decade, the dramatic violence associated with the Klan often eclipsed these efforts in the public eye. Members of the Klan targeted blacks, Jews, Catholics, foreigners, and anyone, including white men and women, who violated the group's rigid standards of societal morality. Local Klan leaders planned much of the violence ahead of time.[28]

It is difficult to gauge the Klan's impact on Alabama's more general tradition of vigilante violence. Hooded activity certainly did little to deter imitation. In at least one instance, five white teens went on a spree of terrorism inspired by the KKK. Calling themselves the "Tombstone Gang," the boys planted tombstones along with Klan-style letters of warning in front of three Gadsden homes. Eventually they confessed, but as was usually the case with their adult role models, local authorities failed to punish them.[29]

Unfortunately, though, violence and intimidation were not restricted to mimics; they permeated Alabama. Kluxers flogged a Sylacauga café owner for no apparent reason. A white mob pistol-whipped the operator of a pool room in Anniston, then carried him to nearby woods for a more leisurely beating. A Marshall County mob tore off a woman's clothes when she interposed herself between Guntersville Knights and her husband. On Birmingham's south side, robed Klansmen conducted a door-to-door search for a youth to whom they planned to administer "correction." A group of Clanton thugs attacked and whipped a former state senator as he sat on his front porch reading a book.[30]

Although it is impossible to determine exactly how many of these incidents were directly attributable to the Klan, several observations can be made with a good degree of confidence. First, the revival of the KKK in Alabama coincided with a dramatic increase in mob violence, especially violence directed at the published enemies of the Klan—blacks, Catholics, Jews, immigrants, and the offenders of a variety of moral and community sensibilities. The victims of these crimes often named their assailants as Klansmen or reported that they had worn the garb of the order. In some rare instances, authorities arrested Klan members. In a few later cases, Klansmen were actually convicted of crimes. Still, community approbation, fear, and the inherent secrecy of the society make it impossible to determine the precise number of Klan outrages. Klan violence, though, has almost certainly been underestimated. Most acts of KKK violence were accompanied by warnings to remain silent or move—warnings that were likely to be heeded, given the brutality that had just occurred. More important, the Klan, through the violence it perpetrated, was the single actor most responsible for breeding an atmosphere of unrestrained mob violence in the state.

The violent excesses of the Klan's membership seriously hampered its growing political machine. On at least two occasions, the repeated threat of Klan violence led to suicides. A Cordova man shot himself barely a month and a half after Walker County Klansmen had given him a savage beating. His brother, a Nazarene preacher, blamed the KKK for his death. In another incident, a Birmingham auto dealer took his life because he feared harm from the Klan. A. P. Rich, co-owner of Ahrens-Rich Auto Company, left behind a note explaining how a local attorney and well-known politico had repeatedly threatened him with the order's wrath if Rich failed to repay a debt in full. Rich, who had struggled to pay his creditors in increments before eventually declaring bankruptcy, had been harassed by Walter B. Brower up to an hour before the suicide. Brower, who was a state senator, attributed the charges to unspecified "political enemies," then grew silent on the issue. When asked whether he was a Klansman, Brower replied that this was "an insulting question [that] . . . had no bearing on the case." In fact, he was a ranking member of the Klan.[31]

Early in 1925 Birmingham experienced a rash of hooded violence that, for some, diminished its political appeal. Four disguised men beat one man with a blackjack and pine slabs and ordered him to marry a local woman. In February, hooded men assaulted a doctor who was an ear, nose, and throat specialist. The physician, who suffered a broken nose, several bruises, and lacerations, was confined to bed for over a week. He claimed he could identify his attackers and vowed to handle the matter personally once he recovered.[32]

During a nine-day stretch in March 1925, Birmingham mobs struck six times. Three masked men abducted Joseph Zimmerman from the powerhouse of the Louisville and Nashville Railroad and drove him to Mount Pinson near Tarrant City. Seventh grade boys had previously mobbed Zimmerman as he emerged from a tunnel beneath the girl's restroom at the Inglenook School. After Zimmerman's kidnapping, locals never saw him again, but rumors circulated that he had been beaten and castrated. Three masked and armed men kidnapped an Italian grocer, carried him to Mount Pinson, and beat him into insensibility. Birmingham Klansmen had previously burned two crosses in front of the man's store in protest because he sold alcohol and worked on Sundays. In Fairfield, an unidentified caller advised a mortician to stay open late because a "wop" was about to be flogged. Soon after, sheeted Klansmen flogged the Italian operator of a hotdog stand. Another disguised band of whites beat a black grocer so badly that he, too, was confined to bed. Several days later, five men abducted a truck driver at gunpoint, drove him to Mount Pinson, and lashed him fifty times with a leather strap for failing to support his wife. The men held two pistols against the driver's ribs during the ordeal and threatened to kill him if he whispered a word about the assault. In the final incident of the March spree, a hooded mob, using brass knuckles, badly beat a doctor for having sexual relations with a female patient.[33]

The March 1925 outbreak was shocking even for a city as accustomed to violence as "bad, bad Birmingham" and quickly had negative political consequences. Opposition to the floggings surfaced from a variety of sources, but the consensus was the same: the beatings had to stop. The most vocal criticism emanated from an increasingly agitated cadre of privileged planters and industrialists who were beginning to see that a revitalized KKK represented a political threat. While members of the oligarchy had initially greeted the resurgence of the KKK with enthusiasm and nostalgia, by 1925 they were increasingly losing political positions to partisans of the mask and robe. Criticism of hooded depredations kept pace with the political disillusionment.

Spokesmen for Big Mule and planter interests did their best to voice disaffection with the violence. Victor Hanson, owner of four large dailies, played a leading role. "Some of the [Klan's victims] undoubtedly deserved punishment," the Birmingham News argued after the Joseph Zimmerman flogging, but "the most flagrant guilt on the part of the victims does not justify" mob violence. "Either we have a civilized community, or we haven't."[34]

Other editors in Birmingham followed Hanson's lead. "There never was a mob that didn't claim it was acting in behalf of the law while at the same time breaking it," wrote E. T. Leech of the Birmingham Post. Like other disciples of the materialist New South creed, Leech's criticism was marked by an acute concern with the toll that Klan violence was taking on the city's prospects for attracting northern capital. Ensley's Kiwanis club and other business groups also spoke out against the incidents.[35]

Religious resistance and some legal opposition were more idealistic. Clergymen at the First Christian Church, Eleventh Street Baptist, and the district Methodist conference deplored flogging as abhorrent to basic standards of decency and justice. One Baptist minister, an admitted admirer of the KKK, said, "if this is their method of doing business, then I am ready to change my opinion of them." Two Jefferson County judges also deplored the March violence and ordered a grand jury to investigate the attacks.[36]

Despite these sentiments, many in Jefferson County saw little wrong with hooded violence. A strong Klan spirit imbued many Alabamians and, for that matter, many Southerners as well. Much of the South's pro-Klan sentiment during the 1920s was directly traceable to Dixie's traumatic Reconstruction experience, reinforced by almost continual screenings of *Birth of a Nation*. Hugo Black, who should have been in a position to know, later recalled that the "name Klan [was] magic down there. Thad Stevens and his Reconstruction have never been forgotten."[37]

This "Reconstruction Syndrome"—sentiment that was antiblack, antifederal, antioutsider—was so ingrained and so powerful that its logical consequence was the reflexive defense of an order that many viewed as heroic. Although American communities outside the South nurtured powerful Klans for a time during the 1920s, they did not have a similar reservoir of deep traditional sentiment on which to draw.

Alabama's opposition, although vigorous and quite genuine, was limited in some ways. Jefferson County solicitor Jim Davis pressed a grand jury for indictments and soon had seven in two separate floggings, but both cases were eventually dropped. The *Birmingham News* lamented the results, but a Montgomery jurist was on target in his criticism. Branding Birmingham "the city of attacks," Judge Leon McCord remarked, "The people of Birmingham . . . have no one to blame but themselves [for the lack of convictions] . . . , because the courts are no better than the juries that made them. . . . [Birmingham] is a great, big, strong city despite its people." Inquiries revealed that a dozen other floggings had quietly occurred in the city since the beginning of 1925.[38]

Jefferson County, though, was far from being the only area stung by the Klan's whip and politically divided by its excesses. During the spring of 1925 pro- and anti-Klan factions split politics in Walker County, a coal-rich area northwest of Birmingham, virtually in two. The trouble in Walker began with the flogging of Will Tallant, a twenty-two-year-old white hotel clerk. An outspoken critic of mob violence, Tallant escaped one attempted Klan abduction by leaping from a hotel window. In early March, as Walker Klansmen set up roadblocks on several highways to search out critics of their order, they stumbled upon Tallant. Delighted, thirty Kluxers took him to a wooded area where they administered over a hundred licks with a rawhide whip. During the ordeal, Tallant's assailants further terrorized him by placing a gun in his mouth.[39]

The Tallant beating had an electric effect on Walker. Instead of heeding the Klan admonition to keep quiet under pain of death, the courageous Tallant reported the incident to county authorities. In a tumultuous sequence of events—a federal probe, death threats to Tallant's mother, Klan confessions of guilt, and a spectacular courtroom brawl—three Klansmen were found guilty of the assault. A Walker judge sentenced Homer

Sanderson, Jim Braidfoot, and Will Dupree, "the whipping boss," to six months of hard labor and $1,000 fines.[40]

The Tallant trials belied the fiction that floggings were conducted by lone Kluxers on the lunatic fringe and that mainstream Knights usually knew nothing about the violence. Authorities discovered that Walker Klansmen routinely discussed potential targets of violence at their klavern meetings. Authorities also learned that a host of violent episodes had taken place in Walker—at least six other floggings and a forced "shotgun" wedding.[41]

Serious political and social divisions arose in Walker County, but the Klan eventually emerged intact. Most of the animus directed at the hooded order emanated from a business community disenchanted by the negative attention that rampant Klan violence had brought to their county. Political forces close to Walker's industrial interests led the denunciation of the Klan. Six hundred residents turned out for a mass meeting at which a former state legislator castigated the KKK as "an organization of 'misfits'" who were bound to destroy America unless they were outlawed. He led the adoption of a slate of anti-Klan resolutions and called on all good men in the KKK to resign.[42]

Other county officials joined Walker's business interests in the fight against the Klan. The circuit solicitor quizzed each potential member of the Will Tallant juries about his "stand on the Klan" and disqualified those who belonged to, or sympathized with, the order. Walker's sheriff further infuriated local Knights by deputizing two of their most notable critics, and a county judge voided the Klan's shotgun marriage.[43]

Despite this spirited opposition, the Walker Klan survived largely because it relied on an abundance of community sympathy. By April 1925, county Knights were again holding massive meetings and were setting up roadblocks with impunity to trap critics of their order. In 1926, the first of Will Tallant's convicted assailants gained a mistrial in his appeal, and Tallant left Walker for good.[44]

Will Tallant's case never reached the notoriety of the 1923 flogging of Dr. J. D. Dowling and several later outrages. The limited public reaction aroused by the Tallant assault demonstrated that residents were more concerned with the identity of the victim than with the nature of the crime. Put another way, Tallant's beating failed to elicit the same reaction around much of the state as Dowling's because Tallant did not belong to the elite. The 1925 Tallant convictions should have been considered an epic event in state history. After all, an Alabama court had convicted three Klansmen for flogging. Curiously, the case went virtually unnoticed.

In Walker and elsewhere, though, political opposition to the hooded order was intense. Oscar Underwood, Alabama's senior senator, was eventually forced into an early retirement because of the Klan's political hostility. Underwood nevertheless remained unrepentant. "The days of the Klan are numbered," Underwood predicted in late 1926 as he compared the order to the Know-Nothings and the True Americans, political cadres of nativists both of which had proven to be transitory. He based much of his withering attack on the Klan's affinity for secrecy and intolerance, attributes that he found contrary to the most fundamental principles of democracy.[45]

Prominent jurists also spoke out against the KKK. Judges Walter B. Jones of Montgomery and George Smoot of Clanton were especially incensed by the society's disregard for due process. Jones was the son of a former Bourbon governor, a determined segregationist, and a member of the state's entrenched oligarchy. Grover Hall, editor of the *Montgomery Advertiser* and a spokesman for the planter/industrialist elite, joined in the jurists' complaint. Two patrician justices of the state supreme court also chastised the KKK for interfering in a trial for statutory rape by delivering the following broadside to Etowah County jurors: "Remember, every criminal, every gambler, every thug, every libertine, every girl ruined, every [home] wrecker, every wife beater, every dope peddler, every moonshiner, every crooked politician, every pagan papal priest, every shyster/lawyer, every K. of C., every white slaver, every brothel madam, every Rome-controlled newspaper is fighting the Ku Klux Klan. Think it over. Which side are you on?"[46]

THE CAULDRON OF BIRMINGHAM POLITICS

Notwithstanding such determined opposition, Alabama's Klan strength was more apparent in the state's political arena than anywhere else. A major political fight in 1925 concerned the seat on the Birmingham Board of Education that had been filled by Ensley's R. E. Chadwick. Chadwick had first come under Klan fire for his refusal to vote for the dismissal of Chester Bandman, the Jewish principal of Woodlawn High School. Seeking to punish Chadwick and to remove Bandmen as well as other Jewish and Catholic teachers, local Klan groups pushed for Chadwick's impeachment and offered to replace him on the board with a man reputed to be an Ensley cyclops.[47]

Klan agitation forced the city commission to call for a vote on the issue in April 1925. Meanwhile, the Klan's enemies charged the order with trying to run every non-Protestant out of public education and attempting to control the school board's $3.5 million building fund.[48]

A coterie of privileged planters and industrialists increasingly dominated the opposition to the KKK's political meddling. Such opposition, while white hot in its intensity, was temporary, tied to specific issues, and often highly political. The Ensley Kiwanis Club, Merchants and Business Men's Association, and Real Estate Board came to Chadwick's defense, while the local klavern in Ensley, where Chadwick ran a bank, split. A host of other Birmingham business and political fraternities also backed Chadwick: the Civitans, Kiwanians, Rotarians, American Business Club, and the League of Women Voters.[49]

In a 3–2 vote, which saw Chadwick narrowly retain his seat, both Klan-backed city commissioners voted to oust the banker. One pro-Klan commissioner explained his support by disparaging blacks and Asians. Police Commissioner W. B. Cloe was even more direct. "Klansmen are a good bunch of men or they wouldn't be knocked so much," he said. "Take that raid on the Brookside dance hall, I say 'God bless them.' It may be your sons or daughters who are going to hell. They say the Ku Kluxers don't want the Jews to teach . . . , but . . . if we want Christ and the Bible in our schools, then we must have Christ-like people to teach. . . . What we need here is more love of Jesus Christ."[50]

The board of education fight presaged increasingly tense relations between the KKK and the oligarchy. In some ways, the struggle over Chadwick's seat was a dry run for Birmingham's city elections that, in turn, served as a dress rehearsal for the 1926 state elections. After suffering such a narrow defeat on the Chadwick issue, Jefferson County's klaverns pooled their resources to attempt a virtual coup d'état in Birmingham's upcoming city elections. During the Chadwick fight, the KKK leaked news of its preferred slate for the city commission. By the October 1925 election, though, Klan politicos had replaced two of their three original candidates, most notably with newcomer Jimmie Jones, a protégé of the Klan's new chief political boss, the chameleon Horace C. Wilkinson.[51]

The Klan's opponents, led by Victor Hanson's *Birmingham News* and the *Birmingham Post,* backed Jack Adams for commission president and W. E. Dickson and Edgar Bowron for associates.[52] At stake was control of the city commission and, with it, the school board with its all-important building fund. The League of Women Voters played a prominent role in the election by grilling commission candidates on the Klan issue. Only two candidates in the sixteen-man field proved recalcitrant, both backed by the secret order. Reputed Klan leader John Taylor flatly refused to answer the women's questions, and Joe Lacy clumsily evaded them.[53]

On 12 October 1925, a clear and pleasant day in Birmingham, voters made their choices for city commission. No disorder was reported, although authorities had feared that some might occur. Jack Adams, the anti-Klan choice for commission president, easily outdistanced his five competitors, polling 7,911 votes. Klansman Jimmie Jones came in a distant second, some

3,500 votes behind, but Jones forced a runoff, since Adams had just avoided polling a majority.[54]

The Klan did somewhat better in the races for associate commissioner. John Taylor polled 6,258 votes to come in second in a field of eleven; Joe Lacy placed fourth. Both Klan candidates qualified for a four-man runoff set a week later.[55]

Ample rhetoric preceded the runoff. Klan judge Hugh Locke, Jimmie Jones's campaign manager and a close friend of Horace Wilkinson, borrowed a phrase from Jones's namesake, Revolutionary War hero John Paul Jones, and declared that his man had not yet begun to fight. Victor Hanson's *Birmingham News* countered by celebrating Adams's strong showing as "magnificent [and] highly gratifying" and predicted that his election was "as certain as anything can be. . . . It is inconceivable that a lead of 3,500 votes can be overcome." The pattern of support for the three Klan-backed candidates was virtually identical: Jones, Taylor, and Lacy all did well in East Lake and Pratt City (precincts 10 and 29), but were crushed in old Birmingham east of Twentieth Street (precinct 21).[56]

Perhaps the Klan's strongest weapon was its capacity for rapid political organization. The KKK's decentralized makeup made it ideally suited for political organization. It was organized into klaverns corresponding roughly to neighborhoods or voting wards. Much as the sixteenth-century Huguenots were organized into religious cells that could be converted into military units at a moment's notice, Alabama's KKK was divided into chapters that could quickly and easily become neighborhood political organizations.[57]

Desperate after their initial setback, the hooded political machine shifted into high gear. Klan spokesmen ignored the fact that front-runner Jack Adams had been a lifelong prohibitionist; instead they called him a notorious wet who was in favor of a "wide open town." The slander campaign sounded curiously like the work of Horace Wilkinson, a master politician with few scruples. After the initial polling, Wilkinson held an emergency strategy meeting in his office with Jones, Locke, area cyclopes, and Grand Dragon James Esdale that persuaded a disconsolate Jones to stay in the race. Klan tacticians organized the city into wards to "get out the vote" and assigned local supervision to lecturer Earl Hotalen. Esdale then left for Georgia to give the appearance of Klan nonchalance, but he closely monitored developments in Birmingham by telephone.[58]

In what one newspaper termed "a miracle . . . , the most remarkable election in the history of Birmingham," the KKK scored a huge victory over the Big Mules in the 19 October runoff. Jimmie Jones led all vote-getters and defeated Jack Adams. John Taylor, who polled a close second to

Jones, gained a second seat for the KKK and a majority on the three-seat commission. The third Klan candidate, Joe Lacy, narrowly missed making the election a complete sweep.[59]

Some polling disorder and irregularity was reported at the runoff, including the use of police cars to chauffeur Klan supporters to and from the polls. After the election, many Knights could not disguise their glee. Several hundred Jones backers paraded downtown, pausing just long enough to jeer outside the offices of the *Birmingham News,* the *Birmingham Age-Herald,* and the *Birmingham Post.* The *News* responded by lamenting that vulgar appeals to passion, prejudice, and misinformation "can still excite our people to the point where they lose their cool judgment."[60]

A comparison of the 12 October and 19 October elections shows exactly how successful the Klan campaign was.[61] The vote patterns of all three candidates backed by the order were remarkably similar in both elections. In the runoff, Klan candidates did extremely well in Eastlake (10), Avondale and East Birmingham (46), Gate City (36), and North Birmingham (42). Precinct 21 (Old Birmingham), made up predominantly of older, more established and privileged residents, continued to be a stumbling block for the Klan. In addition to its strongest precincts, the KKK also made significant gains in Woodlawn (34), Pratt City (29), and Ensley (45). Typically, the Klan slate polled well in the outlying areas of the city, those populated by middle-class and some working-class residents or those living closest to blacks. Jones increased his share of the East Lake vote from 43 percent in the initial election to 84 percent in the runoff. Taylor and Lacy also did well in East Lake, piling up 2,133 votes to their opponents' meager 685. In Old Birmingham, Jack Adams still took 73 percent of the runoff vote, while Taylor and Lacy got only 2,249 votes to their opponents' 6,307. Jones showed tremendous strength in those areas that historian Kenneth Jackson has termed "zones of emergence," gaining more than 72 percent of the runoff vote in East Lake, Gate City, North Birmingham, Avondale and East Birmingham, and Wylam.[62]

There was also significant evidence of Klan canvassing between the two elections. Jones made quantum leaps in the week between the regular election and the runoff: 18 percent to 76 percent in Gate City, 23 percent to 73 percent in North Birmingham, 27 percent to 79 percent in Avondale and East Birmingham, and 43 percent to 84 percent in East Lake. Both Taylor and Lacy added huge support in Elyton and West End and also in Ensley.[63]

Yet fratricide followed close upon the heels of victory for Birmingham's KKK. The city's pursuit of the Chinese café raiders in January 1926 left more than one Knight resentful of their freshly elected commissioners. After his arrest and conviction, Avondale cyclops W. J. Worthington threatened to "get" the jobs of Birmingham's public safety commissioner John Taylor and police chief Fred McDuff, both of whom had strong ties to prominent Klansmen. In October 1926, Worthington attempted to make good on his threats by accusing Taylor of allowing prostitution to flourish and charging that McDuff had closed his eyes to bootlegging.[64]

The power struggle reached a climax in a tumultuous city commission meeting at which both Jimmie Jones and Chief McDuff physically threatened the Avondale cyclops. Yet Worthington, whom one editor termed "a self-made savior," loved the limelight. He claimed that, in one month, his Kluxers had made 168 vice "arrests" in order to compensate for the city's laxity. He also predicted that the city commission would hire an assassin to kill him, since the political battle was really a struggle for control between two rival Klan factions, his own and that of John Taylor.[65]

Disgusted by Worthington's antics, commission president Jimmie Jones (figure 11) issued a statement in defense of Taylor and McDuff, as did a committee of police detectives and the Robert E. Lee Klavern. Worthington's assassination prediction failed to occur, but city police did mysteriously discover twenty-five gallons of corn whiskey on his property, a find that effectively ended his brief foray into city and Klan politics.[66]

Wounds between the county sheriff and his chief deputy were also slow to heal after the café raids. At the next election, Henry Hill challenged Sheriff T. J. Shirley for his job at the polls but lost. In order to avoid further friction between the two Klansmen, the Lee Klavern issued a statement of support for both, and Hill got the post of city warden as a consolation prize.[67]

GOLDEN YEARS

Despite its internal cleavages, the KKK was riding high in Alabama. Still, its greatest triumphs lay ahead. In the August 1926 Democratic primary, a number of Klansmen shocked the Big Mule/Black Belt alliance by riding to victory over its candidates. Bibb Graves became the Democratic Party's standard-bearer for governor, Hugo Black for U.S. senator, and Charlie McCall for attorney general.[68]

Of the three major 1926 victories, Black's was the most impressive. Speaking at all 148 Alabama klaverns, and at county courthouses where Klansmen were conspicuously present, Black defeated a strong field that included former governor Thomas Kilby, former state supreme court justice J. J. Mayfield, John H. Bankhead II, the son of one of Alabama's most illustrious senators, and L. B. Musgrove, a millionaire coal dealer. Fittingly, Black won the seat that had long been held by Oscar Underwood. While Klan

11. James Marion ("Jimmie") Jones, Jr., ca. 1925. A political protégé of
the Klan, Jones served several terms as president of the city commission
and, later, as Birmingham mayor. Courtesy Birmingham Public Library
Archives, Portraits.

leaders claimed that Underwood had retired to avoid fighting the Klan,
Black more graciously attributed the move to poor health. To protect himself, Black wrote a letter of Klan resignation that was kept secret from all
but a few.[69]

By 1926, the Alabama KKK held so tight a grip on state politics that
L. B. Musgrove failed to defeat Black even though he was an extremely
wealthy Klansman with the backing of Atlanta's imperial headquarters. As

the national chairman of the Anti-Saloon League, Musgrove was known as the League's "sugar boy," although he had been expelled from his beloved Methodist Church for attending a dance. The richest man in Alabama, Musgrove allegedly offered a quarter of a million dollars to Black and James Esdale to have Hugo withdraw from the race. Black's victory, though, demonstrated Klan power *in Alabama* and not just in Atlanta; the new senator enjoyed strong support in his home state, whereas Musgrove did not. The coal operator's backing derived predominantly from the imperial headquarters in Atlanta, to which he was a major financial contributor.[70]

By winning the primary in solidly Democratic Alabama, Klan-backed candidates ensured themselves of victory in the November general election. Black won the senatorial nomination by polling 63,580 votes, a 33 percent plurality, and led his closest competitor in the five-man field by 19,000 votes.[71] The gubernatorial election was tighter. Montgomery's Bibb Graves shocked political pundits by piling up 50,144 votes, or a 28 percent plurality. He narrowly defeated patrician favorite Charles S. McDowell by 3,800 votes as well as experienced politicos A. H. Carmichael and A. G. Patterson.[72]

Other Knights and fellow travelers rode the Klan wave into office. Montgomery Klansman Charlie McCall became attorney general. George Frey, who shared office space with Alabama grand dragon James Esdale, won his bid for the state legislature. Klan-backed Ben Ray won a place on the state Democratic executive committee (SDEC), as did Hugh Locke, a leading Birmingham Klansman. Klan opponent George Bondurant felt the wrath of the society as he lost his reelection bid for chair of the SDEC. In fact, the only Klansman of note who lost was a state senator who had been scandalized by a Klan-induced suicide.[73]

Bibb Graves and Hugo Black did well in Alabama's urban areas. Black dominated Jefferson County (Birmingham), while Graves also prevailed in the county by a smaller margin. Graves easily carried his home county of Montgomery, while Black placed a close second there. In the older, more Catholic, city of Mobile, both Klansmen did poorly. Black took only 17 percent of the vote; Graves polled a dismal 14 percent.[74]

Although the political ascendance of Alabama's KKK and the state's 1928 bolt against Al Smith have often been labeled the "north Alabama Revolt," this term is not completely descriptive—at least not when applied to 1926. Graves did much better in the eastern hill counties, the Wiregrass, and even the Black Belt than he did in the northern hill counties, the Tennessee Valley, or the west. Black, too, was weak in the west and the Tennessee Valley. Although Black ran well in the northern hill counties, he actually polled better in the Wiregrass and the Black Belt and did best in the eastern hill counties. Counties that went for both Black and Graves were predominantly eastern hill counties and the Wiregrass, not—contrary to popular belief—in the north. Overall, Black carried forty-three of Alabama's sixty-seven counties; Graves captured twenty-five.[75]

Alabama's 1926 Democratic primaries also fit within the "friends and neighbors" concept articulated by V. O. Key. Candidates piled up huge majorities in their home counties and won strong support nearby. According to Key, localism indicated an absence of stable statewide factions.[76] As the schisms of the order indicated, while politically quite powerful, Alabama's KKK was highly volatile. Klan strength was diffuse, perhaps even ubiquitous, but it was certainly not restricted to north Alabama alone.

Hugo Black won an overwhelming 80 percent of the votes cast in Clay County, his home, and also polled heavy majorities in the adjacent counties of Tallapoosa, Coosa, Talladega, and Chambers.[77] Graves recorded one of his highest totals in his home county of Montgomery and also did best in adjacent Macon, Elmore, Autauga, and nearby Butler. One of the few counties that Archie Carmichael won in his disastrous bid for governor was Tuscaloosa, his home county.

Grover Hall, editor of the *Montgomery Advertiser* and future winner of a Pulitzer Prize for his anti-Klan editorials, took some solace in Bibb Graves's Yale Law School and University of Texas credentials. Hall expressed the hope that the new governor would recognize that discrimination by public officials "is a meaner vice than Vice itself." He expressed optimism that Graves's education would enable him to restrain the more bigoted and irrational of his Klan followers but concluded that the new governor would face an uphill battle in any fight for tolerance in Alabama.[78]

By the 1926 elections, the Klan virtually controlled Alabama. The Big Mule/Black Belt team that had grown so accustomed to dominating state politics had been temporarily and shockingly dethroned. Alabama's KKK "elected every officeholder, and an appointee had to be a Klansman or sympathizer," remembered Cooper Green—himself a Klansman, Senator Black's local representative, and a future Birmingham mayor. "Even businessmen had to put TWK (Trade With Klansmen) cards in their windows to keep their customers." A reporter for the *New York Times* concurred: "The Klan was so strong in Alabama in 1926 that practically no one could hold a public office unless he joined it. . . . State, county and city offices were filled with Klansmen." Sylacauga's mayor was a Knight. Coosa County Klansmen held positions as probate judge, circuit court clerk, and sheriff. In fact, all but two of the state's sixty-seven county sheriffs were Klansmen. "Everybody, if they ever expected to win any contest or election . . . be-

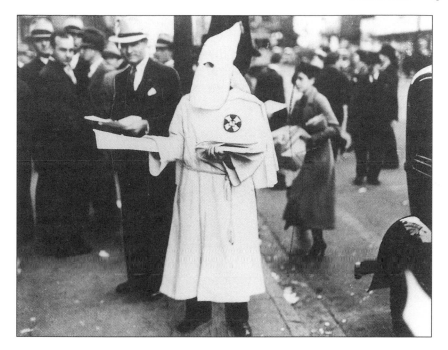

12. Klansman Handing Out Literature in Birmingham, 1927. During the 1920s, Alabama's Klan enjoyed such widespread popular acceptance that public leafletting was not at all unusual. Courtesy Birmingham Public Library Archives, Cat. No. 816.13.79.

longed to the Ku Klux Klan," recalled a Birmingham woman. According to its grand dragon, James Esdale, the secrets of the order's remarkable political strength were its organizational structure and the fact that virtually all of the membership voted (figure 12).[79]

In September 1926, Alabama's state Klan convention provided an ideal opportunity for the order to flaunt its electoral prowess. Four motorcycle policemen led 4,000 Klansmen and women auxiliaries in full regalia in a parade through downtown Birmingham. That night, 2,000 Knights gathered to hear Imperial Wizard Hiram Evans speak. He blasted Oscar Underwood, planter/industrialist opponents of the order, and, to everyone's astonishment, Klan darling Tom Heflin. Three titans and fifty cyclopes attended the wizard's speech, which was aired by WBRC in one of the city's first night radio broadcasts. A Klan band stressed patriotism to region and country, and religious piety, as it played "Dixie," the "Star Spangled Banner," and "Nearer My God to Thee."[80]

The highlight of the evening came when sheeted officials presented lifetime memberships to Bibb Graves and Hugo Black. The "golden passport" was the highest honor that could be bestowed on a Klansman. Prior to the Birmingham ceremony, it had been awarded to just six Knights in the entire country. Graves solemnly vowed that he would be a living exemplar of white Protestant Christian Americanism and promised to cherish his passport forever. He also predicted that the Klan's elite enemies would like nothing better than to see a hooded governor become the most spectacular failure in state history.[81]

Hugo Black was scarcely less fawning. He recognized that Klan support had been indispensable to his victory. "I realize [that] I was elected by men who believe in the principles I have sought to advocate," Black said, "the real Anglo-Saxon sentiment that must and will control the destiny of the Stars and Stripes. I want your counsel . . . I crave your counsel [and] . . . the Anglo-Saxon spirit."[82]

Black, Graves, and Charlie McCall were complex individuals. Practical politicians—or cynically expedient, if a commentator is less polite—all three shared in the nativism of the times, but none was a bigot or "true believer." McCall later waged a legal war against the KKK. Graves saved at least one black inmate from the electric chair, and Black was most paradoxical of all. A Sunday school teacher, he defended Klan murderers in court, railed against immigration as "the melting pot idea," and advised true Americans to "clean house and Americanize all the foreigners." If James Esdale and Hugh Locke are to be believed, he could "make the best anti-Catholic speech you ever heard." Still, long before he reached the bench of the U.S. Supreme Court, Hugo Black spoke up for Jewish educators like Chester Bandman, represented Chinese restaurateurs in court, and opposed violence—all in the face of intense opposition from his Klan brethren.[83]

Success, though, came at the price of rampant violence. Bibb Graves constituted a progressive alternative to the stagnant conservatism of planters and industrialists. Hugo Black later became one of America's leading liberals. Yet some of Alabama's rank-and-file Klansmen were more interested in the violent regulation of community mores than in political reform. More important, many other Alabamians were still in concert with the Klan's most basic emotive impulses: white supremacy, anti-Catholicism, anti-Semitism, nativism, and xenophobia broadly defined. The price of political reform—a high one for Alabama—was one to which men like Graves and Black had to reconcile themselves in order to promote their progressive agendas.

Political success also bred ambition, and ambition soon bred factionalism. In a scene that played out again and again, the Klan achieved victory only to find itself mired in a train of internecine squabbles. Plagued by internal divisions, Alabama's sheeted society enjoyed success but was unable to con-

solidate its power fully or to translate its diffuse strength into a more permanent hegemony.

Intoxicated by the 1926 victory, Grand Dragon James Esdale made the
reckless boast that his order would bolt the Democratic Party in 1928 if
New York governor Al Smith were nominated for president. The head of the
state Anti-Saloon League quickly endorsed the threat. Smelling a rare opportunity to gain voters who might be put off by a bolt, Alabama's Republican Party briefly flirted with the idea of inserting an anti-Klan plank
into its official platform. Eventually, though, the Republicans decided not to
alienate the powerful KKK and passed on the idea. Instead, GOP leaders
leaked word that they were willing to fuse with the hooded order if the
Alabama Klan bolted the Democratic Party in 1928.[84]

The bolting controversy was only the first of James Esdale's problems
in the wake of the sensational 1926 victories. Angry loyal Democrats persuaded Esdale to deny his comments publicly. Soon, though, he was back in
the news. Frederick Thompson's *Birmingham Age-Herald* published a secret
Klan document, written by Esdale, in which he criticized the state's American Legion for political activism and its choice of a Catholic as commander.
Embarrassed again, because many Legionnaires supported Bibb Graves, the
grand dragon charged two reporters with having stolen the document. He
did not, however, deny having written it.[85]

Despite such backtracking, Esdale's headaches were hardly over. In December 1926, he launched a grandiose scheme to bring every Alabama jury
and every state legislator under the Klan's thumb. As governor, Bibb Graves
could theoretically appoint a new member of each three-person county
jury commission every year. Within three years, Esdale hoped to find only
"good and loyal Klansmen in good standing" on the commissions and only
"the right kind of men" sitting on Alabama's juries. He also traveled to
Montgomery to attend the opening caucuses of the state legislature and
tried to recruit every lawmaker who was not already a Knight. Another
development, though, embarrassed Esdale once again. Alabama's public service commission rejected Charlie McCall's attempt to repay Klan support
by making Esdale an assistant attorney general and a special counsel for the
Public Service Commission.[86]

James Esdale was not the only Klansman in Alabama distressed by the
new problems that accompanied political success. In late December, Montgomery mayor William Gunter infuriated Knights all over the state by
granting a place in Bibb Graves's inaugural parade to the American Legion
but not to the KKK. Woodlawn's Klan No. 60, led by Horace Wilkinson,
suggested that the Birmingham klaverns hold their own inaugural for
Graves and wrote Montgomery's Klan No. 3 for its opinion: "We have a

great victory, why should we be barred from all privileges because we are Klansmen? Can a 2 × 4 mayor, of a Jew-owned town prevent 50,000 100-percent Americans from jubilating in our great victory. We say no."[87]

During the 1920s, Alabama Kluxers participated in civic activities, private charity, and public education, including fund raisers to pay for schoolbooks, and jump-started the political careers of two of the state's most noted liberals, Hugo Black and Bibb Graves. Still, for every Hugo Black there was a Horace Wilkinson, eventually one of the most vocal, visible, and reactionary demagogues the South ever spawned. Both Graves and Black, it should be noted, were political opportunists who used Klan strength to further their own careers and could never be mistaken for fanatics or more extreme Kluxers.

Indeed, the presence of some undeniably progressive features of the Klan suggests that there really was no one monolithic KKK during the 1920s—years when, ironically, there was only one official organization on the books. Instead there was a multiplicity of Klans: one that was civic, one educational, one political, even one that was progressive, but also a violent Klan, a reactionary Klan, and a nativist, bigoted, racist, and intolerant Klan. The point is that there were many types of Klans, and many types of people became Klansmen. A more unified Klan mentality flourished during the 1940s, 1950s, and 1960s, years when there were actually a number of official Klan groups. Such an analysis helps explain the endless civil warfare within the order; it was a patchwork of different people with different agendas. Such an analysis also helps account for the phenomenal growth of the order: as diverse as it was, the Klan offered something for almost everyone.

The issue of violence illustrates these varied motivations. Reported incidents probably constituted only a small percentage of the actual violence that took place. Many victims kept their suffering private from fear, trauma, concern for the safety of loved ones, or a well-founded lack of faith that the authorities would come to their rescue. Jefferson County's March 1925 outbreak, for example, led to the discovery of twelve additional incidents of violence in addition to the six that had first been brought to light. In Walker County, the tumult surrounding Will Tallant's flogging led to the revelation of a host of related abuses, including a forced wedding, midnight shootouts, and a Klan-induced suicide. KKK violence, by its very nature and logistics, required the participation of only a few individuals. That only a few participated directly, though, neither exculpates the majority who may have cheered nor means that the perpetrators belonged on the outer fringes of the Klan cosmos. The few Kluxers who acted did so with, if not the full approbation of their Klan brothers, at least the tacit toleration of some leaders, many members, and much of the broader community.

Violence or its threat was a pervasive part of Klan activity in Alabama, even activity that ostensibly dealt with other matters such as morality. Alabama Klansmen wielded guns at the Brookside dance hall raid, during cross-burnings at houses of ill repute, and at the Chinese café raids. Cross-burning itself so often preceded violence that the cross came to serve as a warning to mend one's ways or suffer the consequences. While it may be unfair to cite violence as the raison d'être of the revised KKK, Alabama's Klan cannot accurately be portrayed as a purely nonviolent civic organization, nor can its violence be attributed to the aberrant conduct of a misguided few. Violence was as inherited a part of the second Klan as its robes. Yet it was a double-edged sword that sometimes cost the order politically.

Alabama's Invisible Empire reached its political pinnacle in 1926. "In many Southern states," one author wrote, "the Klan was not only a potent political force, it was the electorate" Although this statement is undeniably hyperbole, the KKK was unquestionably powerful in Alabama. The Klan controlled the voting machinery in virtually every Alabama county. At one point, nearly every one of Alabama's county sheriffs was a Klansmen, and Klan leaders routinely got out the vote against nonmembers. Just two weeks after the Chinese café raids, a Klan-elected and Klan-controlled Birmingham City Commission outlawed restaurant booths where patrons "necked" and "petted." Some of the most prominent Alabama politicians were members of the order: state supreme court justice John C. Anderson, Jefferson County court reporter A. B. Hale, Jim Folsom's later legal counsel Ira B. Thompson, attorney Crampton Harris, Jefferson County judges William E. Fort, Horace Wilkinson, and Hugh Locke, Sheriff T. J. Shirley, state representatives Walter Brower, George Frey, and James A. Simpson, A. G. Patterson, Hollis Black, Hugo's nephew, future Birmingham mayor Cooper Green, both of Alabama's U.S. senators, its governor, and its attorney general.[88]

Years later, Alabamians recalled the power and pervasiveness of the KKK during the mid-1920s. "We had the best people in the state," James Esdale fondly remembered. Clifford and Virginia Durr said that "almost every [Alabama] politician was a member of the Klan." "Just about everybody, including the police," supported the Klan, another Alabamian remembered. Many others have since concurred. A Birmingham attorney remarked, "When I say powerful, they took over the state. You couldn't be an officer, couldn't win an election unless you were a member of the Klan, that was true of [the] counties and the cities."[89]

Although these years were golden for Alabama's KKK, by the time Bibb Graves entered the governor's mansion, cracks were beginning to form in the order's foundation. They were small at first and barely perceptible: factional cleavages, violent excesses, petty political squabbles. Still, unheeded

13. Manifestation of Klan Strength, 1924. As the 1920s drew to a close, large open air celebrations and initiations like this 1924 ceremony in Fayette County became increasingly rare. Courtesy Birmingham Public Library Archives, uncataloged.

and left to grow, these lines of dissension possessed the power to undermine the whole movement in Alabama.

By the end of 1926, the individuals in Alabama who most desperately wanted to see the demise of the revised KKK were its erstwhile supporters, the state's Big Mule/Black Belt alliance. While these oligarchs, many of them the physical descendants of Reconstruction Klansmen, initially welcomed the revitalization of the sacred old order (figure 13), by 1924 they had clashed politically and publicly with the Ku Klux upstarts. The oligarchy won the first round in New York, thanks mostly to the influence of Oscar Underwood, Forney Johnston, and B. B. Comer. Still, the victory cost Underwood the rest of his political career and presaged renewed confrontation over prizes such as Birmingham's city commission and its board of education. With its stunning triumph in the 1926 elections, the KKK could lay claim to having accomplished something for which Alabama's Republicans, anti-Redeemers, and Populists had only hoped. They had vanquished the powerful and entrenched planter/industrialist machine. In 1927, the proud oligarchs would begin to strike back with a vengeance.

6

The Year of the Whip

Klan revival brought fresh mob violence to the state—an epidemic even by Alabama's distinctive standards. Yet even on those occasions when Klansmen were identified by their regalia, police failed to arrest and juries failed to convict. Because of widespread approval, sympathy, and fear, Alabamians almost never punished Klan lawlessness. Perhaps more troubling, much of the violence was planned by Klan leaders in advance.[1] Curiously, the patricians who spoke out so passionately against hooded violence later in the 1920s were nowhere to be found during the early years of the decade. Until their devastating electoral defeat at Klan hands in August 1926, the oligarchy saw little wrong with the occasional Klan flogging—or even regular ones. Thereafter, the oligarchy's outlook changed considerably.

While hooded violence had been occurring at alarming levels since the Klan's 1915 revival, all hell broke loose in 1927. State, local, regional, and finally national press attention became riveted on the scandalous state of affairs in Alabama. Law and order, the world was told, had taken a holiday in the Deep South state ever since a Klan-elected and Klan-controlled slate of candidates had swept the state's elections in November 1926. Now, insulated by friendly political officials, the Klan ran wild. What resulted was variously termed an "epidemic," an "explosion," and an uncontrolled "rash" of lawlessness and violence. Men, women, blacks, whites, natives, foreigners, city dwellers, and country folk alike, whether young, old, poor, or prosperous, were whipped, flogged, scourged, and terrorized. The litany of reasons stretched from racism and nativism to a raw and unmitigated religious intolerance. Yet the vigilantism was dominated by acts aimed at the regulation of local morality and mores. What ensued shamed a state, shocked a region, and mesmerized a nation.

RACIAL AND ETHNIC VIOLENCE

By any standard, Alabama witnessed an explosion of mob violence after 1915. The year 1927 has been singled out, though, as the zenith of a disgraceful state flogging epidemic. The actual number of Klan beatings can only be guessed at; most likely the true number will never be known. Many victims never reported their assaults because of the sheer terror and primordial trauma involved. Some fled, others feared a repeat performance, still others, embarrassed and ashamed, blamed themselves. Some simply realized the futility of reporting the outrage to public officials controlled by the Klan. Attorney General Charlie McCall estimated that seventy floggings took place in Alabama during the summer of 1927 alone. Later, he guessed that ninety-three such attacks had occurred during an eighteen-month span. The *Montgomery Advertiser*, though, correctly realized that "no living man [really] knows how many midnight floggings have occurred in this State."[2]

Klan floggings were brutal. They usually involved abduction, often from the sacred security of the home, sometimes even from the victim's own bed. The psychological toll of such a primeval violation is difficult to measure, but the cost must have been great. Second, Klan floggings differed categorically from the benign images conjured up when the words "flogging" or "whipping" are used today. Floggings, horrific affairs, were often animalistic assaults that used tree limbs, leather belts, rawhide whips, heavy wooden canes, branches, sticks, baseball bats, and even, on at least one occasion, an automobile fan belt. Victims were beaten at gunpoint; some had guns forced into their mouths to keep them from screaming. Some were pistol-whipped to ensure compliance. Floggings caused welts, bruises, blood clots, bleeding, broken bones, the loss of teeth, and lengthy hospital stays for many Alabama victims. Some lapsed into comas, suffered nervous breakdowns, or were permanently maimed; at least a few died. Klan floggings were savage, and the victims took their psychological and physical scars to the grave.

People of color, long the favorite targets of Klan terrorists, temporarily took a backseat to other Alabama victims during the 1920s. Still, African Americans comprised a considerable percentage of the secret society's victims. There are significant differences between the outbreaks of Ku Kluxism during Reconstruction, the 1920s, and the era that followed *Brown v. Board of Education*.[3] The situation of black victims was comparable, though, in all three periods.[4] Blacks made up the preponderant share of Klan victims during the 1860s and the 1960s. Although they were fewer in number during the 1920s than white moral offenders, the incidence was still out of proportion, given their representation in the general population. Such

continuity across the eras of Ku Kluxism muddies the picture of chrono-
logical periods and adds to the complexity of the Klan phenomenon.

One of the worst floggings of the 1927 spree was the July beating of
Arthur Hitt. Hitt was, by all accounts, an honest, hardworking old black
man who had tilled an especially rich piece of farmland north of Birmingham for four decades. His grandmother, an emancipated slave who had
gotten the land from her master upon manumission, had left the land to her
grandson when she died. The sixty-acre tract consisted of a tree-shaded glen
with a road that ran close to a railroad track flanked on both sides by rows
of brightly colored flowers. Wooded hills surrounded Hitt's house, which
was wrapped in green vines with a shady arbor. A cornfield and a spring
of pure water lay close by. Locals fondly described Hitt as "a white-man's
nigger"—a man who was content to work his land in peace and quiet. Hitt
did not realize, though, that beneath one of his hillsides lay a rich deposit
of gravel worth a small fortune.[5]

In the summer of 1927 several whites offered Hitt $900 for the land. Tax
assessors had conservatively appraised the farm at $6,000, and the place had
sentimental value for Hitt, and so he politely but firmly refused. Several
nights later two white men appeared at his door and told Hitt that his closest white friend was stuck down the road with a stalled car. As the elderly
black emerged from the house to help, the men struck him on the head with
pistols, shoved him into a car, and drove him to a deserted grove where fifty
white-robed Knights waited. The Klansmen bloodied the old man so viciously with a belt buckle that he could still barely walk a month later. They
accused him of making moonshine, of letting a white girl ride in his truck,
and of being too wealthy for a black man. "You get out of this country,"
they warned him, "we don't want niggers around here." When the Kluxers
finally untied him, Hitt collapsed, unconscious.[6]

Three days later, after being threatened with another beating, Arthur
Hitt sold his farm for $600, one-tenth of its worth. He moved his family to
nearby Village Springs and began life over as a tenant farmer on a small plot
of land. Hitt lived in constant fear of death, with the mob's final words still
ringing in his ears: "Nigger, you will be killed if you mention this affair."
White friends soon learned that the new name on the farm's deed belonged
to none other than W. J. Worthington. When confronted, the Avondale cyclops insisted that he had paid a "fair price," but within weeks he began
excavating gravel for sale to the railroads.[7]

The Hitt flogging provoked an avalanche of anti-Klan reaction from a
Big Mule/Black Belt press still smarting from the recent electoral defeat.
Grover Hall led the way by asking, "How long, O Lord, how long" Alabama

would be ruled by the mask and lash. "It is perfectly outrageous that . . . any . . . person should be bullied and frightened into sacrificing the fruits of a lifetime of toil in order to save his life," he wrote. Hall described Hitt as a shell of his former self—nervous, frightened, at times babbling, blank, and incoherent.[8]

James Chappell of the *Birmingham News* took up the attack in one of Victor Hanson's other newspapers. "Today it may be a defenseless negro who is robbed of his property rights," Chappell warned, striking the sensitive chords of New South materialism. "Tomorrow it may be some defenseless white man . . . [or] some big property." Arthur Hitt, Chappell wrote in displaying his own fidelity to traditional race relations, was "an ignorant, frightened black man . . . , the kind of negro that decent law-abiding white people of the South know is indispensable to the South's progress and prosperity." Chappell went on to describe the assault as "hideously mean . . . , foul, wrong . . . , venomous . . . , [and] dastardly" and closed with admonitions about divine retribution. "The man . . . who most needs to comprehend [this]," he warned, "is the Hon. Bibb Graves."[9]

Frederick Thompson's newspapers called the flogging the most shocking case that had yet come to light. A north Alabama paper concurred by noting that the assault would do incalculable harm to Alabama's business prospects.[10] Nevertheless, Hitt's flogging was replicated in Colbert County a short time later.[11]

Blacks in Alabama became targets of Klan violence for much less than rich farmland. Emory and Lily Cobb, parents of eight, worked a 207-acre cotton and truck farm in Blount County for over fifteen years. Aroused by rumors that Lily was an adulteress, rumors that her husband passionately denied, fifteen hooded Klansmen came calling. When the men broke into the Cobb home, a midnight shootout ensued. Emory repulsed the Kluxers with his shotgun, but his wife fell mortally wounded. He ran to the nearest house to get help, but local blacks were so cowed by the Klan that they refused to lend him a car. By the time Cobb found a doctor it was too late. His wife died the following day.[12]

Events after the tragedy looked promising for those interested in law and order. Authorities arrested a suspected Klansmen who had sought the services of an Oneonta doctor for a gunshot wound on the same night as the slaying. Local police talked of fifteen more arrests while Emory Cobb fled to Cleveland in terror even before his wife had been buried.[13]

Still another incident occurred in Marengo County. Luman Greathouse, a black teen regarded as hardworking (according to local whites), asked for and borrowed some wire from his employer's car. Unbeknownst to Greathouse, his boss had just sold the car. Four whites, enraged at the boy's effrontery, took him out and gave him such a terrific beating that he ran a fever of 109 degrees, lapsed into a coma, and died. The local solicitor denounced the fatal flogging as "a menace to civilization" and later oversaw several arrests and indictments.[14]

Individual blacks obviously found themselves in a precarious position in Klan-controlled Alabama, but so did whites who violated the fundamental tenets of traditional race relations. In 1927, the famed liberal Clarence Darrow traveled to scenic Fairhope, Alabama, originally a Utopian community. The lawyer planned to stay at the home of friends and agreed to give two speeches in nearby Mobile. At the Lyric Theater, Darrow shocked white sensibilities with what amounted to racial heresy by condemning lynch law and urging interracial cooperation. Later, speaking before an all-black audience, he recommended cooperation with peaceful whites and active resistance to terrorists.

> Resist your white masters. . . . I see you pray, but to what good? . . . Your God must be white considering the way he treats you. No doubt there will be a "Jim Crow" law in your heaven. You have some [white] friends not afraid to sit at the table [and share a drink] with you . . . , [but] you will have to help yourselves. . . . [Defy] the white man who calls himself your friend. How has he manifested his friendship? By hanging [you] and burning you, by making you do his work . . . use his backdoor . . . and sit in the rear of the street car. The only front place the white man has ever given you is in the battle line. There you can stop the bullets but when you return home you can't [even] use the sidewalks.

Obviously accustomed to the license of northern courtrooms, Darrow failed to gauge the inflammatory nature of his remarks. In two brief talks, he managed to violate almost every sacred custom of the white South. He mingled with blacks, deplored white supremacy and vigilante justice, disparaged religion, flouted prohibition, and went so far as to encourage black resistance openly.[15]

News of the poison Darrow was spreading reached the local KKK within minutes of his second speech. Klansmen printed handbills depicting Darrow as an "outside agitator" bent on fomenting strife between the races, and they made plans for a tar-and-feathering party. Talk circulated that Darrow would be lynched. Local civic leaders, fearful for the well-being of their well-known visitor, got word of the Klan plot to Darrow and his hosts. Concerned citizens even called Birmingham to implore James Esdale to intervene in order to prevent a riot. The plan worked. While local clergymen and editors castigated Darrow as evil incarnate and the meddling emissary of a morally bankrupt North, plainclothes detectives ushered the attorney onto a train headed for Chattanooga and safety.[16]

Despite the fact that Alabama's revised KKK targeted white moral offenders more often than blacks, most people of color still regarded themselves as Klan enemy number one. They realized that, while "immoral" whites might temporarily displace them as a favorite target, the order would always retain a special disaffection for them. A July 1927 Klan assault vividly reinforced this belief. Twelve masked men beat a Crenshaw County black repeatedly on the head and flogged him for buying liquor from a white man. Nearby, men in Klan uniforms lashed two black lumber workers for immorality. Robed Crenshaw vigilantes enticed a fifty-year-old black sharecropper from his farm by posing as federal agents and beat him so badly that he almost died. Sheeted Klansmen flogged a black Talladega doctor and a black pharmacist for treating whites, a transgression that presented an ongoing problem during the decade, and Calhoun Kluxers gave one local black seventy-five lashes.[17]

On some occasions black Alabamians of rare constitution took up arms. Faced with a midnight band of invading Klansmen, a black Centre farmer fired buckshot at them. The next day a prominent white merchant was reported dead. Recognizing that discretion is sometimes the better part of valor, the farmer fled Cherokee County.[18]

Alabama Kluxers also violently repressed immigrants during the 1927 epidemic. One thing foreigners undoubtedly failed to include in their sense of the American dream was the vision of grown men draped in sheets determined to blunt their claims to freedom, democracy, tolerance, and the pursuit of happiness. Nativist attitudes shared a primitive kinship with racist notions about blacks. In 1920s Alabama, immigrants occupied a place on the social scale just barely above the cellar customarily reserved for blacks. Foreigners constituted a basic, seemingly immutable threat to white Anglo-Saxon culture, seeming almost as alien to Alabama's native white landscape as blacks. Deviation from majority norms had to be countered in order to preserve a subculture and its cherished way of life.

In a climate of moral, ideological, and ethnic homogeneity, persons of foreign extraction had to tread lightly regardless of their character, religion, political affiliation, or desire to be assimilated. Those who did not do so found themselves, like their black cousins, obliged to pay an awful price. Dan Mitchell was one such careless alien. Greek by birth, a commercial artist by trade, Mitchell offended the fragile sensibilities of Clay Countians when he married an American woman. In July 1927 Klansmen flogged Mitchell for the offense. Afterward, a hooded party paraded around the couple's home. When Kluxers attempted to beat Mitchell a second time, he was ready. Responding in kind to the violent cultural mores of his new home, Mitchell dispersed attacking Klansmen by firing a shotgun into their midst.[19] A Jefferson County Greek purchased a home for $6,000 only to have an angry mob inform him that he would never be able to occupy the house as long as he lived. Birmingham Knights flogged the German owner of a grocery store and his teenage daughter because, after having been warned not to do so, he allowed her to wait on blacks.[20]

ATTACKS ON WOMEN

During the flogging frenzy of 1927, Alabama Kluxers routinely beat women—mostly for violating social conventions and moral ideals but sometimes for being racially tolerant. The Klan's targeting of female victims, aside from contradicting its own doctrine on chivalry, was revealing about some of the men who belonged to the 1920s order. Women, it should be remembered, had only just received the franchise in 1920. The flapper, despite her paucity, terrified some males. The automobile and birth control forbode growing female autonomy, divorce rates were up, and more women were entering the workforce.[21] Gender relations, like racial and ethnic purity, came under a withering assault during the 1920s. Some members of the Klan rode to ensure that the clock would be turned back to a simpler time, a purer time, when women knew their place, when "darkies" were content, obedient, and happy, when foreigners were invisible, and when northern agitators stayed at home.

One 1927 assault that received a great deal of attention was the attack on Bertha Slay, a white woman in Florence. Midnight raiders tied her husband and sister to chairs and took Mrs. Slay from her bed to the front yard. There, they bent her over a barrel and whipped her with such gusto that they exhausted themselves. After resting a while, her assailants traded their tree limbs for an automobile fan belt. Despite her suffering, Mrs. Slay refused to "confess" to taking part in a neighborhood scandal. Before departing, the mob warned that they would drive her from the community if she reported the incident.[22]

The assault stimulated more comment than many other floggings because the victim was a native white female—not a male, an immigrant, a Yankee, or a black. An enraged editor in Covington County denounced the act as uncivilized and demanded that southern gentlemen take up arms to protect white womanhood from the depredations of hooded mobs. "Where are they now . . . , [the] men . . . , the pride of the Southland[?]" he asked, "men whose honor is worth more to them than their life's blood. . . . Do they sleep . . . ? Is the spirit of the Old South waning?"[23] Grover Hall rushed to lead the planter/industrialist assault on the KKK's peculiar notions of chivalry. Recognizing the potential embarrassment to Klan politicos when its Knights beat women, Hall in his eagerness found himself for once at a loss for the right words. He called the attack "appalling," the work of a "gang of hooded demons . . . , fiends . . . , hiding their cowardly faces behind masks . . . , hooded brutes . . . , heartless ruffians . . . , carloads of beasts," and then proposed that someone coin a new word to describe such flogging. "Every blow of the lash . . . on the body of a defenseless . . . woman is a blow at . . . [the] State and [the] law," Hall argued. "So long as masked men may go into an Alabama home to . . . satisfy . . . their lust for cruelty . . . so long will Alabama harbor anarchy and barbarism . . . shame and humiliation . . . [and the] cries of the farm wife of Florence."[24]

The attack of a white woman brought reproach from other sources. The *New York Herald-Tribune* observed that the Slay flogging was nothing more than the invariable consequence of "two bitterly inexcusable" Alabama practices, mob interference in private morality and the legal use of masks.[25] Even Bibb Graves emerged from the protective cocoon of his silence to announce dramatically that "flogging in Alabama must cease." The governor promised to look into the case but, when pressed for specifics, refused to elaborate.[26]

News of other female victims followed. Eight masked Knights kidnapped and flogged a seventeen-year-old girl in Florence and threatened to kill her parents if she reported the attack. Gowned men lashed a bedridden teenager and her mother for allowing a black man in St. Clair County to teach them how to drive. In Clanton, sheeted thugs repeatedly terrorized "Aunt Decky," the elderly widow of a Confederate veteran, to force her to sell a restaurant. Her appeals to police and politicians fell on deaf ears.[27] A Holiness preacher led a Klan crew to the home of two divorcees who had recently married each other. The preacher led a prayer, then directed the flogging of both and took up a collection of $3.50 and a bottle of ointment for the blood-stained woman.[28]

Perhaps the most dramatic example of the Klan's inverted notions of piety was the thrashing of Fannie Clement Daniels in Luverne. As the self-appointed custodians of community morality, Klansmen targeted individuals, often women, who violated local behavioral norms. The norms, for the most part, were the products of a narrow evangelical Protestantism that reflected conservative theological concerns about personal morality—drinking, dancing, gambling, sloth, infidelity, spousal abuse, and the like.[29]

The Klan visited Fannie Daniels twice. The seventeen-year-old Ms. Daniels had been briefly married to a much older man from Birmingham whom she had met through a "Lonely Hearts Club." When her father died, Fannie got a divorce and moved back to Crenshaw County to care for her elderly mother. After several months, she took up with a young farmer, thereby feeding the appetite for local gossip. On their first visit, Klan members only talked to Fannie and her mother, but during a second encounter, this time at midnight, they broke down the front door, wrenched a shotgun from Fannie's mother, roughed up the old woman, and demanded that her daughter dress suitably to go in search of her boyfriend. As Fannie changed clothes, several of the hooded men refused to leave her bedroom, preferring instead to leer at her. Growing impatient, the men threw her across the bed, hiked up her dress, and whipped her. Then they took her to the living room for more questioning. When she showed signs of being unrepentant, one of the men hit her across the face with the back of his hand. Another called out from the back, "Give her some more, she ain't had enough."[30]

Attacks such as these brought virulent condemnation from the anti-Klan press; Grover Hall led the way. "There was a time when the flogging of a woman would have been the equivalent of a death sentence," wrote the editor of the *Montgomery Advertiser.* "Today a Southern mob would just as soon torture a woman as a man. All that is necessary . . . is idle gossip. . . . we'll bend her over a barrel and beat hell out of her, we neo-Southern gents!" Hall's editorial allies in Birmingham and the Black Belt accused 90 percent of Clanton, including business owners, of going along with the KKK's intimidation of a Confederate widow. Chilton County businessmen, red-faced at the accusation, denied the charge and maintained that the lawless element in their county accounted for only a small minority of the population.[31]

While Alabamians debated the meaning of these attacks—misogyny, barbarism, anarchy, new ethical standards, the death of chivalry—an editor in Tennessee drew attention to the obvious sexual component of the Alabama floggings. He argued that the Klansmen who participated were not only brutes, cowards, and moral fanatics but also sadistic sexual perverts. The excessive piety characteristic of the mobs, according to the journalist, merely concealed the underlying sexual nature of the act from others as well as themselves. Indeed, in the floggings of Fannie Daniels and another Crenshaw County divorcee, Kluxers took pains to disrobe the women before the floggings so that the lash would strike naked flesh.[32]

THE VIOLENCE OF MORALITY

Hooded attacks on women were closely related to the most popular form of Klan assault during the 1920s, attacks on the violators of community morals. Those who participated in these attacks did so for a variety of reasons. Some were sadistic. Some earnestly believed that they were improving society through the application of the lash; still others were moral authoritarians bent on elevating themselves to the status of a moral elite. Some became drunk with the power of deciding who would be lashed, when, where, and for what. Still others were anxious about the new Freudian ethics or so consumed with guilt and shame that they displaced it onto others. For many, a variety of motivations were at work. Regardless, those Knights who actually wielded the moral lash often acted with the knowledge, acquiescence, and even encouragement of their Klan superiors and many sympathizers in the wider community. They were clearly not just a few troubled individuals working in isolation.

Alabama's moral climate in 1927 was a far cry from that of today. Birmingham, for instance, harbored long-simmering tensions between those devoted to older agrarian notions of piety and a more cosmopolitan segment of mercantile leaders. Battles over dancing, blue laws, and Sunday movies had been waged sporadically but with much emotion. In 1927, ministers and lay moralists condemned Sunday movies as a "threat to American Christian Civilization" and won the city's second referendum on the issue. One of Bibb Graves's first acts as governor was to send state policemen to "clean up" Jefferson County's taverns. In an environment that was hypersensitive about personal morality, some Klansmen felt justified in breaking civil laws to punish the violators of God's law. Many others in the community agreed.[33]

In the summer of 1927, five Jefferson County Kluxers flogged teenager Eaton "Mule" Murchison in what was obviously a Klan sting. As Murchison parked with a girl and another couple on a lonely Midfield road, nightriders called him out, took him to a thicket, and administered twenty-five licks to his back with a heavy leather strap. The robed men then returned Murchison to his car, summoned a police car to drive the girls home, and released the two boys. Montgomery liberal Virginia Durr recalled being so afraid of Klan raids on young couples "necking" that she and her future husband did their courting in a garage.[34]

Violators of prohibition and other laws were favorites for Klan floggers during the 1927 craze. In August, five masked men charged a couple with bootlegging. In the ensuing shootout, Knights wounded a black bystander. In Birmingham, sheeted thugs attacked one man three times in the course of a few weeks. On the first two occasions they kidnapped and flogged him; on the third, they shot him in the stomach.[35] Four men abducted one Jefferson County man from his bed and lashed him for drinking, beating his wife, and having relations with his invalid daughter. Eight hooded marauders beat an Eastaboga man so badly for gambling that he nearly died. Calhoun Klansmen whipped a black man for bootlegging and stole forty-six dollars from him for good measure.[36] Sometimes Klansmen killed two birds with one stone by combining ethical regulation with nativism. In August 1927, for example, Calhoun Knights beat an immigrant restaurant owner for having an affair with a local woman.[37]

The contradictions inherent in the idea that masked mobs could consider it appropriate to beat people for moral misconduct struck at the very core of Grover Hall's being. From his acidic pen flowed a river of abuse aimed at people he regarded as sheeted hypocrites. Hall took special issue with what he termed the "misplaced emphasis" of Alabama law enforcement that could crack down on drinking and gambling but turn a blind eye to hooded terrorism. He suggested flogging convicted floggers as one possible solution. Exercised to a lather by the morality floggings, Hall also took on the Klan politicians whom he held responsible. He reproved Charlie McCall as a moral crusader who remained indifferent to Klan terror, reproached Bibb Graves as the author of "pretty speeches" on morality but a man completely unmoved by the sufferings of nonconformists, and scolded Senators Hugo Black and Tom Heflin as eloquent men who, if they had ever condemned a hooded gang, did so only "in the sweet hour of prayer in their private chapels."[38]

Other groups distanced themselves from the work of the Klan's morality police. The Freemasons, themselves not renowned for tolerance, denounced hooded mayhem. In 1925 the Masons had joined the KKK in a spectacular open air celebration in Prattville, but in 1927, Alabama Masonic leader O. D. Street condemned Klan violence as contrary to essential Masonic principles and vowed that none of his men would mock patriotism or blaspheme religion by participating in the outrages. An editor echoed Street's reprimand by noting that the very people who appointed themselves the violent monitors of ethics paradoxically claimed that they were acting in the name of virtue.[39]

Still, plenty of Alabamians agreed that the vigilantism and perhaps hypocrisy were preferable to the greater evil of immorality. Some naively compared Klan assaults to the whippings they had received as children. Others felt that the local community had a right, indeed a civic responsibility, to regulate personal conduct. Some evangelical adherents felt that it was their moral duty to correct the ethical shortcomings of their neighbors—by force if necessary. Still, the use of violence to regulate morality raised questions that eventually drew church leaders into the public debate. The KKK was predominantly Baptist and Methodist, but a number of Protestants were uneasy about using the lash to preach virtue.[40]

14. Grover C. Hall, Sr., ca. 1930. Grover Hall, a consummate political conservative, could be quite pragmatic, even mercenary at times, in his opposition to the Klan. Courtesy Birmingham Public Library Archives, Portrait.

Grover Hall (figure 14) mobilized religious opposition by rebuking the *Alabama Baptist* and the *Alabama Christian Advocate* for their silence on the matter. The newspapers, respectively the official state organs of the Baptist and Methodist churches, had up to 1927 furnished not a "word of pity and compassion . . . , a hint of regret . . . , no call—not even a faint whisper" that the Klan's violence was intrinsically un-Christian. Hall did note, somewhat derisively, that the *Alabama Baptist* had run yet another anti-Catholic "thrust at the Pope" but wagered that no Jew or Knight of Columbus had taken part in a Klan flogging.[41]

Others followed Hall's lead. Victor Hanson's *Birmingham Age-Herald* sharply noted the paucity of religious editorials against hooded outrages and accused religious editors of having yellow streaks. A north Alabama Methodist expressed his disappointment that the *Christian Advocate* had failed to damn Klan flogging and had instead dismissed Hall's attacks as politically inspired. He defied anyone to show him a scriptural passage in which Christ had "robed himself with a mask and [gone] forth to preach salvation with a lash in one hand and a fiery emblem of vengeance, intimidation, and fanaticism in the other."[42]

The verbal barbs of Hall and his sympathizers eventually roused some of Alabama's more conscientious religious figures to action. A Highland Methodist minister took issue with the Klan's use of the cross at its beatings. Five other Protestant pastors followed suit. From his pulpit at the Southside Baptist church, as well as a guest column in the *Alabama Baptist,* the idealist Dr. J. E. Dillard sternly repudiated masked violence. Three Montgomery preachers echoed his words. Even Dr. L. C. Branscomb, president of the Alabama Anti-Saloon League, issued a statement opposing flogging. The last denunciation was significant, if curious, because it emanated from a prominent political ally of the KKK.[43]

Hall greeted these statements with undisguised pleasure and called upon bankers, editors, judges, and politicians to join the pulpit. What he did not mention, though, was that the churches' denunciations of violence came principally from pulpits in Birmingham and Montgomery, the hubs of planter/industrialist political power.[44]

Many members of the cloth were not only unmoved by moral violence but actually supported it. James Esdale later estimated that over half of Alabama's Protestant ministers and their congregations were either members of the KKK or fellow travelers. Other commentators have made higher estimates. Dr. L. L. Gwaltney, editor of the *Alabama Baptist* and a frequent target of Grover Hall's rhetorical attacks, defended the Klan's existence and its mask. Gwaltney extolled the original KKK, blamed the rise of the revised order on the Knights of Columbus, apologized for its excesses, and argued that, despite its warts, secret organizations such as the Klan had a history of granting more freedom to the common people. A Troy bank cashier urged Gwaltney not to pay attention to Hall's juvenile attacks. "Bad boys have always liked to annoy their God-fearing elders," he explained. "So sit steady [and] don't worry about rocks thrown from the outside."[45] The pastor of Ensley's First Methodist church defended the robed monitors of morality and criticized Victor Hanson for distorting public perceptions of the Klan. After one especially brutal flogging, another Methodist minister all but congratulated the sheeted terrorists.[46]

Support for the Klan that came from the pulpit showed that many Alabamians agreed with the order's most basic ideas and also reflected the order's close ties to Protestantism. Much of the work was carried out by the Methodist minister Earl Hotalen. The Reverend Hotalen crisscrossed the state, presiding at Klan galas, picnics, and tent revivals. On one occasion he presented Billy Sunday, the renowned evangelist, with a lump sum of money on behalf of Mobile Klan No. 108. Hotalen defended the doctrine of white supremacy, describing it not as inimical to other races but as essential for the preservation of an unpolluted heritage. He also did much to define the KKK's concerns apart from organized terror: the Klan, he said, stood for chivalry, free public schools, free speech, a free press, the separation of church and state, patriotism, and Bible study. Hotalen claimed that Klansmen wore robes, not to disguise the identities of those committing crimes, but to symbolize the purity of Jesus Christ. The KKK would unmask, he vowed, only when "our Lord, the Prince of Peace, shall come again . . . , when Satan . . . shall have been bound in chains, and when bootleggers . . . , rapists, thugs, gamblers, crooked politicians, and murderers no longer encumber the earth."[47]

A serious blow to Protestant solidarity with regard to the Klan was struck late in 1927 by the Alabama Baptist Convention, the largest denominational organization in the state and a powerful political interest group. The condemnation—a short, simple, and direct statement—denounced flogging and called upon all Christians to do the same. Grover Hall and other patrician editors enthusiastically welcomed the statement as a turning point in the fight against the Klan.[48]

Not all of the 1927 violence directly concerned the policing of local virtue. A number of attacks occurred because of the violently permissive atmosphere that Klan vigilantism had inspired. There did indeed appear to be a moratorium on law and order in the state, a culture of pervasive chaos. In such a climate anything from personal disputes and petty jealousies to racial, sexual, religious, and ethnic control was fair game for adjudication at the end of a Klan whip. Masked men attacked John Bolton of Jefferson County not once or twice but three times. The mobs blindfolded him, whipped him with a cat o'nine tails, kicked him, bludgeoned his skull with pistol butts, and eventually burned his house to the ground. No clear reason for the attacks was ever discerned. Disguised men abducted two men from a convict lease camp in Rosedale, spirited them to a remote area, and flogged them. A Jefferson County grand jury later indicted a dozen men, including the camp warden. In July, at the height of Alabama's flogging epidemic, for no discernible reason Walker Kluxers attacked a Colorado couple on a walking trip to Miami.[49]

UNFAVORABLE NATIONAL PUBLICITY

Alabama's flogging rash became big news in the summer of 1927. Articles on the Klan's reign of terror appeared everywhere: in the *New York Times,* the *New York Herald-Tribune,* and the *Chicago Tribune,* in magazines such as

Time, Collier's, Outlook, the *Literary Digest,* and a host of other national publications. Alabama's KKK terror became so widely known that one Missouri family, on the way to a vacation in Florida, stopped a Montgomery traffic cop to ask whether it was safe to travel through the state at night.[50]

Still, wretched public relations were no laughing matter to Alabamians who cherished economic progress and capital investment. When Randolph officials announced that eight new floggings had taken place in their county alone, a Birmingham newspaper concerned with New South materialism blasted Governor Graves for allowing a lawless atmosphere to pervade the state.[51]

Pro-business newspapers in the other southern states were, themselves, not likely to look favorably on Klan excess that jeopardized regional prospects for attracting capital. A North Carolina editor praised Georgia's law enforcement against Ku Kluxism but disparaged Alabama's. The *Atlanta Constitution* balefully asked when Alabama's barbarism would end, and its editor observed, "The whole state of Alabama is on trial." Alabama became the target of regional rage from Knoxville, Greensboro, Columbia, Charlotte, Baltimore, Richmond, Nashville, and a host of other southern cities.[52]

State and regional uproar led to a national outcry against the Alabama situation. A Massachusetts paper attributed the Alabama crisis to backward social development that manifested itself in an unfathomable ignorance of the basic legal, political, and civil rights guaranteed to all Americans. The *New York Times* called for a national campaign to pressure Alabama officials to end the epidemic but expressed doubt that southern writers would heed the call. The *Literary Digest* termed the Alabama situation a "national scandal," while other national publications concluded that moral repression was the exclusive province of the South and principally of Alabama.[53]

One notable exception to these essentially accurate but chauvinistic assessments came from the pen of a Chicago editor. "There should be little temptation to throw stones," he wrote. After all, the KKK was hardly confined to any one state, even Alabama, and the "abyss of ignorance and bigotry" that produced such violence was also not the monopoly of any one state or region. "It exists," he astutely pointed out, "in more or less extent," everywhere.[54]

Blacks, by definition interested parties, adopted a curious position on the Alabama flogging epidemic. During the summer of 1927 it became obvious that blacks (at least for the moment) no longer held the primary attention of whip-wielding white mobs. Whites occupied center stage and specifically whites who in some way fell short of the almost superhuman moral demands made of them by overly enthusiastic evangelicals. Klansmen ter rorized whites while people of color watched, from their unique vantage point, with a mixture of sympathy, empathy, bemusement, cynicism, satisfaction, and an acute awareness of irony. Black leaders had long warned whites that unchecked vigilantism would eventually retard any sense of decency and that even whites would one day fall victim to the mob. Alabama's acceptance of mob justice for blacks had led to a general erosion of the sanctity of law, a New York editor concluded, even for whites. Mob rule had finally consumed the state. White disregard for black due process "now stunted . . . [any white] sense of justice." "It was formerly the impression that so long as mobs whipped, hanged, and burned Negroes . . . , lawlessness would recognize the sanctity of the color line," the *Pittsburgh Courier* remarked, "but now the South is learning [that] this sort of thing is contagious . . . , that the mob that burns a Negro today will not hesitate to burn a Caucasian tomorrow." A black editor in Washington, D.C., was equally critical: "As long as the Southern lash descended only upon black shoulders, little or no protestation was voiced. . . . the graveness of the situation never dawns upon the Nordic as long as he and his own are not threatened."[55]

The flogging of a white did occupy the center of attention in Alabama in 1927: the case was that of Jeff Calloway, a mentally impaired orphan from Blount County. The Calloway flogging, and the trial of seven Klansmen that followed, provided the climax to Alabama's summer orgy of violence. Strangely enough, it was sufficient to stem the tide of adverse national publicity that the state had suffered and actually to reverse it.

THE CALLOWAY AFFAIR

The attack on Jeff Calloway took place on the hot summer evening of 16 June. Klansmen from Blount County and two Jefferson County klaverns had converged on the Antioch Methodist Church on Blount's Straight Mountain to hear sermons by three Klan ministers. While the meeting took place, young Calloway stood outside the church laughing, talking, and drinking with several teenage friends. When the meeting adjourned, enraged Klansmen, stimulated beyond control by exhortations to oppose the "whiskey evil," seized Calloway at gunpoint, loaded him into a car, and drove just over the Jefferson line. During the ride, they stuck a gun in his ribs and beat him. Once at Mount Pinson, the Kluxers tied the young man to a tree and beat him so savagely that he lost consciousness, developed blood clots, and later suffered a nervous breakdown. As they beat him, Calloway's tormentors laughed, told jokes, and took turns drinking his whiskey.[56]

Calloway's assault quickly became the cause célèbre of 1927, perhaps because he was so young or because he was an orphan, or because he was at least the eighth such victim in Blount County in two years. Alternatively, the reason might have been that the Klansmen had just come from church or that the mob had passed within fifty yards of the sheriff's office on their way to Mount Pinson. Physical proximity to legal authority exposed the Knights' preference for violence rather than actual enforcement of the law. They were—inevitably—accused of hypocrisy because they had only just attended church.[57]

The backlash that greeted the flogging exceeded the outrage over all the other 1927 beatings. Grover Hall again took the lead in criticizing the KKK for the attack. In perhaps the most famous of his Pulitzer Prize–winning editorials, entitled "The Glove of the Beast—Will the State Pick It Up?" Hall chastised the Klan's most prominent elected officials for the violence of its rank and file. He reserved special condemnation for Bibb Graves, Hugo Black, Tom Heflin, and Charlie McCall and movingly described "grotesque figures" clad in Klan regalia falling upon a teenage orphan who "had made his [own] way almost from babyhood." "The probability is that [Calloway] committed no serious wrong," Hall reasoned. "But it does not matter. What does matter is that human beasts feel free to fall upon a fellow man . . . , whisk him away, kick him, curse him, and then beat him unmercifully."[58] Subsequent editorials bashed Alabama editors for remaining silent on Klan violence. Hall noted that only five newspapers ran negative editorials about the Calloway incident, twenty-five specifically provided no denunciation, and only 5 percent of the state's papers had even reported the assault. He called for press and pulpit to wrestle with the issue raised so viscerally "by the blood and groans of all the uncounted Jeff Calloways in Alabama."[59]

James Chappell of the *Birmingham News* followed Hall's line of attack. In an emotional piece entitled "Alabama's Shame—What Will the Governor Do?" Chappell joined his close friend and colleague in demanding that Bibb Graves take the lead in identifying and punishing the "brigands" responsible for the beating. Chappell called upon Governor Graves to break whatever bonds still "shackle[d] him to [the] forces of anarchy" and recommended that Graves outlaw the concealment of auto tags, a ruse commonly used by KKK floggers. Chappell also questioned the sincerity of the governor's opposition to violence and asked the memorable question: "Why is it that Col. Graves persists in folding his hands . . . in this slumber and sleep of his? Can it be that Alabama which once boasted government by the law must now admit that it only has government by the lash?"[60]

Smaller weekly papers, especially from the Black Belt and its environs, followed the example set by Chappell and Hall. An editor in Opp called the KKK the nation's "greatest menace." Denunciations came from Opelika and Centreville, where angry newsmen focused on the adverse effect that hooded violence was bound to have on Alabama's prospects of attracting commerce. A Dadeville editor took Calloway's floggers to task for their "ridiculous ignorance" of due process and trial by jury. Sheffield's paper concurred and described as "perverted" the idea that happiness derives from meddling in the private affairs of others. Florala and Headland editors branded Klan floggers hypocritical "bigots." A Florence newspaper called on the Klan's good men to resign, and a Demopolis paper declared that it was "unconscionable" for Knights to commit perjury to protect accused floggers.[61]

The *New York Times* joined the fray by calling Bibb Graves the "darling of the Klan," describing Charlie McCall as obsessed with slot machines, and denounced the whole state of Alabama as fixated on the "monomania" of prohibition. "Isn't the root of the trouble," a *Times* editor asked, "to be found in the grotesque magnification of the prohibition law . . . , [the] cardinal statute" in Alabama?[62]

Although the Calloway affair triggered strong opposition to the Klan, it also caused many to defend the order reflexively. The pastor of the Blount County church where Calloway had been kidnapped registered only mechanical disapproval of the assault but praised the KKK for "greatly . . . keeping down drinking and disturbances at our public gatherings . . . [and] the whiskey evil which has heretofore prevailed." A Montgomery merchant applauded Calloway's punishment. The *Fayette Banner* called Calloway a "drunken bully" whose "good whipping" at the hands of the KKK was well deserved: "Just because of a 'poor little orphan,' . . . full of booze and trying to bulldoze a whole community which was worshipping, . . . Alabama is pictured as a state to be avoided."[63]

Some apparent condemnations of the attack were, upon closer inspection, actually apologies for the Klan. A Midland man maintained that the KKK still had a good platform even if Klansmen did not always live up to it. An Evergreen newspaper called the flogging "regrettable" yet insisted that the Klan would apprehend "the real" floggers. Newspapers in Athens and south Alabama agreed. A Colbert County editor regretted the violence but suggested that Calloway probably deserved the beating anyway.[64]

Bibb Graves, perhaps rocked by the maelstrom of protest, at last looked as though he were ready to act. The governor assigned two plainclothes detectives to the case, called a well-known opponent of mob law to convene a special grand jury, and assigned the case to Charlie McCall.[65] Still, Graves's actions may not have reflected an intent to act. McCall had been swept into office on the same Klan wave as Graves and, like the governor, owed his political allegiance to the secret order. The attorney general had shown no interest in crossing the Klan—at least not yet. He had confined himself to cracking down on gambling, drinking, and other personal vices, joining James Esdale's libel suit against the *Birmingham Age-Herald,* and even attempting to name the grand dragon to his staff. Graves's choice of McCall to oversee the Calloway case represented, at the least, no great move in the direction of law and order. At the most, it was a calculated attempt to ensure light treatment for the accused Klansmen. Graves's assignment of handpicked policemen was equally suspect, because the ranks of the state police were rife with avowed Klansmen, many of them appointed by the governor himself. Graves lost what little credibility he may have had when the state announced that it was delaying the arrests of fifteen suspects for eight days until the grand jury had had a chance to convene. The move, a most irregular one, was greeted with derision by legal pundits, who recognized that the delay would give Klan defendants a golden opportunity to perfect their alibis.[66]

Local authorities did arrest seven Klansmen, six of them from Tarrant City, and Charlie McCall praised the grand jury's investigation. McCall proved instrumental in procuring arrests; he called over a hundred witnesses into a packed Oneonta courtroom. The young attorney set the county "abuzzing" with his prosecution of the case.[67]

McCall's obvious change of heart (and change of political allegiance) marked a serious shift. Up until the Calloway trials, he had shown himself to be a solid Klan politician. Yet his transformation in July 1927—perhaps because he found violence repugnant or because he hoped in the future to win Big Mule political support—marked a clear and unmistakable change, one that would have serious consequences for Bibb Graves and Alabama's KKK.

Meanwhile, Blount County was in an uproar. Residents were enraged that their county was receiving negative national attention because of the misdeeds of Kluxers from another county. When the indictments came down, Oneonta's newspaper virtually screamed the fact that the defendants were from Jefferson County. Blount citizens held a mass meeting to deplore the assault, sympathize with Calloway, pledge their intention of cooperating with police, and deny that their county was lawless. Oneonta residents went even further. They asked state lawmakers and the city council to pass antimasking legislation and enacted an ordinance prohibiting the concealment of automobile tags.[68]

Rumors circulated that Charlie McCall would go easy on the Klan defendants, that he might even use James Esdale as an assistant in the case. What the attorney general did next, though, surprised almost everyone in the state. McCall released a bombshell of a letter to Esdale claiming that the state had incontrovertible evidence that members of the Klan had beaten Calloway. He demanded that the grand dragon turn over the names of all the Knights involved.[69]

McCall's letter, published in virtually every newspaper in Alabama and many others around the country, sent shock waves through the KKK. The Montgomery klavern, home to both McCall and Governor Graves, denounced violence. Blount's cyclops publicly blamed the flogging on Kluxers from Jefferson County. John Wade explained that a group of Tarrant and Ensley Klansmen had brought Calloway to him directly after the church services, but that he had told them to turn the boy over to the local sheriff for breaking the prohibition law.[70]

As fractures within the KKK became increasingly obvious, state Klan leaders struck back. James Esdale announced that he would personally oversee a hooded investigation of the flogging. In Blount County and in Birmingham Knights distributed leaflets arguing that the assault on Calloway had been just punishment for his irreverence and alcohol consumption. "These whiskey drinkers were talked to, pleaded with, and prayed to . . . in order that the church-going, God-fearing people might worship their God in a befitting manner unmolested," the flyers asserted. "The little orphan that you've been reading about is a full grown man, and if he is big enough to drink liquor, and tote a .38 or .44, he is old enough to know better than to attempt to break up a protracted meeting."[71]

In August 1927 the Calloway cases opened to a packed audience of over a thousand people, more than three times the capacity of the county courthouse. Spectators traveled to the county seat of Oneonta in cars and buggies, by foot and on horseback, to see the historic event.[72] At the helm of the defense team was Horace Wilkinson, the gifted Klansman who was a close friend of Bibb Graves and also one of the nation's foremost constitutional lawyers. The choice of Wilkinson was an unmistakable sign that the governor's sympathies lay with the Klan. Wilkinson was Graves's right-hand man and played a major part in his election in 1926 and would again in 1934.[73]

On the first day of the trial of Klansman Eugene Doss, Wilkinson and the lead prosecutor, Attorney General Charlie McCall—both young, talented, forceful, and ambitious—clashed verbally and on a number of occasions almost physically. But it was James Esdale who stole the show. Esdale played a prominent part in the legal drama. He ignored a state subpoena to appear and finally yielded only after being threatened with a contempt charge. The grand dragon, whose legal offices adjoined Wilkinson's in Birmingham, proved an elusive, recalcitrant, and intractable witness. He denied all knowledge of the flogging and even of routine Klan business. Esdale frustrated McCall at every turn. When asked whether he had sent a Klan investigator to Oneonta, Esdale replied, "I don't know." When McCall asked what right he had to send an investigator, the grand dragon answered, "The same right I have to send you." "You have no right to send me anywhere," the attorney general snapped. "I have sent you," responded the imperturbable Esdale.[74]

Wilkinson used his rich legal talent to slow the inexorable legal process, but his efforts were ultimately of little avail. The state's case, built around the confessions of three self-avowed Klan floggers, was simply too strong. Wilkinson filed demurrers, motions to quash the indictments, and pleas of abatement, and he raised an endless succession of objections on technical grounds. Judge O. A. Steele, though, repeatedly overruled the Klan lawyer. Wilkinson did win some small victories; he established that Calloway had indeed been unruly and intoxicated, and he showed that the beating had not been premeditated.[75] Still, Wilkinson could not refute the state's strong case. Judge Steele did not appear to be sympathetic to the Klan and, at one point, interrupted Wilkinson to ask if the "klavaliers" were an elite whipping squad. Wilkinson exploded in protest, and the judge quickly withdrew the question.[76]

Other Klan officers, taking their cue from Esdale, were also less than forthright in answering Charlie McCall's questions. Dr. L. S. Fennell, suspected cyclops of the Tarrant klavern, told the court that he had resigned just prior to the Calloway attack and did not know who had taken his place. Ordered to produce records and membership lists, Fennell appeared in court empty handed.[77]

Still, the prosecution had perhaps the strongest case ever mounted against Klansmen in an Alabama court. Three members of the flogging crew, "tired of lying," confessed to the assault and turned state's evidence. As the trial wore on, other Klansmen repeatedly threatened their lives. One informant alone reported fifty threats. Finally, McCall advised the trio to "repel with force" any further Klan threats.[78]

Twelve peers of the defendant Eugene Doss—eleven Blount County farmers and a bank cashier, who served as foreman—deliberated for seventeen hours before finding Doss guilty of assault and battery and kidnapping. Judge Steele sentenced Doss to the maximum eight to ten years in prison. Horace Wilkinson filed notice of appeal and asked for a $5,000 bond.[79]

Steele's conduct was especially noteworthy and inspiring. Years earlier he had rebuked a Jefferson County jury that acquitted the floggers of a prominent Birmingham physician. In the Doss case, Steele applied the maximum sentence, fined a cyclops for speaking out against press coverage of the trial, and lectured the defendant in no uncertain terms at his sentencing. "Every lick that you and the members of your flogging party hit Jeff Calloway was a blow at the personal liberty of every citizen of the State," Steele told Eugene Doss. "There is no mitigation and no justification for your crime. You have defied the fundamental principles on which government was founded. . . . You do not look like a bad man, but you have some very bad ideas." [80]

Lee A. Clayton was the next defendant. Unaccustomed to losing in Alabama courtrooms, Horace Wilkinson did everything he could to win an acquittal. He called 120 witnesses and fired off a barrage of protests, demurrers, pleas, and objections. Eventually the case became a personal war of wills, not only between Wilkinson and McCall, but also between Wilkinson and the judge. [81]

The testimony of several Kluxers who had taken part in the flogging was again fatally damaging to the Klan's case. J. T. Hughes described the beating in detail, stated that Lee Clayton had been present with a pistol, and named each participant in the flogging. Oliver Tidwell affirmed Hughes's testimony and furnished details about the klavaliers, a special flogging crew. A local woman spoke about the night's sermons at Antioch Methodist Church, which included invective against liquor and teen sex, and thereby also helped the state's case. [82]

Clayton's jury returned a verdict of guilty, and Steele gave him the same sentence as Doss. Recognizing that it would be futile to have additional trials in Blount County, Wilkinson made a deal. If the state changed the kidnapping charge to "inciting riot," five other Tarrant Klansmen would plead guilty: Amos Covington, Peter Carlisle, Chester and Clifton Clayton, and Dr. L. S. Fennell. All received six-month sentences and $500 fines. [83] Afterward, Charlie McCall vowed to be as relentless as his foes. "I shall not let up," he swore, "I'm going to give them hell, for that is the same thing they have given their victims." [84]

The Calloway convictions were historic. At the time, tabloids mistakenly described them as the first convictions of Alabama Klansmen ever won. True, it was the first time that an Alabama court had convicted Klansmen of flogging under state law. Klansmen had of course been convicted earlier, during Reconstruction, of flogging and other outrages, but these cases had been tried in federal courts under federal law. There had also been previous convictions of Alabama Klansmen in state courts under state laws but for offenses other than flogging. Furthermore, Alabama's state court had handed down convictions in other flogging cases involving individuals not proven to be Klansmen. [85]

The conviction of acknowledged Klansmen for flogging had a remarkable effect. Hundreds of Alabama floggings were immediately forgotten. Politicians, editors, ministers, and civic leaders of all kinds hailed the Cal-

loway convictions as the end of Klan terror in Alabama. Grover Hall called
the convictions "a magnificent triumph . . . over the forces of anarchy and
darkness . . . , [one] that marks . . . a new day in Alabama." The *Birmingham
Age-Herald* likened the event to the fall of the Bastille and celebrated the
end of masked tyranny: "It is not a casual revolt, it is a revolution against
intolerable oppression and injustice. . . . History was made in Oneonta. . . .
the fabric of intimidation and terror woven by the Ku Klux Klan has
crumbled before the onset of legal justice." Almost immediately, formerly
hostile editors began lavishing praise upon Charlie McCall as the un-
crowned king of Alabama. Grover Hall, who had repeatedly impugned
McCall's character and his Klan motives, now lauded his "acumen, courage,
energy . . . [and] conscientious devotion." Planter newspapers in south Alabama called the convictions "the most exhilarating piece of news that has
emanated from Alabama" and asked Alabamians to ratify them in the court
of public opinion. Lee County officials, acknowledging the convictions' importance, changed the theme of their upcoming county fair from "Klan
Day" to "Shrine Day."[86]

Following the convictions, Alabama's anti-Klan editors declared that
their victory against the KKK was complete. Editors of the *Birmingham
News* called themselves "men of moral perception and courage" for their
part in killing the Alabama KKK. The *Age-Herald* applauded grassroots animus against the order and declared that Alabama is "free from the grip of
sinister forces. . . . The day of the new independence is at hand."[87]

Other Southerners were just as ready to declare victory in the war
against the Klan. Atlanta and Charleston editors concluded that Alabama had
vindicated itself. An editor in Columbia, South Carolina, also interpreted
the convictions as the end of the Alabama Klan. "When a politician deserts
a ship," he remarked wryly, "it is indubitably sinking."[88]

Former critics on the national scene likewise concluded that Alabama's
KKK was now dead and welcomed Alabama back into the family of civilized states. A Minnesota paper likened Victor Hanson to Emile Zola because of his defense of human rights. The *Chicago Tribune*, a bitter critic of
Alabama's lawlessness, applauded Hanson's papers for providing inspiration
to freedom-loving newspapers everywhere and for defeating the Alabama
Klan with unusual courage and eloquence. A black Chicago paper concurred with the white paper, while the black *Pittsburgh Courier* celebrated
with a backhanded compliment: "Even the most ignorant person can learn
something once in a while, and the most backward sections occasionally
give evidence of increased enlightenment."[89]

For all practical purposes, the war against the Ku Klux Klan in Alabama
was apparently over, waged to a successful conclusion—or so most people

thought. The year 1927 had been a memorable one in Alabama history. The state had plunged into national disrepute for its toleration of Klan excess— traceable, in the eyes of most observers, to the order's political sweep of the November 1926 elections. A state with a Klan governor, Klan senators, and Klan officials in virtually all local positions had proved to be a haven for those members of the organization who felt inclined to punish other human beings for their differences—religious, racial, ethnic, and moral. In such an environment, those compelled by a perverted version of the evangelical mandate ran amuck. State opposition to the whip began in the office of Victor Hanson and with the pen of Grover Hall. It spread to Hall's fellow editors in Birmingham, Mobile, and the Black Belt and from there diffused throughout the region and the nation. Alabama had literally become the scourge of the country. The state became as renowned for pervasive violence as for the propensity of its officials to look the other way.

The situation changed, however, with the conviction of Jeff Calloway's floggers. Three Klansmen, by acknowledging their membership in the order and their participation in the crime, had made the state's case unbeatable. The county, infuriated by the notoriety it inherited due to the actions of terrorists from another county, resolved itself to act. An attorney general, repelled by the Klan's affinity for moral regulation and disenchanted by the order's political leadership, drove himself and the disaffected locals to convict. An upstanding judge, steadfastly determined to punish wrongdoers, made the convictions count. By the end of the summer of 1927, an obscure orphan named Jeff Calloway seemed to have killed the Ku Klux Klan in Alabama.

7
Elite War on the Klan

People all over the country were anxious to quell the Klan in Alabama in part so that the state would conform to national standards. By 1926 the KKK was dead or dying fast in most states but not in the Deep South.[1] In fact, it had seen a resurgence in Alabama. With its sweep of the 1926 elections, the Klan had scored a stunning political triumph over its Big Mule/Black Belt antagonists. The political conflict between Klan and oligarchy allowed the hooded order to extend its influence far longer in Alabama than in other states. During the 1920s, Alabama became the arena in which the oligarchy and the Klan waged a political battle royal. In the politically charged atmosphere, events such as the 1924 national convention, the 1926 state elections, and Oscar Underwood's retirement acquired new meaning.

Considered within the same context, the conviction of Jeff Calloway's floggers marked a major victory for the Big Mule/Black Belt coalition. National and regional editors took their cue about Alabama conditions largely from the patrician press. Both national and regional editors first noticed the "epidemic" of violence in Alabama only after Victor Hanson's newspapers had spoken of one. Now, in the fall of 1927, the victory of good over evil in Alabama was more apparent than real. Actually, the Klan's death was a figment of wishful oligarchical thinking and not reality. The Calloway convictions were undeniably a serious setback for Alabama's KKK but hardly amounted to the death of the secret society. The conflict between Alabama's Klan and anti-Klan forces during the 1920s, usually depicted as a struggle between good and evil, between light and darkness, is more complex.

Patrician mouthpiece Grover Hall took the lead in declaring the Klan dead in Alabama. "Wherever the State goes into action against floggers," Hall declared in the pages of the *Montgomery Advertiser,* "Klansmen are indicted and convicted—because they are guilty."[2] Yet Hall was far from the only social critic to sound the death knell. The KKK had suffered such a series of setbacks around the country that by 1926 it was generally assumed to be defunct everywhere. Legislatures in Massachusetts, Connecticut, and North Carolina dealt severe blows to the Invisible Empire. The U.S. Supreme Court upheld the right of Kansas to outlaw the KKK. Pennsylvania's woes became front page news replete with tales of internal strife, lynchings, fatal rioting, and the kidnapping of a four-year-old girl. Even those who defended the order on the ground that it maintained traditional values were hard-pressed to excuse such misconduct. In Indiana, scandal surrounding the grand dragon and the death of one of his lovers led to the rapid decline of a KKK that had been politically powerful. Grover Hall gleefully reported on a "cesspool of political corruption" in Indiana and other Klan setbacks around the country. In fact, much of his rhetoric was aimed at trying to place Alabama on the roll of states that had effectively exterminated the Klan.[3]

Alabama's Klan membership was indeed falling. In 1925, fully 115,000 men had been members of the secret order; in 1926, membership was down to 94,301. By 1927, the number had fallen to just 10,431. Many equated the membership decline with the society's complete demise, but the KKK still had tremendous political strength in the state despite losses in the rank and file.[4]

To some extent violence was responsible for the drop in membership in Alabama by 1927.[5] As in the Reconstruction years, some "good" Klansmen, perceiving the order's commitment to violence, quit in disgust. But this explanation does not fully account for epidemic Klan violence in Alabama from as early as 1921, nor does it explain the role that Klan leaders played in planning, organizing, and later covering up vigilante acts. Why did the Alabama KKK suddenly lose members in 1927 if violence had been a characteristic feature since at least 1921? One likely possibility is that Big Mule/ Black Belt political opposition to the Klan that specifically *publicized* violence was the major reason for the Klan's membership decline—not the violence alone nor a sudden aversion to vigilantism on the part of many "good" Klansmen. Such opposition gained momentum in Alabama only after November 1926, precisely the time when Klan membership took a turn for the worse.

Still, the decline in numbers of dues-paying Klansmen, despite appearances, did not necessarily mean that Alabama's Klan had breathed its last. The vigorous resistance of planters and industrialists might injure the KKK as a political power, but its focus was primarily political and did not extend to all spheres.

ALABAMA POLITICS

As noted above, planter/industrialist opposition to the Klan was a function of Alabama's ancient division between privileged whites and their poor white adversaries. For decades, Alabama politics had been dominated by the Black Belt oligarchy and their industrial allies. Violence, terror, repression, and disenfranchisement had long since destroyed the African American as a viable political entity in the South. During the 1920s the KKK allied itself with some unions, farmers, women, evangelical Protestants, and Prohibitionists to become part of a formidable coalition that backed politicians who owed their allegiance to the Klan rather than to the oligarchy. Bibb Graves was the foremost representative of this new cadre.[6]

By any measure, Graves's reform agenda in Alabama was impressive. By southern standards it was remarkable; for Alabama it was miraculous. Graves's progressivism, though, was purchased at a price—a monetary debt for the state and a decline in power for the oligarchy. The cost seemed more than financial to planters and industrialists and far more damaging.[7]

The planter/industrialist tandem had run Alabama and other southern states since Reconstruction. Traditionally, these conservative Democrats had kept public spending on the social, educational, health, and public sectors at atrociously low levels. Meanwhile, members of the oligarchy, such as the celebrated Bankheads of Jasper, had made fortunes and built political dynasties on revenues from some of the most unsavory aspects of the Redeemer program, such as convict lease.[8] Despite the vested interests of the Redeemers in maintaining the status quo, those who wanted to push Alabama forward viewed the perpetuation of such conditions as intolerable.[9] While Alabama lurched along unsteadily—far behind other states in terms of education, public health, and most social services—the Bourbons prospered. In the eyes of Alabama's old conservative oligarchy, Bibb Graves's attempts at reform made his program anathema, and he became a pariah.

David Bibb Graves began his political career in Alabama's house of representatives in 1898 as a delegate from Montgomery County. He served two terms, quickly becoming identified with the Joseph F. Johnston wing of the Democratic Party, which opposed schemes to disenfranchise poor whites and periodically produced challenges to patrician power at the turn of the century. In 1916 Graves gained election as chair of the state Democratic executive committee. During World War I, Graves led an Alabama regiment in Europe as a colonel. Soon after the war, he ran for governor. While his campaign was unsuccessful, it did make him more recognizable to voters.[10]

By 1926, Graves had recognized the Klan's potential as a way of challenging the oligarchy's stranglehold on state politics. Still, he was a long shot in the governor's race. Lieutenant Governor Charles S. McDowell, Jr., of Eufaula, who had patrician backing, was the obvious favorite. Graves ran on a progressive platform but was challenged by other self-proclaimed progressives such as A. G. Patterson, president of the Alabama Public Service Commission, and Archie H. Carmichael, a noted lawyer from Tuscumbia. Graves ran best in the hill counties of east Alabama and worst in the Black Belt. Buttressed by the Klan, veterans, organized labor, and some educational and professional groups, the "little colonel" shocked political pundits by winning the Democratic nomination for governor and, in effect, the election.[11]

Once in power, Graves launched an extensive program of reforms that further alienated the state's fiscally conservative oligarchy. At the start of his administration he raised taxes and earmarked $400,000 for a reform-minded fact-finding study. The new governor also secured passage of a $600,000 emergency appropriation for public schools that targeted the state's subpar rural schools.[12] He bolstered educational reform by forcing the state to increase spending and to set aside $20 million to ensure that the public school year lasted at least nine months in towns and seven months in the countryside. The move passed, again over strong oligarchical opposition, largely because it was reminiscent of attempts by poor whites to escape the Bourbon dragnet of disenfranchisement through literacy tests and educational qualifications.[13]

The reform package of course exhibited inconsistencies in line with the character of the era. Whites got more than blacks, and males got more than females. Despite the sexual and racial inequities, the appropriations represented a dramatic increase in spending on education for people of both colors and sexes in Alabama.[14]

Public health was another area in which Graves's reform irritated the oligarchy. A massive health program in fifty-four of the state's sixty-seven counties enabled health officers to give all children of school age regular medical examinations and vaccinations. The program targeted smallpox, tuberculosis, hookworm, and pellagra, long the bane of southern existence.[15]

Graves (figure 15) made inroads on railroad monopolies by launching an aggressive program of highway and bridge construction. Alabama's few roads and bridges had been allowed to deteriorate in order to preserve railroad control over the shipment of essential goods and raw materials. Graves presented a serious challenge to the railroad allies of the planters and their dominance of freight transportation by passing a $25 million bond issue in April 1927 and by successfully lobbying the federal government for $6 million in matching funds. His program also called for the construction of a

15. Governor Bibb Graves, 1930s. Although Graves stood for economic liberalism in Alabama, he often closed his eyes to the reign of terror imposed by some of his hooded political backers. Courtesy Alabama State Department of Archives and History.

state docks in Mobile and the improvement of the city's seaport and net-work of supporting waterways.[16]

Graves's most incendiary move may have been his support of organized labor, the most obvious adversary of Alabama's industrialists. The governor led a movement that outlawed the barbaric convict lease program in 1928, earning Alabama the dubious distinction of being the last state in the Union to take this step. Abolition of the medieval system cost patricians such as the Bankheads a million dollars in net profits each year. The governor also cracked down on other labor abuses through the efforts of reformers such as Julia Strudwick Tutwiler and Mrs. A. M. Tunstall. Reform led to the earmarking of $500,000 for juvenile homes and to a 60 percent increase in the pensions of Confederate veterans and their wives.[17]

There was bad blood between the Klan and the oligarchy on another issue, namely the retirement of Oscar Underwood. Senator Underwood, a revered public figure in Alabama, had run for president in 1912 and 1924 and when he retired cleared the way for the senatorial election of Klansman Hugo Black. While the oligarchy smarted from this development, Hiram Evans poured salt on its wounds by describing Underwood's "forced retirement" as one of the Klan's greatest achievements. From his retirement home in Virginia, Underwood celebrated the 1927 Calloway convictions with Victor Hanson but warned the publisher that it would be premature to dismiss the Klan as a force to be reckoned with. Underwood argued that Alabama's legislature would have to kill the KKK effectively and permanently. He also lamented the fact that many of Alabama's "leading people [were] not making the stand against the Ku Klux Klan that ought to be made." "Of course," Underwood wrote, the KKK "must go down in the end . . . , but the splendid battle you are making will always stand in the forefront of Alabama history."[18]

THE ANTI-KLAN CAMPAIGN
OF THE OLIGARCHY PRESS

Victor Hanson had indeed been waging a splendid battle against the secret order—at least in the eyes of the planters and industrialists for whom he spoke. Hanson's editorials had slowly led to the realization that there was a masked threat to law and order in Alabama. Frederick Thompson's dailies followed Hanson's lead, as did some of the state's smaller weeklies, especially in the Black Belt.[19]

Hanson, a devout conservative, stood squarely in the Big Mule camp. He had resisted strikes, courted northern investment, and spouted probusiness sentiment for years. In addition to owning three of the state's largest newspapers, Hanson sat on a number of company boards. He had little sympathy or patience for Bibb Graves's reforms or for the plain folk who made up much of the governor's following.[20]

In 1927, Hanson, James Chappell, and Grover Hall mapped out their anti-KKK strategy in the publisher's Birmingham offices. Hanson felt strongly that a direct attack on the hooded order would result in a reflexive and unproductive defense of Klan principles such as temperance, public education, family values, Protestantism, Americanism, ethnic integrity, and traditional morality. Instead, Hanson advised his editors to attack the Klan indirectly by casting aspersions on the society's less defensible aspects: its violence, its mask, its secrecy, and the beating of women. By avoiding a direct attack on the Klan itself, one that they feared might backfire, the patricians hoped to use the Klan's more unsavory aspects to embarrass the KKK politically. "This can best be done by not attacking it as an organization," Hanson cautioned. "Attack lawless acts . . . ; attack the mask. All of this is a gradual process . . . , a process of attrition. . . . I believe it is the best and wisest way to destroy the [political] power and influence of the Klan." "If we can identify the Klan so thoroughly with lawlessness and with brutality and outrage that honest men will be ashamed of their membership . . . If through the years we can wear down the influence of the Klan," Hanson argued, "we shall have accomplished big things. . . . if there is going to be a time when a smashing, direct fight against the Klan . . . would be effective, we are far away from that time in Alabama today."[21]

Hanson chose Grover Hall to lead the oligarchy's opposition to the Klan because the editor had special gifts. Born in Henry County in 1888, Grover Cleveland Hall had been named after a Democratic president and, appropriately, became a lifelong adherent of the conservative wing of that party. He served newspaper apprenticeships in Dothan, Enterprise, Pensacola, and Selma before arriving at the *Montgomery Advertiser* as an associate editor in 1910. Hanson, with whom Hall had become close, made him editor of the paper in 1926. Two years later, Hall won the Pulitzer Prize for his anti-Klan editorials of 1927 and gained other rewards from the oligarchy for his political loyalty and resistance to the Klan. Conservative governor Benjamin Meek Miller appointed Hall probate judge in the 1930s. Frank Dixon placed him on the state personnel board when he became governor in 1939. Conservatives also backed a successful Hall run for circuit judge. A devoted servant of the oligarchy, Hall developed friendships with conservative notables other than Miller and Dixon—men such as Walter Jones, Joe Bonner, Marion Rushton, future governor Chauncey Sparks, Colonel Harry Ayers, Alabama Power's Thomas Martin, Charles McDowell, and John Bankhead. Hall's in-laws were also among the oldest Black Belt planters in the state.[22]

H. L. Mencken, the acerbic editor of the *Baltimore American Mercury,* was an admirer of Hall. Mencken had first been introduced to Hall's writings by Sara Haardt, his wife, who was a native of Alabama. Mencken's frequent praise of Hall is ironic, given that Mencken is best known for his ruthless criticism of the South. Mencken encouraged Hall to write pieces about a "revolt of the civilized minority" in Dixie against fundamentalism, evangelicalism, the Klan, and related devices that had, Mencken felt, so long retarded intelligent progress in the South.[23]

Scholars have long portrayed Grover Hall as the champion of light over the forces of darkness in Alabama, a gallant knight errant of enlightenment, clad in white, with a pen his Excalibur, who fought against the evil that was the KKK of the 1920s.[24] Grover Hall possessed many admirable qualities, but he was also a complicated man. Economically, he was a staunch conservative with little use for government activism or social programs. He was also a states'-rights enthusiast and a close associate of confirmed racists such as Frank Dixon, Walter Jones, and Forney Johnston. In addition, the most fundamental tenets of his beloved state Democratic Party can hardly be termed enlightened, much less a source of light over darkness. Throughout his long tenure at the *Advertiser,* Hall did not use his pulpit to challenge any entrenched views.[25]

Men like Grover Hall were probably not driven to oppose the Klan solely for political reasons. Still, Hall, the *Advertiser,* and the other oligarchy papers were also probably not impelled to resist purely from a love of justice, fair play, and the American way. Most likely such beliefs were part of their motivation. Another motive, at least as strong, was the realization that lawlessness was the Achilles' heel of the Klan's political machine in Alabama— the same machine that had temporarily displaced the oligarchy as the most dominant political force in the state. Patrician editors could, and did, use the existence of hooded violence as a weapon to attack the Klan as a political entity.

Hall was relentless. He commented almost daily on new Klan beatings and delighted in publishing all the anti-Klan copy he could find. An astute political animal, he took pains not to insult every member of the sheeted fraternity lest he alienate potential converts. He repeatedly qualified his statements, almost pandering to a "good" segment of the Klan, and constructed a stark and somewhat artificial dichotomy between "good" and "evil" Klansmen.[26]

The *Advertiser* editor faced internal and external challenges. Many outside the oligarchy berated his attacks as more harmful to Alabama's national image than the Klan's violence. Although this critique was obtuse, it contained a kernel of wisdom. Hall's critics realized that he was the focal point of state opposition to the Klan and that regional and national editors took their cues from him as to the seriousness of the situation in Alabama.[27]

The most serious fault line of internal dissension, one that threatened to undermine the oligarchy's campaign against the Klan, was a difference of opinion between Victor Hanson and Grover Hall on the liquor issue. To the editor, prohibition was an inherent part of Alabama's Klan problem. The KKK's political strength, Hall felt, was largely due to its fixation on narrow issues of personal morality. An obsession with prohibition consumed many

16. Victor Hanson, ca. 1927. As the state's leading newspaper mogul, Hanson articulated Big Mule/Black Belt interests in the pages of the *Birmingham News,* the *Birmingham Age-Herald,* the *Birmingham Ledger,* and "Old Grandma," the *Montgomery Advertiser.* Courtesy Birmingham Public Library Archives, Portraits.

Alabamians and embodied conservative religious directives. Hall saw little difference between the violence of the Klan's morality police and the dry position itself. One fed off the other, and the two were largely indistinguishable. Accordingly, Hall often disparaged the Anti-Saloon League as the "white trash of [the state's] second-rate pulpits."[28]

Victor Hanson (figure 16) felt differently. By 1927, the publisher had not yet made up his mind on the alcohol issue, but he believed that prohibition was a fact of life that Americans were going to have to live with for some time to come. Hanson feared that editorials against Klan lawlessness would be seriously compromised if his editors also encouraged Alabamians to break any law, including prohibition. A campaign to repeal the Eighteenth Amendment even struck the publisher as untimely. Hanson viewed the fight against Alabama's KKK as essentially political and was reluctant to alienate potential converts by offending their sensibilities on the liquor issue. The publisher had no objection, he told his star editor, to mounting a campaign for repeal "at a proper time, when it would not interfere with [the] big things we are trying to do" against the Klan. "I hope I have made myself clear," Hanson instructed Hall, "I do not want to put any hobbles on your mind or any shackles on your typewriter, but I do think it important that our three papers keep a fairly good liaison and use the same compass."[29]

In explaining his position to the temperamental editor, Hanson betrayed an unabashed elitism and showed that he held the average Alabamian in fairly low esteem. He saw his editors as guiding common Alabamians "through the wilderness and priest-ridden ignorance to which our people now seem utterly lost." "I fear that, just as a starving man can be injured by too much food administered too rapidly," Hanson confided, "the treatment must be a sparing administration of intelligence gradually applied." "I think we must not excite too many of their prejudices at once," he cautioned Hall, "but must work at it very slowly and tactfully, violating as little as possible their sacred taboos."[30]

Hall's hostility to prohibition was not long in becoming apparent to the Klan's press allies. The *Evergreen Courant,* the *Andalusia Star,* and the *Alabama Baptist* all blamed Hall and Hanson for Alabama's wretched national image and charged that the wet faction's desire to repeal prohibition had caused it to denounce Klan violence. Other editors reflected a strong popular sentiment that favored the firm, even violent, repression of moral wrongdoing or nonconformity in Alabama. The *Alabama Christian Advocate* accused Grover Hall of making flogging victims look like "little saints—near Godworthy to be canonized." "We don't know any of them," its editor admitted, "but from [our] reports they were menaces to their several communities."[31]

Occasional slips in editorial writing betrayed the underlying political thrust of the oligarchy's campaign. Grover Hall spoke of a "constituency" in defending his editorial war on Klan violence. In denouncing one 1927 flogging, James Chappell wrote that the *Birmingham News* regarded the KKK as a bunch of insolent political upstarts. When Jeff Calloway's assailants were convicted by a jury in Blount County, the *News* lamented that Klan politicos would bear no accountability for the violent tendencies of their backers.[32]

Hanson's *Birmingham Age-Herald,* edited by Charles A. Fell, also did its part in the war against the KKK. Fell was hostile to the 1920s Klan but fondly nostalgic about the Reconstruction order and its aims. The newspa-

per infiltrated klavern meetings, earning the special scorn of Klan leaders. "The basis of its stories are infamous lies, willfully and maliciously
made . . . , as black a lie as ever was written," Alabama Klansmen complained. "Space will not permit the naming of all the infamous lies this
newspaper is publishing, but their articles are a series of lies from beginning
to end. Lies. Lies. Lies."[33]

Smaller Black Belt papers representing political alliance with the Big
Mules joined the campaign. The *Dothan Eagle* and the *Selma Times-Journal,*
newspapers for which Grover Hall had once worked, denounced Alabama's
reign of Klan terror. Stung by the sensitive charge that they were tarnishing
Alabama's image, the papers defended their participation as well worth a
public relations problem if they could achieve their aims.[34]

Some representatives of the "country press" resented the big-city machinations of the oligarchy papers in trying to impose their cultural values on
rural people as part of their war on the Klan. The *Roanoke Leader*'s editor
denied that he was a Klansman or an apologist for flogging but took issue
with the condescending approach of the patrician campaign against sheeted
violence. He admitted that the urban dailies had performed a service by
focusing attention on flogging but felt that they had gone too far; they had
performed a disservice to Alabama by exaggerating the rash to foster the
impression that a law-and-order crisis was taking place on the Klan's political watch. He particularly resented an arrogant tone that he detected in the
elite press. "The . . . people of Alabama [are] not . . . fools or lawless folk
[that] . . . have to be educated by incubator methods into the realization
that mob law is pernicious," he argued somewhat sanguinely, "nor . . .
jerked up by the hair . . . to be made to do their duty." A Prattville minister
lambasted the *Montgomery Advertiser* for its war on Klan lawlessness and for
encouraging people to flout the prohibition law—precisely the charge that
had so worried Victor Hanson. The pulpit and country press declined to
follow the urban lead in resisting the Klan, the preacher explained, because
of this disturbing double standard and because they were suspicious about
the political motives of papers like the *Advertiser,* the "staunch and loyal
friends of liquor . . . , the greatest curse that ever blighted humanity."[35]

THE OLIGARCHY'S OPPOSITION

Resistance to the Klan was waged by more than just Victor Hanson,
Frederick Thompson, and the planter press. Many other members of the
oligarchy who were not involved with the press got into the act. Anti-Klan
sentiment, predictably, was centered in the traditional political strongholds
of the Big Mules of Birmingham, the Lesser Mules of Mobile, and the

planters of the Black Belt, with a kind of regional headquarters in Montgomery.

Members of the oligarchy were, of course, concerned with regaining political preeminence in a state that they had long considered their own. Still, other issues surrounding Klan mayhem also alarmed them. Many members of the oligarchy, especially the industrialists, worried that excessive lawlessness would cripple the state's ability to attract business. Strict adherents of the New South creed, these businessmen correctly assumed that Alabama's dreadful reputation around the country would do little to help the state's prospects for outside capital. Other oligarchs opposed the 1920s Klan for reasons that can only be termed antifederal, namely a rigid resistance to the possibility of federal intrusion into the state's pattern of race relations. The Redeemer oligarchy of course had reason to fear federal interference. The memory of Reconstruction, accompanied by the temporary loss of political power to black and white Republicans, was enduring and emotional— and powerfully motivated resistance to any further involvement by Washington in the race question.[36]

Some of the biggest Mules and planters in Alabama joined their press allies in battling the KKK. In 1927, John H. Bankhead II issued a dramatic public condemnation of the order. Bankhead deplored "a reign of hooded outlawry" and laid responsibility for state anarchy on the doorstep of the politicians who had profited most from Klan support. He charged Klan officers with planning violent acts, aiding criminal perpetrators, and obstructing justice. The reason for Alabama's crisis, according to Bankhead, was the overwhelming success of the KKK at the polls in 1926 and the political protection that it had enjoyed ever since. He called upon Governor Graves to disband the order and took special pains to castigate Senator Tom Heflin. While not expressly defending the anti-Catholicism, anti-Semitism, and nativism of the Klan, Bankhead dismissed such threats as basically irrelevant. He also praised the original KKK and its motives, and bragged that the order had comprised Alabama's best men. Bankhead parroted traditional mythology surrounding the original Klan, dismissing its terrorism as the work of irresponsible ruffians who took over only after the "best men" had left. Many of Alabama's oligarchs exhibited this tendency to denounce the 1920s Klan while praising the Reconstruction order.[37]

Bibb Graves usually took refuge in silence. After Bankhead's declaration, though, the governor leaked word that he refused to dignify the schemes of his political foes with further comment. Meanwhile, Grover Hall feted Bankhead's missive and tried to portray the author as just another interested civic-minded Jasper attorney rather than the scion of one of the oligarchy's most powerful political dynasties.[38]

Bankhead's appeal was echoed by the eloquent voice of Judge Walter B. Jones of Montgomery. A determined white supremacist and the son of a former governor, Jones later took a leading part in Alabama's resistance to racial integration. In 1927, he issued an extensive public attack on the Klan as part of a grand jury charge. "Every voice in Alabama should be lifted in protest against the cowardly outrages. . . . From the bench . . . , the press . . . , the pulpit . . . , the streetcorner and office should swell a mighty chorus of protest and condemnation [against the] . . . unholy vengeance upon helpless citizens, and . . . the majesty and dignity of our state," he said. "I call upon every Alabamian . . . to speak out against the unspeakably cruel outrages which have disgraced our state. . . . law and order . . . will battle to the last ditch in defense of the constitutional rights . . . secured to them by the shedding of so much holy blood, and the glorious sacrifices of some of the noblest patriots who ever lived."[39]

Jones particularly deplored the KKK's propensity to take violent action on the basis of rumors of moral misconduct. He objected to the Klan's antediluvian practice of summary judgment and vigilante justice. He denounced "a court which meets in dark and hidden places . . . , whose judges and jurors are shrouded and hooded from head to foot . . . , where no voice is heard in defense . . . , where the idle tattle and filthy gossip of scandalmongers is given [full] credence . . . , a court that is ashamed . . . for the rising sun to dawn upon its sessions."[40]

Former U.S. congressman L. B. Rainey contributed to the oligarchy's crusade against the Klan from Dadeville. He took special pains to discount politics as a motive for his criticism ("I have touched the purple robes of political victory and found that touch was cold"), but more telling than his disclaimer was the fact that Rainey aimed his indictment at Bibb Graves and called upon the governor to lead a fight against mob violence. "The backbone of the creature that threatened Alabama has been broken. . . . , the bridge that carried you into the state's White House has [fallen]," Rainey wrote. "The whole rear of your political ship has been busted." He also praised Attorney General Charlie McCall as an eagle who had set aside personal ambition to soar above the state's political swamps, and he celebrated the death of Alabama's KKK, for which he found clear evidence in the Calloway convictions.[41]

Still, no one issued as strong an indictment as John Bainbridge, a Black Belt Democratic activist whose family had seen over six generations of political service. In typical Redeemer fashion, Bainbridge damned the second Klan while eulogizing the first with its aim of preserving white supremacy. The revised order, according to the planter, was a sorry outfit masquerading under the name of a venerable old organization "like an ass in a dead lion's skin." "There it stands," Bainbridge declared, "a band of exploiters, hypo-crites, and hoodlums, cowed officials, barren minds, failures, fanatics . . . , a challenge to the heirs of reconstruction . . . , the straight thinkers carrying on Alabama's commerce." Bainbridge was so incensed by the damage that Klan lawlessness was doing to Alabama's chances of importing capital that he vowed to vote for "a black, republican Catholic on a bolshevist platform, pledged to annex Alabama to Haiti or to Hell itself" in preference to any "malodorous . . . , trash-pick[ing] Klan nominee." Bainbridge foamed at the mouth as he defined those who made up the "unwashed barbarianism" of the second KKK. Here were "cowardly recruits [who] drift into the Klan ranks as naturally as slime oozes to the gutter . . . , sorry . . . , craven . . . , cowardly . . . , miserable . . . , wretched . . . , hypocritical . . . , the hysteri-cal Pharisee . . . foe[s] to advancing liberal civilization . . . tightening its slimy coil around [Alabama's body politic] . . . , an Army of greasy political illiterates . . . [the] misinformed fanatic and sheeplike joiner." He also de-nounced the order's leaders as greedy failures able only to exploit the "ster-ile intellects . . . [of the] feeble-minded joiners" who signed on. Yet the planter reserved special opprobrium for Tom Heflin. He ridiculed the senator as "Admiral Heflin," commander of an antipapist armada on the Coosa River, and "the most noisy vent of a somewhat flatulent body politic." Bainbridge castigated moral police squads as bands of "brave tom-tits" who indulged their Freudian fantasies to "spank some neighborhood [Mary] Magdalene" and recommended a liberal use of buckshot as a good remedy. He took special pains to cast the Klan problem in national terms and called for the heirs of Redemption to overcome the upstart Klan challenge to their political power.[42]

Devotion to the New South tenet of improvement through the infu-sion of outside capital was a central component of the oligarchy's campaign against Alabama's KKK. Material improvement and profit were dear to the hearts of many members of the oligarchy, and they chafed uncomfortably as they watched hooded ruffians contribute to Alabama's already benighted image. During the late nineteenth and early twentieth centuries, a number of southern governors had prostituted their states in order to industrialize, sentencing their people to lives of profound hardship in convict lease camps and company-owned towns. Illiteracy, tenancy, disease, vice, exploitation, and miserably low wages followed the Redeemers' campaign to bewitch northern and English investors by offering enticements such as subsidies, tax incentives, land grants, corporate welfare, and a favorable antiunion cli-mate.[43] Black Belt members of the oligarchy were also concerned about the issue. Since most planter wealth was tied up in land, any activity that de-pressed its price was anathema.[44]

New South types all over Dixie worried about the negative image that the South, and Alabama in particular, were acquiring in the country as a whole. A Georgia editor warned of the evils of Ku Kluxism, fundamentalism, intolerance, and "placid provincialism" in blunting the South's material attractiveness. A Tennessee editor echoed the admonition. The *Baltimore Manufacturer's Record,* the leading mouthpiece of New South materialism, flatly warned that southern businessmen should recognize that every Klan whipping "is a drawback to the material prosperity of their section." The admonitions that James Bowron, an executive of the Tennessee Coal and Iron Company (TCI), addressed to a Wahouma klavern in 1927 reflected such resistance to the Klan. Bowron expressed concern over Klan "practices" such as secret membership and the wearing of masks but told the Knights that he "approved quite extensively of their principles."[45]

An unsettling dilemma faced the planter/industrialist cabal in mounting opposition to the Klan on the basis of politics and economics. How could the opponents possibly reconcile their affection for the Reconstruction Klan of their fathers while denigrating its 1920s successor? The solution was to cast the two orders as separate, unrelated, and almost mutually exclusive. This idea has proved remarkably enduring.[46]

Alabama patricians often spoke of a glorious Reconstruction KKK while disparaging the 1920s order. One old member of the 1860s Knights of the White Camellia had nothing but contempt for Alabama's new Kluxers. He called the 1920s Klansmen "would-be imitators" of the Reconstruction Klan and "hairy-necked hoodlums" who were 180 degrees off the track. The former Camellia remembered his spiritual cousins in the Reconstruction KKK, however, as the "surviving flower of Southern chivalry" engaged in the noble work of preserving southern civilization from the "tyrannies and outrages of alien and negro usurpations . . . , the barbarous vengeance of ignorant black freedmen, fired by the incendiary counsels of south haters . . . and negroes under tutelage by evil-hearted adventurers from the North."[47]

Grover Hall concurred in this dark Dunning School assessment. He praised the Reconstruction Klansmen as an ancient band of chivalrous knights who saved the South from utter racial and political ruin. Montgomery federal district court judge Henry D. Clayton also reproached the 1920s Klan while lauding the Reconstruction order. A former U.S. congressman and the author of the Clayton Antitrust Act, he praised the original Kluxers for rescuing southern civilization from carpetbag and scalawag vultures backed by the "bristling bayonets" of the federal government who imposed hell on a prostrate Dixie in the interest of "ignorant negroes in brutal numbers." While the secret society had once served the South gloriously, Clayton reasoned in 1927, "there is no place for the Klan in Alabama now."[48]

Inconsistencies in patrician attitudes toward the two Klans can best be understood if we consider the political aims of both orders. The 1920s Klan in Alabama, and in other southern states, posed a serious challenge to the political hegemony of the Big Mules and their privileged planter allies. Not surprisingly, it incurred the wrath of men like Judge Clayton, Judge Jones, Victor Hanson, and Grover Hall. The Reconstruction Klan, it should be remembered, was the creature of Conservative Democrats, the very political and familial relatives of the planters and industrialists. To remain consistent politically, Alabama's 1920s enemies of the Klan had to be somewhat inconsistent logically. These patricians usually sidestepped the disturbing fact that the two Klans used similar methods, regalia, ritual, violence, and language to attain some similar ends.

Montgomery during the 1920s was the capital not only of the state but also of Big Mule/Black Belt resistance to the Klan. Ironically, Bibb Graves directed state government from the same city, making Montgomery a town almost torn apart by civil strife. Anti-Klan insurgence existed everywhere. Judges Walter Jones and Henry Clayton sat on their county and federal benches in the city, and of course Grover Hall presided over the *Montgomery Advertiser.* Considerable opposition to the Klan also emanated from Frederick Thompson's *Montgomery Journal.*[49]

During this period, Montgomery politics provided a frequent forum for conflict between the Klan and its detractors. Mayor William Gunter, a twelve-year incumbent, was a confirmed oligarch and an outspoken enemy of the sheeted organization. In 1927, the KKK tried to unseat Gunter by pushing the candidacy of J. Johnston Moore, a local druggist and Klan cyclops. Bibb Graves, James Esdale, and reactionary evangelist Bob Jones canvassed Montgomery for Moore, while hooded leaders alluded to underworld elements exercising influence in municipal government and vowed that Moore would clean up vice in the city.[50] Still, Montgomery remained a bastion of anti-Klan strength. Voters rejected Moore's candidacy 2 to 1 and ratified Mayor Gunter's pledge to have government "of, for, and by the people" rather than by an invisible empire.[51]

Oligarchy and Klan also clashed in Montgomery over Bibb Graves's inaugural. Gunter and the city council opposed a Klan parade in support of the new governor, passed a city ordinance to prohibit masks, and refused to issue a parade permit. The mayor also swore to deputize anyone he could find to mobilize a city army to block a Klan parade. Montgomery Knights exacted revenge on Gunter by kidnapping and flogging his son.[52]

The controversy over the inaugural was not the last time Montgomery became a battleground. Joe Bonner, disciple of the Big Mule/Black Belt faction, opened his 1927 bid for the state supreme court at the county courthouse. Mayor Gunter introduced Bonner who, in turn, announced that resistance to the KKK was the central issue of his campaign. He disparaged James Esdale's attempts to control the selection of Alabama jurors and dramatically indicted the secret fraternity on a list of ten counts ranging from flogging to "pernicious political" activity.[53] Other political opponents of the order followed suit. One Montgomery judge pardoned a man who admitted slaying a policeman during a Klan parade by blaming the secret order for the chaos. The judge also depicted the KKK as a group that pandered to a "cheap patriotism" in order to terrorize people because of accidents of race, creed, and color.[54]

The city's pulpit responded to its patrician leadership, although its complaints against the order were noticeably more elemental. Dr. Donald McGuire of the First Presbyterian Church attacked Klan violence during the summer of 1927 as barbaric, inhuman, and a fundamental contradiction to the laws of God and society. He also indicted public officials as either incompetent or conniving—or both. The Reverend H. V. Carson of Trinity Presbyterian joined McGuire. Taking a page from William Jennings Bryan, he vowed that the Klan would not crucify the free people of America upon a fiery cross. Carson described masked mayhem as a stench rising to the nostrils of God, a voice of blood crying out from the soil of Alabama, and called the flogging of women in particular so revolting that the "moon has hidden its face in shame and . . . a veil of clouds . . . hide the stars."[55]

An older city with more Catholics, Mobile was also a center of hostility to the Klan. The port city served as the home of smaller industrialists who were the political allies of Birmingham's Big Mules and the Black Belt planters. City commissioners used an antimasking ordinance to block Klan parades and passed resolutions calling for universal opposition to the KKK and more action from Bibb Graves and Charlie McCall.[56]

Perhaps the most compelling evidence as to the war's political nature lies in the timing of the crusade. An epidemic of masked violence had not simply materialized out of thin air in 1927, whatever the oligarchical hysterics might say to the contrary. Alabama had experienced consistent Klan violence from at least 1921 and a good deal of it even earlier. The state had an even longer tradition of generic vigilante violence. While planter/industrialist partisans screamed about an explosion of Klan violence in 1927, they knew full well that the "explosion" was at least six years old. Pro-Klan editors had never had reason to denounce the violence, but oligarchy editors were not sufficiently alarmed until after November 1926. Thereafter, oligarchs "discovered" a flogging epidemic that led to unprecedented criticism of Alabama government—a Klan-controlled government. This shocking political upset roused previously quiescent patricians from their slumber and spurred them to take action against the Klan as a political rival.

From 1921 to 1927 literally hundreds of floggings went unnoticed and undenounced in Alabama. In 1927, the patrician press fostered the mythology that a new flogging epidemic was directly and solely attributable to the Klan's political success.[57] The implication was that the Klan had to be defeated at the polls. More important, the explanation ovelooked an important cause of the violence, the persistence of public approval for vigilantism and the KKK.

The situation actually differed considerably from the oligarchy's depictions of a sudden 1927 epidemic. Klansmen flogged so many Alabamians between 1921 and 1927 that no one knew for sure how many people had been assaulted. At least a hundred people were flogged in Alabama during the first few years of the decade and twenty in Birmingham alone during 1921 and 1922. Authorities documented several hundred Klan floggings around the state between 1921 and 1927; some estimates put the number at between 600 and 800. New York and Massachusetts newspapers agreed that Alabama flogging from 1922 to 1927 had constituted a virtual "orgy." An Alabama newspaper admitted that there had been "scores if not hundreds" of masked whippings in the state since 1921, and another editor wrote that "no living man knows how many midnight floggings have occurred in this state in the past half dozen years." *Collier's* estimated the number of Alabama Klan floggings that had taken place between 1924 and 1927 alone at 700. In another piece, the magazine pointed out that 1927 Alabama still had over 500 unsolved flogging cases stemming from the group's 1915 revival. Georgia's Julian Harris, son of novelist Joel Chandler Harris and Pulitzer Prize–winning editor of the *Columbus Enquirer-Sun*, argued that "the truth is, there has been, if anything, a decrease in the number of [Alabama] floggings."[58]

In 1927 Alabama's oligarchy resurrected many cases that had gone unreported and others that police and grand juries had ignored for years. Over 100 Crenshaw County indictments, handed down in the fall of 1927 only at Charlie McCall's instigation, included many floggings that had actually taken place years earlier. Talladega Klansmen had viciously flogged a Catholic druggist in 1921, breaking his jaw and knocking out most of his teeth, but criminal charges were not preferred until the critical year of 1927. One black woman had been slain by Blount Klansmen in 1925, but her case did not receive significant attention until 1927.[59]

An analysis of Talladega County's 1927 indictments provides some perspective. A grand jury indicted a hundred defendants for fifty-six acts of

; that had taken place over a four-year period. Over 90 percent of cks were expressly attributed to the KKK. In addition, county s had dynamited two black homes and burned a white home, a school, a church, two dance halls, and a number of barns. Some victims had been flogged so severely that their clothing was embedded in their flesh. Some were afraid to talk to authorities; others fled. Of the fifty-six assaults—thirty-five on whites and twenty-one on blacks—only three had actually occurred during the so-called flogging epidemic of 1927. Nine took place in 1926, twenty-five in 1925, eighteen in 1924, and even one in 1921.[60]

Prior to November 1926, patricians had shown distressingly little concern about Klan floggings. Only after most state and local offices had been lost to Klan-backed politicos did the matter become important, even critical. Klan apologists of the time were aware of the inconsistency. Governor Graves remained silent even when mountains of criticism landed on his desk. On one occasion, though, he confided to a fellow Klansmen that the reason his political opposition reported floggings with such relish was to discredit the KKK—not as an order but a rival at the polls. A Talladega Klan observer concurred. In 1927, "suddenly the press that had seen nothing to condemn when . . . [William Joseph] Simmons' Klan whipped somebody, roared with resentment of what they called FLOGGINGS . . . [and] painted everything else the Klan did as being mighty bad. That attitude was the result of a realization that a block vote by . . . many Klansmen could destroy the oligarchy."[61]

While state political ascendance offered the oligarchy powerful reasons for resisting the Klan, fear of the federal government and a concern with maintaining traditional forms of racial control were also factors. During 1927 the specter of an invasive central government was still ubiquitous. Most of the threat came from outside the region. Northern observers, burdened by their own affinity for regional chauvinism, often simplistically argued that Northerners held a monopoly on virtue and Southerners a monopoly on vice. A call for federal intervention, legitimate or not, was not far behind. In 1927, the *New York Age* demanded federal involvement in Alabama because, in its opinion, organized government had utterly collapsed under the weight of Klan domination. A black editor in St. Louis agreed. He declared that federal interference was warranted because black property rights were habitually violated in Alabama.[62]

A more serious threat of federal intrusion loomed in the U.S. Congress. Illinois Republican Martin B. Madden joined the *Chicago Tribune* to call for federal intervention in Alabama. Madden was particularly distressed by violations of Fourth Amendment property rights and Fourteenth Amendment guarantees of due process and equal protection. Alabama's 1927 floggings constituted one of the blackest pages in American history, Madden declared as he demanded an inquiry by the Justice Department. So pervasive was the pollution of lawlessness in Alabama, Madden said, that state and local officials must be either unwilling or unable to maintain law and order; the crisis demanded federal action. "It makes the blood boil to read the details of those fiendish persecutions," Madden reported to his fellow congressmen. Alabama must "hang her head in shame, if she be not shameless."[63]

The planter/industrialist press occasionally buttressed political opposition by hinting at the disaster that federal action against Alabama's Klan might bring. J. A. Coleman, editor of the *Green County Democrat,* was a strong opponent of the 1920s KKK as well as a devoted advocate of states' rights—a combination that was not unusual in Alabama. His biggest fear was that rampant vigilante violence would eventually lead the federal government to meddle in Alabama. This threat was especially relevant in a county such as Greene, which was 83 percent black and where white elites had long since worked out mechanisms to repress blacks. James Chappell of the *Birmingham News* also supplemented political antagonism toward the KKK by warning that the power of the federal courts might be invoked if things went on as they had. Even Grover Hall showed himself not averse to falling back on the tried-and-true anti-federal theme on occasion. Hall warned that national criticism of Alabama's Klan lawlessness might lead to federal interference. Rejecting Congressman Madden's call for federal intervention, Hall relied on classic states'-rights verbiage. A federal invasion "would be humiliating . . . [and] of a doubtful legal expedient," he wrote. "Alabama should be allowed a free hand in working out this problem. It is an Alabama problem; . . . the [Klan] evil should be . . . destroyed by the people on whom the responsibility principally rests."[64]

On occasion, the talented editor of the *Advertiser* was able to fuse both strains into a kind of hybrid opposition. After bellowing longer and louder than anyone else about the need for strict law enforcement against Klan floggers, Hall finally got the chance to celebrate the event that he had longed for. When the sentences in the Calloway cases finally came down, though, he had a curious reaction. Judge O. A. Steele sentenced the first two defendants to the maximum penalty of eight to ten years; Horace Wilkinson's plea bargain won token sentences of six months for the remaining five defendants. At the precise moment of apparent victory, though, Hall abandoned his die-hard pose. He criticized Steele's first two sentences as "excessive" and called the five lighter sentences "adequate." His elaborate explanation contained an element of antifederalism but also hinted that he was more committed to political opposition of the Klan than to combating vigilantism. "The people are [not as] . . . interested in seeing the men serve long penitentiary sentences," he wrote, "as they are in seeing them brought to justice and made to feel the power of the law. What really counts is the demonstration by the *State* of its power."[65]

Federal power was a thorny issue. It is clear that Southerners have habitually camouflaged their racism behind the verbiage of states' rights and not very subtly. Pledges to abolish slavery, integrate schools, and end mob violence from within have moved at a ponderously slow pace. In such cases, federal intervention has been not simply the prerogative of the central government but its duty when the protections of the U.S. Constitution needed to be defended. On the other hand, some Northerners have shown a disturbing propensity to attach moral superiority to their calls for federal involvement in Dixie. Rare, indeed, was the insight of the famed attorney Clarence Darrow, himself nearly a victim of the Alabama Klan: "Lynchings and discrimination against the Negro are a disgrace to the North and South alike. In Chicago, St. Louis, and Springfield, Negroes are accorded the same unjust treatment and . . . horrible riots as [in Alabama]."[66]

8

Limits of the Oligarchy's Campaign

The anti-Klan campaign mounted by Alabama's oligarchy had definite limitations. There were problems with having oligarchs speak for common Alabamians. Grover Hall and company, however loudly they decried Klan atrocities, did not represent many of the plain folk upon whom the Klan depended for support, acceptance, and the occasional acquittal. Patrician resistance, in the eyes of many Alabamians, was also imbued with the ambition of the planter/industrialist clique to regain political ascendance in a state its members had long considered their own.

Perhaps the most obvious difficulty was a racial double standard. White victims just seemed to count more than blacks. County and state prosecutors, in the rare instances when they did prosecute floggers, usually targeted those who had attacked whites. The Klan extortionists of Arthur Hitt's farm never came to trial, nor did the Marengo County floggers who killed Luman Greathouse or the murderers of Lily Cobb. The Kluxers who lashed black doctors for treating white patients also escaped justice. The *Pittsburgh Courier*, a leading black newspaper, addressed the problem of color blindness. "In reality [Alabama] is awakening only in the cases of white people who have been flogged," the paper pointed out, but the "Negro still remains the [ultimate] test of American justice, chivalry, and fair play. When he is treated squarely . . . , then everyone is sure of justice."[1]

Incidents that seemed certain to become disasters for the Klan had a strange way of turning out rather well. Much of the reason may have been the oligarchy's tendency to overstate the successes and popular bases of its anti-Klan crusade. If the planter/industrialist press was to be believed in 1927, for example, James Esdale's fall from grace was a foregone conclusion. Schisms, scandals, and lawsuits had rocked the Klan leader. Rumors circulated that Bibb Graves and Charlie McCall, with other Klan heavy-weights, had endured all they could stand of Esdale and were plotting his ouster. Yet soon after the convictions in the Jeff Calloway case, 300 local Klan officers from across south Alabama met to give their blessing to Esdale and his reign, a vote of confidence punctuated by attacks on the patricians and Judge O. A. Steele.[2]

After the Calloway convictions, an allegedly dead KKK suddenly took on new life. Actually, Alabama's Klan had never been in anything like the desperate straits that Grover Hall had identified in 1927. In fact during the fall of 1927 the sheeted society racked up political victory after political victory, even apart from Bibb Graves's seemingly ineluctable reform program. Klan power pervaded the state. Hooded agitation led the Birming-ham City Commission to sponsor a cleanup of Gate City moonshiners in which gowned thugs operated freely. In other states, Klan political power led to corruption, embezzlement, and financial irregularity. In Alabama, a New York editor observed, political power was used mainly to "protect murder [and] bloodshed . . . , [to] create a supergovernment," and to guar-antee immunity from criminal prosecution.[3]

LEGISLATIVE LIMITS

Persistent Klan power was most clearly seen at the statehouse, where the governor's reform package rolled to victory after victory over the oligar-chy's plaintive wails. Support from Klan-backed legislators from counties all over the state was critical to Bibb Graves's successful efforts at progressive reform. Ironically, without the help of Klan-elected lawmakers, much of Graves's reform program would never have become reality.[4]

The hooded political machine pursued more than just reform, however. The domination of state law was a wonderful way for Klan politicians to protect even the most questionable acts of their constituency. State senator Travis Williams of Franklin County proposed a stiff antimasking statute that promised to emasculate the order's ability to terrorize people. Williams, acting on behalf of the planter/industrialist alliance, was joined by Mont-gomery's Taylor Goodwyn, a planter ally, in the lower house. The pair pro-posed a combination bill that made the wearing of a mask in public pun-ishable by a $100 fine and a year in jail and made masked flogging a felony punishable by five to twenty years in prison.[5]

Klan-backed politicians leaped forward to defend the mask and, in effect, the violence of many of their rank-and-file constituents. A day after the house judiciary committee reported the bill favorably, intense lobbying by James Esdale, Bibb Graves, Great Titan Bert Thomas, and J. Bibb Mills, superintendent of Alabama's Anti-Saloon League, led the committee—bizarrely—to reverse its own report. House representatives killed the bill by a vote of 50 to 42; the senate concurred 16 to 13.[6]

Editors speaking for the oligarchy raged against the mask. Grover Hall termed the mask "a source of unmitigated evil . . . , a menace to life and limb, and a reproach to civilized society." He blamed Bibb Graves for the bill's death and denounced the governor as "either wanting in perspicacity" or bound so tightly to the hooded order that he could not move. Charles Fell of the *Age-Herald* concluded that Alabama was the battlefield between two armies, the "minions of the moon and [the] lovers of sunlight." The bill's defeat was a "denial of love, a denial of faith—a denial of God!" he lamented. Frederick Thompson's *Mobile Register* and James Chappell of the *Birmingham News* depicted the fight as a litmus test that Graves had flunked before the entire world. In a stinging editorial entitled "The Grand Dragon Whips the Governor to a Frazzle," Chappell concluded that Esdale's will was superior to that of Graves, that the Klan controlled the state politically, and that the bill's death would cause every flogger to drink the governor's health before applying the lash.[7]

Successful Klan lobbying against the bill won Alabama's robed order the enmity of editors all over the South who spoke for the oligarchy. A Charleston critic termed the mask a public menace, a Charlotte editor remarked that Alabama's continued toleration of the mask was "a pity," and the *Atlanta Constitution* reiterated its claim that the whole state was on trial. Commentators from North and South Carolina deplored Alabama's violence but expressed confidence that, if the order unmasked itself, it would no longer be blamed for outrages that it did not commit.[8]

Stung by the criticism, Klan leaders proposed a weaker substitute bill. The measure, sponsored by a Shelby County senator and a Randolph County representative, stipulated that the mask could be used provided that each cyclops kept a log showing who had checked one out. No provision was made for an outside audit of the cyclopes' records, nor were there restrictions about the types of activities at which the mask could be worn. Flogging, though still illegal, was not a felony but a misdemeanor carrying a maximum sentence of ten years. An addition to the bill changed its status and cut the penalty.[9]

Politicians allied with the KKK stood solidly behind the milder substitute bills as they did most of Governor Graves's reform bills. Graves, Esdale, Bert Thomas, and Bibb Mills again lobbied heavily for the measure. They were joined by Esdale's law partner, George Frey, a state senator and a Klansman. Lawmakers declined to reconsider the original bill, tabling it by a senatorial courtesy vote of 28 to 0. Shelby County senator L. H. Ellis introduced the Klan's milder substitute bill by revealing that he effectively tolerated violence for moral offenses: "While I . . . do not advocate such affairs, I firmly believe that everyone who has been attacked has committed a moral offense. . . . those who were flogged had given definite provocation [and] . . . the men who participated . . . stood high in the communities in which they resided." Montgomery's Taylor Goodwyn, cosponsor of the failed harsher measure, suggested that Alabama's lawmakers should also vote to remove the stars from the American flag but leave the stripes as a symbol of her degeneration. Both substitute bills passed and were promptly signed into law by Bibb Graves.[10]

Planters and industrialists were predictably unhappy. The *Selma Times-Journal* called the substitute bill "as mild as mother's milk," while a former editor of the *Alabama Christian Advocate* said that the measure was worse than no law at all. Grover Hall dubbed it "a flabby compromise." A critic in Clarke County pointed out that people who did things that were morally correct did not usually wear masks to conceal their identities.[11]

Fresh from this victory, hooded political strategists forced the issue of whether Alabama should annul its minority primary system. A number of Klan allies had been swept into office over oligarchy adversaries in 1926 under the minority-rule system and thus had a vested interest in its continued deployment. Senators Heflin and Black joined Graves, Esdale, and the KKK in leading the friendly legislators opposed to changing the system and again tasted success at the statehouse.[12] Grover Hall greeted the Klan victories with uncharacteristic despair: "The Klan wanted the mask [and] . . . the minority-rule primary law saved. The Klan saved both. . . . This is the government under which Alabamians, once proud . . . lovers of liberty, now live, and against which it is useless to contend."[13]

Alabama's KKK had at long last had enough of Grover Hall and his interminable criticism. Fed up with opposition from the patrician press, Klan leader Horace Wilkinson drew up two revolutionary libel bills to muzzle press criticism of the sheeted order. The Wilkinson bills—introduced in the state senate by the reliable George Frey and backed by Governor Graves and James Esdale—called for $25,000 fines on newspapers that criticized public officials or injured the state's reputation in any way. The measures were clearly aimed at the oligarchy press, and only by sheer accident did they fail to become law. Klan lobbying resulted in the favorable reporting of the bills out of committee over the strenuous objections of legislators tied to planter/Mule interests. But when a dozen lawmakers left the senate chamber to hear the final hour of house debate, oligarchy senators quickly pushed through adjournment of the legislative session, automatically killing the bill.[14]

The Klan's attempt to muzzle Alabama's press was serious business. It struck at the very core of the First Amendment and outraged the robed order's adversaries. State representative Taylor Goodwyn characterized the measure as "a rank weed in the Garden of Liberty," while Grover Hall denounced the "craven wretches . . . , masked anarchists, [and] slinking beasts" who could back such a "malicious, tyrannical [and] outrageous" legislative scheme. Hall argued that flogging was the only organized crime that enjoyed official protection. He rejected the idea that his editorials were detrimental to Alabama's reputation.[15]

Hall had a point. Attempts to muzzle the press did little to improve Alabama's already benighted national image. A Chicago editor observed that the bills made a mockery of free speech and free press, and he dubbed Alabama's affliction one of the most remarkable in the history of American politics. The *New York Times*, concurring that the bills' main purpose was to cater to Alabama's passion for moral absolutism, suggested renaming the state "Heflinia."[16]

LEGAL LIMITS

The shortcomings of an opposition to the KKK that was politically motivated were painfully apparent at the state assembly. Lawmakers knew where the sympathies of their constituents and patrons lay, and for many of them in 1927, it was not with the oligarchy. Setback after setback greeted the planter/industrialist coalition at the statehouse, but still greater defeats awaited them in the county court. Grand juries—the friends, neighbors, and peers of Klansmen—were called upon to indict hooded mobs. Petit juries made up of these same people were obliged to convict them. The system was inherently flawed. Because societal sympathy for the Klan far outstripped that acknowledged by the Big Mule/Black Belt press, indictments were difficult to come by, and convictions almost impossible. After the Calloway convictions, the event that was mistakenly supposed to have signaled the death of Alabama's KKK, one disappointment after another followed in the state's courtrooms.

Randolph County had suffered a reign of terror. Late one night several men called Lon Royston, a sixty-year-old crippled man, out of his house to sell them cigars and gasoline. When Royston emerged, they pulled out pistols, forced him into a car, and drove to a thicket. Three other cars filled with gowned Klansmen followed behind. At the thicket, fifty Kluxers gave Royston fifty stripes for beating his wife, all the while demanding a confession. Royston, whose wife denied that he had ever abused her, finally confessed "to keep them from killing me." Giggling, the satisfied Knights drove away. Royston later asked the local solicitor for permission to arm himself and was told to buy two pistols and shoot to kill should the sheeted men return. In a similar incident, nightriders caned a woman who had separated from her husband and was the mother of four; they charged her with having had improper sexual relations. Klansmen also beat a Randolph man for refusing to allow his wife to visit her sick mother. As in the previous floggings in Randolph, over fifty Knights participated, strong evidence that the act was part of an organized campaign and not the work of a few troubled minds. Other Klan attacks took place in Randolph, including the beating of two black women who had been stripped naked and an incident in which a man was forced to run a gauntlet around the bases at a Roanoke baseball field.[17]

Randolph grand jurors admitted that at least seventeen Klan floggings had occurred in their county, but they concluded that there was insufficient evidence to return even one indictment. Instead, they passed the buck to state laws against the wearing of masks and the concealment of automobile tags. The grand jurors attributed their failure to return an indictment to an atmosphere of intimidation that undermined their ability to gain hard evidence. National observers, though, condemned the jury's inaction as pathetic. Closer to home, Grover Hall deplored Randolph's kangaroo Klan courts where people could be condemned on the basis of mere gossip. Ironically, Hall also called for state interference in localities that were powerless through choice, fear, or complicity. A confirmed critic of national interference in state affairs, Hall apparently saw nothing wrong with state intervention in places like Randolph that could not, or would not, cope with the Klan situation on their own.[18]

While grand juries in Etowah, Talladega, Butler, and Marengo Counties indicted a few persons in 1927 for hooded floggings, ultimately the results there were as fruitless as those in Randolph. It seemed to matter little whether the presiding judge sincerely opposed masked violence or openly supported the secret sect. Judge O. A. Steele admonished an Etowah grand jury to stand up and do its duty in the face of almost certain reprisals, but R. F. Elmore, a judge in the seventeenth circuit, revealed his Klan sympathies when he addressed a Marengo grand jury. The jurors were looking into several floggings, including that of Luman Greathouse, a black teen who had died as a result of a hideous beating. "As far as the Ku Klux Klan is concerned," Elmore said, "they stand for just what you and I stand for . . . , the constitution . . . , white supremacy . . . , [the] chastity of women . . . , the public school and education . . . , not for anything unlawful." Judge Elmore's charge, as remarkable as it was, virtually contradicted Steele's. Still, when suspected Klansmen went to trial before juries composed of their neighbors, support and sympathy usually overwhelmed the facts and guaranteed that they would be acquitted.[19]

Hugo Black, for example, used his talents to get "Chum" Smalley acquitted of 1920s murder charges even though he knew that Smalley had killed an innocent black man. During the trial, Black even shed a tear. Years later he admitted that his actions had been "inexcusable," but, he explained, "Chum was my friend." As extensive as Black's legal talents were, acquittal was all the more likely in a society that was reluctant to punish KKK violence.[20]

The collapse of law enforcement in Jefferson County, home of the Big Mules, was especially revealing. The plain folk in Jefferson who made up jury pools were not as moved by the oligarchy's resistance to the Klan as many industrialists were. After his amazing success in the Calloway trials, Charlie McCall targeted Jefferson, enlisted the aid of Mobile's Bart H. Chamberlain, one of the finest prosecutors in the state, and called over a hundred witnesses before a grand jury.[21] The attorney general also charged the hooded assailants of a man who had operated a barbecue stand, had twice been lashed by sheeted gangs, and had had his stand burned to the ground. McCall, Chamberlain, and Jim Davis, an energetic local solicitor, also pursued the case of a Jefferson man who had been beaten twice and shot during an ambush.[22]

Prosecution of the Arthur Hitt case annoyed the local Klan because it singled out W. J. Worthington—the former cyclops of the Avondale KKK, the leader of the 1925 Chinese café raids, and a wealthy member of an old Alabama family. Worthington, a prosperous real estate agent, resigned as head of the Avondale lodge in 1927 to become a rank-and-file member. During the emotional ceremony marking his resignation, he predicted that no one would be admitted into heaven who did not wear the robes of the Ku Klux Klan. Worthington's name appeared on a county deed just days after Hitt had been kidnapped, brutalized, and frightened into selling his farm for less than one-tenth of its worth. In addition to leading the Chinese café raids, Worthington had irritated city commission president and Klansman Jimmie Jones over the enforcement of prohibition in Gate City, had led an attempt to overthrow city police chief Fred McDuff and to replace him with a Woodlawn cyclops, and had participated in a liquor raid on the home of newspaper czar F. I. Thompson. Klansmen, furious over the focus on Worthington, repeatedly threatened the county prosecutor with violence. Jim Davis began carrying a gun and assigned a police guard to Arthur Hitt.[23]

Davis pressed ahead by summoning James Esdale to appear before the Jefferson County grand jury, along with Worthington, to procure the membership rolls of lodges in the Birmingham area, and to question the grand dragon about a series of phone threats that his office had received. In response, Bert Thomas issued a statement claiming that the KKK had not been involved in the Hitt affair and that the black man had been beaten over a dispute with moonshiners. When written threats to Davis failed to call him off, a pair of burly Klansmen visited the prosecutor. Davis responded by taking steps to bring federal charges against the Klan.[24]

For a while the efforts of Davis, McCall, and Chamberlain appeared likely to bear fruit. A grand jury returned eighteen indictments covering eight floggings. Authorities arrested Worthington for kidnapping as well as for attempting to bribe grand jurors. Police also arrested Worthington's lawyer (a Klansman) and another Tarrant City Knight for attempted bribery and refusal to answer questions before the grand jury. The pair had reportedly attempted to bribe a witness into testifying that he had helped flog Hitt in a private dispute over moonshine. The indictments also called for the arrest of two Tarrant City Knights who had previously been involved in the Jeff Calloway cases.[25] Despite these encouraging signs, the local community was simply not interested in prosecuting the KKK. Grand jurors admitted that sympathy and intimidation had made their task difficult.[26]

Then the cases simply fell apart. Formidable Klan attorney Horace Wilkinson threw a wrench in the works by appealing the Calloway convictions. One of the best lawyers in the country, Wilkinson questioned the formation of the Calloway juries as well as the definition of kidnapping spelled out in the state code. The KKK also contracted Wilkinson to defend the Jefferson County Kluxers. He successfully moved for a postponement of the Jefferson trials until the state supreme court had ruled on the Calloway appeals. Prosecutors were faced with the additional burden of addressing juries that were friendly to the KKK. All but ten people in the 125-person venire called for jury duty were themselves avowed members of the Klan.[27]

Some observers had foreseen the problem of sympathy for Klan defendants. Several grand jurors had warned that little would actually be accomplished unless the county's ordinary citizens became aroused. An editor for the New York World agreed by noting that it "is impossible for justice to rise above its fountainhead."[28]

Aside from the Calloway convictions, efforts at legal resistance to the Klan had been a bust. Juries in Randolph, Talladega, Marengo, Etowah, Calhoun, and Jefferson Counties had been abject failures. Community sympathy revealed that there was little popular support for battles against the Klan. Even in Lauderdale County, where Bertha Slay's floggers had been convicted, their sentences had been so absurdly light that other floggers were probably encouraged rather than deterred. Despite the crimes that had taken place all over the state, grand juries in sixty other Alabama counties remained virtually silent.[29]

THE DEBACLE AT CRENSHAW

Alabama's most devastating legal disappointment came in Crenshaw County. Charlie McCall had won the opening round of his anti-Klan fight in the Calloway cases. The KKK dominated the middle rounds, punctuated by Horace Wilkinson's postponement triumph in Jefferson County. Late in 1927, McCall and Wilkinson, representing patrician and Klan, clashed in what was to be the decisive legal battle of the oligarchy's campaign against the hooded order. The site was Luverne, the county seat of Crenshaw in south Alabama.

McCall and Wilkinson's personalities dominated the event. Both were young, exceptionally energetic, tough, articulate, insatiably ambitious, and fully committed. They knew each other well, disliked each other intensely, had both served in the state attorney general's office, and knew Alabama's judicial system intimately. Both were members of the KKK, veterans of war, utterly fearless, and mostly self-made men.[30] McCall's odyssey to Luverne had been rather remarkable. Until his curious conduct in the summer of 1927, he had behaved as befitted a faithful Klan servant.[31]

The situation changed, though, in the summer of 1927. By attacking the hooded order in the Calloway cases, Charlie McCall had violated the most sacred obligation of a Klan member. After his shocking defection, previously hostile planters and industrialists described the attorney general as an "energetic, brilliant young firebrand." Political observers speculated on the reasons for his reversal—political opportunism, treachery, a need to grandstand, a revulsion to violence, perhaps a love of honesty—yet no one was quite sure why McCall had bitten the gloved hand that fed him. "That flogging business was too much for any white man to stand," McCall said. "It wasn't civilized. What kind of man is it that whips human beings until they bleed? What kind of man is it that would whip a dog that way?"[32]

McCall's hatred of Klan vigilantism was probably genuine. Still, his political aspirations fit nicely with his distaste for violence. The fact that McCall ran for governor in 1930 by seeking Big Mule/Black Belt support strongly suggests that perhaps law and order were not the only things on his mind in late 1927. After Oscar Underwood's retirement from political life, the position of Klan political enemy number one in Alabama remained unfilled. The state's flogging epidemic gave an ambitious young lawyer like McCall the perfect opportunity to fill the void.

The attorney general behaved like a man possessed in Crenshaw. Boasting that he had secured enough evidence for at least eighty indictments, McCall implored Governor Graves to send investigative aid and to call for a special grand jury. The governor obliged. A judge empaneled a grand jury for 10 October consisting of fourteen farmers, three small merchants, and one Ford dealer. McCall predicted that there would be over a hundred felony convictions and spoke of at least twenty assaults and kidnappings, some of them fatal.[33]

Once the grand jury convened, though, the KKK fought McCall each step of the way. For several days, James Esdale ignored his subpoena, then finally arrived in Luverne. Cecil Davis, a former great titan for the south Alabama province, flatly refused to answer McCall's questions, called them "irrelevant," and explained that to respond would violate a higher oath to the Klan. Judge A. E. Gamble jailed Davis five days for contempt, which only made him a hooded martyr. George H. Thigpen, the current great titan for the southern province and also Alabama's state superintendent of insurance, followed Davis's example. Thigpen escaped a contempt charge by stipulating that he could not answer McCall's questions because he did not know the answers.[34]

Some observers were outraged by this brazen display of recalcitrance. Grover Hall noted that it was colossal hypocrisy for Klansmen to denounce Roman Catholics as answerable to a higher foreign power while they themselves provided the best example available of such treason. The *Mobile Register* argued that Alabama was a higher power than any fraternal organization, and a Birmingham editor denounced loyalty to a secret oath. A *Chicago Tribune* writer demanded that Cecil Davis be jailed for treason and asked the state to outlaw the KKK.[35]

Charlie McCall's determination, though, paid off in a way that even he had not envisioned. Crenshaw's grand jury handed down 102 indictments involving 45 persons, all but 1 of them members of the KKK. The report listed over twenty acts of flogging as well as assorted atrocities and compared Crenshaw's reign of terror to the Spanish Inquisition. Perhaps most important, the report did much to dispel the myth that Klan violence emanated from the troubled minds of a few Knights on the lunatic fringe. The jurors chastised James Esdale and Cecil Davis as well as local Klan leaders for presiding over the "barbaric terrorism of the rule of mask and lash." They laid responsibility and knowledge directly to the "evil leadership" of the KKK, which, they said, was "at war with the constituted authorities." The report capped more than a week of testimony and included indictments against four individuals who had attempted to intimidate grand jury witnesses into remaining silent. Jurors reserved special condemnation for the "yellow deeds, diabolical schemes . . . , and cowardly torturing attacks" that had been hatched in the presence of Klan leaders behind lodge walls. Judge Gamble, in his instructions to the grand jurors, compared flogging to a cancer eating at Crenshaw and declared that the county stood naked before the world as one of its most lawless corners.[36] Planter/industrialist editors rejoiced at the report. One patrician called it "the most hopeful scrap of paper that had made its appearance in Alabama in many moons." Grover Hall rejoiced the most loudly, toasting Charlie McCall as a man underrated by many.[37]

McCall's investigation brought to light a number of ghastly incidents that had previously been unknown. Crenshaw Klansmen had savagely flogged one couple because the husband and the wife had both been previously married. The mob, witnesses said, was led by Baptist preacher L. A. Nalls. He had officiated at the couple's wedding and had apparently officiated at their flogging as well. After the brutal affair, conducted in front of the couple's young children, Nalls had taken up a collection for the bleeding woman. He offered her $3.50, a jar of ointment, and some pastoral words of wisdom: "Sister, you were not punished in anger this evening; you were punished in a spirit of kindness and correction to set your feet aright and to show your children how a good mother should go." Nalls fled to Texas when news of the indictments came down. In another incident, Crenshaw Knights flogged one black so ferociously that he nearly died. When his white employer protested that the victim had always been peaceable and hardworking, they burned his barn. Kluxers also beat a seventeen-year-old divorcee for dating a farmer and tried to bludgeon a pair of sisters who were spinsters. The women dispersed one masked mob with their shotgun, but Kluxers returned in their absence and shot their furniture full of holes. Crenshaw's Klansmen also targeted G. T. Miller, one of their own. A third grade dropout, Miller had served time in a federal penitentiary for shooting a deputy during a bootlegging raid. When he was released in 1926, he joined the Crenshaw KKK, but his robed brethren beat him twice for tipping off people whom the Klan intended to flog.[38]

While the Reverend Nalls hightailed it to Texas, in the week after the indictments Crenshaw authorities arrested only twenty-four of the county's thirty-seven indictees. Luverne's mayor identified five of the worst Klan offenders as two local blacksmiths, a barber, a bricklayer, and a shoe repairman. He described a sixth as the village drunk who had been intoxicated until 1924. "Ever since he's sworn off," Mayor J. H. Reddock explained, "he's been all hell in favor of virtue."[39]

McCall's initial success soon proved to be illusory. Crenshaw, a Klan-controlled county, obstructed his investigation at every turn. Bibb Graves, exasperated by his loose cannon and increasingly pressured by Klan notables to do something, pulled state support out from under McCall. Vowing to put a stop "once and for all" to flogging in Alabama, McCall told the public to report all future floggings directly to him. It would be a waste of time, he suggested, to go to the local authorities or anyone else in the Klan-ridden state government. Reports from around the state soon flooded McCall's office. Klansmen retaliated by shooting at one man from ambush, piercing his hat in three places. Reports detailed beatings, threats, and the forced sales of homes and businesses for pennies on the dollar. In just a few days, the attorney general compiled a list of seventy new floggings to investigate after Crenshaw. For Bibb Graves and the Klan's leaders, Charlie McCall had gotten completely out of hand.[40]

Meanwhile, justice moved at a glacial pace in Crenshaw. Three defendants fled the county, and rumors floated around Luverne that friendly deputies had tipped the men off before their escape.[41]

McCall faced other obstacles. Members of his staff spotted three men spying on his hotel room. McCall requested help from the governor to deal with rampant hooded intimidation but learned that men claiming to be state policemen had already been in contact with the witnesses. Graves sent Walter K. McAdory, the chief of the state police, to Luverne, ostensibly to aid McCall, but relations between the men were openly sour.[42]

Perhaps most unsettling to McCall was intimidation by the local KKK. Robed mobs visited prospective witnesses and persuaded many to quit their jobs, leave their homes, and flee the county. Complaints flowed into the governor's office, but Graves denied that any intimidation had occurred. McCall pressed the governor on the issue and enlarged a small fissure into a wide rift when he scolded Graves for being derelict in his duty.[43] An irate Charlie McCall divorced himself from Graves and instructed witnesses to use deadly force against Klansmen who tried to intimidate them. "This monkey business . . . is taxing my patience," McCall announced as he called for contempt and obstruction of justice charges against Klansmen. "Your home is your castle." McCall himself, who had boxed professionally for two years without defeat, began carrying a long, steel blue revolver.[44]

The governor decided to deal with his unruly subordinate by tightening McCall's purse strings. Klan notables, holding Graves responsible for McCall, had put pressure on the governor. After a major KKK huddle in Montgomery that included James Esdale, Bert Thomas, and Cecil Davis, the governor summoned McCall to the capitol. Graves asked the attorney general how much money he intended to spend, then informed him that $15 per case would be sufficient and capped the maximum at $1,500 for the 102 Crenshaw indictments. A furious McCall replied that he needed at least

$100 per case, or $10,000, but the governor refused to budge. Graves also took issue with McCall's employment of local counsel and instructed the attorney general that a "reign of terror" had never existed in Crenshaw County or for that matter in any other Alabama county. The enraged McCall vowed to use local counsel even if he had to pay the attorney's fees out of his own pocket. McCall then made details of the meeting public, expressed disgust with Graves, and declared that any funds used to blot out Alabama's shame would be money wisely spent. Graves, as usual, declined to make any comment other than to describe the encounter as "a routine administrative matter." Yet Grover Hall managed to comment on his own behalf and on that of the reticent governor when he expressed surprise at Graves's sudden passion for frugality.[45]

Whenever Bibb Graves is mentioned in studies dealing with Alabama history, he is usually called the liberal governor of a state that has seen precious few progressives.[46] His reputation for economic liberalism is well deserved. Still, Graves's public career, like that of Hugo Black, his contemporary, has elements that are difficult to reconcile with his progressivism. To be sure, Graves backed a number of progressive projects during his two terms and was, relative to other Alabama governors before and since, a liberal godsend. He was interested in health, education, labor, prison reform, roads, welfare, and old-age pensions. The price of Graves's reform, though, was high—the official toleration of hooded crime. His record regarding the KKK and its predilection for violence was poor.

Clearly, Bibb Graves was in a difficult spot. The KKK was the well from which he drew his political power. It was his resource, and Graves felt that it had to be protected even in its excesses. In 1927, he did everything in his power to ignore, if not actively obstruct, justice in a state that needed responsible governance as much as it needed economic reform.

Graves's attitude toward Klan violence was negligent at best and actively collusive at worst. Although he took credit for the Calloway convictions, and promised to spare no effort to combat flogging, he became increasingly obstructionist as McCall showed himself genuinely zealous. Graves knew that the KKK flogged Alabamians; he admitted as much in his private correspondence. Yet he believed that he was in an untenable position politically. Protection of the Klan's dark side was the price that Graves felt he had to pay to receive the KKK blessing and vote, the price that he and Alabama had to pay for a badly needed program of reform. For Graves, flogging was the lesser of two evils. Entrenched, inert, oligarchical conservatism was the greater. Graves consequently ignored the pleas of flogging victims, denied reality, hamstrung McCall, and never answered the letters written by individuals such as F. M. Vann, the former cyclops of the Roanoke klavern. Vann had quit the Klan because of its violence. When Vann asked the governor to make a state inquiry into eight specific and detailed acts of terror, Graves remained silent. "Coolidge himself could not have been more silent," Grover Hall remarked. His words, unfortunately, were true.[47]

As Graves's silence became oppressive, state and national commentators questioned his sincerity. The *Nation* viewed his few public statements on flogging as "probably . . . a nice gesture and nothing more," while black editors regarded his rare utterances as public relations ploys meant for national consumption. The *Pittsburgh Courier* and the *New York World* joined Birmingham's press in calling on Graves to announce what he planned to do about the flogging epidemic. Other southern editors rebuked Graves for his refusal to deal with flogging.[48]

Still, the governor took all the sustenance he needed from individuals such as the Reverend Dr. H. H. McNeill of Prattville. A Klan apologist, McNeill praised the governor's "manly good sense" in maintaining a silence that he compared favorably to Cal Coolidge's. The reverend accurately attributed much of the attacks on Graves and Klan floggers to the oligarchy's political motives, but he also excused vigilantism on the ground that instate criticism of it was politically inspired. McNeill explained Charlie McCall's treason as that of a "raw youth" whom the Big Mules were using politically. McCall would be dropped like "a hunk of mud," McNeill declared, as soon as he had served their purposes.[49]

Matters came to a head on 20 October 1927, when McCall publicly resigned from the KKK. Calling the Klan "the greatest menace," the attorney general announced that he could no longer belong to an organization that was "at war with constituted authority," that was directed by a "lawless leadership," and that condoned, planned, and encouraged the commission of violent crime (figure 17). McCall asserted that the order had not only refused to assist him but had actually shielded criminals from the law. He charged Klan leaders with blocking investigations by inspiring further terror and banishing members for testifying in court.[50]

McCall's letter was an amazing statement. When he joined the ranks of the oligarchical enemies of the Klan, though, he did so mainly on the ground that the order's leadership had obstructed justice. In his resignation, he defended basic Klan doctrines, praised the Anglo-Saxon race and its "tall, sun-crowned men," and advocated stricter immigration laws that would preserve America's ethnic integrity from assault by "a polyglot and unassimable people."[51]

Fallout from the bombshell was considerable. Grover Hall placed the attorney general on an honor roll and called for all "good men" in the Klan to resign. Tuscaloosa Klansmen did just that; 150 of them adjourned sine die in support of McCall. Meanwhile, Bibb Graves issued what had by now

"RESOLUTIN'!"

RECKON I HAD BETTER RESOLVE TO ABANDON THE LASH!

MASKED FLOGGERS

New Year's Resolutions 1928

RESOLVED: — THAT DURING THE COMING YEAR I WILL DO ALL IN MY POWER TO PUT EACH AND EVERY ONE OF ALABAMA'S MASKED FLOGGERS BEHIND THE BARS WHERE HE BELONGS — THAT OUR STATE MAY BE REDEEMED FROM TERRORISM Signed C. McCall

CHARLIE McCALL

INK

GEE TEE MAXWELL

17. Political Cartoon of Charlie McCall, 1927. Swept into office in 1926 on the same tidal wave of Klan popularity that elected Bibb Graves and Hugo Black, Attorney General Charles C. McCall soon turned on the hooded order and launched a series of legal offensives against it. Courtesy Birmingham Public Library, Tutwiler Collection of Southern History. Originally published in the *Birmingham News*.

become his standard response. He described McCall's dramatic resignation as only "a personal matter that does not concern me."[52]

McCall obviously sensed the difficulty of trying a case in a county as infested with the Klan as Crenshaw. He hired F. P. Bricken, a well-liked local attorney, and chose Shelby Gregory to stand trial first, probably because of the severity of the charge against him.[53] A Crenshaw Klansman, Gregory had allegedly been the ringleader in the fatal flogging of Annie Mae Simmons, a black woman. McCall most likely selected him as the first defendant because the elderly African American woman had died from her beating in July 1925. The choice, though, proved to be a serious mistake. Annie Simmons's color was more important in Crenshaw than her death. As one defense attorney later explained in open court, because she was black, her death was of no consequence.[54]

Other problems besides race occupied McCall. Horace Wilkinson arrived in Luverne to head the defense team. Wilkinson, a former Birmingham judge, was immensely talented and quite committed to the cause of white supremacy. McCall and Wilkinson had split two flogging cases, in Blount and Jefferson Counties; the Crenshaw cases would be the rubber match between the rivals.[55]

Wilkinson led a four-man defense team that was cheered at every point by a partisan courtroom crowd. He began Gregory's defense by arguing that the state's case was groundless and should be dismissed. Judge A. E. Gamble denied the motion, and Wilkinson proceeded to construct an alibi by introducing Gregory's father, who swore that he and his son had been eating watermelon at the time of the flogging. Wilkinson's participation was revealing. He was Bibb Graves's chief political lieutenant, and his very presence, not to mention his active involvement, suggested where the governor's sympathies truly lay.[56]

The state's case should have been more than sufficient to convict Gregory had the local community been in a mood to adjudicate fairly. The defendant had previously confessed to the fatal flogging, describing how he and four other unmasked Knights had forced Annie Mae Simmons into an automobile at gunpoint, had driven to a nearby cornfield, had flogged the woman with shingles, and had warned her not to let the sun go down on her in Crenshaw County. McCall also introduced three blacks who had witnessed the kidnapping and the flogging.[57]

Wilkinson attacked Gregory's confession by claiming that he had been browbeaten, cursed, threatened, cajoled, and reduced to a state of blathering incoherence by systematic sleep deprivation. Gregory told a rapt courtroom that Charlie McCall had threatened to break his neck and fry him in the electric chair and had later tried to bribe him. On cross-examination Gregory admitted that he had actually come to the attorney general for money. McCall put jailers on the stand to refute the charges, but the damage had been done.[58]

In a remarkable turn of events, Horace Wilkinson placed a state policeman on the stand to corroborate Gregory's claims against the attorney general, forcing McCall to respond with one of his own. Still, the court had been treated to the bizarre spectacle of two state policemen disagreeing publicly about an attorney general's alleged threats and bribe offers. The move came after an unusual huddle at the defense team's hotel in which James Esdale and state police chief Walter McAdory had met with Horace Wilkinson behind closed doors.[59] The defense further damaged McCall's case by blasting him for "butt[ing] in[to]" Crenshaw's affairs. Of course, there was considerable irony in state officials' being tarred with a local version of home rule.[60]

Wilkinson put the final touches on the Klan's case by giving the jury of eleven farmers and an oil dealer a peg on which to hang an acquittal. In another miscalculation, Mcall had charged Gregory with kidnapping—not murder or even flogging. Wilkinson, a renowned constitutional lawyer with an eye for detail, argued that state law specified that kidnapping meant taking a victim against his or her will for the purpose of either imprisonment or removal from the state. The defendant, as Wilkinson pointed out, had taken the woman not for either of these two reasons but only—allegedly—to beat her.[61]

As James Esdale, state Klan leaders George Thigpen and Cecil Davis, and Bibb Mills, the Anti-Saloon League superintendent, moved conspicuously around Luverne, the jury retired to deliberate. The next morning the foreman announced that Shelby Gregory was not guilty. A packed courtroom stood and thundered its applause. Dismayed by the community's frank display of support for the Klan, Charlie McCall refused comment. Later he weakly maintained that the state had not lost any ground.[62]

McCall by this time knew better. The Gregory trial showed that a strong state case had little chance against a community united in its sympathy for the KKK. If McCall did not know going into the trial that he faced insurmountable obstacles in Crenshaw, he soon learned. Public opinion overwhelmingly favored the Klan defendants. Spectators cheered the defense team's every point and greeted the acquittal with a rousing ovation. Intimidation and bribery permeated the proceedings, as did spying on state counsel. Local authority was paralyzed. Apparently, no arrests or prosecutions of Klansmen preceded McCall's invasion and the grand jury's indictments. Like many of his counterparts around Alabama, the current sheriff was a member of the KKK. His predecessor, former Klansman Pat McQueen, denied that Crenshaw even had a serious problem. State police and their chief freely colluded with the defense; some, incredibly, testified for the defense. McCall became the focus of attention as the defense team cast aspersions on his political motives and his respect for local sensibilities. One defense lawyer had articulated what many in the county were obviously thinking, that the Klan's murder of a human being was "of no . . . consequence" because the victim had been black.[63]

The crowning indignity came soon after the acquittal. McCall saw confirmation of his worst suspicions about Bibb Graves: indications that the governor or someone in his office was colluding with Klan leaders to thwart the state's case. In a raid on the home of Luverne cyclops Ira B. Thompson, McCall discovered evidence strongly suggesting that Graves and state policemen were helping the KKK to derail his case. The raid, backed by a subpoena, had been aimed at recovering the membership records of the Luverne klavern. Instead, McCall stumbled on a letter from James Esdale to Ira Thompson about McCall's prosecution. Esdale had written: "I think it is high time that something be done to bring the attorney general to his senses and let him know that the people of Alabama elected him to run the attorney general's office and not spend all his time . . . working up police court cases against the Ku Klux Klan." Esdale assured Thompson that he planned to talk to the governor personally about the matter. "I have the utmost confidence in Col. Graves, and feel sure that he will lend us his full cooperation in the future as he has so nobly done in the past," Esdale wrote. "Personally, I feel that Col. Graves' attitude toward the attorney general is about the same as ourselves."[64]

More damning, though, were additional documents that McCall found in the cyclops's effects, including copies of official state police reports to the governor about the Crenshaw cases. The papers, locked in Thompson's safe, furnished strong evidence of a state conspiracy to stymie McCall. Perhaps more troubling, shortly after Esdale's promise to visit Graves, the governor had called McCall on the carpet, chastised him for hiring local counsel, denied that a reign of terror existed, and tried to cripple him by slashing his budget. Despite the nature of McCall's charges, and their implications, Graves and his police chief remained silent. They never even denied the charge that the state and the KKK had colluded to foil McCall.[65]

Not an individual who readily capitulated, McCall tried again by calling G. T. Miller to trial. Miller had been an alleged participant in the fatal Simmons flogging, but McCall tried him for the beating of Travis Bozeman. Having learned the worth of black lives in Crenshaw, McCall this time chose the flogger of a white person.

The second Crenshaw trial was as disappointing as the first. Although McCall stayed in the background and let F. P. Bricken handle the proceedings, what should have been an open-and-shut case could not be won. Crenshaw County was simply in no mood to convict Klansmen. The state supplied evidence and eyewitnesses to Bozeman's 1926 flogging. Prosecutors charged that Miller and other Klansmen had lured their victim to a church meeting only to waylay him later. A dozen masked men gave Bozeman fifty stripes, admonished him for drinking liquor and spending his father's pension, and ordered him to find work. A confident Horace Wilkinson argued that the state case was flawed because, technically, the charge should have been "white-capping" rather than kidnapping. The point was enough to win an acquittal and another standing ovation from a court full of Klan sympathizers. Years later, Miller admitted taking part in two fatal Klan floggings.[66]

Furious, McCall prepared to leave the county. Calling state police "frenzied" in their desire to aid the defense, McCall formally withdrew the rest of the state's cases. Before leaving, though, he expressed keen disappointment that local opinion had so strongly favored the Klan that it was blind to justice. McCall, as well as both the pro- and anti-Klan press, realized with the failure of the strong Crenshaw cases that it would be virtually impossible for the state to gain guilty verdicts elsewhere.[67]

In the aftermath of the disaster, a number of theories were advanced to make sense of the Crenshaw developments. A reporter for *Collier's* explained community support and acquittals as reflecting a desire to attain moral elitism by monitoring the ethical shortcomings of one's neighbors. "Nothing crazier ever happened in any house of maniacs than happened in Alabama," William G. Shepherd wrote. "This spirit . . . made up of the most poisonous mixture of ideas opinions and emotions that could ever gas and gag a community . . . set the law aside [and] . . . created an anarchy wilder than any Russian ever dreamed of. . . . It did not call itself evil, it called itself the organized GOOD of the community, [but] it had no mercy, kindness, sympathy, or understanding. It tolerated nothing which dissented from it. . . . Indeed, it was a tyrant above control."[68]

Other comments followed. A Luverne attorney surmised that the whipping fever managed to sift out the county's "yellow cowards" and degenerates. A local businessman mused that the whip-wielders had become giddy with power and addicted to morality enforcement and their own illusions of moral elitism. Ira Thompson admitted that he had been too busy to lead the local klavern properly, that bad men had seeped into his hooded ranks, and that he had lost control. Treasurer of a local Masonic hall, a board member of the Methodist church, the captain of a state artillery unit, and the local cyclops, the civic-minded Thompson was, by his own admission, overwhelmed. "I had too much to do. I couldn't keep the thing going straight," Thompson explained. "I always talked against violence. But some of the boys got out of control." There was no legitimate reason to flog anyone, he said: Luverne had no Jews, no foreigners, and only two Catholics, a pair of old women that everybody loved. Mayor J. H. Reddock agreed that

Thompson was responsible but attributed the cause to his political ambition, not his full calendar. He added that Thompson had removed any barrier to Klan membership in order to swell his voting base for a failed 1926 run for mayor. "He took in riff-raff," Reddock remarked. "No wonder he's in trouble now. . . . he couldn't control the men. . . . They weren't the kind of fellows one could control." Sheer obstinacy was also a factor. Crenshaw's former sheriff denied that the county had a serious problem.[69]

Editorial opinion gloomily agreed that Alabama's Klan was strong enough to subvert the ends of justice. It implicitly recognized as well that societal acquiescence was behind the order's success. What anti-Klan editors did not see as clearly, perhaps, was that opposition mounted on political competition would not undermine this wellspring of support.

While Grover Hall mourned the collapse of justice in Crenshaw and criticized Bibb Graves, the pro-Klan press celebrated. Hall's lament was drowned out by the Klannish *Andalusia Star*, which dubbed Charlie McCall a publicity seeker and a dupe of Roman Catholic interests. A Luverne editor applauded the acquittals as a slap in the face for McCall and as evidence that Crenshaw's populace was perfectly able to run its own affairs. The states'-rights rhetoric that Alabamians had used for years to disparage the encroachment of the federal government had so saturated the public that it applied to state and local relations as well. "The general opinion is that Crenshaw can run her own affairs, including the courts"—he spat out the words—without the unwanted intrusion of outside state agitators.[70]

Regional reaction alternately criticized McCall for giving up the Klan fight and sympathized with his plight. *Atlanta Constitution* editors worried that the dark secrets divulged in Alabama had analogues in other southern states. They found it especially unnerving that a state attorney general had accused Klan leaders of aiding and abetting violent perpetrators, intimidating witnesses, planning and ordering the floggings, and later obstructing justice. North Carolina and Tennessee editors condemned the acquittals, while a Georgia critic observed that the thermometer of justice in Alabama had fallen below zero.[71]

Northern onlookers were thoroughly disgusted. The *New York Times* held local attitudes responsible for retarding the impulse toward justice and for stunting Alabama's march toward progress. Another New Yorker mocked Bibb Graves's appearance before a national police convention as the height of hypocrisy. Others attributed the work of Klan committees to a puritanical fixation on prohibition and sexual irregularity. According to the *Chicago Tribune*, Graves remained silent, ordinary Alabamians were unaroused, and repeated acquittals occurred because most folks thought the victims had "something coming to them" anyhow. Baltimore newsmen depicted the trials as a colossal waste of time, given the enormous sympathy for the Klan

Klansmen of Birmingham, Ala.
Dec. 15- 1927
Municipal Auditorium

18. Celebratory Klan Dinner at Birmingham's Municipal Auditorium, December 1927. By the end of 1927, Alabama's KKK had much to be thankful for, including a series of victories in the state's courtrooms. Courtesy Birmingham Public Library Archives, Cat. No. 49.55.

in Crenshaw. Another critic pictured the Alabamians who tolerated Klan abuse as stubborn, shrewd, simple, and fiercely independent folk who resented outside intrusion above all else. Because Charlie McCall had failed to understand them, he had been destined to fail. "The . . . acquittal was written before the first case went to trial," Harold Stephens wrote. "Your hidebound rural Alabamian, whose advocacy of local government amounts to prejudice, deems the enforcement of laws by the State an arbitrary transgression on his rights and liberties. The State officer is a stranger, and in rural Alabama the motives of all strangers are questioned. . . . perhaps . . . [McCall] did not [fully] understand [this]. . . . before he left he understood." [72]

Yet legions of Alabama Klansmen and sympathizers remained impervious to written assaults from within the state or outside it. Just before Christmas, the state Klan held a celebration in Birmingham to commemorate the Crenshaw verdicts (figure 18). Charlie McCall dismissed the event as a fleeting gesture, but it spoke volumes about the societal aid and comfort that

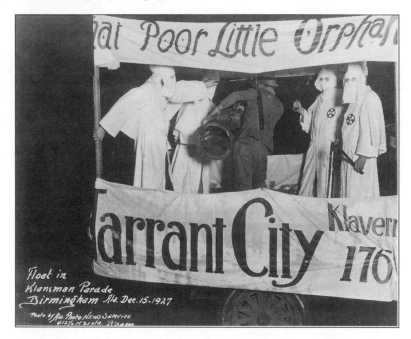

19. "Poor Little Orphan" Float, December 1927. Tarrant City's Klan proudly exhibited their float commemorating the beating of the Oneonta orphan Jeff Calloway and
their eventual legal victory. Courtesy Birmingham Public Library Archives, Cat. No.
49.56.

sustained the order. Hooded leaders expected 25,000 to 50,000 participants,
but continuous rain reduced the ranks to about a thousand die-hard individuals. The hardy souls who withstood winter rain to parade, distribute
pamphlets, dance, and eat dinner at the Municipal Auditorium represented
many other Alabamians who were equally pleased that the Klan had won
out in Crenshaw County. A sheeted troupe of WKKK women performed
a dance, and other gowned participants rode a macabre float dubbed "Poor
Little Orphan" that depicted the Jeff Calloway flogging (figure 19).[73]

After the parade, though, news arrived of another Klan triumph over
patrician adversaries. Horace Wilkinson had the Jeff Calloway convictions
overturned at the state supreme court. As two convicted Klan floggers
walked free into Alabama's sunlight, the limits of resisting the KKK in the
state became even plainer than it had been with the dramatic collapse at
Crenshaw.[74]

Still, the 1927 war against Alabama's KKK had other limitations. Little of it challenged the fundamental precepts of the Klan, its prejudices, or
its basic intolerance. Like most patrician enemies of Alabama's Klan in the

1920s, J. M. McCary was a staunch admirer of the Reconstruction Klan. He praised it as representing "the most exalted principle which the citizens of America have ever . . . support[ed] . . . , the absolute and eternal divorce of the white man and the negro from sexual contact." The Reconstruction Klan existed, McCary explained, to resist the African domination guaranteed by the Fourteenth Amendment. The amendment, he wrote, was "a bare-faced fraud" on behalf of Africans "who were but shortly removed from naked, driveling paganism and savagery . . . to negroize Congress" and bolster black suffrage for the northern Republican Party. The essential Reconstruction question was: should the Caucasian, "who has conquered a continent from the red savage and excluded the yellow pagan . . . , share it with the black, in whom both traits are fundamental?" Still, the 1920s Klan, for McCary and many others, had fallen into the hands of "men who have neither the principle nor the intelligence to direct the mighty moral force" at their command and to resist a "gospel of equality of colors."[75]

During the climactic year of 1927 Alabama paid the price for its brief political and economic experiment with reform. Bibb Graves marked a radical departure from the stultifying conservatism of Alabama's entrenched planter/industrialist regime, but the violence and terror that came with Klan ascendance was the high price of reform in Alabama: official tolerance of intolerance, ethnic bigotry, moral authoritarianism, racial repression, misogyny, religious proscription, antilabor vigilantism, and the violation of democratic and constitutionally guaranteed rights of due process, equal protection, free speech, free press, free religion, and private property.

The Klan's "better men" were powerless to control a violent element that may well have been a minority.[76] The actual number of people who conduct terrorism is small, almost of necessity. A question more important than size is whether the few reflect the views or acquiescence of other members or of the broader society. In Alabama the few clearly did so. A Chicagoan perhaps envisioned eventual public rejection of the Klan when he advised Alabamians not to content themselves with merely destroying the mask but to go much further "to root out the sources of the Klan's power, the narrow and purblind sectarianism, the savage race prejudice, and the spirit of intolerance."[77]

9

Race over Rum, Romans, and Republicans

Despite the obvious vitality the Alabama Klan demonstrated in 1927, and the apparent inability of its opponents to persuade petit juries, the order's enemies pronounced it dead yet again in early 1928. The announcement, not unlike its predecessors, was largely the function of wishful thinking. Alabama's Klan was to have, perhaps, its finest hour in 1928.

The year witnessed one of the most ferocious clashes in modern political history. The KKK—combating a rapidly thinning membership, declining revenues, diminishing influence, and an anemic moral stature—plunged headlong into the political fray that would finally rip apart the Democratic Party. The party had been seriously divided since at least 1924, when a northern, "wet," urban, ethnic, and prolabor wing collided with its rural, farm, Anglo-Saxon counterpart in the South. After a record number of ballots, the national convention had passed over the principal figures representing the two factions—New York governor Alfred E. Smith and the "Great Commoner," William Jennings Bryan—in favor of an obscure compromise candidate.

In 1928, Alabama's hooded political strategists used a caustically divisive campaign to resuscitate the order, at least politically. In fact, the open splitting of the Democratic Party over Al Smith's nomination gave the KKK the perfect tool with which to stage a comeback in the Deep South. Smith's 1928 nomination at Houston exposed some of America's darkest prejudices in bold relief. His Catholicism, Tammany Hall connection, immigrant background, and political wetness promised the most divisive campaign since the Populist wars of the 1890s. Rum, Romanism, nativism, and Tammany became critical national issues in 1928. Still, in Alabama, and in much of the rest of the South, the race question eclipsed all of these.

The issue of race had always been of paramount importance for the

South. Its centrality, in fact, has been the South's most essential and enduring feature.[1] By the eve of the 1928 presidential election in Alabama, race had again loomed larger than any other conceivable bone of contention. Catholicism, liquor, and Tammany, still hot topics, had all undergone fundamental changes in Alabama, transformations that set them apart from their counterparts elsewhere. In the Deep South race had, by November 1928, grafted itself onto all other issues, bending them, twisting them, and contorting them into something decidedly and distinctly southern in flavor. Liquor was dangerous in Dixie, not just because of its adhesion in the popular mind to domestic discord and sloth, but because it threatened to send a savage race out of control. Catholicism was evil in Alabama, not merely because of its affiliation with foreign dominance and because it carried the odor of unwashed immigrants, but because Romanists supposedly planned to use the African as a foot soldier in the coming race war. Alliance with Republicans was ominous in Alabama because it recalled the dark specter of Reconstruction, Radical politics, federal domination, and, worst of all, black rule.[2]

Because of its primal nature, race irrevocably altered the main issues of 1928.[3] By the midpoint of the presidential campaign, Alabama's regular Democrats and its Hoovercrats had largely forsaken talk of liquor, foreigners, and the Pope in favor of the jugular issue, white supremacy. Both loyalists and bolters showed an insatiable appetite for race-baiting. In Alabama all other issues became peripheral or were so altered by race that they were no longer separable. The Klan thrived in this climate. The presidential campaign exposed the deep and indelible racial fault line in Alabama's soil that had long carried the very lifeblood of the KKK.

KLAN PROBLEMS

Although the Klan in Alabama was not yet dead in early 1928, it was experiencing considerable difficulty. Membership had plummeted from 115,000 in 1925 to 10,400 at the end of 1927. With the decrease came a crippling loss of revenue. By 1928, the secret society had also experienced serious blows to its self-imposed capacity for moral leadership.[4]

Klan woes in 1928 were national in scope. In fact, the only three states that had not yet suffered membership declines were Oklahoma, Virginia, and Florida. The New York Supreme Court declared that the KKK was "a suspect body," and South Dakota Klansmen canceled a speech by Tom Heflin because they could not attract a large enough audience. Klan troubles were so serious, even in Alabama, that hooded leaders were forced to demand that dues be paid in advance.[5]

In response, the order became increasingly defensive. Alabama's state newsletter ranted and railed against the "entire newspaper press, the Roman Hierarchy, the Jewish interests and the misinformed Protestant public . . . [who have] misrepresented, misquoted, double-crossed, hissed, ridiculed and hindered" the KKK. "[Do] you still hang back because you don't know exactly what becomes of every cent of the money you pay for dues?" one Klan leader asked his Alabama brethren. "The law of our land holds that every man is innocent until proven guilty. Have you been as kind to your Klan officials?"[6]

Other problems beset the KKK as well. Dissension threatened to break up the organization for good. Knights looked at each other with increasing suspicion as fears of internal treachery escalated. In Birmingham, one Klansman offered to sell the minutes of klavern meetings to several newspapers. Embezzlements of between $300 and $26,000 also became public knowledge. Rivalry between W. J. Worthington's Avondale den and the Robert E. Lee Klan threatened to erupt into full-scale riot. Trouble was averted at the last minute because four of the Avondale Knights "lost their nerve." A brawl between the rival chapters did break out, though, in which Kluxers used brass knuckles on each other.[7]

A rift between Bibb Graves and James Esdale also developed regarding the character of the governor's reform program. Early in his administration, the Klan had performed reliably in helping the governor push his progressive programs forward. In 1928, though, Graves and Esdale had a falling out and did not speak for a time as rumors of the governor's imminent resignation from the sheeted society circulated widely. Graves was enraged that the KKK had failed to "function properly" in support of his $20 million bond issue for education. The unpleasantness highlighted increasing friction between Graves's liberalism and the endemic conservatism of much of the KKK's membership and leadership. Imperial Wizard Hiram Evans joined the fracas from Atlanta by upbraiding Alabama's Kluxers—not for failing to support the bond more enthusiastically but for "being on the wrong side" of it in the first place. The governor, meanwhile, was increasingly worried that his progressive record would be obscured, and his future reform plans jeopardized, as Alabama's Klan became smaller and more exclusively reactionary.[8]

The feud was important partly as it bore on the likelihood of Graves's continued legislative success but also as it reflected the Klan's ability to exercise its will in the legislature on issues important to it. Big Mule/Black Belt power was concentrated in the legislature, and the KKK had to rely on lawmakers such as Jefferson County's George Frey, Shelby's L. H. Ellis, Randolph's L. B. Ware, and, of course, the ubiquitous political operative Horace Wilkinson.

A bitter voice rose from the mists of the past to lament the Klan's plight. "There now remains only the bleaching bones of a long-since dead and disintegrated carcass of a one-time splendid movement," William Joseph Simmons declared from his south Alabama exile. "The Klan . . . has forfeited my respect—and those who have brought about its ruin have my supreme contempt. . . . It has degenerated into a pseudo-political organization without even a political conscience."[9]

In response to such criticism, to rejuvenate its sagging rolls, and to refill its coffers, the KKK instituted a new degree of membership in January 1928. The K-Trio Degree became mandatory for all U.S. klaverns by 22 February. It involved a name change and the abandonment of the visor portion of the hood. At a dollar a head, K-Trio was an obvious attempt to raise money and increase membership by appeasing Protestants who could not (in Hiram Evans's words) "stomach the mask." It was also a ploy to minimize criticism about Klan floggings and a rather naked effort to beat state and local enemies to the punch by unmasking the organization voluntarily.[10]

The actual effects of K-Trio, though, were largely unanticipated. Institution of the new degree exposed the order as a moneymaking enterprise and underscored its growing desperation. The loss of anonymity with the unmasking hastened the departure of many Knights who did not want their identities to become public knowledge. The oligarchy's massive publicity about Klan violence prompted even more members to leave the order. By doing away with the visor, the Klan forfeited much of its ability to enforce morality by physical violence and thereby accomplished more than strict laws or vigilant press coverage had to this end.[11]

At a Montgomery klorero, Hiram Evans and Earl Hotalen spoke along with Nathan Bedford Forrest, grand dragon of the Georgia Klan and grandson of the famous Civil War general and Reconstruction Klan wizard. After the speeches, 1,500 local officers from around the state took the K-Trio Degree, paid their dollar, and detached their masks. Evans upbraided the Alabama realm for its excessive violence, for its destructive factionalism, and for the insatiable ambition of some of its leaders. In response, the Klan contingent promised to steel itself for battle over the possible Democratic nomination of Al Smith.[12]

A mask shower followed the K-Trio conclave. The idea, which originated at a Birmingham Klan Association meeting, was to mail discarded masks to the most prominent opponents of the hooded group. Victor Hanson emerged by far and away the big winner. Charlie McCall also received a number of masks. One Kluxer sent the attorney general a mask on which he had sketched a crude drawing of a skull and crossbones with the simple message "Sorry I voted for you." Marie Bankhead Owen, matriarch of the planter/industrialist dynasty and director of the Alabama Department of Archives and History, rushed to acquire the mask for the state collection.[13]

While Marie Owen responded to the unmasking with a curator's instinct, others responded with contempt. Chief among the latter group were members of the oligarchy. Grover Hall and the *Montgomery Advertiser* greeted the unmasking as the final death throe of the Alabama Klan. The *Birmingham News* concurred, as did Julian Harris's *Columbus Enquirer-Sun*. The *Birmingham Age-Herald* followed suit by portraying K-Trio as a "stroke of despair" and a mere "raffling scheme." Three members of Montgomery County's state legislative delegation likewise pronounced the Klan dead. One of them, R. Tyler Goodwyn, the Big Mule/Black Belt author of failed unmasking legislation in 1927, remarked simply, "No hood, no Klan. A crumbling column in the Pagoda of Intolerance."[14]

Other observers, especially outside the South, were not so sure. A New Jersey paper and the venerable *New York Times* agreed that the Klan was done for, but another New York editor argued that the degree was a move to gear up for the 1928 presidential election. Others realized that a Klan spirit could not be killed off simply by doing away with the mask. A Connecticut editor insisted that a leopard could not change its spots even if it lost its mask, and an upstate New York paper agreed that the KKK should "strip off its intolerance" if it truly wished to change. Veteran Klan observer Stanley Frost pointed out that 90 percent of the former Kluxers he knew remained sympathetic to the order's goals even after they formally resigned. Although many of these individuals were no longer members in good standing, they were still members in spirit. A journalist in Decatur, Alabama, contributed to the atmosphere of cynicism by concluding that the unmasking really meant nothing more than lower laundry bills for Klan members.[15]

In fact the Alabama KKK had not died. The national Klan experienced significant problems, and Alabama's order was hardly immune from them. Alabama's hooded membership had suffered many casualties as a result of Grover Hall and the oligarchy's war. Yet the Klan endured and at times even thrived. Like a cat with nine lives, the Alabama Klan defied death again and again to keep coming back—albeit on a markedly smaller scale. K-Trio did not spell the end any more than the Calloway convictions had done or the Jefferson, Marengo, Lauderdale, Talladega, and Crenshaw County indictments or the fractures, fissures, and scandals. The spirit of the Klan was far too resilient to fade away so easily. By October 1928 national Klan leaders, invigorated by the presidential campaign, had rescinded K-Trio and the unmasking and were calling these measures "a mistake."[16]

ANTI-CATHOLICISM AND THE ELECTION OF 1928

In fact, Alabama's KKK was licking its lips in 1928. Al Smith's nomination as the Democratic candidate for president would resuscitate the order, albeit temporarily, as no other event ever had. Klan leaders frequently spoke of a "papal menace" and fifth column "Popish plots" to undue America from within.[17] They even targeted the Boy Scouts of America for investigation because of its affiliation with Catholic parishes and schools. They denied that the Klan was dead and looked forward to proving their mettle in life-and-death conflict with Al Smith, the scion of the "Papal monster."[18]

Alabama's Klan had been severely shaken by the negative publicity of 1927. That fact should not be obscured. Membership had fallen off dramatically because of the constant and strenuous opposition of the oligarchy. In this respect, the patrician political machine and its press allies had waged a successful campaign. For the reduced number of Klansmen who remained in 1928, though, it was business as usual. Bert Thomas resigned as titan and klaliff but remained on the realm's finance committee and continued to serve as director of the Junior KKK. Governor Graves rewarded Thomas for his political allegiance by appointing him state inspector of gasoline for north Alabama, a post that paid the tidy sum of $200 per month. George Frey, a state legislator from Birmingham, replaced Thomas as great titan.[19]

Al Smith's presidential candidacy increasingly dominated Klan thought and action. Alabama's KKK attempted to have the state Democratic executive committee send an instructed delegation to Houston with orders to oppose Smith's nomination. The plan shocked Washington insiders but became a moot point when it failed to materialize.[20] Instead, Klan leaders put together a slate of delegate candidates for the national convention. The list allegedly included Harry Ayers, an Anniston publisher, and the politicos Dempsey Powell of Greenville and Borden Burr of Birmingham. The order also backed state senator Watt T. Brown of Ragland against incumbent national Democratic committeeman Walter Moore.[21]

The announcement of a Klan slate amounted to the opening salvo of Alabama's 1928 civil war. Planter and industrialist spokesmen responded firmly. George Bondurant, U.S. bankruptcy court referee and a power in Birmingham politics, debated hooded speakers at a Wahouma Klan meeting. St. Clair County's Klan founder came out in support of industrialist Walter Moore for a seat on the national Democratic committee over the Klan's preferred choice. "I brought the Klan to Ragland," the former cyclops intoned, "and I'm ashamed of it." A candidate for circuit judge hotly objected to attempts to link his name with the Klan slate for Alabama's Democratic primary: "I am not much of a person for a personal difficulty, but if I could find out the identity of the person [who made the allegation] . . . one or the other of us will get a good licking before the sun sets. . . . if it is a woman, of course, I would have to pass her up." Klan leaders urged their followers to vote for Klan-backed candidates "down the line" in the May 1928 primary and in all county races. To hedge their bets, hooded leaders handed out blank poll watcher's certificates to their Knights. A Birmingham city commissioner dutifully signed the forms, granting official authorization in advance.[22]

State Klansmen joined with the Anti-Saloon League and the Women's Christian Temperance Union (WCTU) for the May primary. The results demonstrated that the KKK was not yet dead in Alabama—at least not politically—and that its interest in prohibition had strong support. Most of the Klan slate achieved election as delegates to Houston. In the race for a place on the national Democratic committee, Klan-backed Watt Brown swamped Big Mule Walter Moore by 22,000 votes.[23]

In Houston, Al Smith won nomination easily as the Democratic party's 1928 standard-bearer. Party leaders chose Senator Joseph T. Robinson of Arkansas—a dry southern Protestant and the Senate minority leader—to balance the ticket as Smith's running mate.[24]

Smith's status as the national party's nominee gave the South a delicate problem to solve. On the one hand, a vote against Smith would be a vote against the Democratic Party. Since Reconstruction, southern whites had vested their most sacred interests in a strong Democratic Party. The "Solid South," to most post–Civil War Southerners, represented the best chance of ensuring racial purity and guarding against the encroachment upon, and erosion of, white supremacy. In most southern states, including Alabama, Democratic solidarity was understood to be one of the loftiest ideals of the day. Any deviation was regarded as a perversion, anathema, an act that threatened to subvert white supremacy, racial integrity, and the southern way of life.

Although the Democratic Party had weathered serious independent challenges in the 1880s and in the Populist revolt of the 1890s, Al Smith's candidacy presented entrenched Democrats with a far more urgent crisis. Smith personified almost all that southern Democrats found repugnant in 1928. Besides being the governor of a "damned Yankee" state, he was, in the eyes of Southerners, part of dirty, corrupt machine politics in New York City. He was an ardent antiprohibitionist, a relative liberal on the race issue, and, perhaps worst of all, a Catholic. Some Southerners held their noses and voted for the papist anyway in the interest of party unity, but many simply could not bring themselves to commit the act. Fully realizing that their stance would be understood as treason in the face of hallowed party solidarity, they nonetheless concluded that voting for the "man" was more important than voting for the party.

Alabama delegates cast only one vote for Al Smith in Houston.[25] Yet once he had been nominated, Alabama's oligarchy was locked into supporting him. Maintenance of the party standard was supremely important to these entrenched Democrats, whoever the nominee might be. Most members of the SDEC felt that stability in Alabama, and most especially the cherished values of white supremacy, would be threatened by an appeal that went beyond the boundaries of the party directly to the masses.

Alabama's KKK responded to Smith's nomination as if its very life were imperiled. Klan leaders mobilized by declaring that their worst fears had finally materialized: the Roman Catholic political machine had flung down the gauntlet in a life-and-death challenge to "Protestantism and Americanism." For many Kluxers the two were interchangeable. They warned that Catholics would use every means at their disposal—propaganda, mind control, hoarded gold reserves, and Jesuit assassins—to win. "The Romanists have girded their loins for battle," an Alabama Klan leader said, "and they are ready . . . to challenge the sacred right and heritage of the true founder and builder of America—The Protestant . . . to say whether or not this Nation shall be governed by the American people who are the Protestants . . . or . . . by an invisible force and power that lives [outside] . . . our barriers."[26]

From Atlanta, Hiram Evans promised to banish any member of the Invisible Empire who voted for Al Smith. Evans vowed to use the KKK to spread the "truth" about the New Yorker: that his election would be tantamount to "bossism, nullification [of prohibition], alienism . . . [and] priest rule." After the KKK had finished with Smith, Evans confidently predicted, he would be unable to win election in New York as dog catcher.[27]

Alabama's Klan, smelling an opportunity, quickly mobilized. Asked whether the secret order planned to take an active part in the election, hooded evangelist Earl Hotalen responded, "You bet your immortal soul it will." Klan senator J. Thomas Heflin, the figure who would prove to be most prominent in the fight against Smith, informed Alabamians that the Vatican was plotting to take over America through Al Smith and that Jesuit assassins, with "murder in their hearts and mean looks on their faces," were plotting his own assassination. "I am fighting the Roman Catholic hierarchy," Heflin boomed as he praised the original KKK. "I discovered it. I'm fighting it and I'm going to continue to fight it."[28]

Atticus Mullin, political columnist for the *Montgomery Advertiser*, reacted bitterly to the speech. "Heflin's hold on rural audiences was never more plainly shown," Mullin complained. "Eyes stuck out on stems as he related 'hellish Catholic plots' . . . and how he would keep on foiling the villain as long as his good tongue was not palsied." Mullin marveled that Heflin actually elicited tears of rage from some listeners as he told Romanist atrocity stories and how Catholic assassins stalked him on the streets of Washington "as if he were a wild beast." "They fell for it," he jeered, "hook, line, and sinker." [29]

Bourbon Democracy's response to the Smith nomination, while not openly hostile, was scarcely warmer than the Klan's. "No candidate other than a resurrected Thaddeus Stevens," according to historian Wayne Flynt, "could have worse offended Alabama Democrats." Privately, members of the oligarchy admitted that they were merely "playing the game" in order to protect the party and white supremacy. They still found Smith's lineage and views obnoxious to the most essential principles of their venerable old party.[30]

HOOVERCRATS AND THE KKK

So divisive was the Smith candidacy that many lifelong Democrats swore to vote for Herbert Hoover and without declaring themselves Republicans. On 13 August 1928, a group met at Birmingham's Tutwiler Hotel to organize the Alabama Anti-Smith Democrats. Klansmen Horace Wilkinson and Hugh A. Locke assumed leadership of the bolters (figure 20). Wilkinson led adoption of a resolution branding Al Smith a "political traitor" and wasted little time in beating the drum of racial discord. "I recently returned from a trip up North," Wilkinson reported, and "I am sick and tired of having these liquor-loving papers down here frighten the people with the negro question. Up North all negroes are for this alleged nominee of the Democratic party. . . . Alabama newspapers . . . [should not] . . . lead these people to vote for a man who stands for social equality." Other Klan-backed speakers hurled insults at Victor Hanson's *Birmingham News, Birmingham Age-Herald,* and *Montgomery Advertiser,* all staunch supporters of Smith. Attendees denied admittance to one reporter because he refused to sign a placard declaring opposition to Smith. They roughed up another reporter and threatened to turn him over to the Klan for punishment.[31]

Women were conspicuous at the Klan-influenced rally. WCTU leaders were quite visible. One woman traveled throughout the hall handing out copies of the *Rail Splitter,* a vulgar anti-Semitic and anti-Catholic tabloid from Illinois, which she called "our little paper."[32]

Jefferson County judge and Methodist deacon Hugh Locke attacked Alabama's patrician press as the "bloodhounds of the liquorcrats" and warned

20. Political Cartoon Depicting the 1928 Bolt. Courtesy Birmingham Public Library, Tutwiler Collection of Southern History. Originally published in the *Birmingham News.*

that Smith's election would mean the dictatorship of Victor Hanson in Alabama. He also cautioned listeners about the lies of the Bourbon press and blasted the papers for prostituting the freedom of the press "bought with the blood of our forefathers."[33]

Other speakers contributed to the Klannish, anti-Catholic, and antiblack tone of the bolt. Members of the powerful Anti-Saloon League showed up; their secretary cruised the hall soliciting donations. Montgomery evangelist

Bob Jones called Birmingham the most typical Anglo-Saxon city in America and pointed out that large northern cities were made up mostly of unwashed "foreigners." "If Catholic Al Smith is elected," the preacher warned, "the gates to immigration will be thrown open. I had rather see a saloon on every corner . . . than to see the foreigners elect their candidate." The minister closed by asserting that "God Almighty" had called Southerners to be His chosen people and to save the country from the wickedness of its big cities. The Reverend A. J. Barton, a member of the Southern Baptist Convention's social service committee, preached against the pollution of American civilization by decadent European values. "They say we are intolerant," Barton remarked, but "I have never been so happy in all my life as I am in supporting Herbert Hoover. He is not a negro lover." Horace Wilkinson read his committee's resolutions against the wet forces and their affinity for racial equality. "No man believing as Smith does regarding . . . liquor . . . and the negro need expect the vote of Alabama," he concluded. "Alabama Democrats who believe in white supremacy will deliver the vote for Hoover." [34]

Although immigrant bashing was prevalent in 1928 Alabama, and in much of the rest of the country, it applied only to the new immigrants from southern and eastern Europe. Like many of their ancestors in Britain and Germany, America's Anglo-Saxon Protestant stock harbored deep prejudices and hostility toward Catholics.

Wilkinson, Locke, and Tom Heflin—Klansmen all—comprised the ruling triumvirate of the Alabama bolters. Another prominent Klan figure, though, proved to be quietly uncooperative with either side. Heflin courted Hugo Black throughout 1928 but to no avail. While Black did not openly bolt, he and Bibb Graves refused to campaign for Al Smith in Alabama. Repulsed by Smith's candidacy, both the senator and the governor understood traditional Democracy's power and their debt to the KKK too well to offend either cause. [35]

Of all the speakers who took the stump in 1928, no one was more visible, colorful, or outrageous than Tom Heflin. Dubbed "Cotton Tom" for his early and frequent support of the southern crop, Heflin hailed from the tiny town of Louina in east Alabama's Randolph County. He was one of seven brothers; two were doctors, two judges, and two Methodist ministers. He had gotten his start in politics as mayor of Lafayette and later served as a state legislator and U.S. congressman. In 1920 he won office as a U.S. senator upon the death of John H. Bankhead, Sr. Heflin had a special knack for mimicry, storytelling, and the absurd. He dressed in what has been described as "sartorial splendor": a black or cream-colored Prince Albert coat, a double-breasted vest, a broad-brimmed white hat, a high formal collar with a sash tie, and a corset. He owed much of his political success to the KKK but repeatedly denied membership until 1937, when his knighthood became public knowledge. Heflin specialized in religious and racist prejudice and was Alabama's best-known demagogue. The Klan, in turn, sheltered his membership, campaigned for him, and praised his "magnificent and courageous fight[s]" against the evil forces of Rome.[36]

Two major incidents, both of which took place on the hallowed floor of the U.S. Senate, brought Heflin into extreme disrepute early in 1928. The first involved an angry exchange with Democratic senator Joseph Robinson of Arkansas. Robinson, the Senate's minority leader and the party's 1928 nominee for vice president, rebuked Heflin publicly for a particularly nasty speech against Catholics. An embarrassed Heflin shot back that he would like to see Robinson return to Arkansas and preach tolerance for Catholicism. Himself now fairly lathered up, Robinson retorted that he would repeat the speech not only in Arkansas but in Alabama as well. It was then that Heflin uttered his infamous threat, "If you do, they will tar and feather you." Adding insult to injury, Heflin called on Robinson to resign as minority leader.[37]

The remark, unwise even by Heflin standards, threw the Senate into an uproar. A furious Robinson said, "That is illustrative, my friends, of how a good man can go wrong, and how far he can go wrong, and what a fool he can make of himself after he has gone wrong." The following day, Robinson offered his resignation, but the Democratic caucus voted 33 to 1 to keep him on as leader.[38]

In Alabama, the Klan's opponents leaped at the opportunity to criticize the sheeted order's favorite son. Mayor William Gunter invited Senator Robinson to speak in Montgomery, Mobile's city council censured Heflin, and Grover Hall branded the affair "an outrageous and humiliating incident." The most memorable comment, though, came from the pen of Julian Hall, the anti-Klan editor of the *Dothan Eagle* and a nephew of Grover: "And there you are—the senior Senator from our Great State talking like a half-civilized moron to a fellow Senator on the floor of our greatest lawmaking body! Oh, memories of Morgan! Oh, shades of Pettus! Oh, features of Underwood! Oh, Heflin! Oh, Hell!"[39]

Four months later, Heflin virtually duplicated the Robinson fiasco by attacking Maryland senator W. C. Bruce. Weary of Heflin's attacks on Baltimore and Washington newspapers, which he called the tools of Rome, Bruce denounced the Alabama senator's "squalid and inflammatory bigotry . . . , loose and lavish inaccuracy . . . , natural instinct for scurrility . . . , deranged intellect," and obvious affection for the KKK. Heflin responded by accusing the Maryland senator of taking lessons from the "Roman Catholic machine" and worshiping at the political altar of the Pope. Such histrionics understandably earned Heflin the derision of many national journalists. H. L. Mencken regarded the Klan senator as "one of my delights. He makes the *Congressional Record* [a] beautiful thing."[40]

Anti-Catholicism, initially the dominant issue of the campaign in Alabama, was the dominant issue nationally as well. Al Smith was the son of Catholic immigrants and the political product of Irish-Catholic Tammany Hall. It is impossible to separate anti-Catholicism completely from nativism or the liquor issue, but the Hoovercrats in Alabama and elsewhere made much headway by speaking of dark Popish plots, papal domination, Catholic immorality behind convent walls, stockpiles of arms, Roman corruption, and American subordination to a foreign potentate and his hellish designs. American politics had a long tradition of opposition to Catholicism, but never before had the issue gained such widespread currency.[41]

From the outset, Alabama Klansmen urged voters to oppose Smith because he was a Catholic. Klan speakers warned voters to "ignore the nice sugar-coated pill of religious tolerance" in order to avoid the "iron-rule of Rome." The Hoovercrats missed no opportunity to amplify the nativism quotient of their appeal by consistently speaking of "Roman" Catholicism, not merely Catholicism. Asked why Alabama's KKK was fighting so hard for Republican Herbert Hoover, one Knight responded, "Because Mr. Hoover is a *Christian* American." The response spoke volumes.[42]

Some in Alabama considered Catholics not only un-Christian but un-American as well. Klansmen and other members of the anti-Smith faction worried that a vote for Smith would be a vote to subsume state to church and to destroy democracy in favor of papal authoritarianism and would violate the most revered American principles.[43]

Foremost among the anti-Catholic speakers was a man who had made a career out of fighting the "Roman Catholic menace" wherever it existed. Tom Heflin had gained notoriety years earlier by charging, without any basis in fact, that the Catholic Knights of Columbus were attempting to drag the United States into war with Mexico in order to further the interests of the Vatican. While Heflin's senatorial colleagues laughed, and editors smiled at the absurdity of the charge, many average Americans took the allegation seriously. Stung by criticism, Heflin (figure 21) responded, "If intolerance means that I am going to continue to give the truth to the American people . . . , then I am intolerant."[44]

In 1928, Heflin's anti-Catholic attacks became obscene. He spared no method, adjective, invective, innuendo, or slur in a campaign that verged on mania. So ferocious were his attacks, so vulgar the accusations, so grossly was reality distorted, that the lines between fact and fiction probably be-

21. Senator J. Thomas Heflin, ca. 1928. Courtesy Birmingham Public
Library Archives, Portraits.

came blurred even in Heflin's own mind. "God deliver this nation from the
rule of Al Smith and all [the] . . . Pillage, plunder, and graft [of the] Roman
Catholic political machine," Heflin prayed. "Gird your loins for political
battle the likes of which you have not seen." Such a declaration was the
customary introduction to a battery of Heflin charges against Smith and
Catholics in general: they were agents of the Pope of Rome; the pro-Smith
press was "Romanized"; the Jesuits planned to seize all the major cities in
America, poison Heflin, plunge the United States into foreign wars, and use
brainwashing and genocide to convert all Protestants.[45]

Still, Heflin did not reserve all of his bluster and bigotry for Klan gatherings. On the floor of the U.S. Senate he said, "I drove from cover the most
insidious . . . dangerous and deadly political machine . . . in any country on
earth—the Roman Catholic political machine. . . . I have taken my stand
for my country against the invisible government of the Pope of Rome, and

I am going to uncover it in the United States in spite of what the Jesuits may do with dagger or poison. . . . I bare my chest to all. . . . I defy these evil, un-American forces of Rome. I do not fear them. I have not got time to consider what may happen to me. I am ready to accept whatever comes. The people of my State are too high-minded . . . , [too] grounded in the principles of Martin Luther . . . to bow their knee to this veiled, insidious monster . . . who has his habitat in Tammany Hall."[46]

Some around the country praised Heflin. The *Fellowship Forum,* a national Masonic organ based in Washington, D.C., lauded Heflin and the KKK for its yeoman service against the Roman church. "It has been a long time if . . . ever," the *Forum's* editor wrote, "when an American senator had the nerve to stand up in the Senate Chamber and tell the truth about the papal conspiracy." A Texas Klansman urged "Brother Heflin" to keep up the fight. "Don't stop," he pleaded, "until those mule-colored emissaries of the 'Dago on the Tiber' take to the woods." A Maryland Klansman who was convinced that Heflin was Christ-like, remarked: "When Satan's darts are at you hurled, look ever to Jesus for renewed strength, and [know that] the Ku Klux Klan are ever ready to stand with you."[47]

While Heflin led the charge, other members of the anti-Smith faction followed closely behind. The fact that Catholics made up only 3 percent of Alabama's population and were outnumbered by half a million Baptists alone made little difference. The only limit to the charges against the Catholics, it seemed, was the human imagination. "Having stopped the progress, withered the civilization, and destroyed the intelligence and culture of every people she has controlled," a KKK leaflet argued, "Rome now aims her brutal, arrogant and unholy propaganda at the sacred circle of the American . . . Protestant home." More typical charges referred to papal domination of the American government, the erosion of core American values, the use of American soldiers in Vatican wars, Roman control of the federal judiciary, repudiation of the U.S. Constitution, a new tidal wave of Catholic immigration, and official acknowledgment of papal infallibility. One of the wilder stories claimed that Al Smith's election meant the conquest of America by Catholics and its colonization as "another Ireland." Another rumor detailed the systematic genocide of all non-Catholics by the Knights of Columbus, the Vatican's shock troops, who were, according to the Alabama KKK, sworn to kill all Protestants "by drugs and deadly poisons."[48]

Alabama's Bourbon oligarchy defended itself and the Democratic standard-bearer against the Klan's anti-Catholic bigotry. According to Grover Hall, the same spirit of intolerance that would deny Al Smith the presidency could perform any other crime in the name of religion that fanatics had committed in the past. "Today the bodies of dissenters are safe from the flames but we burn the souls of men instead," Hall wrote. "We must accept Smith, his Catholicism included, or stop lying to our children about religious liberty in the Land of Opportunity for all." Montgomery judge Leon McCord reserved particular odium for reactionary evangelist Bob Jones. McCord compared the preacher to Judas Iscariot and accused him of selling out his party, perverting his religious mission, fomenting intolerance, and prostituting his frock for Klan silver. The jurist praised Woodrow Wilson's personal secretary as a trustworthy Catholic who had known and protected the secrets of American government during World War I. "No one asked the religion of the boys overseas when America needed her sons" in the Great War, McCord reminded voters.[49]

Although loyal Democrats fought against being tarred by the anti-Catholic brush, some of the venom invariably dripped onto them. Tom Heflin heard jeers and ridicule in the U.S. Senate, but Klansmen and women in twenty-five other states rallied to hear his words.[50]

NATIVISM AND LIQUOR

Because most American Catholics were of Irish, Italian, or eastern European descent, the immigration issue was indelibly imprinted on the Catholic issue. Along with concern about papal domination came the worry that people only one generation removed from the old country would not harbor the same loyalties to American government, values, or society as the northern and western European stock that had emigrated to the United States in earlier years. The anxieties reflected the powerful insecurities of an earlier generation of immigrants whose memories of their own odyssey to America were remarkably short-lived. Several sensational events—not the least of which were the Red Scare of 1919–1920 and the trial of Sacco and Vanzetti—cemented the idea in the popular imagination that all aliens favored anarchy. Given any rein at all, they were likely to attempt a violent overthrow of the republic. In this respect, the second Klan was typical of the preparedness and patriotic societies spawned by World War I and quite different from the Reconstruction order.[51]

Antialien propaganda made up a large part of the 1928 campaign in Alabama. Klan circulars routinely referred to "wops . . . , dagoes . . . , [and the] beggerly [and] illiterate" character of Catholic countries. "The only way that the [Roman Catholic] Hierarchy can be maintained," one Alabama Klan leader announced, "is by continually pouring on the fuel of ignorance. That can only be done by opening the flood gates of immigration and allow[ing] the illiterate and criminal immigrant of Southern Europe who . . . knows nothing but Rome." At one Hoovercrat rally, Horace Wilkinson, a Klansman and the leader of an American Legion post, took the stump to denounce Al Smith, Catholics, Tammany Hall, Alabama's patrician press, and Democratic delegates at Houston with "foreign-sounding names." He captivated listeners by skillfully tying dread of the alien to Rome, Catholicism, and Al Smith.[52]

Yet Alabama's Democratic loyalists invoked the same xenophobia that was being used by the Klan. The *Birmingham News* intimated that Klan-led anti-Smith politicians were actually bankrolled by "forces alien to this state's life." F. D. McArthur, a spokesman for the regular Democrats, refuted Wilkinson's nativist fire by using antialien fire of his own. McArthur ridiculed Wilkinson's "southern" lineage by pointing out that, while six of his own uncles had died for the Confederacy, Wilkinson's Michigan grandfather had fought for the Union. Further mocking the Klan leader's attacks, McArthur said that if the gates of immigration had been shut "just a little earlier, Horace would not have been with us," as his other grandfather was a Swedish immigrant. "In solving Southern problems," McArthur observed, "it seems to me that a person who undertakes this should have a Southern viewpoint." Both the *Birmingham News* and the *Age-Herald* heartily endorsed McArthur's nativistic speech.[53]

Reaction to the "new immigration" was not the only issue that amplified the importance of Al Smith's Catholicism. The battle over prohibition also played a part and became virtually inseparable from the religious issue. Smith followed predominant Catholic culture on the question. Catholics, traditionally far less concerned with issues of personal morality than evangelical Protestants, generally regarded alcohol consumption as a harmless vice if it was a vice at all. While most responsible Catholics considered drunkenness, spousal abuse, and excess as deplorable as evangelicals did, Catholics did not attach the same stigma to social drinking. This essential difference was largely the product of divergent views about theology and religious service. While evangelicals emphasized faith, personal morality, and the narrow attendant monitoring of their neighbors' behavior, Catholics concentrated on broader issues of social justice, social service, and ensuring one's salvation by performing "good acts." For many Protestants, though, the alcohol issue was laced with profound social implications, impinging, as it sometimes did, on spousal and child abuse and the welfare of the family as a social unit.[54]

Most prominent Alabama evangelicals lined up with the KKK, the Anti-Saloon League, and women temperance activists on the liquor question. Methodists argued that the 1928 election was not about Tom Heflin, the Klan, Catholicism, or any other issue apart from alcohol. Still, the Methodist

Alabama Christian Advocate enthusiastically defended Heflin and embraced the Klan. Prominent Methodist minister Bob Shuler warned that, if Smith were elected, the Democratic Party would become the "party of Rome and rum for the next hundred years." Other preachers urged their flocks to "vote as you pray" or "vote as Jesus our Captain would have us vote." The Baptists sponsored speeches by the superintendent of the state Anti-Saloon League and railed against "boss-ridden city masses—largely foreign and thirsty." One Birmingham WCTU member, the wife of a Baptist preacher, believed that all women who planned to vote for Smith were "emissaries of the Devil." "It is useless," she sobbed, "to pray that the wicked will change their votes." Meanwhile, the Alabama KKK charged that patrician leaders were drunks, imported famed New York reverend John Roach Straton to speak against Smith and liquor, and distributed jingles about "the nigger . . . , the Jap . . . , [John J.] Raskob . . . , [and] the cork."[55]

The Alabama Klan seemed to be utterly consumed with the liquor issue, nativism, and religious intolerance. Witness the following KKK poem:

Alcohol Al for President,
    I stand for whiskey and bad government.
My platform is wet and I am too,
    And I get my votes from Catholic and Jew.
The ignorant wop and the gangster too,
    Are the trash I expect to carry me through.
And when I land in the White House chair,
    They can all be damned, for all I care.
I'll rule the people and Pope will rule me,
    And the people's rights you will never see.
And the Protestant heretics who vote for me,
    I'll reduce to abject slavery.
I'll take down the flag from the public schools,
    And put up the cross for the ignorant fools.
The Bible in the schools shall not be read,
    But instead we'll say masses for the dead.
And the flag you love shall be put down,
    And put up instead the Papal crown.
Then the Pope of Rome shall rule the homes,
    And bring back the glory that once was Rome's.
And every knee shall bow to me,
    Because I shall rule your destiny.
And every one that dares to rebel,
    I'll send his soul to eternal hell.
And this is the plank on which I stand,
    And hope to rule this glorious land.

So all for AL and AL for all,
    And booze for all and that is all.[56]

Despite the vulgarity of such tactics, it is clear that the Klan and many supporters felt they held the moral high ground in 1928. Alabama Knights claimed they used the cross "to constantly remind us that Christ is our criterion of character and His teaching our rule of life." They added fire to signify that "Christ is the light of the world" and to illuminate the Klan path as one that "dispel[s] ignorance, superstition and intolerance and enable[s] one to walk mentally and spiritually without falling into the pitfalls of sin." Despite the inherent contradictions in the KKK position, there is little doubt that these men and women genuinely believed in the moral correctness of their cause.[57]

Nationally, Al Smith's forces adopted a wet position on the liquor issue buttressed by persons such as Clarence Darrow, the famed criminal defense attorney and champion of human rights. "The story of Prohibition in America should be a warning to all intelligent people of the dangers of intolerance and bigotry," Darrow wrote. "In a mad desire to enforce an obnoxious statute . . . a psychology of hate and bitterness has been cultivated which makes any act of cruelty possible." Senator W. C. Bruce of Maryland, Tom Heflin's adversary, attacked prohibition and the Klan as the "twin cherries" that flourish wherever sectarian illiberalism prevails, "blighting, demoralizing, and corrupting."[58] Still, Alabama's Smith supporters were far drier than their national allies. Rather than openly espouse repeal, Alabama loyalists attacked Herbert Hoover for being a crypto-wet.[59]

Alabama's KKK did more than just rail against demon rum. As part of their strategy for the election, Horace Wilkinson and Hugh Locke negotiated a pact with state Republicans to list twelve leading Democrats as Hoover electors. The move, endorsed by state Republican boss O. D. Street, was apparently designed to soothe the troubled consciences of Alabama Democrats who could now vote for twelve anti-Smith Democrats instead of actual Republicans. The GOP agreed not to run any candidates in order to free the bolters to vote Democratic locally and still be able to vote Hoover for president. Women, prohibitionists, and moral conservatives made up the Klan slate, including George H. Malone, the Dothan banker; Mary T. Jeffries, president of the Alabama WCTU; and Zue Musgrove Long, the sister of L. B. Musgrove, the Klansman, millionaire, and prohibition leader.[60]

O. D. Street, a Republican and Masonic leader, was especially active in 1928. Although he opposed Alabama's entrenched conservative Democracy, his own perspective was a long way from enlightened tolerance. Street's anti-Catholic bigotry was so raw, in fact, that it earned him the official censure of the Republican party's national chairman. At least one Birmingham newspaper refused to accept his paid political advertisements against Al Smith, branding them "reprehensible . . . inaccurate propaganda." Undaunted, Street printed and distributed (most likely with Horace Wilkinson's help) 200,000 copies of a circular entitled "Governor Smith's Membership in the Roman Catholic Church and its Proper Place as an Issue in this Campaign." The Republican boss echoed Klan arguments by claiming that Catholics stood for state subordination to Rome and opposition to religious liberty, free thought, and virtually every other fundamental tenet of American republicanism. Most objectionable, though, was a shocking imprint that accompanied Street's circular. The picture depicted a scene from the Spanish Inquisition in which priests were cutting off a Protestant woman's breasts. The caption read: "She nursed a heretic child."[61]

While Street conspired with KKK strategists to fan the flames of intolerance, local klaverns took more concrete action. At a summer 1928 rally in Wahouma's Nathan B. Forrest den, hooded speakers deplored the "steamroller tactics" used to nominate Al Smith, and they lynched the New Yorker in effigy. One Klan leader held a Smith mannequin before the crowd of 200 men, women, and children and asked what they wanted to do with it. "Lynch him! Lynch him!" the mob chorused. The Klansman then cut the dummy's throat with a long knife, and mercurochrome spurted forth, simulating blood. As the macabre display went on, klavaliers tied a noose to the doll and dragged it around the hall for spectators to kick and shoot. When the crowd had been worked into a frenzy, another Kluxer took the podium to swear that lynching was too good a fate for Smith. In November, the hooded speaker promised, Smith would be lynched with "good Christian votes." The exhibition revealed how ingrained violence and intolerance had become in the social milieu of the Alabama Klan and illuminated the Klan's idea of "family values."[62]

Other Klan members were actively involved in the campaign. Walker County Knights launched a wave of intimidation. Three shotgun-wielding men traveled in disguise around the traditional Republican and Klan stronghold, warning Smith supporters to stop campaigning or "there [would be] blood." They threatened a Democratic candidate for alderman as well as the local sheriff and the county solicitor. Birmingham's Robert E. Lee Klavern, which comprised a number of civic leaders, adopted the more genteel course of urging Democrats to bolt the party without fear of political retribution by the SDEC.[63]

Dixie, though, hardly held a monopoly on the venom of bigotry. Tom Heflin spoke to KKK groups in over half of the states. He earned more than $10,000 from these speeches, "imbecile yawpings" before what a Pittsburgh

22. Horace C. Wilkinson, 1930s. Courtesy Horace W. Weissinger.

editor called the "denizens of Moronia" throughout the country. The sum exceeded his senatorial salary. In Syracuse, New York, Heflin told 10,000 listeners that he was fighting to prevent the American presidency from becoming the "tail to a Roman Catholic kite." At an Albany klavern, he denounced Al Smith as a Roman Catholic, a Tammanyite, and a "soaking wet." A Pennsylvania senator concurred by speaking against immigration: "Somebody owns this country. Either we own it or they do; and we got here first."[64]

One of the more intriguing aspects of the 1928 battle was Horace Wilkinson's pioneering use of hate-sheet campaigning in Alabama. While Wilkinson used hate sheets extensively for the KKK in 1928, the leaflet served his own varied political purposes in later years. U.S. congressman Lister Hill fell victim to the method in 1928. Miffed by Hill's endorsement of Al Smith, Wilkinson issued a circular charging that Hill was a closet "Romanist" who appointed Catholics to West Point. Wilkinson (figure 22), a Baptist deacon and a Klan notable, leaked another rumor that Victor

Hanson had enticed Mississippi's Theodore Bilbo to Birmingham to tell stories about Herbert Hoover that depicted him as a "negro-lover." While it is true that the Birmingham publisher contacted the Mississippi governor about a pro-Smith speech, Wilkinson doctored Hanson's telegram to mention a $1,000 fee and a specific request to race-bait Hoover. A furious Hanson published both the original and bogus telegrams in the *Birmingham News* and unsuccessfully demanded an apology from the KKK's political leadership—Wilkinson, Heflin, and Hugh Locke. Bourbon investigators eventually traced the doctored telegram back to the offices of Horace C. Wilkinson.[65]

THE OLIGARCHY'S RESPONSE

Traditional Alabama Democrats did not sit still while the Hoovercrats took the political battle to them. The KKK/Hoovercrat forces had a distressing penchant for reducing the political debate to personality, creed, nationality, and downright mudslinging. Yet the oligarchy hardly worked to keep Alabama politics on an elevated plane. In fact, the 1928 campaign in Alabama degenerated to the very basest level of modern political discourse. Neither side was noticeably more guilty than the other.

Planters and industrialists matched their adversaries in intensity, viciousness, and the willingness to pander to the lowest common denominator. The oligarchy was somewhat hamstrung because it pleaded the case of a man it found every bit as repugnant as the Hoovercrats. Although the Big Mule/Black Belt coalition detested Al Smith in principle, he was the guardian of all that they cherished in 1928—party regularity and the racial status quo.

The campaign was so fierce in Alabama that almost every traditional Democratic heavyweight weighed in against the Klan. Congressmen William Bankhead, George Huddleston, Henry Steagall, E. B. Almon, Lister Hill, and John McDuffie took the stump for Smith. William B. "Buck" Oliver not only spoke for the planter/industrialist clique but also took charge of Al Smith's Alabama campaign. Other patrician heavyweights also enthusiastically participated: John Bankhead II of Jasper, Judge Leon McCord, Mayor W. A. Gunter, and former congressman Henry De Lamar Clayton II, also of Montgomery, Wilcox judge Benjamin Miller, Edmund W. Petus II of Selma, former governors William "Plain Bill" Brandon and Thomas Samford, and out-of-state personages such as Josephus Daniels, the former cabinet member and famed North Carolina journalist. A host of lesser Bourbon lights also actively campaigned for Smith: state representatives Tyler Goodwyn of Montgomery, Travis Williams of Russellville, future Dixiecrat Samuel Hobbs of Selma, Chief Justice J. C. Anderson, Anniston's W. L. Harrison, former Klan attorney general Charlie McCall, and A. H. Carmichael, an unsuccessful 1926 gubernatorial candidate who provided some of the most scintillating speeches on behalf of Al Smith and traditional Alabama Democracy.[66]

A number of prominent women also got involved on the patrician side. Marie Bankhead Owen opposed Hoover because he was a Quaker, demonstrating that religious discrimination was not the sole province of the bolters. Mabel Jones West, a figure well known in Birmingham politics, endorsed Smith, as did Dothan's Maude Kelly and the wife of former governor Charles Henderson. Traditional Democrats also relied on the press support to which they had become accustomed from Victor Hanson and Frederick Thompson.[67]

On the same night that Klan politicos organized the Anti-Smith Democrats at the Tutwiler Hotel, 2,500 supporters of Smith rallied at Fair Park. Patrician speakers included virulent opponents of the Klan such as Oscar Underwood and Major Harwell G. Davis. Smith's Alabama adherents blamed the KKK political machine for Underwood's failure to become president in 1924 and for Davis's inability to win election as governor and U.S. congressman.[68]

The *Birmingham News* implied that the Klannish Hoovercrats were actually Republicans in Democratic clothing. Comparing the disloyalty of the bolters to that of Reconstruction scalawags, the journal identified parallel threats to party solidarity. In an apparent swipe at Wilkinson, Locke, and Heflin, one editor argued that a "few designing politicians [not] unwilling to sell their birthright for a mess of pottage have striven to amalgamate [the] forces of discontent . . . only for personal profit." Although editorials portrayed the triumvirate as pawns on the chessboard of master GOP strategists, the Klansmen clearly led the bolt for their own reasons. The newspaper also noted that the Reverend Bob Jones "unmasked himself and his associates" as Klan sympathizers when he revealed that he objected to Smith's candidacy primarily because of the New Yorker's Catholicism.[69]

Hanson's *Birmingham Age-Herald* joined its cousin paper in attacking the Hoovercrats. Casting aspersions on the extent of Hoover's dryness, and accusing the KKK of "pulling down the pillars of democracy and knifing the party" in the back, the newspaper called the bolters "Catholic-baiters and hatred-mongers." "The old Klan spirit of proscription dominates the anti-Smith leaders," Charles Fell argued, "with former Klan officials and sympathizers sowing the seeds of intolerance, hatred [and] . . . religious bigotry." In closing, the editor ridiculed the bolt faction's "lust for witch-burning" and reproached the group's "Christian appetite for hatred."[70]

Patrician strategists trained many of their biggest guns on Tom Heflin, the Klan's darling. As Alabama's senior senator, Heflin was a major embarrassment to the state's traditional Democrats. While the Klan politicos Hugo Black and Bibb Graves did not win any points with the patricians by sitting out the 1928 civil war, their silence effectively distanced them from Heflin's risky gambit. The flamboyant Heflin was an extremely large man, a virulent racist, self-servingly inconsistent, and identified with prohibition, anti-Catholicism, Negrophobia, and, "at least in some circles, with political buffoonery." He had gained the colorful nickname "Tom-Tom" by banging on podiums and his breast with his hamlike fists to drive his points home. Heflin had once enforced his own understanding of segregation by gunning down a black man on a streetcar in Washington, D.C. Grover Hall described him as a man of "slender talents . . . , utterly commonplace. . . . We do not know whether Tom is out of his head, or whether he is a mere simpleton. He is one or the other." James Chappell theorized that Heflin was "burning with an inner and . . . unhealthy fire." A Montgomery editor characterized him as a "callous and wretched demagogue," and Montgomery mayor Bill Gunter called him the "Klan Krusader" as he refused to permit Heflin to use the city's auditorium. The incensed senator arrived in Montgomery anyway and Klan leaders had to ask Bibb Graves to call out a state police squadron to protect him. In September, the SDEC officially condemned the senator. He responded by taking the ultimate step, vowing publicly to "vote against Al Smith, so help me God!"[71]

Rough treatment was nothing new to Heflin. A Massachusetts audience pelted him with rocks and bottles in 1928. In Fort Payne, Alabama, a crowd used eggs and rotten oranges. City fathers blocked the demagogue from speaking in Portland, Maine, and Asheville, North Carolina. The *New York Sun* described most American opinion toward the Alabama senator as "one of undescribable loathing," while a fellow senator called Heflin's ravings about Catholics "the flimsiest bubble that ever found lodgement in an empty head." Another colleague responded to Heflin's warnings about a Catholic assassination plot with mock concern: "The army should assign troops to surround the Capitol. The navy should send a large part of the fleet into the Potomac. The Marines should be called [out] . . . to protect his precious life." Curiously, white Alabamians were hardest on the Klan lecturer. A former Alabamian residing in Oklahoma observed that "in the good old days . . . buffoons practiced their tricks in saloons and grog shops instead of the U.S. Senate. . . . But, alas for poor old Alabama, let us hope that [in] time . . . the braying of the ass will be heard no more on the banks of the Tallapoosa and the Tombigbee." A self-described white Alabama Methodist was even more direct. He effectively, if crudely, expressed his disgust with the Alabama Klan's biggest mouthpiece. "Say listen," he wrote Heflin. "A yellow dog will piss against a post but would take one smell at you and run along. You a Southerner, an Alabamian—God no, a thousand NOES. . . . Back to the shit from whence you sprung."[72]

RACE AND THE 1928 CAMPAIGN

Despite its intensity, the patrician response to Heflin did not define Alabama politics. The patricians' own appeal to racial prejudice ultimately dominated the 1928 contest. Loyalists had already shown themselves not averse to fighting intolerance with intolerance. Marie Bankhead Owen had attacked Herbert Hoover's candidacy on religious grounds. Other patricians had defended Smith's wetness by accusing Hoover of being just as wet and had resorted to nativist prejudice to tap into Alabama's abundant reserves of xenophobia.

Still, everything paled before the oligarchy's use of race to discredit Hoover. The Hoovercrats—led by the KKK's Wilkinson, Locke, and Heflin—were themselves of course the last persons to object to race-baiting. Consequently, while the rest of the country concentrated on rum, Romans, foreigners, and Tammany, by the fall of 1928 race had effectively subsumed all other competing issues in Alabama. An average Alabamian described the 1928 struggle as a "family affair . . . , a family fight." Both Smith's Alabama supporters and detractors allowed themselves to be consumed by the race issue. Unfortunately, Alabama's presidential campaign was eventually reduced to a vulgar contest in race-baiting.[73]

The Hoovercrats were, of course, adept at playing the race card. Klansmen, evangelicals, and prohibitionists pointed to the existence of Ferdinand Q. Morton as a priori evidence that, if elected, Al Smith would turn the national civil service over to blacks. It made little difference that a Republican governor had appointed Morton head of New York's civil service or that the African American's credentials were impeccable. He held a law degree from Harvard University and had served with distinction as an assistant district attorney in New York City. The Hoovercrats took out full-page advertisements in Alabama's county newspapers criticizing Smith for his racial liberalism. Klan speakers railed that Smith "not only loved negroes but bootlicked 'em and admitted it." L. L. Gwaltney, editor of the *Alabama Baptist,* adopted a pro-KKK attitude on the race issue. He called 10 million blacks in Dixie reason enough for his opposition to Smith. "To give [them] free access to liquor—to place this passion inflamer in the hands of a child race not far removed from their savage haunts in the jungles of Africa," Gwaltney wrote, "would be to court tragedy unspeakable." Methodist minister Bob Shuler, introduced by Hugh Locke to a crowd of 5,000, spoke at Birmingham's Municipal Auditorium. After making perfunctory denouncements of Catholicism, Tammany Hall, national Democratic chair John J. Raskob, and the "liquor-controlled press," Shuler shifted gears to his main topic—tarring Al Smith with the racial brush. He denied that Herbert Hoover was personally responsible for the racial integration of the Commerce Department and declared that Smith's only hope of election was to cater to "Harlem negroes." Meanwhile, Horace Wilkinson distributed thousands of hate sheets around the state with titles such as "Al Smith, the Negro Bootlicker" and "Al Smith, the Negro Lover."[74]

Race-baiting sprang naturally from the rump group's Klan roots. Their charter defended the bolt because the Democratic Party had nominated a candidate who failed to represent the most fundamental principles of the party—namely the maintenance of white supremacy. Al Smith, the Hoovercrat leaders claimed, was a "menace to the white . . . race," an advocate of social equality, and a threat to racial integrity. In November, Tom Heflin spoke to the largest Birmingham crowd ever assembled and spent the bulk of his time linking Smith with racial intermarriage, racial impurity, and general leniency toward the black race.[75]

Rank-and-file Kluxers and Alabama's Klan leadership did all they could to tarnish Smith's candidacy by raising the race issue. The state's Klan publications routinely referred to Smith's "love" for blacks, his appointment of over 800 blacks to public offices in New York state, his association with antisegregationist and former heavyweight boxing champion Jack Johnson, rumored plans to name an African American to his cabinet, and the fact that Tammany Hall drew support from Harlem, the "Negro heaven . . . [and] black belt of New York City." They printed and distributed racist leaflets about the New York governor under such headings as "Nigger, Nigger, Nigger," "Smith's Negro Babies," "Tammany and the Negro," and "More Nigger." A favorite Klan conspiracy theory held that Smith's election would initiate a Catholic overthrow of American government and white supremacy. Klan campaign workers in Alabama worked hard to link Catholicism, liquor, and Tammany with the black race. A Kluxer wrote Tom Heflin to applaud his crusade against Smith and complain that in his "Romanized [home]town," one could see "the Nuns lined up" to vote along "with the niggers, Dagoes, gamblers, macks, and pimps." Heflin responded by challenging Alabamians to "choose ye this day whom ye shall serve, the God of white supremacy or the false god of Roman social equality."[76]

In September, the Alabama KKK released its official position on Al Smith and the race question:

Although Al Smith's skin may be white, his heart is as black as that of any African that roams the jungles. . . . Smith was raised with the negroes. He lived with the negroes. He moves and associates with the negroes now. He eats with the negroes. Therefore, we cannot say that he is the equal of the negro, because the negro is better than he is. Any white man that makes the negro his equal is not as good as the negro. Yet—for what some hair-brained Democrats call "party loyalty" and "Southern tradition," they would ram an animal like this into the highest office. . . . Yes, Smith believes in negro equality. He thinks the negro is just as good as he is and is entitled to all the rights and privileges that he might be entitled to. A white man that feels that way towards the negro is no better than the negro. That's the reason we charge that, although Al Smith's skin may be white, he has the heart of a black man and we say that he is as black in his heart and soul as the blackest negro that roams the cotton fields of Alabama.[77]

The planter/industrialist press howled in response to this propaganda, the kind that could "inflame ignorant persons against [Smith and] . . . induce Klan dupes to give the big-wigs in the Klan money." Patricians' logic, though, allowed them to overlook their own racism while condemning the Klan for stooping to racial and religious prejudice. In fact, Alabama's entrenched Democrats had more years of experience appealing to race than their upstart rivals. While the loyalists' appeals were more subtle and sophisticated, in the end they were no less lethal and certainly no more tolerant.[78]

At a north Alabama rally, loyalist speakers responded to KKK demagoguery with their own brand of Negrophobia. In doing so, they betrayed the fact that the Hoovercrats were not alone in being racially intolerant. "We have a white man's government in Alabama, and we are going to keep it unless federal bayonets again tear our heritage from us," F. D. McArthur stated. An oligarch told horror stories about a giant black man who had headed a Hoover reception line in Washington. Someone else spoke of a Montgomery woman who had quit her job in Herbert Hoover's Commerce Department because she could not stand to work alongside blacks.[79]

The scene repeated itself across the state as loyalists took the stump to advocate white supremacy and antifederalism. Former governor Thomas Samford of Opelika remarked succinctly, "It is a white man's party and we are white men." Major Frank Dixon, a future governor and a Dixiecrat leader, cautioned that Hoover's election would reconstitute "Negro rule" of the sort seen during Reconstruction and would again bring "the black heels of the ex-slaves down on the throats of Southern men and women." In Montgomery, regular Democrats exhorted their fellow citizens to work for the preservation of Anglo-Saxon civilization. Tyler Goodwyn, the author of a failed anti-KKK bill, explained that his resistance to the hooded order in no way amounted to racial progressivism: "You ask what my party stands for, my answer it shall be / It stands for the rule of white men, white men like you and me." Goodwyn also worried about possible encroachment by the federal government. A Hoover victory, the lawmaker asserted, would "light a spark . . . [and] start a [federal] blaze more destructive than Sherman's." [80]

Other loyalist Democrats reasoned along racial lines (figure 23). Hugh Mallory, a confirmed Redeemer, appealed to religion to buttress his argument for party regularity and white supremacy. "God meant Alabama to be a white man's state," he explained to a Selma audience, "and the Democratic party has been His instrument in keeping it a white man's state." Congressman John McDuffie told a Dothan gathering that Herbert Hoover had achieved nomination with the aid of 122 black delegates while "not a black face disgraced the Democratic convention." Benjamin Miller, another future governor, agreed with McDuffie: "There was not a seat for a [single] nigger at Houston. . . . No nigger helped nominate Al Smith. He was nominated by more than 900 Anglo-Saxons." From his sickbed in Tuscaloosa, former governor Bill Brandon rose to appeal to white supremacy. Arguing that the Hoovercrats were really Republicans, Brandon warned of "negro domination . . . , the perils of Republican misrule . . . , the slimy trail of the carpetbagger," and a second Reconstruction. "I believe in white supremacy and the rule of [the] white man," Brandon declared in explaining his support for the New York governor. Victor Hanson's newspapers quoted anonymous Klansmen as being disgusted with the secret order for supporting a "negro lover" such as Herbert Hoover. [81]

Antifederal sentiment informed the patrician appeal for regularity much as it had the patricians' war against the Klan. Because of the South's chronic bouts with a "Reconstruction Syndrome," race could never be completely divorced from fear, hatred, and mistrust of the federal government. The same aversion to the central government that fueled 1928 appeals for party regularity also shaped the resistance that the oligarchy had thrown up against the Alabama Klan. An overwhelming concern with federal intrusion and home rule eclipsed other considerations. The 1928 campaign showed that Alabama remained fascinated by race and federal domination.

Again and again in 1928, patricians referred to the specter of federal interference in matters of race as reason enough to remain true to the Democratic Party. State chairman Buck Oliver made this appeal ad nauseam in a major Birmingham speech. Oliver reminded Alabamians that Tammany Hall had insulated the South from the 1890s "force bill," predicted that federal registrars would swoop down on the South if Herbert Hoover won,

23. Racial Control Through Convict Leasing. Alabama was one of the first states in the Union to adopt convict leasing before the Civil War and in 1928 became the last state to abolish the practice. Courtesy Birmingham Public Library Archives, Cat. No. 21.8.4.5.21.

and spoke ominously of a Republican antilynching bill. If Hoover were elected, Oliver assured his audience, the Republicans would use "federal bayonets to 'put the black heel on the white neck'" just as they had during Reconstruction.[82]

While Birmingham editors praised Oliver's statement as "compelling . . . , lucid . . . , [and] an epochal utterance," they failed to see any connection between the patrician appeal to racial prejudice and the Klan's use of race and religion. In fact, despite Oliver's repeated insistence on the need to safe-guard white supremacy and eschew federal intervention, these same jour-nalists gushed and rhapsodized over his speech. "It is a carefully thought out passage that scorns to wave the red flag of prejudice," the Hanson editors wrote. Instead it "pleads like angels trumpet-tongued against . . . the resort to witch-burning, and the hospitality to evil which the malcontents are urging with such vociferousness."[83]

Following Buck Oliver's lead, other planter/industrialist leaders echoed the call for party regularity to avoid federal intrusion into southern race relations. Congressman George Huddleston made the antifederal appeal in Birmingham. Victor Hanson's press echoed it, as did Congressman Henry Steagall and Tuscumbia's Archie Carmichael. Anti-Hoover circulars habitu-ally spoke of the perils of black Radical Republican misrule, Reconstruc-tion, and federal bayonets, thereby fusing conservative Democratic concerns with the issues of race and the federal government.[84]

The racial nature of the 1928 conflict was amplified by an eleventh hour appeal from Mabel Jones West, president of the Alabama Women's League for White Supremacy. Proving that the Klan, Hoovercrats, and men in general had not cornered the market on racial prejudice, Mrs. West spectacularly repudiated the KKK, endorsed Al Smith, and chastised the secret order for its promotion of religious proscription. Declaring that the Klan, to which she had once belonged, had allowed itself to be "prostituted," Mrs. West followed the lead of other loyalist Democrats by pandering to racial bigotry while criticizing the Hoovercrats for catering to religious bias. "When the time comes when we must choose between the Ku Klux Klan and . . . white supremacy," she said, "let the Ku Klux Klan go to the devil." De-scribing her former membership in the WKKK as "humiliating," she de-clared, "I am not afraid of the Ku Klux Klan. . . . And that includes Jim Esdale and Horace Wilkinson."[85]

Other female loyalists were equally outspoken on race. One Alabama woman, a federal employee, was so distraught over the desegregation of Herbert Hoover's Commerce Department that she appealed to South Caro-lina demagogue Cole Blease for assistance. Especially distasteful to the Ala-bama woman was the thought of having to use the same bathroom as blacks. "Think of a Secretary of Commerce having to stoop to niggers . . . [and] nigger politicians . . . to win," she complained. "I wonder how Mr. Hoover would like to have the women of his family use the same toilet that colored people use. . . . We call these colored people 'Hoover's chocolates' and all wish we could make him eat them."[86]

Perhaps most ironically, Bourbon leaders imported the notorious Theodore G. Bilbo to lecture the Hoovercrats on tolerance. Bilbo, known simply as "the Man" in his native Mississippi, was one of the South's most consummate racists and a demagogue without parallel. Arriving in Birmingham just days before the election, the Mississippi governor did not even wait for his actual speech to begin lecturing the Hoovercrats on the unseemliness of their appeals to religious bigotry. In the ultimate example of the pot calling the kettle black, Bilbo unabashedly denounced Alabama's KKK, the WCTU, the Anti-Saloon League, and evangelicals for their "ignorance and prejudice" against the Catholic church. "Why[,] the Pope can't even control Italy," Bilbo scoffed. "All this stuff about Catholicism is food for fools. . . . Tom Heflin . . . is more to be pitied than blamed." In his formal speech on 5 November, before a capacity crowd in Birmingham's municipal auditorium, the Mississippian blasted Herbert Hoover for being a "negro lover" and for doing everything he could to abolish racial segregation in Washington. Bilbo denounced Horace Wilkinson, Hugh Locke, and Tom Heflin by name as "willful, malicious, pusillanimous, dastardly, premeditated, pluperfect, damnable, perfected liars" and anticipated the Klan's opposition with the boast that he was "a charter member of the Ku Klux Klan—of Bilbo Klan No. 40." Yet the sheeted order, Bilbo stated, was now dead, and if Southerners wished to preserve white supremacy, they had to move beyond loyalty to the KKK. As a contingent of Confederate veterans dramatically ringed the stage, Bilbo got to the heart of the matter:

> Just as sure as Hoover is elected Tuesday you can get ready for trouble with the negro in the South. . . . The Republican party of the North is the negro party of the South. It is Street's party and Locke's party and Wilkinson's . . . Republican 'nigger' organization of Alabama. . . . If you . . . desert to the Negro Republican party you will live to regret it. And there will be blood spilled—the blood of your children, some of them yet unborn."[87]

On the eve of the election, loyalists predicted that Al Smith would carry Alabama by more than 50,000 votes. Shockingly, though, the election was almost too close to call, with Smith just edging Hoover in Alabama, 127,796 votes to 120,725. Over 83 percent of the state turned out to vote, but the Black Belt made the difference by giving the Democratic candidate a 10,200 majority. Some pointed to vote fraud in the Black Belt as the only reason that Al Smith carried the state at all.[88] Nationally, Hoover crushed Smith. In a result that illustrated the national complexion of religious prejudice, Smith fared worse than any other Democrat in American history. He captured only eight states to Hoover's forty and lost five on the periphery of the so-called Solid South: Virginia, Tennessee, North Carolina, Florida, and Texas. In the popular vote Hoover overwhelmed Smith by 6 million votes and even won New York. A jubilant Tom Heflin crowed, "I told you so." Hugh Locke and L. B. Musgrove actually voted for Hoover, but Heflin's nerve failed him at the last moment, and in a weak attempt to protect himself from the SDEC's wrath, he abstained.[89]

The 1928 bolt of fanatical Klan racists and prohibitionists like Wilkinson, Locke, and Musgrove was fundamentally related to the revolt of fanatical segregationists in 1948. Although the patricians were loyalists in 1928 and bolters in 1948, the two Democratic revolts were actually quite similar. They showed that national party solidarity was too weak a glue to hold Alabama ideologues inside the Democratic Party when vital interests were threatened. When push came to shove on race, as in 1928 and 1948, extreme segregationists such as Wilkinson, Locke, and the KKK bolted the party.

After the election, Alabama's KKK demonstrated that it still had some life left. Patrician leaders, who initially thought Judge O. A. Steele had lost his bid for reelection, blamed the Klan for "flogging him off the court" because he had presided fairly at the famous Calloway trials. A few days later, the loyalists learned that Steele had survived by the barest of margins. One triumphant Klan candidate showed that the KKK would still be a force to contend with in some localities by promising to give the secret order "first consideration" as long as he held office. Klan leader Horace Wilkinson withstood patrician attempts in court to have him ousted as state boxing chairman and Birmingham's assistant city attorney.[90]

As in 1926, east Alabama provided much of the revolt against Black Belt democracy.[91] The "North Alabama Revolt" concept faced some qualifications in 1928. Herbert Hoover did best in the northeastern counties but also had significant support in the east central portions of the state and some even in the southeastern Wiregrass. In contrast, he made a dismal showing in the western counties—north, central, and south. Walker County, traditionally a northwestern center of Republican strength, stayed within the regular Democratic fold in 1928, perhaps in reaction to the Klan-like intimidation of Smith supporters there. Limestone, Lauderdale, Colbert, Lawrence, Marion, and Lamar Counties—all of them in north Alabama—also rejected the KKK's 1928 candidate. More surprisingly, Jefferson County went Republican for the first time in its history, with voting patterns that paralleled those in the 1925 Klan-dominated city election. The patricians prevailed in the older downtown precincts, while Hoover, the Klan-backed candidate in Alabama, controlled Eastlake, Woodlawn, Wylam, Pratt City, Gate City, and Avondale—all centers of KKK strength.[92]

Despite the claims of both Alabama sides in 1928, neither advanced the cause of progressivism—that of Bibb Graves or any other type.[93] Indeed, Graves's cooler relations with Klan leaders underscored the growing distance between his economic liberalism and the indigenous reaction of many in the shrinking KKK and presaged the day when he would discard the order altogether. After 1928 it became increasingly clear that the Klan and its more intolerant backers had been a passing phase for politicians like Bibb Graves and Hugo Black.

10

Disloyalty, Revenge, and the End of an Era

The 1928 presidential election had active political fallout in Alabama. While Bourbon elites celebrated their success in delivering the state's electors to Al Smith, they grieved the larger Republican triumph and realized how narrowly their own state had escaped. Still, the bareness of their victory did not prevent the oligarchy from issuing yet another round of declarations that the KKK was dead. This time the pronouncement was far more accurate, especially in a political sense.[1]

For a while the Klan leaders of Alabama's Hoovercrats did some celebrating of their own. Their neck-and-neck race proved that the politics of prejudice was alive and well in the Deep South. Such a remarkably close vote in a Solid South state was a powerful testament to the ability of politicians to prey upon the deepest insecurities of their fellow Alabamians. By threatening to cost a party the loss of Alabama in a national election, the KKK's leading strategists, perhaps for the first time, began to realize the potential of waging a politics based almost exclusively on racial fear and hatred.

Although Tom Heflin, Hugh Locke, and Horace Wilkinson most likely felt cheerful about the future, for two of them the 1928 election actually marked the zenith of their political careers. While the trio clung to the politics of intolerance after 1928, they increasingly fought a rearguard action that even they eventually recognized as untenable. Hugo Black and Bibb Graves, though, were rewarded for the discretion they displayed in 1928. While Heflin and Locke's political stock plummeted, Graves and Black moved further from the Klan and consequently thrived. Wilkinson marched to his own drummer. After 1928 Wilkinson increasingly concentrated his efforts on dominating politics and patronage in Birmingham.[2]

By the time Heflin's political career ended, as it effectively did in 1932, Alabama's 1920s Klan was largely a thing of the past. The KKK continued to exist in Alabama into the 1930s, 1940s, and beyond, but it was reduced to something inherently different from the 1920s order. The Klan had never risen or fallen on the likes of Tom Heflin—quite the reverse—and as long as racial intolerance continued to beat in the breast of the Alabamian, the order could expect to exist on some level. By 1932, though, a distinctive epoch of hooded ascendance in Alabama had come to an end.

In 1928, the omnipresent issue of race in Alabama had reshaped national issues—liquor, Tammany, immigration, and Catholicism. During the Great Depression, problems endemic to that crisis were also transformed in Alabama. Economic issues were paramount in the tumultuous 1930s, and mounting class friction led the Communist Party to move its southern headquarters to the industrial city of Birmingham. The Red specter alone was not responsible for the Klan's more meager sustenance, though. As before, the regional obsession with race superimposed itself on the Communist phobia—altering, distorting, and fundamentally changing it. Ultimately, the product of this union allowed the KKK to survive in Alabama at a diminished, but still important, level. The Klan at this stage of its development has not received due attention.

REVENGE OF THE OLIGARCHY

Almost as soon as the ink had dried on the last 1928 ballot, Alabama's Big Mule/Black Belt alliance began to plot retaliation against the KKK. Bolting was serious business in a place like Alabama. The state's Democratic Party stood for white supremacy—first, last, and always. To flout that party, to step out of it and publicly challenge it, was to jeopardize and subvert the very foundations upon which civilized society rested. Reckless behavior, much of it motivated by simple political and financial ambition, had to be dealt with—swiftly, severely, and decisively—lest it set an example for others to follow. To many within the planter cabal, the only prudent option seemed clear: Tom Heflin and Hugh Locke had to be barred from running as Democrats in 1930. They had to atone for their Hoovercrat sacrilege by being expelled from Alabama's Democratic Party.[3]

Soon after the 1928 bolt, Locke (figure 24) filed formal notice of his intention to run for governor in 1930. Locke, a well-known Methodist judge whom one scholar has described as "a progressive gone rancid," decided to manage his own campaign. Heflin was also obliged to run for reelection. Throughout the state, voters speculated whether the state Democratic executive committee would bar the bolters from the 1930 primary.[4]

24. Hugh A. Locke, 1930. Courtesy Birmingham Public Library Archives, Portraits.

Edward C. Boswell, a Geneva County member of the SDEC, first suggested expelling the wayward Kluxers. The anti-Klan suggestion was noteworthy because the Genevan was later the sponsor of Alabama's infamous Boswell Amendment to the state constitution. The measure protected disenfranchisement by requiring voters to read, understand, and "explain" selected passages of the Constitution. In 1945, the amendment became synonymous with southern intransigence after the Supreme Court struck down the all-white primary in *Smith v. Allwright*.[5]

Klan politicos mobilized to fight expulsion in what would become their penultimate battle against the oligarchy. The patricians succeeded in preventing Heflin and Locke (dubbed "Heflox") from running as Democrats in 1930 and thereby threatened to drive another stake into the Klan's political heart. Realizing that the KKK was seriously imperiled, Bibb Graves and

Hugo Black broke the silence that they had maintained in 1928 and became actively involved in a movement to oppose expulsion. Graves traveled to Washington to confer with Senators Heflin and Black, while Gaston Scott, one of his chief lieutenants, helped organize resistance back home. Both Governor Graves and Hugh Locke had served as former chairs of the SDEC, the same body that was now considering expulsion. Horace Wilkinson directed the Klan's Heflox forces in Birmingham and, in 1929, Hugo Black released a formal statement contesting expulsion. In fact, Black was so alienated by the SDEC's contemplated action that he seriously considered bolting the party. Happily for his own career, he confined his efforts to verbal protests.[6] Jouett Shouse, chair of the national Democratic Party, spoke against expulsion in Alabama, but his involvement only aggravated the situation by allowing the planter/industrialist clique to complain of outside interference in state affairs.[7]

Initially, some patricians opposed expulsion on the grounds that Heflin, Locke, and their Klan ilk could be better dealt with in a fashion less disruptive to the party. Yet after the Klan-dominated state legislature refused to abolish the double-choice primary system in 1929, patricians almost unanimously favored putting up the bars.[8]

On 16 December 1929, just one year after the presidential election, the issue formally came before the SDEC. S. A. Lynne of Decatur, former speaker of the state house of representatives, submitted the motion for expulsion. John D. McQueen, a noted Tuscaloosa attorney and future chairman of the party, seconded the motion as Edmund W. Pettus II, chairman of the SDEC, echoed it. Ben Ray, a Horace Wilkinson/KKK protégé, spoke long and strenuously against expulsion, but when the votes were finally tallied, the SDEC had expelled Heflin and Locke from the party of their fathers by a margin of six votes.[9]

Victor Hanson's editors waxed poetic about the majesty of the move. It was "the only wise and brave course to take," Charles Fell of the *Birmingham Age-Herald* declared. By not putting up the bars the party might have avoided later strife, but it also would have "los[t] its soul for all time." Instead, expulsion demonstrated that Alabama's Democratic Party clung to "the path upon which its feet ha[d] always walked, the path of honesty, the path of loyalty, the path of the just which is as the shining daylight that shineth more and more unto the perfect day."[10]

True to their nature, the Klan-led bolters did not take the SDEC decision lying down. Tom Heflin blasted the twenty-seven committee members who voted to bar as "drunkards, reprobates, thieves, culprits, minions . . . of the Pope . . . , grafters . . . , and hirelings of the liquor interests." "We have fallen upon strange times," the Klan senator roared, "when money from the

Roman Pope and Tammany Hall can corrupt the sovereign state of Alabama." Locke, usually more restrained than his KKK partner, was barely less vocal in this case. After branding the expulsion a "blasphemous . . . un-American . . . absurdity," the hooded judge vowed that the vote meant subservience to Tammany, rampant immigration, and subscription to the "extreme liquor views of Al Smith . . . of the liquor interests, by the liquor interests, [and] for the liquor interests."[11]

Others rallied to the standard set by the Klan duo. In Washington, Hugo Black condemned the expulsion as "fundamentally un-American." Montgomery judge Charles E. McCall requested a formal advisory opinion from his son, the attorney general. The junior McCall, apparently still in the service of the patrician clique, endorsed the SDEC move.[12]

Alabama's Ku Klux Klan, feeling the political strain, showed signs of serious internal dissension. James Esdale lamely denied that the KKK was involved in politics in any way, while other Klan leaders urged their faithful to speak out against the "unfair, un-Democratic, un-American, subversive . . . smokescreen . . . of the State Autocracy Executive Committee." "And just to whisper you a secret," one KKK communication told the rank and file, "we intend to lick our enemies until they can't stand up." Perhaps most alarming to the SDEC was Horace Wilkinson's announcement that he planned to file suit on behalf of the scorned candidates. Crampton Harris, exalted cyclops of the Robert E. Lee Klavern and Hugo Black's law partner, agreed to assist Wilkinson.[13]

The battle shaped up to be a titanic confrontation between entrenched Alabama Bourbonism and the upstart Klan Democrats. Forney Johnston, son of a former governor and a close associate of Klan enemy Oscar Underwood, provided legal representation for the SDEC. Some Knights tried to distance Heflin from Locke in a desperate move designed to pacify the Bourbons. They argued that the Birmingham judge should be expelled, but not the senator, since Locke had actually voted for Republican Herbert Hoover, while Heflin had merely abstained. Klan attorneys, though, continued to fight on behalf of both candidates.[14]

The KKK based its suit on the premise that the SDEC, in barring Heflin and Locke, had treated voters in a categorically different manner from candidates. That is, in adopting a loyalty oath requiring candidates to swear that they had supported the national ticket in 1928, the committee had failed to require a similar pledge from its primary voters. Citing this difference as prima facie evidence of bias, Klan attorneys sought an injunction to prevent the Democratic Party from holding its August 1930 primary. Four months before the primary, Hugo Black wrote Horace Wilkinson to offer his support for the attorney's logic. Wilkinson welcomed the support in 1929 but later used the letter against Black in an election pitting the senator against Thomas Kilby, the Klan lawyer's oldest political patron. This development occurred only after Black had broken with the KKK and Wilkinson had moved on to other things.[15]

Tom Heflin was overjoyed to have Wilkinson's services. "I have read and re-read your last brief and argument," Heflin wrote. "I do not see how you could improve on it. It is as clear as a bell and as strong as horse radish." Senator Walter George of Georgia also expressed confidence in Wilkinson's legal logic, and legal pundit Ben Ray characterized it as "very shrewd . . . , thorough, logical, and weighty." Such expressions of confidence were soon justified when the Klan's attorney won the second round of the expulsion bout in appellate court. Crampton Harris, Wilkinson's chief aide and a fine lawyer in his own right, attributed the victory to the "shrewd and penetrating nature of Horace's strategy."[16]

Flushed by the initial victory, Heflin asked Wilkinson not only to win before the state supreme court but to pressure the justices into publishing an early decision. "Adroit and masterful diplomat that you are, can't you do something to bring the matter to a head this week?" the senator asked. "You know how anxious I feel about it."[17]

Alabama's highest tribunal, though, sidestepped Wilkinson's logic by interpreting the issue as a strictly political matter. Wilkinson applied for a rehearing but was denied.[18] "Mr. Horace Wilkinson now has his answer . . . [and] in conclusive form," an industrialist editorial rejoiced. "The bars against . . . Heflin [and] . . . Locke are up . . . , set by the Democratic State Committee and . . . kept up by the commonwealth's most august tribunal." An editorial in the *Birmingham News* gleefully advised the two Klan candidates to stop their "childish protests," accept the verdict graciously, and "learn how to lose."[19]

While it was clear that Alabama's KKK was on the ropes, the order's political leadership refused to throw in the towel. Consulting with Heflin, Wilkinson proposed that the KKK/Anti-Saloon League coalition take their case directly to the people. The Klan's chief political boss and legal strategist, Wilkinson suggested that Heflin and Locke run for senator and governor, respectively, as "independent Democrats." Alabama grand dragon James Esdale opposed another bolt as futile, but Wilkinson went over Esdale's head to Atlanta to receive the imperial blessing of Hiram Evans. Heflin and Locke prepared to run as "Jeffersonian Democrats," with Wilkinson as unofficial campaign manager for both.[20]

Like the 1926 and 1928 elections in Alabama, a breakdown of the 1929 expulsion vote supplies some evidence of the need to qualify the concept of a north Alabama revolt in some respects.[21] Historian Mills Thornton suggested, in an important and seminal 1968 article, that the Klan/Anti-Saloon League revolt of the late 1920s was in effect "a recrudescence of Populism." Several features of this argument are, perhaps, open to another interpretation. It is true that some Black Belt representatives on the SDEC voted to bar the Klan bolters, but two of Jefferson County's five committee members and both Mobile County delegates voted *against barring*. They did so although Birmingham and Mobile were the homes of the Big Mule and Little Mule political allies of the Black Belt aristocracy. Montgomery County, a hub of Black Belt power, also split its two votes, while a Marengo County SDEC member from the Black Belt actually voted against expulsion. As in the 1926 and 1928 elections, Heflin and Locke gained strong support in east Alabama: the northeastern counties of Jackson, DeKalb, Etowah, and Calhoun and Clay County in the east central part of the state. Some north Alabama committee members (from Morgan, Marshall, Cullman, and Cleburne and two from Lamar) actually voted against Klan wishes by favoring expulsion.[22]

There are other indications that the Klan revolt was not simply confined to north Alabama farmers. The KKK was strong in several urban areas— Birmingham, Montgomery, and Mobile—as well as in south Alabama counties such as Lee, Crenshaw, and Marengo. It is also difficult to accept the notion of the 1920s KKK as a simple "recrudescence of Populism." The 1920s Klan, unlike the 1890s Populists, was not dealing with overtly economic and agrarian issues such as supply, credit, commodity prices, freight rates, planter-merchant exploitation, country-store monopolies, corporate concentration, and so forth. Nor were the 1920s Knights anywhere near liberal, especially on matters of race and federal activism. The Populists were economically liberal, especially for their time period and region, and racially pragmatic. Populists allied with black voters and called for massive federal involvement in the economy to level the playing field, things the 1920s Klan never dreamed of. Furthermore, if a scholar hoped to transfer the later liberalism of Hugo Black and Bibb Graves to the 1920s KKK, it would easily be outweighed by the enduring conservatism of Horace Wilkinson, Hugh Locke, Tom Heflin, and others. Heflin, inexplicably described by one scholar as "a natural leader of the underprivileged, down-trodden, low-income masses," got his political baptism in 1896 as the candidate of entrenched and privileged Democracy—fittingly enough, *against* a Populist candidate.[23]

SWAN SONG FOR THE KKK: THE 1930 ELECTION

As the KKK/Heflox forces prepared for their 1930 run at the governor's mansion and a U.S. Senate seat, the Big Mule/Black Belt combination also began to sort out its ticket. The planters and industrialists selected Jasper's John H. Bankhead II—son of a former patrician senator and a loser in 1926 to Hugo Black—to retire Tom Heflin from the Senate. Bankhead "rejoiced" to learn that he had been chosen for the honor, while Heflin responded with his usual bravado. "For God's sake, let me in there with old John," he said, "Why[,] John hasn't got any more chance to go to the United States Senate than a mouse-colored mule has to operate an airplane. You can bet I'll feast on his bones in November."[24]

Bankhead handily won the senatorial primary over Frederick Thompson, a patrician publisher, but the gubernatorial primary was more contentious. Planter/industrialist bosses favored Wilcox County judge Benjamin Meek Miller. A die-hard fiscal conservative, Miller contrasted sharply with out-going progressive governor Bibb Graves. The *Montgomery Advertiser* dubbed him "Old Economy" for his vaunted parsimony and praised him for using oil lamps on his south Alabama farm rather than having electricity installed. Instead of running solely on an economy platform, though, Miller made opposition to the dying KKK his central campaign issue. "If you are satis-fied with the rule of the Ku Klux Klan," Miller announced, "don't vote for me. Vote for any of my opponents." A leader of the Montgomery Chamber of Commerce was jubilant: "When you vote for Miller, you don't have to spell Democracy with a 'K.'"[25]

The Klan issue had already been a major one for Charlie McCall who, at about this time, was beginning to feel the cold steel of a patrician knife in his back. McCall had risen to the rank of attorney general in 1926 with strong KKK backing only to turn on the sheeted society and launch an ag-gressive legal campaign against it. Observers differed in estimating McCall's motives for the sudden and dramatic transformation. Even if McCall had been moved primarily by notions of justice and equity, he almost certainly expected a political payoff somewhere down the line. Instead, Grover Hall notified McCall in print that the oligarchy had forsaken him for Miller. Hall even had the temerity to call McCall a "Klan darling" after he had repeatedly praised the attorney general's yeoman service against the Klan in 1927. When McCall realized to his horror that the patricians had betrayed him, he reacted with outrage by describing them as "buzzard's vomit from [the] . . . Ditch over . . . Montgomery."[26]

Alabama's KKK committed a serious mistake in 1930 by dividing its bloc vote among several candidates for the Democratic nomination. While it is safe to conclude that former Klansman Charlie McCall received negli-gible backing from the order, three other gubernatorial candidates shared hooded support: Watt T. Brown, Jeff Carnley, and W. C. Davis, Graves's lieu-tenant governor. The balkanization of Klan political power was an error about which Hiram Evans had warned the Alabamians in 1928. Still, the blunder was repeated.[27]

In addition to Bankhead and Miller, the patricians chose Anniston's Hugh D. Merrill as their candidate for lieutenant governor. The Klan-supported Jeffersonian ticket for the general election consisted of Heflin for senator, Locke for governor, and Dempsey Powell for lieutenant governor. For the first time since the 1890s, Alabama's Democratic primary promised not to be equivalent of actual election.[28]

Some northern black journalists, unfamiliar with the intricacies of Deep South politics, mistook appearances for reality. They denounced Alabama's Klan-backed rump party as the racists in the 1930 campaign yet failed to realize that the regular Democrats, despite their sophistication, were just as committed to the principle of white supremacy.[29]

After dissipating their bloc strength on several primary candidates, the Alabama Klan lined up behind Heflin and Locke for the general election. Along with the name "Jeffersonian Democrats," the Heflox ticket adopted the symbol of a liberty bell with the words "white supremacy" on it. Traditional Alabama Democracy had long used a rooster with "white supremacy" as its logo. The Jeffersonian tag was an attempt to invite comparison with old Populists even though Alabama's Jeffersonian People's party of the 1890s had waged self-conscious class warfare against "the interests," had sought federal involvement, and had attempted to forge a biracial voting coalition. Klan reliable Hugh Locke described his rump party as "Progressive Democrats," while Heflin rashly predicted a 150,000-vote margin of victory.[30]

The press greeted the Heflox ticket with derision despite a January 1930 rally in Birmingham's municipal auditorium that attracted over 5,000 people. Atticus Mullin of the *Montgomery Advertiser* attempted to throw a wet blanket over the rump party by airing rumors that Locke would be sacrificed to the SDEC in the hope that Heflin could run as the sole Democratic nominee for Senate. Mullin also published a second rumor: that James Esdale wanted to yank KKK support from under Heflin and Locke in favor of two new candidates. The *New York Times* speculated that Alabama's Republicans would fuse with Heflox, eliminating the two-party system and making the GOP "a mere appendage" of the Klan.[31]

The KKK promised to be a major issue for the last time in 1930. Patrician assessments notwithstanding, the Klan's political juggernaut had not yet been fully disarmed. Understanding this point, Benjamin Miller made opposition to the hooded order his marquee issue, denouncing one opponent for "sucking the biggest teat at the Klan-ridden capitol." When news leaked that William B. Bankhead might also be challenged for his congressional seat, the Bourbons immediately suspected the Klan. KKK publications, meanwhile, urged the rapidly dwindling faithful to support Heflin in his re-election attempt. Anyone who voted against Heflin, "the great Patriot of the Twentieth Century," a Klan editorial argued, would be "hated and despised forever by all true Americans." "This is no time," an Alabama Knight declared, "for foolish talk about [party] regularity . . . irrelevant issues, or . . . personalities." [32]

Klan involvement in 1930 was personified by the secret order's chief political strategist, Horace Wilkinson. He served as Heflin's campaign manager and his hand was evident once again in several scandals. Wilkinson, who had pioneered hate-sheet campaigning in Alabama politics, pursued it again in 1930. Just before the election, posters appeared all over the state promising $250 rewards for evidence of electoral fraud. They were mysteriously signed by a "National Secret Service." Absentee voters also received stern warnings about electoral fraud that bore the imprint of the National Secret Service. No such organization existed, of course, much less exercised jurisdiction in state elections. Investigators soon learned that Wilkinson was behind this latest and "lowest form of political skullduggery." [33]

By 1930, Tom Heflin's Washington colleagues regarded his speeches as tiresome, his tactics revolting, and his mind suspect. Yet he launched into the bid for reelection with all of the vigor he had demonstrated in 1928. After describing "Meekus Miller" as "an old wart hog," he turned his attention to his own opponent. "My God!" he boomed, "What got it into John Bankhead's head that he was FIT to go to the Senate of the United States?" The Klan senator appealed to white supremacy and religious prejudice, but his words rang less true against Bankhead, an Alabama Methodist, than they had against Al Smith, a Catholic New Yorker. Heflin declared that Alabama's Democratic Party was controlled by Tammany Hall, Catholics, liquor, and forces inimical to white supremacy. He accused national party chairman John J. Raskob of being a Catholic cardinal in disguise and charged that Bankhead and Miller were bankrolled by "the tainted dollars of the Roman Pope [to] . . . swallow their Protestant convictions and crawl on their bellies like serpents before the Pope, and kiss the cardinal's ring." He also relied on a Wilkinson hate sheet that roasted the twenty-seven SDEC members who had voted for expulsion as agents of a "wet-Catholic" conspiracy. [34] Behind his customary bombast, though, a worried Heflin spoke of possible election fraud by the Big Mule/Black Belt combination. He apparently also contemplated jettisoning Hugh Locke to run alone. Although Locke received some inside Klan pressure to withdraw, he steadfastly continued his run for governor. [35]

The Klan-backed rump party negotiated a deal with Alabama's Republican Party that was reminiscent of 1928. State GOP patronage referee O. D. Street and U.S. district attorney C. D. Kennamer agreed not to run Republican candidates for senator or governor in 1930. The move, designed to "tear up [Alabama's] Democratic party for the next 50 years," seemed the more expedient because Street coveted a federal judgeship that had become vacant with the death of Montgomery's Henry D. Clayton. Street spent a night at the White House discussing the judgeship with President Hoover, then returned to Alabama, where he announced the latest Republican covenant with the political wing of the KKK. In return for the elimination of Republican resistance in the general election, Senator Heflin reportedly agreed to vote favorably on Street's nomination for judge. The deal allowed Heflox to compete for 50,000-odd Republican votes in Alabama without having to commit party treason again by overtly fusing with the GOP. The arrangement was struck despite Heflin's celebrated crack that he could detect federal Republican officeholders upon crossing any county line in Alabama "because they smelled so much like negroes."[36]

The patrician faction attracted a formidable group of supporters to its 1930 standard, including former governors W. D. Jelks, Charles Henderson, Thomas Kilby, and Bill Brandon, publishers Victor Hanson and Frederick Thompson, Congressmen Lister Hill, Henry Steagall, Buck Oliver, E. B. Almon, George Huddleston, and William Bankhead, SDEC chair Edmund Pettus II, and SDEC members Borden Burr, Frank M. Dominick, W. L. Harrison, John D. McQueen, and Samuel Hobbs, and others. Three Alabama politicians, elected with considerable Klan support, all broke with the hooded order for the 1930 election—a clear sign of the order's imminent demise—Senator Hugo Black, Lieutenant Governor W. C. Davis, and Democratic national committeeman Watt T. Brown.[37]

Of the three defections, Black's was the most serious. Although the senator had remained silent in 1928, and openly opposed expulsion in 1929, he finally broke with the Klan in 1930. The rupture came early in the year when Black and Texas Democrat Tom Connelly urged Heflin to drop the Catholic issue. "But he won't listen," Black sadly reported. "He has a glassy eye and is now suspicious of me. I believe he may go crazy. Poor fellow. If he had just gone along without raising the issue he could have ended his days in the Senate peacefully." Political insiders suggested that Black, apart from his concern for his colleague's health and political orientation, also defected from the Klan political machine because he feared that Heflin would challenge his own seat in 1932. Washington observers reported that Heflin, dry as a chip politically, was drinking heavily.[38]

Benjamin Miller, the dry son of a Presbyterian minister, charged that all three Klan candidates—Heflin, Locke, and Dempsey Powell—used alcohol. He also tagged the Klan-backed Jeffersonian Democrats as crypto-Republicans, or at least fellow travelers, and denounced the KKK at every opportunity.[39]

Big Mule/Black Belt editors clamored around Bankhead and Miller. Editors who had once supported Klan candidates now stayed aloof or came out openly for the regular Democrats. Only 19 county weeklies of the state's 151 newspapers endorsed the Klan's rump party. Victor Hanson's *Birmingham News* published editorial after editorial celebrating the death of the state's KKK. Grover Hall, responding to Heflin's paranoia about Jesuit assassins and Catholic plots, and his fear of being poisoned, challenged the senator to submit to a psychiatric examination. The *Birmingham Age-Herald* castigated Heflin for making his faction the hostage of "Republican guerrillas [bent on] defil[ing] the house of his fathers" and upbraided state GOP leaders for allowing their party to become the tail on a Klan kite. Planter devotees charged that Heflin was a fair-weather prohibitionist, a coward for not actually voting for Herbert Hoover in 1928, and a sworn enemy of the female voters to whom he now appealed. They published Heflin quotations about "henpecked husbands" being nagged by "female cranks" and his criticism of the "crazy movement" for women's suffrage. On at least one occasion, Heflin had suggested that any man who voted for female suffrage should be required to wear a dress.[40]

Traditional Democrats found the most objectionable aspect of Heflin's candidacy the damage that his tenure in the Senate did to Alabama's national image. The heirs of Bourbon Democracy were hypersensitive about Alabama's reputation largely because they sought to import northern capital while keeping the federal government at bay. A Klan demagogue of Heflin's stripe, representing the state before the eyes of the nation, did little to encourage disciples of the New South Creed or to ease their anxiety about federal meddling in their racial customs. "[Heflin] has made Alabama ridiculous," a national journalist observed. "The guffaws of the forty-seven states have not been directed at him alone unfortunately. . . . Alabama has come to be an object of some wonder; what kind of people can inhabit that state?" John Bankhead agreed that Heflin had made the state an object of mockery as he pledged to resurrect Alabama's image and attract badly needed investment (figure 25).[41]

Bankhead, who laid claim to an almost royal lineage in Alabama politics, got down and dirty in 1930. He declared that Heflin's sole legislative accomplishment in a thirty-five-year career had been the passage of a Mother's Day bill—a measure easier to pass "than one endorsing the Ten Commandments." Stung by the Klan candidate's charges that he was a Catholic sympathizer, Bankhead stooped to a milder anti-Catholicism of his own. He

25. Political Cartoon of Tom Heflin, ca. 1928. Courtesy Birmingham Public Library, Tutwiler Collection of Southern History. Originally published in the *Birmingham News*.

pointedly denied that he had been educated in parochial schools, boasted that he had given ten hours and ten dollars to the Methodist church for every one given by Heflin, and declared that Heflin would "bootlick the Pope" if he thought it might gain him some votes.[42]

Bankhead and the patricians, accustomed to more subtle and sophisticated forms of character disparagement, were irritated no end by the tenor of the 1930 campaign. "No campaign has ever been conducted in Alabama on so low and indecent a basis as this one," Bankhead complained, directing his remarks at Heflin and Horace Wilkinson. "They have stopped at nothing short of physical murder . . . , spreading falsehoods . . . , frauds and forgeries . . . , character assassin[ation] . . . , slanderous and irresponsible . . . , indecent and vile and libelous . . . [accusations] in the gutter of mud and slime." Hugo Black later agreed that "Horace followed me around [in 1930] . . . and accused me of everything except murder" because the senator broke with the Klan to support Bankhead and Miller. Bankhead especially objected to the Klan's charges that he had sold thousands of dollars of worthless stock.[43]

The patrician then did his best to elevate the vulgar level of the campaign by accusing Heflin of being insane and a traitor to his state. "I brand Heflin as a character assassin, a creature more detestable and despicable than a man-killer," Bankhead declared.

> The only extenuating circumstance is the unfortunate state of his mind. It is impossible to doubt that he is a crazy man. . . . It is impossible for Heflin to be mean and vicious enough to manufacture [these lies] with a cool brain—I am obliged to believe they emanate from feverish and scrambled brain cells. . . . His mind is wobbly, the people of Alabama will not send to the United States Senate a traitor to his party . . . a traitor to his people, a character assassin, or a demented man.[44]

Mabel Jones West, former Klanswoman and current president of the Alabama Women's League for White Supremacy, illustrated well the kinship of intolerance that the KKK and the patricians shared. Mrs. West had long been reactionary in matters of race, but in 1930, as in 1928, she fought against the Klan and its candidates for their "foolish and fanatical assaults" on Catholics.[45]

The 1930 elections, like the presidential election of 1928, elicited strong popular participation in Alabama. Of the state's 357,000 registered voters, 252,000 cast ballots with disastrous results for the Jeffersonian Democrats. Bankhead defeated Heflin by a whopping margin, 151,000 votes to 101,000, while Miller swamped Locke in the governor's race by 59,000 votes. The loss was Heflin's first since the start of his career in 1896. U.S. congressman George Huddleston beat Hollis Parrish, the only other Klan-backed candidate.[46]

Patrician editors celebrated Jefferson County's "weed[ing] of its garden of Democracy" because it returned to the traditional fold after its 1928 hiatus. James Chappell of the *Birmingham News* greeted Bankhead's victory by musing that Heflin "never was a great credit to the state but he was at least respectable up until 1926. After that something happened to him and he became . . . intolerable." Chappell and other members of the traditional Democrats blamed the influence of the KKK.[47]

The Big Mule celebration was tame compared to the reaction in the Black Belt. A Centreville crowd dug four graves so as to bury in effigy the leaders of the 1930 rump movement: Wilkinson, Heflin, Locke, and Dempsey Powell. "The defeat of Wilkinson's [Klan] candidates," a veteran political observer wrote, "will remove him as a power in Alabama politics." Wilkinson, though, was a consummate politician. In the 1930s he shifted gears, leaving the Klan behind and becoming the patronage-dispensing boss of a powerful Birmingham political machine. True to form, Miller had an inaugural parade that featured just two cars in order to conserve fuel. Miller raised eybrows even more by bringing his favorite cow to Montgomery to supply the governor's mansion with milk and butter.[48]

Voting patterns in 1930, again, did not completely bear out the notion of a north Alabama revolt. As in 1926, 1928, and 1929, the patterns suggest instead an east Alabama revolt against the Black Belt.[49] Heflin won only two counties—Winston and Escambia—in what can properly be called west Alabama. He prevailed in five east Alabama counties and lost by less than a hundred votes in five others. Moreover, the bulk of his support was in Alabama's east central hill counties—not the north. Locke's pattern of support was virtually identical.[50]

Reactions to defeat varied in the rump/KKK camp, revealing that perhaps rumors of campaign dissension had not been without basis. At the very least, Hugh Locke weathered substantial lobbying from within the KKK faction to give up the race. In defeat, Heflin and Locke parted ways again. Locke and Hamp Draper, head of the state convict department and KKK director of the Heflox campaign in central Alabama, offered their congratulations to the oligarchs and expressed their determination to return to the regular Democratic fold. Heflin, stubbornly unrelenting, stood in stark contrast. With Horace Wilkinson whispering advice in his ear, the old senator insisted that there had been vote fraud and vowed to contest the election in the U.S. Senate.[51]

Heflin's promise of a federal investigation only poured fuel on the fire raging between the KKK and Alabama's regular Democrats. Victor Hanson's press empire wore the patrician heart on its sleeve over this sensitive matter. The *Birmingham Age-Herald* pleaded with Heflin not to do this "shabby and ignoble thing" but instead to accept defeat. "For the sake of the good name of Alabama it is to be hoped that [Heflin will] . . . not persist in his absurd insinuations of elections frauds," wrote an editor for the *Birmingham News*. "No matter how groundless the charges . . . , a senatorial investigation . . . would be distasteful to the people of Alabama, and it would give the state a great deal of undesirable publicity." The *Birmingham Age-Herald* concurred, betraying an almost unnatural fear of the central government. Grover Hall and the *Montgomery Advertiser* chimed in by recalling the political horrors of Reconstruction, raising the issue of white supremacy, and hinting that the nightmare might be revisited because of Heflin's proposed folly. "The only time the foes of the Democratic party ever came to control of affairs in Alabama," Hall wrote, "was when they summoned the Federal Army to give them the strength . . . to subdue an unconquerable people . . . the most infamous episode in the long history of the Anglo-Saxon in the Western World, . . . to occupy this conquered province . . . , seize the power and treasure of our people [and] . . . form a cruel and cowardly alliance with the untrained children just released from slavery."[52]

To wage his controversial protest, Heflin again turned to the Klan adviser Horace Wilkinson, "my chief counsel [and] the best lawyer in my State by miles." In earlier years, Heflin had provided a model for Wilkinson. He was older, more experienced, and politically successful, having served in the U.S. House of Representatives prior to being seated in the Senate for eleven years. As the Klan senator increasingly relied on Wilkinson's legal brilliance and political counsel, though, the younger man began to exercise undue influence over the older demagogue. After their shared struggles in the vanguard of the Klan's political movement—the 1928 bolt, the 1929 expulsion movement, and the 1930 election—Heflin leaned heavily on Wilkinson. In turn, the younger Klansman delivered political advice, legal counsel, moral support, and an endless supply of bombast. Determined "never [to] die satisfied until I see you take the oath of office as a U.S. Senator," Wilkinson urged Heflin to claim that the 1930 election had been stolen from him by the oligarchy. The alleged fraud smacked of the old Populist days in Alabama when Reuben Kolb had been cheated out of at least two gubernatorial elections by the Redeemers. As Wilkinson had expected, less privileged whites, many of whom bitterly remembered the 1890s battles, rallied to the cause of their new tribunes. "The time is right for . . . a political revolution in Alabama" against the Black Belt, wrote one farmer. "The farmer is the *worst sufferer* and [yet] he has the *most votes*."[53]

Before the Klan candidate and his attorney could plead their case, they first had to reach the Senate floor—something Alabama's patricians worked to prevent. Hugo Black, whose break with the KKK was now complete,

voted not to allow a Senate hearing on the fraud charges. Yet Nebraska senator George Norris, Heflin's old ally from the Senate farm bloc, facilitated
the Alabamian's efforts. An enraged Heflin denounced Black, his "one-time
friend," and branded the 1930 election "the biggest and most scientifically
conducted steal in the history of politics. . . . the trail of the serpent of corruption is over it all."[54]

During 1931 and 1932, Horace Wilkinson virtually controlled every
move that Heflin made. At one point, the fallen senator told a reporter for
the *New York Times* that he had actually been reelected by a clear majority
of at least 100,000 votes. A furious Wilkinson censured the old demagogue
and instructed him that, in the future, he should check with the Klan attorney before talking to anyone. Heflin dutifully agreed.[55]

The fraud hearings brought the conflict between Alabama's patricians
and its KKK to the floor of the U.S. Senate. Wilkinson questioned over 300
witnesses before a Senate subcommittee, while John Bankhead called 257
witnesses in his own behalf. Wilkinson boasted that he had 1,200 more witnesses to call, submitted a fifty-two-point summary of alleged frauds, and,
in a memorable three-hour oration, categorized preliminary proceedings as
"the most brazen parade of perjury that ever stalked the corridors of the
Federal Building" in Birmingham. The Senate eventually decided to continue recognizing Bankhead (figure 26) as Alabama's senator by a vote of
63 to 19. Before the final tally was taken, though, Wilkinson made one last
effort on behalf of his old Klan ally. "The alleged primary was an illegiti-
mate political monstrosity, sired by hate, damned by corruption, utterly in-
capable of providing a human being morally fit to occupy a seat in the
Senate," he railed. "That political crime should not receive the approval of
any body charged with [the] preservation of political liberty. . . . Like the
Pharaoh in Biblical history, Mr. Bankhead stiffened his neck and hardened
his heart."[56]

Heflin's appeal effectively marked the end of his political career and of
the 1920s Klan that he had so ably represented. Observers differed in their
views of the Klan senator at the time of his political passing in 1932. H. L.
Mencken lamented that the "new Senate . . . will show some gifted clowns,
but there will still be a large vacuum . . . where the Hon. J. Thomas Heflin
of Alabama used to sit, [and] howl, and have his being." Years later, a maud-
lin appraisal of the Klan lecturer appeared, one that failed to take stock of
the damage wrought by Heflin's oppressive racial, religious, and nativist bigotry. The author hoped that readers would remember Heflin "as a son of the
soil—as Southern as the fig—as rich in the stuff that composes humor and
good fun as a Samuel Clemens or a Joel Chandler Harris. . . . I can charge

26. John H. Bankhead II, ca. 1930. Courtesy Alabama State Department of Archives and History.

his faults, when they are visible to me, to his times and to the moods of the people. A host of his ideas are not for today, but for his yesterdays, they were real." [57]

THE PERSISTENCE OF KU KLUXISM

The overwhelming 1930 verdict against the Heflox ticket was a serious blow to the Alabama KKK. Undefeated in thirty-five years of campaigning, Heflin was never again to win public office, although he tried several times. The unsuccessful fraud hearings marked the end of the Alabama Klan's political career as well. The Klan's role as a political entity had sustained it as an organization during the final years of the 1920s when it had faced so many challenges in other areas—financial, membership, and ethical. Now, however, the gigantic umbrellalike 1920s KKK was clearly a thing of the past in Alabama.[58]

During the first years of the new decade, the KKK persisted in local affairs on a nonpolitical level. Although the order's opponents had been hoping, praying, and preaching since 1927 that Alabama's secret order was dead, a Ku Klux spirit was plainly alive even at the end of 1932. Despite repeated setbacks, the Alabama Klan survived at a significantly reduced but still important level.

For the most part, the Klan spirit lay just beneath the surface of things. Still, it was discernible in the occasional parade, the odd cross burning, the isolated flogging, and the sporadic act of intimidation. During the height of Al Smith's campaign in Alabama, at the very time the Klan's political enemies were declaring it dead, an angry mob of Knights visited a black Baptist preacher from Dexter Avenue in Montgomery to terrorize him for questioning Jim Crow. The pastor had offended local sensibilities by instructing his flock to withhold advertising revenue from white newspapers until they addressed blacks as "Mister" and "Mistress," as they did when whites were mentioned in the paper. In the Klan stronghold of Walker County, two men kidnapped and flogged a nineteen-year-old woman for impersonating the daughter of a local man. Jefferson County's Klan Association attracted 500 Knights to its December 1929 meeting and had crowds as large as 1,500 in 1930. The KKK kept some ties to the Anti-Saloon League and waged a 1930 crackdown on Colbert County moonshining that led to the hasty resignations of the sheriff, the county prosecutor, a justice of the peace, and several deputies and county commissioners.[59]

During its decline, Alabama's KKK also sponsored over 200 religious revivals that attracted on average (according to bloated Klan estimates) over a thousand people per night. Boaz, Mobile, Gadsden, and Ensley proved to be hot spots. Imperial officers in Atlanta arranged for the Alabama realm to serve as a laboratory for their experiment in religious recruitment. The process took the following form. First, Grand Dragon James Esdale enlisted a local Klan lodge to sponsor tent revivals lasting anywhere from a week to a month. During the meetings, hooded evangelists appealed for new members and held special WKKK and Junior KKK meetings to recruit women and children. Robed leaders bragged that the revivals boosted recruitment substantially. In one south Alabama town, which was home to only twelve dues-paying Klan members in 1928 and had not held a klonkave in over eight months, 186 new members enlisted as a result of the revivals. Local organizers also reinstated a hundred delinquent Knights and converted a vocal critic of the order into a Klan officer.[60]

The threat of hooded violence also persisted. In rural Jefferson County, five men flogged a Hanceville mail carrier in 1929, leaving him with welts and a black eye. Seven men flogged a black man in Blount County; authorities made arrests but later dropped the cases.[61] During the height of the emotional 1930 election, the Birmingham KKK gained national notoriety by threatening the life of Oscar DePriest, a black U.S. congressman from Illinois. A native of Florence, Alabama, DePriest had embarrassed Alabamians by reporting that his family had left the state after a lynching. In June 1930, Congressman DePriest planned to address a southern convention of Mosaic Templars in Birmingham. A Klan response was almost axiomatic whenever local racial sensibilities had been bruised; in this case the response was electric. Birmingham klaverns staged a 2,500-man parade through the mostly black north side of town. Robed Klansmen sang "Happy Days Are Here Again," distributed leaflets, and fired pistols, shotguns, and machine guns into the air. Klan broadsides announced a message that was repeated all over the country: "Alabama is safe for white supremacy. . . . It is a good state for good Negroes, but a bad state for bad Negroes." Kluxers highlighted the sensational protest by burning DePriest and a white Communist in effigy and burying them under placards reading "He believed in social equality."[62]

The protest caused a national uproar, but it also demonstrated that some elements of the Klan would remain active during the depression decade. Knights were still capable, even likely, to rise at a moment's notice if provoked by threats to white supremacy—Communist, northern, or indigenous. A black editor in Indianapolis called Alabama's Kluxers the "Knights of the Kerocene Kan" for their incendiary display, and a Harlem group threatened to kill "each and every white living human being down there" if one hair on DePriest's head was harmed. A shell-shocked black Chicagoan, who had been visiting Birmingham relatives during the incident, published an eyewitness account of the Klan intimidation in several northern papers. "This is a frightful section of the uncivilized world," he concluded, the "mobbers and lynchocrats . . . [are] becoming more bloodthirsty each day."[63]

Alabama Klansmen, aroused by the insolence of the black response, wired DePriest to repeat their message that Alabama was "a white man's state" and that his presence was not desired. The Mosaic Templars took heed and changed their convention site to Little Rock, while Klan hate sheets in Alabama lambasted DePriest as "the coon congressman from Chicago . . . a common lyin' nigger . . . and a black son of Ham." "Real white men have real respect for the negro who knows his place and keeps it," one Alabama KKK member explained, but "all decent white men—and for that matter all decent negroes—despise the 'nigger' who arrogates to himself a social and political position for which he is not endowed by nature." "God put the reins of government in the hands of the white races," another Alabama Klansman reasoned, "and God gave the servant's position to the negro. The elevation of Oscar DePriest to Congress is a defiance to God, an insult to white culture, [and] a threat against white supremacy. . . . [He] is as morally rotten and degenerate as it is possible for an impudent, lying, debased, cowardly, lustful, criminal 'nigger' to be."[64]

Perhaps the most disturbing aspect of the DePriest affair was not the Klan parade, its guns, or even the group's epithets. The most troubling moment came when the Birmingham City Commission publicly endorsed the Klan's actions and sentiments. The city commission, controlled during the 1930s by none other than Klan politico Horace Wilkinson, rescinded a city permit allowing DePriest's speech in order to "safeguard 'white supremacy.'"[65]

Sporadic Klan violence continued in 1931, although there was far less of it than there had been during the 1920s. Pickens County blacks were plagued by a series of masked floggings. In an ironic twist, Pickens authorities invoked a local version of the states'-rights argument against Alabama officials when pressed on the matter by the B. M. Miller administration. The county solicitor blamed the violence on local sympathy for the Klan but demonstrated that localism was ingrained by denying that his bailiwick required assistance from the state.[66]

State authorities did prevent vigilantism on a few occasions. In 1931, they interceded in time to prevent lynchings in Huntsville and Scottsboro. A Sumter County mob did lynch a black man on Independence Day, though, precipitating a race riot in which three more blacks and two whites died. State interference led to the replacement of county deputies with state police and a local judge and solicitor with a Mobile magistrate and state prosecutor. Yet justice seemed oddly served as authorities indicted twenty African Americans, some of whom were later put to death, while not a single white was arrested.[67]

Although the Klan lay relatively low by 1920s standards, it persisted in such a climate. Klan parades and depredations still occurred during the first few years of the 1930s, letting the state's residents know that, despite the economic hardships of the depression, a small hard core of Klan loyalists was still not too busy to hate. On New Year's Day 1930, Klan notices appeared around Alabama as well as in Mississippi and Arkansas. The posters announced a Klan plan to ship people of color out of the South and suggested that interested parties send five dollars and contact a Montgomery resident for details on how to start their own klaverns. In the fall of 1931, robed Kluxers paraded through Birmingham's black north side to protest several black-on-white rapes and two murders. Later that year, Klan chapters held an old-time spectacular at East Lake Park that was reminiscent of the 1920s and featured fireworks, a barbecue, souvenirs, and a speech by Imperial Wizard Hiram Evans. Men, women, and youth who were Klan members turned out in full regalia.[68]

In 1931, Alabama's Invisible Empire reorganized. At a Birmingham klorero, James Esdale finally stepped down as the realm's grand dragon. Esdale had become increasingly alienated by Hiram Evans's 1930 decision to give his blessing to the Heflox rump party. The grand dragon and the imperial wizard had also butted heads over their reactions to the 1929 expulsion controversy. Hamp Draper, head of the state prison system, stepped in as interim leader of Alabama's KKK, taking the title "imperial representative," and Bert Thomas agreed to serve as secretary. Hugh Locke also played a leading role in the reorganization.[69]

Despite their 1930 election victories, the patrician faction was not about to abandon its crusade while the hooded group still posed any threat. State legislators formally condemned Tom Heflin in 1931 for his negative impact on the state's image and his destructive charges of electoral fraud. Planters and industrialists also struck at Horace Wilkinson by attempting to limit him to only one public office. The skilled Klan attorney, though, repeatedly triumphed over his antagonists in state court.[70]

During the early 1930s, Alabama's KKK turned its attention to local politics and to irritating the state's new governor. Horace Wilkinson led the Klan's political remnants. Wilkinson gained control of Birmingham politics when he placed on the city commission Lewey V. Robinson and William O. Downs, two trusted clients. Bill Downs had a Klan history. He had served as the exalted cyclops of an Ensley klavern and as Jefferson County's sheriff. Jimmie Jones, the other member of the three-man commission, had already served a Klan apprenticeship under Wilkinson's eye and had originally been elected commission president in 1925 with substantial hooded backing. Later in the 1930s, Jones would break away from Wilkinson's orbit and cater to the Big Mules through a policy of retrenchment that slashed the city budget, fired employees, and cut badly needed services. Birmingham's KKK scored a political victory in 1931, though, when it successfully promoted a bill that lengthened the terms of its loyal commissioners to six years.[71]

Klan infighting in city politics illustrated in microcosm the order's last death throes at the state level. Governor Benjamin Miller had won election in 1930 largely by denouncing the KKK. Once Miller was in power, the secret order's remnants made it their mission in life to harass him. Sixteen Klansmen launched an anti-Miller crusade by attacking William F. Feagin, the governor's right-hand man; apparently there was no shortage of ammunition. Miller's nepotism was so excessive that even fiscal conservatives such as Julian Hall criticized the favoritism as public waste. Hall published a "Shame Sheet of Alabama" in his *Dothan Eagle* that listed the names of prominent beneficiaries of Miller's largesse, including Hall's own future bride. He was joined by the pro-Klan *Abbeville Herald*. Horace Wilkinson got into the act by attacking Miller's abysmal labor record. The new governor had done little to endear himself to plain folk by making remarks as sensitive as "a dollar a day [is] enough for any working man." At one point, Wilkinson accused the Miller administration of misappropriating $7 million in state funds and proposed that an independent accounting agency audit state books with the proviso that Miller resign if he was found guilty.[72]

The Alabama KKK savored the opportunity to cast a few final stones at the new governor. "Gov. Feagin and Economy (?) Miller are ruining our state. Petty jealousies, interdepartmental feuds and official spite work are bringing shame to our State Capitol," Klan critics charged. "Trust funds are being shamelessly diverted into whose pockets no one knows . . . school teachers have become the unpaid victims of high handed racketeering. . . . Our highways are becoming mudholes and gullies. Our State law enforcement department has been abolished so that negroes assault and murder our white women with impunity, bootleggers flourish, corruption goes unindicted and Russian Communists organize their program of violence and destruction among negroes and ignorant whites." "It is high time that all real klansmen gather again," one Knight advised, "recruit their strength to the very maximum and remind the world by their deeds that klansmen are intolerant of such depravity, incompetence, extravagance and waste as now disgrace the State of Alabama."[73]

In 1932, Horace Wilkinson performed his final political services for the Klan before he shifted to concentrate all of his efforts and energies on consolidating his own political power in Birmingham. During the 1930s Wilkinson would become a power unto himself in the city as he headed up his own private political machine. Wilkinson and Tom Heflin campaigned vigorously against Hugo Black in his 1932 senatorial reelection attempt against Thomas Kilby. The Klan duo sought to make up politically for Black's abandonment of the order, but Wilkinson also owed a private political debt to Kilby. The campaign featured some of Wilkinson's dirtiest tactics. Wilkinson also opposed incumbent George Huddleston, an old Klan foe, as the "pink dean of the do-nothing-but-draw-a-salary bloc" in Congress and said he spoke with a forked "alien tongue."[74]

One after another, solid cases against Klan criminals also fell apart in front of petit juries—a familiar phenomenon in Alabama's love/hate relationship with the secret order. Horace Wilkinson managed to have the landmark convictions against Jeff Calloway's Klan floggers overturned in 1929 at the Alabama Supreme Court. He won on the technicality that the Blount County grand jury had been improperly drawn. Prosecutors decided to drop the Arthur Hitt flogging case for good. The black farmer in Jefferson County had been terrorized into surrendering his farmland, and the patrician press had gained considerable political mileage from the incident. After numerous delays, Jefferson County authorities also dismissed strong cases against a host of other Klan floggers. Despite a mountain of evidence, Blount County jurors acquitted every Klan murderer of Lily Cobb, a black woman. The Oneonta newspaper did its best to help the case along by describing the defendants as "businessmen and . . . good citizens" who had never run afoul of the law before. Upon news of the acquittal, the local editor celebrated the jury's decision as one that would "meet [with] the approval of the people of the county." When one exceptional Alabama jury found a pair of floggers guilty, Judge H. P. Heflin, brother of the infamous senator, imposed the paltry penalty of a $100 fine. Actions such as these prompted some to gloat over the limits of an elite political opposition that did not challenge Klan fundamentals or folk support for the group. "What has become of that flogging fanfaronade that was so flamingly played up by the 'big papers' and their satellites?" an editor for the *Coosa River News* snickered. "Couldn't work juries, boys?"[75]

Klan leaders themselves realized that the anti-Klan campaign had been inspired, in part, by "political motives." From time to time the patrician press all but admitted the charge by letting it slip that their editorial crusade against the flogging epidemic had begun in 1927. The floggings had been a major problem since at least 1921 but had failed to elicit significant public outrage until the KKK swept the 1926 elections. Likewise, until he bolted, Alabama elites had little problem with the unseemliness of Tom Heflin's bigotry.[76]

Curiously, some patricians such as Grover Hall depicted themselves (and were depicted) as cutting-edge liberals. Hall, though, never lost an opportunity to criticize Alabama's economically liberal Bibb Graves and his educational, health, and social reforms; he called them "a sickening story" or "Ku Kluxism's latest gift to man in Alabama." Julian Hall lampooned Graves's progressivism as a "wild debauchery of spending by a be-Kluxed Governor and a be-Kluxed Legislature." The Hall family also praised Congressman Lister Hill for fighting against a federal antilynching bill, maintained close ties to such "peg-legged bigot[s]" as Frank Dixon, and worked overtime to stimulate further industrial development by currying external investment even at concessions disastrous to Dixie.[77]

The 1930 election, and its tumultuous aftermath, marked the end of the Klan's 1920s heyday in Alabama. Still, a resilient Klan spirit existed after 1930.[78] Such an ethos could transcend lost elections and doomed political battles. Its endurance was evident in the marches, galas, and floggings that still occurred after 1930 whenever white supremacy was threatened. It lived on in Alabama after 1930 much as it did between 1874 and 1915, at a subterranean level. Yet it never completely disappeared.

The Klan persisted in Alabama largely because of an intractable race issue. Southern politics and society had long turned on the issue of race. Even through the ferment of 1928—Al Smith, alcohol, Tammany, and Catholicism—white supremacy remained the paramount issue in Alabama. "It's great to be a Romanist, isn't it?" one Alabama Klan leader had observed during that campaign. "They make 'saints' out of niggers . . . and then say their prayers to them." A Klan leaflet attacked Victor Hanson, Al Smith's press spokesman in Alabama, calling him the publisher of "filthy papers . . . [that] love the nigger so [much] that they do not want to charge any of their race with any crime that portrays the animal instinct of the new arrivals from the Ape family . . . , [even] the nigger of the savage type." "There is no need to discuss the question of white supremacy," a Knight explained. "Every Klansman is a white man and will never consent to our civilization being mongrelized or contaminated."[79]

Black suffrage, for the KKK, violated the most fundamental tenets of white supremacy, since it treated the races as equal. Black voting was, for the Klan, an abomination, a sin, a revolting menace to the republican form of government. If accomplished under black leaders, it would be a testament to and a function of "their inferior mentality and character . . . and would degrade our government." If, instead, black voters followed white leaders, only "demagoguery and corruption" would result. Either way, Klan members and many other white Alabamians felt, viable black suffrage would ruin politics by forcing the two major parties to respond to black interests in order to compete for a black vote. The only acceptable course, the Alabama KKK argued, was to abolish the constitutional provision of black suffrage. To this end, Alabama Klansmen used the words "coon" and "nigger" nineteen times in their September 1929 newsletter and invoked the primitive fear of interracial sex as the inexorable product of black suffrage.[80]

As long as the race issue and its related antifederalism remained central in

Alabama, the KKK promised to live on at some level. As the scenes, screams, and dramas of the late 1920s passed, along with its giant mainstream Klan, remnants of the once mighty order showed signs of rallying around the race issue. An Order of the Black Shirts met at the Montgomery Courthouse, 100 strong, to revive Ku Kluxism under a different name and to speak of communism, a new threat on the horizon. Five hundred Klansmen paraded in Birmingham to warn Communist agitators against trying to proselytize the African American.[81] Just as the issues of 1928 had become warped by the irrepressible race issue, so antiradicalism (a new rallying point for the fewer but more purely reactionary Klansmen of the 1930s) promised to become altered by race. Remnants of the Alabama KKK lobbied to repeal the Fifteenth Amendment, the suffrage key that would permit the black male to "lay black hand[s] upon white flesh."[82] Until the Deep South could overcome such primeval fears, the Klan would always be a threat to reappear in different forms.

1930s Causes Célèbres

Scottsboro and Hugo Black

During the 1930s Alabama was one of the most repressive spots in America. Many observers have persisted in believing that nothing much happened in the state during the 1930s, but poverty and political oppression dominated the decade. Like people elsewhere, Alabamians starved. Poverty, heartache, misery, and despair accompanied the hard times. Farm families endured a seemingly inexorable downward shift in mobility as they had for over a half century prior to 1929. As the economy lurched to a standstill, urban workers in the industrial center of Birmingham and the mill towns of north Alabama joined the agricultural workers.[1]

Much else occurred. The Ku Klux Klan persisted and, on occasion, even thrived under profoundly adverse conditions. A north Alabama rape case, that of the "Scottsboro Boys," mesmerized human and civil rights defenders the world over as its drama unfolded in a Decatur courtroom. The case and its subplots cast a dark pall over the state throughout the decade.[2]

Other events contributed to the state's growing reputation for infamy. Federal officials pinpointed Birmingham as the city in America hardest hit by the depression. In 1930, the paralyzed industrial giant became home to the southern branch of the Communist Party and its official party organ. Alabama sharecroppers erupted in protest against the medieval conditions under which they labored and lived. Community, landlord, vigilante, and government backlash against the croppers was so excessive that Alabama's Black Belt became a magnet for international criticism. The nation's single largest industrial conflict, hatched in the textile centers of north Alabama, eventually engulfed over 400,000 workers across the country. A series of shocking incidents, gothic in their horror, disgusted a nation and caused

Alabama to be likened to Adolf Hitler's fascist state: the Birmingham assault of Jewish Communist Joseph Gelders; a triple lynching in Tuscaloosa; the public murder and mutilation of Claude Neal by an Alabama mob near Florida; the repression of farm tenants in Tallapoosa, Lowndes, and Dallas Counties; and an international scandal surrounding the appointment of Hugo Black, the former Alabama Klansman, to the Supreme Court.[3]

So ingrained were class and racial oppression, so rampant the terrorism, so firm the ties between business, government, and the Klan, and so powerful the aversion to outside interference that Alabama came to seem the most benighted piece of turf in America during the 1930s. It had the worst record of any state in the country on human and civil liberties and certainly one of the most wretched records in the annals of Western democracy.[4]

Not only did the Klan survive in such a climate, at times it even flourished—a daunting prospect for any enterprise during the Great Depression. The Klan—a different Klan from the gigantic middle-class order of the 1920s—reinvented itself throughout the 1930s mostly as an instrument for the perpetuation by business and government of the status quo, lopsided with respect to both race and class. In Alabama, this status quo came under attack from urban workers, poor farmers, "uppity niggers," unionists, a handful of Communists, and the ever-present "outside agitator."

Though the KKK functioned in Alabama throughout the 1930s, this was an era largely separate from the 1920s. Birmingham Klansmen threw parties, cut watermelon, served coffee and doughnuts, and staged pie-eating contests. Mobile's Gulf Coast Knights held oyster and fish fries. A Huntsville lodge sponsored a three-day gala replete with a barbecue and parades. Klaverns were also active in Talladega, Anniston, Baldwin, Bayeau La Batre, Evergreen, Robertsdale, Atmore, Brewton, Ensley, Collinsville, Selma, Alexander City, and scores of other Alabama towns and hamlets.[5]

Not all Klan activities were benign. In Alabama, 1930s hooded activity revolved around a handful of basic themes: the Scottsboro cases, repression of urban radicals, subjugation of insurgent Black Belt croppers, the squashing of organized labor, and the Hugo Black cause célèbre. Although many agreed that depressed economic conditions made it less likely that people would "throw [ten dollars] away on an over-sized night shirt," the "lost Klan" did operate between 1930 and 1954 and has received little attention from scholars. Between thirty and forty-four new chapters sprang up around Alabama during the 1930s. In the war against the Left, the Klan contribution blended so thoroughly with police, state, and corporate violence that it is now impossible to separate them completely.[6]

SCOTTSBORO AND THE KLAN

The Scottsboro case festered like a great open sore during the 1930s and permitted the small KKK on a few occasions to do more than just subsist. The case contained a number of ingredients certain to sustain interest and emotion in Alabama: communism, outside intervention, summary justice, and, above all, the primordial taboos of interracial sex and social equality.

The drama began in March 1931 when Jackson County deputies arrested nine young black males in Paint Rock Valley near Scottsboro and charged them with raping two white women.[7] Alabama justice, notoriously lethargic in cases of white-on-black crime, moved with lightning speed in this instance. Within six days, a grand jury had indicted the Scottsboro Boys (as they now began to be called), and local officials called a special session of circuit court to expedite their prosecution. An all-white jury found eight of the boys guilty. The presiding judge sentenced them to a mass execution in July and burst into tears.[8]

The cases quickly became a cause célèbre for a host of reasons: the questionable "efficiency" of Alabama justice; the involvement of Communist defense attorneys in the form of the International Labor Defense fund (ILD); the systematic exclusion of people of color from Alabama juries; the staging of a trial in the midst of a potential lynch mob of several thousand angry whites that included more than a few Klansmen; brutalization of the black prisoners; and the protests of Albert Einstein, Theodore Dreiser, and others. Alabama jailers kept the boys in primitive conditions, starved them for up to a week at a time, deprived them of exercise and fresh air, and routinely imposed solitary confinement on them. Beatings, teargas, and threats were common. Some guards required the boys to call them "Massah." One especially brutal guard who relished the harsh treatment advised the prisoners to "tell your Jew friends in New York. Write the ILD all about it. Bring 'em down here and we'll give 'em the same stuff."[9]

The National Association for the Advancement of Colored People (NAACP) tried to enter the fray by importing Clarence Darrow, the famed trial lawyer, and Garfield Hays of the American Civil Liberties Union (ACLU). The Communist ILD, recognizing the organizing potential in the cases, jealously warded off NAACP involvement. In March 1932, the Alabama Supreme Court upheld the circuit court's conviction despite ILD appeals and the judge's refusal to ask jurors whether they were racists.[10]

The cases became Alabama's albatross. Already subjected to criticism from much of the known world, the state retreated even further into what some have called a "siege mentality" or a "closed society."[11] Patriotic Ala-

27. Large Gathering of 1920s Klan Leaders. Scenes like this one, common during the 1920s, became rarer during the depression years. Courtesy Birmingham Public Library Archives, Cat. No. 25.38.

bamians responded by becoming absolutely, rigidly, and often irrationally defensive in the face of any criticism from outside the state. Such a mindset made Klan involvement likely. It also supplied a ready-made defense of mob action (it could be blamed on "outside agitation") and excused law enforcement of questionable vigor once the crime had occurred.

As usual in Alabama, race was at the heart of things. ILD communism was most repellent in Alabama because it threatened to level the races. The Communists preached the heresy of interracial cooperation and provided free legal defense for black males accused of having raped white women and thereby breaking the most sacred taboo in southern society.

The race threat was not the only ingredient certain to attract the attention of the Alabama Klan, however. The Invisible Empire also entered the Scottsboro affair as a function of an abiding anti-Semitism. Both ILD counsel were New York Jews. On one occasion, 200 hooded Klansmen surrounded attorney Samuel S. Leibowitz on a Decatur street. In another, a thug grabbed Joseph R. Brodsky by the coatsleeve as he tried to make his way through the Klan mob that maintained a vigil outside the county courthouse. "Come on, yah Jew bitch!," he screamed in Brodsky's face, "We'll show you how to defend nigger rapers." The Jewish attorneys remained intrepid in the face of repeated Klan threats. Threatened with tarring and feathering, flogging, and murder, Leibowitz responded, "Mobs mean nothing to me. Let them hang me; I don't care. Life is only an incident in the Creator's scheme of things, but if I can contribute my little bit to see that justice is served then my mission is fulfilled."[12]

Curiously, anti-Semitism reached its nadir inside the Scottsboro courtroom. Illustrating the connection between community sentiment and Alabama justice, county solicitor Wade Wright made repeated anti-Semitic statements in open court. He railed against "fancy New York clothes" and the "Jew language" and repeatedly made various slurs. At one point, he urged jurors to show the Communist lawyers that "Alabama justice cannot be bought and sold with Jew money from New York."[13]

Despite the ubiquitous presence of Klansmen and their threats, the Communists did not merely sit and await their fate at the end of a Klan rope. They implored a series of Alabama governors to protect them but got nowhere. George W. Chamblee, a native Southerner and a member of the ILD defense team, unsuccessfully begged Benjamin Miller to provide protection for the defendants and their counsel by trying to push the governor's xenophobic buttons. He stressed the national shame that would befall Alabama if any of the boys were lynched. Answering a county sheriff, the state attorney general, and the trial judge, who had advised against sending state guards, Chamblee warned the governor of the "disgrace [that would be] brought down on the good name of the State." Despite the cautionary words, and Chamblee's certainty that the presiding judge was "intimately connected" to the KKK, the governor refused to send protection. Instead, he noted his preference for local authority and the "law-abiding spirit" of the local citizenry.[14]

Alabama's KKK did not limit its Scottsboro activities to north Alabama. During the 1930s, Birmingham klaverns routed meetings of blacks and Communists protesting Scottsboro and the treatment of black radicals such as Angelo Herndon. At one large 1932 rally, held under Communist party auspices, Klansmen dispersed a crowd of 2,000 by dropping hundreds of leaflets from a nearby building: "Negroes of Birmingham, the Ku Klux Klan is watching you. Tell the Communists to get out of town. They mean only trouble for you, for Alabama is a good place for good Negroes and a bad place for Negroes who believe in racial equality." The scene was repeated a number of times with admonitions against social equality and advice for blacks to report radical activity to the Klan's local post office box.[15]

These incidents, and the intrinsic injustice of the Scottsboro cases, prompted a barrage of national and international criticism; rallies for the Scottsboro boys took place all over the globe. References to possible federal intervention, though, only fueled Alabama's growing defensiveness.[16]

Outside protest was a constant source of pressure on Alabama officials, who already felt under siege. Opponents of the state's draconian legal system sometimes used the bad press as a weapon in their Scottsboro struggle. Allan Knight Chalmers, chair of the southern-based Scottsboro Defense Committee (SDC), repeatedly cited negative national opinion as he sought to pressure Alabama governors into pardoning the boys. In 1936, he complained about solitary confinement, third-degree confessions, and Klan vigilantism, and he warned Governor Bibb Graves, now in a second term, that such practices would be "a further stain . . . [and] lasting reproach" on Alabama's good name that "will not be easy to wipe out." The SDC, Chalmers declared, would wait only "a reasonable time for a positive reply" and was fully "prepared to carry the situation much further."[17]

"Carry the situation further" was a euphemism for the nightmare that had plagued Alabama elites since at least 1866, namely the specter of federal involvement, not only in Scottsboro, but in Alabama race relations generally. Such a disaster had to be avoided at all costs even if it meant that Alabama elites would have to combat Klan violence themselves. The interest of outside groups—the ACLU, the NAACP, the ILD, and the SDC—sustained anxiety on this score.[18]

Anxiety reached a fever pitch when an organization based in the South flouted regional customs to endorse federal intervention in Alabama. In 1934, Nashville reverend Will Alexander's Commission on Inter-racial Co-operation (CIC) endorsed the Costigan-Wagner federal antilynching bill. A few other noted Southerners—Tar Heel journalist Virginius Dabney and Texas congressman Maury Maverick—also defied regional convention to support the measure. The bill twice passed the House only to fall prey to Southern intransigence in the Senate owing to the efforts of Richard Russell of Georgia, Carter Glass of North Carolina, South Carolina's "Cotton Ed" Smith, Mississippi's Pat Harrison and Theodore Bilbo, and others. North Carolina senator Josiah Bailey spoke for many when he fumed that the bill was only "the forerunner of a policy studiously cultivated by agitators not for the purpose of preventing lynching, but . . . to introduce the policy of Federal interference in local affairs . . . [and] a civil rights bill [like that] which Thad Stevens tried to put upon the South." Although the bill was ultimately defeated, it kept Southerners mindful of the federal threat and significantly influenced elite Alabama's resistance to the KKK.[19]

Outside criticism and the specter of federal intrusion intensified Alabama's innate defensiveness. Hypersensitive elites, at first predisposed to imprison the Scottsboro Boys and throw away the key, began to reverse themselves and push for a pardon. The heightened sensitivity brought the KKK a new round of denouncements somewhat different from the political opposition to the 1920s order. Practical elites, at first concerned only with punishing the black youths, became obsessed with paroling them, condemning the Klan, and thereby minimizing national criticism and the chance of federal encroachment on race.

Within months of the first Scottsboro trial, over 2,000 written protests had found their way to Montgomery. Rallies were staged as far away as Geneva, Switzerland. "Outside agitators," in the form of the Communist Party, the ILD, the National Committee for the Defense of Political Prisoners (NCDPP), the ACLU, the NAACP, the SDC, and a host of other organizations descended upon the state.[20]

To be accurate, Alabamians who entertained the notion that the state still had much of a good name left to preserve by 1935 were engaged in a form of self-delusion. Nevertheless, a group of loyal Alabamians tried its best to salvage Alabama's reputation. It is noteworthy that the small committee of influential Alabamians who fought hardest for the release of the Scottsboro Boys were dyed-in-the-wool conservatives known for their vehement opposition to the Alabama KKK. Accordingly, condemnation of the Klan became a notable feature of their crusade. Grover Hall and James Chappell, of the *Montgomery Advertiser* and *Birmingham News,* respectively, led the group.

Noted Klan opponents Forney Johnston and the Reverend Henry M. Edmonds were prominent figures, as was Anniston textile magnate Donald Comer, the son of a former governor.[21]

Many members of the elite were on the defensive. Zebulon Judd, dean of Auburn University's school of education, rejoiced when the boys were convicted early, objecting only to the "pestiferous interferences from the outside world." Birmingham columnist John Temple Graves II agreed that the social and economic questions raised by the ILD outweighed the issue of actual guilt or innocence. The *Jackson County Sentinel* openly mused that a wholesale lynching of the boys might be more desirable than Scottsboro's continued toleration of the "filthy insinuations . . . [of] outsiders." Frank Owsley, a history professor at Vanderbilt University, intimated that continued "outside interference" in the Scottsboro affair could only lead to a violent backlash from the Klan. Grover Hall wailed about the "bellow[ing] and stink[ing]" of Communist influence in Scottsboro. Disparaging the mercenary motives of the ILD, Hall wagered that if the cases did not hold organizing potential for the CP, "all children under ten in this hated capitalistic republic could be chloroformed like surplus kittens without exciting a murmur of protest from any Communist agitator."[22]

The transformation of Grover Hall on the Scottsboro question shows how a desire to shield the state from external criticism and from possible federal interference, and to perpetuate the racial status quo at the same time, was connected to resistance to the Klan and the advocacy of parole. For six full years Grover Hall had been an unapologetic proponent of conviction. His *Montgomery Advertiser* had staunchly supported the state's prosecution of the Scottsboro Boys. Then, in a 1937 editorial entitled "Throw Away This Body of Death," Hall suddenly called for a gubernatorial pardon in order to liberate Alabama from further reproach. The following year Hall repeated the plea for clemency, not because the boys were innocent ("for the . . . Scottsboro culprits . . . are [certainly] not innocent"), but because the "reputation in civilized countries of our beloved State of Alabama is worth more than the 'honor' of two 50-cent prostitutes." "This Scottsboro thing," Hall confided to Governor Graves, "has done more to injure Alabama in the public mind, outside of Alabama . . . than any other experience it has had before."[23]

Grover Hall took immense pride in his 1920s war against the Klan—and with good reason. The movement had been quite effective in diminishing the order's membership and political influence. During the 1930s, leading progressives such as Montgomery's Virginia Durr regarded Hall as the panoplied champion of Alabama enlightenment who contrasted starkly with the bigotry of the Klan. Yet Hall's resistance to the order and his search for a Scottsboro pardon were rooted in pragmatism. While damning Klan involvement in the Scottsboro affair, Hall simultaneously expressed his certainty of the boys' guilt, opposed black jury service because the race was "not yet prepared," referred to the defendants publicly as "gorillas" and privately as "fool niggers," and engaged in an advanced form of Alabama xenophobia by deploring "kept agitators" and "outside interferences." Hall worried incessantly about how he could parry outside attacks, pursued a pardon (not to redress an injustice but to rid Alabama of embarrassment), and expressed his complacency with the current state of southern race relations. "In Alabama," he wrote, "Negroes and whites understand how to get along together, but whites elsewhere . . . do not seem to be . . . satisfied with the arrangements."[24]

Hall's practicality was further evidenced by his willingness to trade the rape of "two alley cats . . . on a gondola in High Jackson [County]" for a pardon. He was convinced that the boys were guilty but believed that the preservation of the state's reputation far outweighed in importance any concerns with justice. In addition, Hall retained a strong affection for states' rights and for fiscal conservatives such as Benjamin Miller and Frank Dixon. He opposed the Tennessee Valley Authority (TVA) because, in providing electricity to poor hill-country residents, it threatened to cut into Alabama Power Company profits. He repeatedly attempted to trip Bibb Graves and Hugo Black, Alabama's two leading New Deal liberals.[25]

In 1938, other enemies of the Klan echoed Hall's advocacy of a parole, notably James Chappell and Forney Johnston. Chappell thought the Scottsboro debacle "a curse . . . , a body of death" thrust on an unlucky state by the evil machinations of outside agitators. He also feared that Scottsboro would trigger a Klan backlash and perhaps even more national criticism of Alabama's antediluvian racial customs. Yet Chappell failed to realize that Alabama's prejudices, not "outside" malevolence, were responsible for the state's latest public relations crisis.[26]

Forney Johnston was, unlike Hall and Chappell, a die-hard white supremacist. Many in Alabama considered Johnston tolerant because of his part in Oscar Underwood's historic battle against the KKK. As Underwood's 1924 presidential campaign manager, Johnston had placed the senator's name in nomination with a famous attack on the Invisible Empire. His pursuit of a Scottsboro pardon, though, does little to substantiate the view that he was enlightened. Johnston's personal correspondence illuminates his racial views and motives for seeking a pardon. It shows that Johnston was an unreconstructed bigot and the proprietor of an extreme set of racial attitudes.

Johnston doubted the boys' guilt, but he did not pursue their liberation for reasons approximating justice, equity, or any other abstract principle. His goal was the mercenary retention of state control over race. In a 1938 plea for parole addressed to Governor Graves, Johnston called the prisoners "gorillas . . . , coons . . . , African cro-magnons . . . , scum . . . , tramps . . . , transient trash . . . , convicted morons . . . , [and] chimpanzees." They have "ugly natures . . . , complete ignorance . . . , and are manifestly sub-normal." He wrote:

> These tramps were not citizens of Alabama. They were transient trash from some other commonwealth . . . and the colored race at large. This State owes them no free board . . . , nor is there any reason why the stench of their existence should be perpetuated in the Confederacy when the North yearns for them. Good lord, think of keeping them here to proliferate and exude like cancer cells their sordid jungle reactions in the penitentiary when the benevolent North is baring a bosom for them. . . . The [SDC] did what, so far, has proved an extraordinary job in suppressing the four who were released. They may even succeed in substituting habit and mimicry for the natural reactions of those chimpanzees, though I doubt it. . . . How on earth could the governor miss seeing . . . that he could . . . put this responsibility for their good conduct on the negro race and its organized benefactors. There has been no such opportunity since Father Abraham turned them loose. . . . These tramps were transients when they ran counter to our laws. . . . The State of Alabama should not . . . make itself the perpetual sponsor of these prisoners as if it owed them or the general public a special duty for their basic natures and impulses. . . . [We could be] . . . rid of them as a perpetual problem and a perpetual reminder of a shocking drama, sordid, perplexing and interminable.[27]

Bibb Graves, accustomed to fielding political arguments against the Klan, resisted political requests for a pardon. Things came to a head, though, in late 1938. Grover Hall confronted the governor with the quintessential logic underlying the two-pronged movement that opposed Klan vigilantism and favored a Scottsboro pardon:

> Who cares whether Norris kills Patterson? I don't. Who cares whether Weems picks fights with all and sundry? I don't. Who cares whether Patterson loves long knives and "gal men"? I don't. I don't care if they kill off one another. I don't care what they do—so long as they do it in another State, preferably Ohio and New York. I don't care if they eat one another without benefit of pepper sauce. I do not know whether they are guilty or innocent of the rape of two cut-rate prostitutes. I do not care. What I do care for is . . . that the character of Alabama and its people is at stake before the world and that these moronic beasts are the most expensive guests that Alabama is now entertain-

ing. Give them to other States! . . . If these wretches turn out badly it will not be Alabama's fault. It will redound to the credit of our State if we release them . . . even [if] . . . they turn out badly.[28]

Hall and his allies simultaneously opposed three things: Communist criticism, Klan vigilantism, and the continued imprisonment of the Scottsboro Boys. "Communism is acid stuff," Hall wrote, referring to Scottsboro, "indefensible by any rule of logic. . . . But Ku Kluxism is a poor antidote. . . . Ku Kluxism is a first cousin to Communism. It is neither quite as stupid nor quite as nasty . . . , since it is native and basically patriotic."[29]

Such logic pacified some blacks who might otherwise have become more insistent in their demands for Scottsboro and racial justice. Robert R. Moton, Booker T. Washington's successor as principal of the Tuskegee Institute, strenuously avoided taking a public stand on Scottsboro but cautioned blacks to be on guard against the wicked machinations of "agitators from the outside" who were bent upon "creating ill will and suspicion between the races." The Reverend P. Colfax Rameau, Ph.D., a longtime associate of Birmingham's Big Mules, reassured nervous whites that his people would resist the sirenlike Communist call for social equality. A black African Methodist Episcopal bishop did the same. G. Lake Imes, secretary at Tuskegee and Grover Hall's personal choice to succeed Moton, went even further. He traveled to Kilby Prison to pressure the Scottsboro Boys, unsuccessfully, to fire their northern Communist lawyers in favor of native Alabama counsel. He also assured the Alabama blacks, somewhat incredibly, that "we can look to the white man in the South for justice—it makes me feel proud to be a citizen of Alabama."[30]

THE AFFAIR OF MR. JUSTICE BLACK

Apart from Scottsboro, the single most dramatic episode for Alabama's depression-era KKK actually concerned events that had taken place a decade earlier. The state's embarrassing romance with the KKK was laid bare for national scrutiny in the 1937 appointment of Hugo Lamar Black to the U.S. Supreme Court.

Black's appointment was supposed to be, for President Franklin Roosevelt, an act of sweet revenge. Instead, it became one of his most trying episodes. FDR had suffered embarrassment and frustration when his "court-packing" scheme backfired in 1937. Incensed by growing congressional opposition to his programs, Roosevelt wanted to avoid a repeat performance of the high court's 1935 rejection of the National Industrial Recovery Act. His plan for a batch of additional justices whom he himself would appoint met with widespread criticism, though, and failed in Congress. In selecting Hugo Black to replace a retiring justice, FDR secretly believed that he had painted his conservative southern senatorial antagonists into a corner. As a member of the Senate, Black was virtually certain to be confirmed. As an outspoken New Deal liberal, though, and the author of a wages and hours bill, Black was definitely not a member of the conservative southern "senatorial club."[31]

Black excused himself while his peers considered his appointment. His confirmation was hasty but not uneventful. His peers approved him 63 to 16, but a fistfight was narrowly averted in a Judiciary Committee session when Black's relationship to the Alabama KKK was mentioned. Only six hours of debate ensued, during which Black remained conspicuously silent as other senators swore that he had never been a member of the Klan. As soon as he had been confirmed, Black resigned from the Senate and set sail for Europe with his wife.[32]

While the Blacks retreated across the Atlantic, a scandal of epic proportions broke in the press back home. Ray Sprigle of the *Pittsburgh Post-Gazette* penned a six-piece series setting forth Black's Klan past in full and gory detail. Sprigle, armed with Republican money and several private detectives, had uncovered extensive evidence of Black's involvement in the Alabama KKK. Among other things, he revealed that Black had joined the Klan in 1923 and had resigned in 1925 just prior to his run for U.S. Senate. Technically, Sprigle showed, Black was still a member of the Klan. He had accepted a "grand passport" (an honorary lifetime membership) at a 1926 celebration of the KKK's electoral triumphs in Alabama. Perhaps most damaging was Sprigle's revelation that Black and Bibb Graves had sat mute while Hiram Evans railed against blacks at the 1926 celebration. "There isn't a Negro in Alabama that dares open his mouth and says he believes in social equality," the imperial wizard had crowed. "Any time they propose to produce equality between me and a . . . Negro they are simply going to have to hold a funeral for the Negro."[33]

While Black's relationship to the Alabama Klan was common knowledge among state politicians, it was stunning news to the rest of the country. Affiliation with Alabama's KKK conjured up images of bloody repression at the very time the country was being exposed to the Scottsboro trials and a series of Alabama lynchings. It was unthinkable to many that a member of the U.S. Supreme Court could once have worn the robes of the Ku Klux Klan—and in Alabama of all places.[34]

Paparazzi hounded Black and his wife in Paris and London. Made virtual prisoners in their hotel room, the Blacks (figure 28) booked public passage aboard a New York luxury liner, then slipped back into the States aboard

28. Mr. and Mrs. Justice Black, 1930s. Hugo Black and his wife, Josephine Foster Black, appear uncomfortable as they prepare to embark on a trip. Courtesy *Birmingham News*.

a Norfolk mail steamer. A British tabloid wryly noted that Black had left England "klandestinely." Meanwhile the Blacks met the press in Norfolk with a terse silence. The episode proved a major embarrassment for FDR.[35]

The Black affair rapidly became a public relations nightmare. Critics of the New Deal from the Right, opponents of the Klan from the Left, and shocked moderates damned Black in a variety of dialects. Raymond Moley, a former "brains truster," said that there had been worse appointments, he just could not "remember where or when." Herbert Hoover declared the Supreme Court "one-ninth packed," and Socialist leader Norman Thomas regretted that Black had not "openly and manfully" condemned the Alabama Klan. *Collier's* denounced Black's "sorry betrayal" of FDR and predicted that, as a Supreme Court justice, he could only "embarrass his friends." Pundits dubbed Black's home state "Klalabama," called Washington, D.C., "Ku Kluxville on the Potomac," and joked that the new justice could save money by dying his Klan robes black to sit on the high court. "The true purposes and character of the Ku Klux Klan were well understood when Hugo L. Black first joined, when he resigned, and when he reentered," one editor wrote. "He was not an innocent boy blundering into an evil organization." Catholics bitterly rejected the protest that some of Black's best friends were Catholic and cited the comment of a Southerner about Black's 1921 conduct in defending a Klan gunman who killed a Catholic priest: "Shoot a priest or shoot a 'nigger,' it's all the same in Alabama." [36]

The barrage continued. The *New York Herald-Tribune* accused Black of "deliberate double-dealing," cast aspersions on his character, and lamented that he had forsaken FDR and his fellow senators "because he was afraid to jeopardize his ambition by a single act of common honesty." *Commonweal* demanded his immediate resignation. Another New York editor branded the new justice "a humbug and a coward," while the pro–New Deal *New York Post* mocked Black's claims that he counted Jews and Catholics among his friends: "We might reply in kind that one of our best liberal friends was a Klansman but we still don't think he ought to be on the Supreme Court." The *Boston Post* called on Black to resign by offering their logic that "one who associates with bigots, bids for their support, takes the bigots' oath and then is so craven that he allows his friends in a crisis to deny it all, can't clear himself by asserting it was all contrary to his real character." [37]

Black did gain some support amid the maelstrom of protest. Most of his backing came from three surprisingly different sources: the KKK, President Roosevelt's staunchest New Deal allies, and Alabamians of all stripes—even Black's fiercest erstwhile enemies. While some have argued that Klansmen were not happy with Black's appointment, in fact they were pleased at least initially. Knights noted Justice Black's appointment with pride and extrapolated that the Alabamian had been schooled in the KKK. It was not until later, when Black showed a stronger inclination toward the prevailing ideology of New Deal liberalism, that the KKK disowned him. In fact, in 1937, leading Klansmen were instrumental in trying to conceal his hooded past. Hiram Evans claimed that Black had never been a Kluxer, not even a sympathizer. Black's old KKK friends in Alabama were also loyal. Bibb Graves, who was then in his second gubernatorial term and had just named his wife to Black's vacant Senate seat, admitted that he, himself, had been a member of the order but claimed that he could not recall seeing Black at any Klan functions. "When you quit paying dues, you quit being a member," the governor explained. Birmingham postmaster and future mayor Cooper Green, another former Klansman and an aide to Black, told the same story.[38]

Stalwart New Dealers defended the appointment as much for the president's sake as for Black's. William Allen White, the famed editor of the *Emporia Gazette,* wrote that FDR had hit a "veritable three-bagger" by naming a liberal, a Southerner, and a member of the Senate whom fellow senators could only confirm. Roosevelt himself had been delighted with Black's selection. "They'll have to take him," he rejoiced about his conservative southern enemies in the Senate. As it turned out, FDR was right. "Even 'Cotton Ed' Smith, of South Carolina, who 'God-damned' the nomination all over the place when it was first announced, didn't have the courage to stand up and vote against a fellow Senator from the Deep South," a Roosevelt aide concluded.[39]

Once the Klan scandal broke, some New Dealers continued to stand behind FDR's choice. John L. Lewis of the new Congress of Industrial Organizations (CIO) and Edward Keating, the Irish Catholic editor of *Labor,* defended the appointment. Progressive Nebraska senator George Norris complained that Black was being attacked because he was a vocal New Deal liberal. Harold Ickes acidly returned hostile press questions by quipping, "I really think the greatest expert on the Ku Klux Klan is [former] President Hoover. I refer you to him. He accepted their support [in 1928]. Nobody criticized him." Perhaps *Washington Star* columnist Jay Franklin put it best: "If Hugo L. Black had been a labor-baiter, a trust corporation attorney, a man who had amassed a fortune and achieved political prominence as a result of helping the banks, utilities and corporations to loot . . . Alabama and stifle competition by strong-arm monopolies, he could have engaged in devil-worship . . . , practiced polygamy . . . , hunted down run-away sharecroppers with his bloodhounds, and eaten babies for breakfast, for all that his conservative critics would care."[40]

As a New Deal administrator, an Alabamian, and Black's brother-in-law, Clifford J. Durr had a variety of reasons to support the new justice in his darkest hour. Still Durr, himself a noted champion of civil liberties, allowed his support to become so colored by personal bias that thirty-four years later he was still able to write a pure apologia on Black's behalf. In 1971 and in 1937, Durr defended Black's affiliation with the Klan as "an act of conformity," not an act of "bigotry," and as something that the struggling young attorney did to cater to poor-white working-class clients, "the Union people." Durr's wife, the colorful Montgomery liberal Virginia Foster Durr, defended Black's Klan association in much the same way. Still, joining the KKK was something neither Durr would ever have done, no matter how suffocating the pressure to conform or how intense their political ambition.[41]

The most extraordinary support for Black came, not from old friends, but from old enemies—many of them Alabama's leading opponents of the Klan. Alabama's reflexive xenophobia proved so potent that even confirmed enemies of Black, the KKK, FDR, liberalism, and the New Deal were able to put these "petty" issues aside when the state's good name was in jeopardy. Grover Hall, who had habitually opposed Black and had taken him to task for silently tolerating the KKK, helped Alabamians of all stripes close ranks in the face of an outside attack. Hall and the *Montgomery Advertiser* showed themselves willing to subsume, at least temporarily, their elemental animus for Black, the KKK, and his liberal economic philosophy in order to insulate the state's good name. Hall argued, in his inimitable style, that Black's critics around the country would refuse to "see any good in him [even] if all other human beings regarded him as the greatest law-giver since Moses." Harry Ayers of the *Anniston Star,* a devout adversary of the Klan and a states'-righter, followed suit. John Temple Graves II of the *Birmingham Age-Herald,* another outspoken Klan opponent and a staunch white supremacist, managed to find good in the former Klansman by applauding some of his early dissents in favor of states' rights. Even economic reactionaries and old adversaries of the Klan such as John Bankhead II set aside old differences with Black to close ranks in the face of an outside threat to Alabama's name. So powerful was the defensive urge that old bitter differences vanished like driftwood in a gale.[42]

The fact of the matter, though, is that the pressure on Black was largely pointless. The most virulent criticism might embarrass Roosevelt, but it served no practical purpose. FDR was powerless to remove Black once the Senate had confirmed him. Even if the president had possessed the legal authority to remove Black, it was a political impossibility, given the backlash that he had just suffered for tampering with the Supreme Court. The Senate was also powerless. Impeachment required a criminal act, and as one editor pointed out, being a member of the KKK may have been in bad taste, but it was not illegal.[43]

Bowing to the intense pressure of friend and foe alike, and probably feeling no small debt to the president, Black at last decided to issue a public statement. He chose the medium, method, forum, and format with care. There was no press conference, no media free-for-all, and no uncomfortable questions from an army of aspiring Ray Sprigles. Instead, Black decided on a radio address, thereby removing himself physically from his audience.[44]

The long-awaited event took place on 1 October 1937, before an estimated 85 million listeners, an international radio hookup second only to that assembled for Edward VIII's abdication of the English throne. In the final days before the address, Black remained in total seclusion, working and reworking what he would say with help from no one but Clifford Durr. On the appointed evening Black spoke from a friend's Washington living room. A nervous Franklin Roosevelt arranged to be incommunicado. Black's remarks were brief. He used only eleven of the thirty minutes allotted. He spoke clearly, deliberately, and unapologetically about his relationship with the Ku Klux Klan in Alabama. He admitted to having joined the Klan in 1923 but said that he had resigned in 1925 and had never rejoined. The "grand passport" was honorary and meant nothing. He did not endorse racism or bigotry of any kind. He had a number of Jewish, Catholic, and black friends, and he regarded his Senate record on that score as enough to satisfy any critic. This was to be his first and last statement on the matter. When the address ended, as far as he was concerned, the matter was closed.[45]

Many listeners found Black's statement unsatisfactory to say the least. He admitted a Klan affiliation but failed to apologize for it or even to explain it. Furthermore, he failed to denounce Klan violence or to condemn the KKK's notorious record in Alabama. Black also failed to explain his silence in the Senate and in Europe while friends had made political fools of themselves on his behalf. He did not indicate why he had never informed FDR that there might be a problem. Nor was any resignation offered. In sum, many of his critics were unimpressed. One skeptic called it "too damned clever . . . , the plea of a man caught with the goods."[46] Curiously, the individual who most appreciated Black's address was the Machiavellian Franklin Delano Roosevelt, the man who stood to lose the most from the affair. While FDR's closest advisers gritted their teeth and wrung their hands, the president declared Black's speech "a grand job." "It did the trick," he assured his inner circle, "You just wait and see."[47]

The president was correct again. Three days later, as Hugo Black formally took his seat on the court, a Gallup poll showed that 56 percent of all Americans favored his appointment. Before his speech, the figure had been much lower. Soon after, FDR helped Americans forget the matter by delivering his famous "Quarantine Speech" in Chicago, which hinted at possible American involvement in an imminent world war.[48]

Black's refusal to fill in anything more than the bare outlines of his membership in the KKK paralleled his earlier decision to join the Klan. It was the epitome of political expedience. Hugo Black had never been a racist or a bigot, but he had joined a bigoted organization. It is true that on a few occasions, Black had endured the ire of some of his hooded brethren to speak up for blacks, Jews, and other targets of repression in Alabama. It is also true, though, that Black's mere membership in the order reflected tolerance of prejudice, a closing of his eyes to violence. He had even defended two murderers in court in order to secure popular election so that he could promote his version of political reform. He was also to back reform in the nation's highest court.

To some extent, Black's conduct may have been the product of guilt, expiation, or even retribution. On more than one occasion, he had swallowed his enlightened convictions when faced by the reality of electoral politics in Alabama. His determination to weather all kinds of personal vituperation in 1937 in order to dispense justice from a protected position may have reflected attrition or revenge against the Alabama voters who had long owned his political soul. When FDR tapped him for the Court, Black had been preparing to accede to the Deep South's attitude toward race and federal intervention by voting against the Wagner-Costigan federal anti-lynching bill.[49] For Alabama, the Hugo Black cause célèbre put the state's KKK in a national spotlight even more glaring than Scottsboro.

It should also be noted that Black's subsequent career shocked his critics, alienated most Alabamians, and incensed the KKK. He became one of the brightest lights ever to grace the high court, especially in the field of civil rights. Justice William O. Douglas, himself a legendary figure in the area, predicted that ultimately "none [would] be rated higher" than Black in the realm of civil rights. Alexander Bickel wrote about a "Hugo Black majority" on the court, and legal scholar Tony Lewis observed that "if any member of the Court saw his philosophy become doctrine . . . it was not the Chief Justice [Earl Warren] but Justice Black." The phrase "Mr. Justice Black, dissenting" became a standard in the Alabamian's early years on the court as he consistently pushed his brethren leftward to break new ground in safeguarding civil liberties. He set a record for lone dissents, and he paid a high price at home for his stand. Calhoun County has still not erected a public memorial to its most famous son. Ashland, his hometown, refused to participate in the 1989 celebration of the centennial of Black's birthday.[50]

One of the most regrettable aspects of the Hugo Black affair was the intolerance displayed by some American liberals. In their premature condemnation of Hugo Black's appointment to the Supreme Court, some liberals violated the most fundamental hallmarks of liberalism: tolerance of diversity and dissent. In 1937, Justices Louis Brandeis and Harlan Stone greeted Black's appointment inappropriately. Without first giving Black a chance, Brandeis snubbed him and Stone declared that Black lacked proper legal preparation and could not write. The famed federal judge Learned Hand told the press, Hugo Black "isn't my idea of what a judge is at all."[51] By the time of the 1954 decision in *Brown v. Board of Education,* though, liberals, opponents of the New Deal, and formerly proud Alabama Kluxers had all changed their minds about Hugo Black.

During Black's first few years on the Court, ironically, the KKK was his chief public defender. In 1937, certain that Black would make them proud, Alabama Klansmen delighted in taking liberal critics of the new justice to the woodshed for violating their vaunted birthright of toleration: "Many . . . profess to stand for Americanism and . . . [also] condemn a Klansman because he does not agree with their views. That is not Americanism; that is bigotry and intolerance, prejudice and hatred, and has no place in our country."[52] They might have felt differently if they could have seen the future.

12

The Threat of Urban Radicalism

While the Scottsboro and Hugo Black affairs kept Alabama's KKK in a state of excitement during the 1930s, much Klan activity also centered on Birmingham, a place of intense unrest during the Great Depression. Much of the unrest concerned the arrival of the southern Communist Party headquarters in the city. The Communists set up shop and began publication of their official party organ, the *Southern Worker,* in 1930. They soon had several hundred members on their rolls. Birmingham was especially valuable to the Communist effort in the South and other parts of Alabama because it served as a convenient launching point for organizing drives among south Alabama's impoverished sharecroppers. Affiliated Communist groups such as the International Labor Defense also set up operations in the city, and the Communist Party actually ran candidates for public office in Alabama in 1932 and 1934. Although the party was hopelessly unsuccessful politically, it was able to organize members in Birmingham, especially among workers in the mining and metal industries, and domestic service. The fledgling Communist Party was 80 percent black in Alabama and comprised a number of quite militant, sometimes violent black women in Birmingham.[1]

In a state defined by its xenophobia, communism epitomized an alien threat. "When the Communists entered the Magic City," one historian has written, "they entered a world unaccustomed to 'Reds' outside the pale of mythology." Most Alabamians associated communism with godless atheism, southern European radicalism, or turmoil in the North Carolina textile mills—three decidedly negative reference points for most natives of Alabama.[2] Two northern white Communists—Tom Johnson of Cleveland and Harry Jackson of San Francisco—set up a beachhead in the city with the assistance of an Italian immigrant metal worker named J. J. Giglio. The three soon began to alienate many citizens with their calls for social equality and economic reform.[3]

After passage of the 1935 National Labor Relations Act, Birmingham became a headquarters for other labor organizers as well. The Roosevelt administration had declared Birmingham, for years a bastion of antiunion activity, the city hardest hit by the depression, but after 1935, 50,000 workers, over 67 percent of them black, joined unions such as the United Mine Workers (UMW) and the largely Communist International Union of Mine, Mill and Smelter Workers.[4]

By the end of the decade Birmingham organizers had as many as 3,000 mostly black men on its rolls who were, if not full-fledged members, at least workers willing to give the Communist Party a chance. These workers included a number of black radicals who later became active organizers for the new Congress of Industrial Organizations after the organization's birth in 1935: Hosea Hudson, Andy Brown, Ebb Cox, and Henry O. Mayfield. Famous black Communist Angelo Herndon got his start as an eighteen-year-old home-grown Communist organizer in Birmingham, and fellow black Birmingham Communist Al Murphy built the largely Communist and predominantly black Share Croppers' Union in Alabama's Black Belt.[5] Atlanta's Klan *Kourier,* the Invisible Empire's official organ, named Birmingham Dixie's "hub of alien radicalism." The Communist Party technically signed on about 8,000 Alabamians statewide—actually quite a small number, given the unparalleled economic turmoil that confronted blacks and whites, farmers and workers, during the 1930s.[6]

Birmingham desperately required relief. In an overly optimistic move consistent with the prosperity and conservatism of the 1920s, Birmingham dissolved its welfare department in 1929. Until the depression, Birmingham's community chest had provided for 800 families a year. By 1932, it had to support almost 10,000 persons. Over one-quarter of the city's 108,000 eligible workers were unemployed. Most of those fortunate enough to find work held only part-time jobs at substandard wages. Full-time workers at U.S. Steel made the lordly sum of ten to fifteen cents an hour, usually in the form of scrip redeemable at overpriced company stores. The scene was ripe for a radical alternative.[7]

BIRMINGHAM COMMUNISTS AND THE KKK

The Communist Party entered Birmingham with shrill calls for class solidarity across racial lines, unemployment insurance, relief work, and criticism for Alabama's timeless lack of enthusiasm for funding schools. The *Southern Worker* bruised local sensibilities by rudely rejecting the effort of Jasper Boy

Scouts to relieve depression-era distress by salvaging toys for the needy: "We don't want slop, we want UNEMPLOYMENT INSURANCE!"[8]

The remnants of Birmingham's KKK responded almost instantly with anti-Communist circulars, parades, radio warnings, and violence. Birmingham's Klan, though small, was a vocal and visible force during the decade. Largely because of the Klan, the city became a regular on the ACLU's list of the nation's leading centers of repression, cities where violence was "continuous, not incidental."[9] Without doubt, the component of southern communism that most stirred the blood of Alabama's Kluxers was the Communist pursuit of social equality. In its propaganda and its terror, the KKK consistently cited the Red predilection for racial equality as the radicals' number one offense.[10]

The hooded fixation on social equality was but one more manifestation of southern history's central theme. Class issues were important and related—especially during the Great Depression—but they did not possess the unique ability of race to alter issues. Not only was the racial bogey clear in the Klan reaction to Birmingham's smattering of Communists, it was also plain in the pressure applied by community leaders. The Communist Party, known colloquially as the "nigger party" and a collection of "nigger lovers," endured constant charges that it was spreading a cancerous racial heresy. Internally, the Communist Party, like other attempts at biracialism, wrestled with strong black-white tensions. Most impressive, though, was the ability of the southern race issue to alter, amplify, and regionalize virtually any already controversial issue. During the 1920s, Alabama's KKK had helped make Catholicism, liquor, and nativisim something uniquely southern by magnifying each of these independently controversial issues with a corresponding racial menace. During the depression, Alabama's KKK again regionalized the class threat intrinsic to communism by obsessing over the related threat it presented to race relations.

Klansmen made their position on communism and race crystal clear. From the Klan's headquarters in Atlanta, the imperial wizard Hiram Evans warned Birmingham blacks to stop "breathing [the] hot communistic airs" of racial equality or there would be trouble. "The negroes are made to believe that the communists practice complete racial and social equality," the *Kourier* complained. They "dangle before the ignorant, lustful and brutish negroes . . . a tempting bait . . . that negro men should take white women and live with them, declaring this is their God-given right under a Communist regime." The issue was especially compelling in Birmingham, where four of every five Communists were black. Appearing in 1930 before the congressional Fish committee, charged with investigating communism, John G. Murphy, a Birmingham Klan kligrapp, explained the KKK position unequivocally: "Our organization [is] interested in the [Communist] proposition purely from the fact . . . that they [are] teaching social equality." [11]

Birmingham Klansmen burnt crosses, beat organizers, broke up meetings, and waged a war of attrition and intimidation against the city's Reds as well as any others who might have had loose ties to the Party but were actually more interested in material relief than ideology. On one occasion, local Knights burned white Communist Party organizer Tom Johnson in effigy along with a black congressman. Birmingham's city commission president, former Klansman Jimmie Jones, appeared publicly with robed Knights and police to disperse radical meetings and to quiz individual Communists about their stand on social equality. [12]

Reflexive Klan repression erupted into full-blown community hysteria in the summer of 1931. The occasion for the deterioration was the kidnapping and murder of several young Mountain Brook women by a disturbed black man. During the ordeal, in which the perpetrator carjacked the women's vehicle and held the occupants in the woods for four hours, he occasionally spouted Communist propaganda and swore revenge on the white race for exploiting black labor. Finally, the man shot the three women, killing one. Simmering tensions boiled over and gave way to a summer reign of terror in which Kluxers, police, and corporate enforcers wreaked havoc on the city's black population. Before the outbreak was over, white mobs, with apparent Klan involvement, had burned and bombed black businesses, shot several blacks at random, and assaulted many others. Authorities imposed a 10:00 P.M. curfew for black neighborhoods and arranged for the electric company to extinguish street lights early. [13]

Racial fears were also present in the KKK's anti-Semitism. Business leaders remarked that "Russian Jews of the low intelligence type" comprised the leadership cadre for Alabama's black Communists. Vigilantes forced Rabbi Benjamin Goldstein, a supporter of the Communist ILD, from his post at Temple Beth-or in Montgomery and, eventually, from the state. Threatened with economic boycott and Klan intimidation, Montgomery Jews asked for Goldstein's resignation and condemned "outside interference" in Alabama's racial affairs. Local anti-Semitism was a function of the Klan's broader hatred of Jews in the 1930s, largely stemming from Jewish influence in Hollywood and its relation to race,

> the most putrid and evil smelling business in the United States. . . . The White Slave business is respectable . . . compared to the . . . oceans of filth ladled out by the greasy hawk nosed merchants of Hollywood. . . . The Jews, parasites, filchers, usurers always, have found . . . an ideal vehicle for the coin-

ing of the dirtiest kind of dollars and the pleasurable debauchery of the morals of the young. . . . Competing children of Israel squabble in the garbage
heap of literature for . . . decaying morsels . . . [of] "art." The viler the subject, the better. . . . American youth is being crucified by the Jews through
their movies as surely as they martyred Christ two thousand years ago. You
can't touch a Jew without both losing money and being defiled. . . . Almost
every high official of the Russian Soviet government is Jewish. . . . Jews provide the brains [and] the funds . . . for worldwide communis[m]. . . . [The
film] industry [is] controlled by Jews who with their flashy clothing and
greasy black ringlets stage orgies which have become nationally famous. . . .
Hollywood certainly needs a Hitler! . . . [The] trend . . . is toward . . . building [Negroes] up to social equality. Because the Jews fraternize with the negroes they [think] . . . it is ideal for American white people to do the same
thing, [but] . . . [w]hite Americans are disgusted at moving picture africani-
zation. . . . The only art at which a negro excels is the beating of a "tom-
tom" in the jungle.[14]

Communists and Klansmen in Birmingham actually had more in common with each other than they probably realized. Specifically, they shared
the tendency to overestimate the extent of biracial solidarity in the southern Communist Party.[15] Powerful factors traditionally worked against any
kind of interracial cooperation in the South. Vigilante violence and social
opprobrium exercised powerful external forces, while internal cleavages
constituted another impediment. The *Southern Worker* consistently exaggerated the extent of biracial unity in Birmingham's tiny party in an attempt
to encourage greater solidarity. The paper twisted any remote example of
interracial cooperation into a declaration of perfect black-white unity.
Meanwhile, the Klan also harbored an exaggerated fear of what the Communist Party represented.[16]

The Communist pipe dream of biracial unity remained unfulfilled
largely because of the inertia conferred by the racial division that confronted radicals all over the South. Birmingham factory owners, faced with
the prospect of biracial insurgency from leftists and labor, reminded disgruntled whites, "You may not be making a lot [of money] but you're still
making more than the niggers." Internal divisions in Birmingham were
practically guaranteed by the presence of several former Klansmen in the
city's thin Communist ranks. Because of the economic emergency that
confronted them during the 1930s, a few 1920s Knights shed their robes in
order to join the Communist Party, but they did not abandon ingrained
racist attitudes as easily.[17]

Actually, the exaggeration of biracial unity reduced the party's already
slim chances of succeeding in Birmingham. Incidents suggesting interracial

solidarity, embellished by the *Southern Worker* for maximum effect, further excited a nervous white population. Fearing that their worst racial nightmares were on the verge of coming true, many Alabama whites were willing to grant a freer rein than usual to the Klan. The result was disastrous for Birmingham's few radicals. Klansmen beat, flogged, kidnapped, terrorized, intimidated, and killed Alabama radicals. Much of the abuse was directed toward Birmingham's Communist organizers and was conducted with obvious police and corporate cooperation. The city, already renowned as "bad, bad Birmingham, the murder capital of the world," was, according to watch groups like the ACLU, a place where brutality had soaked into the fabric of the culture. In 1930, Klan terrorists dynamited the house of an Italian-born Communist. Later, hooded thugs kidnapped and beat white Communist leader Tom Johnson and Eugene Braxton, a young black organizer. The KKK, the police, and the Tennessee Coal and Iron Company responded jointly to Communist demands for unemployment insurance by inflicting a series of beatings. Other Klan assaults occurred with the apparent connivance of Birmingham police after Knights had spent days tailing the movements of Red organizers.[18]

Two of the most savage assaults occurred during the summer of 1935. Four members of the White Legion, a Klan-related outfit devoted to the repression of radicals, snatched Robert Wood from a Birmingham street corner. After taking a savage beating on this occasion and on several others, Wood finally left Alabama. Birmingham police beamed their car lights on Blaine Owen moments before vigilantes kidnapped him. The men assaulted Owen and other radicals much as they had Wood, with rawhide whips, blackjacks, and revolvers. Owen, who survived such a beating, recorded the details of his assault in the *New Republic:*

> Smash! It came, though I had known it would come, as a surprise. My lip was numb as I took a deep breath and tried to double up as it came again. This time it caught me on the cheek and I could feel the small surface of a yellow gold ring crushing the skin against the bone. There was a salt taste to the thick blood. . . . A sharp knee dug into my stomach and I gasped . . . I thought I would never again get air into my lungs. . . . "Blaine Owen," he said. "Think you're smart, don't you Blaine Owen." He dragged it out, gloating over the victim, like a jackal. "You've got too much hair you god damn nigger lover." "How do you like this?" he wanted to know, the sound coming choked and jagged from somewhere deep in his throat as a handful of hair was torn out and stuffed into the thick blood clogging of my mouth. . . . "Putting out a god damn Red paper, you low bastard," he said. Again his knee came up sharply and I thought my nose was surely broken this time. . . . I dug my face into my crooked arm [and] watched my white sleeve darken slowly, as the

blood dropped on it from my mouth and nose. I spat more blood and hair onto the sleeve and the floor before his heels dug into my head . . . the scalp coming off on the sharp corner of the leather.[19]

The assaults followed a formula: surveillance, abduction, beating, the drive to a lonely spot, more beating, and warnings to keep quiet, leave town, and stop stirring up blacks—all on pain of death. Ample evidence exists to implicate the Birmingham police, company guards, the White Legion, and the KKK. Communists also feared the police department's "Red Squad" and a corporate goon squad directed by private detective Milt McDuff. So organized was the campaign of antiradical repression that Klansmen from time to time bragged openly about their collusion with police and corporate guards. Antiradical violence also took place in Mobile, Montgomery, Huntsville, and Tuscaloosa.[20]

It is difficult to argue that the Communists did not receive fair warning. The KKK did everything in its power, including taking out local advertisements, to warn those who insisted on challenging the bounds of social equality. "Communism will not be tolerated. . . . Ku Klux Klan Rides Again," read one flyer that robed Knights distributed on Birmingham's street corners. An accompanying sketch depicted a Reconstruction-style Kluxer on horseback. "Negroes Beware. Do not attend Communist meetings," another leaflet cautioned. "Paid organizers for the communists are only trying to get negroes in trouble." During one anti-Communist parade through Birmingham's black neighborhoods, 500 Klansmen distributed the following warning: "Foreign and Northern agitators are in Birmingham teaching social equality among whites and blacks. Alabama laws guarantee the supremacy of the white race by prohibiting mixed marriages. A vast majority of Southern Negroes know that social equality doctrine is 'bad business' and are advising their friends to leave alone the Communists and their like. The agitators should be sent to the North, or to Russia. See that they go!"[21] Alabama Klansmen sent one threat directly to ILD headquarters in New York. "You Negroes are invited to Alabama," it read. "We want your scalp[s] along with the nine [Scottsboro Boys] we already have."[22]

Klan, police, and corporate violence plagued Birmingham during the 1930s, making it one of the most notorious antilabor scourges in America. Phalanxes of policemen and Klansmen routinely and violently dispersed Communist meetings. Arrests and vigilante violence were frequent and often overlapped. Kluxers distributed counterfeit notices calling off Communist meetings or supplying incorrect locations. As white Communist Party presidential candidate William Foster prepared to visit Birmingham in 1932, he received a chilling Klan notice. "Your presence in Birmingham,

Alabama . . . is not wanted. Send nigger Ford." The threat referred to James Ford, his black running mate and an Alabama native. On May Day 1933, Klansmen, White Legionnaires, and Birmingham police fought a pitched street battle with 3,000 hunger protesters. At Communist-led gatherings the next day, several black women asked organizers when the next rally would be so that they could "whup them a cop."[23]

Things got even worse in 1935. Police and vigilantes used teargas and clubs to break up a solidarity march of Communists and union miners on behalf of striking black women. Vigilantes assaulted white Communist Boris Israel twice and beat a black member of the Young Communist League (YCL) so badly that he nearly died. Birmingham police slew a black youth, and an off-duty policeman shot and killed a black man in an Ensley café as "a prank." Police and Klan-like vigilantes arrested and beat a number of black Communists, male and female. One organizer was beaten three times. In closed-door sessions that often lasted for hours, they employed blackjacks, leather straps, clubs, and rubber hoses to beat the radicals into repeated spells of unconsciousness. Black Communists Clyde Johnson and Helen Longs were two such victims. Antiradical toughs and police beat them into periodic senselessness while quizzing them all night about radical activities. Whenever the pair came to, the beatings would resume until they blacked out again. When a black New York Communist arrived to investigate, vigilantes flogged him into unconsciousness.[24]

The collaborative nature of KKK, police, and corporate "establishment violence" was apparent in the conduct of public officials. Commission president Jimmie Jones, a card-carrying member of the American Federation of Labor (AFL) and a former Klansman, dispersed Communist rallies flanked by Klan advisers. When Birmingham Klansmen burned crosses, marched, and issued threats against a black congressman's visit, the city commission publicly backed the sheeted group in the interest of preserving white supremacy.[25]

Perhaps Birmingham's most notorious form of antiradicalism was the Downs Ordinance. The measure, sponsored by city police commissioner William O. Downs, called for the fining and imprisonment of persons possessing more than one copy of a "radical publication." The law, ostensibly aimed at publications advocating the forcible overthrow of constituted government, allowed authorities to terrorize almost anyone. A former Jefferson County sheriff and Klan cyclops, Downs was undoubtedly influenced by the reactionary Klan attorney Horace Wilkinson, who had been a political mentor for him and for Jones. Yet the former Klan political strategist and legal gun distanced himself from distractions such as the KKK during the 1930s in order to protect his hold on city politics and patronage.[26]

The Downs Ordinance was par for the Wilkinson-controlled city commission of the 1930s. An ultraconservative body, it rejected federal relief, somehow managed to operate in the black during the unprecedented economic crises of 1932–1933, and outlawed bread lines because they were "unseemly." The commissioners—Jones, Downs, and Lewey Robinson—insisted on practicing a policy of fiscal economy and lethal retrenchment and remained seemingly oblivious to the depression even during its darkest days.[27]

The ordinance allowed police and vigilantes to run amuck. Klansmen and police assaulted one black three times on the pretext of searching his home for radical material. Sixteen Klansmen burst into the home of one militant black, briefly searched for literature, then stripped and flogged his two grown daughters. Authorities supplemented the ordinance with vagrancy arrests and gained a steady stream of friendly hearings in Judge H. B. Abernathy's Ensley courtroom. Angelo Herndon, the Atlantan who became perhaps the most famous black Communist of the 1930s, was arrested for radicalism for the first time in Alabama.[28]

In 1935, beleaguered Reds received a backhanded assist from the unlikeliest of sources. When state lawmakers copied the Downs ordinance, *Dothan Eagle* editor Julian Hall defended the right to free speech. Grover's nephew, Julian Hall wrote in large letters on the front page of his newspaper, "We advocate the overthrow of Alabama's government by violence. We urge the citizens to arm themselves with shillalahs, set out to Montgomery and whale hell out of the members of the Alabama legislature." "After these ex-statesmen are thoroughly subdued," the younger Hall continued, "we advocate that the government of Alabama be changed from a so-called democracy to one of communism. Blood will be shed, of course, but capitalism and the curse of private profits must be destroyed." The authorities did not arrest Hall, of course, but the editorial received national attention.[29]

One of the greatest ironies of the congressional Fish committee hearings on radical activity, held in several cities during the 1930s, was the plaintive wail in Alabama for federal assistance to fight communism. The congressmen—who interviewed Klan members, corporate leaders, Birmingham's police chief, and a special state investigator—heard a surprising cry for federal help from Birmingham. Like a number of other states'-rights enthusiasts, Alabamians most strictly adhered to the doctrine when it served their interests.[30]

One of the most troubling aspects of Birmingham's antiradical terror was its official and composite character. The mosaic of forces lined up against Birmingham's radicals made it difficult, if not impossible, to distinguish between Klan terror, corporate repression, antilabor violence, and police brutality. All of these interests worked in concert for the same general objective, preservation of the political, economic, social, and racial status quo.

At one time or another during the 1930s, Birmingham's KKK, TCI, AFL, American Legion, city police, and county deputies worked in concert to thwart communism. One local klavern held its meetings in the local AFL hall, seemingly under the auspices of the more conservative branch of labor. Editors of the *Southern Worker* deplored AFL "prostitutes" and their "bastard sheet," the *Birmingham Labor Advocate*, for its treason against true working-class insurgency, blasted TCI's "reign of persecution" as unparalleled in the country, and charged that the subsidiary of U.S. Steel virtually "owned the city." Big Mule industrialists employed African American spies to infiltrate Communist Party cells and hired Milt McDuff's notorious detective agency. Jefferson County's sheriff made "more money than the President of the United States" by commissioning company guards as county deputies. TCI guards pistol-whipped miners who handed out Communist leaflets. The miners' head wounds had to be stitched. "We don't need to call the police to run you bastards out of the county," one guard/deputy boasted. "We are better shots than the police."[31]

Police and Klan terror was even more overt than TCI's. They raided the homes of suspected Communists separately and together, uniformed and not. Kluxers helped police arrest Communists for vagrancy, relying on Judge H. B. Abernathy to sentence offenders to a year on a chain gang. City police chief Fred McDuff and G. C. Giles, his chief detective, assured radicals that they would be arrested for vagrancy every ten days until they left the state. At one vagrancy trial, Klan members loitered in the courthouse hallways and promised bystanders that "if this jury fails to convict these [five] Red bastards, we will convict them with a gun." Releasing four black Communists from the Birmingham jail, a police sergeant warned: "You Goddamn niggers get out of that gate and get out of town. You damn Reds better not be caught in Birmingham any more. If you do, it will not be good for you."[32]

Several vignettes provide a sample of KKK/police collaboration in depression-era Birmingham. Three police officers and thirteen Klansmen went on a rampage that targeted the homes of at least four black Communists. The men ransacked homes in search of radical literature and mercilessly beat their occupants. Failing to find one suspected Communist at home, the vigilantes satisfied themselves by beating two women and threatening another "dirty black bitch" with violence. Capturing and beating Steve Simmons, the vigilantes lectured him: "You Goddamn black nigger, you know you can't have social equality in this country. We ought to kill you, you black sonofabitch." In 1935, robed Knights "arrested" one black radical for transporting thirty gallons of liquor by automobile, an action supported by Police Commissioner Downs. In the ensuing controversy over the matter, Birmingham's police chief suspended Officer T. E. Lindsey for taking part in the Klan raid. The chief suspended the patrolman a second time, along with another officer, when they were wounded by a shotgun blast in another 1935 Klan raid on Steve Simmons's home. Despite the suspension, Police Commissioner Downs publicly defended the joint KKK/police action. When rumors circulated that the Klan planned to "shoot up" a Communist rally, eighty Birmingham policemen "safeguard[ed]" the blacks who attended by forcing them to walk a gauntlet of rifles, pump guns, and mounted machine guns. A week later, sixty Klansmen disrupted a Communist-sponsored rally at a black theater by pelting the stage with stink bombs. As cooperation between Klansmen and police proliferated, some Birmingham Knights gloated about their joint crusade against communism. An even greater public relations faux pas occurred in 1938 when Jefferson County's sheriff-elect twice lamented that Klan numbers were dwindling and wondered aloud how police would now "get things done."[33]

Klan vitality against urban radicalism encouraged imitation, most notably from the White Legion. The Legion, described by contemporaries as a "Birmingham section of the Klan . . . in modern dress" and a "rechristened Ku Klux Klan," apparently enjoyed official sanction. White Legionnaires held their meetings in the Jefferson County courtrooms of Judges H. B. Abernathy and Romaine K. Boyd, publicly supported Commissioner Downs and his sedition ordinance, backed Bibb Graves's second run for governor, and generally operated with the "approval of [Birmingham's] political powers." Before one May Day rally, Birmingham police announced that they had 1,500 White Legionnaires prepared to assist them. Legionnaires indulged in antiradical vigilantism along with their Klan brethren, supported legislation to prevent attorneys who were not natives of Alabama from "embarrassing our courts" by representing Alabamians, and backed a measure to ban the employment of teachers who were sympathetic to communism or atheism.[34]

During the 1920s, Alabama's KKK had several times united with labor unions in temporary political coalition against the Big Mules and planters. The broad-based Klan had also furnished much of Bibb Graves's backing for his program of reform. The 1930s Klan, and its spiritual cousins such as the Legion, were a smaller, more cohesive, and more militant group that was not as interested in unseating the oligarchy or in supporting reform. Its members, some of them AFL members, targeted Communist unions and the racially inclusive CIO along with any other perceived threat to the racial status quo. Robert S. Gulledge, director of the White Legion, embodied the close connections between anti-CIO vigilantes and the KKK. He was a former strikebreaker from Gastonia, North Carolina and the Kentucky coal mines, as well as a kleagle in the Alabama KKK.[35]

Birmingham's black radicals did not sit on their hands while Klansmen, Legionnaires, company detectives, and police tormented them. The Communists distributed their own handbills warning Kluxers and police to "keep their filthy hands off our brothers." Steve Simmons, a black Communist from north Birmingham, survived three Klan assassination attempts and routed two of the hooded mobs with a shotgun.[36]

Black resistance to the Klan, it should be noted—and for that matter the militancy of lone Jews, Catholics, and poor whites—antedated the arrival of the Communist Party in Birmingham. Acts of resistance were usually isolated and more a product of personal resolve than of concerted action or a general feeling of radical solidarity. Alabama's tradition of black and white physical resistance to the KKK hearkened back to Reconstruction. Still, more than any other factor including social opprobrium and internal factiousness, Klan terror was the single most important thing in stunting the growth of Birmingham's Communist Party.[37]

Another reason the Communist Party failed to take off in the American city hardest hit by the depression was the almost uncanny ability of Party organizers to alienate virtually everyone in the South—even people who might have been able to tolerate it. The *Southern Worker* attacked, at one time or another during the decade, FDR, the New Deal, the AFL, the CIO, the UMW, the CIC, socialists, liberals, Samuel Leibowitz, Alabama interracialists, the federal government, the black press, Clarence Darrow, Arthur Garfield Hays, the ACLU, and the NAACP. The state AFL, in particular, responded to Communist criticism by resorting to racist condemnation of the radicals. The *Birmingham Labor Advocate* called the Communists agitators who "openly preach social equality for the Black race" and declared that "any man who seeks to disturb the relations between the races is a dangerous character and should be squelched NOW."[38]

Birmingham's Communists almost guaranteed their own failure by attacking the most sympathetic groups they could find. This excessive suspicion alienated southern liberals and labor unionists of both colors. It also increased the isolation of Alabama's few Communists, making them even easier prey for the KKK.[39]

Eventually Birmingham's embattled Communists realized that, while their calls for social equality appealed to the city's depressed black working class, their traditional impiety did not. By 1936 Birmingham's Communist Party, feeling the sting of the Klan whip regularly, appealed to the South's endemic religiosity. Remarkably, a drawing of Jesus Christ appeared in the July issue of the *Southern Worker* along with a caption that sought to infuse some of the inherently socialistic elements of Christianity with regional religious preferences. The editors cleverly used a sketch of Christ to create a wanted poster replete with the following caption:

Jesus Christ. WANTED—For Sedition, Criminal Anarchy, Vagrancy and Conspiring to Overthrow Established Government. Dresses poorly, said to be a carpenter by trade, ill nourished, has visionary ideas, associates with common working people, the unemployed and bums, Alien—believed to be a Jew—ALIAS "Prince of Peace," "Son of Man" "Light of the World" etc. Professional agitator, red beard, marks on hands and feet the result of injuries inflicted by angry mob of respectable citizens and legal authorities.[40]

RADICALISM AND THE KKK
IN OTHER ALABAMA CITIES

Birmingham was not the only city in Alabama in which radicals were suppressed during the 1930s. Montgomery featured a social climate that, if it did not actively encourage Ku Kluxism, did nothing to discourage it. The city was older and sleepier than Birmingham, and it lacked the industrial city's almost frenetic pace of change. The few Communist meetings that took place were small underground affairs among blacks and white intellectuals, unlike Birmingham's provocative open air meetings. As the state capital, though, Montgomery was Alabama's logical political center and a bastion of old patrician opposition to the Klan. Whites addressed blacks as "boy" or "girl." Some Catholics, Jews, and Greeks enjoyed the warmth of southern culture without ever feeling completely accepted. Religious and ethnic minorities bore the monikers of "Yankees, outsiders, [and] damn Yankees." Montgomerians addressed one local Jew, albeit affectionately, as "the foreigner" even though he had lived in the city for over thirty years. "We stood somehow not altogether as 'white folks,' but between black and white," a Montgomery Jew remembered years later. He added that Montgomery's ubiquitous prejudice was milder than the raw bigotry he experienced in some northern cities.[41]

Two other factors probably limited KKK activity in Montgomery. As the urban center of a predominantly agrarian area, it suffered less from the traumas of the 1930s than industrial Birmingham. The city also featured an eclectic oasis of philosophical, literary, and social intercourse in its Unity Club. The club, confined to fifteen influential and semipermanent members, was an extraordinary gathering in which liberals such as Clifford Durr and

Gould Beech associated with moderate Charlie Dobbins and the more conservative Grover Hall and Marion Rushton.[42]

In spite of its relative insulation, Montgomery was not completely immune to the Red hysteria of the 1930s. After the shooting of three Mountain Brook girls by a deranged black radical, Montgomery succumbed to a wave of insurrection panic reminscent of antebellum days. As Klan backlash spread southward, rumors circulated in Montgomery that carloads of blacks were approaching the city with stockpiled weapons and dynamite. Klan activity followed the hysteria. The KKK was also visible at Bibb Graves's second inaugural in 1935 and in the neighboring hamlet of Prattville, which boasted several hundred new Knights by the end of the decade.[43]

Montgomery's blacks were used to dealing with the Klan. The city achieved national prominence, of course, during its 1950s boycott of segregated municipal transportation, but the famous bus boycott had deep roots. Black community leaders cultivated an indigenous aptitude for economic boycotts as early as 1919. During one outbreak of sheeted activity following World War I, Montgomery blacks had responded to several lynchings by organizing a boycott of newspapers, insurance companies, and other white-owned businesses. The pattern repeated itself during the 1920s. During the depression, blacks boycotted a merchant's store after he beat a young black boy with a hoe for drinking out of a whites-only water fountain.[44]

Mobile also saw some Klan activity during the 1930s. The port city was the site of a number of state Klan meetings and the home of several active lodges. Hiram Evans spoke at a state klorero in Mobile as did a number of other sheeted luminaries. Bowing to a local antimasking ordinance, Klansmen conducted their state parade unmasked. A KKK representative, speaking in Mobile, praised area dens for keeping the African American "in his place" and described the Invisible Empire's struggle with communism in life-and-death terms. "The lines are drawn," he told a rapt audience of Mobile Kluxers, "and the KKK will either run communism out of the country or will be run out by the Communists."[45]

While 1930s Klansmen mostly engaged in rhetorical exercises in Mobile and Montgomery, the scene in Tuscaloosa was far more serious. Controversy began in the summer of 1933 when police arrested three blacks for the rape and murder of a twenty-one-year-old white woman. The ILD immediately sent attorneys to Tuscaloosa, but Judge Henry B. Foster sought to coerce two of the three defendants into firing their Communist lawyers. One defendant, Dan Pippen, Jr., refused. Judge Foster, a confirmed opponent of labor, engaged in questionable conduct during the following weeks. Despite Pippen's protests, the judge refused to allow ILD lawyers to represent the blacks. The local KKK, already quite active, quickly gained momentum. Rumors circulated that the "communist Jew" attorneys would be lynched by the Klan. Fearing for their lives, disguised ILD attorneys eluded angry Knights under cover of the night with the help of militiamen. A Tuscaloosa mob, with apparent police and Klan complicity, attacked the three black defendants, killing two, including Pippen. One of the three—shot, beaten, and burned alive—somehow survived. In Birmingham, Communist speakers levied murder charges against Judge Foster, Tuscaloosa County's sheriff, and several deputies for allegedly handing the defendants over to the Klan.[46]

White Tuscaloosa—already up in arms because of what it perceived as black rape, murder, insolence, and the unwarranted intrusion of outside agitators—exploded. A Citizen's Protective League, with apparent KKK involvement, ran wild. Vigilantes destroyed black homes, churches, and businesses, attacked individual African Americans with impunity, prevented blacks from voting, and forced them to vacate homes that were "too good for niggers." A climax was reached when vigilantes descended upon Dennis Cross, an eighty-four-year-old semiinvalid, took him from his sickbed and lynched him on a golf course for the rape of a retarded white woman. Afterward, a white undertaker received a call informing him that "there's a dead 'nigger' down the road. You'd better [go] pick him up." Curiously, Cross had been slated to testify in a murder trial involving a white love triangle. A subsequent investigation by the Alabama Inter-racial Council concluded that he had been "completely innocent" of the rape.[47]

The Tuscaloosa outbreak illustrated the essentially cyclical relationship between Klan violence, Alabama's xenophobia, and public toleration of the order. After the triple lynching, Communists in Alabama appealed to President Roosevelt and the Justice Department. Calls for federal intervention were amplified by northern appeals for justice that were accurate about the heinous nature of Klan violence but not quite as diligent in analyzing problems outside the South in matters of civil liberties. The partly chauvinistic criticism alienated many Southerners, including some who genuinely abhorred Klan terror. One Pennsylvanian complained to Governor Graves about Alabama's "unprotected environments" in which any black could fall victim to the KKK. "Prejudice, race hatred and everything that is bad applies to the State of Alabama," the Pennsylvanian wrote as he informed Graves that Northerners considered Alabama to be the worst state in the Union for "mob violence . . . , lynching," and the "K.K.K. and other clans." He proposed that Alabama solve its problems by educating its "illiterate white people down there who have no more conscious [sic] than some kind of a wild animal" and advised the governor to direct the education campaign to protect his own name "even if you don't care what happens otherwise."[48]

A number of Alabamians responded to the criticism by combating Klan vigilantism. Realizing that blatant Klan violence would bring the state more harm than good, and fearing the prospect of federal intervention, a group of loyal Alabamians condemned the KKK. Denunciation of the Tuscaloosa tragedies brought further condemnation of the sheeted order, but the Communists were almost universally blamed for "stirring up" Tuscaloosa's citizenry. Alabama's attorney general had virtually predicted the Tuscaloosa affair by warning ILD lawyers not to agitate Klansmen and locals. "If you step beyond certain bounds," he had warned the lawyers, "I do not know how you will be treated. No one can tell what will happen."[49] Tuscaloosa's KKK reacted differently from many Alabama elites. It stridently defended its actions, condemned the "meddling . . . , arrogant . . . Jew lawyers" of the ILD, and invested in community support by delivering Christmas baskets to Tuscaloosa's needy.[50]

Elite and folk elements were evident in Tuscaloosa's acquiescence to Klan terror. Dr. J. R. Steelman, a sociology professor at the University of Montevallo, visited Tuscaloosa a year after the three lynchings to investigate the outbreak. Steelman, who held advanced degrees from the University of North Carolina and Vanderbilt University, was shocked to find himself accosted in his hotel room at midnight by a band of fifteen Klansmen. The party demanded to know Steelman's business, accused him of being a Communist agitator, searched his luggage for radical literature, and expressed concern that he might be a "Community-ist" upon discovering that he carried with him a student paper on the New Deal. The Klansmen were disappointed to learn that Steelman was a native Southerner and an Alabama professor, credentials that hardly qualified him as an "outside agitator." Determined not to release their prey prematurely, the group phoned Judge Henry Foster twice in the wee hours of morning. When Foster, who may have been somehow associated with the local KKK, reassured the Knights, they adjourned to the street for further deliberations. A furious Steelman, still clad in his nightclothes, caught up with the Kluxers near a rail depot and lectured them on tolerance. Forty masked Klansmen, in clear violation of the state antimask law, searched Steelman's car while two uniformed policemen lounged in plain view. Before he left town, Steelman learned that Tuscaloosa's KKK included city police and county deputies, that virtually no official protection had been afforded blacks during the 1933 terror, and that Dennis Cross had indeed been innocent of the rape for which he had been murdered. Meanwhile, newspapers around the state derided the KKK as "a hooded band . . . of outlaws" and pleaded for stricter law enforcement locally.[51]

Professor Steelman admitted that he could not account for the KKK's ability to flourish openly in a university town that might have been expected to be an oasis of enlightened thinking. He identified racial fear and insecurity as the linchpins for official toleration of the Klan and warned, "Unless the Tuscaloosa community overcomes its present hysteria and learns how to view the race problem with more sanity and balance, it is in danger of being stigmatized in the eyes of the nation."[52]

The same xenophobia that Alabamians used to discredit "outside agitators" in the 1960s was exploited with frightening efficiency during the 1930s. The charge was part of a persistent theme that allowed privileged Alabamians to block attempts at biracial politics in the 1870s and 1880s, Populist reform in the 1890s, later black-white labor organization, communism and the CIO in the 1930s, and civil rights during the 1950s and 1960s. Constant reference to the perils of "outside agitation" served an important and powerful purpose for these privileged white Alabamians from Reconstruction onward. For many plainer whites, the charge amply justified vigilante violence against biracial threats.

THE GELDERS INCIDENT

No event during the 1930s more clearly illustrated the connections between community acquiescence, xenophobia, and the persistence of Klan terror than the 1936 flogging of Joseph Gelders. Ironically, the Klan was not directly or discernibly involved in the attack. Yet it was part and parcel of a systematic campaign of terror waged against Alabama's urban radicals, a campaign for which the KKK claimed principal responsibility.

Alabama's criticism of the Gelders assault also transcended any other 1930s episode, but it did not ultimately produce concrete results. The Gelders case contained wrinkles that probably contributed to the volume of Alabama's outpouring of sympathy for the victim. Joseph Sydney Gelders, unlike most victims, was not black and was not technically an outside agitator. He was a homegrown Communist, born and bred in Birmingham. He had taught physics for six years at Alabama's beloved state university in Tuscaloosa. His Jewish lineage and creed, though, and of course his affinity for Marxism, afforded the basis on which he could have been regarded as an alien. For pure brutality and notoriety, the Gelders flogging was unmatched. In 1935, Gelders had moved to New York City to assume the secretaryship of the Communist-affiliated National Committee for the Defense of Political Prisoners. He returned to Birmingham in 1936 to oversee NCDPP operations locally and, specifically, to lobby for the release of a Communist with tuberculosis who was serving time for possessing radical literature. Gelders traveled to Bessemer, along with two area ministers, but was the only member of the delegation whom the mayor refused to see. An old school chum, working in the Bessemer district attorney's office, warned Gelders that vigilante elements were threatening to take his life.[53]

Late on the evening of 24 September 1936, as Gelders returned to his Southside home, three men attacked him. The first assailant slugged Gelders from behind with a blackjack. When the Communist turned to defend himself, two other men joined the attack. The trio quickly overpowered Gelders and loaded him into a nearby car. As they drove sixty miles to Chilton County, Gelders's attackers beat him, kicked him in the face, and cursed him as a "damned radical" and a "nigger lover." The assault became so vicious that several times the abductors checked Gelders's pulse to see whether he had died. Eventually, he feigned unconsciousness to avoid more beating. Eighteen miles west of Clanton, Gelders's assailants stopped to refuel and to rendezvous with a fourth individual. When a curious bystander got too close to the car, one of the men removed a hat shielding Gelders, pointed to his bloody and disfigured face, and said, "Look at that, ain't that a mess?" A few miles later the four men stopped the car, removed their prisoner, stripped him to his socks and underwear, and beat him with a belt, a blackjack, a baseball bat, and the automobile's running board. The flogging was so severe that Gelders suffered two black eyes, a broken nose, swelling of the head, a ruptured heart muscle, and assorted welts, bruises, and lacerations. He also lost several teeth. Later, authorities found a sawed-off baseball bat with Gelders's hair still attached to it. Sometime during the ordeal Gelders blacked out but not before the men threatened to "fill him full of lead" if he reported the flogging or stayed in Alabama. When he came to, Gelders crawled to a nearby farmhouse. A Maplesville doctor, apparently cowed by the local Klan, refused to treat him, but Gelders finally persuaded a farmer to drive him to the hospital in Clanton.[54]

Initially, Alabama reaction was impressive. Governor Graves phoned Gelders at Clanton, sent two state bodyguards, and held a meeting with Birmingham detectives, county deputies, and Joseph Gelders himself, who had left the hospital against his doctor's orders. The governor also announced a reward of $200, assigned a state detective to the case, and assured the press: "We want to get to the bottom of this thing. . . . Gelders is a human being. They can't get away with those things in this state."[55]

National criticism was overwhelming. Revolted by Alabama's repeated Ku Klux violations of civil liberties, editors and social critics cut loose. New York's ILD headquarters and the Communist-led Workers' Defense

League filed official protests. Arthur Garfield Hays announced a $500 reward from the ACLU. The *New Republic* called Alabama "hysterical and reactionary." Numbers of ordinary Americans, disgusted by Scottsboro, the KKK, and a myriad of vigilante assaults, branded the state "appalling . . . backward . . . , a disgrace . . . , a refuge for thugs and criminals . . . , [and] a barbaric, medieval state where free men can no longer walk safely [or] . . . express a critical opinion." Gelders, himself, ruefully admitted that he had come back to Alabama because "civil liberties ha[d] been more ignored [in the state] than anywhere else in the country."[56]

The attack could not have occurred at a worse time for Alabamians concerned about federal intrusion into race relations. Debate over the Wagner-Costigan antilynching bill was reaching a crescendo in Washington. With this threat to home rule in the background, the most prominent Alabamians denounced the assault almost with one voice. Grover Hall called it "one of the most bestial, outrageous affairs in the long history of Alabama." The *Mobile Press* declared that Alabama was "not going to have its good name blackened by would-be Fascists." James Chappell, in a *Birmingham News* editorial entitled "It Can't Happen Here," said that "only by showing the world that it is utterly and thoroughly opposed to floggings [will] . . . Alabama ever be able to lift its head in pride." Chappell also warned that the attack would become a rallying point for more outside agitation and perhaps even federal interference. A cartoonist for the *Birmingham Age-Herald* published a sketch of Gelders's floggers trampling on civil liberties that found currency around the nation, and Birmingham's chief of detectives expressed his determination to oppose organized vigilantism. "I don't care who they are or what organization they may belong to," G. C. Giles told the press with obvious reference to the KKK. "If I get my hands on them I'll leave no stone unturned to . . . guarantee their conviction. It is a form of cowardice I have hated all my life." As a native Southerner who well knew the region's hypersensitivity to criticism from the outside world, Joseph Gelders let it be known that he wanted investigation and arrest by Alabama police, prosecution by Alabama attorneys, and conviction by an Alabama jury.[57]

State calls for swift justice had a powerful and pacifying effect—indeed almost a hypnotic one—on outside critics. An optimistic ACLU related its pleasure at the state's response. The *New Republic,* bastion of liberal New York opinion, concurred. Its editors heaped lavish praise on Alabama's press and elites for their stern posture and publicly apologized for having insinuated that Alabama had historically let vigilantes off easy.[58]

Back in Alabama, though, that was exactly what was happening. City police and county deputies dragged their feet at first, then actively worked to cover up the affair. Detective chief G. C. Giles, who had publicly expressed his determination to punish vigilantism, confided that he did not "expect too much enthusiasm" out of his own men because of Gelders's radical political orientation. He also privately admitted that he was opposed to arresting the radical's assailants even though he knew exactly who they were. Instead, he recommended "a good talking to." State detective James H. McClung, apparently the only law enforcement officer involved who was actually interested in prosecution, ran into stone walls whenever he tried to secure local police cooperation. A Birmingham gasoline salesman gave police the license plate number of an individual he had seen throwing away Gelders's wallet and a sawed-off baseball bat; he was told to forget about the information. Frustrated, he took the information to county deputies but received the same response. Birmingham police chief Luther Hollums and police commissioner W. O. Downs met privately with TCI's chief of security. After the meeting, Walter J. Hanna—a state militia captain, a close friend of Hollums, and a prime suspect in the flogging—kept a noticeably lower profile.[59]

The posture of state law enforcement was matched by Alabama elites. Birmingham businessmen met—not to track down Gelders's assailants but to organize resistance against "outside agitators." Grover Hall, the recipient of a Pulitzer Prize and a prominent opponent of the Klan, kept mum about the secret corporate effort even after Virginia Durr had brought it to his attention. Evidence mounted that those responsible for the attack had close ties to TCI, but Victor Hanson's *Birmingham News* defended the steel giant from complicity and reminded readers that TCI had recently pumped $31 million into the Birmingham District. TCI's attorney, allegedly a former beneficiary of Klan political support, issued the dubious disclaimer that the steel company had no private detectives or labor spies on its payroll, then lectured national critics on the sanctity of states' rights. The climax came when two separate grand juries refused to hand down indictments despite a mountain of evidence implicating two TCI agents and state guardsmen. Jefferson County solicitor George Lewis Bailes, a former Klansman, virtually guaranteed that the jury would not indict when he deliberately sabotaged his own prosecution. During his presentation Bailes ignored the assault and instead stressed that Gelders was a Jew, a Communist, and a supporter of the Scottsboro Boys. A grand juror later admitted that Bailes's efforts had been critical, as had the jury's belief that Gelders was "an agitator." Birmingham and Selma editors quietly endorsed the jury's failure to return indictments by reasoning that most of Alabama wanted the case closed anyhow. Bibb

Graves himself ended the matter decisively by ignoring Gelders's pleas for a special state or federal prosecutor to replace the conniving local solicitor—and by declaring that there would be "no outside lawyers."[60]

The sour fruit of Alabama's tolerance of vigilantism brought the federal intrusion that many citizens had feared in the first place. The experience, like most instances of federal interference, reinforced Alabama's conviction that Klan and vigilante violence had to be curbed if federal encroachment was to be avoided. In 1937—exasperated by the actions of local police, prosecutors, and Governor Graves—Joseph Gelders abandoned his hope of having Alabama achieve an in-state conviction and appealed to the federal government for help. For Gelders, the final straw came when Graves responded to his assertion that George Bailes was "a babe in the hands of fascist elements" by publicly insisting that the prosecutor (his former campaign manager for Jefferson County) had behaved correctly.[61]

Federal involvement came in the form of hearings before a U.S. Senate committee on free speech and labor rights. At the hearings, much that had been learned during earlier investigations was set forth for national consumption. Testimony confirmed that TCI detectives had been involved in the Gelders flogging, that local police and county deputies had blocked the investigation, and that the county solicitor had sabotaged his own case before the grand jury. A local labor organizer explained that community action in the Gelders matter had been less than vigorous because TCI had invested millions in Birmingham and was the employer of all but two of the state guardsmen assigned to the district. State detective James McClung echoed these findings in speaking before the committee and noted that TCI "owns about fifteen-sixteenths of the country" around Birmingham.[62]

13

Farm, Factory, and Hooded Persistence

Most of Alabama's rural Communists, like their urban counterparts, were black. It was a good bet that they, too, did not know the difference between Stalin and Trotsky or between Lenin and Marx, nor did they much care. They were starving during the 1930s. Times were hard.

It is difficult to determine exactly whether city dwellers or farmers had it worse in Alabama during the Great Depression. Certainly, both were in a bad way, but farm families perhaps had two slight advantages. First, they were accustomed to poverty. Their economic history had been a stultifying record of steady downward mobility since at least 1865. Also, it was more difficult to go completely without food in the countryside. Even after worse came to worst, farm people had recourse to the meager produce of a family garden.[1] Much as in the city, though, poverty in the countryside bred desperation, and desperation bred experiments in communism. Radicals in the Alabama hinterland also guaranteed that the KKK would remain present and active.

So abject was Alabama's farm poverty, so complete the system of subjugation under which tenants lived, and so dismal their prospects for change that some 5,000 rural Alabamians actually turned to the Communist Party during the 1930s. Most were attracted by the Communists' determination to abolish hunger rather than by the ideological bases of radical doctrine. Birmingham became a center of Communist activity during the decade and served as the jumping-off point for attempts at organizing Alabama's sharecroppers. Hosea Hudson and several other organizers got their starts as Communist workers in Birmingham and, as the decade progressed, spread the radical word throughout Alabama's countryside.[2]

The vast majority of Alabama's farm Communists consisted of black tenants. While white farmers should logically have been as ready to embrace the alien standard of communism, they were retarded by social convention, ostracism and violence, and their own racial biases. Race conquered all in the South. The southern Communist Party, even during the depths of the worst economic crisis in American history, remained essentially black.

The trend largely held across Alabama, despite a few isolated examples involving whites and the Communist tendency to exaggerate them as evidence of indigenous white radicalism. While charges of racial treason and social opprobrium blunted the appeal of communism for poor whites, violence remained the most powerful weapon of those determined to snuff out radical insurgency among people of color.

Race was also the central issue for those threatened by rural communism. Communist promises of social equality undermined the Party's appeal among poor whites. More important, the racial threat posed by communism served as a strong adhesive to glue landlord, Klansman, and peace officer in a lethal combination. Left untended, the Red position on race threatened to transcend the economic emergency of the 1930s and leave a harmful and lasting imprint on southern social customs. White fear on this score constricted the spread of radicalism, fueled its violent repression, and, for many, assured that antiradical vigilantism would be tolerated. Down on the farm and inside the factory, Alabama whites instinctively closed ranks whenever they believed that traditional race relations were in jeopardy.

The Communists openly pushed their appeal to blacks in many ways, as in the lyrics of a 1930s song in Alabama's countryside:

No mo' KU-KLUX-KLAN with their burnin' crosses
   No mo' chain-gang, we's not dogs no'-ho'ses
The NAACP, God no' Moses
   Can stop us blackies fightin' the bosses
Negroes ain' black—but RED!
   Teacher Lenin done said
Brothers all oppressed an' po'
   Ain't it so?
Sho!—No Mo', No Mo'[3]

An extensive KKK document, written by a Clarke County attorney in response to such songs, showed just how large the race issue loomed in rural Alabama. The document, distributed to Klan lodges throughout Alabama, Georgia, and Mississippi, called for lynching in response to black rape, repeal of the Fourteenth and Fifteenth Amendments, a ceiling on black education, antimiscegenation statutes, the establishment of white supremacy by law, and the expulsion of "outside agitators" who advocated equality for blacks. Special Klan vituperation was reserved for Communist organizers who jeopardized the allegedly "cordial" traditional relationship between Black Belt whites and blacks by preaching notions that could only result in "injury and untold harm to the poor ignorant Negro":

If the blacks do not wish to live under the rule of whites, let them return to their native land. . . . his position as a slave was better than anything he had ever known at home. . . . We owe the Negro nothing, we found him a naked, snake-worshiping savage and conferred upon him all the polish of civilization that he is competent to receive . . . and supplanted his serpent fetish with the Christian faith. Having lifted him out of savagery, we are under no obligation to bear him over our shoulders. . . . reading, writing and arithmetic . . . is as much as they can absorb to advantage. A Negro crammed on Latin [or] Greek . . . is a ruined Nigger! . . . no matter how many books you rub into his head, Nature created him INFERIOR . . . and if ever the white man lowers his level to that of the Negro . . . THE CRIME AGAINST CIVILIZATION WILL BE PUNISHED. . . . Negroes with a suggestion of intellect are usually . . . mongrels in whose veins flow the blood of some depraved white man. The pure blood blacks who have exhibited intellectual and moral qualities superior to those of the monkey are few and far between and yet the pure-blooded Ethiop is generally much safer . . . than the "yaller Nigger" who appears to inherit the vices of both races and the virtues of neither. I am not an advocate of "lynch law" but I have red blood in my veins and I believe it is no more contemptible to string up a Negro in the face of high heaven than it is to pounce upon an unprotected white woman and defile her. . . . the proper thing to do is to crack their necks with the least possible delay. . . . we must see to it that the Negro makes no Haitian hell of the United States.[4]

THE KLAN AND RURAL COMMUNISM

Klan and Communist clashed first in Tallapoosa County. In July 1931, simmering tensions erupted into violence when 800 black sharecroppers affiliated with the Communist Share Croppers Union (SCU) went on strike. Landlords precipitated the strike by demanding that tenants supply the labor to build a new sawmill—at fifty cents a day for men, twenty-five cents for women. Strike objectives included the restoration of cash advances, the right to sell cotton at any time during the year and not just at fall harvest when supply was high and prices low, a nine-month school year and a school bus for tenant children, and cash wages for cotton.[5]

On 15 July 1931, Tallapoosa sheriff Kyle Young and a "posse" of landlords and nightriders descended on an SCU meeting near Camp Hill where they beat and dispersed eighty croppers. Later, the meeting's remnants gathered at the home of Tommy Gray, a local black radical. Vigilantes followed and resumed the beatings at the Gray house, fracturing the skull of Gray's wife. Apparently on the brink of committing wholesale slaughter, the mob was blocked by the intervention of a shotgun-wielding Ralph Gray. The elder Gray, known affectionately as "Brother Ralph," was something of a folk hero among the black community for having bested a white landlord in a fistfight. Seeing Ralph Gray and his shotgun, the raiders retreated.[6]

Tensions escalated the following day. A group of whites, led by Sheriff Young and Dadeville's police chief, attacked a meeting of 150 black croppers. SCU sentries exchanged fire with the raiders, and Ralph Gray, standing guard, was hit in both legs. Gray continued to fire from his seated position and hit Sheriff Young in the stomach. Raiders and unionists rushed their wounded to safety. That night, a white mob of landlords, deputies, and Klan-like vigilantes arrived at the Gray house. Tommy Gray later recalled that one member of the mob "poked a pistol in Brother Ralph's mouth and shot down his throat." The mob then burned the house to the ground and carried Gray's corpse to the Dadeville courthouse where, for hours, local whites gathered to kick and shoot his lifeless body.[7]

The aftermath of Ralph Gray's murder proved to be tumultuous. Authorities arrested forty black croppers as Dadeville's police chief published his desire to "kill every member of the 'Reds' . . . and throw them into the creek." Constituted authority took a holiday as KKK mobs ran wild. Klansmen beat black sharecroppers, burned their homes, and fired into their cabins. It is difficult to determine exactly how many croppers were killed, injured, fled, or "laid out" in the woods Reconstruction-style. Black informants also plagued the local SCU. On one occasion, a black preacher informed authorities that a female Communist was hoarding dynamite. White nightriders attacked her and broke her spine.[8]

The black Communists near Tallapoosa, a militant lot, fought back determinedly. Croppers wounded two deputies but suffered at least eight casualties of their own. White authorities eventually summoned Robert Moton, the principal of Tuskegee Institute, to help quell the disturbance. The Communist ILD sent two attorneys to Camp Hill, where they arranged for the release of thirty arrested blacks who were being held without sufficient evidence of wrongdoing.[9]

There were smoldering embers in Tallapoosa County for some time. Periodically, the embers burst into flame. In 1932, Klansmen and landlords ran amuck following a confrontation between black SCU leader Cliff James and several deputies. Landlords, seeking to remove James from the local labor equation, sent a posse to attach a mule and a cow as payment for debts. James and several SCU comrades repulsed the posse with shotgun fire as its ringleader vowed to return and "kill all you 'niggers' up in a pile."[10]

A second white crowd did return, and in the ensuing battle three black Communists died and four deputies were wounded. Terror reminiscent of 1931 reigned for the next four days while Klansmen and landlords shot and beat blacks on sight. Authorities convicted six croppers for attempted murder, and county officials arrested anyone who sheltered the unionists. In 1933 the union attributed at least five assassination attempts on SCU members to the KKK and police. On one occasion, a black informant's bullets just missed Tommy Gray as he sat fishing on the banks of the Tallapoosa River.[11]

These episodes both fueled and obstructed Alabama radicalism. Black Belt communism was a revolt against the inherently oppressive circumstances of agrarian life in the South. Communism was a function more of hunger than of ideology, but it was also an attempt to defeat the racism, bigotry, and inequity endemic to tenant life. Violence alienated and united black radicals and also raised the stakes. Insurgency clearly might mean death.

Klan activity was not uncommon throughout rural Alabama during the 1930s as landlords and croppers clashed. Yet the situation differed from that in the 1920s. Instead of massive open air celebrations, and civic and fraternal activity, the small 1930s Klan served as the blunt instrument of planters who wanted to retain control of black labor at traditionally low wages.

Russell County in east Alabama became a scene of intense conflict in this regard. During one 1930s raid, six Klansmen in search of a cropper broke down a cabin door. Posing as U.S. deputies, the Knights took the cropper's wife to a graveyard to debate her fate. When six other Klansmen failed to rendezvous as planned, they released her. Nearby, a black farmer was routing the six Knights with his revolver. After one of the Kluxers was shot three times, his confederates took him to a local hospital. Police charged him with impersonating a federal officer but later evidently dropped the charges.[12]

The KKK targeted small farmers in Alabama who refused to plow crops under in order to reduce supply and raise commodity prices. Klansmen lit fiery crosses in Montgomery County, and Attalla Knights prevented a black barber from moving into a white neighborhood. A Chilton County landlord killed one of his female tenants for trespassing on his pastureland, a Dale County landowner shot three tenants for being insolent, and a Hayneville mob lynched a black youth.[13]

The 1930s Klan was especially active in Crenshaw County, an area of intense economic dislocation. A Luverne Klansman earned a flogging and a double load of buckshot in his back for warning black croppers who had been earmarked for a "dressin'." "They beat the hell out of you with a wide leather strap with holes in it," he later said when asked to explain the procedure. Eventually he got revenge by assaulting two of his former comrades.[14]

The actions of Alabama's government and press figures did little to deter Klan repression of rural communism. Attorney General Thomas Knight warned radical attorneys to stay out of local affairs and likely encouraged Klan vigilantism by declaring that communism had to be stamped out of Alabama "by armed force if necessary." There were also open press calls on the KKK to deal with disorderly blacks. The *Dadeville Record* asked the Klan to "quiet disturbances among our Negroes in Tallapoosa County" and, likewise, to work against "outside interferences." Grover Hall censured the Dadeville editor but also blamed "outside agitators" for Alabama's violence. Governor Graves offered rewards for the arrests of Emelle blacks who had defended themselves against a lynch mob.[15]

Hall and others who exhibited insular resistance stood in marked contrast to two social pariahs, Aubrey Williams and Gould Beech. As the publisher and the editor, respectively, of the *Southern Farmer*, they fought the Klan and promoted liberal racial and farm policies in 1930s Alabama. Congressman Martin Dies, the Texan who chaired the House Un-American Activities Committee (HUAC), branded Alabama's Williams "the most dangerous man in America."[16]

Convulsive outbreaks of rural terror following Camp Hill were but a prelude to an explosion of agrarian unrest and Klan reaction in the middle 1930s. The farm terror won, for Alabama's already soiled reputation, a fresh wave of criticism from beyond its borders. Vigilante terror concentrated in the counties affected most by an SCU strike for wages of a dollar a day, those in the Black Belt and on its periphery: Dallas, Hale, Lowndes, Macon, Montgomery, Sumter, Chambers, Randolph, and Lee.[17]

While economic issues were undoubtedly important considerations, they took a backseat to the bogies of biracial activism, black improvement, and social equality. The bulk of antiunionist sentiment and violence was geared toward short-circuiting the explosive racial potential in the conflict even more than preserving a system of economic repression. Ironically, white backlash intensified when the Communists exaggerated the extent of interracial cooperation. This tendency fueled hysteria, vigilantism, and broad societal toleration of violence more than it encouraged actual black-white cooperation.[18]

White inertia with regard to economic cooperation with blacks was, to say the least, considerable. Native whites who considered placing class interests above racial loyalty were constantly reminded of the high price of such treason. Klan propaganda reminded plain Alabamians that Communists promised blacks everything from political control to white mistresses. At one Klan meeting in east Alabama, a sheeted leader was even more explicit:

> The Communist preach[es] absolute equality of race. He goes to where you are . . . , puts his arm upon your shoulder and with that arm still warm . . . , puts that same arm around the niggers . . . and says to them: "Don't you know you can sit in the front seats of street cars and have a white wife?" . . . Niggers are picketing a white store . . . to force [it] to hire nigger help. If any of you would go into that store and buy merchandise from a nigger clerk, then God have mercy on your dirty soul. . . . No real white man would take his picture with a nigger. . . . Any man who would do that . . . God have mercy on his rotten filthy soul. . . . I would [sooner] climb Stone Mountain to kiss the ——— of a mosquito. . . . We got to keep the nigger in his place. We'll show them that the Klan is riding again.[19]

If the racial heresy charge failed, Klansmen resorted to out and out terror. Klan marches became common affairs in east Alabama during the middle 1930s. Black Belt Kluxers warned rural blacks, "We won't allow you Negroes of this county to get as far ahead of us as those damned Negroes of Tallapoosa." The KKK rode almost nightly in Phenix City's black neighborhoods of Sugartown and Stillwell's Quarters. Russell County Knights whipped one black girl so badly that she nearly died. Corpses turned up regularly; the bodies of three blacks were found in shallow graves dug on the banks of a creek. In what had become a distressing pattern, local police did little or nothing to stop the terror. Anxious Alabama editors, aware of northern scrutiny, cautioned against continued violence.[20]

At one Russell County cross burning, a robed KKK leader told terrified blacks:

> Listen here, you niggers, all of you. . . . We're down here on business. There's been too many complaints from white folks about how you damn niggers is been cuttin' the fool and it's got to stop—got to stop right now, or else! This cross is being burned here tonight for a little warning to each and every one of you. There's been too much cussin' when white folks was walking down the streets of this heah quarter; too much liquor drinkin', fightin' and hell raising in general. . . . It's got to stop I tell you and right now, too. Now we don't wanna hafta come back down heah . . . 'cause if we do, we gonna take

about a dozen of you goddamn niggers . . . and flog the hell outtin' you. . . .
mind your p's and q's or get ready to take some durned bad medicine![21]

Concerted violence occurred throughout the Black Belt in response to
the sharecroppers' strike. Macon County vigilantes shot at several croppers
from ambush and forced wholesale evictions of tenant families. Police and
Klan beatings occurred, and one landlord killed a black cropper with no
subsequent inquiry. Camp Hill's 800 striking tenants faced constant KKK
harassment. Lee County authorities arrested black croppers for handing out
circulars, and landlords in Chambers shot at black strikers without fear of
arrest. Montgomery police detectives forced strike leaders to leave their
city.[22]

Lowndes County was a hotbed. Alabama's 1935 SCU strike began on
J. R. Bell's plantation, where black sharecroppers quit work in search of a
raise to one dollar a day or one dollar per hundred pounds of picked cotton.
Bell summoned Sheriff R. E. Woodruff of Hayneville, who arrived with a
posse of whites and informed the croppers that "poor Mr. Bell" could not
afford to pay more than forty cents a day. Disgusted, strike leader Willie
Witcher turned to leave, muttering that the explanation was nonsense.
The sheriff ordered Witcher to halt, but the cropper ignored the command.
Woodruff then fired five times, hitting the cropper in the legs. Running to
the fallen man, the sheriff pistol-whipped him, screaming, "I'll kill you, you
black son of a bitch." "You might kill me," Witcher answered from where
he lay, "but you'll never scare me." The words became a rallying cry, and the
Lowndes strike held.[23]

In Lowndes County, there ensued a reign of terror similar to that in Tallapoosa. The struggle exemplified the economic element of southern racism.
Black tenants—simultaneously occupying a low place on both the class and
racial totem poles—represented a potentially huge problem for wealthier
whites who had once been motivated and organized to alter area labor relations. In the countryside it had been considered essential that black labor
be retained but at levels that preserved white economic and racial control.
The Reconstruction Klan had served to maintain the labor status quo in
Alabama's countryside, and the 1930s Klan functioned in much the same
way. In this respect, race and class were indelibly connected in the Deep
South.

Lowndes sheriff R. E. Woodruff, at the head of a group of Klan-like
vigilantes, kidnapped black sharecroppers, flogged them until they were
senseless, and then dumped them in area swamps. Three days after the incident at the Bell Plantation, Jim Press Merriwether interrupted the beating of three black women. Before leaving, though, the vigilantes shot and

wounded Merriwether. Later, they returned with reinforcements, carried him away, and riddled his body with bullets. That night, whites visited Merriwether's home, hung his wife from a tree several times before cutting her down, and flogged another black woman who had come to stay with the new widow. Grover Hall's *Montgomery Advertiser* blamed the Lowndes trouble on outside Communist agitators.[24]

The terror in Lowndes was at least matched by the KKK in neighboring Dallas County. Selma police and county deputies were conspicuous in mobs that kidnapped, beat, flogged, tortured, and killed SCU croppers during 1935 and 1936. During one stretch, Dallas whites flogged at least twenty-six SCU members. Law enforcement openly connived with Black Belt vigilantes by arresting strikers and releasing them to hungry mobs. In one week, Selma nightriders abducted and flogged a unionist a day in what croppers described as the "return of Klan terror." All "hell broke loose," a black Communist later recalled. Hosea Hudson, a radical more accustomed to Birmingham than to Selma, wrote about the spree: "The deputy sheriffs and the Ku Klux . . . was terrorizing and beating and arresting Negroes. Negroes was coming up missing." Indeed, local residents whispered that Klansmen had killed some black tenants, encased their bodies in concrete, and dumped them in the Alabama River.[25]

The unrest spread to nearby areas. In Greensboro, whites lured the leader of a Hale County SCU from a cotton field. Friends found his body a few days later filled with bullets. Whites also riddled a car with bullets as it carried northern organizers across Sumter County's Gorgas bridge near Livingston.[26]

In the summer of 1935, Dallas County officials arrested five SCU organizers, held them incommunicado, and then apparently released them to Klansmen. The vigilantes bound, stripped, and horsewhipped them, then held a flame to their wounds. Birmingham Communist Party leaders sent two men to investigate. They were in Selma only two hours before police arrested them for vagrancy and released them to vigilantes who gave them the same treatment. The ILD sent another investigator; he too was flogged upon reaching Selma. Blaine Owen, an intrepid white Communist, journeyed to Selma with a black companion. Police arrested the pair when they reached Dallas County and, within two hours, tried to release them to waiting Klansmen. When the Communists resisted their "liberation," a deputy forced them from the safety of their cell at gunpoint. "You all kin git ready to write yer own funeral," a vigilante assured them. "You all done all the talkin' you're agoin' to in Dallas County—stirrin' up your niggers! A dollar a day for cotton choppin'! . . . they ain't a nigger in this county whose life is worth a goddamn nickel when we git through cleanin' up this here union.

You dirty, goddamn trouble-makers . . . nigger lovers." Whites tied the pair to a tree and horsewhipped them while holding a torch to their wounds. At the county line, a Kluxer told them, "Next time you all hit Dallas County, ain't nothin'll stop us from killin' you."[27]

Klan, police, and vigilante terror surrounding the SCU strike in 1935 shocked the sensibilities of an increasingly cynical nation. The ruthless acts, for many, violated the most fundamental principles of American life. Due process was flouted, laws were ignored, and constituted authority was absent or, worse yet, conspired in the commission of atrocities. To many Americans, Alabama's rural anti-Communist program was violently repugnant.

Criticism poured into the state, reflecting, echoing, and even eclipsing that during the Scottsboro trials. "It is fast becoming the opinion of [all] civilized people" a New Yorker observed, that "Alabama is a region where barbaric feudalism still exists. . . . human life has very little value in Alabama. Certainly the spilling of blood is of far less consequence than the maintenance of profits." A paralyzed World War I veteran pleaded with Alabamians "in Jesus' name" to stop the brutality and deplored their "bestial state." "God, oh God," he cried. "I never fought for this." A Philadelphian called for the impeachment of Dallas County's sheriff and other "thug[s] and worker-whipper[s]." "Is that the way you [in Alabama] uphold law and order," he asked, "by beating, lynching, and whipping the white and black workers of your state? How long [do] you think you can get on like this?" Another outraged observer suggested that the state adopt a hangman's noose for its official symbol: "Alabama is inhabited by, or better still, governed by brutes . . . in whom [the] . . . instincts of . . . justice and civilization do not exist." The Catholic Interracial Council deplored the mayhem. Northern editors compared Alabama's Klansmen to Nazis. Will Rogers quipped that Adolf Hitler "doesn't want to be führer, he wants to be a kleagle." *Hammer Magazine* in Leipzig, Germany, reciprocated by praising the southern Klan. American Communists denounced Alabama's KKK, White Legion, and Black Shirts as variants of a global fascist strain. A Chicago editor agreed that Alabama's Ku Klux repression was as "reprehensible and degrading as . . . fascism or nazism to liberty-loving people" all over the world.[28]

The response from northern blacks was varied. Some ridiculed Klan terror as anachronistic. Although the attempt was made in good faith, it was much easier to be cavalier about the Klan from the safe confines of a New York office than from the cotton fields of Alabama. Some northern blacks tried to frighten southern authorities with warnings about biblical vengeance: "The white man is so drunk with power, conceit, and deceit, that his civilization must be completely destroyed. . . . When it comes to dealing with black folks he do[es] not even know the meaning of the word[s] [fair play]. But mark you; you are going to learn."[29]

Black Belt croppers responded with their own brand of humor:

It say in the Bible how Lawd he make man
　　But who in the hell make de Ku Kluck Klan?
Shaped like a tadpole, smell like a skunk,
　　Hide in the midnight sheet, like chintz in a bunk.
Ku Kluck Klan, Ku Kluck Klan,
　　Lowest down creeper in de lan'.[30]

NATIONAL CRITICISM

Two incidents amplified outside criticism of Alabama during the mid-1930s SCU strike. One was the murder and mutilation of Claude Neal, a black man accused of raping and killing a white girl. The Neal lynching was a horrific affair. It featured official approval, police connivance, public approbation, interstate mob cooperation, and sadism of the basest sort. Authorities moved Neal to Alabama from a Pensacola jail after a sheriff announced that he had "never wanted to kill a negro so bad in his life." Alabama whites abducted Neal from the Brewton jail, took him just over the Florida line, and tortured him for the better part of a day with red hot pokers and homemade spears. The frenzied mob amputated Neal's fingers and toes, then cut off his genitals and made him eat them. During the spectacle, they repeatedly stabbed and hanged him only to cut him down just before he suffocated. After he died, Neal's lynchers dragged his corpse behind a moving car for hours and left it on public display. Several newspapers advertised the lynching for days prior to the actual event, and an Alabama sheriff assured whites that they would not be molested by law enforcement before, during, or after the killing. Neither Governor Benjamin Miller nor his Florida counterpart sent the militia to prevent the lynching, but afterward Miller sent the guard to quash black protests of the incident.[31]

The other major incident that increased outside censure of Alabama at this time involved a group of visiting Communists. At the pinnacle of the SCU strike, the National Committee for the Defense of Political Prisoners sent a delegation of five to Alabama to investigate its vigilantism. The national group, which was affiliated with the Communist Party and the ILD, had several well-known members, such as Upton Sinclair, John Dos Passos, Lincoln Steffens, Sherwood Anderson, Granville Hicks, Rockwell Kent, and Joseph Gelders.[32]

The delegation first visited Birmingham, where it tried to provoke a test case of the Downs ordinance. On the steps of city hall, the Communists handed out copies of the *New Republic,* the *New Theatre,* the *New Masses,* the *Nation,* and the *New York Daily Worker,* but police refused to arrest them. The officers did rough the Reds up a bit, though, then invited them in for a talk with Birmingham's chief of police and its public safety commissioner. Commissioner William Downs, a former county sheriff and Klan cyclops, advised the radicals to "go back North and leave the 'niggers' to the South which has taken care of them since the Civil War." A courteous Downs informed the delegates that "he was just as good a liberal as any of [them]" but that "every time a nigger comes back here from up North we have to give him a dose of castor oil to rid him of bad ideas and bring him back to his senses." Police Chief Luther Hollums was also stiffly polite, patronizing, and at times rather frank about Alabama race relations. "This literature isn't unlawful," Hollums told the visitors, "but it contains what offends some people. Besides, the ignorant working people shouldn't be allowed to read such literature. It stirs them up. Why, before these radicals began scattering such stuff, the nigger would come holding up his hands when a white man called to him. Now the niggers are uppity." Then the chief smiled and made a thinly veiled threat of Klan violence: "We have a certain element here, some anti-radicals that do things we don't always approve of. If you continue to distribute such literature here I won't be responsible for what may happen to you."[33]

Sobered, the Communists drove to Montgomery in hopes of meeting with the governor. Near Clanton, a car overtook the visitors and riddled their car with bullets. Miraculously, no one was hurt. The Communists demanded police protection, but Governor Graves reacted in the hypersensitive manner that had earned Alabama national scorn. He denied protection, detained the radicals for eight hours, accused them of shooting up their own automobile, and declared the whole incident to be "a frame-up for publicity."[34]

Criticism of the state's handling of the NCDPP shooting only added to the public censure to which Alabama was being subjected because of the sharecroppers' strike. Northern critics called the governor's statement the "natural reaction" of a former Klansman, termed the episode "incredible in a civilized country," and called for immediate federal action. A New York activist remarked, "Once more, Alabama has confirmed the widespread impression that she is unable to govern herself peacefully." The ACLU's Arthur Garfield Hays blasted Bibb Graves, while other critics pointed to the governor's refusal to provide police protection as an "open invit[ation]" for more KKK attacks. Meanwhile, a succession of Alabamians and Southerners applauded Graves's tough stand against the Yankee press and condemned the gall of "visiting meddlers . . . invaders [and] irresponsible radicals."[35]

Although Benjamin Miller and Bibb Graves were often on opposite sides of the fence politically, as 1930s governors they responded in similar ways to antiradical repression and outside scrutiny. Politicians and their constituents in Alabama found it more important to maintain familiar customs than to respond to criticism for violations of civil liberties.

During the 1930s, Alabama's industrialists enjoyed a close, almost intimate, relationship with state and local law enforcement personnel and public officials. Foremost in the minds of these allies was fear of the radical "outside agitator." These "outsiders," it was believed, sought to exploit a disastrous economy in order to corrupt peaceable and complacent blacks, make them into disciples, and agitate for class and racial revolution. Because such fears were so widespread, Klansmen, White Legionnaires, and antiradical and antiblack forces of their ilk moved in easy and fluid alliance with many in leadership positions within Alabama's state and local governments.

These ties were particularly strong during the administration of Benjamin Miller (figure 29), a conservative probusiness governor during 1931–1935. Alabama's UMW, encouraged by National Industrial Recovery Act codes of fair labor conduct, challenged Big Mule hegemony for the first time since 1921. Miller responded to the almost hysterical appeals from industrialists about blacks, Communists, and "outside agitators" by sending in the National Guard to crush the strike. During the labor trouble, General John C. Persons of the state militia functioned as Miller's eyes and ears in the Birmingham District, largely through military spies. Persons also served as president of Birmingham's First National Bank and was a staunch antifederal white supremacist. In crushing the black, radical, and outside triple threat that the coal strike presented, Persons acted as the liaison between the governor; his assistant John Peach; and leading Big Mules such as Henry and Charles DeBardeleben, of DeBardeleben Coal and Alabama Fuel and Iron, respectively; Milton H. Fies, vice president at DeBardeleben; Robert Gregg, president of TCI; A. B. Aldridge of Alabama Power; Hugh Morrow of Alabama By-Products; Preston H. Haskell of ABC Coal and Coke; Donald Comer of the Avondale Mills; Robert Jemison, Jr.; antilabor attorneys Borden Burr and Forney Johnston; and assorted sheriffs, police chiefs, and local politicians. Their phone conversations and correspondence were studded with frantic references to "trespassers," "outsiders," "outside agitators," "invaders," "communists," "interference," and "Negroes." On one occasion, the adjutant general soberly informed Governor Miller that Charles DeBardeleben was preparing for the coming carnage by equipping a private army with sawed-off shotguns and submachine guns. On another occasion,

29. Governor Benjamin Meek Miller, 1931–1935. A lifelong member of the planter–industrialist oligarchy, Miller made opposition to Ku Kluxism the marquee issue in his 1930 bid for the governorship. Courtesy Alabama State Department of Archives and History.

Milton Fies told the governor exactly where the DeBardelebens wanted the state militia deployed. Miller asked General Persons to get Big Mule publisher Victor Hanson to lobby so that Alabama's congressmen would become actively involved in the strike, which he did.[36]

The same ties and phobias were apparent during the Great Textile Strike of 1934. To his credit, Governor Miller resisted intense pressure from industrialists before he sent in the state guard to crush yet another labor uprising. Miller found himself under pressure from H. D. Agnew and Donald Comer of the Avondale Mills; Scott Roberts, president of the Alabama Cotton Manufacturing Association; George Lanier of Westpoint Manufacturing; east Alabama's H. V. Carter and John Denson; Exchange clubs; Kiwanis clubs; merchants' associations; the American Legion; and a number of local politicians; law enforcement figures; and mill owners. Much of the appeal was couched in terms of threats from "Communists" and "outsiders." On one occasion, an impatient Scott Roberts threatened the governor with electoral reprisal if he did not act to aid the industrialists.[37]

During Bibb Graves's second term (1935–1939), these ties loosened considerably. Graves functioned as a friend to Alabama labor and twice refused to send the militia against labor. Still, he remained adamantly opposed to outside influences, "outside lawyers," and, especially, Communist agitators.[38]

ORGANIZED LABOR AND THE KKK

During the 1930s the KKK also targeted the newly formed Congress of Industrial Organizations largely because of the intrinsic racial threat it represented. The UMW's John L. Lewis, along with the Amalgamated Clothing Workers' Sidney Hillman and the Ladies Garment Workers' Dave Dubinsky, formed the CIO after simmering tensions led to an open break with William Green's AFL at its 1935 Miami convention. The new CIO represented a decidedly liberal alternative to the more staid "bread and butter" unionism of the AFL. Lewis's group, like the mine workers' union, advocated a visible and active role for black workers, immigrants, and the unskilled and pursued a pattern of industrial organization in contrast to the AFL's more exclusive craft policies. During the second half of the 1930s, the CIO launched "Operation Dixie," an effort to organize large numbers of southern workers in industries such as coal, steel, textiles, and rubber making. Of mixed success, the efforts predictably stimulated southern fears of social equality, racial intermarriage, and "outside agitators."[39]

Klan repression of Alabama labor was part of the state's long tradition of using vigilantism to beat back any attempt at biracialism based on common class interests. Reconstruction Republicans, the Knights of Labor, 1880s independents, 1890s Populists, the UMW, and steel and railroad strikers had all encountered vigilante violence designed to thwart their attempts at biracial class activism. During the 1930s, Communists, the CIO, and other left-wing groups that promoted black-white unity also fell prey to Klan terror. Like their predecessors, depression-era challengers to Alabama's racial status quo found themselves confronted by hooded terror, charges of racial treason, and stiff societal hostility toward "outside agitators."[40]

It is difficult now to determine how much the Klan, the vigilantes, the police, the landlords, and corporations were separately responsible for the repression of the 1930s, and that is precisely the point. The lines blurred; overlap and cooperation existed. Hooded persistence during the 1930s was part of a stubborn legacy of vigilante reaction against outsiders. The xeno-phobic epithet "outside agitator," despite its adhesion in popular culture in the 1960s, did not originate with Bull Connor. It was an old and established part of the Alabama lexicon, used by people accustomed to dealing harshly with any foreign threat.[41]

In synch with southern anxieties, the KKK declared war on the CIO. "We shall fight horror with horror!" one Klan leader announced in response to CIO plans to organize southern blacks and whites. "The CIO is infested with Communists," Imperial Wizard Hiram Evans declared from Atlanta, "The Klan will not sit idly by and allow the CIO to destroy our social order . . . without swift punishment."[42]

Heeding the imperial wizard's words, Klan leaflets appeared in Birmingham proclaiming that the "CIO Is Communism. Communism will not be tolerated. Ku Klux Klan Rides Again." Klan leaders denounced "alien" CIO leaders and the imminent "industrial war" they were trying to foment. "We did not feel that we would have to fight the Ku Klux Klan," a 1930s textile organizer in Alabama said. "We felt it was dead and buried, but no sooner had we stepped into the field than [out] they came with the Night Shirts and fiery crosses." Klansmen accused John L. Lewis of being a crypto-Communist for parting company with the more staid AFL and favoring biracial organization.[43]

KKK activity did not end with Communists and the CIO. Any threat to the color line was fair game. John Altman, a Pickens County attorney and Democratic veteran, accused William Mitch, a leader of the Birmingham UMW, of preaching racial heresy, exactly "what the Communists preach on Negro equality." Mitch, though, pointedly discouraged both Communists and Klansmen from joining his union. At Birmingham's epic 1938 meeting of the Southern Conference for Human Welfare (SCHW), which marked the high tide of regional reform, Klansmen red-baited the liberal gathering. Mabel Jones West, an old hired hand for the Ku Klux Klan who had vacillated between supporting and opposing its candidates during the 1920s, attacked the SCHW as a Communist meeting and charged that its delegates were having interracial sex—a potent charge that would also be revived during the 1960s.[44]

The depression turned Birmingham into a seething cauldron of economic disaffection in which Klansmen functioned as the blunt instruments of the status quo. Strikers bombed a milk company and several laundries. Vigilantes kidnapped the son of a union leader and wreaked havoc on unionists much as they had against Communists. In 1935, vigilantes and company guards waylaid a UMW march, killing one miner and wounding six.[45]

Police involvement in the antilabor violence was clear. In 1937, the city civil service board fired Officer P. L. Stapp for two "unwarranted assaults" on north Birmingham workers. During the hearings, it was learned that Stapp had killed seven persons during his tenure with the police department and had often been embroiled in controversy. Stapp's brother, a police sergeant himself, threatened to kill blacks who testified for the board. "Now that P. L. Stapp has been fired from the police force," a radical editor quipped, "it is not known whether TCI or Republic Steel will make him a special deputy or whether he will become a plantation riding boss[, as he is] . . . fitted for any of those jobs."[46]

Violence against labor proliferated in this culture. Company guards at Thompson Steel shot the wife of a black worker because he attended a union meeting. An Alabama National Guardsman, "sickened" by the violence, acknowledged that militiamen had nailed one black man to his own front door by his thumbs.[47]

In Birmingham, after 1934, Horace Wilkinson and the KKK sometimes found themselves on opposite sides of the fence when it came to organized labor. While the 1930s Klan worked to hinder unionization, labor leaders considered "Boss" Wilkinson to be labor's "first-class . . . ever-dependable fighting man." Through his newspaper, the *Alabama Herald,* Wilkinson supported prolabor politicians such as Governor Bibb Graves and Senator Hugo Black, New Deal projects, TVA, FDR, and the UMW. During the decade, Wilkinson and the patricians continued to fight, with the political boss now posing as an anticorporation demagogue against entrenched commercial interests, and working through Representative John Arnold to unnerve the oligarchy at the state legislature. Victor Hanson, Governor Benjamin Miller and state senators James A. Simpson and Eugene "Bull" Connor were the prime targets of most of his attacks.[48]

During the second half of the 1930s, Wilkinson battled against civil service reform in order to keep his hold over patronage and city jobs. The contest reached especially intense levels when, as city commissioners, several former protégés forsook Wilkinson to ally with the oligarchy: Bull Connor, former Klansmen Jimmie Jones and John Taylor, and their ally, former WKKK leader Mabel Jones West.[49]

Wilkinson's Birmingham machine included labor, but it cannot be said that Wilkinson abandoned his racism. He still functioned as the leading race-baiter in the state, and much of his opposition to the Big Mules was studded with references to race. He fought patrician efforts to institute civil service because, as Wilkinson's *Alabama Herald* said, the program would guarantee "a nigger or a communist" jobs over Alabama whites. With irony fit for the ages, Wilkinson also mercilessly race-baited former pupil Bull Connor. "In due time," the *Alabama Herald* predicted, "the NAACP will . . . recognize [Connor's] distinguished service . . . [on behalf of] negroes . . . , and if intelligence tests are not too high . . . [will award Connor] the Sengambian Service medal and the Caucasian Double Cross."[50]

While the oligarchs led the opposition to Klan excesses during the 1930s, much as they had during the 1920s, they were essentially in concert with the Klan's antilabor sentiments during the depression. Labor recognized Governor Miller and SDEC chair and Mobile lawyer Gessner T. McCorvey as determined enemies. The Big Mules sponsored publication of the *Southern Outlook*, a tabloid that specialized in antiblack, anti-Semitic, and antiunion copy. The local CIO dubbed Big Mule governor Frank Dixon (1939–1943) a "peg-legged bigot whose creaking cork leg is moved to take each step at the command of Birmingham's industrial barons." The state legislature could never "pass enough anti-labor bills to please him." Dixon was involved with the Christian Americans, a "semi-fascist" antiunion group that was known colloquially as an "anti-labor KKK."[51]

Klan activity was a part of north Alabama's Great Textile Strike of 1934, which eventually became the single largest industrial work stoppage in American history because it involved over 400,000 workers. The *Huntsville Times* called the strike "illegal and unjustified," blamed "outsiders" for the discord, and charged that the whole thing "smack[ed] of communism." A Klan-like vigilante outfit sprouted up and was soon implicated in the kidnapping and beating of Huntsville's textile organizers.[52]

Still, CIO organizing efforts received a boost from more than just their own organizers and SCHW liberals. Labor organizers counted three former Klansmen as allies during the 1930s: Bibb Graves, Horace Wilkinson, and Hugo Black. In 1936, and again in 1937, Alabama governor Bibb Graves flouted a long tradition among state executives of using the militia to crush strikes when he refused to send troops to textile strikes in Talladega and Huntsville. Graves had no use for "outside agitators," Communists from the NCDPP, or "outside lawyers," but during the decade he functioned as an ally of organized labor, FDR, and the New Deal. Graves "frequently sided with organized labor" during the 1930s, according to historian Wayne Flynt. He created a state department of labor in 1935 that oversaw child labor and wage and hour laws, and mediated labor disputes. He appointed a union bricklayer to head up the new labor department and Molly Dowd, a textile organizer, to participate in dispute mediation. "In fact," Wayne Flynt has written, "Graves played as large a role in Montgomery as Roosevelt did in Washington to create a vigorous, politically assertive labor movement in Alabama."[53] Horace Wilkinson did "more than . . . any other man" in the state to assure Graves's second gubernatorial election in 1934 over Big Mule candidate Frank Dixon. The political boss also supported labor, as did former Klan senator Hugo Black, the author of the Black wages and hours bill.[54]

There was extensive repression of the CIO in Gadsden. As in the Joseph Gelders assault, KKK involvement was not absolutely discernible. Yet as in the Gelders case, Gadsden's violence was extralegal, shared a primal kinship with antilabor Klan repression, enjoyed considerable community acquiescence, and prompted much national criticism.

Gadsden, Alabama, was considered by many to be the toughest antilabor city in America. The seat of Etowah County, Gadsden was home to three large plants: Goodyear Tire and Rubber out of Akron, Ohio; Dwight Textiles of Massachusetts; and Cleveland's Republic Steel. The plants employed about 8,000 workers, easily the bulk of Gadsden's workforce. Labor surpluses, the 1930s economy, hierarchical community relations, and an unrelenting suspicion of outsiders made the town nearly impregnable to unions. Sent to Republic Steel, which was 25 percent black, one veteran organizer reported that he left Birmingham with the eerie feeling that it would be his "last earthly undertaking."[55]

Trouble existed in Gadsden's textile and steel industries, but the rubber industry became the focal point of resistance to the new CIO. Antilabor violence erupted in 1936 when Goodyear announced a massive production shift from Akron to Gadsden. Alarmed by the vigilante violence, United Rubber Workers of America (URW) strategists sent union president Sherman Dalrymple to Gadsden. Locals pelted him with eggs, jerked him from a platform in midsentence, and beat him with clubs and fists until he sustained a concussion and fled town. Antilabor vigilantes assaulted at least twenty other individuals while the county sheriff, who had handed Dalrymple to the mob, did nothing. The U.S. Department of Labor, the National Labor Relations Board (NLRB), and the state labor department investigated. Rather than producing the desired effect, though, the investigations merely created more local support for vigilantism. Threats increased, and the city passed ordinances against communism, union meetings, and biracial gatherings. A courageous Methodist preacher found himself ostracized when he protested the laws. In June 1936, a crowd of 500 trashed the local URW office and assaulted its hysterical occupants as deputy sheriffs and city police looked on. After the mob completed its work, police provided first aid and offered the unionists transportation out of town. A fresh round of federal intervention, in the form of hearings by the LaFollette committee, revealed that police had collaborated with vigilantes, that Goodyear had paid vigilantes to attack unionists, and that spies infested the URW locals.[56]

Gadsden reaction was again sharply defensive. Goodyear set up a violent company union led by Jimmy Karam, a former football player for Auburn University. Karam declared that "Stalin is the head of Russia and John L. Lewis is trying to be the same thing here" as he denounced "outside unions and outside interference." Karam's men beat URW members daily, emboldened by a city commissioner's thinly veiled threats against "outside agitators." Vigilantes assaulted two Communists from Birmingham and mobbed an NCDPP delegation consisting of Joseph Gelders and several outraged Birmingham ministers.[57] Gadsden's antiunion climate and hypersensitivity led to a third round of federal intervention when the NLRB documented rampant violations of civil liberties.[58]

Three stages of federal involvement were usually more than enough to adjust the attitudes of even the most intransigent jurisdiction—at least temporarily. Not so in Gadsden. Determined to run their own affairs as they saw fit, local vigilantes launched a new wave of terror. Early 1938 saw the beating of a unionist and the local union president. The president evidently saved his own life by cutting three of his assailants with a work knife. Violence continued for several more years. In February 1941, vigilantes beat one organizer so badly that he required eighty-six stitches to close fifteen head wounds and lost consciousness for several hours. A sickened onlooker described it as "the most unmerciful beating I have ever seen." In 1942, the Fifth U.S. Circuit Court of Appeals upheld an NLRB ruling against Goodyear. The following year Gadsden's textile, steel, and rubber industries, mostly as a result of federal intervention, succumbed to organization.[59]

External pressure against Alabama's Klan and antilabor vigilantes accelerated in the wake of Gadsden. A New York editor branded Alabama's KKK the "anti-labor Gestapo." The U.S. Supreme Court struck down an Alabama statute against peaceful picketing that had been upheld by Tuscaloosa judge Henry Foster. The LaFollette committee ranked Alabama as the number one antilabor state in the nation and reported that Alabama companies spent more on arms and ammunition than did those in any other state.[60]

RACE, ANTIFEDERALISM, AND THE PERSISTENCE OF THE KLAN

The KKK may have been, as Alabama journalist Gould Beech remarked, "in bad odor" during the 1930s, but it most certainly existed in his state. The organization clearly lacked the political clout and overt acceptance that it

had enjoyed during the 1920s, but it persisted in Alabama because of a resilient Klan spirit, a Ku Klux ethos that imbued the state's culture. "It would
be easier to level down the mountains with a toothpick than to destroy . . .
Klan teaching and the principles back of it," a knighthawk accurately observed during the 1920s. Throughout the 1930s, the Klan *Kourier's* masthead
declared, "Once a Klansman, Always a Klansman." Community attitudes
were as vital as actual members who remained in the order. As long as ordinary Alabamians accepted Klan excess as the price of racial stability, the
KKK continued to exist.[61]

At the end of the 1920s, Alabama had only about 5,500 Klan members
left. Though the numbers of active, dues-paying, uniform-wearing Klansmen probably fell during the 1930s, Alabama kept a climate favorable to Ku
Kluxism. Ku Kluxism and a basic propensity for vigilantism were part of
Alabama's social fabric. Imitators of the sheeted organization proliferated.
The White Legion sprang up in Birmingham, affiliated with the KKK, and
was headed by Klan members. The Alabama Black Shirts—another home-
grown fascist outfit devoted to the repression of blacks, unionists, and
Reds—also took root during the decade. In 1939, an embryonic Klan clone
was born in Montgomery. Three men, including an Opelika bankruptcy
referee, assumed leadership of the group and sought 10,000 members at ten
dollars a head. Joseph Starnes, a U.S. congressman from Alabama, represented
this group when he proposed legislation to register and fingerprint every
immigrant in the country. During the depression the KKK occasionally
went for the same targets as its 1920s counterpart: immigrants, Jews, Catholics, prostitutes, and moral nonconformists. The state's penal department remained a bastion of Klan strength during the decade. Green K. Fountain,
the Klan warden of Atmore Prison, was so renowned for his skill that he
was known as "the whipping boss . . . , an artist" with a seven-pound whip.
In hamlets throughout the state, friends and neighbors listed former Klan
members among their communities' top leaders.[62]

The 1930s Klan existed in an atmosphere of local acceptance, if not actual support. It built on this foundation by devising forms of paranoia that
would serve the extreme Right for years to come. One popular depression-
era Klan conspiracy theory focused on "internationalism" and an excessive
fear of global plots. Klan leaders sought to pass their mantle on to a younger
cadre of "shock troops" for the coming race war.[63]

Even as things change, some elements remain the same. Rarely can one
pinpoint completely unbroken themes throughout history. By the same token, dramatic and complete breaks with the past seldom occur. Dialectical
change—the struggle between thesis and antithesis and its resolution in a
new synthesis—is much more likely. The history of the KKK is an example.

Even as the 1920s Klan died, some elements of continuity—violence, persecution of blacks, Jews, Catholics, aliens, and outside agitators—continued.

Alabama's 1930s Klan was not averse to invoking the legends of Reconstruction and the 1920s in order to claim legitimacy. Individual klaverns invited surviving Reconstruction Klansmen to speak to 1930s Knights about the order's enduring values and timeless goals. At the height of Birmingham's Communist hysteria, theater owners repeatedly showed a revised version of D. W. Griffith's classic tale of the Reconstruction South, the *Birth of a Nation*. Advertisements for the Robert E. Lee Klavern accompanied the screenings. Perhaps the most overt theme of continuity, though, was the order's persistent preoccupation with race. During the 1930s, Birmingham's Klan flooded the streets and radio waves with warnings about the perils of social equality and communism. Flyers with Klansmen on horseback warned blacks to stay away from Communists and other racial heretics. Viewing one such flyer, a white Birmingham woman said to a friend, "Looks like Reconstruction days, doesn't it?"[64]

Some career Klansmen served their hooded apprenticeships during one Klan era and sometimes achieved prominence during another. Dr. E. P. Pruitt, a leader of Alabama's KKK after World War II, belonged to the hooded order through the 1920s and 1930s. During the 1930s, the Graves political machine pushed Matt Murphy to challenge Montgomery judge and Klan critic Leon McCord for his seat on the national Democratic committee. McCord won, but Murphy went on to prominence during the 1950s and 1960s as one of the Alabama Klan's top legal guns. Robert S. Gulledge had several connections. As head of the White Legion in depression-era Birmingham, and as a Klan kleagle in the 1940s, Gulledge reflected the spiritual affinity between groups such as the Legion and the prototypical KKK.[65]

The fact that the KKK survived in Alabama at a time when many other business enterprises failed suggests that more was behind it than klectokens, robe sales, and hate literature. In fact, a number of factors contributed to the order's persistence. Foremost was, of course, race. The primordial and obsessive nature of the race question made it the single most dominant issue in southern history, generally, and in the Klan's resilience specifically. Race consistently overshadowed every other competing factor in Alabama history. The utter ubiquity and unmatched intensity of race was the most important ingredient in the South's regional distinctiveness.

During the 1930s, the race question was everywhere in Alabama. It was so pervasive that all political discourse was eventually reduced to its impact on race. Virtually no political problem existed in total seclusion from this one issue. "The Klan is waging no war on Negroes, but we are against social equality," the secretary of the Lee Klavern explained, for example, and "that is what the Communists are preaching. We are trying to educate Negroes to the dangers of listening to agitators who are preaching doctrines that can only lead to trouble."[66]

The middecade shift of black voters from the party of Lincoln to the party of Roosevelt increased the intensity of feeling surrounding the race question in Alabama. Fearful that the national Democratic Party might pander to a northern black vote, Alabama Klansmen and other southern Democrats bitterly concluded that "a Darkey Drives the Donkey Now." The 1930s Klan showed some important differences from the 1920s version, but its imperial wizard summed up its enduring contribution best in 1937: "It is a question of White Supremacy. That is all this great Klan fight is. It is a question of White Supremacy."[67]

The specter of federal involvement was powerfully linked to Alabama's concerns about race. Since the 1860s, Southerners had resented, feared, and resisted the federal government because of its impact on race and politics. During the 1930s, the federal threat never left southern consciousness even when it ceased to be at the forefront.

Ample evidence existed to fuel Alabama's fear of the central government. The New Deal brought unprecedented governmental involvement into the lives of Southerners. With federal dollars, though, came federal strings. Minority groups—the National Negro Congress (NNC), the NAACP, and various types of Communists—also caused periodic alarm by calling for federal investigations of the KKK by Congress, the president, and the Justice Department. Unrelenting NAACP pressure eventually forced HUAC to look into the Klan. The LaFollette committee, the NLRB investigations, U.S. Supreme Court reversals in the Scottsboro cases, and the occasional Labor Department or congressional inquiry also kept the antifederal fire burning in Alabama throughout the decade.[68]

The single most important progenitor of anxiety, though, was the Wagner-Costigan federal antilynching bill. The measure, backed by the NAACP, the NNC, and many New Dealers, called for a fine of $5,000 or five years' imprisonment for local and state officers who failed to protect prisoners from lynch mobs. Conniving peace officers could receive sentences of up to twenty-five years, and individual counties could be required to pay up to $10,000 in indemnities to the families of lynch victims.[69]

Although the bill passed muster in the House twice, it eventually failed in the Senate because of stiff southern opposition. Alabama's KKK blamed lynchings on the incitement of "Northern and New York liberals," Grover Hall blasted federal intrusion, and future Dixiecrats such as Alabama governor Frank Dixon called the measure "dangerous . . . , disastrous . . . , unwarranted . . . , [and] unwise." In one breath Dixon blamed the North for poverty, and poverty for southern lynchings; in the next breath, he denied that the South had a lynching problem.[70]

Official condemnation of the 1930s Klan might have led an observer to conclude that the vigilante group could not survive in Alabama. "There is no place in Alabama for vigilantes," Grover Hall thundered. The "stupidity of the ox and the stupidity of the Ku Kluxer . . . are on a par." The *Birmingham News* published a ten-point list of prerequisites for membership in the KKK, featuring intolerance, illiberalism, anticonstitutionalism, un-Americanism, and the like. Harry Ayers wrote eloquently about toleration for Catholics and Jews and condemned the Klan. Montgomery editorials alternated between contempt for communism and contempt for the hood. A Huntsville editor concluded that there "is no justification whatever for any Klan organization in this state. We don't want its stigma upon us."[71]

This resistance was well meaning, sincere, and effective, to a point. Still, it did not call into question some of the most basic reasons that many Alabamians tolerated the KKK. While Colonel Ayers railed against the Klan, he was a states'-righter to the core. One Clay Countian rejected the KKK because he considered masks to be "unmanly." In the place of masked floggings, though, he recommended public lynchings. The *Montgomery Advertiser* and Governor Benjamin Miller emphasized that many members of the order were good men. The editor of the *Birmingham Age-Herald,* after bashing the Klan for a few paragraphs, praised Jimmy Colescott, the new imperial wizard, for his 1940 order to unmask and concluded, "Bring the Klan into the open, and very few persons will wish its death." An editor of the *Birmingham News* criticized the 1930s order but praised the Reconstruction KKK as "a composing influence" that saved the South from racial "chaos."[72]

In two of the clearest statements of the economic reasoning behind some resistance to the Klan, the *Montgomery Advertiser* and the *Birmingham News* repudiated the KKK so that Alabama could continue to receive New Deal relief. The South, finding itself dependent on federal largesse, perhaps for the first time, realized that Klan mayhem was potentially very costly. Grover Hall, an ardent states'-rights advocate, sought federal aid in 1939 to regulate differences in freight rates and to prop up Dixie's sagging agricultural system. "If the South yields" to the KKK, Hall warned, "if ignorance cows intelligence, if self-appointed vigilantes substitute terror for the due process of law . . . , the South will find itself ostracized by the enlightened opinion of the world. . . . [The realization of our economic] demands . . . is dependent upon the good will of the nation and the political influence the South is able to enlist." In the midst of the Great Depression, the *Birmingham News* was even more blunt: "At a time when the South is . . . seeking much from the nation, it would be disastrous to fall victim to Ku Kluxism."[73]

The Klan's chief enemies in Alabama did not challenge the order's views on race. In his 1934 run for governor, future Dixiecrat leader Frank Dixon enlisted the Klan issue as a weapon against Bibb Graves. When Lister Hill defeated Tom Heflin for Alabama's vacant Senate seat in 1937, observers as astute as John Temple Graves II interpreted the Hill victory as a blow against Ku Kluxism. Hill, though, was opposed to federal antilynching bills and wedded to states' rights. In effect he was constrained by the same electoral shackles that had fettered Hugo Black while he was in the Senate. Benjamin Miller, a vocal foe of the KKK, was not above joining forces with the 1930s Klan in order to keep alcohol out of the hands of blacks.[74]

Weak or nonexistent law enforcement against the Klan also contributed to its persistence. Alabamians let the Klan get away with much because they sympathized with the order's goals. Its ability to escape punishment, though, further promoted its survival. Two Jefferson County grand juries, despite abundant evidence, refused to indict Joseph Gelders's assailants because of his Jewish heritage, radical politics, and the less than earnest efforts of city police, county deputies, and the circuit solicitor. Tuscaloosa police and at least one judge evidently exacerbated a volatile situation by tolerating the KKK's breaking of the law. Tuscaloosa police allowed masked Klansmen to parade in their streets and to frisk suspected radicals in contradiction to state law. Birmingham police routinely looked the other way or participated when the Klan attacked radicals. A jury in Coffee County returned an acquittal after eight masked men stripped and flogged a woman in 1940. Gadsden police allowed mobs to torment labor organizers. Authorities watched passively or actively helped as Klansmen, landlords, and vigilantes forcibly preserved the racial and economic status quo in the Black Belt.[75]

The situation in Henry County provided a striking example of one community's refusal to punish vigilante violence despite the risk that the federal government would interfere in state race relations. Two grand juries refused to hand down indictments in a 1937 lynching even though the local sheriff virtually delivered the victim to his fate and then named ten members of the mob in open court. Grand jurors also refused to impeach the sheriff. In response, Governor Graves, who was also concerned by debate over a federal antilynching bill, declared that "lynch law shall not prevail in Alabama." Nervous editors tried to stave off federal involvement by touting the efficiency of state law enforcement. The sheriff's defense attorney claimed that Alabama "has been making good progress in educating the law to take its course" and admonished outsiders to "let us deal with our crimes . . . without interference." Alabama's attorney general stressed that the state needed to impeach Henry's sheriff or federal intrusion might occur as a result. "If the State doesn't enforce constitutional clauses on lynching," Attorney General A. A. Carmichael cautioned, "Congress is going to do something about it by passing an anti-lynching bill." Ultimately, though, the Alabama Supreme Court refused to overturn the sheriff's acquittal or to force the grand jury to indict the lynchers.[76]

The KKK showed every sign of persisting in a state that could not generate strict legal punishment for crimes committed by Klansmen and other practitioners of vigilantism. It did so although such excess posed a serious threat to the credibility of states' rights and the preservation of home rule on race. As long as resistance to the order stopped at the door of the Alabama courthouse, the life and work of the order seemed likely to continue.

14
World War II and Postwar Alabama

The Klan reemerged strongly in Alabama shortly after the end of World War II. This outbreak of the Klan strain has been difficult to explain. The period 1946 through 1949, a period half as long as Reconstruction in Alabama, has received insufficient attention. Nevertheless, the Klan that grew in Alabama during this time shared a number of features with its counterparts in earlier days. Indeed, although the Alabama KKK gathered marked momentum after 1945, the secret society and its engine of racial divisiveness were sores that festered throughout World War II.

While scholars have done a good deal to elucidate southern racial violence during the war, the postwar period has received far less attention.[1] World War II was a watershed in southern economic history, but it also exerted a profound effect on the course of race relations in the South. Black activism, assertiveness, and agitation for voting rights all accelerated in the wake of war. After 1945, a cadre of progressive southern white politicians appealed with some success to a new biracial coalition of working-class whites and a small but growing black electorate. This progressive cabal was so successful in Alabama that the state soon boasted of having a progressive governor, two progressive senators, and the South's most liberal congressional delegation.[2]

Progressive electoral success in wartime and postwar Alabama was accompanied by a tense racial atmosphere and an increasingly violent backlash from the forces of white supremacy. The Klan rode again in this climate, targeting not only assertive blacks but also whites who challenged conventional notions of morality. Elite Alabamians from a variety of backgrounds responded in a number of ways.

RACE AND WORLD WAR II

The stresses and strains that accompany any war breathed life into the 1940s KKK. Economic dislocation, competition for jobs and housing, and insecurity about the future strained the already frayed relations between the races. Women and blacks, asked in 1941 to replace white men in American industries, found that peace brought a change in their duties. When they were banished from the factory, resentment grew.[3]

Relations between the states and the federal government also changed considerably. Southern states received an inordinate share of federal largesse during World War II. In return, they were expected to abide by federal standards in the workplace rather than regional ones. Historian Bruce Schulman has shown how deficit military spending led to the rise of a new cohort of southern politicians after World War II. These were politicians motivated more by economic progress than by race. During the war, many blacks left the South to pursue economic opportunities in the North. The southern labor force became less rural, more highly skilled, and more exclusively male, and the region profited when it received military bases and plants. Wages increased 40 percent from 1939 to 1942 and continued to rise during the war years. The National Wage Labor Board isolated southern industry by banning wage differentials on race so that black wages could rise. Southern manufactured employment also increased 50 percent. In 1941, President Franklin Roosevelt narrowly averted an embarrassing march on Washington by mortgaging the future of race relations in the defense industry. The result of that promise, the Fair Employment Practices Committee (FEPC), while not the boon that had been anticipated by some, heralded inclement weather for conservative southern whites. Two years later, a rash of race riots unseen since 1919 erupted around the country.[4]

The war affected southern race relations in other ways. Nervous racial moderates tried to mitigate black calls for civil rights by stressing the contributions of African Americans to the war effort. Yet growing prosperity only highlighted segregation as a problem that had remained untouched by economic improvement. Some whites also found it difficult to reconcile American participation in a war for democracy with continuing inequities in the treatment of blacks at home. Anxiety on this score hinted at serious repercussions to come. "Operation Dixie" and the political action committee of the CIO also threatened the ramparts of southern conservatism.[5]

Alabama race relations became even more tense than usual. In February 1942, Fort Deposit whites lynched a black for arguing with his white employer. Governor Frank Dixon refused to acknowledge that an actual lynching had occurred. Instead he warned that the KKK might ride again if the federal government did not allow southern states a free hand in controlling their black populations.[6]

Desegregation of the armed forces contributed to heightened domestic race tensions. One native Alabamian, an Air Force officer stationed in Colorado, reported that northern whites were just like "rebels" on the race issue. He expressed his dismay about military desegregation to his close friend, Charles B. Crow, a nephew of the patrician matriarch Marie Bankhead Owen. "Someday [desegregation] is going to be the cause of some of us being court-martialed," he predicted. "I am willing to do anything necessary to help win this war but . . . place a negro on the same social plane. . . . If they want to have negro outfits let them . . . train them in the north if they love them so much." Crow congratulated the airman for his support of progressive senator Lister Hill and commiserated with him on the race issue. "Thank God I am not in that situation," he wrote. "Maybe they will hurry up and get those [black] troops over [to] the southwest Pacific and let the Japs get them!"[7]

During the war, Mobile experienced severe racial tensions. Union molders and machinists refused to work alongside blacks. In May 1943, Mobile's dockyards exploded in riot when twelve black workers were promoted in compliance with a six-month-old FEPC directive. Whites attacked blacks with pipes, clubs, and tools until U.S. Army troops, the U.S. Coast Guard, state and local police, and Alabama National Guardsmen arrived to restore order. In 1944, the scene was nearly repeated at a U.S. Army post nearby.[8]

Furious over federal involvement by the Army and Coast Guard in quelling the Mobile riot, Chauncey Sparks, the new governor of Alabama, decried outside intrusion into the state's racial affairs. His remarks revealed that, like many white Alabamians, Sparks was far more comfortable with traditional race relations and favored offering only practical educational opportunities for blacks:

We would not have any [race problems] but for influence over which we have no control. If self-seeking politicians, misguided philanthropists and outside influences would quit trying to regulate matters which are entirely local, we would have no future difficulty, . . . if we can be let alone and zoot-minded propagandists do not misinform.

. . . future race rioting . . . will have its roots buried in inflammatory negro newspapers . . . ambitious politicians and misguided and emotional missionaries who place shibboleths above reality. The South does not need to be taught morality by prosecutions, by . . . committee [or] by [the] preachments . . . [of] some unreasonable agitator. . . . when the negro quits chasing rain-

bow ends and butterflies, such as social equality and the abolishment of segregation and confines his attention to fundamentals, such as industry, education . . . [and] economic security, the better off he will be and the less successful the agitators will be.[9]

During the early 1940s, Alabama's buses and streetcars became moving theaters in which racial tensions were acted out in violent and often
dramatic ways. Increasingly assertive blacks, individuals whom one black
scholar has termed "baaad niggers," challenged segregation in public transportation long before anyone ever heard of Rosa Parks. In 1942 alone, Birmingham bus and streetcar officials recorded eighty-eight incidents involving blacks who took whites-only seats as well as 176 racial incidents of
other sorts, including eighteen brawls between passengers, twenty-two fistfights between passengers and white drivers, and thirteen arguments over
other indignities habitually afforded to people of color. Blacks were often,
according to one scholar, "profane and militant" in challenging transportation segregation. Black women, as in the 1930s, showed a particular willingness to test the boundaries of Jim Crow, sometimes even engaging in fistfights with white males and gun-toting bus drivers. On 15 August 1942, the
inevitable happened in Mobile. During an argument, a white bus driver
shot and killed a black army private as he was returning to his barracks.[10]

Southern white supremacists were not about to surrender their way of
life without a struggle. Horace Wilkinson, one of the South's leading racial demagogues and a former Klan leader, sounded the trumpet of regional
alarm. Speaking to a Birmingham Kiwanis Club in 1942, Wilkinson horri-
fied listeners with stories about blacks who ignored Jim Crow, "stole" the
jobs of white steelworkers who had gone overseas, and threw kisses to white
schoolgirls. He told appalled whites about a Birmingham bus driver who
had pointed to a group of blacks and predicted, "Right there, mister, is
where our next war will break out, and it may start before this one is [even]
over." "If there is room for a National Association for the Advancement of
Colored People," Wilkinson bellowed, "there is need for a League to Maintain White Supremacy."[11]

After the war, the atmosphere in Alabama continued to be tense. Klan
violence greeted black assertiveness, voting registration, and a progressive
political challenge to Big Mule/Black Belt hegemony. While relatively liberal politicians lost gubernatorial elections to race-baiters in Georgia, Texas,
and Mississippi, James E. "Big Jim" Folsom defeated Handy Ellis in Alabama's 1946 primary. The Folsom victory demonstrated that a more liberal
appeal to a biracial alliance of blacks and plain whites could result in vic-

tory. Electoral success combined with expanding black voting registration efforts and the NAACP's legal challenge to segregation.[12]

As soldiers, black and white, returned home, worried Alabama whites battened down the hatches of white supremacy. Because of intense segregationist protest over plans for interracial viewing, Birmingham became one of only two cities to miss out on the 315-city "Freedom Train" tour featuring "the nation's most priceless" collection of historical artifacts. Alabamians also passed the Boswell Amendment. An extraordinary measure, Boswell required the reading, understanding, and explaining of the U.S. Constitution as the basis for voting. It gave white registrars the perfect tool with which to deny blacks the vote.[13]

Violence accompanied the tough talk and legal impediments. In May 1946, Athens, Alabama, exploded in race riots. Nearly a hundred persons, mostly blacks, were injured. Similar episodes occurred around the South as returning GIs, many of them black and armed with state poll tax exemptions, threatened to make politics less certain at home.[14]

After the war, President Harry Truman's civil rights package lent additional impetus to the rejuvenation of the KKK. Truman's program—which called for a permanent FEPC as well as for laws against lynching, segregation, and the poll tax—presented the greatest federal intrusion into southern race relations since Reconstruction. The South, ever protective of home rule, mobilized to fight the president. In 1948, disgruntled southern Democrats formed a third national party, the States' Rights Democrats, or "Dixiecrats," and prepared to block Truman's bid for reelection.[15]

Communism and the emergence of the cold war also bolstered the Klan. When peace finally came, Soviet Russia and the United States filled the vacuum of global influence left by older imperial powers such as Britain, France, and Germany. As the new superpowers hurtled along a collision course, which seemed as ineluctable as it promised to be destructive, cold war rhetoric became the new postwar parlance. Strategic and economic factors shaped the development of the cold war for policymakers, but for average Americans, differences were reduced to their lowest common denominator. Politicians found the language of ideology, which could be easily understood and parroted at the popular level. The postwar world was divided in black-and-white terms between capitalism and communism, democracy and tyranny. Almost subconsciously, American patriotism became increasingly defined as loyalty to democracy and to the capitalist economic creed.[16]

In Alabama, anticommunism had long been used as a weapon. Vigilantism aimed at black activists, racial liberals, and labor unions usually accompanied the red-baiting. Anti-Communist rhetoric had been used with frightening efficiency against 1920s unionists and depression-era unionists, radicals, and defenders of the Scottsboro Boys.[17]

The cold war, though, had a two-edged effect on Alabama's KKK. While Klan leaders quickly gauged the potential in posing as America's guardians against fifth column subversion, racist violence also became a liability in the new war of propaganda between East and West. By 1946, many Americans had become sensitive to the fascist impulse. Grisly tales of Dachau ovens, Auschwitz gas showers, and painful experimentation on human guinea pigs shocked and sickened an entire generation. The Nazi Holocaust left the KKK vulnerable to charges of being a breeding ground for Nazis in sheets. As a result, postwar Klansmen found themselves greeted by reflexive national opposition that had not threatened earlier Klans until several years into their respective careers.[18]

Postwar opposition to the Klan also reflected the order's heritage. By 1946, old excesses had etched themselves so indelibly into the fabric of Klan lore that any new group bearing the same name was bound to carry heavy baggage. The stigma included a collective memory of lynchings, beatings, floggings, castration, branding, poisoning, assassination, rape, mutilation, and tarring and feathering along with a host of negative images: congressional inquiries, muzzling acts, hypocrisy, unfavorable publicity, and scandal.

POSTWAR KLAN RESURGENCE

Formal revival of the Ku Klux Klan took place in Atlanta on 27 March 1946. One night later, eight crosses burned in Birmingham to mark the resurgence of the order in Alabama. During World War II, Alabama's KKK had shrunk to just four chapters and a thousand hard-core members. Yet it had never entirely disappeared.[19]

Imperial Wizard Jimmy Colescott had let the order go bankrupt in 1943 when a visit from federal auditors resulted in a demand for $685,000 in back taxes. "It was that nigger-lover Roosevelt and that Jew Morgenthau who was his Secretary of the Treasury who did it!" he insisted. Still, Colescott had maintained that the audit did not mean the KKK was completely dead. Mark Etheridge, astute editor of the *Louisville Courier-Journal,* agreed. "Of course, as the imperial wizard points out, the Klan is not actually dead," Etheridge wrote. "Such a spirit, rooted in the still-strong impulse to evil in mankind is hard to kill, is capable of springing full-fledged into vitality again."[20]

Leadership of the postwar Klan was disputed almost immediately. Atlanta physician Samuel A. Green registered the Association of Georgia Klans as a corporation because Georgia's fifty-cent annual fee had been paid each year on Hiram Evans's 1920s Knights of the Ku Klux Klan, Inc. Although headquartered in Atlanta, Green's group organized 20,000 Kluxers in Alabama and other southeastern states. He also emphasized continuity: "The Klan has never been dead and the Klan is never going to die."[21]

As the dominant postwar Klan, Green's organization concentrated on the race question. "The niggahs . . . got all the good jobs while you were in uniform," Green told returning white veterans. "I'll tell you this, no CIO or AFL carpetbagging organizers or any other damned Yankees are going to . . . tell Southerners how to run either their businesses or their niggahs." On another occasion, Green asserted, "There ain't a nigger that's the equal of a white man. If God wanted us all equal, He would have made all people white men."[22]

A rival group soon sprang up in Alabama. Dr. E. P. Pruitt took the title "chairman of the board" for the Federated Ku Klux Klans, Inc., while William Hugh Morris, a well-known roofing contractor, settled for the title of "director." The pair filed incorporation papers in July 1946, but the group had already been operating for several months. Morris declared the purpose of his new Klan group to be the "protection of . . . white womanhood and white supremacy." "All we want to do," he said, "is keep the colored man in his place." Pruitt seemed to be as dedicated to these precepts as his partner. He had previously advocated the abrogation of the Fourteenth, Fifteenth, and Nineteenth Amendments and the denial of civil rights to blacks, Catholics, and Jews. Curiously, Pruitt viewed his position as paternalistic rather than prejudicial. "The Klan don't hate nobody!" he insisted. "In fact, the Klan is the good nigger's best friend. I've delivered many a nigger baby without charging a cent for it. My nigger maid even washes my Klan robe for me."[23]

Morris and Pruitt organized their order with gusto. Birmingham, as it had so often been, was the easiest area in Alabama to organize—probably because of postwar residential and occupational competition between the races. An older white resident greeted news of the Klan's rejuvenation by rejoicing: "This will teach the niggers to stay put in their place. If they don't, we'll stack 'em up like cordwood." A young NAACP worker, apprised of the increase in KKK activity, asked where he could buy a bulletproof vest.[24]

Klan organizers sponsored rallies in Gadsden, Montgomery, Centreville, Brent, Tarrant, West Blocton, and other areas. Talladega Klansmen tried to palliate concern over the increase in sheeted activity by dressing up as Santa Clauses and presenting a 107-year-old black man with a new radio. Although a hooded leader cited the act as prima facie evidence that the Klan did not hate blacks, a Will Morris speech at Notasulga belied his words. As the home of the Tuskegee Improvement Association, Macon County was an area of significant turmoil during the 1940s. African Americans, perhaps galvanized by their 1930s forays into rural communism, attempted to increase their presence on county voting rolls. Addressing 200 Macon Klansmen, Morris outlined a Communist plot in which "modern carpetbaggers" allegedly planned to use black "puppets" to set up "colored republics" in the Black Belt. At a rally in Bessemer, a masked orator echoed his warning.[25]

The seeds of racial intolerance fell upon fertile soil. Within three years, the Federated KKK could make the inflated claim of having 30,000 dues-paying members in Alabama and 7,000 in Birmingham alone. Nationally, Klan officials claimed an exaggerated 1 million members across twenty-eight states, but the vast majority of 1940s Kluxers were concentrated in the South. Although membership was only a fraction of what it had been during the 1920s, robed officials were pleased with the postwar resurgence and argued that their 1940s membership comprised a purer and more select group.[26]

Others were less certain. Readily acceding that the rolls enumerated a smaller and more dedicated cadre, many observers commented on the obviously low socioeconomic status of those who joined. *Newsweek* noted that the ranks of the 1940s order were filled with the "backward and the frustrated, the poor and the disappointed of the Deep South." An observer in Greenville, Alabama, concurred, linking the secret society to the state's grinding poverty and illiteracy. The *Montgomery Advertiser* and a Jewish woman from Butler County were less diplomatic. They preferred the term "white trash" to describe the majority of postwar Klansmen, "the kind . . . that feels the need to assert its supremacy by means other than superiority." Virginia Durr agreed that they were "so low down themselves they need someone beneath them to kick." Whatever the words chosen, the 1940s Klan clearly attracted a membership of more humble social origins than the broad 1920s order.[27]

The low caliber of the postwar Klansmen was apparent throughout Alabama. The W. O. Dycus Klavern met every Friday night in an old shack eight miles north of Pell City that had boarded windows, beat-up benches, kegs that passed for tables, and a dirt floor littered with cigarette butts. Whereas Hugo Black, Bibb Graves, Crampton Harris, Cooper Green, Charlie McCall, and other high-profile politicians could be found in Alabama's 1920s klaverns, Tuscaloosa's 1940s branch was characterized by poor organization, raunchy storytelling, appalling ignorance, and sheer confusion. Tuscaloosa's post–World War II lodge was made up primarily of industrial and skilled blue-collar workers, some public employees, and a few small merchants. Its cyclops was a salesman, and its meetings were studded with diatribes against blacks and Jews. Speaking about the Boswell Amendment, one hooded member said, "I don't give a damn how bad that rascal [U.S.] Supreme Court up there wants to kick it out, they can't until somebody makes a protest—and God pity the damned Negro that makes a test case of this just law." Another Klansman expressed his unhappiness when he saw black dishwashers talking with white waitresses and watched the races sharing Tuscaloosa's elevators. "I think [once we] get a good organization going here," he suggested, "we should just plain go out and get them." Meeting as the "Tuscaloosa Social Club" at the county activities building, the sheeted society planned parades, rallies, and mysterious midnight rides where members were required to perform unknown duties and were sworn to eternal secrecy.[28]

While its social origins were lower and its agenda more purely militant than those of the 1920s Klan, the post–World War II Klan did share the bolting tendency with the 1920s order. In 1948, much as in 1928, Alabama's KKK sided with the far right wing of the Democratic Party. Alienated by President Truman's civil rights program, the States' Rights Party met in Birmingham in July 1948 to declare war on Truman and any other politician remotely concerned with civil rights. Founded by former Klansmen Horace Wilkinson and Hugh Locke, and by the staunch patrician white supremacists Frank Dixon and Gessner McCorvey, the party was especially well organized in Alabama, where it counted on the strong support of the industrialist/planter machine. In 1948, Bull Connor ran an antifederal campaign for governor as a Dixiecrat candidate. Corporation attorney James Simpson challenged Lister Hill for his senatorial seat backed by fellow Dixiecrat Sidney Smyer, whose speeches reminded people of Klan rallies. The "KKK element" of Wilkinson and Locke was consistently tied to the States' Rights Party, and a gallery of privileged segregationists, mostly Big Mules and Black Belt planters, populated the rump party: John Temple Graves II, Donald Comer, Marie Bankhead Owen, Handy Ellis, Marion Rushton, Congressmen Walter Givhan and Samuel Hobbs, the journalist Thomas Abernathy, the Dothan banker Wallace Malone, the insurance magnate Frank Samford, Jr., and the Selma planter Sam Englehardt.[29]

Horace Wilkinson's states'-rights verbiage tied together virtually every southern fear: "President Truman . . . is now training federal police to enforce [civil rights], federal police to go in[to] each hamlet of the country and impose the will of a strong federal government upon the people." "Federal police!" Wilkinson exclaimed. "What could be more un-American? We must face the race question frankly and fairly as we have learned to face . . . venereal disease. . . . The first step towards a Communized America is the invasion of States' Rights. . . . [an invasion] determined to make life in each State conform to a Washington pattern. . . . [We aim] to prevent the establishment of a Federal Gestapo, empowered to interfere in the lives of our people and create a police State on the pattern of Moscow."[30]

Overlap between the KKK and the Dixiecrats, at least in terms of ideology, was considerable. In fact, many Alabamians saw the 1940s Klan as the poor uneducated instruments of Dixiecrat politicians and their patrician allies. "The Klan is not a spontaneous expression," racial moderate Charlie Dobbins wrote in the *Montgomery Examiner.* "It is artfully contrived by leaders who want either money or political advantage."[31]

Men such as Horace Wilkinson and Hugh Locke had made a career out of seeking both. During the 1940s, Wilkinson turned to publishing hate sheets as a new way of cashing in on racial tensions. His increasing obsession with race accompanied his reconciliation of long-standing differences with Alabama's oligarchy. During the 1940s, the former Klansman functioned as the most active spokesman on behalf of his erstwhile enemies. At one point, Wilkinson declared that he would rather "die fighting for states' rights than live on [Harry] Truman boulevard in a nigger heaven."[32]

Editors across the South blamed the "hate promoting utterances" of Wilkinson and Bull Connor, his protégé turned enemy turned ally, for aiding and abetting the rejuvenation of Alabama's 1940s KKK. A national magazine termed Klansmen the "disappointed crackpot fringe of the States' Rights party." A Chicago editor was even more blunt. He informed his readers that the "fools and hoodlums" of the KKK had been given the green light by Alabama's more privileged Dixiecrat leaders. Meanwhile, hate sheets such as the *Trumpet,* the *Militant Truth,* and Wilkinson's *Southern Outlook* and *Alabama* spewed bigotry and fomented racial discord. The Big Mules heavily subsidized them.[33]

The Alabama Klan stood behind the States' Rights Party in letter and in spirit. Klan leaders regularly boasted that the secret order backed the Dixiecrats "100 per cent." "The Dixiecrat movement is a good thing for the protection of the South," Dr. E. P. Pruitt declared. Like his Dixiecrat allies, Will Morris often blamed "outside meddlers trying to cram social equality down our throats" for the South's racial woes. Bull Connor, never a formal Klan member but long a sympathizer, announced his Dixiecrat candidacy for governor by borrowing the KKK notion of a Communist plot involving African American dupes.[34]

Klan-Dixiecrat collusion stretched to other fronts as well. When Mobile blacks organized a league to fight the Boswell Amendment, Klan director William Morris, "in the interests of white supremacy and common sense"—apparently the two were synonymous—wrote a circuit judge to protest the granting of a charter. Asked to elaborate on his appeal to hooded audiences, eccentric Klan chaplain Lycurgus Spinks relied on vintage states'-rights rhetoric: "I just tell 'em they are entitled to every bit of bounty that the government is passing out—but that the government ain't got no right at all to be meddling in their business." When Henry Wallace, the 1948 presidential hopeful of the Progressive Party, swung through Alabama, Kluxers arranged a hostile reception.[35]

Roosevelt's secretary of agriculture and former vice president, Henry Wallace was a pariah in the South for his racial liberalism. Gadsden Kluxers led a mob of steelworkers who pounded his car with pipes and bats and tried to drag the candidate from the car. Police officers stood by and did nothing. A shaken Wallace fled Gadsden without getting out to speak. As his driver whisked him to safety, he muttered to himself, "Now I've seen the eyes of fascism." In Birmingham, he fared little better. Police Commissioner Bull Connor (figure 30) greeted him by vowing to enforce the city's segregation ordinance at Progressive Party rallies. Connor obviously meant business. Only a year earlier he had jailed Wallace's running mate, a U.S. senator, for entering a Birmingham building through a "colored-only" entrance.[36]

Bull Connor's relationship to the KKK is an intriguing subject. Without question he knew Klansmen, associated with them, sought and accepted their support, and habitually let them have their way with people of color. Still, no one has been able to demonstrate that Connor ever actually joined the Klan—unlike other arch-conservative racists such as Horace Wilkinson and Hugh Locke. Evidence exists that Connor allowed, even aided and abetted, the Klan's terrorism of African Americans and white racial liberals. At the very least, he did much to foster a climate of permissiveness that Klan terrorists used to their advantage. He was presiding over the city's police force in April 1956 when Klansmen attacked black balladeer Nat King Cole and also in May 1961 when Birmingham police gave the KKK fifteen minutes to beat the biracial "Freedom Riders." After he retired, a former acting police chief admitted that there had been several Fairfield Klansmen on Birmingham's police force in the 1960s, and many other sympathizers, but as for "Bull, I don't think he ever joined the Klan or nothing, but he certainly concurred in their efforts."[37]

VIOLENCE AND REACTION

Blueprints for Klan violence were translated into action after World War II. Most Alabama violence was aimed at black challenges to white supremacy, political control, social exclusion, and job and housing opportunities. Still,

30. Theophilus Eugene ("Bull") Connor, 1940s. As Birmingham police commissioner, Connor was obviously sympathetic to the Klan whether or not he was formally a member. Courtesy Birmingham Public Library Archives, Portraits.

an enduring moral authoritarianism reminiscent of the 1920s also marked Klan violence in 1940s Alabama.

Rhetoric led to acts of violence. Robert S. Gulledge, a Klan kleagle and head of the 1930s White Legion, told a 1947 gathering in one breath that the KKK was not racially intolerant and in another that the Klan mission was an effort to "save the Negro from his own folly." Gulledge termed black attempts at educational, residential, and voting rights direct affronts "to every white, Protestant, Gentile, Democrat in Alabama."[38]

Violence sometimes followed such remarks.[39] The mere threat of Klan violence was often enough to bring about a mass exodus of black residents or the scrapping of plans to move into nicer neighborhoods. In 1947, Klansmen held a hate rally at Enon Ridge, a black subdivision in Birmingham. Sylacauga Kluxers put on a similar demonstration. The KKK also sent threats to NAACP workers and black war veterans in Birmingham.[40]

One of the Kluxers who took a lead in postwar Klan violence was Robert Chambliss, an employee at a garage run by the city of Birmingham. Immortalized in the annals of the Klan as the 1963 bomber of Birmingham's Sixteenth Street Baptist Church, during the 1940s Chambliss was busy serving his apprenticeship as a hooded terrorist. An admitted member of Robert E. Lee Klavern No. 1, Chambliss visited a black insurance agent and threatened to blow up his home. He also gained notoriety by earning an indictment for flogging and for smashing the camera of a reporter at a Klan rally while police officers impassively looked on. Mayor Cooper Green called Chambliss on the carpet and threatened to fire him, but Chambliss responded with a threat of his own to sue the city.[41]

Robert Chambliss was an example of a "career Klansman," an individual who remained active in the KKK during the 1940s, 1950s, and 1960s. A true believer in white supremacy, he donned a hood in the 1940s and continued to intimidate and harm people for the Klan through the 1960s.

In 1948, most Klan violence revolved around black desires to vote in the upcoming presidential election. After experiencing only frustration in their attempts to register, Tuskegee blacks staged a sit-in at the Macon County board of registrars. Klansmen retaliated by burning crosses at black homes, while the African American community followed up the protest with a boycott of white-owned businesses and an appeal to Alabama governor Jim Folsom. Leading Birmingham blacks also entreated the governor to investigate the slaying of six black males by city police officers, assaults on several NAACP representatives, Klan terrorism, and a number of unsolved Klan bombings. Birmingham police commissioner Bull Connor dismissed the petition as the obvious work of Communists.[42]

Meanwhile, racial tensions grew more strained. Fifty cars packed with Klansmen in full regalia paraded through Brighton, a black neighborhood near Bessemer. Hooded men burned eight crosses in Gadsden, including one in front of the mayor's home and several others at black businesses and the homes of NAACP members. Cross burnings and Klan parades also took place in Anniston, in Talladega, and at the University of Alabama. As Klansmen paraded through a black neighborhood in Talladega, the local police chief noted approvingly of the scene that "it was orderly." Several miles outside of Birmingham, highway patrolmen and sheriff's deputies directed traffic as 200 Klansmen initiated new members.[43]

Not all 1948 violence related to voting, though. Some came in response to black economic aspirations. Klansmen burned a cabin on the Coosa

River because black laborers had built it. Sheeted raiders also broke a Massachusetts student's windshield in Sumter County because it had a Henry Wallace bumper sticker on it. One Klan preacher threatened blacks because he thought they were being made the tools of Communist subversion.[44]

The most sensational act of KKK intimidation in 1948 occurred on 10 June. Over a hundred robed Klansmen raided a Girl Scout camp in Bessemer. Kluxers ransacked the tents of two white female instructors, accused them of teaching communism, and informed them that they had just twenty-four hours to vacate the premises. The two young women, who had been working with twenty-one black Girl Scouts as part of a two-week training course, were badly shaken. They immediately canceled their course and fled.[45]

Instead of making arrests, Jefferson County deputies publicly endorsed the raid. The county's chief deputy conducted an impromptu survey of ninety-two local residents and concurred with the majority's judgment that the Klan visit had produced "a good effect" because "folks around here don't like Negroes and whites living together."[46]

Klan leaders were similarly unrepentant. William Morris argued that the white women should not have been sleeping in such close proximity to blacks. Dr. E. P. Pruitt denied that the Federated KKK had participated as an organization but insisted that the raid had been a good thing. "If I saw a mad dog or a snake I would shoot it," he explained. "And some people act like mad dogs and snakes."[47]

When the Klan terrorized an organization expressly devoted to the preservation of Americanism and womanhood—allegedly two of the KKK's most inviolate tenets—it met with swift and widespread opposition. Newspapers in Alabama and other states were quick to condemn the raid. The *Birmingham News* described it as "unspeakable, despicable," the *Birmingham Age-Herald* as "horrifying," and the *Montgomery Advertiser* as "contemptible." The *Birmingham Post* also registered its disapproval, while Birmingham's leading black paper dubbed the raiders the "hooded Knights of cowardice." Editors in Georgia, Texas, and other states deplored the escapade, and a Tennessee newspaper called the act "one of the most vicious, dastardly and stupid outrages" that the Klan had perpetrated in years.[48]

Civic and religious groups joined the press in condemning the Klan. The Young Men's Business Club, the Alabama department of the Veterans of Foreign Wars (VFW), the Girl Scout Board, the Birmingham Pastors Union, the Birmingham Baptist Pastors Conference, and the Birmingham Methodist Association all denounced the raid.[49] Additional opposition came from prominent businessmen such as Donald Comer and Frank B. Yielding.[50]

Political opposition accompanied the outrage. Governor Folsom asked

Jefferson County's solicitor for a full report. Alabama's speaker of the state house of representatives castigated the event as "un-American and unlawful." The state's small Progressive Party joined the opposition. Even Alabama's tiny Communist Party published a ringing condemnation.[51]

Of infinitely more concern to many Alabamians was criticism from beyond its borders. The national director of the Girl Scouts sent shock waves through Alabama when she raised the specter of federal involvement by asking U.S. attorney general Tom Clark to look into the matter. The National Negro Congress also caused a stir by calling for Alabama's KKK to be dissolved. Yet by far the most persistent critique came from Abraham Berkowitz, a Jewish attorney in Birmingham. Calling the chief deputy's approbation of the incident as offensive as the raid itself, Berkowitz demanded that Alabama's attorney general begin proceedings to revoke the Klan's corporate charter. He also drafted eight unsolicited ordinances designed to outlaw the KKK and submitted them to startled Birmingham officials. While Mayor Cooper Green, himself a 1920s alumnus of the secret order, considered the proposed laws, Berkowitz endured Klan death threats. Finally, growing weary of the city's inaction, he informed Alabama's attorney general that he planned to initiate revocation proceedings as a private citizen if the state and city refused to act. "Experience proves," Berkowitz said, "that only the pitiless light of continued exposure can [defeat] . . . the type of cowards who prowl at night. . . . [The KKK] exists for no lawful or useful purpose."[52]

One of the most curious aspects of the Girl Scout raid was the absence of censure from organized labor. In stark contrast to other groups, labor unions remained silent despite prodding from a miffed NAACP. William Mitch, president of District 20 of the UMW, perhaps revealed one of the reasons for labor's sluggishness when he informed his rank and file that they would have to choose between Klan membership and belonging to the miners' union. Some Kluxers belonged to steelworkers' unions; a few were actually card-carrying members of the Socialist Party, an almost uniquely southern combination.[53]

Despite Mitch's urgings, and the enmity that had existed between the KKK and labor during the 1930s, Alabama unions took a different position on the 1940s Klan. Labor's silence was a complicated issue. It is clearly misleading to discuss Alabama "labor" in monolithic terms. While some miners were plainly involved in hooded violence, in the 1930s organized labor had usually found itself on the receiving end of the Klan whip.[54]

Despite the almost certain participation of miners and other workers in Klan depredations, the animus between labor and the Klan had continued through World War II. The Klan especially disliked the relatively new CIO.

Founded in 1935 by John L. Lewis, the CIO stood for biracial, inclusive, industrial, and liberal labor policies in contrast to the more staid and exclusive tenets of the AFL. In 1942, Alabama Klansmen had flogged unionists and burned crosses for weeks in anticipation of a CIO representation election at a steel plant in Tuscaloosa County.[55]

After World War II, CIO organizers launched "Operation Dixie," a campaign to organize Alabama and the other southern states. In response, a Covington County newspaper practically solicited Klan violence to block the organization of several textile mills. Authorities reported the outbreak of nearly twenty attacks on southern unionists. A Lanett mob hurled bricks bearing the inscription "Vote No for CIO" through the windows of local businesses known to be sympathetic to the group. At the Avondale Mills, Klansmen kidnapped and flogged a disabled CIO organizer crippled by wartime service. In Sylacauga, masked men beat CIO organizers who distributed leaflets at the Beacon Manufacturing Company. Evergreen Kluxers ambushed a car carrying two CIO organizers, riddled it with bullets, then burned it. A Montgomery deputy sheriff joined the Klan war against labor by assaulting yet another CIO organizer. Because the CIO was a pioneer in biracial unionism, 1940s violence aimed at the group included an important element of racism.[56]

MORALITY ENFORCEMENT

As 1949 unfolded, Klan violence increasingly targeted blacks and poor whites who had offended the order's fragile moral sensibilities. By the end of the year, a rash of violence unseen in Alabama since the heyday of the 1927 nightriders had descended upon the state. The sheer intensity of the terrorism in June suggests that it was most likely the product of a planned crusade rather than the spasmodic work of a few independent-minded extremists. The nature of the violence—reflecting an obsession with morality and local mores—was strikingly reminiscent of the 1920s Klan's moral authoritarianism.

Within one two-week period, Klansmen burned eighty-nine crosses and assaulted over twenty Alabamians. Buoyed by the words that the KKK's Reverend Alvin Horn uttered against the "return of carpetbagger government [and] Negroes running things," Kluxers burned crosses in Tarrant, Warrior, Tuscaloosa, and Gadsden. Special attention was devoted to Horn's own bailiwick of Talladega. There Klansmen burned crosses and staged nocturnal motorcades through black neighborhoods, prompting the president of a black college to complain to the state attorney general and to contact civil rights attorneys. Local police did nothing to interfere with the Talladega intimidation even though hooded Klansmen concealed their license plates in clear violation of state law. Birmingham Klansmen also vandalized the new 210-foot tower at a black radio station.[57]

William Morris practically announced a campaign against immorality in advance. At an April 1949 rally, Morris informed the public that his Klansmen were ready to "ride," a euphemism for hooded terror. He later boasted that he had over 200 men patrolling Jefferson and Walker Counties in search of ethical offenders—"honky-tonk operators, common brier-patch prostitutes, and people of that type."[58]

Alabama Klansmen wreaked vengeance on individuals they regarded as moral reprobates, many of them poor whites. Edna McDanal was one of the first to feel the Klan's wrath. On 10 June, a year to the day after the Bessemer Girl Scout raid, over a hundred armed Knights broke into McDanal's Jefferson County home. Kluxers tore from her hands the shotgun that she was trying to load, slugged her over the head with a blackjack, and dragged her outside to witness a cross burning. As McDanal looked on in horror, Klansmen took turns threatening her with beating, hanging, and burning at the stake. A willful woman, she snatched the hoods off several of her tormenters and later identified them—including one Baptist minister. The vigilantes charged her with selling liquor and pornography, prostitution, statutory rape, and dancing nude on her front porch. She threatened to call the police, but one of her assailants laughed and told her that several of them were the law. Another said, "Damn the law. . . . we are going to burn you and string you to the cross." Residents later testified that three preachers were in the Klan mob and that Graysville's police chief led the Klan procession away from McDanal's house with his siren wailing. While the macabre spectacle went on, weirdly illuminated by a fiery cross, one of McDanal's neighbors watched with delight. Later he explained that McDanal was an immoral woman and that the Klan cross "sure was pretty."[59]

On the same night, pistol-wielding Klansmen burned a cross at a café close to the McDanal home. As the local police chief looked on, hooded Kluxers warned the café's Greek owner that he must stop serving blacks. "You've got to keep those niggers down," one of the men explained. Another said that the Klan was tired of having Catholics run the town. "Furthermore," one Klansman said, "you're going to clean up those niggers here, cussing and raising hell inside and outside." J. F. Shaffer—an alderman and assistant policeman who was reputed to be a Klansman—arrived at the scene just moments too late to do anything.[60]

Similar acts followed. Four nights later, Klansmen abducted Billy Guyton Stovall, a navy veteran, from his home and covered his back with welts.

They charged Stovall with failing to support his family, because his wife had taken a part-time job. Stovall himself worked full time at a pipe company, had another part-time job, and attended school three nights a week. In Sumiton, two Klansmen assaulted a reporter for the *Birmingham Post* who was doing a story on hooded vigilantism. One of the men took aim at the reporter's head with a hammer. Later, the pair offered to buy the reporter a fried chicken dinner and proposed that he forget all about the incident.[61]

Other violence occurred during the summer spree, much of it directed against whites accused of moral transgressions. At Pumpkin Center, Kluxers flogged two men and a woman because she had given birth to three children out of wedlock. An Assembly of God minister removed his hood to pray over the victims before their beatings. Walker County Klansmen assaulted an elderly miner who was out of work because he had broken his back. He suffered a nervous breakdown. In nearby Dora, Klansmen kidnapped and terrorized three couples as they sat in their living room watching television. They beat some and simulated the hanging of others by throwing nooses over tree limbs, placing them around the victims' necks, and pulling the hysterical individuals almost off the ground. One young woman who several times believed that she was about to die, later identified her assailants. Klansmen also flogged two coal miners in Lacy's Chapel and whites in Homewood and Boston, Alabama. They burned crosses in Munford, Brighton, Rosehill, and Pineywood, on Birmingham's northside, and in front of the palatial Mountain Brook home of Clarence B. Hanson, publisher of the *Birmingham News*. Over a hundred Walker County Klansmen hijacked one car, held a gun to the driver's head, and accused him of bootlegging, gambling, and failing to support his family. Two weeks later, 200 masked men stormed a nonunion mine, beat several of its occupants, and threatened to "blow [their] guts out" if they reported the incident. A number of Birmingham residents left town after receiving Klan threats, while Dr. E. P. Pruitt denied that his Klan had been involved in the June spree—at least as an organization. "I don't look like any damned hoodlum—do I?" he asked. "Those days are gone."[62]

Clay County was also afflicted. Despite Klan threats, two courageous Methodist ministers investigated a rash of violence and concluded that Clay's 800 Klansmen had flogged 30 people in six months. Race seemed to make little difference. Robed thugs beat a black man who had earned five medals in World War II and several whites accused of having premarital sex. Three masked men fired gunshots into the ceiling of a black restaurant and shot at a black farmer as he ran for his life through a corn patch. Nightriders used hickory sticks, blackjacks, and pistol barrels to beat whites who tested area mores and blacks who pushed the boundaries of Jim Crow. A Birming-

31. Cross-burning in Autauga County, Late 1940s. Alabama's post–World War II Klan tar-geted blacks as well as whites who challenged conventional morality. Courtesy Boone Aiken.

ham newspaper captured the almost surreal atmosphere by reporting that fear "freezes the heart and stills the tongue" in Clay County. "Nobody trusts anybody" (figure 31).[63]

Although most of the Klan's 1949 terror was restricted to the mining district around west Jefferson and Walker Counties, with the notable excep-tion of Clay, some other instances dotted the state. Two avowed Fayette County Klansmen kidnapped and flogged a white youth with hickory branches, breaking his nose in the process. Coosa County vigilantes showed little respect for the color line by tying blacks and whites to the same tree to horsewhip them both. Near Mobile, three robed men lashed a cabinet maker at gunpoint. Kluxers burned four crosses around the county. Tuscaloosa's Klan chapter flogged one black, raided the home of another, and conducted a seventy-five-car motor parade through the black quarter of town. Klansmen also burned crosses in Cullman, Pike, and Shelby Counties.[64]

15

Federal-State Interaction in the 1940s

Alabama's 1949 rash of Klan violence provoked many responses. Reaction came from the federal government, elite Alabama, and the nation at large. Whatever the particular source, the interplay between national criticism, federal involvement, and state reaction to the Klan continued to be strong.

WASHINGTON AND ALABAMA

The Bessemer Girl Scout raid planted the first seeds of possible federal intervention in the mind of U.S. Attorney General Tom Clark. During the summer of 1948, Clark had discussed the possibility of Justice Department involvement in Alabama with the national director of the Girl Scouts. The next summer, as reports of the state's epidemic Klan violence reached his desk, Clark decided to act. He ordered an FBI probe into Alabama and placed the KKK on the department's list of subversive groups.[1] Buoyed by the hope of federal interference in Alabama, the Tuskegee Civic Association also called for a congressional probe. To their astonishment, its leaders had their prayers answered. Led by Brooklyn Democrat Emmanuel Cellar, a House subcommittee launched an official inquiry into Alabama's KKK situation.[2]

National support for the congressional action was plentiful. A Gadsden native, transplanted to Philadelphia, concluded that if Alabama "can't stop the Klan, then we'll see what the Federal Government can do." *Commonweal*'s national editors also chimed in: "Unfortunately this kind of violence is not new, and as yet the South has not demonstrated that Klanism is a local crime which it has in hand. If now Alabama is ready . . . [to] enforce adequate laws, there need be no federal interference. . . . If not, federally enacted civil rights legislation is the alternative [that Alabama] brings on itself." For nervous Alabamians, congressional and FBI probes merely hinted at the undesirable possibilities that Klan excess might entail.[3]

During the House hearings, congressmen displayed acute concern about the extent to which local law enforcement was responding to Klan activity. Herbert Levy, staff counsel for the ACLU, disclosed that thirty of Jefferson County's fifty deputy sheriffs were either avowed Klansmen or sympathizers. Furthermore, local deputies had several times helped Kluxers elude state police. "I think it is time for the Federal Government to step in and do something," he concluded. An NAACP representative echoed the call for federal action. New York's Anti-Nazi League publicly petitioned Governor Folsom to revoke the Klan's charter.[4]

Federal intrusion struck at the very nerve center of Alabama's being. States' rights lay at the heart of the Alabama body politic, and the actions of the attorney general, the FBI, and the House of Representatives rudely awakened some in Alabama. The most immediate concern for many was the possibility that the federal government might interfere with state race relations in response to the Klan's excesses. White Alabamians feared the passage of President Truman's 1948 civil rights package—a sweeping program calling for federal laws against Jim Crow, lynching, the poll tax, and job discrimination. A number of state elites, now jolted from their lethargy, closed ranks to oppose the central government. Realizing that the only way to prevent almost certain federal encroachment was to combat the Klan themselves, Alabama's elites bargained for time. Political, religious, legal, press, and civic elites vowed to erase Klan violence from within Alabama but stressed that their campaign would take time. The disparate opponents of the Klan often called for patience.

Such demands for patience both preceded and followed the 1949 episode and provided a bulwark against change that was almost as strong as "massive resistance" itself. The Reverend Martin Luther King's famous "Letter from the Birmingham Jail" was composed as a response to such frustrating pleas for patience on the part of Birmingham's religious elites.[5]

The elites that waged war on Alabama's KKK differed in their motivation. Some were metropolitan newsmen, others were economic liberals like "Big Jim" Folsom, and still others were county-seat elites. Many were only tactical opponents of the order, groups of citizens fearful of federal invasiveness. Some journalists and clerics were repelled by hooded violence but could not sit by and watch the sudden disruption of regional race patterns. Businessmen feared the negative effect that Klan violence and continued national criticism would have on state commerce. Some politicians feared electoral reprisal if they took too broad a stand against the order. Few critics, though, mounted a comprehensive resistance that challenged the most fundamental tenets that underlay the Klan—segregation, white supremacy, states' rights, or the even more general racism and intolerance.[6]

Alabama's press corps led the 1949 fight against the Klan. The *Birmingham News* argued that local action would be the most effective mode of opposition but cautioned that results should not be expected overnight. Birmingham's *Age-Herald* concurred, while a Tuscaloosa editor chastised the sheeted order for attracting unwelcome federal attention. Editors of the *Montgomery Advertiser* suggested that Alabama could improve its own shortcomings without federal intrusion and noted that it was only human to resist pressure from outsiders.[7] A Memphis editor echoed its sister state's pleas against the central government's plan to "butt into what is going on in Alabama" and advised Alabamians to frustrate federal involvement "in the only way they can"—by eradicating Klan hoodlumism themselves.[8]

Political figures added their voices to the states' rights argument against the Klan. Attorney General A. A. Carmichael, Birmingham judge Robert J. Wheeler, and the chair of a joint veterans' committee complained that Alabama could solve its own problems without the benefit (or the drawbacks) of outside help. U.S. congressman Laurie Battle, who had helped get the federal ball rolling in the first place by asking Tom Clark to look into the Klan, backtracked in order to avoid appearing to be too enthusiastic an advocate of federal action. Battle assessed damage control to his career and warned of a dangerous connection between Klan excess and national support for President Truman's civil rights package. The state legislature demanded that the U.S. Congress cease its "deplor[able] . . . , wholly unnecessary, unwarranted, and unjustifiable" probe into Alabama's Klan violence and complained that racial violence in Ohio and Missouri had not received the same attention. Lawmakers exaggerated the efficiency of state law enforcement and the determination of Alabamians to stamp out Klan violence as reasons for a laissez-faire policy.[9]

Perhaps the most interesting protest was made by the witnesses who actually appeared before the U.S. House subcommittee. So deeply ingrained was the impulse to defend states' rights that three Alabamians asked for federal patience in allowing their state to solve its own Klan problem—despite the fact that they themselves had been victims of the order. Congressman Samuel Hobbs, a leading Alabama Dixiecrat, adopted a classic states'-rights position to argue eloquently against federal meddling. Using India's caste system and the Nazi Holocaust as rough analogues, Hobbs conceded the barbarity of flogging, but concluded that Congress "has just as [little] . . . power over India as we have over Alabama."[10]

To make good on their pledge to eradicate vigilantism from within, Alabama elites launched a war on the Klan from several fronts—legal, political, religious, press, and civic. A grand jury in Jefferson County demanded that Federated Klan director William Morris turn over his membership rolls. When Morris refused, a Birmingham judge clapped him in jail. The grand jury also returned indictments against seventeen defendants covering forty-five counts of Klan flogging. Among the indictees were four law enforcement officers: Brookside's police chief and a patrolman, Flat Creek's constable, and Coleman A. "Brownie" Lollar, a special Jefferson County deputy sheriff. The grand jury also indicted a Holiness preacher, a football coach from west Jefferson, a former head of the state AFL, and Brownie Lollar's brother, the exalted cyclops of an Avondale klavern. The solicitor boasted that the surface had "hardly been scratched," and a grand jury in Walker County followed suit by looking into a dozen floggings.[11]

The state legislature also drew blood in the fight against the Klan. Tuscaloosa senator Henry Mize sponsored a bill to outlaw masks. Actually, the bill was a revised version of a similar measure that had failed to become law during the 1920s. This time, though, the state senate voted 23 to 3 for it, and the house followed 84 to 4. Five minutes later, Governor Folsom signed the bill into law.[12]

Before the vote, Klan leaders had tried various strategies to defeat the bill. Dr. E. P. Pruitt unsuccessfully courted Folsom, assuring him that "your enemies are my enemies. My friends are your friends." In an attempt to steal the legislature's thunder, Pruitt unilaterally ordered all Alabama Klansmen to unmask. When Will Morris publicly challenged the wisdom of Pruitt's order, the Birmingham physician tersely replied that he, not Morris, was the head of Alabama's Invisible Empire. The difference of opinion opened what would, by year's end, become a wide and debilitating split.[13]

Morris chose a more direct route by informing legislators that the KKK was interested only in regulating prostitutes, liquor dealers, and other blights on Alabama's moral landscape. Morris's new chief ally, Talladega preacher Alvin Horn, said he would "rather be hung from the balcony over the steps where Jeff Davis took his oath than to have the mask" stripped away. A high school teacher, representing Clay County in the house, reckoned simply that he was voting against the measure "because the Klan doesn't want it, and I don't want to do anything the Klan doesn't want." Senator Mize, Montgomery's mayor, the Veterans of Foreign Wars, the Alabama Local Government League, and the state CIO supported the bill.[14]

A Birmingham attorney asked Governor Folsom to rescind the Klan's charter, but Folsom passed the political hot potato to his attorney general and instead launched a propaganda blitz against the Klan. During the summer of 1949, "Big Jim" castigated the sheeted terrorists as "would-be

Hitlers . . . , a renegade bunch of hooded cowards . . . , [and] a disgrace" and warned the Klan to "watch its step" in his state. He also called for legislative authority to create an Alabama bureau of investigation in order to ferret out KKK leaders. Folsom ordered the highway patrol to crack down on night-riding and hinted that he might even employ state revenue agents to audit Klan accounts. Himself no stranger to financial irregularity, Folsom declared that he had no intention of allowing vigilantes to run Alabama. In one of his many colorful speeches, he insinuated that beneath their masks the "white" Klansmen might really be "outlaws, Communists, Chinamen or Indians." The governor also issued a virtual carte blanche to resist robed marauders with physical force. "Your home is your castle," Folsom told the people of Alabama. "Defend it any way necessary."[15] Attorney General A. A. Carmichael, who had insisted that Washington allow Alabama to combat the Klan alone, branded Kluxers as "bums, hoodlums and cutthroats." He promised to help the governor wage war on the KKK and announced that state detectives had uncovered proof positive of the Klan's involvement in a number of floggings.[16]

Encouraged by Folsom and Carmichael's example, lesser politicos came out against the masked society. Mobile's mayor deplored the Klan, while a grand jury investigated hooded terror near the port city. The president of the Jefferson County Commission announced that the courthouse could no longer be used to hold meetings of hate groups. Montgomery's city commission informed Lycurgus Spinks that his Klan splinter was not welcome in the capitol. Civic, fraternal, and labor groups—including the League of Women Voters, Montgomery's Junior Chamber of Commerce, the Young Democrats, and the state AFL and CIO—vexed the Klan by backing black voter registration. Even the tiny Alabama Communist Party got involved by blaming the Dixiecrats and Bull Connor for sheeted violence.[17]

Some elites drew timely parallels between Klan and Nazi-style fascism. The editors of a Montgomery newspaper understood the connection well: "We are too much interested in washing the faces of other nations to be properly aware of the dirt behind our own ears. How a Veteran who risked his life to stop the terror of Hitlerism can come home today to play Hitler himself, we cannot understand." At one time or another during Alabama's anti-KKK crusade, the *Birmingham News,* the *Tuscaloosa News,* the *Jasper Mountain Eagle,* the *Anniston Star,* and several veterans' groups all compared Ku Kluxism to Nazism. Newsmen in Chicago, Atlanta, New York, and elsewhere made the same connection in writing about Alabama's Klan woes.[18]

Alabama editors realized that, in order to stave off the central government, they had to demonstrate state determination to resist Klan lawlessness, not just fascism. Grover Hall, Jr., of the *Montgomery Advertiser,* whose father and uncle had been in the vanguard of the fight gainst the KKK during the 1920s and 1930s, became a strong antagonist of the post–World War II Klan. "We thought we had outgrown such . . . frightful deeds often inhuman in nature," Hall wrote. "Apparently we have not." "The Klan claims to be Christian," he continued. "If it is, you may be sure that its main emphases are not the Christianity of Christ. It is anti-Jewish; and Christianity was founded by a Jew. It is anti-racial . . . in open violation of Christ's tolerance. . . . It claims to be a true exponent of 'true Americanism,' but forgets that America is made up of heterogeneous national and racial groups, and . . . constitutional and statutory law. . . . It is anarchy in action. It thrives on ignorance, intolerance, prejudice, and hate."[19] For a Birmingham journalist, the whole "misguided and ignoble movement" boiled down to one thing: "Alabama is bigger than . . . the Klan."[20]

Editors in Chicago, St. Louis, Norfolk, and elsewhere took up Alabama's attack. An Atlanta editorial observed that differences in the names of white supremacist groups meant very little: "They all smell alike. They are all violently anti-negro, anti-Catholic, anti-Semitic, [and] anti-liberal. . . . Violence and mystic hokus pokus are their stock in trade."[21]

Civic and fraternal groups joined the press assault. Donald Comer—textile baron, Dixiecrat, and son of an Alabama governor—headed a blue-ribbon committee of 500 to fight the KKK. Comer's steering committee brought an eclectic mix of Alabama elites together: Methodist and Episcopal bishops, the president of the state Baptist convention, leaders of Alabama's AFL, CIO, and UMW, the president of the Alabama Power Company, and the executive of a powerful savings and loan.[22] Birmingham's Junior Chamber of Commerce, the Elks, Kiwanians, Young Men's Business Club, League of Professional and Business Women, Council of Church Women, and First National Bank rallied their disparate forces against Ku Kluxism. Vicariously stung by the June lashing of a World War II sailor, veterans' groups in Florence and Tuscaloosa passed anti-Klan resolutions. The VFW, Disabled American Veterans, and the American Legion offered a $3,000 reward for the arrest of hooded thugs. At the Legion's 1949 state convention, Tuscumbia attorney Howell Heflin (later a U.S. senator) addressed the problem. Heflin's speech, a forceful one, was ironic inasmuch as his uncle, J. Thomas Heflin, had been a 1920s Knight and one of the most virulent bigots ever seen in Alabama. The junior Heflin, though, demonstrated that he was related to his infamous uncle more by blood than by sentiment. He called for the abolition of masks and "the spirit which hides behind the mask, the spirit of lawlessness, malice and prejudice . . . [which the] Klan . . . [uses to] desecrate the symbol of Calvary with the fire of hate."[23]

Religious resistance to the KKK went hand in glove with press and civic discontent. It was driven by church elites and populated primarily by main-stream denominations that attracted middle- and upper-class whites. Fringe evangelical sects appealed more to lower- and working-class groups and poor whites and exhibited a closer proximity to the 1940s Klan.[24] Baptists, Presbyterians, and Episcopalians sat on Donald Comer's committee, but most inspiring were the courageous actions of two Methodist preachers and their bishop in investigating a particularly nasty spree of Klan vigilantism in Clay County.[25]

Others wondered aloud how religious people could belong to the KKK and still profess to believe in Christianity. A Clanton man termed the obvious contradiction "a pity." A Huntsville resident worried that religious Europeans would think Southerners hypocritical because their pastors "don hoods and go out with the lawless gangs on their beast-like march of terrorism, thuggery, and savage acts." Noted Atlanta columnist Ralph McGill wrote that any preacher who had forsaken Christian doctrine to chase the Klan cross was marching in the steps of Nazi stormtroopers. "Try to imagine the Nazarene in a Ku Klux robe going in a mob to terrify helpless persons," McGill challenged Alabamians. "The Klan prostitutes the cross by burning it to advertise the threat of violence." A speaker for the Atlanta Christian Center mused that a "time of confusion and darkness" had descended on Alabama when its churches relied on hooded terrorists to furnish order and financial support.[26] Montgomery editor Charlie Dobbins, a fierce enemy of the KKK and the Dixiecrats, observed that the involvement of clerics in the Klan was sadly consistent with a long tradition of religious persecution that had its roots in the Crusades, Islamic jihads, Spanish Inquisition, and Protestant Reformation. Dobbins, who was repelled by Klan violence but still firmly opposed dramatic racial change, wrote that "people have committed murder thinking they were doing God's will, people have been burned at the stake by religious fanatics who thought they were serving the Lord."[27]

The little popular opposition to the Klan that could be found in Alabama was less genteel. Folk victims favored fighting fire with fire. After one navy veteran was flogged, he bought several guns, taught his wife how to use them, and vowed to kill the next batch of hooded intruders who entered his home. Friends egged him on by promising bounties of $100 for every Klansmen he shot, and they swore to flog Klan terrorists. Some victims were likely encouraged toward violent opposition by Jim Folsom's folksy pronouncement that every man's home was his castle and by a sheriff's advice that they "shoot to kill" if necessary. In any case, a disabled miner in Walker County whom Kluxers had forced to witness a friend's lashing took the advice to heart. Purchasing a shotgun, he swore to "blow as many _ansmen] as I can into damned small bits" and invited nightriders to return if they wanted to "taste [his] supercharged ammunition." A twelve-year-old Munford boy did more than just talk. Incensed by a cross burning in his father's yard, the lad defied Klansmen and incurred death threats by knocking the cross over and dousing it with water. The one-armed mayor of the appropriately named Iron City (on the Georgia-Alabama line) traded gunshots with parading Klansmen and engaged in a thirty-five-mile chase that ended with the arrest of a Florida Klan lord in Dothan, Alabama. Northern black newspapers solicited physical resistance by chastising war veterans for allowing themselves to be terrorized by people in bedsheets after having endured the hell of Axis bombs and shells.[28]

Alabama Klansmen reacted angrily to the resistance being mounted against them. Increasingly confronted, not just from enraged outsiders, but from Alabamians with clout, the KKK lashed back. Most distressing was the sudden animosity of politicians whom the order had considered friendly, or at least indifferent, prior to the federal government's involvement in Alabama affairs. Branding the legislature's mask law "discriminatory and unconstitutional," E. P. Pruitt shook his fist at Montgomery's capitol, swore that the Klan would fight back, and promised political death to the bill's sponsor, Henry Mize of Tuscaloosa. "That boy [has] washed himself up politically," Pruitt predicted. "He is too young to know anything about the race problem anyway." A Klan admirer scolded "Large Jim Janitor" Folsom. "What are you trying to do, turn traitor like Horseshit Truman?" he asked, "Don't turn against your people and try to curry favor. . . . Hurrah for the K.K.K." [29] Especially objectionable to Alabama Klansmen was John Buchanan, the morally outraged and outspoken pastor of Birmingham's large Southside Baptist Church. Knights red-baited other critics.[30]

Elite opposition to the KKK led to the rise of the Reverend "Dr." Lycurgus Spinks, a bizarre personality by any standard. With his shoulder-length mane of silver hair, Spinks looked more like a snake-oil peddler than a minister. He had bestowed the title "doctor" on himself because he once made a living by delivering lectures on "sexology" to male-only and female-only audiences. In a decade of travel through Arkansas and the Carolinas, Spinks had sometimes soberly billed himself as the reincarnation of George Washington. In 1947, he made an ill-advised bid for the governor's mansion in Mississippi and captured only 1.2 percent of the vote. He also ran two equally dismal campaigns for tax collector in the Magnolia State.[31]

By 1949, Spinks's odyssey had brought him to the heart of Dixie. Recognizing the potential in leading a popular revolt against Alabama's elites,

Spinks presented himself as a Klan folk hero. Appearing in Talladega and Tarrant City, Spinks promised to see that "some of those birds down in Montgomery are retired to their country estates" for passing the nefarious mask law. Flushed by the moment, the reverend waved a Confederate flag and boasted that Alabama's KKK would soon have 150,000 members ready to vote as a bloc against unfriendly politicians. At the time, Alabama's actual Klan strength was at least 120,000 members shy of Spinks's estimate. Calling the state attorney general's war on the KKK the "biggest joke in Alabama," Spinks vowed that Alabama Kluxers would unseat every politician arrayed against it, depicted the order as the last and finest bastion against communism, and claimed that the Klan was to be thanked for America's decline in lynchings.[32]

A week later Spinks was less impressive. He announced that 2,500 unmasked Klansmen would march in Pell City to demonstrate the impotence of the Mize antimask law. Spinks learned, though, that the average Alabama Klansman had little desire to appear unmasked in broad daylight or perhaps that he was not the charismatic leader he thought himself. He led a disappointing cluster of only fifty-eight men through a steady drizzle.[33]

More important than Klan rejoinders was what non-Southerners had to say about elite Alabama's struggle against the robed band. Some elites hoped for relief from national pressure for federal intervention in Alabama. They were not disappointed; praise for Alabama's war on the Klan poured in. Newspapers in Louisville, Nashville, Chattanooga, Atlanta, Columbus, Raleigh, Jackson, Dallas, New Orleans, Little Rock, Roanoke, and elsewhere in the South weighed in with strong editorials lauding Alabama.[34] More important, northern papers responded favorably. The *Chicago Defender* named Jim Folsom to its honor roll of the fifteen most outstanding men and women in America and noted that Alabama "is showing . . . the whole country that law may not be ignored here without grave risk of stern punishment." The *New York Times* and the *New York Herald-Tribune* also heaped praise on Alabama, as did newspapers from Baltimore, Cleveland, Hartford, Milwaukee, Des Moines, and other northern cities. U.S. attorney general Tom Clark was moved to announce that he found Alabama's opposition to be highly "gratifying." Most important, though, the House committee on Klan violence cut its Alabama inquiry short after hearing only four witnesses.[35]

Alabamians rejoiced at this obvious sign of federal withdrawal. Still, the National Negro Council offered a lone voice in dissent. Feeling the federal retreat to be a response to mere rhetoric, the council bitterly compared the congressional move to Pontius Pilate's washing of his hands.[36]

LIMITS IN 1949

In some ways the opposition to the Klan by Alabama's elite could not have been improved upon. Some journalists and clerical figures, in particular, provided an impassioned, sweeping rejection of the order, its goals, and its methods. The result was the effective start of an assault on the popular bases of support and tolerance for the order. Yet a large part of elite opposition was rooted in a self-interest that was less fundamental and more practical. Obsessed with the need to sustain white supremacy by means of state control, some participants in Alabama's war on the Klan were, in reality, staging yet another southern rebellion against federal encroachment.

Despite the declarations and resolutions, committees and investigations, and statutes and denouncements, the Ku Klux Klan was still a thriving concern in Alabama when the 1940s drew to a close. Almost wherever anyone cared to look, the results of opposition were mixed. After successfully infiltrating a local klavern and running a fascinating series of articles, the *Tuscaloosa News* refused to deal a lethal blow to the Klan by publishing the membership rolls it had procured. Birmingham officials equivocated over Abraham Berkowitz's package of proposed ordinances to outlaw the KKK, then turned them down flat. Another of Berkowitz's propositions also inspired misgivings in Alabama's elite adversaries of the Klan. In 1948, Berkowitz and New York's Anti-Nazi League had independently broached the idea of revoking the Klan's state charter. In rapid succession, Governor Folsom assigned the politically risky task of personally killing the Alabama Klan to his underling, Attorney General A. A. Carmichael, who dodged responsibility by placing the problem in the lap of the state legislature. A politician of some skill, Carmichael did so with flourish and ceremony, castigating the Klan as made up of people "as far from decency as east is from west . . . villainous, scoundrelly, [and the very] . . . antithesis of decency." Not to be outmaneuvered, the lawmakers informed Carmichael, upon consideration, that actually the proper party to press for revocation was the attorney general. The charter was never revoked.[37]

While Governor Folsom criticized the Klan, he was reluctant to violate regional taboos by accepting the New York league's outside offer of help against the Klan. Folsom opposed the 1940s Klan, but some of his top aides were 1920s Knights or individuals who reminisced nostalgically about the Reconstruction order.[38]

Moderate Charlie Dobbins offered measured resistance to the Klan and its Dixiecrat allies, but he also opposed President Truman's civil rights package. Dobbins favored Dwight Eisenhower because he thought Eisenhower would preserve segregation, and he rejected a bolt from the Democratic

Party because he thought it would harm southern prospects of attracting investment and would in the end only attract Communist agitators.[39]

Fear of electoral reprisal from racial conservatives hindered some Alabama politicians who might, in other climes, have fought even harder against the Klan. Hamstrung by their fears, men like Folsom, Carmichael, Lister Hill, and John Sparkman trod more carefully where race was concerned than they did with regard to the economy.[40]

Only two trials resulted from Jefferson County's seventeen sensational indictments. Both were unsuccessful. Placed by witnesses at fourteen separate floggings, and positively identified by four victims, Brownie Lollar should have furnished the perfect target for prosecution. He was the proprietor of a small coal mine, held a county commission as special deputy sheriff, and made extra money guarding cars at the Adamsville Klan meetings over which his brother presided. Taking the stand for two hours in his own defense, Lollar committed perjury by denying that he was a Klansman. Later he admitted that he belonged to Robert E. Lee Klavern No. 1. Despite repeated eyewitness identifications and the testimony of three former Klansmen, who placed Lollar at numerous assaults, the jury deliberated only one hour before finding him not guilty. Lollar's attorneys relied on a parade of nineteen character witnesses, an alibi about attending a baseball game that several Klan buddies supported, and nude photos of a woman standing in a cornfield who was said to be Edna McDanal.[41] Even a letter of explanation bearing Lollar's return address, sent to the mother of one victim of morality regulation, did not seem to make a difference to the jury. "We are sorry that this had to be done but it has went on so long till it had to be stopped," the letter explained. "He wasn't hurt but if we haft [sic] to come back he will remember it for a long time. Please help us to stop all of this. He will be watched every day. God bless you."[42]

The trials proved to be a study in Klan misconduct even under the close official scrutiny of the court. Klansmen roamed the courthouse halls, openly carried pistols, threatened newsmen, and intimidated witnesses. When one female witness accused a Holiness minister of being a Klan flogger, he got up and slapped her across the face. The judge sentenced him to a day in jail but rescinded the judgment when the preacher wept and asked to be forgiven.[43]

The trial of a second Klan defendant was similar. KKK attorneys decided to use the same strategy for A. Byrd Carradine, an admitted member of Adamsville's Stonewall Jackson Klavern, that had proven so successful for Lollar. Carradine also claimed to have been at a baseball game, and his attorneys paraded virtually the same set of character witnesses to swear that he was a good citizen. Spice was added to the Carradine trial when Ervin

Leon Key appeared. A former Klan brother, Key had fled to Houston but turned state's evidence despite frequent Klan death threats. He swore that Carradine had been present at a number of floggings that had been planned in advance at the Adamsville lodge. Despite his testimony, and although he was identified by three different victims, the proceedings for Carradine were declared a mistrial, and he went free.[44]

After the spring indictments coughed and sputtered in actual trials, Jefferson County's next grand jury declined to return any flogging indictments. To make matters worse, revelations about the summer grand jury were less than reassuring. Holding the immediate future of Alabama justice in their hands were one avowed Klansman, an illiterate, a convicted felon who should have been ineligible for jury duty, and five others who had police records. The county prosecutor was a former Klansman himself, as was the presiding judge.[45]

While events in Alabama gave new meaning to the phrase "a jury of one's peers," a disturbing double standard emerged. Alabama's anti-Klan indictments were issued only in the cases of white victims. "Nobody cared much what the Ku Klux Klan did to Negroes, until the nightgowned riders started beating up . . . white men and women," a black editor observed. "Now . . . Kissing Jim Folsom . . . is raising a mighty hubub." The *Memphis World* agreed. "What would have been the attitude of Alabama authorities had the floggings . . . been limited only to Negroes?" he asked. "Somehow we can't help thinking that the aroused citizens of that state would still have been sleeping."[46]

Perhaps more troubling than the racial double standard on victims was the one for perpetrators. During the 1940s, city and county police were nothing less than incompetent or unwilling to pursue Klan criminals. The few arrests in 1949 came only at the behest of an empaneled grand jury. Yet when a group of black teenagers dressed up in hoods and sheets and formed their own "Klan" to keep neighborhood women from dating white men, Ozark police reacted instantaneously. Suddenly, the courts worked too. Ironically, the only Klansman convicted in Alabama during the 1940s was an African American.[47]

Without question, though, the incident that most dramatically demonstrated the mixed character of Alabama's battle against the Klan was the case of William Hugh Morris. Circuit judge Robert Wheeler sentenced the Klan leader to jail on 7 June 1949 for refusing to produce membership records for the Federated Ku Klux Klan. At first Morris, a balding moon-faced man, seemed to enjoy his role as a Klan martyr. Receiving candy, cards, flowers, and visits from well-wishers throughout the state, he basked in his newfound celebrity and exuded bravado. "I'd rather see this jail rot down around me than give up the sacred secrets" of the Klan, he declared. Morris also claimed that he was so comfortable in his cell that he was prepared to stay a hundred years if necessary.[48]

As Birmingham's hot summer wore on, though, Morris grew less comfortable, received fewer visits, and rapidly grew weary of playing the martyr. He hired Hugh Locke to represent him and filed an appeal. Locke, a former Klansman and longtime confederate of Horace Wilkinson, denied having any affiliation with the 1940s Klan, though he had been a 1920s Knight. Losing the Morris appeal 4–2 at the state supreme court, Locke proved increasingly irascible in his old age. At one point, he informed a startled justice that his logic evaded every point of the law. After the loss, he threatened to appeal to the U.S. Supreme Court.[49]

Morris gained release in late July on his pledge that he would retrieve the membership lists at his home. Soon after he was freed, though, Morris informed the court that the rolls had been stolen by a black civil rights attorney and a Communist accomplice. Unimpressed by the tale, Judge Wheeler remanded Morris into custody on 2 August. Back in jail, an angry Morris issued a statement in which he charged that Wheeler, Attorney General A. A. Carmichael, and county solicitor Emmett Perry were former Klansmen. He also accused the attorney general of "peeping Tom tactics" for installing a hidden dictaphone in a Masonic lodge and ridiculed the solicitor as a "crumb-grabbing" publicity seeker.[50]

Morris's intransigence won him few friends outside the sheeted society. Despite a stream of Hugh Locke appeals, including another setback at the state supreme court, Morris languished in jail for two months. During his tenure behind bars, Samuel Green, the grand wizard of the Association of Georgia Klans, died. Morris hinted at his possible succession to Green's throne but also realized that he had to be free in order to attain it. He agreed to provide the grand jury with as complete a membership list as his memory would allow.[51]

Morris's list of twenty-eight names was little more than chicanery. The majority of those listed were 1920s Knights, officials of the organizations whose identities were more or less public knowledge, and Klansmen who had already acknowledged membership. An assistant attorney general aptly termed the list "worse than useless," but it was enough for county authorities to release him on 21 September.[52]

HOODED DISSENSION

While the Will Morris drama entertained Alabamians, it had an unforeseen effect on Klan solidarity. Tempted by Samuel Green's untimely death, and

Morris's temporary absence, ambitious Klan leaders decided that the time was ripe to seize hooded power. The upshot was a splintering of the Alabama Klan that hindered its effectiveness. A paradox resulted from the schism. Though it went by several names in the 1940s, the various groups that made up the Klan attracted basically the same kind of member: frustrated, economically depressed, white, mostly blue-collar supremacists. The single 1920s Knights of the Ku Klux Klan, Inc., had appealed to people with diverse socioeconomic status and personalities.

The first signs of hooded discord came in 1949 with the resignations of two leading Alabama Klansmen, Dr. E. P. Pruitt and kleagle Robert Gulledge. Upon resigning, both affirmed their faith in white supremacy and "our Protestant, Gentile creed," but Pruitt condemned vicious elements that had "wormed their way into the Klan . . . to go out and whip people."[53]

Smelling an opportunity, the irrepressible Lycurgus Spinks decided to act. After visiting Will Morris in jail to pledge his undying loyalty, Spinks stabbed him in the back. He arranged for Klan leaders from six states to meet in Montgomery to announce a new Knights of the KKK of America with himself as its head. Sam Roper, a Georgia policeman who had outmaneuvered Morris to become imperial wizard of the Georgia Klans, threw his considerable weight behind Spinks. Roper announced that Morris's Federated KKK was virtually defunct, while Spinks planned an unmasked parade near Birmingham. The parade was a fiasco, but somehow Spinks managed to talk Morris's wife into attending.[54]

Other breaks came in rapid succession. The Reverend Alvin Horn, another onetime Morris ally, deserted his incarcerated chief to lead a rogue movement of four klaverns near Talladega. Along the Georgia-Alabama line, a group calling itself the Original Southern Klans, Inc., organized with a twenty-three-year-old at its helm. Two of Sam Green's former lieutenants actually ran things, though, prompting rivals to denounce it as "a bolshevik Klan." The Original Klansmen made their home in Phenix City, Alabama, where they burned a thirty-five-foot cross, published two issues of a newspaper, tried to create a Klan radio station, and stormed a Russell County jury box in midtrial. The group claimed that its goal was to maintain the "Southern white man's political superiority" and to make sure "the Negro stay[s] in his place, which he is going to do as long as there is a Klan."[55]

Threatened by this factionalism, Will Morris's first order of business upon his release was to reconsolidate his position in Alabama. To restore credibility, he claimed that state prosecutors had tricked him into supplying the twenty-eight Klan names he had published to secure his release. "I wouldn't be a Judas Iscariot and go back on my Klan oath," Morris assured his members. He next appeared at a school meeting to drum up local support for his embattled outfit.[56]

The Lycurgus Spinks problem took care of itself. Appearing in Washington, D.C., on "Meet the Press," Spinks made a national spectacle of himself by arguing that Jesus Christ was a Klansman, that the hooded group had never flogged anyone, and that the KKK was the best friend southern blacks ever had. Sam Roper demoted Spinks to honorary chaplain and public relations counsel, then eased him out of the Association of Georgia Klans altogether. Spinks had once claimed an astronomical membership of 650,000 for his splinter, but Will Morris's allies dismissed the eccentric preacher as "wizard over himself and one other guy."[57]

In December 1949, Morris reestablished himself by combining forces with Bill Hendrix's powerful Southern Knights of the KKK and Tom Hamilton's Association of Carolina Klans. The trio met in Montgomery, with Klan representatives from fourteen mostly southern states, and agreed that they themselves would be the ruling triumvirate of a new Ku Klux Klans of America. Sam Roper and his Association of Georgia Klans were notably absent.[58]

ALABAMA SOCIETY AND THE KU KLUX SPIRIT

White Alabama had mixed feelings about the 1940s Klan. While many decent Alabamians deplored the order's violence, they also felt nostalgic toward the Reconstruction Klan and even the 1920s order. Some had been members during the 1920s or had family, friends, and associates who had been involved in the gigantic order. Many disapproved of the Klan's methods but approved of its basic aims. Others saw it as a costly venture that risked economic loss or federal intrusion in race relations or both. While some elites cherished the memory of their grandfathers' Klan and had pleasant associations with the Klan of their fathers, they did battle with the Klan of their own time. They opposed the Klan of their brothers lest it jeopardize the white supremacy to which many less extreme Southerners still subscribed.

A number of sincere opponents of the 1940s order felt this way. John Temple Graves—Dixiecrat, Birmingham journalist, and adversary of the 1940s Klan—advised his readers to tread carefully in opposing the order. "We must remember," Graves wrote in the *Birmingham Age-Herald,* "that in the 1870s the Klan served us as no other organization could . . . [and] many good citizens also belonged to the Klan when it was revived in the 1920s." Grover Hall, Jr., was an ardent critic of the 1940s Klan. Yet he shared with his father and Temple Graves fond memories of the Reconstruction order.

In fact, by 1949, the *Montgomery Advertiser* seemed to have forgotten the intensity of the senior Hall's war against the 1920s Klan. "To call a man a fellow Klansman in 1927 might be a salutation of fraternity," Grover junior wrote with obvious respect, "whereas today [it] . . . would be an insult." Prominent Alabamians such as U.S. congressman Joseph Starnes lauded the Klan as "just as American as the Baptist or Methodist Church."[59]

To complicate matters even further, some 1920s and 1930s Kluxers reenlisted during the 1940s. By the 1940s, many alumni had reached positions of leadership within government, business, and society. Birmingham mayor Cooper Green was a 1920s Knight. So was Emmett Perry, Jefferson County's chief solicitor; George Lewis Bailes, a circuit judge; Hugh Locke, the former judge who represented Will Morris; Dixiecrat leader Horace Wilkinson; and, if Morris is to be believed, Judge Robert Wheeler. Bert Thomas, a Klan titan during the 1920s, served as Governor Folsom's director of the state conservation department. Will Morris also revealed that Folsom's attorney general, A. A. Carmichael, had donned a sheet during the 1920s. When first confronted with the Anti-Nazi League's demand for revocation of the Klan's state charter, Folsom had run the idea past his chief counsel Ira B. Thompson, a 1920s Crenshaw County cyclops.[60]

Ku Kluxism permeated Alabama. Both physical and mental continuity made legal efforts to combat the 1940s Klan difficult at best. Before 1949 was over, a few observers had begun to appreciate the dilemma. One Birmingham woman urged state officials to crack down on the KKK as "a thing of prejudice and ignorance and hate" as she confessed that "we common people . . . are morally responsible for the Klan!" A disgruntled Gadsden resident refused to believe Governor Folsom's claims that he actively opposed the order: "Don't tell me the government is *trying* to find a way to stop them. Either you can or you don't want to." A St. Louis journalist argued that Alabama's KKK "has been able to exist only to the extent that its prejudices [are] the prejudices of a substantial part of its community."[61]

The *Montgomery Alabama Journal* described Ku Kluxism:

It's largely a matter of attitude . . . of [the] men who have charge of law enforcement. That is the main thing needed today. Our state officials have been trifling with the subject for over a year. The whole present executive administration is studded with Klan leaders of yesterday. They have talked and at the same time secretly condoned. We were told a year ago that the law authorities knew all about a notorious Bessemer raid and would soon make arrests and round up the offenders. It was all bosh because cowardly police officials had no intention of offending [them]. . . . Alabama got into its present mess because we had no backbone in law enforcement . . . from the governor on down. . . . this new anti-masking law . . . means absolutely nothing if the officials continue to sit and let matters take their own course. A mere law is futile in the hands of officials who are Klan-minded. . . . even laws would be useless so long as there was a great body of citizenship that was Klan-minded. Klan-mindedness include[s] many of those not-Klan members, those who d[o] not wear masks, but [are] secretly sympathetic with its covert and cowardly methods. Klan-mindedness [means] a man could still be a Klansmen with all its evils and not wear a mask.[62]

Some Alabama police tolerated and even colluded with the KKK. County deputies and city policemen directed Klan parades, provided security for rallies, had police commissions and Klan memberships simultaneously, guarded Klan cars, and stood by in silence as Klansmen burned crosses, wielded guns, or paraded with faces masked and car tags concealed A New York investigation learned that over half of Jefferson County's deputy sheriffs, and some Birmingham policemen, were either Klansmen or overt sympathizers. Harassed by state police, Klansman and deputy sheriff Brownie Lollar crowed that it would have been an entirely "different story" if county deputies had been involved. Lanett police routinely deputized Klan members and used Klan posses to hunt down black suspects in Chambers County.[63]

After the notorious 1948 Girl Scout raid, Jefferson County's chief deputy praised the action publicly, and Sheriff Holt A. McDowell told reporters that it was "a good thing." So anemic was McDowell's "pursuit" of KKK floggers, that critics termed him "bungling . . . [and] either fail[ing] . . . miserably . . . or refus[ing]" to arrest masked terrorists. McDowell dragged his feet, reasoned that the Klansmen had not actually trespassed on private property since they had not been warned beforehand, dismissed the prospect of police action until Kluxers repeated the raid, and said he was not even sure the hooded terrorists were members of the Klan. Flogging victims later revealed that they had reported other attacks to the sheriff but that nothing had ever been done. Instead, McDowell advised victims not to tell their stories publicly because they might jeopardize ongoing investigations.[64]

Some in Alabama law enforcement openly supported the KKK. Tuscaloosa's Klan hall was home to at least three city policemen. In response to criticism of Clay County's 1949 flogging spree, an Ashland policeman retorted, "Well, the Klan has done a lot of good." One Alabamian, who moved to Atlanta and joined the police force and the KKK, explained that he did so because of the threat to America that blacks and Communists posed.[65]

Support for the 1940s Klan, though, came from more than just policemen and alumni of the 1920s order. The bulk of support resided among many plain Alabamians who backed the secret society for a variety of reasons. Chief among these was race. "Every Southern white woman who has suffered a fate worse than death in the clutches of THE BLACK BEAST," wrote one Klan supporter, "was outraged by an ANTI-KLANSMAN." An Ozark resident in praising the 1940s Klan used a Reconstruction metaphor when he said that it kept the South from being "taken over by the Negro and Yankee carpetbaggers of today." Robed officials themselves enjoyed tarring their critics with the brush of Reconstruction-style racial treason. A fellow traveler of the Birmingham KKK cited racial purity as the order's raison d'être. Approval of Klan raids often followed in the wake of such rationalizations.[66]

For some ordinary Alabamians, morality was as important as race in this respect. A Gardendale woman compared hooded violence to parental discipline and thanked Kluxers for performing a valuable community service. Another Birmingham woman applauded the particularly vicious flogging of Edna McDanal. "How would you like it for some woman to get out in front of your little girls and dance neked [*sic*]" she asked, "When [the Klan] . . . take[s] one out and whip[s] them it is for some disgraceful act. . . . [The Klan is made up of] god-fearing men and god-loving men." Talladegan Vern M. Scott warned Jim Folsom that his opposition to the KKK would cost him considerable "common man support." Besides, Scott reasoned, Klan flogging was justified because it was aimed against persons "of [the] most questionable character" and was welcomed by locals who were grateful that "such persons had been dealt with." In its preoccupation with morality the 1940s begged comparison with the 1920s.[67]

Whole communities supported the KKK (figure 32). Angered by the flogging indictments of seven of their neighbors, 300 residents of west Jefferson County gathered to protest the "prejudiced" attempt to punish Klan violence. In Selma, the KKK was so accepted that it was listed along with other civic groups in the window display of a large utility's district office.[68]

Mass support found echoes in religion. The majority of the Klan's religious opponents were from mainline denominations, but most of its religious supporters came from fundamentalist sects. One Birmingham preacher defended Klan activity as an insignificant trifle compared with real crimes such as liquor consumption. Some ministers thought church attendance was a more pressing issue than hooded vigilantism. "I am a KKK and proud of it," one Jefferson County preacher declared, "and I say if some of these fat, greasy, panty-waist preachers would get intestinal fortitude enough to preach the Gospel, and keep their mouths out of things they know abso-

32. Planting a Klan Welcome Sign, Late 1940s. Two Klansmen erect a welcome sign just outside Prattville. Even after World War II, Alabama's Klansmen felt comfortable enough in some communities to advertise their existence. Courtesy Boone Aiken.

lutely nothing about . . . , the churches would have more people in them." Fundamentalist churches at Hopewell and Littleton in Jefferson County, as well as Holiness churches at Pinson and Massey Line, received friendly Klan visits and regular donations during the 1940s much as mainstream chuches had during the 1920s. A Church of God minister asked his flock to make room in their pews to welcome Klan visitors. One Holiness preacher earned an indictment for his part in several floggings. Another intimidated Walker County flogging victims into remaining silent. The efforts of mainline Protestants to combat hooded vice caused special concern for ministers who were sympathetic to the violent fraternity. Welcoming twenty-five masked Klansmen to his Wylam church, Pastor H. L. Tully feted the KKK and denounced his urban middle-class counterpart at Southside Baptist for criticizing the secret order. A 1920s Knight, Tully defended morality-based Klan violence in the 1940s as "deserved" and listed alcohol and Roman Catholicism as still the two greatest menaces to America.[69]

Support sprang from the ideological roots of the fundamentalist tradition. Captivated by literalism, compelled by fatalism, and obsessed with the personal morality of their neighbors, some of Alabama's more rigid evangelicals looked to confirm their own status as moral elites by finding others wanting. For those already predisposed to join a movement like the KKK, moral imperatives gave strong impetus to the impulse to police aberrant behavior.

Most police and religious opposition to the 1940s Klan came from the highest levels of those institutions. Any resistance that occurred at the popular level was usually violent itself. An important reason for mass identification with the Klan, even as late as 1949, was the educational and economic backwardness of the state. In Alabama, as in other southern states, fears and tensions were orchestrated from above but were commonly fueled and expressed at a popular level.[70]

By the end of the 1940s the Ku Klux Klan had once again sunk its roots deeply into Alabama's soil. Despite its indifference to other crops, Alabama's red clay was particularly fertile for the familiar Klan seed. The 1940s Klan, though, was a hybrid phenomenon that blended attributes of the Reconstruction Klan, the 1920s order, the depression-era Klan, and the post-1954 KKK. The 1940s incarnation remained an essentially southern and racist phenomenon, as the Klans of the first and second Reconstructions, and the Great Depression, had been before it. Unlike the original Reconstruction version, it was far from just a rural phenomenon. Although there were outbreaks of Ku Kluxism in the rural areas of Clay, Walker, Cullman, and Shelby Counties, the KKK also took root in Montgomery, Mobile, Tuscaloosa, and Birmingham. As with the 1920s order, much of the violence in the 1940s was directed at whites who challenged society's fragile notions of acceptable moral conduct. Yet the mainstream religious and antielitist agenda that had so distinguished the 1920s Klan was notably absent during the 1940s, as was the order's old political clout and closeness to veterans' and patriotic groups. The post–World War II Klan was much smaller, less diverse, and politically much weaker than the Klan of the 1920s.[71]

Epilogue
"To Wither Away"

A full examination of the Ku Klux Klan phenomenon in Alabama generally confirms most of the Populist-Civic School theses that have been advanced in studies of other states and regions. Alabama's 1920s KKK was both a rural and an urban phenomenon. Its tremendous and diverse membership supported a political machine that articulated a progressive program on behalf of many average Alabamians who had traditionally been ignored by the state's entrenched Democrats. Although we have no detailed membership list for Alabama, the 1920s Klan was clearly an umbrella organization that appealed to a wide variety of whites, many of them average persons of middle-class origin. The prejudices of Alabama's hooded Knights clearly resonated with ordinary Alabamians who never joined the order and even with the Klan's more patrician adversaries.

It is also evident, though, that Alabama's 1920s Klan was significantly more violent than the versions of the hooded order that have been studied thus far—most of them in nonsouthern regions of the country. Violence was as integral a part of the order in Alabama as its thirst for political power. It was as central as the society's Americanism, civic activity, and diverse complexion. The violence stemmed from deep-seated anxieties about differences—racial, religious, ethnic, and moral. Moreover, the Alabama case makes it plain that much of the violence, while perpetrated by a handful of Knights, was premeditated and endorsed, or at least tolerated, by many others within the organization and, later, beyond it.

The opposition of Alabama's powerful Big Mule/Black Belt oligarchy ended a distinct 1920s era of the Klan by about 1929. Initially nostalgic for the old order and receptive to the new Klan's principles, the patricians in 1926 awakened to the political threat that the Klan represented when candidates backed by the hood swept the state's elections. Within three years, the forceful, sincere, and intense opposition of the oligarchy and its press allies reaped dividends. The 1920s version of the Klan faded from view largely because of effective resistance from the oligarchy.

Still, 1920s opposition often fell short of full resistance to the Klan's program with respect to race and other forms of intolerance. Much of it was "pragmatic opposition" that stemmed from political rivalry, fear of federal interference with race relations, or concern for the region's continued material attractiveness. The opposition was intense, genuine, and quite effective in ending the Klan's political life. Most of it, though, was not a "principled opposition" that challenged the order's most fundamental tenets.

Perhaps most ironically, the second Klan was progressivism at its most extreme. It was the Progressive movement and period carried to its logical conclusion, to its endpoint, after being intensified by the unprecedented experience of world war. Born in 1915, the organization was the physical child of the Progressive era. It was its spiritual offspring as well. Like the Progressive movement, it was for whites only—only more so than any other part of it. Like the Progressive period itself, the revised Klan was dominated by native, middle-class, Protestant whites who felt that they had not received their due from politics or society. Like progressivism, the 1920s Klan was so variegated, so diverse, and so multifaceted that today it defies easy explanation or broad labels such as "conservative" or "liberal." Like progressivism, the Klan centered much of its efforts and energies on civic matters, patriotism, and politics. Like a critically important wing of the Progressives, furthermore, some 1920s Knights focused on issues of morality, temperance, and the social control of immigrants, blacks, labor unions, and other groups thought to harbor the potential for upheaval. For both the Progressives and, later, many of the Klansmen, these groups fundamentally threatened white, middle-class America and its most traditional customs and values. On this score, especially, the Klan became the logical extreme of its Progressive predecessor, a type of progressivism that had been warped and distorted by the traumatic prism of World War I. At times throughout the country, and often in Alabama, the second Klan degenerated into a morally and socially repressive, violent outfit that far outdid the prewar and wartime patriotric societies in the extent and the character of its vigilantism. In so many ways, the 1920s Klan both mimicked its Progressive predecessor and brought the Progressive period to its logical, and sometimes ugly, conclusion.

The notion that nothing of consequence happened with regard to the Klan between 1930 and 1954 obviously does not hold in the case of Alabama. The 1920s version of the Klan died, but the order itself continued to exist in one form or fashion until the *Brown v. Board* decision breathed life into it. A close examination of the 1930s and 1940s in Alabama reveals that these years were not barren, nor were they years of Klan dormancy.

While the Klans that existed during this "bridge" period were decidedly different from the order in the 1920s and after 1954, as well as from each other, they also exhibited some important elements of "qualified continuity." The depression-era Klan—markedly smaller, less political, and more militantly antiradical than the 1920s order—shared the 1920s infatuation with blacks and Jews as threats to stability. The small 1940s Klan virtually ignored Catholics, Jews, politics, and civic activity and was strenuously opposed by the veterans' and patriotic groups that had supported the Klan of the 1920s. Yet the post–World War II Klan, like the 1920s group, concentrated on blacks and threats to moral conformity. It was tiny compared to its counterpart in the 1920s, but like the 1930s order, it viewed itself as the protector of the hearth from a Communist threat. Like other versions, it opposed racial change, this time in the form of direct threats to voting patterns and segregation in a variety of areas.

During all of these years, Klansmen and Alabamians continued to be consumed by race, haunted by fear of the federal government, and determined to oppose the KKK mainly for practical reasons. Race is so much a part of the history of Alabama and the South that, like air and water, its presence and its importance are sometimes easy to forget. To do so, though, is to proceed at extreme peril. All of the different Klan epochs in Alabama had race as their central issue. Devotion to white supremacy among non-Klan members was a powerful force as well. Alabama politicians bowed to state attitudes on race and perennially opposed federal activism. The "Reconstruction Syndrome"—antiblack, antifederal, and antioutsider—endured as a feature of all of these separate epochs.

Whites in Alabama dreaded the idea of federal intrusion into their racial affairs. Fear of federal involvement blinded many so badly that they denounced it as unwarranted encroachment and saw Southerners as the blameless victims of a grasping central government. Many whites interpreted any federal act other than the dispensation of dollars as "meddling." In this climate of fear and resentment, Klan activity was a dangerous double-edged sword. While it certainly perpetuated southern racial customs, excessive Ku Kluxism increased the likelihood of a federal invasion that might disrupt those very customs.

The answer, for some Alabama elites, was a "pragmatic opposition" to the KKK that sought to forestall federal intrusiveness, mitigate national censure, and encourage black concessions on civil rights. The pragmatic nature of the opposition did not make it ineffective. Still, that nature did prevent it from setting an example for ordinary Alabamians by challenging the order's most fundamental principles. Many average Alabamians supported the order out-right or at least tolerated it. Their acceptance of it was especially evident in the decisions of juries that confronted Klan crimes.

In examining the role played by public officials, it is important not to underestimate the constraints imposed by the political realities of time and place. Caution should also be exercised, however. We must be careful not to grant every southern politician who ever confronted the race issue com-plete immunity from the weight of historical responsibility. But we must also steer clear of a stark, and necessarily arbitrary, dichotomy between "good" and "evil" politicians distinguished on the basis of race. In the South, almost every politician bowed to the powerful realities imposed by segregation; some just bowed a little lower and a little more often.

As the Klan in Alabama ebbed and flowed, a Ku Klux spirit persisted. "Ku Kluxism" was something broader and deeper than the activities or membership of the KKK. It included a mindset in Alabama as a whole that accommodated the Klan and its violence. Many who were not formal mem-bers of the group tolerated hooded vigilantism or looked the other way. Fear of any concept foreign to white Alabama culture gave the Klan's sup-porters, tolerators, and even some of its opponents a common cause. It was the glue of "xenophobia" that bound separate incarnations of the Klan to-gether and allowed plain folk who were not themselves members of the order to tolerate it for so long. Many elites as well were essentially unmoved by racial, religious, ethnic, moral, and political intolerance.

Ultimately, average Alabamians best expressed popular feelings about the KKK. "We are . . . responsible for the Klan!" an Alabama woman admitted to Governor Jim Folsom, "Please . . . use your position to fight this thing of prejudice, ignorance and hate. . . . give our children the heritage their fa-thers fought for. I'm not a Jew, Catholic, or Negro, just an American, [and] I'm sick to death of the Ku Klux Klan!"[1] Another ordinary Alabamian put the matter as well as anyone else: "The people themselves in Alabama are responsible for the Ku Klux Klan. It will also be the people who ultimately must change their way of thinking" if the Klan is ever to wither away.[2]

Abbreviations

ARCHIVAL REPOSITORIES

ADAH	Alabama Department of Archives and History Montgomery, Alabama
AJA	American Jewish Archives, Cincinnati, Ohio
AJHS	American Jewish Historical Society Brandeis University, Waltham, Massachusetts
AU	Auburn University Archives, Auburn, Alabama
AUSC	Auburn University Special Collections Department Auburn, Alabama
BA	Boone Aiken Papers, Auburn, Alabama
BCA	Blount County Archives, Oneonta, Alabama
BCHS	Blount County Historical Society Blountsville, Alabama
BPLA	Birmingham Public Library Archives Birmingham, Alabama
CU	Oral History Office, Columbia University New York, New York
DUKE	Duke University Special Collections Department Durham, North Carolina
HST	Harry S Truman Presidential Library Independence, Missouri

HUN	Huntingdon College Archives and Special Collections Montgomery, Alabama
ISU	Iowa State University Library, Ames, Iowa
LC	Library of Congress, Washington, D.C.
MADD	Auburn University Microform and Documents Department Auburn, Alabama
MDAH	Mississippi Department of Archives and History Jackson, Mississippi
MMA	Mobile Municipal Archives, Mobile, Alabama
MPL	Mobile Public Library Archives, Mobile, Alabama
PIKE	Pike County Historical Society, Brundige, Alabama
PU	Mudd Manuscript Library, Princeton University Princeton, New Jersey
RBD	Ralph B. Draughon Library, Auburn University Auburn, Alabama
SC	Schomburg Center for the Study of Black Culture New York Public Library, New York City
SHC	Southern Historical Collection University of North Carolina, Chapel Hill, North Carolina
SLA	Southern Labor Archives, Georgia State University Atlanta, Georgia
SPLC	Klanwatch Project, Southern Poverty Law Center Montgomery, Alabama
SU	Samford University Special Collections Department Birmingham, Alabama
TC	Talladega College Archives, Talladega, Alabama
TCHA	Talladega County Historical Association Talladega, Alabama
TCSH	Tutwiler Collection of Southern History Birmingham Public Library, Birmingham, Alabama
TSLA	Tennessee State Library and Archives Nashville, Tennessee
TSUA	Troy State University Archives Montgomery, Alabama
TU	Tuskegee University Archives, Tuskegee, Alabama

UA   University of Alabama Library, Tuscaloosa, Alabama

UAB   University Archives, University of Alabama at
            Birmingham, Birmingham, Alabama

UASC   Stanley W. Hoole Special Collections Library
            University of Alabama, Tuscaloosa, Alabama

UMO   State Historical Society, University of Missouri
            Columbia, Missouri

FREQUENTLY CITED NEWSPAPERS

AB	*Alabama Baptist*
AC	*Atlanta Constitution*
ADW	*Atlanta Daily World*
AG	*Atlanta Georgian*
AJ	*Montgomery Alabama Journal*
AN	*Amsterdam News*
AS	*Anniston Star*
BAA	*Baltimore Afro-American*
BAH	*Birmingham Age-Herald*
BD	*Oklahoma City Black Dispatch*
BL	*Birmingham Ledger*
BLA	*Birmingham Labor Advocate*
BN	*Birmingham News*
BP	*Birmingham Post*
BPH	*Birmingham Post-Herald*
BR	*Birmingham Reporter*
BW	*Birmingham World*
CA	*Alabama Christian Advocate*
CD	*Chicago Defender*
CDW	*Chicago Daily World*
CJ	*Louisville Courier-Journal*
CP	*Centreville Press*
CR	*Columbia Record*
CSM	*Christian Science Monitor*

CT	*Chicago Tribune*
CW	*Chicago Whip*
DE	*Dothan Eagle*
DW	*New York Daily Worker*
FC	*Atlanta Fiery Cross*
FH	*Florence Herald*
FT	*Florence Times*
HI	*Houston Informer*
HP	*Houston Post*
HT	*Huntsville Times*
JG	*Norfolk Journal and Guide*
LAX	*Los Angeles Examiner*
LH	*Lineville Headlight*
LI	*Columbia Lighthouse and Informer*
MA	*Montgomery Advertiser*
MCA	*Memphis Commercial Appeal*
ME	*Montgomery Examiner*
MP	*Mobile Press*
MR	*Mobile Register*
MW	*Memphis World*
NH	*Atlanta Imperial Nighthawk*
NYA	*New York Age*
NYC	*New York Call*
NYH	*New York Herald*
NYP	*New York Post*
NYS	*New York Sun*
NYT	*New York Times*
NYW	*New York World*
OSD	*Oneonta Southern Democrat*
PC	*Pittsburgh Courier*
SA	*Sylacauga Advance*
SLA	*St. Louis Argus*
SN	*Sylacauga News*

SW	*Birmingham Southern Worker*
TJ	*Selma Times-Journal*
TN	*Tuscaloosa News*
TP	*New Orleans Times-Picayune*
TPD	*Birmingham Times-Plain Dealer*
TRI	*New York Tribune*
WP	*Washington Post*

JOURNALS AND OTHER PERIODICALS

AH	*American Heritage*
AHQ	*Alabama Historical Quarterly*
AHR	*American Historical Review*
AJ	*American Journalism*
ALH	*Alabama Heritage*
ALR	*Alabama Law Review*
AM	*Alabama Magazine*
AMR	*American Review*
AQ	*American Quarterly*
AR	*Alabama Review*
ATL	*Atlanta History*
BNM	*Birmingham News Magazine*
CULR	*Catholic University Law Review*
FHQ	*Florida Historical Quarterly*
GLR	*Georgia Law Review*
HJ	*Historical Journal*
HN	*The Historian*
JAH	*Journal of American History*
JBHS	*Journal of the Birmingham Historical Society*
JIH	*Journal of Interdisciplinary History*
JOP	*Journal of Politics*
JSH	*Journal of Southern History*
JSOH	*Journal of Social History*
KM	*Kourier Magazine*

LH	*Labor History*
MVHR	*Mississippi Valley Historical Review*
NAR	*North American Review*
ND	*Negro Digest*
PSCAAH	*Proceedings of the S. Conference on Afro-American History*
RD	*Reader's Digest*
SE	*Southern Exposure*
SH	*Southern Historian*
SHR	*Southern Humanities Review*
UCLR	*University of Chicago Law Review*

Notes

INTRODUCTION

1. Branch, *Parting the Waters*, 684; Garrow, ed., *Birmingham, Alabama, 1956–1963*, ix; Kelley, "New War in Dixie," 367; Feldman, *From Demagogue to Dixiecrat*, vii, 1, 104, 108 (third quotation); Eskew, *But for Birmingham*; Nunnelly, *Bull Connor*, 3 (fourth quotation); Brown, *Max Heldman's Birmingham*, 38–39 (first and second quotations); Ingalls, "Antiradical Violence in Birmingham," 524 (first and second quotations repeated).

2. Mecklin, *Ku Klux Klan*.

3. Mecklin quoted in Moore, "Historical Interpretations of the 1920s Klan," 20.

4. Tannenbaum, *Darker Phases of the South*; Lynd and Lynd, *Middletown*; Fry, *The Ku Klux Klan*; Frost, *Challenge of the Klan*.

5. Hofstadter, *Age of Reform*, 288–89; Leuchtenburg, *Perils of Prosperity*; Hicks, *Republican Ascendancy*; Moore, "Historical Interpretations of the 1920s Klan," 17–38; Hofstadter, *Paranoid Style in American Politics*, 3–40; Hoffer, *True Believer*; Higham, *Strangers in the Land*; Harris, "Manifestations of Fear."

6. Davis, "Some Themes of Counter-subversion," 205–24, and *Fear of Conspiracy*, 61; Harris, "Manifestations of Fear," 3, 9; Cash, *Mind of the South*.

7. Rice, *Ku Klux Klan in American Politics*; Randel, *Ku Klux Klan*; Lipset and Raab, *Politics of Unreason*, 276–77, 530; Harris, "Manifestations of Fear," 9; George and Wilcox, *Nazis, Communists, Klansmen, and Others on the Fringe*, 30; Shannon, *Between the Wars*, 89–91; Moore, "Historical Interpretations of the 1920s Klan," 22–23, 27–28; Bennett, *Party of Fear*, 17; Miller, "The Ku Klux Klan," 215–55, quoted in Moore, "Historical Interpretations of the 1920s," 27; Wade, *Fiery Cross*.

8. Weaver, "Knights of the Ku Klux Klan"; Chalmers, *Hooded Americanism*; Alexander, *Ku Klux Klan in the Southwest*.

9. Jackson, *Ku Klux Klan in the City*.

10. Ibid., xi; Chalmers, *Hooded Americanism*.

11. Coben, "Assault on Victorianism," 604–25; Hawley quoted in Moore, "Historical Interpretations of the 1920s Klan," 28; Wald, "Visible Empire," 217–34; Sims, *The Klan*, 1, 3.

12. Moore, *Citizen Klansman* and "Historical Interpretations of the 1920s Klan," 343–57;

Lay, ed., *Invisible Empire in the West;* idem, *War, Revolution, and the Ku Klux Klan* and *Hooded Knights on the Niagara,* 146–49; Goldberg, *Hooded Empire;* Gerlach, *Blazing Crosses in Zion,* 163–64; Cocoltchos, "Invisible Government and the Viable Community"; Jenkins, *Steel Valley Klan,* 152–64; Cocoltchos, "Invisible Empire and the Search for the Orderly Community," 97, 117; Toy, "Robe and Gown," 178; Akin, "Ku Klux Klan in Georgia." An influential and important piece that preceded Populist School works of the 1980s and 1990s is Thornton, "Alabama Politics," 83–112, esp. 112.

13. Lay, ed., *Invisible Empire in the West,* 3, 9, 217–22; Moore, *Citizen Klansman,* 9, 11–12.

14. The work of Weaver, Chalmers, and Jackson established the size of the second Klan long before that of the Populist-Civic School. See also Lay, ed., *Invisible Empire in the West,* 4–5, 8; Sims, *The Klan,* 2; Osofsky, *Burden of Race,* 262.

15. MacLean, *Behind the Mask of Chivalry,* xiii. See also Frederickson, *Crusaders Against Modernity.*

16. *New York Times,* 15 Aug. 1926; *Birmingham News,* 14, 19 Aug. 1926; Snell, "Fiery Crosses in the Roaring Twenties," 264–68, and "Ku Klux Klan in Jefferson County," 11, 73. "Big Mules" refers to the Birmingham District's large industrial interests. Birmingham's Big Mules and Mobile's "Lesser Mules" were in political alliance with the planter interests of the Black Belt throughout this period.

17. KKK Scrapbooks, no. 257, BPLA; Feidelson, "Alabama's Super Government," 312; *CT,* 14 Nov. 1927; *Guntersville Advocate* and *Thomasville Times,* in *MA,* 22 July 1927; *MA,* 20–22, 31 July 1927; *AC,* 1 Sept. 1927.

18. Bell, "Reconstruction Ku Klux Klan," 241–49.

19. See note 12 above.

20. Eula Mae McGill, Interview with the author, 12 March 1997; Thornton, "Alabama Politics," 83–112; Flynt, "Organized Labor," 163–80.

1. ORIGINS OF THE REVISED KLAN

1. Tindall, *America,* II:1025–26.

2. Ibid., II:823–29.

3. Ibid., II:1022–23.

4. Ibid., II:1028–38.

5. Forster and Epstein, *Report on the Ku Klux Klan,* 15–16; Chalmers, *Hooded Americanism,* 3; Newton and Newton, *Ku Klux Klan,* 51.

6. Tuskegee Institute News Clipping Files: Ku Klux Klan File, reel 11, 1920, TU; *NYA,* 31 Feb. 1920. James Venable has been described as "perhaps the ultimate Klansman"; see Newton and Newton, *Ku Klux Klan,* 580–81.

7. Smith to Moseley, 17 June 1963, in William Joseph Simmons File, and the Minutes of the Alabama Conference of Methodist-Episcopal Church, South, 74th sess., Eufaula, Ala., 5–10 Dec. 1906, and the Simmons File, and the *Journal of the Alabama–West Florida Conference,* Southeastern Jurisdiction, The Methodist Church, 23d sess., Montgomery, Ala., 30 May–2 June 1961, all at HUN. Charlton Moseley has argued that Simmons was born in Munford, Talladega County, not Harpersville, in "William Joseph Simmons," 17–32; *Opp Weekly News,* 13 May, 27 Oct. 1921, 27 July 1922, 23–24 May 1945; *CA,* 20 April 1905, 5 April 1923; Chalmers, *Hooded Americanism,* 28–30, 78; Newton and Newton, *Ku Klux Klan,* 520.

8. Kennedy, *Over Here,* 31, 53, 146; Curti, *Roots of American Loyalty,* 224–25; Higham, *Strangers in the Land.*

9. Kennedy, *Over Here,* 12 and 24 (first quotation), 67 (second quotation), 68–69; Kammen, *Mystic Chords of Memory,* 231; Hawley, *Great War and the Search for a Modern Order,* 50.

10. Pencak, *For God and Country,* 36, 314; Kennedy, *Over Here,* 69, 81–82; Vaughn, *Holding Fast the Inner Lines,* 98, 216, 296 n. 43, 328 n. 3; Hawley, *Great War and the Search for a Modern Order,* 29; Mohl, *American Legion Story,* 68–69.

11. Chalmers, *Hooded Americanism,* 118; Curti, *Roots of American Loyalty,* 235–36; Zelinsky, *Nation into State,* 105; Kennedy, *Over Here,* 291, 363; Bodnar, *Remaking America,* 86–89; Hawley, *Great War and the Search for a Modern Order,* 50, 127–28.

12. Chalmers, *Hooded Americanism,* 31; *Report of the Alabama Council of Defense;* Owen, *Alabama Department of the American Legion.*

13. Jackson, *Ku Klux Klan in the City,* 7; Fry, *Modern Ku Klux Klan,* 84–85, 140. On the Reconstruction KKK, see Trelease, *White Terror.*

14. Rice, *Ku Klux Klan in American Politics,* 13.

15. Forster and Epstein, *Report on the Ku Klux Klan,* 15; Newton and Newton, *Ku Klux Klan,* 117–18; Lay, ed., *Invisible Empire in the West,* 7.

16. Simmons to Daugherty, 28 Sept. 1921, in U.S. Congress, House, Committee on Rules, 67th Cong., 1st sess., *Hearings on the Ku Klux Klan Before the Committee on Rules,* 74, 128, 169; Newton and Newton, *Ku Klux Klan,* 520.

17. KKK File, reel 13, 1921, reel 18, 1923, TU; *East Tennessee News,* 17 Nov. 1921; *Atlanta Independent,* 18 Jan. 1923; *Savannah Tribune,* 4 Jan. 1923; *HP,* 28 Aug. 1923; *Federal Press Bulletin,* 22 Sept. 1923; *MA,* 28 Aug. 1923, 10 Sept. 1925; *NH,* 5 Jan., 9 July 1924; Snell, "Ku Klux Klan in Jefferson County," 11, 73, and "Fiery Crosses in the Roaring Twenties," 264–68.

18. Tindall, *Emergence of the New South,* 150–55.

19. Leuchtenburg, *Perils of Prosperity.*

20. KKK File, reel 11, 1920, TU; *MA,* 10 May and 13, 16 Oct. 1918; *BAH,* 15 June 1918, *BN,* 25 Jan. 1921; *NH,* 13, 27 June, 19 Sept., 5 Dec. 1923 and 23, 30 April, 7 May, 25 June 1924.

21. Wade, *Fiery Cross,* 150; Snell, "Ku Klux Klan in Jefferson County," 13; Newton and Newton, *Ku Klux Klan,* 52, 216.

22. Underwood to Cooper, 8 May 1924, Oscar W. Underwood Papers, ADAH; KKK Scrapbooks, vol. 1, BPLA; *BN,* 23 Sept. 1923.

23. Underwood to Cooper, 8 May 1924; *BN,* 13 Oct. 1918 (quoted), 23 Sept. 1923; *MA,* 28 Jan. 1921; *BAH,* 25–28; Jan. 1921; *BI.* and *BN,* 25 Jan. 1921.

24. Milner to Tampa, Florida Rotary Club, 27 Feb. 1917, Milner Family Papers, BPLA.

25. Simmons, *Klan Unmasked,* 23–28.

26. *NH,* 4 April 1923, 21 Feb., 23, 30 April, 14 May 1924.

27. Virginia F. Durr, Interview, Oral History Project, p. 7, CU; V. M. Scott Reminiscences, 1988, p. 4, TCHA.

28. Simmons, *Klan Unmasked,* 23–28.

29. KKK File, reel 11, 1920, TU; *Brooklyn Eagle,* 6 Jan. 1921 (second quotation); *CD,* 21 Dec. 1918 (first quotation); *NYA,* 28 Sept. 1918; *Richmond Planet,* and *New York World,* 10 Oct. 1920; *Advocate,* 10 Feb. 1920.

30. *NYT,* 15 Aug. 1926; *BN,* 14, 19 Aug. 1926. Esdale's claim was almost certainly inflated. The figure of 115,000 seems reasonable, although other scholars put it lower. Wayne Flynt put it at 95,000 in Rogers et al., *Alabama,* 431–32. Whichever figure is used, it should be remembered that many women, children, and perhaps older parents and in-laws also belonged to "Klan families" physically and/or sentimentally and that these numbers are not included in strict estimates of membership.

2. THE CIVIC, EDUCATIONAL, AND PROGRESSIVE KLAN

1. *NH,* 6, 20 June, 11, 25 July, 8 Aug., 26 Sept. 1923 and 9 Jan., 7 May, 10 Sept. 1924; *MA,* 22 Sept., 6, 13 Oct. 1918, 18–19 Oct. 1919, 30–31 Jan. 1921; *Cleveland Advocate,* 10 Feb. 1920 in KKK File, reel 11, 1920, TU; *BAH,* 25–30 Jan. 1921; *BN,* 28 Jan. 1921.

2. Talladega County KKK File, KKK Research Files, SU; *SA,* 4, 24 Feb., 10–13, 22 May, 21 June, 26–29 July, 18, 27–30 Oct. 1925, 20, 27 Oct. 1926; Snell, "Ku Klux Klan in Jefferson County," and "Fiery Crosses in the Roaring Twenties," 267–68; *Messenger,* 25 Feb. 1925.

3. James Stanley Laird Diary, 25 May 1918, SU; V. M. Scott Reminiscences, 1988, TCHA; E. C. Sharp, Interview, pp. 2–3, UAB.

4. Chalmers, *Hooded Americanism,* 79; Jackson, *Ku Klux Klan in the City,* 82–83; Snell, "Ku Klux Klan in Jefferson County," 9–11, 64–70, 76–77, and "Masked Men in the Magic City," 256–76; *SLA,* 15 July 1921; *HI,* 9 July 1921; *BAA,* 1 July 1921.

5. *BN,* 15 May 1925, 28 Feb. 1926; *NYT,* 16 May 1925, p. 22.

6. Invitation to Nichols Picnic in DeKalb County, SC 3320, SU; KKK Collection, BCHS; V. M. Scott Reminiscences, 12, TCHA; Clay, Lee, Shelby, and Talladega Counties KKK Files, William R. Snell Research Notes, hereafter cited as KKK Research Files, SU; *NH,* 9, 16, 30 May, 16 June, 4, 18 July, 1, 22 Aug., 5, 19 Sept., 3, 24 Oct., 28 Nov., 26 Dec. 1923 and 27 Feb., 16, 23 April, 14 May, 4, 18 June, 16 July, 6 Aug., 1 Oct. 1924; *SA,* 24 Aug. 1921; *Goodwater Enterprise,* 26 Aug. 1921; *Ashland Progress,* 29 May 1924; *Talladega Daily Home,* 5–7 June 1924; *SN,* 10 April 1924; *Shelby County Reporter,* 20 Sept. 1923; *OSD,* 31 July, 14 Aug. 1924.

7. *SLA* and *Charlotte Observer,* 3 July 1920; *MA,* 16 Sept. 1921, 3 Feb., 18 March, 14 June, and 13 July 1923; *BN,* 19 Dec. 1971, p. C-50; *BAH,* 27 Jan. 1922; Elovitz, *Century of Jewish Life in Dixie,* 323 n. 17; Snell, "Ku Klux Klan in Jefferson County," 9, 21.

8. *MA,* 28 Jan. 1921, 19 Aug. 1922, 22–24 Aug. 1923; *AG,* 18 Oct. 1923; *BN,* 25 Jan. 1921; *AC,* 28 Jan. 1921; *NYC,* 27 Feb. 1921; and Snell, "Ku Klux Klan in Jefferson County," 60–61, 70–73.

9. *MA,* 28 Jan. 1921, 19 Aug. 1922, 22–24 Aug. 1923; *AG,* 18 Oct. 1923; *BN,* 25 Jan. 1921; *AC,* 28 Jan. 1921; *NYC,* 27 Feb. 1921; and Snell, "Ku Klux Klan in Jefferson County," 60, 72–73.

10. Ala. KKK Newsletter 5:7 (March 1927): 2–4, box G192, folder "Ku Klux Klan, 1927," Alabama Governors Papers, David Bibb Graves, ADAH; Bibb County KKK File, KKK Research Files, SU; *CP,* 21 April 1927.

11. Official Document, Knights of the Ku Klux Klan, Realm of Alabama, 4 (June 1926): 7, box 16, folder 11: Ku Klux Klan, Association Records, ADAH, hereafter cited as Ala. KKK Newsletter; E. C. Sharp, Interview, pp. 1–4, UAB; 26 Aug. 1926, clipping, Aiken Papers, BA; KKK File, reel 23, 1925, TU; Lee County KKK File, KKK Research Files, SU; *MA,* 9 May 1925; *BAH,* 1 Nov. 1925; *Montgomery Journal,* 16 Oct. 1926; *Troy Messenger,* 25 Feb. 1925; *Opelika Daily News,* 30 Oct. 1925; Snell, "Fiery Crosses in the Roaring Twenties," 266.

12. *MA,* 27–28 Sept. 1921, 28 March, 21 June, 17 Dec. 1923.

13. *MA,* 27–28 Sept. 1921, 28 March, 21 June, 17 Dec. 1923; *NH,* 16, 23 July 1924.

14. KKK Collection, BCHS; Clay and Talladega Counties KKK Files, KKK Research Files, SU; *OSD,* 17 July 1924; *Advance,* 11 Jan. 22, 24 Feb. 1922 and 2 Jan., 13 Feb. 1924; *LH,* 18 Dec. 1924; *NH,* 12 Sept. 1923.

15. Esdale to Graves, 2 March 1926, box 192, folder: Ku Klux Klan, "KKK" File, Graves Papers, ADAH; KKK File, BCHS; Clay County KKK File and Talladega County KKK File, KKK Research Files, SU; *OSD,* 7 Jan. 1926.

16. 19 March 1925, clipping, Boone Aiken Papers, BA; V. M. Scott Reminiscences, 1, 12, 16, TCHA; Vern M. Scott to author, 21, 25 Jan. 1993, in the author's collection; Talladega County KKK File, KKK Research Files, SU; *NH,* 16 April 1924; Shepherd, "Whip Wins," 10–11, 31–32, and "Whip Hand," 8–9, 44–45; *AC,* 15 Sept. 1927; *MA,* 12 Oct. 1927.

17. 19 March 1925, clipping, Boone Aiken Papers, BA; V. M. Scott Reminiscences, 1, 12, 16, TCHA; Scott to author, 21, 25 Jan. 1993 in the author's collection; Irving M. Engel, Interview, 1969–70, tape 1, p. 37, AJA; Virginia F. Durr, Interview, p. 6 (quoted), CU; Palmer Weber, Interview, p. 8, CU; Talladega County KKK File, KKK Research Files, SU; *NH,* 16 April 1924.

18. *NH,* 23, 30 May, 13, 27 June, 1, 8 Aug., 5 Sept. 1923 and 14 Feb., 12 March 1924; Rice, *Ku Klux Klan in American Politics,* 23. On the poor-white concern with education after 1901, see McMillan, *Constitutional Development in Alabama.*

19. Talladega County KKK File, KKK Research Files, SU; *SA,* 4, 24 Feb., 10–13, 22 May, 21 June, 26–29 July, 18, 27–30 Oct. 1925, 20, 27 Oct. 1926; Snell, "Fiery Crosses in the Roaring Twenties," 267–68, and "Ku Klux Klan in Jefferson County," 100–2; *Messenger,* 25 Feb. 1925.

20. N. A. Barrett City Commission Scrapbooks, micro. no. 19, BPLA.

21. *In re Opinions of the Justices in re School Appropriations Act,* 215 Ala. 524 (1927); Ala. KKK Newsletter 4 (June 1926): 4, 6, box 16, folder 11, Association Records, ADAH; *TWK Monthly,* Feb. 1925 in KKK Scrapbooks, vol. 1, BPLA.

22. V. M. Scott Reminiscences, 4, TCHA; *AC,* 17 Dec. 1920, 23 Aug. 1923; *MA,* 17 Dec. 1920, 26 Dec. 1921; *MCA,* 25 Dec. 1921; *NH,* 5 Sept. 1923; Jackson, *Ku Klux Klan in the City,* 7; Chalmers, *Hooded Americanism,* 78; Snell, "Ku Klux Klan in the City," 64–65, 69; Brownell, "Birmingham, Alabama," 40.

23. Evans, "Where Do We Go from Here?"; Snell, "Ku Klux Klan in Jefferson County," 32–33, 47, 69.

24. Ala. KKK Newsletter 5:7 (March 1927): 2–4, box G192, folder "Ku Klux Klan, 1927," Graves Papers, ADAH; Bibb County KKK File, KKK Research Files, SU; *CP,* 21 April 1927.

25. NAACP Papers, pt. 7, ser. A, reel 1, 19 Feb. 1919, MADD and LC; KKK Collection, BCHS; Talladega County KKK File, KKK Research Files, SU; Snell, "Ku Klux Klan in Jefferson County," 36–39, 57; Newton and Newton, *Ku Klux Klan,* 320; *OSD,* 3 Jan., 31 July 1924; *Selma Journal,* 19 Feb. 1919, *SN,* 13 April 1923, *SA,* 21 Dec. 1923; *The Palladium* (yearbook), 63, TSUA. The yearbook was and is a student publication and as such should not be construed as reflecting the official policies or practices of the State Normal School (as Troy State University was then known) or of TSU today.

26. NAACP Papers, pt. 7, ser. A, reel 1, 19 Feb. 1919, MADD and LC; KKK Collection, BCHS; *The Palladium* (yearbook), 63, TSUA; Talladega County KKK File, KKK Research Files, SU; Snell, "Ku Klux Klan in Jefferson County," 36–39, 57; Newton and Newton, *Ku Klux Klan,* 320; *OSD,* 3 Jan., 31 July 1924; *Selma Journal,* 19 Feb. 1919; *SN,* 13 April 1923; *SA,* 21 Dec. 1923.

27. KKK Scrapbooks, vol. 1, BPLA; Ala. KKK Newsletter 4 (June 1926): 7, box 16, folder 11, Associations Records, ADAH; *TWK Monthly,* Feb. 1925; *Prattville Progress,* 24 Sept. 1925, clipping, file: KKK-Prattville, Aiken Papers, BA.

28. Ala. KKK Newsletter 5:7 (March 1927): 2–4, box G192, folder "Ku Klux Klan, 1927," Graves Papers, ADAH; Bibb County KKK File, KKK Research Files, SU; *CP,* 21 April 1927.

29. Newman, "Hugo Black Manuscript," ch. 6 n. 10. I thank Wayne Flynt for sharing this manuscript with me.

30. *NYT,* 18 April 1927; Snell, "Ku Klux Klan in Jefferson County," 140–44.

31. *BAH,* 9 Jan. 1927.

32. Ibid.

33. Snell, "Ku Klux Klan in Jefferson County," 146, 149–50.

34. Newman, "Hugo Black Manuscript," 332–33.

35. Shepherd, "Whip Hand," 10, 44–45; Rice, *Ku Klux Klan in American Politics,* 65–66; Owen, *History of Alabama,* IV:1087.

36. "The New South," *Nation* 125 (24 Aug. 1927): 173; Newman, "Hugo Black Manuscript," 139–40.

37. *BAH,* 23 Feb. 1927; *AC,* 9 March 1927; Newton and Newton, *Ku Klux Klan,* 187; Snell, "Ku Klux Klan in Jefferson County," 151–53.

38. Owen, *History of Alabama,* III:741; *NYT,* 18 April 1927, p. 16, and 11 Feb. 1927, p. 44; *NYHT,* 11 Feb. 1927.

39. Newton and Newton, *Ku Klux Klan,* 366–67.

40. Ala. KKK Newsletter, quoted in *MA,* 30 July 1927.

41. Esdale to Davis, 16 May 1927, box G192, folder "Ku Klux Klan, 1927," Graves Papers, ADAH.

42. V. M. Scott Reminiscences, 1988, p. 15, TCHA; *MA,* 23 July 1927; Snell, "Ku Klux Klan in Jefferson County," 144–45, 153. I address this subject in more detail in Chapter 3.

43. Thornhill to Graves, 22 Sept. 1927, box G192, folder "Ku Klux Klan, 1927," Graves Papers, ADAH; *BAH,* 23 Feb. 1927; *NYT,* 18 April 1927, p. 16.

44. *MA,* 11 Aug. 1927.

45. Holliman to Underwood, 18 Aug. 1927, box 41, folder 3, Oscar W. Underwood Papers, ADAH; KKK File, reel 28, 1927, TU; KKK Scrapbooks, no. 257, BPLA; Feidelson, "Alabama's Super Government," 311; *NYW,* 15 July 1927; *CR,* in *MA,* 15 July 1927; *General Laws (and Joint Resolutions), 1919,* hereafter cited as *Alabama Acts;* Feldman, *From Demagogue to Dixiecrat,* 25.

46. Weir to Graves, 23 March 1927, Elliott to Graves, 18 April 1927, Graves to Scheffer, 23 March 1927, Standifer to Davis, 3 March 1927, Welch and Dozier to Graves, 8 March 1927, Tipton to Graves, 15 June 1927, Thornhill to Graves, 22 Sept. 1927, Webb and Dozier to Graves 8 March 1927, all in box G192, folder "Ku Klux Klan, 1927"; see also Bailes to Graves, 29 Sept. and 7 Oct. 1927, box G192, folder "Law Enforcement, 1927–1928," all in Graves Papers, ADAH.

47. Graves to Scheffer, 23 March 1927, Thornhill to Graves, 22 Sept. 1927, box G192, folder "Ku Klux Klan, 1927," Graves Papers, ADAH.

48. Snell, "Ku Klux Klan in Jefferson County," 153–54.

3. THE MORAL AND RELIGIOUS KLAN

1. The only book-length treatment of prohibition in Alabama is Sellers, *Prohibition Movement in Alabama.* See also Ownby, *Subduing Satan,* 74–77.

2. This issue is discussed in much of Barbara B. Diefendorf's *Beneath the Cross.*

3. KKK Collection, BCHS; Clay, Shelby, and Talladega Counties KKK Files, KKK Research Files, SU; KKK File, reels 4, 8, 9, 11, 13, 15, 18, and 20, 1916–1924, TU; *SN,* 19 July 1923; *SA,* 11 July 1923; *Shelby County Reporter,* 12 June 1923; *Greensboro Watchman,* 8 June 1922; *OSD,* 3 Jan., 1 May, 31 July 1924; Baimonte, *Spirit of Vengeance,* 151.

4. KKK Collection, BCHS; Clay, Shelby, and Talladega Counties KKK Files, KKK Research Files, SU; KKK File, reels 4, 8, 9, 11, 13, 15, 18, and 20, 1916–1924, TU; *SN,* 19 July 1923; *SA,* 11 July 1923; *Shelby County Reporter,* 12 June 1923; *Greensboro Watchman,* 8 June 1922; *OSD,* 3 Jan., 1 May, 31 July 1924; Baimonte, *Spirit of Vengeance,* 151; MA, 8 May 1922,

6 Nov. 1922; 18 April, 13 July 1923. See also Dobbins, "Alabama Governors and Editors," 137. Dobbins reports that when his father, a Baptist minister in Luverne, denounced the Crenshaw County Klan from his pulpit, two deacons dramatically rose and left the church. Dobbins's father resigned and took a pastorate at Camden in Wilcox County.

5. Mildred Ruth Heaton and Lois Cowan, Interview with Linda Jean Tharp, 1 Feb. 1974, p. 4, UAB; Ala. KKK Newsletter 4 (June 1926): 3, box 16, folder 11, Association Records, ADAH; Clay County KKK File, Talladega County KKK File, and Bibb County KKK File, all in KKK Research Files, SU; Snell, "Ku Klux Klan in Jefferson County, 1916–1930," 116, 121, and "Fiery Crosses in the Roaring Twenties," 268–69; Newton and Newton, *Ku Klux Klan,* 302.

6. *BN,* 1 Aug. 1949 (quoted); Roger K. Newman, "Hugo Black Manuscript," ch. 6 n. 21; Newton and Newton, *Ku Klux Klan,* 302.

7. 15 Oct. 1925, clipping, Aiken Papers, BA.

8. *New York News,* 11 July 1921.

9. KKK File, reel 20, 1924, TU; *BAH,* 31 Dec. 1921, 11 June 1922; *BN,* 19 Dec. 1971, p. C-50; *MA,* 14 Sept., 27 March 1922, 25–26 April 1923, 7 March 1924.; *MCA,* 25 Jan. 1923.

10. Lee County KKK File, KKK Research Files, SU; *AC,* 17 Jan. 1925; *BN,* 16 Jan., 23 Feb. 1925, 24 Nov. 1926.

11. E. C. Sharp, Interview, pp. 1–4, UAB; Bibb County KKK File, Shelby County KKK File, and Talladega County KKK File, KKK Research Files, SU; V. M. Scott Reminiscences, 14–15, TCHA; *SA,* 18 June 1924; *Talladega Daily Home,* 14 June 1924; *CP,* 12 May 1921; Newton and Newton, *Ku Klux Klan,* 145.

12. *BN,* 17, 21 Jan. 1925; Snell, ""Ku Klux Klan in Jefferson County," 79–82; Beirman, "Birmingham."

13. Talladega County KKK File, KKK Research Files, SU; KKK File, reel 23, 1925, TU; *BN,* 4 Feb. 1925; *MA,* 29 Jan. 1925.

14. *BN,* 17, 22 Jan. 1925.

15. James Stanley Laird Diary, 25 May 1918, SU; *AG,* 23 Jan. 1923; *BN,* 18 Oct. 1920; *AC,* 12 Feb. 1924; *MA,* 11 Nov. 1923, 21 Feb. 1924; *BL,* 18 Oct. 1920.

16. Snell, "Fiery Crosses in the Roaring Twenties," 269–70, and "Ku Klux Klan in Jefferson County," 79–83, 116, 120.

17. Lee County KKK File, KKK Research Files, SU; *AC,* 17 Jan. 1925; *BN,* 16 Jan., 23 Feb. 1925, 24 Nov. 1926.

18. *NH,* 25 July, 26 Sept. 1923; Snell, "Fiery Crosses in the Roaring Twenties," 269–70, and "Ku Klux Klan in Jefferson County," 79–83, 116, 120.

19. KKK File, reel 25, 1926, TU; *NYT,* 5 Jan. 1926, p. 15; *AC,* 5 Jan. 1926; *BN,* 4–13 Jan. 1926; *BAH,* 4–14 Jan. 1926.

20. *BN,* 5–9, 12 Jan. 1926; Snell, "Ku Klux Klan in Jefferson County," 90–91, 111–13, 123.

21. Snell, "Ku Klux Klan in Jefferson County," 112, 115, 123.

22. *BN,* 5–9, 12 Jan. 1926; Snell, "Ku Klux Klan in Jefferson County," 90–91, 111–13, 123.

23. *BN,* 8–13 Jan., 1 May 1926.

24. *AC* and *MCA,* 12 Sept. 1922; *MA,* 25 July 1921; *BAH,* 11 June 1922; MacLean, *Behind the Mask of Chivalry;* Rothman, *Woman's Proper Place.*

25. *MCA,* 2, 4 June 1926.

26. *MCA,* 22 Aug. 1924; *MA,* 20 Jan., 22–24 Aug. 1923; Blee, *Women of the Klan;* Snell, "Ku Klux Klan in Jefferson County," 55–56, 77; *NH,* 13 June, 3 Oct. 1923, 14 May, 30 July, 29 Oct. 1924; Rogers et al., *Alabama,* 431.

27. Mildred Ruth Heaton and Lois Cowan, Interview, p. 4, UAB.

28. Boxes 23, 24, Percy Family Papers, file: Ku Klux Klan, MDAH; Clay County KKK File, KKK Research Files, SU.

29. KKK Collection, BCHS; *NYT,* 15 June 1925, p. 6; *BN,* 26 Feb., 1, 15 March, 5, 9 April, 15 June 1925, 26–28 April, 3 May 1926, 1 Nov. 1981, p. 1B; *Decatur Daily,* 10 Aug. 1975; *BAH,* 21 June 1925; *OSD,* 29 April, 6 May 1926.

30. Ku Klux Klan File, Percy Family Papers, MDAH; John P. Johnston to author, 2 Feb. 1993, PIKE; *AC,* 9 Oct., 6–7 Dec. 1921; *AG,* 6–9 Dec. 1921, 30 March 1922; *MA,* 5–8 Dec. 1921, 14, 19–20 Feb. 1923; *Cleveland Advocate,* 10 Feb. 1920.

31. *AC,* 5 Sept. 1923; *TRI,* 7 Nov. 1923; Forster and Epstein, *Report on the Ku Klux Klan,* 15–16; Rice, *Ku Klux Klan in American Politics,* 10; Snell, "Ku Klux Klan in Jefferson County," 47; Newton and Newton, *Ku Klux Klan,* 520–21.

32. Esdale, "How to Operate a Model Realm"; Rice, *Ku Klux Klan in American Politics,* 11; *MCA,* 20 Aug. 1924; *NH,* 12 March 1924.

33. *MA,* 23 July 1927; Snell, "Ku Klux Klan in Jefferson County," 144–45, 153.

34. V. M. Scott Reminiscences, 1988, p. 15, TCHA.

4. THE RACIST AND NATIVIST KLAN

1. Feldman, "Lynching in Alabama," 114–41.

2. Oshinsky, *"Worse than Slavery,"* 94–96.

3. Flynt, *Poor but Proud,* 242; McMillan, *Constitutional Development in Alabama,* 230–32.

4. McMillan, *Constitutional Development in Alabama,* 230–32; Tindall, *America,* II:750–52. See also *Williams v. Mississippi,* 170 U.S. 213 (1898), for the Court's reasoning in upholding the Second Mississippi Plan and its suffrage restrictions.

5. *Brooklyn Eagle,* quoted in the *MR,* 26 July 1901, cited in McMillan, *Constitutional Development in Alabama,* 291 n. 43; see also 290–91.

6. *Galveston Farm News,* 20 Sept. 1921.

7. *AG,* 30 March 1922; *MA,* 12 April, 21 May, 4–8 Sept. 1922, and 2–8 Oct. 1923.

8. Cash, *Mind of the South,* 40, 69–70, 109, 112, 131–33, 171–75, 220–21, 251, 258, 365–66; McMillan, *Constitutional Development in Alabama,* 227; Flynt, *Poor but Proud,* x–xii, 212, 215, 217, 260, 362.

9. KKK File, reel 20, 1924, TU; Bibb County KKK File, KKK Research Files, SU; *AG,* 30 March 1922; *MA,* 12 April, 21 May, 4–8 Sept. 1922, and 2–8 Oct. 1923; Kennedy to Lindsey, 8 Feb. 1923, correspondence by author, IV-k-1, box 1, acc. no. 1591, TSLA; *SLA,* 15 July 1921; *HI,* 9 July 1921, 17 May 1924; *BAA,* 1 July, 5 Aug. 1921, *AC,* 4 July 1923; *MA,* and *BN,* 15 May 1923, 3 May 1924; *BR,* 12 March 1921; *AG,* 5 July 1923; *Little Rock Mosaic Guide,* 7 July 1923; *Cleveland Gazette,* 7 July 1923; *NYT,* 4 July 1923, p. 1, 6 July 1923, p. 3, and 22 July 1923, p. 16; *MR,* 5 July 1923; *Savannah Tribune,* and the *CP,* 12 July 1923; *Norfolk JG,* 14 July 1923; *PC,* 14, 21, 28 July, 4 Aug. 1923 and 10 March 1928; *Charlotte Observer,* 6 July 1923; *AN,* 8, 15, 29 Aug. 1923; *NH,* 16 May 1923; Snell, "Ku Klux Klan in Jefferson County," 54; Schieffelin, "Most Unforgettable Character I've Met," 25–28; Jakeman, *Divided Skies.* An excellent study of civil rights in Tuskegee is Norrell, *Reaping the Whirlwind.*

10. *AG,* 30 March 1922; *MA,* 12 April, 21 May, 4–8 Sept. 1922, and 2–8 Oct. 1923.

11. Thompson to Rogers, 14 Oct. 1916, box 117, folder: Convict Dept., 1916–17, Charles Henderson, Alabama Governors Papers, ADAH; Feldman, "Lynching in Alabama," 114–41.

12. *BLA,* 30 July 1921; *Cleveland Call,* 6 Aug. 1921; *MA,* 24–25 July 1921; and *AC,* 24 July 1921.

13. Lynching File, Tuskegee Institute News Clippings File, reel 222, fr. 0007, 1919, TU; *MA*, 30 Sept., 3–4 Oct. 1919; *New York Daily Herald*, 11 Oct. 1919; Feldman, "Ku Klux Klan in Alabama," 62 (quoted).

14. Elovitz, *Century of Jewish Life in Dixie*, 87; *SLA*, 12 May 1922.

15. Miller, "Ku Klux Klan," 207, 217–18, 253–54; *Eagle*, 6, 28 Jan. 1921; *TPD*, 18 Dec. 1920, 5 Feb. 1921; *NYP*, 18 July 1921; Mecklin, *Ku Klux Klan*; Fry, *Modern Ku Klux Klan*; Monteval, *Klan Inside Out*; Evans, "Where Do We Go from Here?" 11–12.

16. Ku Klux Klan File, Percy Family Papers, MDAH; John P. Johnston to author, 2 Feb. 1993; PIKE; *AC*, 9 Oct., 6–7 Dec. 1921; *AG*, 6–9 Dec. 1921, 30 March 1922; *MA*, 5–8 Dec. 1921, 14, 19–20 Feb. 1923; *Cleveland Advocate*, 10 Feb. 1920.

17. Kennedy to Lindsey, 8 Feb. 1923, correspondence by author, IV-k-1, box 1, acc. no. 1591, TSLA; KKK File, reel 20, 1924, TU; *SLA*, 15 July 1921; *HI*, 9 July 1921, 17 May 1924; *BAA*, 1 July 1921, *AC*, 4 July 1923; *MA* and *BN*, 3 May 1924; *MA*, 12 April 1924, Snell, "Ku Klux Klan in Jefferson County," 54; *BR*, 12 March 1921; *AG*, 5 July 1923; *Little Rock Mosaic Guide*, 7 July 1923; *Cleveland Gazette*, 7 July 1923.

18. *BAA*, 5 Aug. 1921; *BR*, 12 March 1921; 19 May 1923; *BN* and *MA*, 15 May 1923.

19. KKK File, reel 20, 1924, TU; Bibb County KKK File, KKK Research Files, SU; *NYT*, 4 July 1923, p. 1, 6 July 1923, p. 3, and 22 July 1923, p. 16; Kennedy to Lindsey, 8 Feb. 1923, correspondence by author, IV-k-1, box 1, acc. no. 1591, TSLA; *SLA*, 15 July 1921; *HI*, 9 July 1921, 17 May 1924; *BAA*, 1 July, 5 Aug. 1921, *AC*, 4 July 1923; *MA*, and *BN*, 15 May 1923, 3 May 1924; Snell, "Ku Klux Klan in Jefferson County," 54; *BR*, 12 March 1921; *AG*, 5 July 1923; *Little Rock Mosaic Guide*, 7 July 1923; *Cleveland Gazette*, 7 July 1923; *MR*, 5 July 1923; *Savannah Tribune* and the *CP*, 12 July 1923; *Norfolk JG*, 14 July 1923; *PC*, 14, 21, 28 July, 4 Aug. 1923 and 10 March 1928; *Charlotte Observer*, 6 July 1923; *AN*, 8, 15, 29 Aug. 1923; *NH*, 16 May 1923; Schieffelin, "Most Unforgettable Character I've Met," 25–28.

20. Kennedy to Lindsey, 8 Feb. 1923, correspondence by author, IV-k-1, box 1, acc. no. 1591, TSLA; KKK File, reel 20, 1924, TU; *SLA*, 15 July 1921; *HI*, 9 July 1921, 17 May 1924; *BAA*, 1 July, 5 Aug. 1921, *AC*, 4 July 1923; *MA*, and *BN*, 15 May 1923, 3 May 1924; Snell, "Ku Klux Klan in Jefferson County," 54; *BR*, 12 March 1921; *AG*, 5 July 1923; *Little Rock Mosaic Guide*, 7 July 1923; *Cleveland Gazette*, 7 July 1923; Bibb County KKK File, KKK Research Files, SU; *NYT*, 4 July 1923, p. 1, 6 July 1923, p. 3, and 22 July 1923, p. 16; *MR*, 5 July 1923; *Savannah Tribune*, and the *CP*, 12 July 1923; *Norfolk JG*, 14 July 1923; *PC*, 14, 21, 28 July, 4 Aug. 1923 and 10 March 1928; *Charlotte Observer*, 6 July 1923; *AN*, 8, 15, 29 Aug. 1923; *NH*, 16 May 1923; Daniel, "Black Power in the 1920s," 368–88.

21. *SLA*, and *Observer*, 3 July 1920; *MA*, 30–31 Jan. 1921, 3 Oct. 1923, *BAH*, 25–30 Jan. 1921; *BN*, 25–28 Jan. 1921; *MCA*, 9 May 1923; Marks, *Farewell—We're Good and Gone*.

22. KKK File, reel 20, 1924, TU; *New York Telegram*, 20 Oct. 1921; *NYW*, 17 Oct. 1921; *AC*, 21 Oct. 1921, 31 March 1923; *BAH*, 14 Dec. 1921; *MCA*, 13 April 1922; *MA*, 25 Oct. 1922, 12 Nov. 1923.

23. *MA*, 12 Nov. 1923.

24. Sledge, "Black Conservatism in the Twentieth-Century South," 8–9, 12.

25. KKK File, reel 25, 1926, TU; *BR*, 6 June 1925; *MA*, 16 Feb. 1926; Snell, "Ku Klux Klan in Jefferson County," 83–84.

26. Evans, "Where Do We Go from Here?" 11–12, and "The Attitude of the Knights of the Ku Klux Klan Toward the Roman Catholic Hierarchy," 116–17; Ellison, "Little Italy in Rural Alabama," 44; Tindall, *Ethnic Southerners*, 44–45.

27. *AC*, 29 Feb. 1924; *MA*, 3 Dec. 1922; Mecklin, *Ku Klux Klan*, 157–205.

28. Evans, "Where Do We Go from Here?" 11–12, and "The Attitude of the Knights of the Ku Klux Klan Toward the Roman Catholic Hierarchy," 116–17; Ellison, "Little Italy in Rural Alabama," 44.

29. *Fourteenth Census of the United States, 1920, Vol. 3: Population,* table 1, p. 54, and table 9, pp. 59–65.

30. Evans, "The Attitude of the Knights of the Ku Klux Klan Toward the Jew," 125, and "Where Do We Go from Here?" 11, 13; Simmons, *Klan Unmasked,* 68; Fry, *Modern Ku Klux Klan,* 120; *NH,* 1 Aug. 1923.

31. Ala. KKK Newsletter 4 (June 1926): 7, box 16, folder 11, Associations Records, ADAH; KKK Scrapbooks, vol. 1, BPLA; *TWK Monthly,* Feb. 1925; William P. Engel, Interview, pp. 143–44, AJA; Irving M. Engel, Interview, tape 1, p. 39, AJA; Charles A. Fell Memoirs, II, pt. 1, pp. 101–28, BPLA; Papers of the NAACP, pt. 1, reel 13, MADD and LC; V. M. Scott Reminiscences, 12, TCHA; Talladega County KKK File, KKK Research Files, SU; *MA,* 29 Sept. 1923; *BN,* 3 March, 24 April 1925; *HI,* 17 May 1924; *Our Mountain Home,* 10 Sept. 1924; Elovitz, *Century of Jewish Life in Dixie,* 86, 222 n. 5; Snell, "Ku Klux Klan in Jefferson County," 274; Cowett, *Birmingham's Rabbi.*

32. Ala. KKK Newsletter 4 (June 1926): 7, box 16, folder 11, Associations Records, ADAH; KKK Scrapbooks, vol. 1, BPLA; *TWK Monthly,* Feb. 1925; *BN,* 3 March, 24 April 1925.

33. *MA,* 28 Jan. 1925; *BN,* 1 April 1925; *MCA,* 5 June 1926; Snell, "Ku Klux Klan in Jefferson County," 119; Oral History of Maurine Slaughter by James L. Sledge III, 5 Nov. 1985, pp. 14–15, SU.

34. *MA,* 28 Jan. 1925; *BN,* 1 April 1925; *MCA,* 5 June 1926; Snell, "Ku Klux Klan in Jefferson County," 119; Oral History of Maurine Slaughter by James L. Sledge III, 5 Nov. 1985, pp. 14–15, SU; *BN,* 1 April 1925 (quoted); Newman, "Hugo Black Manuscript," ch. 6, n. 36. See also Cowett, *Birmingham's Rabbi,* 136; Atkins, *Valley and the Hills,* 133.

35. Oral History of Maurine Slaughter, by James L. Sledge, 5 Nov. 1985, pp. 14–15, SU.

36. KKK File, reel 25, 1926, TU; *MCA,* 6 June 1926.

37. Charles A. Fell Memoirs, II, pt. 1, pp. 101–28, BPLA; Irving M. Engel, Interview, tape 1, p. 37, AJA; Clay and Shelby Counties, KKK Research Files, SU; *LH,* 19 Jan. 1923; Simmons, *Klan Unmasked,* 69–83, esp. 73; Newton and Newton, *Ku Klux Klan,* 187; Evans, "Where Do We Go from Here?" 114–15; Fry, *Modern Ku Klux Klan,* 109.

38. Dozier to Coyle, 1917, box 7, folder 25, Alabama Pamphlet Collection, ADAH; Coyle to Editor of the *BAH,* 16 Dec. 1916; Whiting, "'True Americans,' Pro and Con," 11; Breedlove, "Progressivism and Nativism," 3–4; Eskew, "Demagoguery in Birmingham and the Building of Vestavia," 202; Brownell, "Birmingham, Alabama," 21–48; Newman, "Hugo Black Manuscript," ch. 6 n. 4.

39. Dozier to Coyle, 1917, box 7, folder 25, Alabama Pamphlet Collection, ADAH; Coyle to Editor of *BAH,* 16. Dec. 1916; Eskew, "Demagoguery in Birmingham and the Building of Vestavia," 202 (quoted).

40. Emmetts to Kilby, 1 Aug. 1921 (quoted), in file "Law Enforcement, 1920–23," William W. Brandon, Alabama Governors Papers, ADAH; Fleming, *What Is Ku Kluxism?* micro no. 3824, MADD; Tindall, *Emergence of the New South,* 188–89; Chalmers, *Hooded Americanism,* 79; Mecklin, *Ku Klux Klan,* 157–205; Snell, "Fiery Crosses in the Roaring Twenties," 258 n. 4; Elovitz, *Century of Jewish Life in Dixie,* 323 n. 17; Pruitt, "Killing of Father Coyle," 24–37; *BN,* 19 Dec. 1971, p. C-50.

41. Minutes of the Meeting, 20 Oct. 1925, City of Mobile, Board of Commissioners Minutes, reel 24, MMA; *BAH,* 2 April 1925.

42. *BN*, 22 April 1921; Hamilton, *Hugo Black*, 84. For more on Wilkinson's unusual career, see Feldman, "Horace Wilkinson and Alabama Politics," and *From Demagogue to Dixiecrat*.

43. *Fourteenth Census of the United States: Population, 1920, Vol. 3*, table 1, p. 54, tables 10 and 11, pp. 66–68, and *Religious Bodies: 1916, Pt. 1: Summary and General Tables*, 238–39, and *Religious Bodies: 1926, Vol. 1: Summary and Detailed Tables*, 142–45.

44. Bibb, Clay, and Talladega Counties KKK Files, KKK Research Files, SU; *CP*, 29 March 1923; *LH*, 12 Dec. 1924; *SN*, 19 July 1923; *SA*, 11 July 1923.

45. KKK File, reel 11, 1920, TU; *Advocate*, 29 June 1918; *MA*, 17–18 June 1918; *NYA*, 28 Sept. 1918; *AC*, 4 Nov. 1921; Jackson, *Ku Klux Klan in the City*, 7.

46. *MCA*, 30 Sept. 1922; *MA*, 13 Aug., 4–5 Oct. 1922.

47. *BLA*, 30 July 1921; *TPD*, 16 April 1921; *BAH*, 11 June 1922; *NYC*, 12 May 1921.

48. Thornton, "Alabama Politics," 83–112; Flynt, "Organized Labor," 163–80.

5. THE POLITICAL KLAN

1. Alabama has seen a number of excellent studies of its politics during this era. Three of the older but still classic works are, of course, the relevant sections in Key, *Southern Politics in State and Nation*, Going, *Bourbon Democracy in Alabama*, and McMillan, *Constitutional Development in Alabama*. More recent contributions are Rogers, *The One-Gallused Rebellion*, Hackney, *Populism to Progressivism in Alabama*, and relevant sections in Kousser, *Shaping of Southern Politics*. See also two recent books: Webb, *Two-Party Politics in the One-Party South*, and Letwin, *The Challenge of Interracial Unionism*. A good examination of the political story from 1958 through 1970 is Permaloff and Grafton, *Political Power in Alabama*.

2. Rogers et al., *Alabama*, xvi–xviii; McMillan, *Constitutional Development in Alabama*, 352 n. 81; Thornton, "Alabama Politics," 84 n. 1.

3. These points make a constant theme for McMillan in *Constitutional Development in Alabama*, Flynt in *Dixie's Forgotten People*, and *Poor but Proud*. See also Thornton, "Alabama Politics," 84 n. 1.

4. *Fourteenth Census of the United States, 1920, Vol. 3: Population*, table 9, pp. 59–69; Rogers et al., *Alabama*, 413; Thornton, "Alabama Politics," 84; Key, *Southern Politics in State and Nation*, 36–57.

5. *MA*, 15 May 1920.

6. Stokely to Underwood, 26 Oct. 1923, box 60, folder 1, and Jones to Graves, 7 Jan. 1924, and Johnston to W. H. M , n d , both in box 60, folder 3, Oscar W. Underwood Papers, ADAH; Rogers et al., *Alabama*, 435–37; Allen, "The 1924 Underwood Campaign in Alabama," 176–87, and "The Underwood Presidential Movement of 1924," 93; Flynt, "Organized Labor," 163–80; Peirce, *Deep South States of America*; Sandlin, "Lycurgus Breckinridge Musgrove," 210–11; *MA*, 9, 15 May 1920; Owen, *Alabama Department of the American Legion*.

7. Sandlin, "Lycurgus Breckinridge Musgrove," 213–14.

8. *BN*, 19 Dec. 1971, p. C-50, from Elovitz, *Century of Jewish Life in Dixie*, 323 n. 17; *MA*, 21 Feb., 24 Aug., and 19 Sept. 1923.

9. J. Thomas Heflin Scrapbooks, MFS-652, II, 1924–25, SU; *New York Sun Globe*, 14 Feb. 1924; *TRI*, 16 Feb. 1924; *MR*, 15 Feb. 1924; *Luverne Journal*, 28 Feb. 1924; *Crenshaw County News*, 14, 21 Feb. 1924; *Washington Bee*, 4 April 1908; *WP*, 28 March 1908; Newton and Newton, *Ku Klux Klan*, 5. The only politician listed whose Klan membership is somewhat questionable is Judge Richard Rives. Other prominent politicians such as state supreme court justice Joel Brown were sympathetic to the order; see Thornton, "Hugo Black and the Golden Age," 901–3.

10. *MA,* March 1920, clipping, in ser. L, box 20, Papers of John H. Bankhead, Jr., ADAH; *TRI* to Kilby, 21 Nov. 1922, *NYW* to Kilby, 24 Sept. 1921, International News Service (INS) to Kilby, Kilby to INS, and Kilby to *TRI,* all three on 21 Nov. 1922, and McCue to Kilby, 24 Sept. 1921 (quoted). All correspondence is located in the file "Ku Klux Klan, 1921–22," in the Alabama Governors Papers, Thomas E. Kilby, ADAH. J. Thomas Heflin denied belonging to the KKK, but reliable sources agree that he was a member; see Chalmers, *Hooded Americanism,* 305, and Rice, *Ku Klux Klan in American Politics,* 89–90; *NYH,* 11 Nov. 1923; *TP,* 15 Feb. 1924; Thornton, "Alabama Politics," 95.

11. KKK File, reel 20, 1924, TU; *New York Telegram,* 20 Oct. 1921; *NYW,* 17 Oct. 1921; *AC,* 21 Oct. 1921, 31 March 1923; *BAH,* 14 Dec. 1921; *MCA,* 13 April 1922; *MA,* 25 Oct. 1922, 12 Nov. 1923.

12. Feldman, *From Demagogue to Dixiecrat,* 88; Pruitt, "The Killing of Father Coyle," 24–37. In a recent biography, Howard Ball incorrectly assigned responsibility for the Stephenson trial to Black's law partner, Crampton Harris; see *Hugo L. Black,* 59–60. A more authoritative account of this episode appears in Hamilton, *Hugo Black,* 89–93. See also Newman, *Hugo Black,* 71–88.

13. Hamilton, *Hugo Black,* 89–93.

14. Ibid.

15. *BR,* 27 May 1922; *MA,* 21 May (quoted), 9 June 1922.

16. *AC,* 12 April 1923; *BR,* 7 April 1923; *MA,* 19–20 Feb., 30–31 March, 1–10 April, 27 May, 1, 15–17 June 1923; *NYH,* 11 Nov. 1923. The Dowling case involved several actors who later became important in Alabama's Klan drama. Klan attorneys George Frey and Hugh Locke defended the accused floggers, while Judge O. A. Steele presided fairly. See *MA,* 1 June, 17 June 1923.

17. *BR,* 27 May, 10 June 1922; *BN* quoted in *BR,* 27 May 1922. See also *BN* and *MA,* 22, 25–27, 31 May, 2, 8–9, Sept. 1922; *AC,* 27 May, 10 Sept. 1922; *MCA,* 14 April 1922; *NYT,* 26 May 1922; Snell, "Fiery Crosses in the Roaring Twenties," 262.

18. *BN,* 25 May 1922; *MA,* 26–27 May, 9 Sept. 1922; *NYT,* 26 May 1922; *AC,* 27 May, 10 Sept. 1922; *Gadsden Journal* quoted in *BR,* 27 May 1922. Arlie Barber, the former public safety commissioner in Birmingham, complained, "If the people of Birmingham will stand for this outrage . . . , they will stand for anything," and he called upon the citizenry to oppose all Klan-backed politicians in the upcoming city elections. Sidney Bowie, a former U.S. congressman and the current president of the Birmingham Civic Association, advised potential mob victims to "shoot to kill and see who the party was later." Both Barber and Bowie agreed that it was "just as bad when a poor white man or Negro" was the victim of mob violence. Both men are quoted in *BN,* 27 May 1922. During this period most people, incorrectly as it turned out, placed blame for the attack on the KKK. See, for example, *NYT,* 11 Nov. 1923.

19. *AB,* 11 Jan. 1923, *CP,* 17 Feb. 1921, *SA,* 11 Jan., 22, 24 Feb. 1922, *Opp Weekly News,* 27 Oct. 1921 and 24 May 1945, newspaper clippings in William Joseph Simmons File, HUN; Bibb County KKK File, Greene County KKK File, Talladega County KKK File, KKK Research Files, SU; *BL* and *BN,* 19 May 1924.

20. Papers of Horace C. Wilkinson, reel 1, misc. clippings, SU; *SLA,* 23 June 1922; *BR,* 27 May, 2, 10 June 1922; *MA,* 31 May, 2, 7, 17 June 1922; *AC,* 7 June 1922; Snell, "Ku Klux Klan in Jefferson County," 36–39, 57; *BAH* and *BN,* 17 June 1922. Baptist minister F. J. Washburn added that the KKK was "against the northern agitator and the [NAACP] . . . , which teaches . . . social as well as political equality." Washburn is quoted in *MA,* 31 May and 7 June 1922, and in *BR,* 10 June 1922.

21. Snell, "Ku Klux Klan in Jefferson County," 36 (first quotation); *AC*, 7 June 1922 (second quotation). See also *MA*, 7 June, 17 June, and 8 Sept. 1922. Dr. J. E. Dillard, pastor of Birmingham's Southside Baptist Church, and O. L. Bunn, a leader of the chamber of commerce, blamed police in *MA*, 31 May 1922, for permitting Klan floggings to occur.

22. KKK File, reel 15, 1922, TU, in particular *Jasper Mountain Eagle*, n.d.; *MCA*, 24 Oct. 1923; *BR*, 27 May, 10 June 1922; *MA*, 8, 17 Sept. 1922, 25 March, 8 April, 26 May, 14, 21 June 1923; *SLA*, 22 Aug. 1924.

23. *MA*, 17 Sept. 1922, 19, 30 May, 22 July, 2, 24 Aug. 1923; *SLA* 10, 17 Sept. 1922, 10 Aug. 1923; *Amsterdam News*, 15 Aug. 1923. Selma circuit judge S. F. Hobbs, a Dixiecrat leader during the 1940s, denounced the second KKK but praised the Reconstruction version. See *MA*, 2, 4–6, 8 Oct. 1923.

24. Underwood's statement appears in *BAH*, 29 June 1914, quoted in Snell, "Ku Klux Klan in Jefferson County," 265 n. 15; *Chattanooga Journal*, 21 June 1924; *TP*, 15 Feb., 26 June 1924: *MA*, 8 Nov. 1923, 29 June 1924; Rice, *Ku Klux Klan in American Politics*, 64; Chalmers, *Hooded Americanism*, 80; Newton and Newton, *Ku Klux Klan*, 572 (which also quotes Underwood's statement). See the clippings in Political Scrapbook, 1876–1982, in the Papers of Forney Johnston, ADAH: *NYS*, and *New York Telegram and Mail*, 24 June 1924; *NYT*, *NYS*, *New York Evening Post*, *New York American*, and *NYHT*, 25 June 1924; *WP*, 26 June 1924. See also *MR*, 31 Jan. 1920, Underwood to Hooper, 27 Feb. 1920, Hooper to Underwood, 21 Feb. 1920, McAdory to Hooper, 31 Jan. 1920, Underwood to Jeffries, 11 Oct. 1923, Underwood to Beaseley, 18 Oct. 1923, Underwood to Wooley, 30 Jan. 1924, all in boxes 56, 58, Underwood Papers.

25. Your nephew to Underwood, 14 July 1924, Underwood to Eugene Underwood, Jr., 15 July 1924, and Underwood to Brown, 21 March 1924, all three in box 40, folder 1, and Underwood to Campbell, 30 Aug. 1927, box 41, folder 3, and Beasley to Underwood, 18 Oct. 1923, box 39, folder 8, Tunstall Letter, 28 Jan. 1924, box 60, folder 3 and Underwood to Sumner, 21 July 1927, Underwood Papers, ADAH; C. J. Durr to Mrs. J. W. Durr, 23 June, 1 July 1924, box 4, folder 1, Durr Family Papers, ADAH; Brandon to McCall et al., 13 Sept. 1923, and Brandon to Loveman et al., 3 Dec. 1923, box 169, folder: Oscar W. Underwood, William W. Brandon, Alabama Governors Papers, ADAH; Newton and Newton, *Ku Klux Klan*, 524–25; Sims, *The Klan*, 2 (second quotation); Johnson, "Oscar W. Underwood," 184–203; Rogers et al., *Alabama*, 437 (first quotation); *NH*, 16 July 1924; *MA*, 14 May 1924; *BN* and *BL*, 15 May 1924.

26. Heflin Scrapbooks, MFS 652, 1, Bankhead Speeches, 1922–24, SU; *BAH*, 10 July 1924; Boykin to Mrs. F. Johnston and Family, 25 Oct. 1965 (second quotation), box 22, folder 6, Forney Johnston Papers, ADAH; Mencken to Hall, 26 June 1924, box 67, folder 1 (first quotation), Grover C. Hall, Sr., Papers, ADAH; *TP*, 15 Feb. 1924; *MA*, 16 Oct. 1924; Forster and Epstein, *Report on the Ku Klux Klan*, 15–16; Rice, *Ku Klux Klan in American Politics*, 64.

27. Underwood to Comer, 26 April 1924, Underwood Papers, ADAH; KKK File, reel 20, 1924, TU; *MA*, 19, 30 May, 22 July, 2, 24 Aug., 3–6 Oct. 1923; *SLA*, 10 Aug. 1923; *AN*, 15 Aug. 1923; Snell, "Ku Klux Klan in Jefferson County," 197; on the 1920s KKK in Alabama, see also box 4, folder 1, Durr Family Papers, ADAH; Klanwatch Project, "The Ku Klux Klan: A History of Racism and Violence," SPLC; Cecil L. Davis Letter, 12 June 1924, Great Titan, Realm of Alabama, folder 1, Davis Letters, ADAH; Johnston to author, 2 Feb. 1993, PIKE; McKiven, *Iron and Steel*.

28. Newman, "Hugo Black Manuscript," 304 n. 34.

29. *BN*, 14, 17–18, 20 March 1925.

30. Ala. KKK Newsletter 4 (June 1926): 3, box 16, folder 11, Associations Records,

ADAH; Talladega County KKK File, KKK Research Files, SU; *MA*, 29 April, 11 June, 21 Aug., 3, 20 Nov., 1926; KKK File, reel 23, 1925, reel 25, 1926, TU.

31. *NYT*, 14 Sept. 1937, p. 18 (first quotation); *BN*, 27 April 1925, 3 and 4 March 1926 (second quotation).

32. *BN*, 22 Jan., 10, 21 Feb. 1925.

33. KKK File, reel 23, 1925, TU; *MCA*, 14, 19 March 1925; *CD*, 21 March 1925; *BN*, 11–15 March 1925.

34. *BN*, 15 March 1925.

35. *BP*, 12 March 1925, quoted in Snell, "Ku Klux Klan in Jefferson County," 87 n. 12. See also Snell, 80, 86, 88.

36. KKK File, reel 23, 1925, TU; *BN*, 18–19 March 1925; *MA*, 17 March 1925; BN 24 Feb. 1925, quoted in Snell, "Ku Klux Klan in Jefferson County," 94.

37. Pt. 1, reel 13, NAACP Papers, MADD and LC; Dunne, *Hugo Black and the Judicial Revolution*, 105–6 (quoted); Newman, "Hugo Black Manuscript," ch. 6 n. 51 (which quotes the same statement).

38. KKK File, reel 23, 1925, TU; *BN*, 13–19, 23 March, 2 April 1925; *BAH*, 24 March 1925; *BN*, 13 and 15 March 1925 (quoting McCord).

39. KKK File, reel 23, 1925, TU; *BAH*, 9 April 1925; *BN*, 10–17, 21 March 1925; *AC*, 12 March 1925.

40. KKK Scrapbooks, vol. 1, BPLA; *NYT*, 11 April 1925, p. 9; *SLA*, 10 April 1925; *BN*, 8–10, 14, 27–28 March 1925; *BP*, 10 April 1925.

41. *BN*, 26 Feb., 1, 21, 27 March 1925.

42. *BN*, 22 March 1925 (quoted). See also *BN*, 12 April 1925 and 12, 29 April, 17 June, 3 Sept., 30 Nov. 1926.

43. *BN*, 15 and 17 March 1925 (quoted). See also *BN*, 20–21 March, 17 June 1925.

44. *BN*, 23–24 March, 29 April 1925, 3 Sept., 30 Nov. 1926; *BAH*, 24 March 1925; *BN*, 3 Sept. and 30 Nov. 1926.

45. KKK File, reel 23, 1925, reel 25, 1926, TU; *PC*, 6 Nov. 1926; *NYT*, 29 Oct. 1926, p. 48; *BN*, 24 Nov. 1926; *MA*, 3 Nov. 1925.

46. KKK File, reel 25, 1926, TU; *MA*, 3–4 Nov. 1925; *PC*, 6 Nov. 1926 (quoted).

47. *BN*, 1–7, 20–21 April 1925.

48. *BN*, 1–7, 20–21 April 1925; Snell, "Ku Klux Klan in Jefferson County," 96.

49. *BAH*, 2, 9 April 1925.

50. *BN*, 21 April 1925 (quoted); Snell, "Ku Klux Klan in Jefferson County," 99 (quotes the same statement). See also *BN*, 20 April 1925.

51. *BN*, 7 April, 16 Oct. 1925.

52. Ibid., 16 Oct. 1925.

53. Ibid., 7 April, 24 Sept., 17 Oct. 1925; Snell, "Ku Klux Klan in Jefferson County," 105–6.

54. *BAH*, 13 Oct. 1925. For detailed tables and graphs dealing with the 1925 Birmingham city elections and runoffs, see table 1 of appendix A in Feldman, "Ku Klux Klan in Alabama."

55. *BAH*, 13 Oct. 1925; table 2 of appendix A in Feldman, "Ku Klux Klan in Alabama," 700.

56. *BAH* and *BN*, 13 Oct. 1925.

57. Diefendorf, *Beneath the Cross*, 107–26.

58. *BN*, 24 Sept., 16, 19 Oct. 1925. For more on Wilkinson's career, see Feldman, *From Demagogue to Dixiecrat*.

59. *BAH*, 20 Oct. 1925.

60. *BAH* and *BN*, 20 Oct. 1925; Snell, "Ku Klux Klan in Jefferson County," 107.

61. *BAH*, 13, 20 Oct. 1925.

62. *BAH*, and *BN*, 13, 20 Oct. 1925.

63. *BAH* and *BN*, 20 Oct. 1925; Atkins, *Valley and the Hills*, 133.

64. *BN*, 26 Oct. 1926; *NYT*, 14 Sept. 1937, p. 18.

65. *BN*, 27–28 Oct. 1926.

66. Ibid., 28–29 Oct., 2 Nov. 1926; Snell, "Ku Klux Klan in Jefferson County," 131.

67. Snell, "Ku Klux Klan in Jefferson County," 132.

68. Ibid., 124–42; *NYT*, 11 Aug. 1926, p. 2; 12 Aug. 1926, pp. 1, 4; 13 Sept. 1937, pp. 1, 3; 14 Sept. 1937, pp. 1, 18; *BN*, 8–9 Aug. 1926; Moore to McCall and McCall to White, both 4 Feb. 1925, Burns to McCall, 7 Feb. 1926, McCall to Brice, 13 Feb. 1926, all in Charles C. McCall Letters, ADAH.

69. *NYT*, 11 Aug. 1926, p. 2; 12 Aug. 1926, pp. 1, 4; 13 Sept. 1937, pp. 1, 3; 14 Sept. 1937, pp. 1, 18; *BN*, 8–9 Aug. 1926; Moore to McCall and McCall to White, both 4 Feb. 1925, Burns to McCall, 7 Feb. 1926, McCall to Brice, 13 Feb. 1926, all in Charles C. McCall Letters, ADAH; Snell, "Ku Klux Klan in Jefferson County," 124–42; Newman, "Hugo Black Manuscript," 371 n. 92.

70. Gould Beech, Interview, p. 5, SHC; Newman, "Hugo Black Manuscript," 328 n. 55, 329, 333, 349–50, 372 n. 103; Sandlin, "Lycurgus Breckinridge Musgrove," 102–10; *MA*, 22 May 1925 and 26 March 1926; *BN*, 23 July, 8 Aug. 1926; Hamilton, *Hugo Black*, 120, 127; Newton and Newton, *Ku Klux Klan*, 52; Mize, "Life and Times of James Jefferson Mayfield," 93–94; Johnson, "John H. Bankhead, 2d," 30–58.

71. *BAH*, 10–11, 14 Aug. 1926.

72. *NYT*, 13 Sept. 1937, pp. 1, 3; *BAH*, 13–14 Aug. 1926.

73. *BAH*, 10, 14 Aug. 1926.

74. *Alabama Official and Statistical Register*, 1927, 358–63.

75. *BAH*, 13 Aug. 1926; Thornton, "Alabama Politics," 83–112. For a detailed map dealing with the 1926 elections, see appendix B in Feldman, "Ku Klux Klan in Alabama."

76. Key, *Southern Politics in State and Nation*, 37–41.

77. *Alabama Official and Statistical Register*, 1927, 358–63.

78. *MA*, 14 Aug. 1926.

79. *NYT*, 14 Sept. 1937 (first quotation), 13 Sept. 1937, p. 13 (second quotation); Maurine Slaughter, Interview, p. 14 (third quotation), also p. 15, SU; *NYT*, 13 Sept. 1937, pp. 1, 3; 14 Sept. 1937, pp. 1, 18; Snell, "Fiery Crosses in the Roaring Twenties," 272, and "Ku Klux Klan in Jefferson County," 124.

80. *NYT*, 13 Sept. 1937, pp. 1, 3; *BN*, 3 Sept. 1926.

81. *NYT*, 13 Sept. 1937, pp. 1, 3; 14 Sept. 1937, pp. 1, 18; 15 Sept. 1937, p. 2; Rice, *Ku Klux Klan in American Politics*, 97–98.

82. *NYT*, 15 Sept. 1937, p. 2.

83. Rogers et al., *Alabama*, 431; Newman, "Hugo Black Manuscript," 304 n. 34, 327, 333, 340, ch. 6 n. 36; Cowett, *Birmingham's Rabbi*, 136; Atkins, *Valley and the Hills*, 133.

84. KKK File, reel 25, 1926, TU; Snell, "Ku Klux Klan in Jefferson County," 127; *MA*, 16–17 Aug. 1926; *BN*, 14–17 Aug. 1926; *NYT*, 15 Aug. 1926; Sledge, "Alabama Republicans."

85. Snell, "Ku Klux Klan in Jefferson County," 134–36.

86. *BAH*, 19, 21, 24 Nov., 12, 19–20, 26, 28 Dec. 1926; *BN*, 21, 24 Nov. 1926; *NYT*, 13 Sept. 1937, p. 3.

87. *BAH*, 29 Dec. 1926.

88. Ala. KKK Newsletter 4 (June 1926): 4, box 16, folder 11, Associations Records,

ADAH; Rogers et al., *Alabama*, 433, 437; Newman, "Hugo Black Manuscript," 314 n. 54, 315 n. 59, 320 n. 27, ch. 6 nn. 23 and 77, 354,; Jackson, *Ku Klux Klan in the City*, 82; Huddleston, *In My Father's House*, 76; Dunne, *Hugo Black and the Judicial Revolution*, 112; Rice, *Ku Klux Klan in American Politics*, iii (quoted); *BN*, 29 June, 26 Oct. 1949; *NYT*, 14 Sept. 1937, pp. 1, 18 and 21 Feb. 1948; *MA*, 22 Feb. 1948; *New York Evening Telegram and Mail*, 13 Aug. 1927.

89. Irving M. Engel, Interview, tape 1, p. 39 (fourth quotation), AJA; Virginia F. Durr, Interview, p. 8 (second quotation), CU; E. C. Sharp, Interview with Ralph Compton, p. 2 (third quotation), UAB; Dunne, *Hugo Black and the Judicial Revolution*, 105–6; Newman, "Hugo Black Manuscript," ch. 6 n. 18 (first quotation) and nn. 51 and 77; *BN*, 27 June, 22 Sept. 1949.

6. THE YEAR OF THE WHIP

1. Pt. 10, reel 23, NAACP Papers, MADD and LC; Diary of James Stanley Laird, 25 May 1918, SU; V. M. Scott Reminiscences, 1988, TCHA.

2. KKK File, reel 28, 1927, TU; *BR*, 6 Aug. 1927; *MA*, 10 July and 1 Oct. 1927; *AC*, 15 Sept. 1927; "The New South," *Nation* 125 (24 Aug. 1927): 173.

3. Mildred Ruth Heaton and Lois Cowan, Interview with Linda Jean Tharp, 1 Feb. 1974, p. 4, UAB; see Introduction, note 2.

4. "The N.A.A.C.P. Battlefront: Klan Rule," *Crisis* 35 (Jan. 1928): 12–13; "With the Editor: The Negro Question," *KM* 3 (May 1927): 29–32.

5. Underwood to Kenna, 21 July 1927, box 41, folder 3, Oscar W. Underwood Papers, ADAH; KKK File, reel 28, 1927, TU; *CT*, 14 Nov. 1927 (quoted); *NYT*, 14 July, 10 Aug. 1927; *BR*, 23 July 1927.

6. *CT*, 14 Nov. 1927 (quoted); *BR*, 23 July 1927; *NYW*, 15 July 1927 (second quotation) and also 26 July 1927; *AC*, 22 July 1927; *BN*, 14 July 1927; *BR*, 23 July, 6 Aug. 1927; *FT*, 18 July 1927; *NYA*, 6 Aug. 1927; *NYS*, 9 Aug. 1927; *AN*, 10 Aug. 1927; *St. Louis Star*, 14 July 1927; *NYW* and *St. Joseph Herald*, 15 July 1927; *SLA*, 12 Aug. 1927; *PC*, 23 July 1927; *New Haven Times*, 22 July 1927; *CW*, 3 Sept. 1927.

7. KKK File, reel 28, 1927, TU; *NYT*, 14 July 1927, p. 25, and 18 July 1927, p. 32; *MA*, 14–15, 26 July 1927; *AC*, 22 July 1927; *BN*, 14 July 1927; *BR*, 23 July, 6 Aug. 1927; *FT*, 18 July 1927; *NYA*, 6 Aug. 1927; *NYS*, 9 Aug. 1927; *AN*, 10 Aug. 1927; *St. Louis Star*, 14 July 1927; *NYW* and *St. Joseph Herald*, 15 July 1927; *SLA*, 12 Aug. 1927; *PC*, 23 July 1927; *New Haven Times*, 22 July 1927; *CW*, 3 Sept. 1927.

8. *MA*, 14 July 1927 (quoted); see also *MA*, 28, 31 July 1927.

9. KKK Scrapbooks, no. 257, BPLA; *BN*, 14 July 1927 (quoted) and 27 July 1927.

10. KKK File, reel 28, 1927, TU; *Montgomery Journal*, in the *Geneva Reporter*, 22 July 1927, and *FT*, 18 July 1927; *Cleveland News*, 16 July 1927.

11. KKK File, reel 28, 1927, TU; *MA*, 1, 4 Nov. 1927; *SLA*, 11 Nov. 1927; *Florence News*, 3 Nov. 1927.

12. *MA*, 28–29 July, 9 Aug. 1927; *NYS*, 9 Aug. 1927; *SLA*, 5, 12 Aug. 1927; *PC*, 6 Aug. 1927.

13. *PC*, 10 Sept. 1927.

14. KKK File, reel 28, 1927, TU; *MA*, 29 July (quoted) and 11, 25 Aug. 1927; *NYW*, 12 Nov. 1927.

15. "*Darrow v. Klan*," *Time* 9 (21 March 1927): 12; *Baltimore Negro American*, 19 March 1927; *CW*, 12 March 1927.

16. *CW,* 12 March 1927.

17. V. M. Scott Reminiscences, 12, TCHA; *MA,* 10, 14 Aug. 1927.

18. KKK File, reel 28, 1927, TU; *New York Evening Telegram and Mail,* 13 Aug. 1927; *Washington Tribune,* 7 Jan. 1927.

19. Snell, "Ku Klux Klan in Jefferson County," 172; *MCA,* 15 Aug. 1927; *Minneapolis Journal,* 28 Aug. 1927; *MA,* 31 July 1927; *NYS,* 9 Aug. 1927.

20. Feldman, *From Demagogue to Dixiecrat,* 85; Snell, "Masked Men in the Magic City," 221; *BAH,* 13 March 1927.

21. Allen, *Only Yesterday;* Tentler, *Wage-Earning Women.*

22. KKK File, reel 28, 1927, TU; *NYT,* 11 July 1927, 14 July 1927, p. 25, 18 July 1927, p. 32; *MA,* 10, 14, 20 July 1927; *AC,* 22 July 1927; *NYW* and *St. Joseph Herald,* 15 July 1927.

23. *Covington County News,* in *MA,* 17 July 1927.

24. *MA,* 11–12 July 1927.

25. *NYHT* in *MA,* 21 July 1927.

26. *NYT,* 11 July 1927.

27. Feldman, *From Demagogue to Dixiecrat,* 85; Blee, *Women of the Klan,* 83; KKK File, reel 28, 1927, TU, *NYT,* 22 Aug. 1927; *MA,* 7, 10, 22 Sept. 1927; *AC,* 10 Sept. 1927.

28. Niebuhr, *Christ and Culture,* 102, 190–96, 240, and *Kingdom of God in America;* Niebuhr, *Experimental Religion,* 26–39.

29. Cromartie, *No Longer Exiles;* Noll, *Religion and American Politics* and *One Nation Under God?;* Wald, *Religion and Politics in the United States;* Neuhaus and Cromartie, eds., *Piety and Politics.*

30. KKK File, reel 28, 1927, TU; Shepherd, "Whip Wins," 32; Newton and Newton, *Ku Klux Klan,* 391, 142; *MA,* 2, 20 Oct., 26 Nov. 1927; *ME,* 7 July 1949.

31. KKK File, reel 28, 1927, TU; *MA,* 9, 12 Aug. 1927 and 15 July 1927, quoted in the *Charlotte Observer,* n.d.; *Eufaula Daily Citizen,* in *MA,* 22 July 1927.

32. Shepherd, "Whip Hand," 8–9, 44–45; *Knoxville Journal,* quoted in "The South Aroused Against the Midnight Flogger," *Literary Digest* 94 (30 July 1927): 8–9.

33. Ala. KKK Newsletter 5:7 (March 1927): 2, box G192, folder "Ku Klux Klan, 1927," Graves Papers, ADAH; Brownell, "Birmingham, Alabama," 38–39; Snell, "Ku Klux Klan in Jefferson County," 154–55; *NYT,* 28 July 1927, p. 18.

34. "Alabama Aroused," *Outlook* 147, 9 (2 Nov. 1927): 261; American Periodical Series (APS), III, reel 149, MADD; *NYT,* 14 July 1927, p. 25, and 18 July 1927, p. 32; *MA,* 11, 14–15 July 1927, *NYW,* and *St. Joseph Herald,* 15 July 1927; *New York Telegraph,* 19 July 1927; and *AC,* 11, 22 July 1927; Virginia F. Durr, Interview, pp. 7–8 (quoted), Columbia University Oral History Office, CU.

35. Snell, "Ku Klux Klan in Jefferson County," 172; KKK File, reel 27, 1928, TU; *MA,* 4, 7 Oct. 1927.

36. Snell, "Masked Men in the Magic City," 221; *BAH,* 13 Jan. 1927; *MA,* 10, 13 Aug. 1927; *NYT,* 10 Aug. 1927, p. 11; *NYW, TRI, NYH,* all on 13 Aug. 1927; *AN,* 17 Aug. 1927; *MCA,* 15 Aug. 1927.

37. *MA,* 14 Aug. 1927.

38. Ibid., 4 July 1927.

39. 20 Aug. and 10 Sept. 1925, clippings, folder: KKK, Prattville, Aiken Papers, BA; KKK File, reel 28, 1927, TU; Snell, "Ku Klux Klan in Jefferson County," 163–64; Lay, ed., *Invisible Empire in the West,* 7; *NYW,* 28 July 1927; *Columbus Standard,* 14 July 1927; Robinson, *Born in Blood;* Knight, *The Brotherhood; Prattville Progress,* 24 Sept. 1925.

40. V. M. Scott Reminiscences, 3–4, TCHA.

41. *MA,* 17, 24 July 1927.

42. J. L. Burgess to Editor, *CA,* in *MA,* 15 Sept. 1927.

43. Snell, "Ku Klux Klan in Jefferson County," 159–62, 164, 175–76; *MA,* 24 July 1927. Dillard was an exception; he had actually opposed the Klan as well as police laxity regarding floggings several years earlier. See *MA,* 31 May 1922.

44. *MA,* 19 July 1927; *Baltimore Sun,* in *BAH,* 30 July 1927.

45. *AB,* 21, 28 July, 18 Aug., 1 Sept. 1927 and 2 Feb. 1928; Snell, "Ku Klux Klan in Jefferson County," 161 n. 23, 162; *MA,* 19 July 1927 (quoted).

46. KKK File, reel 28, 1927, TU.

47. Ala. KKK Newsletter 5 (March 1927): 1 (quoted), box G192, folder "Ku Klux Klan, 1927," Graves Papers, ADAH; Lee County KKK File, Talladega County KKK File, KKK Research Files, SU; *Chattanooga Times,* in *MA,* 20 Sept. 1927; *Opelika Daily News,* 2, 10 Aug. 1927; *SA,* 8 May 1927.

48. Committee on Social Service, Report 1927, Alabama Baptist State Convention, Nov. 1927, pp. 15–17, SU; "Moral Lashes for Alabama Floggers," *Literary Digest* 95 (17 Dec. 1927): 32; *MA,* 18–19 Nov. 1927.

49. Talladega County KKK File, KKK Research Files, SU; *NYT,* 18 July 1927, p. 32, 27 July 1927, p. 48, 11 Sept. 1927, p. 17; *Evening Telegraph and Mail,* 18 July 1927; *MA,* 11, 14–15, 20 July and 10, 18 Sept. 1927; *AC,* 22 July and 10 Sept. 1927; *Our Mountain Home,* 22 June 1927.

50. *MA,* 25 Oct. 1927.

51. KKK Scrapbooks, no. 257, BPLA; *BN,* 17 July 1927; *DE,* in *MA,* 22 July 1927.

52. "The South Aroused Against the Midnight Flogger," *Literary Digest* 94 (30 July 1927): 8–9; *AC,* 12 July 1927; *Greensboro News,* 19 July 1927.

53. KKK File, reel 28, 1927, TU. See also E. A. McAllister to Editor, *NYT,* 12 July 1927 in *NYT,* 18 July 1927; *Baltimore Manufacturer's Record,* 28 July 1927.

54. *TRI,* in *MA,* 16 Sept. 1927.

55. *Baltimore Sun,* in *MA,* 12 Sept. 1927; *PC,* 29 Oct. 1927, editorial page; *Washington Eagle,* 12 Aug. 1927.

56. Ku Klux Klan Collection, BCHS; KKK File, reel 28, 1927, TU; *MA,* 5, 10, 12–14, 19–21 July and 3 Aug. 1927; *OSD,* 4 Aug. 1927; *NYW* and *St. Joseph Herald,* 15 July 1927; *TRI,* 19 July 1927; *NYT,* 12 July 1927, 18 July 1927, p. 32.

57. KKK Collection, BCHS; *NYT,* 10 July 1927, p. 7; *OSD,* 18 Aug. 1927.

58. *MA,* 2 July 1927.

59. Ibid., 4, 10–11, 14–15, 17–18, 24, 28, 31 July, 2, 23 Aug., 10 Sept. 1927. See 24 July 1927 for the editorial "Hideous Rule of Mask and Lash." See also KKK File, reel 28, 1927, TU.

60. *BN,* 4 July 1927 (first and second quotations); *BN,* 5 July 1927 (third quotation); Feldman, *From Demagogue to Dixiecrat,* 85 (fourth quotation). See also KKK Scrapbooks, no. 257, BPLA; *BN,* 8–11 July 1927.

61. Bibb County KKK File, Lee County KKK Files, KKK Research Files, SU; *CP,* n.d. July 1927; *Daily News,* 2, 10 Aug. 1927; *Dadeville Spot Cash, Opp Weekly News, Sheffield Standard, Florala News, FH,* and *Demopolis Times,* in *MA,* 17–18 July 1927.

62. *NYT,* 12 July 1927, p. 24.

63. KKK Collection, BCHS; *Fayette Banner,* quoted in *MA,* 18, 25 July 1927; *MA,* 8 July, 12 Aug. 1927; *OSD,* 14 July 1927.

64. *MA,* 31 Aug. 1927. See also the *SN, Evergreen Courant, Athens Democrat, Colbert County Reporter,* and *Florala News,* in *MA,* 17–18 July 1927.

65. KKK Collection, BCHS; *NYT,* 10 July 1927, p. 7; *OSD,* 7 July 1927; *MA,* 5, 19 July 1927.

66. *MA,* 10 July 1927.

67. KKK File, reel 28, 1927, TU; *NYT,* 10 July 1927, p. 7; *AC,* 22 July 1927; *MA,* 11, 19–20 July 1927.

68. KKK Collection, BCHS; Snell, "Ku Klux Klan in Jefferson County," 157; *MA,* 5, 10, 15 July 1927; *OSD,* 14, 21 July 1927.

69. *DE,* 7 Aug. 1927; *MA,* 12, 14 July 1927; *AC,* 12 July 1927.

70. KKK File, reel 28, 1927, TU; *MA,* 8, 19 July 1927.

71. Feldman, *From Demagogue to Dixiecrat,* 84; *MA,* 11 July 1927.

72. *OSD,* 4 Aug. 1927.

73. KKK Collection, BCHS; *OSD,* 4 Aug. 1927; Feldman, *From Demagogue to Dixiecrat,* 105–7.

74. *MA,* 2 Aug. 1927 (quoted); Feldman, *From Demagogue to Dixiecrat,* 82–83 (quoting the same statement). See also KKK File, reel 28, 1927, TU.

75. Feldman, *From Demagogue to Dixiecrat,* 83.

76. Ibid.; *BN,* 4 Aug. 1927.

77. KKK Collection, BCHS; *NYT,* 18 July 1927, p. 32; *TRI,* 2 Aug. 1927; *OSD,* 4 Aug. 1927; *MA,* 2 Aug. 1927.

78. KKK Scrapbooks, no. 257, BPLA; KKK Collection, BCHS; Feidelson, "Alabama's Super Government," 312; *OSD,* 21 July 1927; *MA,* 3, 23, 25, 31 Aug. 1927; *AC,* 4 Aug. 1927.

79. KKK Collection, BCHS; *AC,* 6 Aug. 1927; *OSD,* 21 July 1927.

80. *Doss v. Alabama,* 220 Ala. 30 (1929), and *Clayton v. Alabama,* 220 Ala. 39 (1929); KKK Collection, BCHS; *NYT,* 5 Aug. 1927, p. 1; *TRI,* 5 Aug. 1927; *OSD,* 18 Aug. 1927 (quoted); *DE,* 7 Aug. 1927 (also quoted).

81. *MA,* 6 Aug. 1927.

82. KKK File, reel 28, 1927, TU.

83. *NYT,* 7 Aug. 1927, sec. 2, p. 1, 9 Aug. 1927, p. 14; *MCA,* 9 Aug. 1927; *CD,* 13 Aug. 1927.

84. *MA,* 25 Aug., 18 Oct. 1927 (quoted).

85. *NYT,* 2 Aug. 1927, p. 10; *TRI,* 2 Aug. 1927; *Atlanta Independent,* 4 Aug. 1927; *SLA,* 12 Aug. 1927; *MA,* 5 July, 5 Aug. 1927.

86. Lee County KKK File, KKK Research Files, SU; KKK Scrapbooks, no. 257, BPLA; KKK Collection, BCHS; Feidelson, "Alabama's Super Government," 311–12; *Daily News,* 4, 12 Oct. 1927; *OSD,* 18 Aug. 1927; *DE,* 7 Aug. 1927; *MA,* 4–5, 11 Aug. 1927; *BAH,* 6 Aug. 1927.

87. Charles A. Fell Memoirs, II, pt. 1, pp. 101–28 (first quotation), BPLA; *BAH,* 30 July 1927 (second quotation).

88. KKK File, reel 28, 1927, TU; *AC,* 10 Aug. 1927; *Charleston News and Courier,* in *MA,* 23 Aug. 1927; *CR,* in *MA,* 21 July 1927 (quoted).

89. *Minneapolis Journal,* 28 Aug. 1927; *TRI,* in *MA,* 16 Sept. 1927; *Chicago Bee,* 6 Aug. 1927; *PC,* 29 Oct. 1927, editorial page.

7. ELITE WAR ON THE KLAN

1. Tindall, *Emergence of the New South,* 194–95; Chalmers, *Hooded Americanism,* 4, 84; Rice, *Ku Klux Klan in American Politics,* 92; Wade, *Fiery Cross,* 248–49.

2. KKK File, reel 28, 1927, TU; *MA,* 16 Oct. 1927.

3. KKK File through 1979, MPL; *Knights of the Ku Klux Klan v. State of Kansas ex. rel. Griffith*, 273 U.S. 664; KKK Scrapbooks, no. 257, BPLA; *MA*, 21 Sept. 1927 (quoted); *CR*, in *MA*, 21 July 1927; *Tucson Times*, 26 March 1927; *LAX*, in *Tucson Times*, 26 March 1927; *St. Louis Dispatch*; *BAH*, in *MA*, 4 Sept. 1927.

4. Wayne Flynt gives slightly different numbers in Rogers et al., *Alabama*, 431–33; Snell, "Fiery Crosses in the Roaring Twenties," 275.

5. Bibb County KKK File, SU; Chalmers, *Hooded Americanism*, 83–84; Rogers et al., *Alabama*, 433.

6. Key, *Southern Politics in State and Nation*; Thornton, "Alabama Politics," 83–112; Flynt, "Organized Labor," 163–80.

7. Gilbert, "Bibb Graves as a Progressive," 15–30, esp. 21; Tindall, *Emergence of the New South*, 227–28, 505; Rogers et al., *Alabama*, 423–27.

8. Woodward, *Origins of the New South*, 215.

9. Hyman, *Anti-Redeemers*.

10. Gilbert, "Bibb Graves," 16; Snell, "Ku Klux Klan in Jefferson County," 126–42; Owen, *History of Alabama*, III:206–7. On Graves's early career, see McMillan, *Constitutional Development in Alabama*.

11. Gilbert, "Bibb Graves," 16; Snell, "Ku Klux Klan in Jefferson County," 126–42; Owen, *History of Alabama*, III:206–7.

12. *In re Opinions of the Justices and In re School Appropriations Act*, 215 Ala. 524; Gilbert, "Bibb Graves," 17–18; V. M. Scott Reminiscences, 1988, p. 17, TCHA.

13. *Alabama Acts*, Act No. 17, pp. 26–27, Act No. 18, p. 27, Act No. 294, pp. 284–85, Act No. 382, pp. 442–55, Act No. 415, p. 483, Act No. 498, p. 598; V. M. Scott Reminiscences, 17, TCHA; Gilbert, "Bibb Graves," 19–21; McMillan, *Constitutional Development in Alabama*.

14. *Alabama Acts*, Act No. 632, p. 718; Gilbert, "Bibb Graves," 20–21; Grantham, *Southern Progressivism*; Link, *Paradox of Southern Progressivism*.

15. *Alabama Acts*, Act No. 17, pp. 26–27, Act No. 403, pp. 470–71, Act No. 615, pp. 711–12, Act No. 640, pp. 774–83; V. M. Scott Reminiscences, 18–19, TCHA; and Gilbert, "Bibb Graves," 25.

16. *Alabama Acts*, Act No. 1, pp. 1–14, Act No. 292, pp. 278–84, Act No. 347, pp. 348–408; Gilbert, "Bibb Graves," 23–24, 28.

17. Feldman, "Labour Repression in the American South," 643–64; Gilbert, "Bibb Graves," 21–26; Tindall, *Emergence of the New South*, 505; Flynt, *Poor but Proud*; *Alabama Acts*, Act No. 126, pp. 87–88, Act No. 128, p. 88, Act No. 293, p. 284.

18. Underwood to Campbell, 30 Aug. 1927, box 41, folder 3, Oscar W. Underwood Papers, ADAH; Underwood to Hanson, n.d., quoted in *NYT*, 22 Aug. 1927, p. 22 (quoted); Rice, *Ku Klux Klan in American Politics*, 65; Chalmers, *Hooded Americanism*, 81–82; Rogers et al., *Alabama*, 432–33.

19. Brownell, "Birmingham, Alabama," 44.

20. Ibid.; Owen, *History of Alabama*, III:741.

21. Lovis to Hall, 12 July 1927, Hanson to Hall 19 July 1927, box 67, folder 1, Papers of Grover C. Hall, Sr., ADAH.

22. Grover C. Hall, Sr., Scrapbooks, 1888–1941, no. 1, ADAH; *ME*, 7 July 1949; and Hall to Hanson, 29 June 1926, Hanson to Hall, 6 Dec. 1927, box 67, folder 1, Hall, Sr., Papers, ADAH; Owen, *History of Alabama*, III:727; Tindall, *Emergence of the New South*, 215.

23. Mencken to Hall, 17 April 1926, 29 May 1926, 26 June 1926, and Owens to Hall, 29 Jan. 1925, 15 June 1926, box 67, folder 1, Hall, Sr., Papers, ADAH.

24. Hollis, "Hall Family and Twentieth Century Journalism in Alabama," 119–40, and *An Alabama Newspaper Tradition;* Matthews, "Clarence Cason Among the Southern Liberals," 4; Peirce, *Deep South States of America,* 278.

25. Hall Scrapbooks, no. 1, ADAH.

26. KKK File, reel 28, 1927, TU; *MA,* 17, 21–22 July and 16 Oct. 1927.

27. *MA,* 10 Nov. 1927.

28. Hall to Hanson, 8 June 1926, box 67, folder 1, Hall, Sr., Papers, ADAH.

29. Hanson to Hall, 12 Aug. 1927, box 67, folder 1, Hall, Sr., Papers, ADAH.

30. Ibid.

31. *Evergreen Courant, Andalusia Star, Alabama Baptist, CA,* and Hall's reply, all in *MA,* 31 July 1927.

32. KKK Scrapbooks, no. 257, BPLA; *BN,* 31 July 1927.

33. Ala. KKK Newsletter 5 (March 1927), p. 1 (quoted), box G192, folder "Ku Klux Klan, 1927," Graves Papers, ADAH; Charles A. Fell Memoirs, II, pt. 1, pp. 101–28, BPLA.

34. *DE* and *TJ,* in *MA,* 29 Nov. 1927.

35. *MA,* 17 Aug. 1927, and *Roanoke Leader,* in *MA,* 22 Aug. 1927.

36. Rogers et al., *Alabama,* 241–58.

37. Bankhead to Editor, *MR,* 26 Oct. 1927, "Ku Klux Klan National Clipping File," *Mobile Press-Register,* Clipping Files, MMA; Owen, *History of Alabama,* III:93.

38. KKK File, reel 28, 1927, TU; *NYT,* 28 Oct. 1927, p. 19; *MA,* 27–28 Oct. 1927; *SLA,* 14 Nov. 1927; Owen, *History of Alabama,* III:88–93.

39. *MA,* 12 July 1927 (quoted); Owen, *History of Alabama,* III:943.

40. *MA,* 12 July 1927.

41. *NYT,* 9 Nov. 1927, p. 22 (quoted); *MA,* 8 Nov. 1927.

42. John Bainbridge to Editor, *MA,* 13 Sept. 1927.

43. Flynt, *Poor but Proud,* 115–24.

44. Cobb, "Beyond Planters and Industrialists," 45–68; Woodward, *Origins of the New South,* 140–74; Cash, *Mind of the South,* 153–54.

45. *Enquirer-Sun,* in *MA,* 20 Sept. 1927; *Chattanooga Times,* in *MA,* 4 Sept. 1927; *Baltimore Manufacturer's Record,* 28 July 1927; Norrell, *James Bowron,* 246, quoted in Kelly, "Policing the 'Negro Eden,'" 41 n. 51 (quoted)

46. To my knowledge, every major work on the KKK has strictly subscribed to the idea of three or four distinct and separate Klans: Reconstruction, the 1920s, c. 1954–1968, and late 1970s resurgence.

47. *AC,* 21 Aug. 1927 (quoted); *MA,* 1 Feb., 16 Aug., 28 Oct. 1927; Brownell, "Birmingham, Alabama," 42–44; Owen, *History of Alabama,* III:347–48.

48. *MA,* 28 Oct. 1927 (quoted).

49. *NYT,* 17 May 1927, p. 32; *MA,* 10 July 1927; *BR,* 16 July 1927; Rice, *Ku Klux Klan in American Politics,* 47.

50. Gould Beech, Oral Interview, p. 5, SHC; *PC,* 4 June 1927, sec. 2, p. 7; *MA,* 22 Nov. 1927.

51. *NYT,* 17 May 1927, p. 32; *MA,* 10 July 1927; *BR,* 16 July 1927; Rice, *Ku Klux Klan in American Politics,* 47.

52. *New York Evening Telegram,* 13 Aug. 1927; *CT,* 18 Jan. 1927.

53. *MA,* 22 Nov. 1927.

54. *BR,* 2 April 1927; *MA,* 5, 18 Aug. 1927.

55. KKK File, reel 28, 1927, TU; *MA,* 18 July 1927 (quoted). Carson declared, "Denizens

of the dark and the skunks of the wood are prowling. . . . it is a burning shame." He asked rhetorically, "Shall we strip down the American flag . . . , bury its stars in the tomb of liberty, tear out its white and blue, and leave only its red with which to weave a bloody crown?"

56. *AC,* 25 Feb. 1927; *MA,* 25 Feb., 13 July 1927.

57. KKK Scrapbooks, no. 257, BPLA; KKK File, reel 28, 1927, TU; *BN,* 6 Sept. 1927.

58. "The South Aroused to Midnight Floggers," *Literary Digest* 94 (30 July 1927): 8 (fourth quotation), also 9; *Springfield Republican,* 17 July 1927 (first quotation); *NYT,* 12 July 1927; *MA,* 10 July 1927 (third quotation); and *MA,* in *NYT,* 12 July 1927 (second quotation); *NYT,* 2 Dec. 1927, p. 22; *ME,* 7 July 1949; KKK File, reel 28, 1927, TU; Shepherd, "Whip Hand," 8, and "Whip Wins," 32; Newton and Newton, *Ku Klux Klan,* 5; Tindall, *Emergence of the New South,* 215.

59. V. M. Scott Reminiscences, 10, TCHA; *MA,* 9 Aug., 2, 6, 12, 16, 20 Oct., 3, 22, 26, 29 Nov. 1927; *AC,* 12, 15 Oct. 1927; *ME,* 7 July 1949; *NYT,* 2 Dec. 1927, p. 22.

60. Talladega County KKK File, KKK Research Files, SU; *MA,* 5 Oct., 3 Nov. 1927; Rogers et al., *Alabama,* 432.

61. Graves to Odom, 13 Aug. 1927, box G192, folder "Ku Klux Klan, 1927," Graves Papers, ADAH; V. M. Scott Reminiscences, p. 14 (quoted), also pp. 2, 8, 10, 13, 15–20, TCHA; *Republican,* 17 July 1927; Snell, "Fiery Crosses in the Roaring Twenties," 273, and "Masked Men in the Magic City," 206–27.

62. *NYA,* 29 Oct. 1927; *SLA,* 22 July 1927; *Toledo Times,* 5 Aug. 1927; *NYT,* and *Pittsburgh Post-Gazette,* 22 Nov. 1927.

63. *Pittsburgh Post-Gazette* and *CT,* 22 Nov. 1927 (the quoted statement appears in both). Congressman Madden actually met with three top officials in the Justice Department about the situation in Alabama.

64. Greene County KKK File, KKK Research Files, SU; KKK Scrapbooks, no. 257, BPLA; *Greene County Democrat,* 7, 14, 28 July, 18 Aug., 15 Sept., 6 Oct., 3 Nov., 1 Dec. 1927; *MA,* 20 Nov. (quoted), 5 Dec., 1927; *BN,* 6 Sept. 1927.

65. *MA,* 10 Aug. 1927.

66. *CW,* 12 March 1927.

8. LIMITS OF THE OLIGARCHY'S CAMPAIGN

1. *SLA,* 19 Aug. 1927; *MA,* 16 Sept. 1927; *PC,* 13 Aug. 1927.

2. KKK Scrapbooks, no. 257, BPLA; Snell, "Ku Klux Klan in Jefferson County," 177–78; *BN,* 11 Aug. 1927; *MA,* 12–13 Aug. 1927.

3. KKK File, reel 28, 1927, TU; *New York Evening Telegram and Mail,* 13 Aug. 1927; *TRI,* 18 Jan. 1927; *Baltimore Herald-Commonwealth,* 29 Jan. 1927; *Enquirer,* 24 Jan. 1927; *Macon News,* 24 Jan. 1927; *PC,* 5 Feb. 1927; *BAH,* 9 Jan. 1927.

4. *MA,* 22 July, 5 Aug. 1927; *SLA,* 22 July 1927; KKK File, reel 28, 1927, TU.

5. *PC,* 23 July 1927, p. 5; *NYT,* 19 July 1927; *Evening Telegram and Mail,* 18 July 1927; *Athens Courier,* in *MA,* 17 July 1927; *MA,* 11, 28 July 1927.

6. *SLA,* 22 July 1927; *MA,* 22 July, 5 Aug. 1927; Howington, "John Barley Corn Subdued," 223. Oscar L. Tompkins of Houston, Alfred M. Tunstall of Hale, and Hugh Merrill of Calhoun reversed their earlier votes.

7. KKK Scrapbooks, no. 257, BPLA; quotation of Fell/*BAH* in "The South Aroused to Midnight Floggings," *Literary Digest* 94 (30 July 1927): 8–9 (quoted); *BN,* 11 and 19 July (quotations of Chappell), also 9 Aug. 1927; *BN* in *MA,* 22 July 1927; *MA,* 14 July 1927 (first Hall quotation); *MA* editorial in KKK File, reel 28, 1927 (second Hall quotation), TU.

8. *Chattanooga Times* and *Greenville News,* in *MA,* 21 July 1927; *Charleston News,* and *AC,* in *MA,* 15, 22 July 1927; *Charlotte Observer,* 13 July 1927.

9. *Alabama Acts,* Act No. 520, 9 Sept. 1927, p. 616; *MA,* 20 July 1927.

10. *NYT,* 28 July 1927, p. 18; *AG,* 27 July 1927; *SLA,* 19 Aug. 1927; *MA,* 20 July, 17–18, 31 Aug., 11, 16, 18 Sept. 1927.

11. KKK Scrapbooks, no. 257, BPLA; Feidelson, "Alabama's Super Government," 312; *TJ, Guntersville Advocate,* and *Thomasville Times,* in *MA,* 22 July 1927; *MA,* 20–22 July 1927; *AC,* 1 Sept. 1927.

12. KKK File, reel 28, 1927, TU.

13. *MA,* clipping, c. 1927 in KKK File, reel 28, 1927, TU.

14. *NYT,* 21 Aug. 1927, sec. 2, p. 4.

15. Ibid., 26 Aug. 1927, p. 17; *MA,* 17, 20 Aug., 10, 16 Sept. 1927.

16. *TRI,* in *MA,* 16 Sept. 1927; *NYT,* 27 Aug. 1927, p. 12.

17. *New York Telegraph,* 19 July 1927; *New York Graphic,* 18 July 1927; *MA,* 24 July 1927; *Greensboro Daily News,* in *MA,* 21 July 1927.

18. KKK File, reel 28, 1927, TU; *Nation* 125 (7 Sept. 1927); *NYT,* 18 July 1927, p. 32, 24 Aug. 1927, p. 15; *CW,* 3 Sept. 1927; *Observer,* 24 Aug. 1927; *SLA,* 29 July 1927; *MA,* 17, 24 July, 5, 23 Aug., 8 Sept. 1927.

19. *MA,* 6, 25 Oct. 1927; *AC,* 22 Oct. 1927; *MA,* 1 Nov. 1927 (quoted).

20. *Ware v. State,* 21 Ala. App. 407, 108 So. 645; Newman, "Hugo Black Manuscript," 360–65; Black, *My Father,* 53–54.

21. *NYT,* 27 Aug. 1927, p. 15; *MA,* 7 Sept., 7 Oct. 1927.

22. *MCA,* 27 Oct. 1927; *MA,* 17 Oct. 1927.

23. Snell, "Ku Klux Klan in Jefferson County," 147–48, 173; *NYW,* 28 July 1927; *AC,* 27 July 1927; *MA,* 28 July, 17 Sept. 1927; *HI,* 13 Aug. 1927.

24. *Chicago Bee,* 6 Aug. 1927; *TRI,* 29 July 1927; *HI,* 13 Aug. 1927; *MA,* 11, 29–30 July, 13 Sept. 1927; *BN,* 27 July 1927; *Marinette Eagle,* 9 Aug. 1927.

25. KKK File, reel 28, 1927, TU; *TRI,* 14 Nov. 1927; *AC,* 18 Sept. 1927; *MA,* 14, 17, 22 Sept. 1927.

26. *NYT,* 17 Sept. 1927, p. 3; *MA,* 16 Sept. 1927.

27. APS III, reel 149, MADD; "Alabama Aroused," *Outlook* 147:9 (2 Nov. 1927): 261, *NYA,* 20 Oct. 1927; *AC,* 18 Oct. 1927; *MA,* 18 Sept., 17 Oct. 1927.

28. *NYT,* 17 Sept. 1927, p. 3; *MA,* 5 Aug., 16 Sept. 1927; quote from *NYW,* 28 July 1927. Actually, there was popular failure on this issue as well as stumbling by the elite. Oscar Underwood, who had retired, recognized that the "leading people [in Alabama] are not making the stand against the Ku Klux . . . that ought to be made." Quoted in Underwood to Campbell, 30 Aug. 1927, box 41, folder 3, Underwood Papers, ADAH.

29. *NYT* and *TRI,* 2 Aug. 1927; *Atlanta Independent,* 4 Aug. 1927; *SLA,* 12 Aug. 1927; *MA,* 5 July, 5 Aug. 1927.

30. Feldman, *From Demagogue to Dixiecrat,* 63, 70, 80–95. Luverne boasted that it was "the friendliest city in the South." See Sims, *The Klan,* 129–39.

31. Shepherd, "Whip Hand," 10, 44–45; Rice, *Ku Klux Klan in American Politics,* 65–66; Owen, *History of Alabama,* IV:1087. McCall had joined James Esdale's libel suit against Big Mule publisher F. I. Thompson, cracked down on liquor and gambling violations, and even attempted to appoint the grand dragon to his personal staff.

32. *ME,* 7 July 1949 (first quotation); Shepherd, "Whip Hand," 44 (second quotation).

33. Crenshaw County KKK File and Lee County KKK File, KKK Research Notes, SU; *AC,* 13 Oct. 1927; *MA,* 1, 4–5, 11–14 Oct., 26 Nov. 1927.

34. *AC*, 15 Oct. 1927; *MA*, 11–14 Oct. 1927; *ME*, 7 July 1949.

35. KKK Scrapbooks, no. 257, BPLA; "Alabama's Floggings," *Literary Digest* 95 (29 Oct. 1927): 11–12; J. J. D., "Free Schools and Education," 8–9.

36. KKK File, reel 28, 1927, TU; *NYT*, 11 Oct. 1927, p. 20; *AC*, 16 and 26 Oct. 1927 (quoted); *MA*, 11, 17 Oct., 10, 22 Nov. 1927.

37. KKK Scrapbooks, no. 257, BPLA; "Alabama's Floggings," *Literary Digest* 95 (29 Oct. 1927): 11–12.

38. Newton and Newton, *Ku Klux Klan*, 391, 412 (quoted); Shepherd, "Whip Wins," 32; *MA*, 2, 20 Oct., 26 Nov. 1927; *ME*, 7 July 1949.

39. *MA*, 10–11, 19–26 Oct. 1927; quotation from Shepherd, "Whip Wins," 31–32.

40. Snell, "Ku Klux Klan in Jefferson County," 181 (quoted); *MA*, 6 Nov. 1927.

41. *AC*, 12 Oct. 1927; *MA*, 7, 12 Oct. 1927; *ME*, 7 July 1949.

42. Graves to McAdory, 22 Oct. 1927, Graves to McCall, 21, 22 Oct. 1927, McCall to Graves, n.d., Tilly to McAdory, 6 Oct. 1927, all correspondence in box G192, folder "Law Enforcement, 1927–1928," Graves Papers, ADAH; *MA*, 13–14, 20, 25 Oct. 1927.

43. Graves to McCall, 16 Nov. 1927, Tilly to McCall, 5 Nov. 1927, McCall to Graves, 3 Nov. 1927, all correspondence in box G192, folder "Law Enforcement, 1927–1928," Graves Papers, ADAH.

44. KKK Scrapbooks, vol. 1, BPLA; Shepherd, "Whip Hand," 9; *MA*, 5, 19, 22 Oct. 1927 (quoted), also 22 Oct. 1927; KKK File, reel 28, 1927, TU.

45. KKK Scrapbooks, no. 257, BPLA; *MA*, 3–6 Nov. 1927; "Alabama's Floggings," *Literary Digest* 95 (29 Oct. 1927): 11–12; Patton, "Ku Klux Klan Reign of Terror," 51–55.

46. Tindall, *Emergence of the New South*, 227–28; Rogers et al., *Alabama*, 423–27, 500; Barnard, "Old Order Changes," 164–65; Feldman, *From Demagogue to Dixiecrat*, 85.

47. Graves to Odom, 13 Aug. 1927, box G192, folder "Ku Klux Klan, 1927," Graves Papers, ADAH; *Evening Telegram and Mail*, 13 Aug. 1927; *MA*, 10 Nov. 1927 (quoted), also 23 July 1927.

48. KKK Scrapbooks, no. 257, BPLA; *PC*, 23 July 1927; *NYW*, in *MA*, 24 July 1927; *Chattanooga Times*, in *BAH*, 18 Sept. 1927; Feidelson, "Alabama's Super Government," 312–13 (quoted). A Tennessee editor predicted that Alabamians would "free themselves of this numbing incubus, if not now, later—for the Graves nightmare must pass." The statement appeared in the *Chattanooga Times* and was quoted in *BAH*, 18 Sept. 1927 (from which I quote here).

49. McNeill to Editor, *MA*, 8 Nov. 1927, quoted in *MA*, 10 Nov. 1927 (quoted).

50. *NYT*, 10 Oct. 1927, p. 12; *Boston Guardian*, 22 Oct. 1927; *AC*, 20 Oct. 1927; *MA*, 20 Oct. 1927 (quoted), also 21 Oct. 1927.

51. APS, III, reel 149, MADD; "Alabama Aroused," *Outlook*, 147, 9 (2 Nov. 1927): 261 (first quotation); *MA*, 20 Oct. 1927 (second quotation).

52. KKK File, reel 28, 1927, TU; *MA*, 21, 28 Oct. 1927; *SLA*, 4 Nov. 1927.

53. *MA*, 7 Oct. 1927.

54. *NYT*, 21 Nov. 1927, p. 3, 25 Nov. 1927, p. 23; *MA*, 2 Oct., 25 Nov. 1927 (quoted).

55. Feldman, *From Demagogue to Dixiecrat*, 82–85.

56. *MA*, 23 Nov. 1927.

57. Ibid.

58. *MA*, 24 Nov. 1927; *ME*, 7 July 1949.

59. *NYT*, 21 Nov. 1927, p. 3; 25 Nov. 1927, p. 23; *MA*, 6, 22, 25 Nov. 1927.

60. *MA*, 24 Nov. 1927 (quoted); *ME*, 7 July 1949; KKK File, reel 28, 1927, TU.

61. *NYT*, 21 Nov. 1927, p. 3; 25 Nov. 1927, p. 23; *MA*, 22, 25 Nov. 1927. The same argu-

ment was used in a Florida Supreme Court case to free 1930s Klan floggers, Chalmers to Mitchell, c. May 1997, copy in the author's collection.

62. *NYT,* 21 Nov. 1927, p. 3, 25 Nov. 1927, p. 23; *MA,* 25 Nov. 1927.

63. Shepherd, "Whip Wins," 10, 31–32; *MA,* 5 Dec. 1927.

64. Stephens, "Mask and Lash in Crenshaw," 441; Esdale to Thompson, 14 Sept. 1927, quoted in *NYT,* 2 Dec. 1927, p. 22 (quoted), and *MA,* 29 Nov. 1927 (quoting the same statement). See also *NYT,* 1 Dec. 1927, p. 56; *MA,* 15 Oct., 30 Nov., 1 Dec. 1927.

65. Stephens, "Mask and Lash in Crenshaw," 441; KKK File, reel 28, 1927, TU; *NYT,* 15 Oct. 1927, p. 2; *MA,* 15 Oct. 1927; *AC,* 15 Oct. 1927.

66. *MA,* 25, 29 Nov., 5 Dec. 1927; *ME,* 7 July 1949.

67. KKK File, reel 28, 1927, TU; *NYT,* 1 Dec. 1927, p. 56; *MA,* 27, 30 Nov., 1 Dec. 1927.

68. Shepherd, "Whip Hand," 9.

69. Shepherd, "Whip Wins," 10 (second quotation), 11 (third quotation), also 31–32, and "Whip Hand," 9 (first quotation), also 8, 44–45; *AC,* 15 Sept. 1927; *MA,* 12 Oct. 1927.

70. *MA,* 23 Oct., 30 Nov., 1 Dec. 1927; J. C. McLendon, ed., *Luverne Journal,* to Editor, *MA,* 25 Nov. 1927, in *MA,* 27 Nov. 1927.

71. *AC,* 9, 22 Oct., 1 Dec. 1927; *Commerce BN,* 8 Dec. 1927; *Daily News, MGA,* and *Macon Telegraph,* in *MA,* 5 Dec. 1927.

72. *NYT,* 2 Dec. 1927, p. 22; 5 Dec. 1927, p. 22; *CT,* 14 Nov. 1927 (first quotation); *MA,* 5 Dec. 1927; *Baltimore Sun,* in *Commerce News,* 8 Dec. 1927; Stephens, "Mask and Lash in Crenshaw," 437–38 and 442 (second quotation), also 435–36, esp. 438–39.

73. Snell, "Ku Klux Klan in Jefferson County," 182–84, and "Masked Men in the Magic City," 222; *BAH, BN,* and *BP,* 11–16 Dec. 1927; *MA,* 17 Dec. 1927.

74. *Doss v. Alabama,* 220 Ala. 30 (1929), and *Clayton v. Alabama,* 220 Ala. 39 (1929).

75. J. M. McCary to Editor, *AS,* 22 Aug. 1927, quoted in *AS,* 24 Aug. 1927 (quoted).

76. *MA,* 9 Aug. 1927.

77. *TRI,* in *MA,* 16 Sept. 1927.

9. RACE OVER RUM, ROMANS, AND REPUBLICANS

1. For statements on race's centrality from different perspectives, see Phillips, "Central Theme of Southern History," 30–43; Key, *Southern Politics in State and Nation;* Degler, "Racism in the United States," 102; Williamson, *Crucible of Race.*

2. The *Ala. KKK Newsletter* 7 (Jan. 1929): 2, box 26, folder: Baptist and Catholic Intolerance, Religion, O. D. Street Papers, ADAH, featured a parody of the regular Democratic oath that read in part: "I, Skidmore Turncoat . . . do solemnly and boozefully declare that I will . . . call Republicans 'nigger,' 'Black Radicals,' or 'Trashy Federal Pie Lovers,' or any other name that will express contempt . . . , vote early and often . . . , make false entries, prepare bogus tickets . . . , wear red shirts . . . , be a monkey and board myself . . . a wild jackass and bray for nothing . . . , kick like a Texas bronco, howl like a whipped pup, steal like an insurance president . . . , and lie like hell all in the name of my party. . . . I deliberately swear [by] . . . the forces of Alienism, Alcoholism, Arrogant Romanism, Corrupt Tammanyism, and of disgusting Negroism . . . to stick like a thick tick to a nigger's skin, binding myself under the awful penalty of having my likker cut out . . . and my soul consigned to eternal purgatory, should I never go back on this Cat-lick Demmycrat Obligation. So help me, Al Smith." A self-described "old lady of the South" backed the KKK in its fights because her father had been in the original Klan that "cleansed our public offices of Negroes, carpetbaggers, and

scalawags." "I can very well remember the Reconstruction Days when the White people of the South were oppressed and mistreated by this ungodly corruptible group," she wrote. "I can remember my Father saying the Ku-Klux Klan will never die. 'It was here yesterday, today, and forever.' And I firmly believe God has a working hand through this organization, for if it wasn't for the Ku-Klux Klan in the Recosntruction Days, America would have been a mongrelized nation." "So today God sees the need of a Ku-Klux Klan as never before," she argued, because America has become a "nation full of corruptible filth." "Instead of the carpetbaggers and scalawags of years past," we have to contend with "Communism . . . the N.A.A.C.P. and other Jewish controlled organizations as peddlers to create hate and brainwash the minds of the American people [and] destroy our Christian faith . . . and the American Way of Life." Declaration in KKK-Prattville File, BA.

3. Race evoked the most primal emotions for many Klan families. The "saddest story ever told," according to one KKK pamphlet, was the tale of a young white woman who married a black: "I was my father's future hope, my mother's joy and pride, but I got lost on life's dark road, and there my spirit died. I smeared my all white heritage and left the white man's track, now my descendants for all time shall be forever black. . . . All other crimes may be forgiven when prayer its power fulfills, the scheming crook may find new hope, and even the man that kills. . . . I try to hide from all the stars, the moon, the setting sun; for all man-kind . . . condemn what I have done. My mother sleeps deep in her grave, my dad lies at her side, for both were crushed when I became a common negro's bride." KKK-Prattville File, BA.

4. Edmonds, "Ignorance Is Power," 153–59; KKK File, reel 36, 1930, TU; *WP,* 2 Nov. 1930; *MA,* 7 Feb. 1928; Newton and Newton, *Ku Klux Klan,* 5; Rogers et al., *Alabama,* 433.

5. Ala. KKK Newsletter 6 (April 1928): 1–2, and July 1928, p. 2, box 26, folder: Baptist and Catholic Intolerance, Religion, Oliver Day Street Papers, ADAH; KKK File, reel 31, 1928, reel 36, 1930, TU; *MA,* 7, 10 Feb. 1928, 2 March 1930; *BAH,* 21 Nov. 1928; Newton and Newton, *Ku Klux Klan,* 532; Thornton, "Alabama Politics," 90.

6. Ala. KKK Newsletter 6 (April 1928): 1–2, and July 1928, p. 2, box 26, folder: Baptist and Catholic Intolerance, Religion, Street Papers, ADAH.

7. Ala. KKK Newsletter 6 (June 1928): 1, Street Papers, ADAH; KKK File, reel 31, 1928, TU; *MA,* 22 Jan., 7 Feb. 1928; *BN* and *BAH,* 15 April 1928 (quoted), also *BN* and *BAH,* 31 Jan., 25 Feb. 1928; Snell, "Ku Klux Klan in Jefferson County," 190.

8. Snell, "Ku Klux Klan in Jefferson County," 190 (first quotation); *MA,* 22 Jan. 1928 (second quotation); see also *BN* and *BAH,* 31 Jan. 1928; *MA,* 7 Feb. 1928; KKK File, reel 31, 1928, TU. Governor Graves gave one of his rare but still brief replies when he was asked about rumors that he would be leaving the Klan. He called the rumors "malicious and false." Quoted in *BN* and *BAH,* 25 Feb. 1928.

9. *BN* and *BAH,* 25 Feb. 1928 (both quote Simmons).

10. *MA, BN,* and *BAH,* 22 Jan. 1928 (the quoted statement appears in all three). See also *NYT,* 22 Jan. 1928, p. 1; *BN* and *BAH,* 23 Feb. 1928.

11. *MA, BN,* and *BAH,* 22 Jan. 1928; *NYT,* 22 Jan. 1928, p. 1; *BN,* 23 Feb. 1928, and *BAH,* 22–23 Feb. 1928.

12. Ala. KKK Newsletter 6 (April 1928): 1, (June 1928): 4, (July 1928), 2–3, Street Papers, ADAH; KKK File, reel 31, 1928, TU; *MA,* 22, 26 Jan. 1928; *BAH,* and *BN,* 22 Jan. 1928.

13. Ku Klux Klan File (quoting the scribbling on the mask), Papers of Charles C. McCall, ADAH; Charles A. Fell Memoirs, II, pt. 1, pp. 101–28, BPLA; KKK File, reel 31, 1928, TU; *BAH,* 25, 29 Feb. 1928 (quoting the same statement); *BN,* 25 Feb. 1928; *MA,* 22 Jan. 1928; KKK File, reel 31, 1928, TU; *MA,* 23–24 Jan., 7 Feb. 1928.

14. KKK File, reel 31, 1928, TU; *BAH*, 23 Jan. 1928 (first quotation), also 24 Jan. 1928; *MA*, 23–24 Jan., 7 Feb. 1928; *BAH* quoted in *Columbus Enquirer-Sun*, 2 Feb. 1928 (second quotation); *BAH* and *MA*, 24 Jan. 1928 (third quotation).

15. KKK Scrapbooks, no. 257, BPLA; KKK File, reel 31, 1928, TU; *Columbus Enquirer-Sun*, 2 Feb. 1928. The *Camden Post, Columbus Enquirer-Sun, New York Times*, and *Birmingham News* argued that the Klan was dead. The *Montgomery Advertiser* and *New York Herald-Tribune* thought that K-Trio was a political move for 1928. The *Hartford Courant* drew the analogy with the leopard's spots. The *Albany News* is quoted regarding intolerance. The *Decatur Daily* made the crack about lower laundry bills. All are cited and quoted in "The Klan Goes in for a 'Face-Lifting,'" *Literary Digest* 96 (10 March 1928): 15–16.

16. KKK File, reel 31, 1928, TU; *NYT*, 12 Aug. 1928, p. 12 (quoted); *MA*, 7 Feb. 1928.

17. Klan propaganda included the following: "The Pope called the Devil up on the telephone one day, the girl at central listened to all they had to say. 'I've planned this for many years, and I've started out to kill all who refuse to bow in submission to my will. My army went through Spain, shooting women and children down. We tore up all their Bibles and killed all the Protestants we found. I knew what you would tell me, till a year or so ago, when tho Ku Klux Klan warned me to go more slow. Now that's why I called you, Satan, for I want advice from you. I know that you would tell me just what I ought to do.' 'My dear Old Father Pope, there's not much to tell, for the Ku Klux will make it hotter than I can for you in hell. I've been an old mean devil, but not half as mean as you. And the minute that you get here, I will give my job to you." Ala. KKK Newsletter 4 (June 1926): 4 (quoted above), box 15, folder 11: Ku Klux Klan, Association Records, ADAH. See Ala. KKK Newsletter 6 (April 1928): 2 (first quotation in my text); *MA*, 18 Aug. 1927 (second quotation in my text).

18. Ala. KKK Newsletter 6 (April 1928): 2–3, Street Papers, ADAH.

19. Thomas to All Exalted Cyclopes, 1 Feb. 1928, in *BAH*, 11 Feb. 1928; *BN*, and *BAH*, 31 Jan. 1928; Snell, "Ku Klux Klan in Jefferson County," 191.

20. *NYT*, 10 Aug. 1927, p. 14; *MA*, 7 Aug. 1927; *PC*, 31 Dec. 1927, p. 1.

21. *BN* and *BAH*, 29 April, 7 May 1928; *PC*, 31 Dec. 1927, p. 1.

22. *BN* and *BAH*, 29 April, 5 and 7 May 1928 (first and second quotations), also 29 April 1928.

23. Ala. KKK Newsletter 6 (June 1928): 1, 3–4, Street Papers, ADAH; KKK File, reel 31, 1928, TU; *MA*, 26 Jan. 1928; *BAH* and *BN*, 11 May 1928; Snell, "Ku Klux Klan in Jefferson County," 195–96.

24. Snell, "Ku Klux Klan in Jefferson County," 85–86; Newton and Newton, *Ku Klux Klan*, 525; Rice, *Ku Klux Klan in American Politics*, 85–86.

25. Newton and Newton, *Ku Klux Klan*, 525.

26. Ala. KKK Newsletter 6 (April 1928): 2, June 1928, p. 1 (quoted), July 1928, p. 1, Jan. 1929, p. 4, in Street Papers, ADAH.

27. KKK Scrapbooks, no. 257, BPLA; KKK File, reel 31, 1928, TU; *MA*, 22 Jan. 1928; and "The Klan Goes in for a 'Face-Lifting,'" 16 (quoted).

28. KKK File, reel 28, 1927, reel 31, 1928, TU; *MA*, 18 Aug. 1927 (quotation of Heflin), 26 Jan. 1928 (quotation of Hotalen).

29. *MA*, 18 Aug. 1927 (quotation of Mullin).

30. O'Connor to W. B. Bankhead, 13 Sept. 1928, box 5, folder 13, and the pamphlet *Alabama Democracy, 1930: United Democracy and Party Harmony vs. Heflin Republicanism and Party Disruption*, 21 (quoted), box 3, folder 10, both in the Papers of John H. Bankhead II, ADAH; Flynt quoted in Rogers et al., *Alabama*, 438; "Al Smith," *KM* 3 (June 1927): 12–13.

31. See "Call for Conference of Anti-Smith Democrats," J. F. Hines Papers, SU; *BAH*, 22

July, 14 Aug. 1928 (quoted); *BN,* 14 Aug. 1928; Rogers et al., *Alabama,* 438; Feldman, *From Demagogue to Dixiecrat,* 90 (quoting the same statement).

32. *BAH* and *BN,* 14 Aug. 1928; Feldman, *From Demagogue to Dixiecrat,* 90 (quoted).

33. *BAH* and *BN,* 14 Aug. 1928.

34. *BAH* and *BN,* 14 Aug. 1928 (all quotations); Rogers et al., *Alabama,* 439. All quotations also appear in Feldman, *From Demagogue to Dixiecrat,* 90.

35. Hugh Gladney Grant Diary, 1, Hugh Gladney Grant Papers, DUKE; "Headquarters: Hoover-Curtis Campaign, Agricultural Group," Hines Papers, SU; *MA,* 8 Nov. 1928; Rogers et al., *Alabama,* 439; Newton and Newton, *Ku Klux Klan,* 52; Thornton, "Alabama Politics," 100.

36. Marie Bankhead Owen to J. H. Bankhead II, 30 June 1927, box 1, folder 7, J. H. Bankhead II Papers, ADAH; box 26, folder: Intolerance, and Ala. KKK Newsletter 6 (July 1928): 3 (quoted), both in the Street Papers, ADAH; *BN* and *BAH,* 4 Nov. 1928; Tanner, "Wonderful World of Tom Heflin," 163–66; Rice, *Ku Klux Klan in American Politics,* 89–90; Rogers et al., *Alabama,* 439; Chalmers, *Hooded Americanism,* 305.

37. J. Thomas Heflin Scrapbooks, MFS-652, SU; *MA,* clipping, c. 1928 (quoted), in box 3, folder 10, J. H. Bankhead II Papers, ADAH; *BAH,* 23 Jan. 1928 (also quoting Heflin).

38. *BAH,* 23 Jan. 1928 (quoted).

39. *MA,* clipping, c. 1928 (quotation of Grover Hall), in box 3, folder 10, J. H. Bankhead II Papers, ADAH; *DE,* 20 Jan. 1928, in Hollis, "Hall Family and Twentieth-Century Journalism in Alabama," 125 (quoted); and Thornton, "Alabama Politics," 98–99.

40. *Congressional Record,* Senate, extract, 18 Feb. 1927 (quotation of Bruce), Heflin Scrapbooks, MFS-652, SU; Mencken to Hall, 15 Oct. 1924, box 67, folder 1, Grover C. Hall, Sr., Papers, ADAH; *BN* and *BAH,* 9 May 1928 (quotation of the exchange between Bruce and Heflin); *AC,* 1 Feb. 1927. See also Heflin's comment: "My God! Tolerance with your Roman Catholic friends means meek and humble submission to everything the Roman Catholic hierarchy does or says. It means silence on the part of real Americans." Quoted in 18 Feb. 1927 extract from the *Congressional Record* (see above).

41. Tindall, *Emergence of the New South, 1913–1945,* 188–89; Pruitt, "Killing of Father Coyle," 24–37; Lipset and Raab, *Politics of Unreason;* Hofstadter, *Paranoid Style in American Politics and Other Essays;* Flynt, *Cracker Messiah.*

42. Ala. KKK Newsletter 6 (July 1928): 1 (first quotation), 4 (second quotation), (Oct. 1928): 3 (third quotation), Street Papers, ADAH.

43. Ala. KKK Newsletter 6 (Oct. 1928): 3, Street Papers, ADAH.

44. Box 192, folder: Ku Klux Klan, 1927, Graves Papers, ADAH; "Senator Heflin," *KM* 3 (March 1927): 26 (quoted); *BAH,* 23 Jan. 1928.

45. *Congressional Record,* Senate, extracts, 20 Jan. and 13 April 1928 (first quotation), also 18 Feb. 1927, also McKinney to Heflin, 23 Feb. 1927 (second quotation), all in Heflin Scrapbooks, MFS-652, SU.

46. *Congressional Record,* Senate, extract, 18 Jan. 1928 (quoted), Heflin Scrapbooks, MFS-652, SU; Hugh Gladney Grant Diary, 1, 71, Grant Papers, DUKE.

47. Potter to Heflin, 1 March 1927 (third quotation), Kern to Heflin, 10 Feb. 1927 (second quotation), Heflin Scrapbooks, MFS-652 (first quotation), SU.

48. Ala. KKK Newsletter 5 (March 1927): 2, 4 (second quotation), April 1928, p. 3, June 1928, p. 3, July 1928, and the leaflet "Read, Think, and Act," c. 1928 (third quotation), by a "Christian Patriot," all in box 26, folder: Intolerance, Street Papers, ADAH; Cannack to Heflin, 23 Feb. 1927, McKinney to Heflin, 7 Feb. 1927, Johnson to Heflin, 30 Jan. 1927, Weldon to Heflin, 28 Feb. 1927, all in J. Thomas Heflin Scrapbooks, MFS-652, SU; "Al Smith," and

J.A.J., "Roman Treason Against Our Homes," 21 (first quotation). On the same page, J.A.J. of the *KM* also asked, regarding the Catholic Church, "What shall be done with this unspeakably vile incubus and parasite?"

49. *BAH*, 10 May (quotation of Hall), 5 Sept. 1928 (quotation of McCord).

50. Hugh Gladney Grant Diary, 1, Grant Papers, DUKE; Ala. KKK Newsletter 6 (June 1928): 4, Street Papers, ADAH.

51. Murray, *Red Scare*; Higham, *Strangers in the Land*; Kennedy, *Over Here*, 31, 53, 146; Curti, *Roots of American Loyalty*, 224–25; Hawley, *Great War and the Search for a Modern Order*, 29, 50.

52. Ala. KKK Newsletter 6 (April 1928): 3 (second quotation), (July 1928): 3 (first quotation), (Sept. 1928): n.p. (third quotation), Street Papers, ADAH; Fede, *Italians of the Deep South*; Feldman, *From Demagogue to Dixiecrat*, 35, 60, 81, 92 (fourth quotation).

53. *BAH*, 11–12 Sept. 1928; *BN*, 11–12 Sept., 4 Nov. 1928.

54. *NYT*, 11 July 1927.

55. The Methodist press wrote, "Mr. Heflin is neither a clown nor a demagogue. He is Alabama's senior senator who is holding the liquor men's feet to the fire so that they are scorching   and they are putting forth every effort to belittle him, to humiliate him, to annihilate him." Quoted in "Let Us Keep the Issues Straight," from *CA*, box 5, folder 13, Papers of William B. Bankhead, ADAH; also the Alabama Women's League for White Supremacy clipping (fifth quotation), in box 210, folder: Birmingham City Commission, Benjamin Meek Miller, Alabama Governors Papers, ADAH; Ala. KKK Newsletter 6 (Sept. 1928): 1, 4, (Nov. 1928): n.p. (sixth quotation), Street Papers, ADAH; *MA*, 18 Nov. 1927; *BN* and *BAH*, 8, 10 Oct. 1928; Rogers et al., *Alabama*, 440 (first, second, third, and fourth quotations); Rice, *Ku Klux Klan in American Politics*, 91.

56. Alabama KKK Newsletter 6 (Sept. 1928): 4, Street Papers, ADAH.

57. Ala. KKK Newsletter 7 (Jan. 1929), Street Papers, ADAH.

58. Darrow, "Name Your Poison," 3, 8; *NYT*, 19 Aug. 1927.

59. *BAH* and *BN*, 5 Sept. 1928.

60. "A Resolution Adopted by Conference of Anti-Smith Democrats," 13 Aug. 1928, Hines Papers, SU; box 26, folder: Intolerance, and Ala. KKK Newsletter 7 (Jan. 1929): 3, both in Street Papers, ADAH; *BN* and *BAH*, 22, 31 Aug., 14 Sept. 1928; Rogers et al., *Alabama*, 438.

61. Street to Marshall, 10 Oct. 1928, Ransom to Street, 20 Sept. 1928 (first quotation), *CT*, clipping, 2 Oct. 1928, and "Governor Smith's Membership in the Roman Catholic Church and Its Proper Place as an Issue in This Campaign" (second and third quotations), all in box 26, folder: Intolerance, Street Papers, ADAH.

62. *NYT*, 8 July 1928, p. 2; *BAH* and *BN*, 8 July 1928; Snell, "Ku Klux Klan in Jefferson County," 76–77, 131; Rice, *Ku Klux Klan in American Politics*, 87.

63. Grace Darden, Interview with Scott Gloor, p. 3, 15 March 1979, Docena, Alabama, SU; *BN* and *BAH*, 8 July, 1 Sept. 1928.

64. "Historian" to Editor, 1 May 1928, box 5, folder 13, W. B. Bankhead Papers, ADAH; Ala. KKK Newsletter 6 (April 1928) (fifth quotation), Street Papers, ADAH; *PC*, 9 June 1928 (first and second quotations); Rice, *Ku Klux Klan in American Politics*, 89 (third and fourth quotations); Snell, "Ku Klux Klan in Jefferson County," 199; Tanner, "Wonderful World of Tom Heflin," 172; Newton and Newton, *Ku Klux Klan*, 525.

65. Hanson to Locke, Wilkinson, and Heflin, 2 Nov. 1928, copy in *BN*, 4 Nov. 1928; *BAH*, 19 Oct. 1928; Feldman, *From Demagogue to Dixiecrat*, 128, 175.

66. Marie Bankhead Owen, "Hoover's Religion" statement, 23 Oct. 1928, box 5, folder

14, W. B. Bankhead Papers, ADAH; KKK File, BCA; Ala. KKK Newsletter 6 (Sept. 1928): 1, Street Papers, ADAH; *OSD*, 6 Sept. 1928; *BAH*, 5, 11 Sept., 19 Oct. 1928; *BN*, 5, 11 Sept., 5 Nov. 1928; Snell, "Ku Klux Klan in Jefferson County," 200; Thornton, "Alabama Politics," 84; Dobbins, "Alabama's Governors and Editors," 136–37.

67. Marie Bankhead Owen, "Hoover's Religion" statement, 23 Oct. 1928, box 5, folder 14, W. B. Bankhead Papers, ADAH; *BN*, 5 Sept. 5 Nov. 1928; *BAH*, 5 Sept., 16 Nov. 1928.

68. Underwood to Wooley, 30 Jan. 1924, box 58, Johnson to Underwood, 18 April 1928, box 82, both in Oscar W. Underwood Papers, ADAH; misc. clippings and *MA*, clipping, 22 July 1928, in MFS-851, Papers of Harwell Goodwin Davis, SU; Harwell G. Davis, Interview with Arthur L. Walker, March 1974, Birmingham, Ala., SU; *BAH*, clipping, 10 July 1924, Heflin Scrapbooks, SU; *BAH*, 14 Aug. 1928; Ray, "Harwell G. Davis."

69. *BN*, 14–15 Aug. 1928.

70. *BAH* and *BN*, 14–15 Aug. 1928; all quoted statements appear in *BAH*.

71. KKK File, reel 31, 1928, TU; *MA*, 10 April 1928 (sixth quotation); *MA*, 19 Aug. 1927, quoted in Thornton, "Alabama Politics," 97 (third quotation); Rogers et al., *Alabama*, 439–41 (fourth and fifth quotations); Feldman, *From Demagogue to Dixiecrat* (first and second quotations).

72. Roberts to Heflin, 21 Jan. 1928 (fifth quotation), box 820, folder 57, Papers of J. Thomas Heflin, UASC; quotation from Feldman, *From Demagogue to Dixiecrat*, 94; Hendon to Editor, *BAH*, 20 Jan. 1928, in *BAH*, 23 Jan. 1928 (fourth quotation); *BN* and *BAH*, 9 May, 8 Sept. 1928; Newton and Newton, *Ku Klux Klan*, 262–63, 376, 485; Rogers et al., *Alabama*, 439–41 (first, second, and third quotations).

73. Parker to Editor, *BN*, in *BN* and *BAH*, 2 Sept. 1928.

74. The broadside "Al Smith, the Negro Lover," box 19, folder 4, State Democratic Executive Committee Records, ADAH; "A Resolution Adopted by Conference of Anti-Smith Democrats," 13 Aug. 1928, Hines Papers, SU; *BAH*, 4 Sept. 1928 (third and fourth quotations); Reagen, "Race as a Factor," 8 and 11 (fifth quotation); *CA*, 1 Nov. 1928, p. 8 (first and sixth quotations), p. 9 (second quotation).

75. *Congressional Record*, extracts, 20 Jan., 7 Feb., 13 April, 26 May 1928, Heflin Scrapbooks, MFS-652, SU; "A Resolution Adopted by Conference of Anti-Smith Democrats," 13 Aug. 1928, Hines Papers, SU; *BAH* and *BN*, clippings, 4 Nov. 1928, in box 26, folder: Intolerance, Street Papers, ADAH; *MA*, 17 Aug. 1928.

76. Adam to Heflin, 26 Jan. 1928, box 820, folder 55, Heflin Papers, UASC; Ala. KKK Newsletter 6 (April 1928): 3. See also the unpaginated issues for Oct. 1928 and Nov. 1928, which contain the first, fifth, and sixth statements quoted in my text. The unpaginated issue for September 1928 contains the second, third, and fourth quoted statements. Also see Hassell to Editor, *New York Observer*, 14 July 1928, *BN* and *BAH*, 4 Nov. 1926, all in box 26, folder: Intolerance, Street Papers, ADAH. The Klan charged that the "Roman Catholic Church . . . is after the negro as one of its major steps in dominating the American Republic." Quoted in "Al Smith," *KM* 3 (June 1927); 13, see also 14; Thornton, "Alabama Politics," 101; Hamilton, *Hugo Black,* 245; Feldman, *From Demagogue to Dixiecrat,* 93–94 (seventh and eighth quotations).

77. Ala. KKK Newsletter 6 (Sept. 1928), Street Papers, ADAH.

78. KKK File, reel 31, 1928, TU; *MA*, 4 Sept. 1928; Reagen, "Race as a Factor," 6.

79. *BN,* 11 Sept. 1928.

80. *BAH,* 7 Sept., 8 Oct. 1928; *BN,* 7 Sept., 8 Oct., 5 Nov. 1928; Reagen, "Race as a Factor," 6–7, 12–17 (all quotations).

81. Reagen, "Race as a Factor," 6–7, 12–17 (first, second, and third quotations); *BN*, 5

Nov. 1928 (fourth quotation). There are plenty of other examples. Addressing a crowd of 2,000 at Springville in St. Clair County, Brandon assured his listeners that any "man who supports Hoover is a Republican" and risks "negro domination" as in the days of Reconstruction. Brandon is quoted in *BN* and *BAH,* 7 Sept. 1928. Industrialist newspapers also argued that a vote for Hoover was a vote "to subscribe to [the] . . . use [of] federal authority to enforce the fourteenth and fifteenth amendments." Quoted in *BN* and *BAH,* 3 Sept. 1928. "So long as there is a Confederate soldier with a dangling empty sleeve," explained A. H. Carmichael of Tuscumbia, "we can never vote the Republican ticket." Quoted in Rogers et al., *Alabama,* 440. U.S. Congressman George Huddleston agreed that a vote for Hoover was "a vote to place our State in the hands of 'Republicans,' whom the responsible white people of Alabama have been fighting since the days of Reconstruction." Quoted in Huddleston to Hammill, 4 Oct. 1928, box 210, folder: Birmingham City Commission, Miller Papers, ADAH.

82. *BAH* and *BN,* 2 Sept. 1928 (quoted); Reagen, "Race as a Factor," 6–7, 12–17. Oliver credited Tammany Hall with having rescued the South during the 1890s when the federal government, through Senator Henry Cabot Lodge's "force bill," threatened the South with supervised federal elections, "federal soldiers," a "federal antilynching bill," "federal registration of voters and federal supervision of elections, [and] the frightful specter of negro domination." Quoted in *BN* and *BAH,* 2 Sept. 1928. Oliver also mentioned the perils of "modern-day Reconstruction" and "social equality." Quoted in Reagen, "Race as a Factor," 6–7.

83. Pamphlet by R. B. Evins, *White Supremacy Endangered: The South Must Continue Democratic to Avoid Legislation to Enforce the Fifteenth Amendment* (Birmingham: Jefferson County Campaign Committee, 1928), AUSC; *BAH* and *BN,* 2–3 Sept. 1928.

84. Huddleston to Hamill, 4 Oct. 1928, box 210, folder: Birmingham City Commission, Miller Papers, ADAH; *BN* and *BAH,* 3 Sept. 1928; Rogers et al., *Alabama,* 440.

85. "Anonymous" (Commerce Department employee) to Blease, c. 1928, box 5, folder 14, W. B. Bankhead Papers, ADAH; *BN,* 4, 6 Nov. 1928; *BAH,* 16 Nov. 1928.

86. "Anonymous" (Commerce Department employee) to Blease, c. 1928 (quoted), box 5, folder 14, W. B. Bankhead Papers, ADAH.

87. *BN,* 5–6 Nov. 1928.

88. *Alabama Official and Statistical Register, 1931,* 511–12; KKK File, reel 36, 1930, TU; *MA,* 6 Jan. 1930; *BN,* 14 Sept., 5, 7–8, 10 Nov. 1928; *BAH,* 14 Sept., 17 Nov. 1928, *NYT,* 12 Aug. 1928, p. 12; Rogers et al., *Alabama,* 441; Rice, *Ku Klux Klan in American Politics,* 91; Thornton, "Alabama Politics," 101. Of course, the Black Belt had a long history of manipulating the black vote by force and fraud; see McMillan, *Constitutional Development in Alabama.*

89. Rice, *Ku Klux Klan in American Politics,* 91; *BN,* 7 Nov. 1928 (quoted); *MA,* 6 Jan. 1930; KKK File, reel 36, 1930, TU.

90. *Ex parte Wilkinson,* 220 Ala. 529 (1929); *State ex. rel. Glenn v. Wilkinson,* 220 Ala. 172 (1929); *State ex. rel. Horne v. Wilkinson,* 220 Ala. 38 (1929); *BN,* 9–10 Nov. 1928.

91. *BN,* 7 Nov. 1928 and 5 Nov. 1930. For a detailed map and political cartoons dealing with the 1928 election in Alabama, see appendix C in Feldman, "Ku Klux Klan in Alabama."

92. *BN,* 7 Nov. 1928; Reagen, "Race as a Factor," 10–11.

93. Ben Ray disparagingly called the patrician forces that wanted to oust Locke and Heflin "reactionary forces"; see Ray's address, 3, in the Proceedings of Meeting Held at Municipal Auditorium, 3 Jan. 1930 [*sic*], box 19, folder 3, State Democratic Executive Committee (SDEC) Records, ADAH; Rogers et al., *Alabama,* 435–42; Reagen, "Race as a Factor," 5–19. Grover Hall bragged that Smith's narrow victory in Alabama was "a tribute to the sanity and liberalism of the people of this State . . . the sanity and liberal impulses of our people." Victor Hanson's editors claimed the state's traditional Democratic Party was the "party of

advance . . . progress [and] liberal policies"; see *MA,* 7 Nov. 1928 and *BAH,* 8 Nov. 1928. The Ala. KKK Newsletter 7 (Jan. 1929): 3, Street Papers, ADAH, furnishes evidence that the Alabama Klan leadership considered its organization conservative.

10. DISLOYALTY, REVENGE, AND THE END OF AN ERA

1. KKK File, reel 34, 1929, TU; *MA,* 10 Aug. 1929.

2. Feldman, *From Demagogue to Dixiecrat,* 99–120.

3. Anderton to Childers, 15 Jan. 1930, box 5, folder 16, Papers of William B. Bankhead, ADAH; "Judge Hugh Locke's Statement Regarding the Executive Committee's Ruling," in J. F. Hines Papers, SU; Wynn to No Name, 26 Dec. 1929, box 210, folder: Birmingham City Commission, Alabama Governors Papers, Benjamin Meek Miller, ADAH; *MA* and *NYT,* 17 Dec. 1929, p. 1; *BN,* 3 Oct. 1930.

4. Weissinger to author, 6 Sept. 1991, Papers of Horace W. Weissinger, Birmingham, Alabama, in the author's collection; *BN,* 2 Nov. 1929; Barnard, *Dixiecrats and Democrats,* 50; Snell, "Ku Klux Klan in Jefferson County," 211.

5. *Smith v. Allwright,* 322 U.S. 716, 769 (1944); Thornton, "Alabama Politics," 101.

6. Hugh Gladney Grant Diary, 85, 2 March 1930, Grant Papers, DUKE; Thornton, "Alabama Politics," 107; Rogers et al., *Alabama,* 441; "Heflin Attacked by Peanuts," *KM* 6 (Jan. 1930): 10–11.

7. Thornton, "Alabama Politics," 109.

8. Subgroup 20: E. W. Pettus Adm., 1927–31, ser. A, box 19, folder 1—box 32, folder 12, SDEC Records, ADAH; Thornton, "Alabama Politics," 83–112.

9. Lynne to Brown, 3 Sept. 1929, Luck to Pettus, 21 June 1930, both in box 25, folder 1, and Merrill to Pettus, 19 Dec. 1929, Milner to Pettus, 2 Jan. 1930, both in box 25, folder 7, and the Minutes of the SDEC Meeting, 16 Dec. 1929, pp. 9–33, Jeff Davis Hotel, Montgomery, Alabama, box 32, folders 4–6, all in the State Democratic Executive Committee (SDEC) Records, ADAH; misc. clippings, c. 1929, box 5, folder 16, W. B. Bankhead Papers, ADAH; Rogers et al., *Alabama,* 441; *BAH,* 17 Dec. 1929; *Florence Times-News,* 9 Sept. 1928. For a detailed map and breakdown of the 1929 vote, see appendix D in Feldman, "Ku Klux Klan in Alabama."

10. *BAH,* 17 Dec. 1929 (quoted).

11. *Alabama Democracy, 1930,* 22 (first quotation), box 3, folder 10, J. H. Bankhead Papers, ADAH; "Judge Hugh Locke's Statement Regarding the Executive Committee's Ruling" (third qutoation), Hines Papers, SU; Cason, "Tom-Tom Heflin," 566, quoted in Harper, "'Cotton Tom' Heflin," 402 (second quotation).

12. *BAH,* 21, 24 Dec. 1929.

13. Heflin to Harris 4, 23 April 1930, box 829, folder 61, and Wilkinson to Harris, 23 May 1930, box 829, folder 62, both in the J. Thomas Heflin Papers, UASC; *NYT,* 28 Dec. 1929, p. 9 (quoted) and 29 Dec. 1929, sec. 2, p. 1 (including part of text of first quotation).

14. Weissinger to author, 6 Sept. 1991, Weissinger Papers, copies in the author's collection; Thornton, "Alabama Politics," 92, 95–99, 103–12; Hamilton, *Hugo Black,* 184–85; Newman, "Hugo Black Manuscript," 138–40.

15. Black to Wilkinson, 14 April 1930, in *BN,* 5 June 1932; *BN,* 17 April 1930.

16. Heflin to Wilkinson, 14 April 1930, box 829, folder 61, and Heflin to Wilkinson, 5, 13, and 28 March 1930, Wilkinson to Heflin, 21 March 1930, Harris to Heflin, 28 March 1930, Ray to Heflin, 20 March 1930, Chilton to Heflin, 19 March 1930, Carnley to Heflin, 17 March

1930, all in box 828, folder 60, Heflin Papers, UASC, quoted in Feldman, *From Demagogue to Dixiecrat,* 96 (all quotations).

17. Heflin to Wilkinson, 14 April 1930, box 829, folder 61, and Wilkinson to Heflin, 16 March 1931, box 832, folder 72, Heflin Papers, UASC, quoted in Feldman, *From Demagogue to Dixiecrat,* 96–97.

18. *Wilkinson v. Henry,* 221 Ala. 254 (1929); *BN,* 17 April 1930.

19. Feldman, *From Demagogue to Dixiecrat,* 97 (both quotations); *BN,* 17 April 1930; Hamilton, *Hugo Black,* 184–85.

20. Wilkinson and Harris to Heflin, 23 May 1930, box 829, folder 62, and Heflin to Wilkinson, 8 July 1930, box 829, folder 64, and Wilkinson to Heflin, 1 March 1930, box 828, folder 60, Dawson to Thornton, 17, 21 July 1930, box 829, folder 64, all in Heflin Papers, UASC; *Alabama Democracy, 1930,* 23, J. H. Bankhead II Papers, ADAH; *MA,* 12 March 1930; KKK File, reel 36, 1930, TU; Snell, "Ku Klux Klan in Jefferson County," 211, and "Masked Men in the Magic City," 224; Feldman, *From Demagogue to Dixiecrat,* 97; *BAH,* 17, 21 Dec. 1929; *NYT,* 28 Dec. 1929.

21. *BAH,* 17 Dec. 1929.

22. Thornton, "Alabama Politics," 86–87, 93, and quotation on p. 112; Rogers et al., *Alabama,* 441–42; *BAH,* 17 Dec. 1929.

23. Harper, "'Cotton Tom' Heflin," 390; Tanner, "Wonderful World of Tom Heflin," 165, and "Senator Tom Heflin as Storyteller," 54 (quoted). In a later essay, J. Mills Thornton III, an otherwise excellent historian, advanced an even faultier premise: the idea that the 1920s Klan was a "fountainhead for [Alabama's] liberalism in later decades" (901). See "Hugo Black and the Golden Age," 899–913. Thornton based this highly questionable thesis, implausibly sustained, on the examples of Hugo Black, Bibb Graves, and Richard Rives—three 1920s Klansmen who later became leading liberals. Yet he confuses cause and effect here, incorrectly crediting the KKK with being "a breeding ground" (901) for these liberals and their liberalism when in fact the 1920s Klan did not school Black and Graves in liberalism—quite the opposite. Both men cynically used the Klan and its electoral strength for their own political purposes, abandoning the order almost as soon as it had served those ends: Graves to push his program of state reform and Black to gain election to the U.S. Senate. Rives, like Black, did not exhibit liberal inclinations, especially on race, until he had been released from the electoral shackles of Alabama politics (903). Thornton's fourth major example, Lister Hill, was never a Klansman and had only the most tenuous connections to any political member of the order. Thornton also ignores 1920s Knights who provided Alabama with ultraconservative, even reactionary, doctrines for the next three decades—Horace Wilkinson, Hugh Locke, and Tom Heflin. His assertion that a "particularly striking example of the tendency for former Klansmen to embrace liberal causes in later decades arose during the battles of the Dixiecrat years" (903) is especially suspect, since Wilkinson and Locke served in the vanguard of the conservative 1948 bolters. Likewise, he never explains the plain white 1920s Klansmen, a number of whom populated the thin but violent and active ranks of the KKK during the 1930s and 1940s. Thornton also curiously cites Ben Ray and makes a quantum leap by treating the Democratic loyalists in 1948 as liberal simply because they chose to fight President Truman's civil rights program in Congress and within the Democratic Party rather than outside it. In this 1985 article Thornton also interestingly repudiates his earlier notion, expressed in 1968, that the 1920s KKK was essentially a reincarnation of populism.

24. *PC,* 6 Sept. 1930, p. 8B (quotation of Bankhead); Cason, "'Tom-Tom' Heflin," 598, quoted in Harper, "'Cotton Tom' Heflin," 399 (quotation of Heflin).

25. Hearin to Hill, 7 June 1930, box 37, folder 13, Lister Hill Papers, UASC (third quotation); speeches by John H. Bankhead II and Hugh D. Merrill, in the Minutes of the SDEC Meeting, 86–106, 26 Aug. 1930, box 32, folder 11, SDEC Records, ADAH; Carau to Hines, 24 July 1930, Thompson to Hines, 28 July 1930, and C. M. Stanley, ed., *AJ,* to Hines, 25 July 1930, all in Hines Papers, SU; *Congressional Record,* Senate, vol. 75, part 8, 72d Cong., 1st sess., 26 April 1932, p. 8920; Harper, " 'Cotton Tom' Heflin," 397; Rogers et al., *Alabama,* 497 (first and second quotations).

26. See *Alabama Democracy, 1930,* 5–6, 23, in box 3, folder 10, John H. Bankhead II Papers, ADAH; KKK File, reel 36, 1930, TU; *MA,* 2 March 1930 (first quotation); *BAH,* 11 Aug. 1930; *ME,* 7 July 1949 (second quotation).

27. KKK File, reel 36, 1930, TU; *Alabama Democracy, 1930,* 5–6, 23, in box 3, folder 10, J. H. Bankhead II Papers, ADAH; Locke to Hines, 6 Jan. 1930, Hines Papers, SU; W. B. Bankhead to McReynolds, 18 Aug. 1930, in box 6, folder 2, McVay to W. B. Bankhead, 20 Jan. 1930, in box 5, folder 16, both in the W. B. Bankhead Papers, ADAH; *MA,* 2 March 1930; Snell, "Ku Klux Klan in Jefferson County," 214–16.

28. "Alabama Democracy, 1930," pp. 5–6, 23, in box 3, folder 10, J. H. Bankhead II Papers, ADAH.

29. *PC,* 6 Sept. 1930, p. 8B.

30. *BAH,* 17 Dec. 1929.

31. KKK File, reel 36, 1930, TU; *MA,* 6 Jan. 1930; *NYT,* 28 Aug. 1930, p. 18 (quoted).

32. Mizell to Feagin, 18 March 1931, State Board of Administration Records, ADAH; KKK Scrapbooks, no. 257, BPLA; Kelly to W. B. Bankhead, 7 March 1930, box 5, folder 18, W. B. Bankhead Papers, ADAH; KKK File, reel 36, 1930, TU; *BN,* 23 Nov. 1930; *MA,* 12 March 1930 (second quotation); Rogers et al., *Alabama,* 497 (first quotation).

33. *NYT,* 28 Dec. 1929; *BAH,* 17, 21 Dec. 1929; *BN,* 3, 5 Nov. 1930; Snell, "Masked Men in the Magic City," 224; Feldman, *From Demagogue to Dixiecrat,* 97.

34. Vance, ed., *Washington Fellowship Forum,* to "Fellow American," Jan. 1930, box 26, folder: Intolerance, Oliver Day Street Papers, ADAH; J. L. Thornton, secretary, to Postmaster, statement, 15 Sept. 1930, Hines Papers, SU; *MA,* clipping, c. 1930 (first and second quotations), box 3, folder 10, J. H. Bankhead II Papers, ADAH; *Congressional Record,* Senate, extract, 18 Jan. 1928 (third quotation), MFS-652, Heflin Scrapbooks, SU; Harper, " 'Cotton Tom' Heflin," 399–406; Heflin to Wilkinson, 14 April 1930, box 829, folder 61, and Heflin to Wilkinson, 5, 13, and 28 March 1930, and Wilkinson to Heflin, 21 March 1930, all in box 828, folder 60, Heflin Papers, UASC.

35. Hugh Gladney Grant Diary, 75, in Grant Papers, DUKE; Harper, " 'Cotton Tom' Heflin," 394.

36. Radio speech by John H. Bankhead on Station WBRC (Birmingham), 3 Nov. 1930, p. 3 (second quotation), transcript in box 3, folder 10, J. H. Bankhead II Papers, ADAH; *BAH,* 21–22 Aug. 1930 (first quotation), also 23 Aug. 1930.

37. *Alabama Democracy, 1930,* box 3, folder 10, J. H. Bankhead II Papers, ADAH.

38. Hugh Gladney Grant Diary, 71, 75, 85, 13 Jan. and 2 March 1930 (I quote entries for all dates), Grant Papers, DUKE; "Cash for the Catholics," *KM* 6 (May 1930): 18.

39. Willett to Miller, 26 Feb. 1930, J. J. Willett Papers, SU; *Alabama Democracy, 1930,* 5, box 3, folder 10, J. H. Bankhead II Papers, ADAH; *BN,* 9 Oct. 1930.

40. KKK Scrapbooks, no. 257, BPLA; *Alabama Democracy, 1930,* 20–22 and 34–35 (third quotation), *Congressional Record,* House, extract, 6 May 1913, pp. 1256–57 (second quotation), and transcript of radio speech by John H. Bankhead II, 3 Nov. 1930, p. 2, and transcript of radio address of Marion Rushton on behalf of John H. Bankhead, 10 July 1930, all four items

in box 3, folder 10, J. H. Bankhead II Papers, ADAH; Acuff to W. B. Bankhead and W. B. Bankhead to Acuff, 12 May 1930, box 5, folder 19, W. B. Bankhead Papers, ADAH; *BN*, 3 Oct. 1930; *BAH*, 22–23 Aug. 1930 (first quotation); and Rogers et al., *Alabama*, 441.

41. "Alabama Points a Moral," *Commonweal* 13 (12 Nov. 1930): 29–30, quoted in Harper, "'Cotton Tom' Heflin," 392 (quoted); transcript of radio speech by John H. Bankhead II, 3 Nov. 1930, p. 5, box 3, folder 10, J. H. Bankhead II Papers, ADAH.

42. J. H. Bankhead speech, Minutes of the SDEC Meeting, 26 Aug. 1930, p. 93, box 32, folder 11, SDEC Records, ADAH; "Bankhead, John Hollis," "Bankhead, John Hollis, 2nd," and "Bankhead, William Brockman," in the *Biographical Dictionary of the American Congress, 1774–1971* (Washington, D.C.: USGPO, 1971), 548; Senate Document 92-8, 92d Cong., 1st sess.; Rogers et al., *Alabama*, 441.

43. Transcript of radio speech by John H. Bankhead II, 3 Nov. 1930, pp. 1–5 (quoted), box 3, folder 10, J. H. Bankhead II Papers, ADAH; Feldman, *From Demagogue to Dixiecrat*, 102.

44. Transcript of radio speech by John H. Bankhead II, 3 Nov. 1930, pp. 3–5 (quoted), box 3, folder 10, J. H. Bankhead II Papers, ADAH.

45. Historian Wayne Flynt astutely viewed the patrician politicos as representatives of the "state's traditional conservative leadership," but they saw themselves as the tribunes of "Southern liberality [and] Southern progress"; see *Alabama Democracy, 1930*, 7, box 3, folder 10, J. H. Bankhead II Papers, ADAH. The Alabama KKK viewed itself, correctly, as conservative; see Rogers et al., *Alabama*, 435–42, and the Alabama KKK Newsletter 7 (Jan. 1929): 3, box 26, folder: Intolerance, Street Papers, ADAH; *NYT*, 27 April 1929, p. 1 (quoted).

46. *BN*, 5 Nov. 1930. See also Rogers et al., *Alabama*, 442.

47. *BN*, 5 Nov. 1930 (both quotations).

48. *BN*, 5 Nov. 1930 (quoted); Rogers et al., *Alabama*, 497; Feldman, *From Demagogue to Dixiecrat*, 99–120.

49. *BN*, 5 Nov. 1930.

50. Ibid. For detailed maps dealing with the 1930 elections, see appendix E in Feldman, "Ku Klux Klan in Alabama."

51. *BN*, 5 Nov. 1930; Harper, "'Cotton Tom' Heflin," 408; "Senator Heflin's Contest," *KM* 7 (April 1931): 26; "Bribery and Vote-Buying Testimony in Heflin-Bankhead Contest," *KM* 8 (Feb. 1932): 26; "Bankhead's Election Called Illegal," *KM* 8 (April 1932): 26.

52. *BAH*, 6 Nov. 1930 (first quotation), *BN*, 6 Nov. 1930 (second quotation); *MA*, 2 Nov. 1930 (third quotation).

53. Wilkinson to Heflin, 17 Oct. 1932, and Oden to Wilkinson, 3 Oct. 1932, both in box 833, folder 84; Wilkinson to Heflin, 20 Sept. 1932, box 833, folder 83; Wilkinson to Heflin, 5 March 1934, box 833, folder 91; Heflin to Bankhead, 7 March 1931, box 832, folder 72; Chilton to Wilkinson, 14 May 1931, and Wilkinson to Hampton, 23 May 1931, both in box 832, folder 74, all in the Heflin Papers, UASC, quoted in Feldman, *From Demagogue to Dixiecrat*, 100 (second and third quotations); *Congressional Record*, Senate, vol. 75, pt. 8, 72d Cong., 1st sess., 26 April 1932, p. 8920 (first quotation); Rogers, *One-Gallused Rebellion;* Hackney, *Populism to Progressivism in Alabama;* Webb, *Two-Party Politics in the One-Party South.*

54. *Congressional Record*, Senate, vol. 75, pt. 8, 72d Cong., 1st sess., 26 April 1932, pp. 8919, 8932, 8944; *In Re the Contest of J. Thomas Heflin v. John H. Bankhead*, brief and argument by Horace C. Wilkinson, 72d Cong., 1st sess., Subcommittee of the Committee on Privileges and Elections (1931), 1–85, box 3, folder 11, and *MA*, clipping, c. 1931 (quoted), box 3, folder 10, both in the J. H. Bankhead II Papers, ADAH, also located in the Bledsoe-Kelly Collection, SU; Tanner, "Wonderful World of Tom Heflin," 172; "Senator Heflin Addresses the Senate," *KM* 8 (June 1932): 23.

55. Wilkinson to Heflin, 15 May 1931, box 832, folder 74; Wilkinson to Heflin, 25 July 1931, box 832, folder 76; and Heflin to Wilkinson, 19 June 1930, box 829, folder 63, Heflin Papers, UASC, quoted in Feldman, *From Demagogue to Dixiecrat,* 100.

56. The "right of freedom of choice was politically murdered . . . in Alabama," Wilkinson wrote in the brief for *In re Heflin v. Bankhead,* pp. 76, 84–85, Bledsoe-Kelly Collection, SU, and in box 3, folder 10, J. H. Bankhead II Papers, ADAH. See Dooley, "United States Senator James Thomas Heflin," 94, 210, 214; *Congressional Record,* Senate, vol. 75, pt. 8, 72d Cong., 1st sess., 26 April 1932, pp. 8939–40; Reports on Conditions of Ballot Boxes, 72d Cong., 1st sess. (Washington, D.C., 1931); and *Hearings Before a Subcommittee of the Committee on Privileges and Elections,* U.S. Senate, 3–7 Dec. 1931, both items in box 3, folder 11, J. H. Bankhead II Papers, ADAH; "Bankhead's Election Called Illegal," *KM* 8 (April 1932): 26; "Senate Votes Heflin Out," *KM* 8 (June 1932): 27; Feldman, *From Demagogue to Dixiecrat* (all quotations). Heflin himself spoke for five hours before the Senate on the matter. Heflin reported having told the Alabama oligarchy, "If I accept your skullduggery, your crookedness, and your corruption, and permit you to defeat [the people's] will and crucify me . . . , I would never have any more respect for myself. So help me God, I will fight it to the death" (8921). Heflin told the Senate, in posing as a representative of the masses, that he was "fighting for the humble factory girl who stands all day at the loom and weaves, who was intimidated by the bosses of the mill to vote for Bankhead . . . , for the boys who wear lamps on their caps and go down in the bowels of the earth to dig coal and iron . . . , for the farmer in the furrowed field, the merchant, the clerk in the store . . . , for the school teachers, who were browbeaten in wholesale fashion, telling them . . . if they did not vote for Bankhead they would lose" their jobs (8925). "I am fighting to smash the worst political machine outside of Tammany . . . , the party machine . . . in Alabama. . . . I will fight on and on and on until . . . we break the jaws of the wicked machine and pluck the spoil from its teeth. Corrupt machine politics shall not control my State. . . . Alabama shall be free; my State will walk again with unfettered step . . . and, by the eternal God, every ballot shall be counted as cast" (8944–45). I quote Heflin from the *Congressional Record* cited above.

57. Tanner, "Wonderful World of Tom Heflin," 173 (quotation of Mecklin), 174 (second quotation).

58. KKK Scrapbooks, no. 257, BPLA; "The Decline and Fall of the Invisible Empire," *BN,* 23 Nov. 1930; Thompson, "Ezra Winter's Murals," 32.

59. *KM* 6 (Jan. 1930): 21; "The Road to Success," *KM* 6 (Feb. 1930): 20; "Cash for the Catholics," *KM* 6 (May 1930): 18.

60. KKK File, reel 31, 1928, TU; *MA,* 1 July 1928; *BAA,* 26 May 1928; "Evangelistic Klankraft in Alabama," *KM* 4 (Feb. 1928): 22–23.

61. KKK File, BCA; *OSD,* 5 Dec. 1929; *BAH,* 9, 19 Feb. 1929. Before beating the mail carrier, his five assailants ordered him to "take off your coat, we are going to whale the tar out of you." Quoted in *BAH,* 9 Feb. 1929.

62. KKK File, reel 36, 1930 (quoted), TU; *PC,* 28 June 1930, p. 1; *Dublin Courier-Herald,* 20 June 1930; *Columbus Enquirer-Sun,* and *TP,* 21 June 1930; and *Meridian Star,* 29 June 1930.

63. KKK File, reel 36, 1930, TU (third quotation); *Indianapolis Recorder,* 28 June 1930 (first quotation); *NYT,* 3 July 1930, p. 6 (second quotation). The Harlem group addressed its comments to you "white crackers . . . and your [Ku] Klux friends," in *NYT,* 3 July 1930, p. 6 (quoted); "Jones Is Menaced by Harlem Negro in Insulting Note," *KM* 6 (Aug. 1930): 4–5.

64. KKK Newsletter 7 (Sept. 1929): n.p. (all quotations except the first), Street Papers, ADAH. This issue of the newsletter also described DePriest's congressional service as "a dan-

gerous gesture in the direction of social equality." See also *PC,* 5 July 1930, pp. 2, 8B (first quotation).

65. KKK File, reel 36, 1930, TU.

66. Pratt to Kimbrough, 23 June 1931, box 20, folder: Administration, Board of Convict, 1931, Miller Papers, ADAH.

67. Minutes of the Anti-Lynching Conference of Southern White Women, 1 Nov. 1930, and "Lynchings and What They Mean," 47, 50, by the Southern Commission on the Study of Lynching, and Ames to Mrs. Graves, 14 Nov. 1930, all in box 207, folders: Administration, Board of Convict, 1930 and 1932, Miller Papers, ADAH.

68. KKK Scrapbooks, no. 257, BPLA; KKK File, reel 36, 1930, TU; *BP,* 15 Sept. 1931; *BPH,* 15 Sept., 19 Nov. 1931; *AN,* 8 Jan. 1930.

69. KKK File, reel 38, 1931, reel 41, 1932, TU; *MA,* 15 Nov. 1931 and 8 Jan. 1932. The latter date contains references to Hugh Locke's membership in the KKK; Snell, "Ku Klux Klan in Jefferson County," 210–11, and "Masked Men in the Magic City," 225.

70. *Alabama Acts,* 5 Feb. 1931, no. 19, pp. 29–30; *BAH,* 23 Feb. 1929.

71. Terry to Miller and Jenkins to Miller, both 23 July 1931, Weller to Miller, 31 July 1931, Wheeler to Miller, 27 July 1931, and *BP,* clipping, 29 July 1931, all in box 210, folder: Birmingham City Commission, Miller Papers, ADAH; Weissinger to author, 6 Sept. 1991, Weissinger Papers, copies in the author's collection; Norrell, "Labor at the Ballot Box," 211; "A Great Klan Victory," *KM* 6 (Jan. 1930): 21. An opponent of the Klan effort to extend city commission terms described Jimmie Jones as "tinged with Republicanism, if not an out and out Republican. [Horace] Wilkinson's history in Alabama is too well-known to mention. [John] Taylor and [W. E.] Dickson are either Republicans or weak-kneed Democrats or Hoovercrats at best. And the political ghost of Tom Heflin hovers about them all." Quoted in Jenkins to Miller, 23 July 1931, box 210, Miller Papers, ADAH.

72. Wilkinson to Heflin, 17 Oct. 1932, box 833, folder 84, Heflin Papers, UASC; Pollard to Miller, 9 Jan. 1932, box 212, folder: Convict Department, James C. Kirby, 1932, Miller Papers, ADAH; Mizell to Feagin, 18 March 1931, State Board of Administration Records, ADAH; KKK File, reel 38, 1931, reel 41, 1932, TU; KKK File, BCA; *JG,* 31 Jan. 1931; *MA,* 8 Jan. 1932; *OSD,* 9 Feb. 1928; *BAH,* 10 Dec. 1935; Rogers et al., *Alabama,* 497; Feldman, *From Demagogue to Dixiecrat,* 101–2, 105–6 (second quotation); Hollis, "Hall Family and Twentieth-Century Journalism in Alabama," 126 (first quotation); Dobbins, "Alabama's Governors and Editors," 136–37.

73. Feldman, "Ku Klux Klan in America," 360 (quoted).

74. *BP,* clipping, 29 July 1931 (quoted), in box 210, folder: Birmingham City Commission, Miller Papers, ADAH.

75. KKK File, BCA; *OSD,* 6 Sept. 1928 (first quotation), 15 Aug. 1929 (second quotation), also 9 Feb., 1 March 1928, and 29 Aug. 1929; KKK File, reel 31, 1928, reel 34, 1929, reel 38, 1931, TU; *Coosa River News,* in *MA,* 30 Jan. 1928; *MA,* 21 June, 13 July, 27 Nov. 1928, 17 April 1929, and 8 April 1931; *BAH,* 2, 5–8 Sept. 1928, 26 March, 28 June, 27 Aug., 8–10 Oct. 1929; *BN,* 5–8 Sept. 1928; *PC,* 22 Sept. 1928, p. 8; Snell, "Ku Klux Klan in Jefferson County," 205–9.

76. KKK File, reel 36, 1930, reel 31, 1928, TU; KKK Scrapbooks, no. 257, BPLA; *MA,* 30 Jan. 1928, 2 March, 22 June 1930; *BN,* 5, 23 Nov. 1930; *BAH,* 10 May 1928; and "Evangelistic Klankraft in Alabama," *KM,* 22–23; Rogers et al., *Alabama,* 442.

77. On the patrician claim to represent liberalism, see *BAH,* 23 Jan., 10 May 1928; Alabama KKK Newsletter 6 (June 1928): 1, 3, Street Papers, ADAH; and the *BN,* 19 Dec. 1971,

quoted in Elovitz, *Century of Jewish Life in Dixie,* 87. On the conservatism and antifederalism of the patricians, see M. B. Owen to J. H. Bankhead II, 20, 25 May 1938, box 1, folder 8, J. H. Bankhead II Papers, ADAH; *Alabama (CIO) News Digest,* 25 Feb. 1943; *MA,* clipping, n.d., box 3, folder 10, J. H. Bankhead II Papers, ADAH; KKK File, reel 31, 1928, reel 36, 1930, TU; *BAA,* 26 May 1928; *MA,* 8 May 1928, 22 June 1930 (first and second quotations); *BN,* 9 May 1928; *BAH,* 9–10 May 1928; *DE,* 29 April 1931, quoted in Hollis, "The Hall Family and Twentieth-Century Journalism in Alabama," 125–26 (third quotation), also pp. 120–24, 127–31; *NYT,* 30 Jan. 1931, p. 18, and 28 May 1931, p. 26, quoted in Harper, "'Cotton Tom' Heflin," 409; *Alabama (CIO) News Digest,* 25 Feb. 1943, quoted in Feldman, *From Demagogue to Dixiecrat,* 108 (fourth quotation).

78. KKK File, reel 34, 1929, reel 38, 1931, TU; *MA,* 10 Aug. 1929; *BAH,* 21 Nov. 1928; *SLA,* 1 May 1931; *East Tennessee News,* 30 April 1931; Rice, *Ku Klux Klan in American Politics,* 91.

79. Ala. KKK Newsletter 7 (Sept. 1929): n.p. (all quotations), Street Papers, ADAH. The June 1928 issue of the KKK newsletter, p. 1, condemned the "spasmodic outbursts" of "this degenerate . . . half breed publisher."

80. Ala. KKK Newsletter 7 (Sept. 1928): n.p. (quoted), Street Papers, ADAH.

81. Ibid.; KKK File, reel 41, 1932, TU; *MA,* 9 Feb. 1932; *PC,* 12 July 1930, p. 2; Ala. KKK Newsletter 7 (Sept. 1929), Street Papers, ADAH.

82. Alabama KKK Newsletter 7 (Sept. 1929), Street Papers, ADAH.

11. 1930S CAUSES CÉLÈBRES: SCOTTSBORO AND HUGO BLACK

1. Flynt, *Poor but Proud,* 91, 281–83, 333, and "New Deal and Southern Labor," 63–96; Agee and Evans, *Let Us Now Praise Famous Men;* Mertz, *New Deal Policy and Southern Rural Poverty;* Smith, *The New Deal in the Urban South.*

2. Gould Beech, Interview, p. 4, SHC; Lipset and Raab, *Politics of Unreason,* 276.

3. Leighton, "Birmingham, Alabama," 239, quoted in Ingalls, "Antiradical Violence in Birmingham," 522.

4. Stroudsburg, Pa., to Graves, 15 July 1936, box SG 12187, folder: Communism, Peters to Graves, 17 Aug. 1935, box SG 12165, drawer 103, folder: Communism, 1935, no. 2, and Sanders to Graves, 2 Dec. 1936, Golat to Graves, 24 Nov. 1936, King to Graves, 15 Oct. 1936, and DeMohai to Graves, 27 Nov. 1936, all in box SG 12176, folder: Joseph Gelders, David Bibb Graves, Alabama Governors Papers, ADAH; Statement by Joseph Gelders to the Police," 24 Sept. 1936, box 22, folder H18, reel 20, micro 981, ILD Fund Papers, SC; Isserman to Baldwin, 26 Sept. 1936, and Hays to Graves, 23 Sept. 1936, both in ACLU Records, PU; KKK File, reel 52, 1936, TU; *BAH,* 26 Sept. 1936; *MA,* 25–27 Sept. and 1 Dec. 1936; *BP,* 26 Sept., 20 Oct. 1936; *DW,* 10 Oct. 1936; *NYT,* 26 Sept. 1936.

5. Pruitt to Grant, 19 June 1933, Hugh Gladney Grant Papers, DUKE; KKK File, reel 67, 1940, TU; *KM* 7 (Nov. 1931): 39; 7 (Dec. 1931): 46–47; "Alabama Makes Its Confession of Faith," *KM* 8 (Feb. 1932): 12; 8 (March 1932): 38; 8 (April 1932): 39; 8 (May 1932): 34; 8 (June 1932): 35; 8 (July 1932): 39; 8 (Sept. 1932): 39; 9 (Aug. 1933): 48; 9 (Sept. 1933): 48; 10 (March 1934): 33–34; Snell, "Masked Men in the Magic City," 226; *BN,* 10 Feb. 1937, 7, 14 April 1940.

6. *MCA,* 26 June 1934 (quoted); *Baltimore Evening Sun,* 22 June 1934; *BN,* 19 Dec. 1971, in Elovitz, *Century of Jewish Life in Dixie,* 323 n. 17; KKK File, reel 46, 1934, TU. During the 1930s Dr. E. P. Pruitt, a post–World War II Klan leader in Alabama, was an active member of Robert E. Lee Klan No. 1. See Pruitt to Grant, 19 June 1933, Hugh Gladney Grant Papers, DUKE.

7. Charles N. Feidelson, "Alabama's Dilemma," 25 Aug. 1934, pt. 6, reel 6, NAACP Papers, MADD and LC; Osofsky, *Burden of Race,* 359–64, 369–86. For the most complete account of Scottsboro, see Carter, *Scottsboro.*

8. *NYT,* 8 Nov. 1932, p. 13; *DW,* 28 Feb., 2 March 1935; *SW,* 13 June 1931, Feb. 1936; Kelley, *Hammer and Hoe.*

9. Gelders to Baldwin, 6 Sept. 1936, Delegation of NCDPP, "Report on Georgia-Alabama," ACLU Records, 19 July 1934 (quoted), PU; NAACP Papers, pt. 10, reel 9, and pt. 6, reels 4, 21, LC; *NYT,* 8 Nov. 1932, pp. 11–12; *SW,* 13 June 1931; "Communists to Defend Scottsville [*sic*] Rapists," *KM* 9 (Feb. 1933): 21.

10. *Powell et al. v. Alabama,* 224 Ala. 540 (1931), 141 So. 201 (1931), 286 U.S. 540 (1931); *Patterson v. Alabama,* 224 Ala. 531 (1931), 141 So. 195 (1931), 286 U.S. 540 (1931); *Weems v. Alabama,* 224 Ala. 524 (1931), 141 So. 215 (1931), 286 U.S. 540 (1931); *Norris v. Alabama,* 229 Ala. 226 (1931), 156 So. 556 (1931), 293 U.S. 552 (1935); *Patterson v. Alabama,* 229 Ala. 270 (1935), 156 So. 567 (1935), 293 U.S. 554 (1935), 294 U.S. 600 (1935). The U.S. Supreme Court overturned the death sentences of seven of the boys because of the presence of a Klan mob during the proceedings and the state's failure to try to procure a racially unbiased jury.

11. Potter, *Impending Crisis;* Cash, *Mind of the South;* Silver, *Mississippi.* James Chappell wrote privately of the "popular intellectual defense mechanisms they . . . , the people who vote and pay taxes in Alabama . . . , automatically set up in such cases" of outside attack, even if the rest of the civilized world disagreed with them. Quoted in Chappell to Chalmers, 31 Dec. 1938, cc. to Edmonds, Johnston, Comer, and Hall, box 67, folder 1, Grover C. Hall, Sr., Papers, ADAH.

12. NAACP Papers, pt. 6, reels 6, 7, LC and MADD,; KKK File, reel 67, 1940, TU; the circular by Angelo Herndon, *The Scottsboro Boys: Four Freed! Five to Go!* (hereafter cited as "Herndon Circular"), c. 1931, p. 9 (first quotation), box 5, folder 30, Alabama Pamphlet Collection, ADAH; *NYT,* 8 April 1933 (second quotation); *TN,* 5 Aug. 1940. One mob member screamed in Brodsky's face: "We're just laying for you sonofabitch Reds. Wait till we get you outside." Quoted in *SW,* 13 June 1931.

13. *NYT,* 8 April 1933, p. 30.

14. Chamblee to Miller, 18 Nov. 1933 (quoted), Miller to Chamblee, 20 Nov. 1933, and Callahan to Miller, 14 Nov. 1933, box 223, folder: Law Enforcement, Scottsboro Cases, Benjamin Meek Miller, Alabama Governors Papers, ADAH; Herndon Circular, box 5, folder 30, Alabama Pamphlets Collection, ADAH; *SW,* 25 March 1934, Feb. 1936.

15. Clyde L. Johnson, Interview, 4 April 1976, p. 30, SLA; KKK File, reel 44, 1933, TU; *CD,* 14 Jan. 1933; *NYT,* 8 Nov. 1932, p. 13 (quoted); Snell, "Masked Men in the Magic City," 226.

16. *SW,* 25 April, 1 Aug. 1931, 25 March 1934, Feb. 1936; *PC,* 14 Aug. 1937.

17. Chalmers to Graves, 8 Dec. 1936 (quoted), box 67, folder 1, Grover C. Hall, Sr., Papers, ADAH.

18. Ward et al. to Roosevelt, 22 Nov. 1933, Leibowitz et al. to Roosevelt, 19 Nov. 1933, White to Miller, 14 Nov. 1933; all in box 223, folder: Law Enforcement, Scottsboro Cases, Miller Papers, ADAH; *NYT,* 8 Nov. 1932, p. 11.

19. Costigan-Wagner Federal Anti-Lynching Bill, c. 1935, pt. 7, ser. B, reels 7–11, Gavagan Federal Anti-Lynching Bill, 1936–39, pt. 7, ser. B, reels 17–20, NAACP Papers, MADD and LC; Sitkoff, *New Deal for Blacks,* 291 (quoted), also 272–90, 292–97.

20. *SW,* 18 July 1931. Over 6,000 people attended biracial rallies in Detroit and Philadelphia in 1931, another 500 showed up in Minneapolis, and actor James Cagney presided over a large San Francisco meeting in 1934. At a Brooklyn rally, the sister of one defendant praised

Communists as "the best people with white skins and straight hair to fight side by side with." Quoted in *PC,* 14 Aug. 1937. A number of other rallies occurred in Europe.

21. Chappell to Chalmers, 31 Dec. 1938, Hall to Chappell, 15 Nov. 1938, box 67, folder 1, Grover C. Hall, Sr., Papers, ADAH; Underwood to Edmonds, 28 Oct. 1927, box 41, folder 3, and Underwood to Eaton, 29 Sept. 1927, box 41, folder 4, Oscar W. Underwood Papers, ADAH. Edmonds was the only exception to the general rule of the committee's conservative orientation.

22. *Jackson County Sentinel,* 16 April 1931, and Frank L. Owsley, Sr., "Scottsboro," 267–68, both quoted in Carter, *Scottsboro,* 109–10 (second and third quotations), 119–21 (first and fourth quotations).

23. Hall to Graves, 7 July 1938, box 67, folder 1, Grover C. Hall, Sr., Papers, ADAH. Hall specifically mentioned "outside interferences" as a danger in his 7 July 1938 letter. Hall was a complex man who disagreed strenuously with Bibb Graves on political and economic matters yet by the late 1930s considered him a personal friend. In Hall to Graves, 14 Nov. 1938, box 67, folder 1, Hall wrote: "What I mean to say is that I am in on all the harassment that has made life interesting to you since last I saw you. I am just sorry that we did not think to ask Hitler, Mussolini, Stalin and even Bill Gunter to call you and give you hell. All because I have a pocketful of bibbies and all because I like you as much as any politician I ever knew, in spite of the fact that you require an extraordinarily larger operating capital for your wonders to perform. I think you are a honey, and it affords me special delight to cooperate with others in bedeviling you. I don't give a damn if you do get mad with me—you can't stay mad. You can't even hate your enemies. As a man of sternness and passion you are a phoney."

24. All quotations come from *MA,* editorials by Hall, 10 April 1930, 23 Aug., 29 Nov., and 17 Dec. 1933, 12, 15, 20, 21 May, 18, 19 Aug. 1934, 6, 9 April 1935. The editorials also appear in Grover C. Hall, Sr., Scrapbooks, ADAH; Hall to Chappell, 15 Nov. 1938, Hall to Graves, 14 Nov. 1938 (mentions "morons" and "fool niggers"), Hall to Chappell, 9 Dec. 1938, all in box 67, folder 1, Grover C. Hall, Sr., Papers, ADAH; Dixon to Hall, Jr., 2 Aug. 1944, box 1, folder 1, Berman to Hall, Jr., 20 June 1956, Hall, Jr., to Berman, 28 June 1956, and Hall, Jr., to Childers, 6 March 1957, all in box 1, folder 2, Grover C. Hall, Jr., Papers, ADAH; KKK File, reel 73, 1941, TU; *SW,* July 1937; *PC,* 18 Jan. 1941; *MA,* 28 May 1938; Carter, *Scottsboro,* 117–18; Hollis, "Hall Family and Twentieth-Century Journalism in Alabama," 132–33.

25. All quotations come from *MA,* editorials by Hall, 10 April 1930, 23 Aug., 29 Nov., and 17 Dec. 1933, 12, 15, 20, 21 May, 18, 19 Aug. 1934, 6, 9 April 1935. Hall to Graves, 7 July 1938, box 67, folder 1, Grover C. Hall, Sr., Papers, ADAH. Hall was not always pragmatic on issues of prejudice, though. After a 1938 editorial calling for religious toleration for Alabama's Jews, Hall confided to James Chappell that "for once in my life I have the feeling that I have done some good. . . . You would be amazed at the response I had even from simple people— Gentiles! . . . I mean former Ku Kluxers." Quoted in Hall to Chappell, 9 Dec. 1938, box 67, folder 1, Grover C. Hall, Sr., Papers, ADAH.

26. Chappell to Chalmers, cc. Edmonds, Johnston, Comer, and Hall, 31 Dec. 1938 (quoted), box 67, folder 1, Grover C. Hall, Sr., Papers, ADAH.

27. Johnston to Hall, 17 Nov. 1938, Chappell to Hall, 18 Nov. 1938, box 67, folder 1, Grover C. Hall, Sr., Papers, ADAH.

28. The block quotation comes from Hall to Graves, 14 Nov. 1938, and Hall to Chappell, 15 Nov. 1938, box 67, folder 1, Grover C. Hall, Sr., Papers, ADAH; Carter, *Scottsboro,* 379–83; Hollis, "Hall Family and Twentieth-Century Journalism in Alabama," 132.

29. KKK File, reel 44, 1933, TU; *MA,* 12 May 1933 (quoted).

30. KKK File, reel 67, 1940, TU; Herndon Circular, 14 (second quotation), box 5, folder

30, Alabama Pamphlets Collection, ADAH. On p. 14 Herndon lamented: "When servile crea-tures of that type are at the head of learning [in Alabama] is it any wonder that the road of Negro liberation is beset with damnable obstacles?" See also Carter, *Scottsboro*, 153 (first quo-tation), 154; *TN*, 5 Aug. 1940.

31. Albert Lee Smith Affidavit, 27 Sept. 1937, Born to Durr, 21 May 1938, Durr to Black, 26 May 1938, and Durr to Born, 27 May 1938, all in box 1, folder 3, Clifford J. Durr Papers, ADAH; Arthur M. Hyde Papers, Western Historical Manuscript Collection, State Histori-cal Society of Missouri, Manuscripts, Ellis Library, University of Missouri, UMO; Chalmers, *Hooded Americanism*, 314–16; Berman, "Hugo L. Black," 103–16.

32. Black to Graves and Graves to Black, both 19 Aug. 1937, *MA*, clipping, 18 Aug. 1937, all in box SG 12176, folder: Hugo Black, U.S. Supreme Court, Graves Papers, ADAH; Hamilton, "Hugo Black and the K.K.K.," 108.

33. Green to Durr, 30 Sept. 1937, box 1, folder 3, Clifford J. Durr Papers, ADAH. *NYT*, 13–15 Sept. 1937, p. 1; KKK File, reel 58, 1938, TU; *MA*, 17 May 1938; "BLACK: A Klan Member on the Supreme Court? New Evidence Comes to Light," *Newsweek* 10 (20 Sept. 1937): 9; Leuchtenburg, "Klansman Joins the Court," 12–13 (quoted).

34. Hugh Gladney Grant Diary, 7 March 1934, Grant Papers, DUKE, KKK File, reel 30, 1938, TU. In the *MA*, 17 May 1938, Paul Y. Anderson of the *St. Louis Star Times*, a former Pulitzer Prize recipient, wryly commented that the 1938 Pulitzer Prize had just been awarded "for a story that was printed in the Montgomery Advertiser in 1926."

35. "BLACK: A Klan Member . . . ," 10; Leuchtenburg, "Klansman Joins the Court," 16, 18 (quoted).

36. "Talent Rewarded: Mr. Justice Black," *Catholic World* 146 (Nov. 1937): 129–34 (sixth and ninth quotations); "No Place for Fanatics," *Collier's* 100 (23 Oct. 1937): 74 (fourth, fifth, and eighth quotations); "Judiciary: Nominee Number 93," *Time* 30 (23 Aug. 1937): 13–14; Leuchtenburg, "Klansman Joins the Court," 11 (first quotation), 16 (seventh quotation), 19; Hamilton, "Hugo Black and the K.K.K.," 109, 111 (first, second, and third quotations).

37. "Klansman Black," *Commonweal* 26 (24 Sept. 1937): 483–84 (first and second quota-tions); *NYHT*, 2 Oct. 1937, p. 14 (third quotation); *Boston Post*, 2 Oct. 1937 (fifth quotation); *NYP* quoted in Hamilton, "Hugo Black and the K.K.K.," 111 (fourth quotation).

38. *FC*, July 1941, p. 4; *NYT*, 14 Sept. 1937, pp. 1, 18; "BLACK: A Klan Member . . . ," 10 (quoted); Hamilton, "Hugo Black and the K.K.K.," 108; Chalmers, *Hooded Americanism*, 316.

39. Leuchtenburg, "Klansman Joins the Court," 8 (second quotation), 11 (third quota-tion); Hamilton, "Hugo Black and the K.K.K.", 64 (first quotation).

40. Durr, "Hugo L. Black," 11; Hamilton, "Hugo Black and the K.K.K.," 110–11 (first and second quotations); *Washington Evening Star*, 21 Sept. 1937, quoted in Leuchtenburg, "Klans-man Joins the Court," 27–28 (second quotation). Rabbi Herbert S. Goldstein of Yeshiva Col-lege said, "As a citizen I do not seek the 'pound of flesh' and as a Jew, I do not seek retaliation." The statement, which appeared in *NYT*, 3 Oct. 1937, is quoted in Leuchtenburg, "Klansman Joins the Court," 20.

41. "New FCC Commissioner Durr Receives Oath of Office from U.S. Supreme Court Justice Black . . . ," box 1, folder 4, and Dixon to Clifford and Virginia Durr, 26 June 1934, box 1, folder 3, both in the C. J. Durr Papers, ADAH; Durr, "Hugo L. Black," 7 (first quota-tion); Virginia F. Durr, Interview, p. 7 (second quotation), CU; Newman, *Hugo Black*. See also Ball, *Hugo L. Black*. Despite the recent proliferation of work on Black's life and career, the most definitive work is still that of Virginia Van der Veer Hamilton. The comments of the Durrs revealed the power of Alabama's and the South's "Reconstruction Syndrome." Clifford did not believe that Black had joined the KKK as an act of political expedience, nor did he

attribute its popularity to any connection with a Scottish clan. The "motivation for the Klan re-emergence [in the 1920s] came . . . from the Klan of reconstruction—looked back up on by Southerners as saviours from carpet-baggers and scalawags and the blacks who attained political power." Virginia Durr concurred. She recalled that her maternal grandfather had been a Confederate war comrade of General Nathan Bedford Forrest and, after the war, the founder of a local klavern. She also remembered her uncle talking about "attacking negroes and Yankees with baseball bats" at the polls during Reconstruction." Both Durrs are quoted in Virginia F. Durr, Interview, p. 7, CU.

42. Black to Hall, Jr., 30 Dec. 1944, Hill to Hall, Jr., 9 Jan. 1945, box 1, folder 1, Hall, Jr., Papers, ADAH; Calloway to Editor, *American Mercury*, in "Notes on a Kleagle," *American Mercury* 43 (19 Feb. 1938): 248–49. In "BLACK: A Klan Member . . . ," 10, Bankhead called the issue the "rattling of old bones that have long been dead and dry." See also Durr, "Hugo L. Black," 10, 16; *MA*, 17 May 1938 (quoted); *BAH*, 23 Nov. 1938; KKK File, reel 58, 1938, TU; Matthews, "Clarence Cason Among the Southern Liberals," 4. One Alabama Republican who had been attacked by the Klan insisted that Black was not a "true believer."

43. Durr, "Hugo L. Black," 1, 7, 10–16 (Durr article also in the Alabama Pamphlets Collection, Persons Vertical File, box 1, folder 12, ADAH).

44. Leuchtenburg, "Klansman Joins the Court," 19.

45. *NYT*, 2 Oct. 1937, p. 3; Leuchtenburg, "Klansman Joins the Court," 19.

46. Hamilton, "Hugo Black and the K.K.K.," 111.

47. Ibid., 111 (quoted); Leuchtenburg, "Klansman Joins the Court," 20. Hugo Black was Machiavellian as well. In late 1946, after "Big Jim" Folsom's election as Alabama governor, Black wrote with advice that embodied his sense of a fundamental difference between public action and private behavior: "If flattery fails to swerve you from your course, and if caution enables you to escape traps and pitfalls, your courage will be tested by intimidation, abuse, and fusillades of public criticism. Much of this will come from good people who have been misled. All of these things you can overcome if you get wisdom and understanding. They teach a man to put the public good above personal glory." Quotation from *MR*, n.d. (January 1995), clipping, folder: Alabama Authors, E-H, AUSC.

48. Durr, "Hugo L. Black," 1, 7, 10–16; Leuchtenburg, "Klansman Joins the Court," 21.

49. *MR*, n.d. (Jan. 1995), clipping, folder: Alabama Authors, E-H, AUSC; Leuchtenburg, "Klansman Joins the Court," 26.

50. Ashby, *Frank Porter Graham*, 155, 163; Grundy, *You Always Think of Home*, 149; Leuchtenburg, "Klansman Joins the Court," 22–24 (all quotations). The first hint that Black would eventually become the white South's pariah on racial matters came in the 1940 case *Chambers v. Florida*. Black wrote the Court's unanimous opinion that overturned the conviction of four blacks whose confessions had been coerced by Florida authorities. Later that year, in *Smith v. Texas*, Black spoke for a united Court in setting aside a black man's rape conviction because Texas systematically excluded African Americans from petit and grand juries. See *Chambers v. Florida*, 309 U.S. 227 (1940), and *Smith v. Texas*, 311 U.S. 128 (1940). Also see *ADW*, 5 March 1941, and KKK File, reel 73, 1941, TU.

51. Leuchtenburg, "Klansman Joins the Court," 22–23 (quoted).

52. *FC*, July 1941, p. 4 (quoted).

12. THE THREAT OF URBAN RADICALISM

1. Ingalls, "Antiradical Violence in Birmingham," 521–22; Kelley, "New War in Dixie," 372, 377, 382–83.

2. Kelley, "New War in Dixie," 368.

3. Ibid., 373–74; Ingalls, "Antiradical Violence in Birmingham," 522–23.

4. Leighton, "Birmingham, Alabama," 239; Ingalls, "Antiradical Violence in Birmingham," 522–23; Kelley, "New War in Dixie," 367.

5. Testimony of [Klansman] John G. Murphy, 199, and testimony of [State Detective] Achmed H. Mundo, 185, 187, in United States, House, 71st Cong., 2d sess., Committee on Rules; Subcommittee to Investigate Communist Activities, *Investigation of Communist Propaganda,* 14 Nov. 1930, pt. 6, vol. 1, hereafter cited as *Fish Committee Hearings,* ISU; *SW,* 16 Aug. 1930; *KM* 11 (Dec. 1934): 16, quoted in Ingalls, "Antiradical Violence in Birmingham," 522; Painter, *Narrative of Hosea Hudson;* Kelley, "New War in Dixie," 370, 384.

6. Testimony of [Klansman] John G. Murphy, 199, and testimony of [State Detective] Achmed H. Mundo, 185, 187, in United States, House, 71st Cong., 2d sess., Committee on Rules; Subcommittee to Investigate Communist Activities, *Investigation of Communist Propaganda,* 14 Nov. 1930, pt. 6, vol. 1, *Fish Committee Hearings,* ISU; *SW,* 16 Aug. 1930; *KM* 11 (Dec. 1934): 16, quoted in Ingalls, "Antiradical Violence in Birmingham," 522 (from which I quote).

7. Feldman, *From Demagogue to Dixiecrat,* 104.

8. *SW,* 29 Nov. 1930 (quoted), 26 Sept., 31 Jan., 10 Oct. 1931; Evans, "Communism Rampant," 1, and *KM* 9 (May 1933): 26; "Report of R. F. Hall," district secretary for District 17, CPUSA, Aug. 1937, in *SW,* Sept. 1937, p. 5; Colman to Editor, *Nation,* 30 May 1934, in "The Klan Revives," *Nation* 139 (4 July 1934): 20.

9. Brown to Grant, 30 Nov. 1932, Hugh Gladney Grant Papers, DUKE; Ingalls, "Antilabor Vigilantes in the South," 72–78, and "Antiradical Violence in Birmingham," 521 (quoted), 524.

10. KKK File, reel 44, 1933, TU; *BAA,* 20 May 1933; *SW,* 16 Aug., 1 Nov. 1930; Kelley, *Hammer and Hoe,* 29–32, 92, 141; "Klansmen Help in Investigating Red Activities," *KM* 7 (Jan. 1931): 44; testimony of Lester N. Shannon, 14 Nov. 1930, pt. 6, vol. 1, p. 183, *Fish Committee Hearings,* ISU.

11. Testimony of Murphy, 193 and 199 (fourth quotation), [Police Chief] Fred H. McDuff, 93, 99, 101, 161, 171, 172, and Mundo, 186–87, all on 14 Nov. 1930, pt. 6, vol. 1, *Fish Committee Hearings,* ISU; "Housing Studies: Alabama, 1936," pt. 5, reel 1, and pt. 4, reel 3, NAACP Papers, MADD and LC; "Communism and the Negro," *KM* 8 (Sept. 1932): supp. 5, 23 (second quotation), and "Communists Stirring Southern Negroes," *KM* 9 (Oct. 1933): 19–20 (third quotation), and "The Meeting That Was To Be Just Wasn't," *KM* 10 (Jan. 1934): 29, and "Communists Name Negro for Vice-President," *KM* 8 (July 1932): 26; KKK File, reel 67, 1940, TU; *PC,* 21 Dec. 1940 (first quotation); and *BN,* 23 May, 28 June 1930; *SW,* 16 Aug., 1 Nov. 1930. Murphy also emphasized that the prospect of social equality was "particularly dangerous" in the South. Quoted in "Klansmen Help in Investigating Red Activities," *KM* 7 (Jan. 1931): 44. This was a sentiment echoed by "everyone who testified at the Birmingham hearing" of the Fish Committee, according to Kelley, *Hammer and Hoe,* 29.

12. Testimony of McDuff, 159–61, 14 Nov. 1930, pt. 6, vol. 1, *Fish Committee Hearings,* ISU; *BN,* 28 June 1930; *DW,* 1 July 1930; "Communism and the Negro," *KM* 10 (July 1934): 26; James Marion "Jimmie" Jones Papers, ADAH and BPLA.

13. *Peterson v. Alabama,* 227 Ala. 361 (1931), 150 So. 156 (1931), and 291 U.S. 661 (1934); "Reds Accused as Murder Inciters," *KM* 7 (Sept. 1931): 27; *SW,* 15, 29 Aug., 12 Sept. 1931; *BN,* 7–10 Aug. 1931; *BR,* 15 Aug. 1931; *BAH,* 7 Aug. 1931; *SW,* 12 July 1933; Kelley, *Hammer and Hoe,* 84.

14. Testimony of Murphy, 195–200 (also contains abundant references to "Russian Jews" as leaders of the Communist movement in Birmingham), and McDuff, 93, 94, 101, 14 Nov.

1930, pt. 6, vol. 1, *Fish Committee Hearings,* ISU; Kelley, *Hammer and Hoe,* 87–88 (second quotation); "Klansmen Help in Investigating Red Activities," *KM* 7 (Jan. 1931): 44 (first quotation); "Jewish Pictures Threaten Youth: Filthy Shows Are Propaganda for Communism," *KM* 9 (Sept. 1933): 10–11 (third quotation).

15. KKK File, reel 46, 1934, TU; *DW,* 5 Dec. 1934; *SW,* 6 Sept., 6 Dec. 1930, 17 Jan., 28 March, 25 April, 25 July, 1, 15, 29 Aug., 5, 12 Sept. 1931, 10 June 1933, 20 Jan., 10 Feb., 25 March, July 1934, and April 1937, p. 2.

16. *SW,* 16 Aug., 6 Sept., 11 Oct., 1, 22 Nov., 13, 20, 27 Dec. 1930. A young black sign painter reported having been told repeatedly "Go away, nigger!" while searching for work in Birmingham. Quoted in *SW,* 31 Jan. 1931.

17. Owen, "Night Ride in Birmingham," 67; *SW,* 10 Feb. 1934; Kelley, *Hammer and Hoe,* 28, 61; Wade, *Fiery Cross,* 260 (quoted); Painter, *Narrative of Hosea Hudson,* 334.

18. NAACP Papers, pt. 10, reel 13, LC; testimony of Murphy, 193–200, and McDuff, 92–93, 158, 175–76, 14 Nov. 1930, pt. 6, vol. 1, *Fish Committee Hearings,* ISU; *DW,* 2 April 1930, 3 July 1935; *SW,* 16 Aug., 6 Sept., 1 Nov. 1930, 10, 17 Jan., 26 Sept., and 3 Oct. 1931, 10 Feb., and July, Sept., and Dec. 1934, and Feb., March-April 1936; *BAH,* 30 March 1930; Johnson to All Party Members, 5 July 1930, McDuff Exhibit 2D, p. 150, 14 Nov. 1930, pt. 6, vol. 1, *Fish Committee Hearings,* ISU; Colman to Editor, *Nation,* 30 May 1934 in "The Klan Revives," 20; Ingalls, "Antiradical Violence in Birmingham," 524 (quoted), also 521; Painter, *Narrative of Hosea Hudson,* 66; Brown, *Max Heldman's Birmingham,* 38–39; Mitchell, "Birmingham," 100.

19. Gelders to Baldwin, 14 Aug. 1936, ACLU Records, PU; Blaine Owen Affidavit, 25 Feb. 1937, pt. 15C, p. 6324, United States, Senate, Committee on Education and Labor, 75th Cong., 2d sess., *Violation of Free Speech and Rights of Labor, Hearings Before Subcommittee,* MADD. Parts 3 and 8 took place in 75th Cong., 1st sess., hereafter referred to as *LaFollette Committee Hearings;* Wood to Graves, 21 May 1935, box SG 12165, folder: Communism, drawer 3, no. 1, Graves Papers, ADAH; *SW,* June 1935; *DW,* 3 July 1935; *KM* 8 (April 1932): 39, and 8 (Sept. 1932): 39, and 8 (Oct. 1932): 38, and "A Resolution of Alabama Klansmen," *KM* 9 (Sept. 1933): 4, and 9 (Aug. 1933): 48, and "Action Started by Alabama Klansmen," *KM* 10 (Nov. 1934): 32, and "Birmingham Leads the Way," *KM* 10 (Dec. 1934): 16, and "I.L.D. Beguiles Labor," *KM* 10 (Dec. 1934): 31; Albert W. Dilling, "Red Revolution," *KM* 11 (Feb. 1935): 33; Owen, "Night Ride in Birmingham," 65–67 (quoted); Ingalls, "Antiradical Violence in Birmingham," 525.

20. Huntsville Province No. 8 adopted a formal resolution against the Communist Party's "overt acts of violence, destruction, murder . . . , rape . . . , [rejection of the] worship of God . . . , [and] advoca[cy] of the social and political equality of all races." Quoted in "A Resolution of Alabama Klansmen," *KM* 10 (No. 1934): 32, and "Birmingham Leads the Way," *KM* 10 (Dec. 1934): 16, and "I.L.D. Beguiles Labor," *KM* 10 (Dec. 1934): 31; Albert W. Dilling, "Red Revolution," *KM* 11 (Feb. 1935): 33; Emily Mabel Owen and Jesse Green Owen Affidavits, 28 Dec. 1936, pt. 3, pp. 962–64, Israel Berlin Affidavit, 9 Jan. 1937, pt. 15C, pp. 6315–17, *LaFollette Committee Hearings,* MADD. Section 4092 of the Birmingham Criminal Code allowed Detective J. T. Moser's "Red Squad" to hold suspects for seventy-two hours without a warrant. See Kelley, *Hammer and Hoe,* 72. For a sample of KKK bragging about cooperation with the police against radicalism, see *KM* 7 (Nov. 1931): 39, 8 (April 1932): 39, (Sept. 1932): 39, and (Oct. 1932): 38.

21. Brown to Grant, KKK Flyer, 30 Nov. 1932, Grant Papers, DUKE; *PC,* 12 July 1930.

22. *SW,* 25 April 1931.

23. Helen Long Affidavit, 30 Dec. 1936, pt. 3, pp. 967–69, Joseph Gelders testimony, pt. 3, 775, Jane Speed, Kenneth Bridenthal, and Harriet Flood Affidavits, 12 Jan. 1937, pt. 3, pp. 961,

970–73, Belle W. Barton Affidavit, 7 Dec. 1936, pt. 3, pp. 973–76, *LaFollette Committee Hearings,* MADD; Kelley, *Hammer and Hoe,* 32 (first quotation), 33 (second quotation), also 30–31, 72–74, 85–86, 101, 121–23.

24. Kelley, *Hammer and Hoe,* 123 (quoted), also 73–74, 121.

25. Emily Mabel Owen and Jesse Green Owen Affidavits, 28 Dec. 1936, pt. 3, pp. 962–64, Israel Berlin Affidavit, 9 Jan. 1937, pt. 15C, pp. 6315–17, *LaFollette Committee Hearings,* MADD; Jones Papers, ADAH and BPLA; Rosenbaum and Sederberg, "Vigilantism," 3–6.

26. Bruce Crawford, NCDPP secretary, clipping, box SG 12165, folder: Communism, drawer 3, number 1, Graves Papers, ADAH; *DW,* 13 Feb. 1935; *SW,* July and Nov. 1934; "Birmingham Leads the Way," 28.

27. In *SW,* 29 Nov. 1930, Jimmie Jones said that there "is no necessity for this type of charity." Bread lines are "depressing, conspicuous, and degrading." See also "Birmingham Leads the Way," 28; LaMonte, *Politics and Welfare in Birmingham,* 92.

28. *Barton v. City of Birmingham,* 234 Ala. 20 (1937), 173 So. 621 (1937); Delegation of the NCDPP, "Report on Georgia-Alabama," 19 July 1934, p. 9, ACLU Records, PU, reported that John Herbert Lawson had been arrested three times for calling Abernethy's court a "Jim Crow Court" and a "Kangaroo court" in the *SW,* 18 May 1934; KKK File, reel 46, 1934, TU. See also *MA,* 8 July 1934; "KKK Threatens to Lynch Angelo Herndon," 27 Oct. 1930, pt. 10, reel 9, NAACP Papers, MADD and LC; *DW,* 5 Dec. 1934; *SW,* Dec. 1936; testimony of Murphy, 196, and McDuff, 99, 156, 14 Nov. 1930, pt. 6, vol. 1, *Fish Committee Hearings,* ISU; Cook, *The Segregationists;* Martin, *Angelo Herndon Case and Southern Justice.*

29. *Alabama Acts,* Act No. 161, 31 July 1935, pp. 203–4, Act No. 330, 27 Aug. 1935, p. 756; no. 2 Oversized Scrapbook, Grover C. Hall, Sr., Scrapbooks, ADAH; "Front-Page Revolution," *Time* 26 (2 Sept. 1935): 51–52 (quoted); Hollis, "Hall Family and Twentieth-Century Journalism in Alabama," 125.

30. Testimony of Mundo, 185 and McDuff, 100, 14 Nov. 1930, pt. 6, vol. 1, *Fish Committee Hearings,* ISU; *SW,* 22 Nov. 1930.

31. James W. McClung testimony, pt. 3, p. 793, Kenneth Bridenthal and Harriet Flood Affidavits, 12 Jan. 1937, pt. 3, pp. 970–73, Belle W. Barton Affidavit, 7 Dec. 1936, pt. 3, pp. 973–76, John D. House testimony, pt. 8, pp. 3016–17, *LaFollette Committee Hearings,* MADD; Starnes to Graves, 13 Jan. 1936, box SG 12187, folder: Communism, Graves Papers, ADAH; testimony of Lester N. Shannon, 183, Johnson to Darcy, 11 July 1930, pp. 127 and 159 (sixth quotation), McDuff Exhibits 1R and 1S, and Johnson to All Party Members in McDuff Exhibit 2D, testimony of Murphy, 193–96, and testimony of McDuff, 156, 14 Nov. 1930, pt. 6, vol. 1, *Fish Committee Hearings,* ISU; *Congressional Record,* House, Committee on Rules, 71st Cong., 2d sess., vol. 72, pt. 8, pp. 8810, 8818, pt. 9, pp. 9390–98, and pt. 12, p. 98; *SW,* 16 Aug. 1930 (first, second, third, and fourth quotations); *BN,* 15 Jan. 1937 (fifth quotation); Feldman, "Ku Klux Klan in Alabama," 392 (also has fifth quotation); *DW,* 14 July 1930 (also has sixth quotation), 3 July 1935; Ingalls, "Antiradical Violence in Birmingham," 521; Wade, *Fiery Cross,* 260; Painter, *Narrative of Hosea Hudson,* 220–21; Kelley, *Hammer and Hoe,* 120–22. In "Antilabor Vigilantes in the South," 72, 78, "establishment violence" is interpreted by Robert Ingalls as "a method of social control directed at . . . anyone . . . who . . . threaten[ed] the status quo."

32. *SW,* 10 and 17 Jan. 1931 (first quotation), 16 Aug. 1930, 14 Feb. 1931; Painter, *Narrative of Hosea Hudson,* 187 (second quotation), also 220–21. Hosea Hudson, one of the four blacks released, used the alias Henry Thornton throughout this period.

33. KKK File, reel 49, 1935, reel 58, 1938, TU; *BP,* 10 Oct. 1932, 6 March 1935, 23 Dec. 1938 (fifth quotation); *DW,* 4 Oct. 1932; *SW,* 12 July 1933, Dec. 1934 (first and second quota-

tions), Feb. 1935; *BAH,* 10 Oct. 1932; *MA,* 17 Dec. 1938; Carter, *Scottsboro,* 152–53; Ingalls, "Anti-radical Violence in Birmingham," 524; Painter, *Narrative of Hosea Hudson,* 128 (third and fourth quotations); *KM* 7 (Nov. 1931): 39.

34. KKK File, reel 46, 1934, reel 52, 1936, TU; *NYT,* 30 May 1934; John Howard Lawson, "The Klansmen Ride Again in Alabama," *NYP,* reprinted in the *MA,* 29 May 1934 (first, second, and third quotations); Colman to Editor, *Nation,* 30 May 1934, quoted in "The Klan Revives," 20 (fourth quotation); *Lancaster News,* 1 June 1934; *DW,* 5 Dec. 1934; *SW,* July, Sept., Oct. 1934; Ingalls, "Antiradical Violence in Birmingham," 524; *DW,* 8 June, 15 Oct. 1936; *BN,* and *MCA,* 9 June 1936; *Greenville Democratic Times,* and *Richmond Times-Dispatch,* 10 June 1936; *AC,* 28 May 1936; *Peoria Transcript,* 31 May 1936; *New Republic* 85 (17 June 1936): n.p.

35. *NYT,* 30 May 1934.

36. Kelley, *Hammer and Hoe,* 101.

37. *Mobile Nationalist,* 11 June 1869; *Alabama State Journal,* 13 Feb. 1869; Hamilton, *Alabama,* 40, 46; Bell, "Reconstruction Ku Klux Klan," 211, 288, 293–94.

38. *BLA,* 26 April, 24 and 31 May 1930, quoted in Kelley, "New War in Dixie," 374. The *SW* called Birmingham's black editors "black Judases" and damned them for joining with the "big boss press in denouncing the Communists and crawling submissively before the white boss monster." Quoted from *SW,* 15 and 29 Aug. and 12 Sept. 1931.

39. Testimony of McDuff, 92, 96, 132, 175, and McDuff Exhibits 1 BB and 2 OO, 14 Nov. 1930, pt. 6, vol. 1, *Fish Committee Hearings,* ISU; KKK File, reel 46, 1934, TU; *Southern Labor Review,* 9 May 1934, quoted in Ingalls, "Antiradical Violence in Birmingham," 523; *LA,* 26 April, 24 May 1931, quoted in Kelley, *Hammer and Hoe,* 29, 169; "Alabama Warned of Alien Plotters," *KM* 9 (Feb. 1933): 29; and *Newark News,* 22 Dec. 1932; *BAH,* 7 Aug. 1931; *DW,* 2 April 1930, 5 Dec. 1934; *SW,* 8 Nov. 1930, 2 May, 13 June, 7, 15, 29 Aug., 14 March, 26 Sept., 31 Oct. 1931, 10 Feb. 1934; *SW,* 29 Aug. 1931.

40. Wade, *Fiery Cross,* 258; *SW,* July 1936 (quoted). Birmingham Communists were hard-pressed on the point of their irreligiosity. Hiram Evans held that "Communism is a product of Bolshevism. . . . [It] does not believe in homes but in sex nests. It terminates Motherhood and Fatherhood at birth. It not only does not believe . . . in any God, but is fighting God. Communism is exactly opposed to everything that Americans hold sacred." Quoted in Evans, "Communism Rampant," 1. Even the progressive pastor of Birmingham's Independent Presbyterian Church announced that the Communist "apostles of revolution pretend fellowship for the negro, but . . . are using him as a means to their own destructive ends" as he cited "certain sinister alien influences" among the Communist ranks. Henry Edmonds is quoted in "Alabama Warned of Alien Plotters," *KM* 9 (Feb. 1933): 29, and *Newark News,* 22 Dec. 1932. Apparently, though, the Communist attempt to adapt itself to Alabama's religiosity paid off to some extent. Black churches allowed Communist meetings to be held; see Painter, *Hosea Hudson,* 128–29. Two white ministers published a prolabor, pro–civil rights, antiwar paper called the *Southern News Almanac* and declared themselves to be Christian Marxists; see Kelley, *Hammer and Hoe,* 196. And R. H. Crossfield, the white pastor of Birmingham's First Christian Church, visited Soviet Russia and returned with praise for its Communist society, in "Observations on Russia," 1259–60, 1264.

41. Reminiscences, folder 1, Eugene Feldman Papers, ADAH. Feldman reported that Greeks and Catholics were treated similarly. On one occasion, a Montgomery woman stopped him on the street and said, "Are you a Jew?" When he responded in the affirmative, she said, "My, you're a real live Jew, aren't you?" This exchange appears on p. 9.

42. Minutes of the Unity Club, Jan. 1936 to March 1938, folders 1 and 2, Unity Club Records, ADAH; Pt. 4, reel 11, NAACP Papers, MADD and LC; Delegation of NCDPP,

"Report on Georgia-Alabama," 19 July 1934, p. 12, ACLU Records, PU; Dobbins, "Alabama Governors and Editors," 136–45.

43. *FC,* March 1940, p. 3; KKK File, reel 49, 1935, TU; *SW,* 5 Sept. 1931; *MA,* 6 Jan. 1935.

44. Reminiscences, folder 1, Eugene Feldman Papers, ADAH; Lynching File, reels 221, 222, 1919, TU.

45. KKK Scrapbooks, no. 257, BPLA; KKK File, reel 46, 1934, TU; *Foley Onlooker,* in *MA,* 6 Oct. 1934; *DW,* 24 Oct. 1934; *SW,* 10 June 1933, Nov. 1934; *BP,* 13 Oct. 1934; Snell, "Ku Klux Klan in Jefferson County," 226.

46. NAACP Papers, pt. 6, reel 2, LC; KKK File, reel 46, 1934, TU; *KM* 10 (Jan. 1934): 30–31, and 10 (Feb. 1934): 44; Colman to Editor, *Nation,* 30 May 1934, in "The Klan Revives," 20; Kelley, *Hammer and Hoe,* 88; *BP,* 30 July 1934; *BAA,* 25 Nov. 1933; *MCA,* 12 Nov. 1933; *New York Mirror,* 13 Nov. 1933; *Lancaster News,* 1 June 1934; and *Macon Telegraph,* 25 July 1934; Madison, "Shots in the Dark."

47. *BAA,* 25 Nov. 1933 (first and second quotations). The *BAA* also reported gatherings of as many as a hundred fully dressed Klansmen during the midsts of the Tuscaloosa troubles. See also NAACP Brief for Federal Prosecution Against Tuscaloosa Sheriff, 13 Oct. 1933, pt. 7, ser. A, reel 4, and Ransom et al. to Cummings, in pt. 6, reel 2, and "Killing of Workers," pt. 10, reel 13, and pt. 7, ser. A, reel 8, NAACP Papers, MADD and LC; *BP,* 30 July 1934 (third quotation).

48. Stroudsburg, Pa., to Graves, 15 July 1936 (quoted), box SG 12187, folder: Communism, Graves Papers, ADAH; *SW,* 31 Aug., 20 Sept. 1933; *Tarboro Southerner,* 28 May 1936; KKK File, reel 52, 1936, TU.

49. KKK File, reel 44, 1933, reel 46, 1934, TU; *BN,* 20 July 1934; *BP,* 6 Aug. 1934; *BAA,* 25 Nov. 1933 (quoted).

50. "Jew Lawyers Cause Alabama Lynchings," *KM* 9 (Sept. 1933): 36 (quoted); *KM* 10 (Feb. 1934): 44.

51. KKK Scrapbooks, no. 257, BPLA; KKK File, reel 46, 1934 (second quotation), reel 73, 1941, TU; *BAH,* 28 Nov. 1941; *BP,* 30 July 1934 (first quotation); 28 July 1934 (third quotation), also 25 July 1934; *MA,* 25, 28 July 1934; *BN,* 24 July 1934; *Jacksonville Times-Union,* 25 July 1934.

52. KKK File, reel 46, 1934, TU; *BP,* 30 July 1934 (quoted).

53. Gelders to Baldwin, 14 Aug. and 6 Sept. 1936, vol. 826, ACLU to Graves 25 Sept. 1936, Isserman to Baldwin, 26 Sept. 1936, vol. 924, and Delegation of the NCDPP, "Report on Georgia-Alabama," vol. 925, in ACLU Records, PU; Belle W. Barton Affidavit, 7 Dec. 1936, pt. 3, p. 975, and see pt. 3, pp. 740–807, *LaFollette Committee Hearings,* MADD; Ingalls, "Flogging of Joseph Gelders," 577–78, and "Antiradical Violence in Birmingham," 529; Salmond, *Conscience of a Lawyer,* 162–64.

54. Statement by Joseph Gelders to the Police, 24 Sept. 1936, box 22, folder H-18, micro no. R-981, reel 20, ILD Fund Papers, SC; Joseph Gelders testimony, pt. 3, 780–88, *LaFollette Committee Hearings,* MADD; Ingalls, "Antiradical Violence in Birmingham," 527, 532.

55. King to Graves, 15 Oct. 1936, and Gelders to Graves, 6 Oct. 1936, box SG 12176, folder: Joseph Gelders, Graves Papers, ADAH; *BAH,* 25–26 Sept. 1936; *BN,* 25 Sept. 1936 (quoted), 4 Jan. 1937.

56. Statement by Joseph Gelders to the Police, 24 Sept. 1936, box 22, folder H-18, micro R-981, reel 20, ILD Fund Papers, SC; Isserman to Baldwin, 26 Sept. 1936, and Hays to Graves, 23 Sept. 1936, both in ACLU Records, PU; Sanders to Graves, 2 Dec. 1936 (fifth quotation), Golat to Graves, 24 Nov. 1936 (third quotation), King to Graves, 15 Oct. 1936 (second quotation), and DeMohai to Graves, 27 Nov. 1936 (fourth quotation), all in box SG 12176, folder:

Joseph Gelders, Graves Papers, ADAH; KKK File, reel 52, 1936, TU; *BAH,* 26 Sept. 1936; *MA,* 25–27 Sept. and 1 Dec. 1936; *BP,* 26 Sept., 20 Oct. 1936; *DW,* 10 Oct. 1936 (also has sixth quotation); *NYT,* 26 Sept. 1936; *New Republic* 85 (2 Dec. 1936): n.p. (first and sixth quotations).

57. Statement by Joseph Gelders to the Police, box 22, folder H-18, micro R-981, reel 20, ILD Papers, SC; Gelders to Graves, 6 Oct. 1936, box SG 12176, folder: Joseph Gelders, Graves Papers, ADAH; KKK File, reel 52, 1936, TU; *MA,* 25 Sept. 1936 (first quotation), also 26 Sept. 1936; *BAH,* 25–29 Sept. 1936; *MP,* 29 Sept. 1936 (second quotation); *BN,* 25 Sept. 1936 (third and fifth quotations), 26 Sept. 1936 (fourth quotation), also 30 Sept. 1936, 4 Jan. 1937; Ingalls, "Antiradical Violence in Birmingham," 536; Teel, "African-American Press and the Campaign for a Federal Anti-Lynching Law," 84–107.

58. *New Republic,* 2 Dec. 1936; KKK File, reel 52, 1936, TU; Ingalls, "Antiradical Violence in Birmingham," 530.

59. Borden Burr testimony, pt. 3, p. 743, Ernest D. LeMay testimony, pt. 3, p. 743, Yelverton Cowherd testimony, pt. 804, 806, McClung testimony, pt. 3, pp. 790–92, Carey Haigler testimony, pt. 3, pp. 802–3, James Brooks testimony, pt. 3, pp. 801–2, [Chief of Detectives] G. C. Giles testimony, pt. 3, p. 798, Ben Winston Affidavit, Feb. 1937, pt. 15C, pp. 6319–21, Paul Weller Affidavit, 26 Jan. 1937, pt. 15C, pp. 6317–18, *LaFollette Committee Hearings,* MADD; Gelders to Graves, 6 Oct. 1936, McClung to McAdory, 4 Oct. 1936, Giles to Graves, 29 Oct. 1936 (second quotation), Hirsch to Graves, 23 Jan. 1937, and *BAH,* clipping, 21 Oct. 1936, all in box SG 12176, folder: Joseph Gelders, Graves Papers, ADAH; KKK File, reel 52, 1936, TU; *BP,* 20 Oct., 14 Nov. 1936; *DW,* 5 Nov. 1936; *SW,* Dec. 1936; *MA,* 23 Oct., 13–14 Nov. 1936; *East Tennessee News,* 26 Nov. 1936; *TJ,* in *BAH,* 17 Nov. 1936; *BN,* 16 Jan. 1937; Ingalls, "Antiradical Violence in Birmingham," 532 (first quotation), also 535, 538, 540–41, and "Antilabor Vigilantes in the South," 74–75 (also has first quotation); Barnard, ed., *Outside the Magic Circle,* 311–12. Walter J. "Crack" Hanna commanded an infantry regiment in the South Pacific during World War II and served as adjutant general of the Alabama National Guard during 1954 when martial law was declared in Phenix City following the assassination of state attorney general–elect Albert Patterson by underworld elements. He later founded Hanna Steel Corporation and in 1995 was inducted into the Alabama Peace Officers Hall of Fame; see *BN,* 8 Nov. 1995, p. 5E. Dent Williams was the other militia suspect in the floggings.

60. Barnard, ed., *Outside the Magic Circle,* 311–312 (first quotation). For an example of *BN* defense of TCI and corporate Birmingham, see the *BN,* 16 Jan. 1937, and Ingalls, "Antiradical Violence in Birmingham," 540; KKK File, reel 52, 1936 (second quotation), TU; *DW,* 5 Nov. 1936; *MA,* 23 Oct., 13–14 Nov. 1936; *Knoxville East-Tennessee News,* 26 Nov. 1936. At one point, Bailes pointedly asked the grand jurors: What "are you going to do" besides flog someone "when there's no law to deal with radicals and Communists?" Quoted in Ingalls, "Anti-Labor Vigilantes," 74–75; Graves to Lee, 21 Oct. 1936, box SG 12179, folder: Re Joseph Gelders, Graves Papers, ADAH. The only notable exception to this pattern of denial and silence was the protests of the *Birmingham Post,* edited by E. T. Leech, long an opponent of mob violence. See *BP,* 14, 18 Nov. 1936.

61. Pt. 3, pp. 740–807, *LaFollette Committee Hearings,* MADD; Barlow to Graves, 9 Dec. 1936, box SG 12176, folder: Joseph Gelders, and Gelders to Graves, 5 Jan. 1937 (quoted), and Graves to Chappell, 22 Jan. 1937, box SG 12179, folder: Re Joseph Gelders, Graves Papers, ADAH; KKK File, reel 52, 1936, TU; *MA,* 1 Jan. 1937; *SW,* Oct. and Dec. 1936, March 1937, p. 6; Ingalls, "Antiradical Violence in Birmingham," 537.

62. *SW,* March 1937, p. 6 (quoted); Ingalls, "Antiradical Violence in Birmingham," 537 (which also has the quoted passage).

13. FARM, FACTORY, AND HOODED PERSISTENCE

1. Flynt, *Poor but Proud*, 91, 281–83, 333, and "New Deal and Southern Labor," 63–96, Agee and Evans, *Let Us Now Praise Famous Men.*

2. Kelley, "New War in Dixie," 370, 384; Painter, *Narrative of Hosea Hudson.*

3. Kelley, *Hammer and Hoe*, 29–32, 92, 141.

4. KKK File, reel 46, 1934, TU; *BAA*, 17 Feb. 1934 (quoted).

5. NAACP Papers, pt. 6, reel 2, LC and MADD; *SW*, 27 June, 25 July 1931; Hoffman, "Crusade That Failed," in UAB; Rosen, "Alabama Sharecroppers' Union."

6. Kelley, *Hammer and Hoe*, 40–43; Delegation of NCDPP, "Report on Georgia-Alabama," 19 July 1934, p. 12, ACLU Records, PU; Rosengarten, *All God's Dangers.*

7. James D. Burton, "Radical Activities in Alabama: Report of the State Interracial Commission of Alabama," and "Interracial Cooperation in Alabama," 24 Aug. 1931, pt. 6, reels 2, 4, and pt. 7, ser. A, reel 7, 8, NAACP Papers, MADD and LC; Kelley, *Hammer and Hoe*, 40–41 (quoted).

8. *SW*, 25 July, 1, 29 Aug. 1931; Kelley, *Hammer and Hoe*, 42 (quoted), 40–41, 43.

9. Kelley, *Hammer and Hoe*, 42–43.

10. *SW*, 18 July 1931, 31 Aug. 1933, April 1937, pp. 6 and 13 (quoted); "Alabama Warned of Alien Plotters," *KM* 9 (Feb. 1933): 29.

11. *SW*, April 1937, pp. 6, 13.

12. NAACP Papers, pt. 7, ser. A, reel 7, and pt. 10, reel 23, LC and MADD; KKK File, reel 44, 1933, reel 62, 1939, TU; *MA*, 10 May 1933; *SW*, 6 Dec. 1930, 12 July, 15 Aug. 1933.

13. *Attalla Press*, 27 Oct. 1939; *BR*, 18 Aug. 1931; *SW*, 15 Aug. 1933.

14. Kennedy, "Cussed and Robbed, Shot and Boycotted," 10–11 and 14 (quoted); Sims, *The Klan*, 129–39.

15. Pt. 7, ser. A, reels 7, 8, 30 and pt. 8, ser. A, reel 3, NAACP Papers, LC and MADD; Hall to Chappell, 7 Jan. and 4 May 1935, box 67, folder 1, Grover C. Hall, Sr., Papers, ADAH; testimony of McDuff, 157, 14 Nov. 1930, pt. 6, vol. 1, *Fish Committee Hearings*, ISU; KKK File, reel 44, 1933, TU; *Dadeville Record*, in *MA*, 7 Jan. 1933 (second quotation); *SW*, Dec. 1934 (first quotation); *DW*, 5 Dec. 1934 (also has first quotation). Bibb Graves was far from a labor hero to the Communists. The *SW*, 30 Aug. and 18 Oct. 1930, said Graves's hands still "dripped with blood" for the militia role he played when the state guard crushed the 1920–21 UMW strike.

16. Gould Beech, Interview, pp. 7–9, 15, SHC; Salmond, *Southern Rebel*, 99–103; *NYT*, 5 March 1965, quoted in Dinnerstein, "Senate's Rejection of Aubrey Williams as Rural Electrification Administrator," 136 (quoted).

17. *SW*, June 1935; *DW*, 28 Feb. 1935.

18. KKK File, reel 46, 1934, TU; *DW*, 18 Sept., 24 Oct. 1934.

19. "Communists Stirring Southern Negroes," *KM* 9 (Oct. 1933): 19–20; "Reds Bait Negroes with Wild Promises," *KM* 10 (Oct. 1934): 26–27; KKK File, reel 52, 1936, TU; *BAA*, 15 Feb. 1936 (quoted).

20. *SW*, Oct. 1934 (quoted).

21. KKK File, reel 49, 1935, TU; *CD*, 15 June 1935 (quoted).

22. Colman to Editor, *Nation*, 30 May 1934, in "The Klan Revives," *Nation* 139 (4 July 1934): 20; Jackson, "You Can Kill Me—But You Can Never Scare Me," *Labor Defender* 11 (Oct. 1935): 6; KKK File, reel 46, 1934, TU; *DW*, 18 Sept. 1934, 28 Feb. 1935; *SW*, Feb. 1936.

23. Ingalls, "Antilabor Vigilantes in the South," 72–78, esp. 73. Jackson, "You Can Kill

Me—But You Can Never Scare Me," 6, and "On the Alabama Front," *Nation* 141 (18 Sept. 1935): 329–30 (quoted).

24. Jackson, "On the Alabama Front," 329–30. See also note 21 above.

25. Eckstat to Graves, 29 Aug. 1935, Wood to Graves, 18, 21, and 24 May 1935, Martin and Sebridge to Graves, 15 Sept. 1935, all in box SG 12165, folder: Communism, drawer 3, no. 1, Graves Papers, ADAH; *SW,* March-April 1936; *DW,* 3 July 1935 (second quotation); *SW,* June 1935 (also has second quotation); Robert Wood, southern secretary of the ILD, "Live and Die in Dixie" (Southern Workers' Defense League), c. 1939; Joseph Gelders testimony, pt. 3, p. 775, and Robert Washington Affidavit, 21 Dec. 1936, pt. 3, pp. 965–66, *LaFollette Committee Hearings,* MADD; Kelley, *Hammer and Hoe,* 168; Painter, *Narrative of Hosea Hudson,* 187–88 (third quotation); Feldman, "Ku Klux Klan in Alabama," 419 (first quotation).

26. Eckstat to Graves, 29 Aug. 1935, Wood to Graves, 18, 21, and 24 May 1935, Martin and Sebridge to Graves, 15 Sept. 1935, and Jackson to Graves, 24 Sept. 1935; Dadeville Secretary of SCU to Graves, 4 Sept. 1935; ILD to Graves, c. 1935; Jordan to Graves, 12 Oct. 1935; Gordek to Graves, 30 Aug. 1935; CPUSA, Sec. 2, Unit 28, to Graves, 14 Sept. 1935; Association Against the Advertiser-Communistic-Tuskegee Drive to Graves, 31 Aug. 1935; Tieger to Graves, 23 Sept. 1935, box SG 12165, folder: Communism, drawer 3, no. 1, Graves Papers, ADAH.

27. *DW,* 3 July 1935 (quoted).

28. Eckstat to Graves, 29 Aug. 1935 (first and fourth quotations), Ross to Graves, 25 May 1935 (third quotation), Black to Graves, c. 1935 (second quotation), Armas to Graves, 14 Oct. 1935, and note 17 above, all in box SG 12165, folder: Communism, drawer 3, no. 1, Graves Papers, ADAH; KKK File, reel 44, 1933, reel 67, 1940, TU; *AN,* 17 Aug. 1940; *Raleigh News and Telegraph,* 14 April 1933; *Chicago Bee,* 13 Aug. 1939 (sixth quotation); *SW,* Nov. 1934; *DW,* 23 Sept. 1941; "Germany Steals Klan Thunder," *KM* 10 (March 1934): 5; Hamlett, "Red Menace Real," 9–10; Wade, *Fiery Cross,* 266 (fifth quotation), 268; Kelley, *Hammer and Hoe,* 193, 218–19.

29. Davis to Graves, c. 1935 (quoted), box SG 12165, folder: Communism, drawer 3, no. 1, Graves Papers, ADAH; KKK File, reel 44, 1933, reel 73, 1941, TU; *BAA,* 20 May 1933; *CD,* 14 Jan. 1933.

30. *NYT,* 8 June 1941 (quoted).

31. Powell to Miller, 31 Oct. 1934; Fleming, ILD to Roosevelt et al., 31 Oct. 1934; LeFlore and Johnson, NAACP to Miller, 27 Oct. 1934;, Interview of R. A. Strong, former Escambia County sheriff and Brewton policeman; *Philadelphia Political Digest,* clipping, 2 Nov. 1934, all in box 250, folder: Lynching of Claude Neal, Benjamin Meek Miller, Alabama Governors Papers, ADAH.

32. Delegation of NCDPP, "Report on Georgia-Alabama," 19 July 1934, pp. 8–9, ACLU Records, PU; Crawford, "Bullets Fell on Alabama," 319–20; Ingalls, "Antiradical Violence in Birmingham," 528.

33. Downs is quoted in Delegation of NCDPP, "Report on Georgia-Alabama," 19 July 1934, pp. 8–9 (quoted), ACLU Records, PU. Page 10 of the same report noted that there "seems to be no organized liberal movement in Birmingham and liberal opinion is rare." See also Crawford, "Bullets Fell on Alabama," *Nation* 141 (18 Sept. 1935): 319–20 (second quotation).

34. *Alabama Acts,* Act No. 161, 31 July 1935, pp. 203–4, and Act No. 330, 27 Aug. 1935, p. 756; Crawford, "Bullets Fell on Alabama," 319–20 (quoted); Alfred H. Hirsch Affidavit, 7 Jan. 1937, pt. 3, pp. 976–77, *LaFollette Committee Hearings,* MADD.

35. Kirkhead to Graves, Conroy et al. to Graves, Hays to Graves, Maurer to Graves, all on

31 July 1935 (first, second, third, and fourth quotations), Damon to Graves, 30 July 1935, Pope to Graves, 19 Aug. 1935 (fifth quotation), Rosen to Graves, 9 Aug. 1935, NCDPP to Graves, 30 July 1935, *Danville Register,* clipping, 22 Sept. 1935, p. 6; *Jacksonville Times-Union,* clipping, 7 Aug. 1935 (sixth quotation), all in box SG 12165, folder: Communism, drawer 3, no. 1, Graves Papers, ADAH.

36. Report of the Sub-Committee of State Interracial Commission, 14 Sept. 1932, Persons to Miller, 21, 28 Oct. 1932, Hurst to Persons, 19 Oct. 1932 in folder 11: Communism, 1932–34; Burr to Peach, 19 April 1934, Adjutant General's Reports, 21, 30 April, 16 May 1934, Oldham to Miller and Gregg to Miller, both on 26 April 1934, Persons to Miller, 27 April 1934, Fies to Miller, 15 May 1934, Aldridge to Miller, 30 May 1934, LeMay to Peach, 13 June 1934, Miller to Persons, 15 May 1934 in folder 18: 1934 Coal Miners' Strike; Adjutant General's Report, 13 June 1934, Persons to Miller, 9 May 1934, Fies to Miller, 16 May 1934 in folder 19: 1934 Coal Strike; Hawkins to Miller, 13 March 1934, Aldridge to Miller, 15 March 1934, Davidson to Miller, 19 March 1934, Burr to Miller, 13 April 1934, Roberts to Miller, 4, 17 April 1934, Alabama Mining Comm. to Miller, 16 April 1934, phone conversation of Persons to Miller, 16 April 1934, Adams to Miller, 19 April 1934, Hawkins to Miller, 20 April 1934, Burr to Peach, 20 April 1934, Hammond to Miller, 21 April 1934, Hanson to Black, 12 May 1934, NCDPP to FDR, 28 May 1934 in folder 20: 1934 Coal Strike, all in box SG 19922, Miller Papers, ADAH; Corley, "Quest for Racial Harmony," 39, 64.

37. Agnew to Turner, 24 Aug. 1934, Agnew to Comer, 5 Sept. 1934, Roberts to Miller, 7, 10, 12 Sept. 1934, Miller to Gamble and Miller to Darby, 21 Sept. 1934, Miller to Speaks and Pride, 14 Aug. 1934, Peach to Agnew, 25 Aug. 1934, Miller to Roberts, 7, 11 Sept. 1934, Miller to Lovelace, 1 Sept. 1934, Miller to Griffin, 13 July 1934, Sylacauga Exchange Club, Merchants'Assoc., and Post of American Legion to Miller, 15 Sept. 1934, Kiwanis Club of Winfield to Miller, 13 July 1934, Speaks and Poole to Miller, 13, 17 Aug. 1934, Hoffman to Miller and Stabler to Miller, 21 Sept. 1934, Griffin to Miller, 13 July 1934, Agnew to Miller, Wells to Miller, Lanier to Miller, Chapman to Miller, Carter and Denson to Miller, all on 6 Sept. 1934, all in box SG 19956, folder 6: 1934 Strike Situation, Miller Papers, ADAH.

38. Zieger, *The CIO;* Sullivan, *Days of Hope:,* 129–40, 171–85; Feldman, *From Demagogue to Dixiecrat,* 120–24; Galenson, *CIO Challenge to the AFL.*

39. Graves to Lee, 21 Oct. 1936, folder: Joseph Gelders, box SG 12179, Graves Papers, ADAH; Rogers et al., *Alabama,* 500.

40. Feldman, *From Demagogue to Dixiecrat,* vi–vii, 7–12.

41. Feldman, "Labour Repression in the American South," 362, and *From Demagogue to Dixiecrat,* 195.

42. Wade, *Fiery Cross,* 262 (quoted); Zieger, *The CIO,* 77–80; Sullivan, *Days of Hope,* 94–97; "K.K.K. vs. Labor: A Sampler," *Southern Exposure* 8:2 (1980): 61 (quoting the same passage).

43. Willoughby to Graves, 6 April 1937, box SG 12187, folder: Communism, Graves Papers, ADAH; *BN,* 12 July 1937; Newton and Newton, *Ku Klux Klan,* 5, 133–34; Ingalls, "Antilabor Vigilantes in Birmingham," 77 (first and fourth quotations); Chalmers, *Hooded Americanism,* 5, 316, 320–23 (second and third quotations).

44. Barnard, ed., *Outside the Magic Circle,* 123 (second quotation); *BN,* 28 Oct. 1934; *SW,* Dec. 1934; Huntley, "Iron Ore Miners and Mine Mill in Alabama"; *LA,* 26 April, 24 May 1931, quoted in Kelley, *Hammer and Hoe,* 141 (first quotation), also 29, 142, 148, 169, and 190; Persons, "Sex and Civil Rights."

45. Statement by Joseph Gelders to the Police, 24 Sept. 1936, box 22, folder H18, ILD Papers, SC; Gelders testimony, pt. 3, 775, J. C. Sheehan Affidavit, 11 Jan. 1937, pt. 3, p. 969,

exhibit 370, testimony of McClung, part 3, 793, in *LaFollette Committee Hearings,* MADD; KKK File, reel 46, 1934, TU; *DW,* 3 July 1935; *BP,* 20 Nov. 1934; *BN,* 7 Aug. 1931, 3 Jan. 1937; *BAH,* 3 Jan. 1937; Kelley, *Hammer and Hoe,* 121; Rice, *Ku Klux Klan in American Politics,* 101–4.

46. *SW,* May 1937, p. 13 (both quotations).

47. Delegation of NCDPP, "Report on Georgia-Alabama," 19 July 1934, pp. 9–10, ACLU Records, PU.

48. Feldman, *From Demagogue to Dixiecrat,* 105–11, 117–20.

49. Ibid., 105–6.

50. Ibid., 110, 115.

51. Ibid., 108 (quoted). For more on Dixon's conservatism and general record as governor, consult the Big Mules mouthpiece, the *Alabama Magazine,* 1939–1942.

52. Pendleton, "New Deal Labor Policy and Alabama Textile Unions," 117–18; *SW,* 10 June 1933, Jan. 1937, p. 8; *HT,* 5 Aug. 1934; "Racial Issue Injected into Textile Strike," *KM* 10 (Oct. 1934): 37.

53. Graves to Lee, 21 Oct. 1936, folder: Joseph Gelders, box SG 12179, Graves Papers, ADAH; Rogers et al., *Alabama,* 500 (quoted); Feldman, *From Demagogue to Dixiecrat,* 104–11, 116.

54. Feldman, *From Demagogue to Dixiecrat,* 106–7 (quoted). After some changes, the Black Bill eventually became the Fair Labor Standards Act of 1938.

55. Stewart, "Gadsden Is Tough," 69; Martin, "Southern Labor Relations in Transition," 559–60 (quoted), 545–50, 561–62.

56. Sherman H. Dalrymple testimony, pt. 8, pp. 3000–7, pt. 8, pp. 3000–51, John D. House testimony, pt. 8, pp. 3016–17, pt. 15C, pp. 5206–8 and 6299–6345, in *LaFollette Committee Hearings,* MADD; Martin, "Southern Labor Relations in Transition," 547–56; Kelley, *Hammer and Hoe,* 140–41; Nelson, "The Rubber Workers' Southern Strategy," 319, 328–29; *SW,* Nov. 1936, Jan. 1937, p. 2, and July 1937, p. 13.

57. Kelley, *Hammer and Hoe,* 140–41 (first quotation); Martin, "Southern Labor Relations in Transition," 554 (second quotation).

58. Martin, "Southern Labor Relations in Transition," 557.

59. Ibid., 558–62. The quoted passage appears on pp. 560–61.

60. *Thornhill v. Alabama,* 189 Ala. App. 527 (1940), 189 So. 913 (1940), and 310 U.S. 88 (1940); Chalmers, "Pickets in the Woods," 68–77; *SW,* April 1937, p. 11; *DW,* 26 Oct. 1941 (quoted); *Greenville Independent-Tribune,* 27 Feb. 1940; KKK File, reel 73, 1941, TU.

61. Gould Beech, Interview, p. 4 (first quotation), SHC; *KM* 7 (July 1931): 39 (third quotation) and 10 (April 1934): 48 (second quotation).

62. Brower to Thompson, ed., *MR,* 3 Feb. 1930 (quoted), box 207, folder: Adm. Board of Convict Department, 1930, Bidgood to Miller et al., 7 Feb. 1931, in box 207, folder: Adm. Board of Convict Department, 1931, Pollard to Miller, 9 Jan. 1932, box 212, folder: Convict Department, James C. Kirby, all in Miller Papers, ADAH; KKK File, reel 62, 1939, reel 73, 1941, TU; *DW,* 28 Sept. 1941; *ADW,* 15 April 1939, 22 Sept. 1941; *SW,* Nov. 1934; *KM* 12 (April 1936): 3, and 10 (March 1934): 33, and 10 (May 1934): 35, and 11 (Feb. 1935): 7–8; and An Alabama Klansman, "Should Roman Catholics Be Public School Teachers?" *KM* 8 (Nov. 1932): 19; Terry and Sims, *They Live on the Land,* 292.

63. "Think This Over!" *KM* 6 (Feb. 1930): 1; "Looking Back," *KM* 10 (March 1934): 17–18; "Younger Men Must Rebuild the Klan," *KM* 10 (Jan. 1934): 1, 13; "Internationalists Are Traitors," *KM* 10 (April 1934): 13; and "The Klan of Tomorrow," *KM* 12 (Oct. 1936): 11; KKK File, reel 58, 1938, reel 67, 1940, TU; *AC,* 6 Aug. 1940; *Negro Labor News,* 3 Aug. 1940;

MA, 6 Oct. 1938; *AN,* 17 Sept. 1938; *Macon Telegraph,* and *BAH,* 6 Oct. 1938; *SW,* June and July 1936.

64. Brown to Grant, 30 Nov. 1932 (quoted), Hugh Gladney Grant Papers, DUKE; *SW,* 28 March 1931; *KM* 8 (Jan. 1932): 47; 8 (June 1932): 35; "The Klan of the Reconstruction Era," *KM* 12 (Oct. 1936): 6–7; "The Klan of Yesterday," *KM* 12 (Oct. 1936): 8–10; "The Klan of Tomorrow," *KM* 12 (Oct. 1936): 11; Calloway to Editor, *American Mercury,* in "Notes on a Kleagle," 248–49; Allen, "KKK," *Literary Digest* 124 (9 Oct. 1937): 15.

65. Pruitt to Grant, 19 June 1933, Grant Papers, DUKE; *Pickens County Herald and West Alabamian,* clipping, in Judge Leon McCord Scrapbooks, ADAH; *BP,* 6 May 1935.

66. KKK File, reel 44, 1933; *Des Moines Tribune-Capital,* 17 May 1933 (quoted); "BLACK: A Klan Member on the Supreme Court? New Evidence Comes to Light" *Newsweek* 10 (20 Sept. 1937): 10.

67. "The Negro Goes Democratic," *KM* 12 (Aug. 1936): 20 (first quotation); "BLACK: A Klan Member on the Supreme Court?" 10 (second quotation). KKK editorials lambasted the "Jew Morgenthau" and the "Jew Ickes" as they peached a "crusade" against FDR's cabinet and the New Deal. One cartoon of Roosevelt and the First Lady said: "You kiss the niggers and I'll kiss the Jews. And we'll stay in the White House as long as we choose." These statements are quoted in Wade, *Fiery Cross,* 259 and 275.

68. KKK File, reel 58, 1938, reel 62, 1939, reel 67, 1940, reel 73, 1941, TU; *NYT,* 26 March 1940; *DW,* 28 Sept. 1941; *Bee,* 15 Dec. 1940; *AN,* 10 Sept. 1938; *Atlanta World,* 14 Feb. 1939; *PC,* 18 Feb. 1939, 13 Jan. 1940; *Greenville News,* 11 Jan. 1940; *Negro Labor News,* 3 Aug. 1940; Carter, *Scottsboro,* 380.

69. *SW,* May 1937, p. 10, and July 1937, p. 2; *BN* and *BAH,* 31 Jan. 1937, p. 3; Carter, *Scottsboro,* 380–81; Father Divine Cult correspondence to Dixon, c. 1940, box SG 12248, folder: Anti-Lynching Bill, Frank M. Dixon, Alabama Governor's Papers, ADAH; Shepard to Graves, 29 Nov. 1935, box SG 12187, folder: Communism, Graves Papers, ADAH. James E. Shepard, the black president of the North Carolina College for Negroes, informed Alabama governor Bibb Graves that "no negro born and reared in the South, as I was, relishes this running to Washington for remedies that lie at home" but explained that the cure was not being sought by state elites. Quoted in Shepard to Graves, 29 Nov. 1935, box SG 12187, Graves Papers, ADAH.

70. Dixon to McKellar, 4 March 1940 (second quotation), McKellar to Dixon, 9 Feb. and 5 March 1940, box SG 12248, folder: Anti-Lynching Bill, Dixon Papers, ADAH; "The Lynching Situation," *KM* 6 (Oct. 1930): 11 (first quotation); Sitkoff, *New Deal for Blacks,* 273; Hall, *Revolt Against Chivalry.*

71. Reminiscences, 9–12, folder 1, Eugene Feldman Papers, ADAH; KKK File, reel 46, 1934, reel 49, 1935, reel 58, 1938, reel 67, 1940, TU; *MA,* 6 Oct. 1934, 8 Jan. 1935, 17 Dec. 1938 (first quotation), 8 Jan. 1935 (second quotation); *BN,* 7 April, 11 June 1940; *HT,* in *BN,* 7 April 1940 (third quotation).

72. Oral History of Rubye Denney in Grundy, *You Always Think of Home,* 27 (first quotation); KKK Scrapbooks, no. 257, BPLA; KKK File, reel 46, 1934, reel 52, 1936, reel 62, 1939, reel 67, 1940, TU; *MA,* 8 June 1934, 18 Feb. 1939; *PC,* 14 Aug. 1937; *BAH,* 18 April 1940; *BN,* 9 June 1936 (third quotation), 15 Feb. 1939, 18 April 1940 (second quotation); *AS,* 23 Feb. 1936; Snell, "Ku Klux Klan in Jefferson County," 227; Chalmers, *Hooded Americanism,* 5, 316–18.

73. *MA,* 8 June 1934, 18 Feb. 1939 (first quotation); *BN,* 9 June 1936, 15 Feb. 1939 (second quotation), 18 April 1940.

74. KKK Scrapbooks, no. 257, BPLA; KKK File, reel 46, 1934, reel 58, 1938, TU; *NYT,* 9 Jan. 1938, sec. 4, p. 7; *BN,* 25 Feb. 1935; *MA,* 3 June 1934, 21 Oct. 1938; Thomas to Editor, *MA,* 29 May 1934; *NYT,* 5 March 1965 quoted in Dinnerstein, "The Senate's Rejection of Aubrey Williams as Rural Electrification Administrator," 136; Delegation of NCDPP, "Report on Georgia-Alabama," 19 July 1934, p. 10, vol. 925, ACLU Papers, PU; *KM* 8 (May 1932): 34; 8 (Sept. 1932): 39; 8 (Oct. 1932): 38; "Klan Is Political Issue in Alabama," *KM* 10 (July 1934): 31; Ingalls, "Antiradical Violence in Birmingham," 530; Chalmers, *Hooded Americanism,* 315; Allen, "KKK," 17; Rice, *Ku Klux Klan in American Politics,* 94–98; Newton and Newton, *Ku Klux Klan,* 262–63; Snell, "Masked Men in the Magic City," 226; Hamilton, *Lister Hill,* 84.

75. *Alabama ex. rel. Albert A. Carmichael v. J. L. Corbitt (alias J. Louis Corbitt), Sheriff of Henry County* 4 Div. 948 (Oct. Term, 1936); KKK File, reel 67, 1940, TU; *SW,* April 1937, July 1937, pp. 2, 13; *BN,* 6–7 Feb., 4–5, 19–20, 24 June 1937, 6–7 10, 14 April 1940; *BAH,* 20 June 1937; *MA,* 6 April, 9, 14 June 1940.

76. *BN,* 6–7 Feb., 4–5, 19–20, 24 June 1937; *BAH,* 20 June 1937; Feldman, "Ku Klux Klan in Alabama," 446 (quoted).

14. WORLD WAR II AND POSTWAR ALABAMA

1. Burran, "Racial Violence in the South during World War II"; O'Brien, "Return to 'Normalcy,'" II:231–54.

2. Brooks, "Coming Home and Taking Charge." I am grateful to the author for making this paper available to me.

3. Perrett, *Days of Sadness, Years of Triumph,* 312–16; Chafe, "Social Politics of Race and Gender," 42.

4. Schulman, *From Cotton Belt to Sunbelt,* 72–83, 94–95, 109; LaMonte, *Politics and Welfare in Birmingham;* Scribner, "Federal Funding, Urban Renewal, and Race Relations," 269–95; Salmond, ed., "'Aubrey Williams Remembers,'" 74–76.

5. Sosna, *In Search of the Silent South,* 105–20, and "Democratic Discourse." See also Norrell, "One Thing We Did Right," 65–80; Brooks, "Coming Home and Taking Charge"; Kneebone, *Southern Liberal Journalists and the Issue of Race;* Sullivan, *Days of Hope,* 207–10; Zieger, *The CIO,* 227–41.

6. Dixon to Ames, 5 June 1942, Ames to Dixon, 4 May 1942 and 9 June 1942, box SG 12278, folder 10, Frank M. Dixon, Alabama Governors Papers, ADAH.

7. Powell to Crow, 5 Oct. 1942 (second quotation), box 1, folder 9, and 3 Oct. 1943 (first quotation), box 1, folder 10, Crow to Powell, 4 Nov. 1942 (third quotation), box 1, folder 9, and Owen to Crow 22 June 1943, box 1, folder 10, Charles B. Crow Papers, ADAH; Osofsky, *Burden of Race,* 414–20, 465–68. One northerner confessed that "there are a million of us up North who have the same feeling about Negroes and Catholics that the K.K.K. has." Quoted in Bennet to Folsom, 26 July 1949, box SG 12644, folder: KKK, 1949, no. 6, Folsom Papers, ADAH.

8. Finch to Colvin, 31 July 1942, Stevenson to Green, 6 Aug. 1942, and Haas to Griger, 2 June 1943, in box 1, folder 18, Philip H. Taft Research Notes, BPLA; Nelson, "Organized Labor and the Struggle for Black Equality in Mobile," 952, 967–68; Kelley, "'We Are Not What We Seem,'" 87, 104–5; Burran, "Racial Violence in the South," 104–28; Cronenberg, *Forth to the Mighty Conflict,* 65, 82. Georgia native J. B. Stoner was also active in Alabama during this period. After being expelled from the Tennessee Klan for being too extremist, in 1944 Stone petitioned Congress to pass a resolution proclaiming that "all Jews are the children of the Devil." In 1945 he organized the Anti-Jewish Party and worked to make practic-

ing Judaism a crime punishable by death. "We ought to get all Jews out of our country," he announced, "and I don't mean send them to another county . . . ! I think we ought to kill all Jews just to save their unborn generations from having to go to hell." Quoted in Wade, *Fiery Cross,* 283.

9. Quotation compiled from: transcript of telephone call from Sparks to local Mobile officials, 25 May 1943, Sparks to Davenport, 30 June 1943, Sparks to Lewis, 24 June 1943, and Memorandum: Race Riot Mobile, 25 May 1943. Sparks's statements were well supported; see Barnes to Sparks and Irvine to Sparks, both 28 June 1943, and Haynes to Sparks and Gray to Sparks, both 25 June 1943, all in box SG 12491, folder: Race Riots, 1944, Chauncey Sparks, Alabama Governors Papers, ADAH.

10. See note 8.

11. KKK File, reel 78, 1942, and reel 82, 1943, TU; *CD,* 4 Dec. 1943; *DW,* 10 Aug. 1942; Sullivan, "Southern Reformers," 81–94; Tindall, *Emergence of the New South,* 716, 717 (quotation); Graves, *Fighting South,* 121–25.

12. Sullivan, "Southern Reformers," 81–94.

13. Barnard, *Dixiecrats and Democrats;* White, "Civil Rights in Conflict." I am grateful to Professor White for making this paper available to me.

14. Box SG 12644, folders: KKK, 1949, no. 1-7, Alabama Governors Papers, James E. Folsom, Sr., ADAH; Brooks, "Coming Home and Taking Charge"; Burran, "Racial Violence in the South," 277–84.

15. Feldman, *From Demagogue to Dixiecrat,* 121–46; Ader, "Why the Dixiecrats Failed," 356–59; Frederickson, "Dixiecrat Movement and the Origins of Massive Resistance."

16. Paterson, *On Every Front;* Gaddis, *Long Peace,* 48–71; Leffler, "Truman Doctrine and the Rise of American Globalism," 139–45; Fried, *Nightmare in Red.*

17. Carter, *Scottsboro;* Kelley, *Hammer and Hoe.*

18. Tindall, *America,* II:1225–26.

19. Mason to Heldt, 15 April 1946, Lucy Randolph Mason Papers, DUKE; *CD,* 6 April 1946, clipping, in the Papers of Philleo Nash, HST; KKK File, reel 96, 1946, TU; *Los Angeles Tribune,* 21 Sept. 1946; *NYT,* 22 July 1946; *BAA,* 3 Aug. 1946; *MA,* 29 March 1946, 21 Feb. 1948; *HI,* 6 April, 21 Sept. 1946; *ADW,* 2 June 1948; *MW,* 1 Feb. 1949; Chalmers, *Hooded Americanism,* 336.

20. KKK Scrapbooks, no. 257, BPLA; KKK File, reel 87, 1944, TU; *MA,* and *AC,* 4 Jan. 1944 (second quotation); *BN,* 5 Aug. 1944; and *Kansas City Call,* 23 June 1944; Chalmers, *Hooded Americanism,* 323–24 (first quotation); Wade, *Fiery Cross,* 275 (also has first quotation).

21. KKK File, reel 91, 1945, TU; *BAA,* 15 Dec. 1945 (quoted); Lipset and Raab, *Politics of Unreason,* 276.

22. Chalmers, *Hooded Americanism,* 326 (first quotation); Wade, *Fiery Cross,* 277 (second quotation).

23. KKK File, reel 67, 1940, reel 96, 146, TU; *PC,* 2 March, 21 Dec. 1940; *ADW,* 15 Dec. 1940; *BD,* 21 Dec. 1940; *MA,* 23 June 1949; *BAA,* 18 May 1940; Corley, "Quest for Racial Harmony," 59; Zanden, "Klan Revival," 456–62; Forster and Epstein, *Report on the Ku Klux Klan;* Wade, *Fiery Cross,* 289–90 (second quotation); *NYT,* 22 July 1946 (first quotation); *BAA,* 3 Aug. 1946 (also has first quotation).

24. Wade, *Fiery Cross,* 279 (quoted).

25. Pt. 4, reel 11, NAACP Papers, LC and MADD; *PC,* 4 Oct. 1947; *DW,* 4 May 1947; *Atlanta Georgian,* and *NYHT,* 23 Dec. 1948; *NYT,* 23 Dec. 1949, p. 40; *ADW,* 27 Jan., 23 April 1949; *MA,* 15 March, 27 Oct. 1949 (also has first quotation), also 23 Oct. 1949; *BAA,* 5 Nov. 1949 (quoted); Newton and Newton, *Ku Klux Klan,* 195.

26. *BN,* 28 June, 7 and 23 July, 20 Aug. 1949; *DW,* 6 Nov. 1949; Newton and Newton, *Ku Klux Klan,* 404; Davis and Sims-Wood, *Ku Klux Klan.*

27. Durr to Judge Jones, n.d. (fourth quotation), box 1, folder 5, Virginia Foster Durr Papers, ADAH; "Kluxers on the Prowl," *Newsweek* 34 (11 July 1949): 21–22 (first quotation); Tuskegee Institute News Clipping Files: Anti-Negro Groups File, reel 108, 1949 (second quotation), TU; *MA,* 13 June 1948 (third quotation) and 10 Nov. 1949.

28. Anti-Negro Groups File, reel 108, 1949, reel 112, 1950, TU; *TN,* 27–31 May 1949; *MA, BN,* and *BAH,* 5 March 1950; *TN,* 28 May 1949 (first and third quotations), 30 May 1949 (second quotation), also 27 May 1949. The Tuscaloosa Klansmen also railed against the "Jew-owned" newspapers of Birmingham (quoted in *TN,* 31 May 1949) and called each other "brother" and used left-handed handshakes as security measures. Quoted in *TN,* 29 May 1949.

29. Telegrams and Marion Rushton Letter, 24 June 1949, both in box 2, folder 1, McCorvey to Dixon, 11 Oct. 1949, and Dixon to Wright, 24 June 1949, box 2, folder 7, Dixon Papers, ADAH; Gould Beech, Interview, 9 Aug. 1990, p. 24, SHC, reported that Englehardt preferred to have his county abolished rather than see black politicians control it. See also *BAH,* 17 Dec. 1943, clipping, in Scrapbook no. 20, Sparks Papers, ADAH; *BAH,* 21 April 1948, clipping, in box 6, folder 24, Cooper Green Papers, BPLA; Coleback to Hill, 20 July 1948 (quoted), box 367, folder 31, Lister Hill Papers, UASC; *AS,* 18 July 1948, clipping in box 181, folder 462, Col. Harry M. Ayers Papers, UASC; Feldman, *From Demagogue to Dixiecrat,* 121–68; Dobbins, "Alabama's Governors and Editors," 143. For more on the Dixiecrat Revolt, see Barnard, "Race, Class, and Party," 66–83. Bull Connor argued that Alabama "should be left alone to work out its own race problem in its own way" as he opposed the Truman civil rights proposals. Quoted in *BAH,* 21 April 1948, clipping, box 6, folder 24, Cooper Green Papers, BPLA.

30. "States' Rights Information and Speakers' Handbook," 1948, pp. 4–5, 13, 50–51 (quoted), box 6, folder 15, and "Help Dixie's Cause! An Appeal to the People of Alabama to Help in the Fight to Preserve Our Way of Life," 1948, box 7, folder 10, both in Alabama Pamphlets Collection, ADAH. "Help Dixie's Cause . . . " spoke of a "Police State . . . , a Federal Gestapo . . . on the pattern of Moscow."

31. Civil Rights File, reel 99, 1947, reel 103, 1948, TU; Subgroup 25: McCorvey Admin., 1947–51, box 83, folder 27-box 85, folder 20, and Subgroup 26, Ray Admin., 1951–55, box 86, folder 1-box 87, folder 9, State Democratic Executive Committee Records, ADAH; *ME,* 16 June 1949 (quoted); *BN,* 23 May 1949; *AC,* 18 July 1949; *CD,* 16 July 1949. For more on Wilkinson's career, see Feldman, *From Demagogue to Dixiecrat,* and "Horace Wilkinson and Alabama Politics," 303; Kennedy, *Southern Exposure,* 226–27.

32. *BN,* 22 March 1950, quoted in Feldman, *From Demagogue to Dixiecrat* (from which I quote); Mason to Carlson, 15 April 1946, Mason Papers, DUKE.

33. *AC,* 18 July 1948 (first quotation); "Kluxers on the Prowl," 21–22 (second quotation); *CD,* 16 July 1949 (third quotation).

34. KKK File, reel 96, 1946, TU; *NYT,* 22 July 1946 (second quotation); *MA,* 23 June 1949 (first quotation); Corley, "Quest for Racial Harmony," 59.

35. Pt. 4, reel 6 and pt. 8, ser. B, reel 26, NAACP Papers, LC and MADD; Anti-Negro Groups File, reel 103, 1948, reel 108, 1949, and KKK File, reel 96, 1946, TU; *NYT,* 19 Nov. 1946, p. 6 (also has first quotation), 1 Sept. 1948, p. 13; *CD,* 30 Nov. 1946 (first quotation); *AC,* 28 Sept. 1949 (second quotation); *BAA,* 10 Sept. 1949.

36. 1948 clipping, box 6, folder 24, Green Papers, BPLA; Sullivan, "Southern Reformers," 239 63, 300–33.

37. Connor to Cook, 2, 25 Feb. 1959, 29 May, and 14 Aug. 1959, box 2, folder 16, Eugene "Bull" Connor Papers, BPLA; Ward, "Racial Politics, Culture, and the Cole Incident of 1956," 181–208; Nunnelly, *Bull Connor,* 77 (quoted), also 76, 157, 170, 184; Chalmers, *Hooded Americanism,* 372; Feldman, *From Demagogue to Dixiecrat,* 110–23, 133–42.

38. *CD,* 26 April 1947 (quoted).

39. Motley to Marshall, 15 Aug. 1949, pp. 1–4 in NAACP Papers, part 5, reel 19, group 2, box B-121 and box B-129, LC and MADD; testimony of Leslie Perry, NAACP representative, 147, and Clancy E. Lake, 186, in United States, House of Representatives, 81st Cong., Committee of the Judiciary, Subcommittee No. 3, *Beatings and Cross-Burnings in Alabama Towns,* Investigation, 1949, MADD, hereafter cited as *House Hearings, 1949;* Anti-Negro Groups File, reel 99, 1947, TU; *People's Voice,* 3 March 1947, p. 8; *CD,* 1 Feb., 26 April 1947, 4 June 1949; *BAA,* 18 Jan. 1947; Nunnelly, *Bull Connor,* 3, 36, 76–77.

40. KKK File, reel 96, 1946 and reel 99, 1947, TU; *BN,* 3 Aug. 1946; *ADW,* 6 Aug. 1946; *PC,* 4 Oct. 1947.

41. Testimony of Clancy E. Lake, 197, *House Hearings, 1949,* MADD; *NYT,* 25 Sept. 1949, p. 81; *CD,* 4 June 1949; *TP,* 28 Sept. 1949; and Corley, "Quest for Racial Harmony," 37.

42. Charles C. Gomillion, of *Gomillion v. Lightfoot* fame, led the Tuskegee group, see 364 U.S. 339 (1960); *LI,* 26 Dec. 1948; *ADW,* 25 Dec. 1948; *MA,* 19 June, 3 Nov. 1948; *BAA,* 12 Nov. 1948; Corley, "Quest for Racial Harmony," 47–48; and Nunnelly, *Bull Connor,* 36.

43. *DW,* 30 May, 14 Nov. 1948; *BN,* 18 Feb., 24–25 Aug., 23 Dec. 1948; *PC,* 23 Oct. 1948; *ADW,* 22 May 1948.

44. *JG* and *PC,* 24 July 1948; *BN,* 30 June 1948; *MA,* 12 April 1948. The KKK note informed the owner of the car with the Henry Wallace sticker that "some of us . . . had to go up North during the war and we had to live the way you damn Yankees live. But now the tables have turned. . . . And we expect you to live the way we rebels live." Quoted in *MA,* 12 April 1948. Note the "Reconstruction Syndrome" language.

45. Thompson to Sheldon, 13 Aug. 1948, folder 2, file "Ku Klux Klan, 1948–1950," Folsom Papers, ADAH; Corley, "Quest for Racial Harmony," 49.

46. *AC,* 23 June 1948, *BN,* 12, 17 June 1948 (quoted); *MA,* 12, 23 June 1948.

47. Morris to Whom It May Concern, 22 June 1948, box 8, folder 21, Green Papers, BPLA; Thompson to Sheldon, 13 Aug. 1948, and Littlefield et al. to Horn, 25 June 1948, box SG 12644, folder: KKK, 1948–50, Folsom Papers, ADAH; *NYHT* and *BN,* 25 June 1948; *Columbus Recorder,* 24 June 1948 (quoted); *CD,* 3 July 1948; *MA,* 13 June 1948.

48. *Chattanooga News,* quoted in *Dallas Southern Weekly,* 3 July 1948 (fifth quotation); *BN,* 15 June 1948 (first, second, and fourth quotations), also 25, 29 June 1948; *MA,* 13 June 1948 (third quotation). Some of the quoted passages also appear in *DW,* 4 July 1948.

49. *BN,* 15, 25 June 1948; Velie, "Klan Rides South Again," 14.

50. YMBC to Green, 21 June 1948, Yielding to Green, 23 June 1948, Comer to Green, 7 July 1949, Parler to Green, 27 June 1948, Gordon to Green, 15 July 1949, box 8, folder 21, Green Papers, BPLA.

51. Anti-Negro Groups File, reel 103, 1948; *BN,* 15 June 1948 (quoted), 17 June 1948; *DW,* 4 July 1948.

52. Berkowitz to Green, 15 June 1948, Willis to Green, 17 June 1948, and Green to Berkowitz, 18 June 1948, box 8, folder 21, Green Papers, BPLA; *MA,* 15, 26 June 1948; *BN,* 17 June 1948 (quoted), 25 June 1948; *TP,* 21 June 1948; and *Charleston News-Courier,* 31 July 1946.

53. Palmer Weber, Interview, p. 8, CU; *ADW,* 3 July 1948; *BN,* 24 July 1949; *AC,* 17 May, 9 Sept. 1946; "The Mark of the Beast," *SE* 8 (2, 1980): 1–112; *BN,* 24 May, 4 and 9 July 1948.

Mitch actually ordered his UMW members either to "get out of the Klan or [to] get out of the Union." Quoted in *BN,* 24 July 1949. The NAACP was especially upset about the silence of the Birmingham Federation of Labor, the Birmingham Industrial Urban Council, the Alabama CIO, the AFL, and William Mitch of the UMW. See *ADW,* 3 July 1948.

54. An exception to this relationship was the temporary alliance of the 1920s Klan with farmers, labor, and women that supported progressive causes; see Thornton, "Alabama Politics," 83–112, and Flynt, "Organized Labor," 163–80. In 1930s Birmingham, Horace Wilkinson remained close both to the AFL and the KKK, while Jimmie Jones, a former Klansman and president of the city commission, was an AFL member. The interracial CIO, though, was a perennial enemy of the Klan.

55. "The Mark of the Beast," *SE* 8 (2, 1980): 61.

56. *BAH,* 18 May 1946; Newton and Newton, *Ku Klux Klan,* 133–34; Zieger, *The CIO,* 278–90.

57. Beittel to Carmichael and Beittel to Shores, 18 Feb. 1949; Carmichael to Beittel, 17 March 1949; Beittel to Carmichael 22 March 1949, TC/Adm/4/13/2/74, Adam C. Beittel Papers, TC; pt. 5, reel 20, NAACP Papers, LC and MADD; J. J. Green to Cooper Green, 13 Aug. 1949, box 4, folder 26, Green Papers, BPLA; *MCA,* 22 June 1949 (quoted); *PC,* 17 Feb. 1949; *BAA,* 12 March 1949; *BN,* 23 June, 20 Aug., 26 Oct. 1949; *MA,* 23 Feb., 3 Aug. 1949; *BW,* 27 Sept. 1949; *CD,* and *BAA,* 6 Aug. 1949; "Kluxers on the Prowl," 21–22; *BN,* 19 Dec. 1971, in Elovitz, *Century of Jewish Life in Dixie,* 223 n. 17; Corley, "Quest for Racial Harmony," 55.

58. Anti-Negro Groups File, reel 108, 1949, TU; *BN,* 19 April 1949 (first quotation), 22 June 1949; *CJ,* 23 June 1949 (second quotation).

59. Edna McDanal, Interview, 24 June 1949, Hugh McDanal and J. E. Woods, Interviews, 12 June 1949, Dester Lott and Jerry Ensor, Interviews, 13 June 1949, Mr. and Mrs. Virgil Cook and Mr. and Mrs. Grady Ensor, Cal Notions, and W. E. Mitchell, Interviews, 14 June 1949, and statement of George Bensko to Torrence, 23 June 1949 (first quotation), box SG 12644, folder: KKK, 1949, no. 5, Folsom Papers, ADAH; Anti-Negro Groups File, reel 108, 1949, TU; *BN,* 26 June, 30 Oct. 1949; *MA,* 12–13 June 1949; *Detroit Free Press,* 12 June 1949; Chalmers, *Hooded Americanism,* 335–37; "It Sure Was Pretty," *Time* 54 (7 Nov. 1949): 24 (second quotation).

60. Testimony of Lake, 179–81, 188–91, and Clark Stallworth, 153, 162–65, in *House Hearings, 1949,* MADD; Anti-Negro Groups File, reel 108, 1949, TU; Steve Marshlar Statement (second quotation), John Marshlar, Ms. Willie A. Black, E. B. Brock, Mayor John Bensko, and James Floyd Shaffer, Interviews, all on 23 June 1949, box SG 12644, folder: KKK, 1949, no. 5, Folsom Papers, ADAH; *MA,* 12–13 June 1949 (first quotation), also 14–16, 20–23 June, 6 July, 7 Dec. 1949; *BN,* 15–16, 20–24, 30 June, 1, 5, 23 July, 16 Aug., 27 Oct., 6 Dec. 1949; *NYT,* 16 June 1949, p. 58; *NYA,* 25 June 1949; *NYHT,* 17 June 1949; *LAX,* 16 June 1949; *CD,* 21 Feb. 1949; *Birmingham Weekly Review,* 11 March 1949; *WP,* 20 June 1949, p. 14; *AC,* 2 July, 7 Dec. 1949; *PC,* 2 April 1949; *CJ,* 1 June 1949; Newton and Newton, *Ku Klux Klan,* 537.

61. Billy Guyton Stovall, Interview, 24 June 1949, Roxie Stovall, Interview, 18 June 1949, Case of B. G. Stovall Investigation, 15–20 June 1949, box SG 12644, folder: KKK, 1949, no. 5, Folsom Papers, ADAH. According the testimony of reporter Clarke Stallworth, Roscoe Fowler said, "Call me on the Klan would you, you son of a bitch?" as Glenn Godfrey threw a hammer at his head. Quoted in testimony of Stallworth, *House Hearings, 1949,* pp. 162–63, MADD and *MA,* 21 June 1949. See also *BN,* 21 June 1949.

62. *BN,* 16 June 1949 (first quotation), also 23 July, 27 Oct., 6 Dec. 1949; *MA,* 23 June 1949 (second quotation), also 6 July, 7 Dec. 1949; KKK File, reel 108, 1949, TU; *ADW,* 1, 21

July 1949; *AC,* 2 July, 7 Dec. 1949; pt. 5, reels 19, 20, NAACP Papers, LC and MADD; Allen et al. to Bates, 25 June 1949, William Hamilton, William Rochester, Flossie Rochester, and Emmet Atkins, Interviews, and Martha Gladys Rochester, Interview, all on 23 June 1949, box SG 12644, folder: KKK, 1949, no. 5, Folsom Papers, ADAH.

63. Anti-Negro Groups File, reel 108, 1949, TU; *BN,* 1 July 1949 (quoted), also 4 July 1949; *CD,* and *PC,* 9 July 1949; *AC,* 2 July 1949; *CJ,* 1 July 1949; *MA,* 2 July 1949.

64. *MR,* 8 Dec. 1949, clipping, box 131, KKK-Mobile File, MMA; *NYT,* 19, 21 July 1949; *BN,* 18 July, 14 Nov. 1949; *MA,* 23, 30 June 1949; *ADW,* 24 March, 15 Sept. 1949; *PC,* 2 April, 17 Sept., 31 Dec. 1949.

15. FEDERAL-STATE INTERACTION IN THE 1940S

1. Anti-Negro Groups File, reel 108, 1949, TU; *NYHT,* 17 June 1949; *BN,* 22–23 June, 19 Aug. 1949; *ADW,* 25 June 1949; *MW,* 28 June 1949; *CD,* 25 June 1949.

2. *House Hearings, 1949; WP,* 25 June 1949.

3 A Citizen to Folsom, 21 Oct. 1949 (first quotation), box SG 12644, folder: KKK, 1949, no. 6, *BP,* clipping, folder: KKK, 1949, no. 7, Folsom Papers, ADAH; *ME,* 7 July 1949; "Night-Riding in Alabama," *Commonweal,* 50 (8 July 1949): 309 (second quotation); *ADW,* 7 July 1949.

4. Testimony of Herbert M. Levy, 126–29 (quoted), Leslie Perry, 147, and Stallworth, 160–69, *House Hearings, 1949,* MADD.

5. Salmond, *"My Mind Set on Freedom,"* 74.

6. Gordon to Folsom, 18 June 1949, box SG 12644, folder: KKK, 1949, no. 4, Alabama Governors Papers, James E. Folsom, Sr., ADAH.

7. *CD,* and *BAA,* 6 Aug. 1949; Corley, "Quest for Racial Harmony," 55; *MA,* 3 July 1949. The *BN,* 22 July 1949, declared, "Congress ought to do nothing to discourage the excellent beginning Alabama has made toward crushing [KKK] . . . lawlessness. It should allow the state authorities a chance to follow through."

8. *MCA,* 27 June 1949 (quoted), clipping, box 8, folder 21, Cooper Green Papers, BPLA.

9. Act No. 434, 23 Aug. 1949, pp. 658–59 (quoted), and H.J.R. 73, 24 June 1949 (also contains the quoted passage), both in *Alabama Acts* (Folsom refused to sign the resolution); David K. Niles Memo, 29 June 1949, Official Files, Papers of Harry S Truman, HST; *CD,* 23 July 1949; *CT,* 24 June 1949; *BN,* 17 June, 10 July 1949; *MA,* 25 June 1949 (also has the quoted passage). A veterans' group spokesman said that Alabama would "clean up this situation without help from the outside." Quoted in the *CT,* 24 June 1949.

10. Testimony of Lake, 184–85, 192–94, Paul B. Trawick, 200–8, and Congressman Samuel Hobbs, 264–301, in *House Hearings, 1949,* MADD (quoted copy on p. 274); *NYT,* 30 June 1949; *CD,* 9 July 1949; *CDW,* 7 July 1949; *MA,* 3 July 1949; *BN,* 31 March, 23 June, 22 July, 1 Nov. 1949.

11. Anti-Negro Groups File, reel 108, 1949, TU; Beirman, "Alabama Rips off the Hood," 3; *NYT,* 9 July 1949, p. 28, 10 July 1949, 23 July 1949, p. 24; *BN,* 10 July 1949 (quoted), also 22, 30 June, 9, 11, 13, 18 July 1949; *MA,* 10, 22 July, 7 Aug., 15 Sept. 1949; *PC,* 1 Oct. 1949, p. 11; *AC,* 20 July 1949; *BAA,* 16 July 1949; Newton and Newton, *Ku Klux Klan,* 195.

12. Act No. 139, 28 June 1949, *Alabama Acts,* 165–66; *NYT,* 26–28, 29 June 1949, p. 54; *CSM,* 28 June 1949, p. 3; *BN,* 18–19, 27–29 June 1949; *CDW,* 22–23, 26 June 1949; *CD,* 25 June 1949; *LAX,* 30 June 1949; *MA,* 23, 29 June 1949; *MCA* and *AC,* 18 July 1949; Rice, *Ku Klux Klan in American Politics,* 113.

13. Pruitt to Folsom, c. 1949 (quoted), box SG 12644, folder: KKK, 1949, no. 5, Folsom Papers, ADAH; Middlebrooks, "Alabama Votes to Unmask the Klan," 871; *NYT,* 26 June 1949, p. 33, and 27 June 1949, p. 38; *AC,* 26 June 1949.

14. *WP,* 23 June 1949; *MA,* 19, 22 June 1949 (both quoted passages); *LAX,* 23 June 1949; *BN,* 22 June 1949; Anti-Negro Groups File, reel 108, 1949, TU.

15. *MA,* 7 Nov. 1948 (fourth and fifth quotations), 19 June 1949; *TP,* 27 June 1949 (first quotation); *BN,* 29 Nov. 1948 (also has fifth quotation), 27 June 1949 (sixth quotation), also 13, 21, 28 June 1949; *CD,* 25 June, 6 Aug. 1949; *CJ,* 23 June 1949; *MCA,* 18 June 1949 (third quotation); *TJ,* 7 Nov. 1948 (also has fifth quotation); Chalmers, *Hooded Americanism,* 336–37 (also has sixth quotation).

16. Carmichael to Perry, 18 Oct. 1948, Carmichael to McDowell, 28 June 1949, folders: Jefferson County, Jefferson County, 1949–1950, and Informal Opinions, 1948–1949, Alabama State Records, Office of the Attorney General, ADAH; Carmichael to Folsom, 22 June 1949, folder 3, Ku Klux Klan, 1949, Inauguration–Ku Klux Klan; and also Perry to Folsom, 12 Oct. 1949; Folsom to Graves, 18 Aug., 17 Oct. 1949; Boyd to Price, 15 June 1950; Folsom to Graves, 22 Feb. 1950; Perry to Lyerly, 29 Aug. 1950, folder 15, Law Enforcement: Hooded Groups, Folsom Papers, ADAH; *NYT,* 13 June 1949, p. 13 (quoted).

17. *MA,* 25 Sept. 1949; *BN,* 19 April 1947, 17 June 1948; *DW,* 4 May 1947, 4 July 1948, 25 Dec. 1949; *PC,* 3 May 1947 and 17 Dec. 1949.

18. *NYT,* 24 Feb. 1948, p. 13; *BN,* 22 July 1949, called the KKK "Nazi-style bully boys." See also *BN,* 24 May 1948, 23 May, 22, 26 June, and 22 July 1949; *MA,* 4 Oct. 1946 (first quotation), 21 May 1946 (second quotation), also 11 May, 15 June 1946, 26 March 1948; *CD,* 16 July 1949; *AC,* 6 June 1946, 21 June 1948; *TN,* 31 May 1949.

19. KKK File, reel 96, 1946, TU; *MA,* 5 April 1946 (quoted).

20. Paul B. Trawick testimony, 198–208, *House Hearings, 1949,* MADD; *MR,* 9 Dec. 1949 editorial, box 131, KKK-Mobile File, MMA; *AS,* 7 Nov. 1948, clipping, box 181, folder 462, Harry Mell Ayers Papers, UASC; *ME,* 23 June 1949, printed anti-Klan editorials from: *DeKalb Times, Eufaula Tribune, Talladega Home, SN, Troy Messenger, Centerville Press, Jasper Mountain Eagle, Our Southern Home, Fort Payne Journal, TJ; BN,* 19 June 1949, added anti-KKK editorials from the *Moulton Advertiser, TN, HT, AJ,* and *BP;* see *AC,* 15 May 1946; *MA,* 11, 27 May 1946; *BN,* 6 Oct. 1947, 19 July, 8 Aug. 1949.

21. Anti-Negro Groups File, reel 108, 1949, TU; *MW,* 2 Sept. 1949 (also has the quoted passage); *CDW,* 22 June 1949; *MA,* 7 Aug. 1949; *BN,* 23, 28 June, 4, 17 July, 8 Aug., 25 Oct. 1949; *ADW,* 22 June 1949 (quoted). The Klan told a Jefferson County veterans' group to "stick to the selling of puppies" and leave the investigation of floggings alone. Quoted in *BN,* 17 June 1949.

22. Middlebrooks, "Alabama Votes to Unmask the Klan," 871; *BN,* 19, 23 June 1949; *MA,* 12 Aug. 1949; *CDW,* 4 Dec. 1949; *CT,* 24 June 1949.

23. "Program Convention, 1949," association box 8, Alabama Associations Records, American Legion Records, ADAH; Warner to Folsom, 21 June 1949, folder 3, Ku Klux Klan 1949, Folsom Papers, ADAH; "Sheeted Jerks," *Nation* 169 (2 July 1949): 2; *MCA,* 20 June 1949; *AC,* 6 June 1949; *PC,* 17 Dec. 1949; *BN,* 17, 21–24, 28, 30 June, 2 July 1949; *MA,* 4 July 1949 (quoted); Rice, *Ku Klux Klan in American Politics,* 110.

24. Harrell, *Quest for a Christian America,* 16–17, and "Religious Pluralism: Catholics, Jews, and Sectarians," 66–73; Niebuhr, *Kingdom of God in America.*

25. *Jasper Mountain Eagle,* quoted in *ME,* 23 July 1949; *MA,* 14 July 1949; *BN,* 2 July 1948, 19 June 1949; *AC,* 15 May 1946, 25 Nov. 1948, 14 June 1949; *PC,* 17 Dec. 1949.

26. KKK Scrapbooks, no. 257, BPLA; Hudgins to Editor, *BN,* 27 June 1949 (second quo-

tation), and Westermann to Editor, *BN*, 27 June 1949, both in KKK File, reel 108, 1949, TU; *MA* and *AC*, 4 Jan. 1944; *MA*, 14 July 1949 (first quotation); *AC*, 14 June 1949 (third quotation), 25 Nov. 1948 (fourth quotation). Klan supporters tarred opponents such as Ralph McGill and Jim Folsom with the Reconstruction labels of "carpetbaggers and scalawags" and called Florida senator Claude Pepper a "turncoat Southerner" and Florida governor Fuller Warren a "traitor." Quoted in *MA*, 23 Oct. 1949.

27. *Jasper Mountain Eagle*, quoted in *ME*, 23 July 1949 (from which I quote).

28. Lake testimony, 189–90, in *House Hearings, 1949*, MADD; *BN*, 19 June 1949 (third quotation), also 17 June and 8 Aug. 1949; *MA*, 19 June 1949 (second quotation), also 16 June and 2 July 1949; *NYHT*, 17 June 1949 (first quotation), also 17 April 1949; *MCA*, 18 June 1949; *BAA*, 2 July 1949. Mrs. Stovall said, "I'd do it" in regard to shooting Ku Kluxers. "I'd not mind at all seeing them drop one at a time." Quoted in *BN*, 17 June 1949, and *MA*, 16 June 1949.

29. McLeod to Folsom, 4 July 1949 (third quotation), folder: KKK, 1949, no. 6, Folsom Papers, ADAH; Anti-Negro Groups File, reel 108, 1949, TU; *MA*, 23 June 1949 (first and second quotations).

30. Anti Negro Groups File, reel 99, 1947, reel 108, 1949, TU; *DW*, 4 May 1947; Corley, "Quest for Racial Harmony," 65.

31. Newton and Newton, *Ku Klux Klan*, 536 (quoted).

32. *NYHT*, 25 Aug. 1949, clipping in official files, Truman Papers, HST; "It Sure Was Pretty," *Time* 54 (7 Nov. 1949): 24; *MA*, 21 Aug. 1949; *BN*, 23 July 1949 (second quotation), also 20 Aug. 1949; *NYT*, 24 July 1949 (first quotation).

33. "It Sure Was Pretty," *Time* 54 (7 Nov. 1949): 24.

34. *BN*, 29–30 June, 18 and 22 July 1949; *MA*, 22 June, 3 July 1949; *CD*, 9, 23 July 1949; *JG*, 25 June 1949; *CSM*, 22 June 1949, p. 7.

35. *CD*, 23 July 1949 (first quotation); Fleetwood to Folsom, 22 June 1949, and Lawrence to Folsom, 20 June 1949, box SG 13479, folder: KKK, 1949, and Governor of Idaho Statement, *NYHT*, 19 June 1949, *Manchester Guardian*, 30 June 1949, and *Bismarck Leader*, n.d., clippings, box SG 12644, folder: KKK, 1949, no. 7, Folsom Papers, ADAH; *NYT*, 29 June 1949, p. 54 (second quotation).

36. *CSM*, 22 June 1949, p. 7; *BN*, 30 June 1949; *CD*, 9 July 1949.

37. Ann M. Parker proposed a municipal antimask ordinance but was told by Mayor Cooper Green that, although he thought it a good idea, he could not pursue it, since city commissioners Bull Connor and Jimmy Morgan regarded it as "superfluous." See Green to Parker, 28 June 1949, box 8, folder 21, Green Papers, BPLA; Sheldon to Folsom, 20 Feb. 1948, Folsom to Sheldon, 1 March 1948, Sheldon and Hoffman to Folsom, 19 Feb. 1948, box SG 12644, folder: KKK, 1948–50, no. 2, Folsom Papers, ADAH; *TN*, 27–31 May 1949; *BN*, 13 June 1949 (quoted), also 28 June 1948, 15, 17, 25 and 28 June 1949; *MA*, 21–22 Feb. 1948, 29–30 June 1949; *TP*, 21 June 1948; *CDW*, 3 July 1948 and 14 June 1949; *TJ*, 7 Nov. 1948; *NYT*, 24 Feb. 1948, p. 13; Middlebrooks, "Alabama Votes to Unmask the Klan," 871.

38. Sheldon to Folsom, 20 Feb. 1948 and Folsom to Sheldon, 1 March 1948, box SG 12644, folder: KKK, 1948–50, no. 2, and Thompson to Asch, 14 Feb. 1950, folder: KKK, 1949, no. 7, Folsom Papers, ADAH.

39. *AS*, 29 April 1948, clipping in 1948 Elections File, Charles G. Dobbins Papers, ADAH.

40. Feldman, *From Demagogue to Dixiecrat*, 134, 149, 154.

41. "It Sure Was Pretty," 24; *BP*, 30 Oct. 1949; *BN*, 26–30 Oct., 7–8 Dec. 1949; *MA*, 26–30 Oct. 1949; *Free Press*, 28, 30 Oct. 1949; *AC*, 27–28 Oct. 1949; *CJ*, 27–29 Oct. 1949; *CD*, 5 Nov. 1949.

42. Anti-Negro Groups File, reel 108, 1949, TU; *BN,* 28 Oct. 1949 (quoted).

43. *BN,* 19 June, 26–29 Oct. 1949; *CJ,* 28 Oct. 1949; *DW,* 6 Nov. 1949.

44. *CSM,* 1 Nov. 1949, p. 11; *NYT,* 13 Dec. 1949, p. 39; *CD,* 12 Nov. 1949; *BN,* 1 Nov., 5–9 Dec. 1949; *MA,* 31 Oct., 1 Nov., 6–7 Dec. 1949; *CJ,* 13 Dec. 1949; *CDW,* 6, 13 Dec. 1949.

45. "Hold Everything," *Time* 54 (25 July 1949): 12; *CSM,* 19 July 1949, p. 15; *BN,* 20 July 1949; *MA,* 21 July 1949.

46. Civil Rights File, reel 108, 1949 and Anti-Negro Groups File, reel 108, 1949, TU; *WP,* 22 June 1949; *Birmingham Age,* 2 July 1949; *CD,* 16 July 1949; *JG,* 2 July 1949; *MW,* 23 Sept. 1949 (second quotation); *New York Age,* 2 July 1949 (first quotation).

47. *BD,* 25 June 1949; *CDW,* and *NYT,* 6 Aug. 1949; *WP,* and *BN,* 4 Aug. 1949; *PC,* 13 Aug. 1949; *JG,* 2 July 1949; *MA,* 4–7 Aug. 1949.

48. *NYT,* 8 July 1949, 27 July 1949, p. 48; *BN,* 7 July 1949 (quoted), also 28 July, 1–2 Aug. 1949; *MA,* 20 Sept. 1949 (has the same quoted passage), also 30 July, 3, 19 Aug. 1949; *AC,* 24–25, 29 July 1949; *BAH,* 31 July 1949; *CSM,* 27 July 1949, p. 16, 30 July 1949, p. 12, and 3 Aug. 1949, p. 10.

49. Pt. 5, reel 20, NAACP Papers, LC and MADD; *NYT,* 1, 15, 18 (p. 1), and 23–24 July 1949; *MA,* 31 Dec. 1941, 8, 12–15 July, 1, 6 Aug., 13 Sept. 1949; *TP,* 7 Sept. 1949; *BN,* 10–11, 17 July, 17 Aug. 1949; *AC,* 15 July 1949; *State v. Morris,* 252 Ala. 51 (1949); *Ex parte Morris,* 252 Ala. 551 (1949); *WP,* 23 July 1949, p. 11B.

50. *Morris v. State,* 253 Ala. 497 (1950); *BN,* 5 Aug. 1949 (quoted), also 20 Aug. 1949; *MA,* 5, 19, 21 Aug. 1949; *PC,* 6 Aug. 1949.

51. *MA,* 15, 19 Sept. 1949; *BN,* 20 Aug. 1949.

52. Anti-Negro Groups File, reel 108, 1949, TU; *BN,* 20 Sept. 1949 (quoted), also 22 Sept. 1949; *MA,* 15, 20 Sept. 1949.

53. *NYT,* 22 July 1949, p. 38 (second quotation); *CSM,* 21 July 1949, p. 3; *BN,* 28 June 1949 (first quotation), also 22 July, 19 Aug., 23 Oct. 1949; *MW,* 2 Sept. 1949; *AC,* 3 Aug. 1949; Rice, *Ku Klux Klan in American Politics,* 115–18; Chalmers, *Hooded Americanism,* 335.

54. *NYT,* 22 Aug. 1949, p. 11; *CSM,* 22 Aug. 1949, p. 14; *BN,* 25 Aug., 7, 26 Sept. 1949; *MA,* 19 Aug., 26 Sept. 1949; *AC,* 19, 24 Aug. 1949.

55. Anti-Negro Groups File, reel 108, 1949, TU, information about the Original Klans from the *New Republic; BN,* 22 June, 23 Oct. 1949; *AC,* 23 July 1949; *PC,* 10 July 1948 (second quotation); Newton and Newton, *Ku Klux Klan,* 445 (first quotation), also 273, 301, 454; "Original Klans, Inc.," *New Republic* 97 (17 July 1948): n.p. (also has second quoted passage).

56. *NYT,* 19 Dec. 1949, p. 44; *BN,* 26, 28 Sept. 1949; *MA,* 8, 25, and 28 Sept., 18–20 Dec. 1949; *AC,* 28 Sept. 1949; *CDW,* 4 Dec. 1949; Newton and Newton, *Ku Klux Klan,* 404; Chalmers, *Hooded Americanism,* 339–40; Anti-Negro Groups File, reel 108, 1949 (quoted), TU.

57. Newton and Newton, *Ku Klux Klan,* 536 (quoted); *BAA,* 10 Sept. 1949; *ADW,* 4 Dec. 1949; *MA,* 25 Sept. 1949.

58. Chalmers, *Hooded Americanism,* 339–40.

59. *MA,* 4 Oct. 1946, and *MA,* quoted in *BN,* 22 June 1949 (second quotation); *CT,* 24 June 1949 (first quotation); Wade, *Fiery Cross,* 273. Apparently this brand of opposition to the Klan could be found in other parts of the South as well. A San Antonio woman wrote that "the harm . . . the Ku Klux Klan has done to Dixie is beyond the scope of mention. . . . it has disgraced us." The stupidity of the Klansmen was "not a dumb God-given ignorance as the savages of the 'Dark Continent' possess," the Texan wrote, revealing the limits of her racial enlightenment. "Their's was a man make [*sic*] ignorance an ignorance bathed in prejudice, hatered [*sic*] and deceit . . . , a form of ignorance that is truly dangerous." Quoted in Whitfield to Folsom, 15 July 1949, box SG 12644, folder: KKK, 1949, no. 6, Folsom Papers, ADAH.

60. *CD*, 1 Feb. 1947; *MA*, 22 Feb. 1948; *NYT*, 24 Feb. 1948.

61. Jennie Bartran Gentleman to Folsom, 13 June 1949 (first quotation), box SG 12644, folder: KKK, 1949, no. 4, A Citizen to Folsom, 21 Oct. 1949 (second quotation), folders: KKK, 1949, no. 6, no. 7, Folsom Papers, ADAH; *St. Louis Dispatch*, 19 June 1949 (third quotation).

62. *AJ*, quoted in *BN*, 4 July 1949 (which I quote).

63. John Marshlar and George Bensko, Interviews, 23 June 1949, statement of J. B. Torrance and George Bensko, 23 June 1949, statement of C. A. Lollar and J. W. Chance, 17 June 1949, Report on Raid in Adamsville Fed. KKK, Inc., 17 June 1949, all in box SG 12644, folder: KKK, 1949, no. 5, Folsom Papers, ADAH; testimony of Herbert M. Levy, 129, *House Hearings, 1949*, MADD; *ME*, 23 June 1949; *AC*, 19 June 1949 (quoted); *BN*, 15 June 1948, 17, 20–21, and 26 June 1949; *PC*, 15 Oct. 1949, p. 20; *TN*, 29 May 1949; *LI*, 26 Dec. 1948.

64. Testimony of Herbert M. Levy, p. 129 (first quotation), *House Hearings, 1949*, MADD; *BN*, 21 June 1949 (second quotation).

65. Memo from Green to Brown, 28 Jan. 1951, Taylor to Editor, *BN*, 26 Aug. 1954, both in box 10, folder 23, Jimmy Morgan Papers, BPLA; *MCA*, 27 June 1949, clipping, box 8, folder 2, Green Papers, BPLA; *BN*, 1 July 1949 (quoted), also 9 Sept. 1949; *TN*, 31 May 1949.

66. Pitts to Folsom, 27 June 1949, and Winter to Folsom, 21 June 1949, both in box SG 13479, folder: KKK, 1949, and Flowers to Folsom, 23 June 1949, folder: KKK, 1949, no. 4, 302 to *BN*, and *BAH*, 25 June 1949, folder: KKK, 1949, no. 5, Anonymous to Folsom, 18 June 1949 (first quotation), folder: KKK, 1949, no. 6, all three files in box SG 12644, Folsom Papers, ADAH; *BN*, 7 July 1948, 20 and 24 July 1949; *MA*, 2 July, 7 Aug., 23 Oct. 1949; Harris L. Charles to Editor, *MA*, 14 Nov. 1946 (second quotation). Another Alabamian added that the "Negro shouldn't want to intermarry. . . . Don't place the blame on the KKK" in yet another complaint alleging that social equality would lead to miscegenation. Quoted in Ernest C. Snyder to Editor, *BN*, 7 July 1948.

67. Scott to Folsom, 5 July 1949 (second quotation), box SG 12644, folder: KKK, 1949, no. 8, and Pitts to Folsom, 27 June 1949 (first quotation), box SG 13479, folder: KKK, 1949, both in Folsom Papers, ADAH.

68. X to author, 20 Jan. 1993, copy in the author's collection; *BN*, 24 July 1949 (quoted).

69. Allen et al. to Bates, 25 June 1949, box SG 12644, folder: KKK, 1949, no. 5, Folsom Papers, ADAH; *DW*, 5 Dec. 1948; *MCA*, 23 Nov. 1948; *BN*, 30 June 1948 (first quotation), 1 Aug. 1949 (quoted), also 24 June, 5, 12 July, and 5 Dec. 1949.

70. KKK File, reel 96, 1946, TU; *BN*, 3 July 1949; *AC*, 15 May 1946.

71. Thornton, "Alabama Politics," 83–112.

EPILOGUE: "TO WITHER AWAY"

1. Jennie Bartran Gentleman to Folsom, 13 June 1949, box SG 12644, folder: KKK, 1949, no. 4, Folsom Papers, ADAH.

2. A Citizen to Folsom, 3 July 1949, box SG 12644, folder: KKK, 1949, no. 8, Folsom Papers, ADAH.

Bibliography

PRIMARY SOURCES

Manuscript and Record Collections

Alabama Baptist State Convention Reports. SU.
Alabama Conference of the Methodist-Episcopal Church, South. Minutes. HUN.
Alabama Pamphlets Collection. ADAH.
American Civil Liberties Union Records. PU.
American Legion Records. Alabama Associations Records. ADAH.
American Periodical Series. MADD.
Anti-Defamation League of B'nai B'rith Records. AJHS.
Anti-Negro Groups File. TU.
Association Records. ADAH.
Office of the Attorney General. Alabama State Records. ADAH.
Harry Mell Ayers Papers. UASC.
John H. Bankhead, II Papers. ADAH.
William B. Bankhead Papers. ADAH.
N. A. Barrett City Commission Scrapbooks. BPLA.
Adam C. Beittel Papers. TC.
Bibb County Ku Klux Klan File. Snell Research Notes. SU.
Birmingham Police Department Surveillance Files. BPLA.
Bledsoe-Kelly Collection. SU.
William W. Brandon Papers. Alabama Governors Papers. ADAH.
Chapman Papers. RBD and HST.
City Board of Commissioners. Minutes. MMA.
Civil Rights File. TU.
Tom C. Clark Papers. RBD and HST.
Clippings File. AUSC.
Eugene "Bull" Connor Papers. BPLA.
Clay County KKK File. Snell Research Notes. SU.
Correspondence by Author. TSLA.

Crenshaw County Ku Klux Klan File. Snell Research Notes. SU.
Crime File. TU.
Charles B. Crow Papers. ADAH.
Cecil L. Davis Letters. ADAH.
Harwell Goodwin Davis Papers. SU.
Diary of James Stanley Laird. SU.
Frank M. Dixon Papers. Alabama Governors Papers. ADAH.
Charles Dobbins Papers. ADAH.
Clifford J. Durr Papers. ADAH.
Durr Family Papers. ADAH.
Virginia Foster Durr Papers. ADAH.
Eugene Feldman Papers. ADAH.
Charles A. Fell Memoirs. BPLA.
James E. Folsom, Sr. Papers. Alabama Governors Papers. ADAH.
Hugh Gladney Grant Papers. DUKE.
David Bibb Graves Papers, 1927–1931. Alabama Governors Papers. ADAH.
David Bibb Graves Papers, 1935–1939. Alabama Governors Papers. ADAH.
Cooper Green Papers. BPLA.
Greene County Ku Klux Klan File. Snell Research Notes. SU.
Grover C. Hall, Jr. Papers. ADAH.
Grover C. Hall, Sr. Papers. ADAH.
Grover C. Hall, Sr. Scrapbooks. ADAH.
J. Thomas Heflin Papers. UASC.
J. Thomas Heflin Scrapbooks. SU.
Charles Henderson Papers. Alabama Governors Papers. ADAH.
Lister Hill Papers. UASC.
J. F. Hines Papers. SU.
Arthur M. Hyde Papers. UMO.
International Labor Defense Fund Papers. SC.
Forney Johnston Papers. ADAH.
John P. Johnston Letters. PIKE.
James Marion "Jimmie" Jones Papers. ADAH and BPLA.
Journal of the Alabama–West Florida Conference. HUN.
Thomas E. Kilby Papers. Alabama Governors Papers. ADAH.
Klanwatch Project. SPLC.
Ku Klux Klan Collection. BCHS.
Ku Klux Klan File. BA.
Ku Klux Klan File. BCA.
Ku Klux Klan File. TU.
Ku Klux Klan File through 1979. MPL.
Ku Klux Klan–Mobile File. MMA.
Ku Klux Klan Scrapbooks. BPLA.
Lee County Ku Klux Klan File. Snell Research Notes. SU.
Lynching File. TU.
Maps of Birmingham. TCSH.
Lucy Randolph Mason Papers. DUKE.
Charles C. McCall Letters. ADAH.
Charles C. McCall Papers. ADAH.

Leon McCord Scrapbooks. ADAH.
J. Howard McGrath Papers. RBD and HST.
Benjamin Meek Miller Papers. Alabama Governors Papers. ADAH.
Milner Family Papers. BPLA.
Jimmy Morgan Papers. BPLA.
Papers of Philleo Nash. HST.
Papers of the National Association for the Advancement of Colored People. LC and
     MADD.
Percy Family Papers. MDAH.
Seth G. Persons Papers. Alabama Governors Papers. ADAH.
Photographs and Pictures Collection. ADAH.
Photographs and Pictures Collection. BPLA.
Race Relations File. TU.
V. M. Scott Reminiscences. TCHA.
Shelby County Ku Klux Klan File. Snell Research Notes. SU.
Simmons File. HUN.
William Joseph Simmons File. HUN.
Chauncey Sparks Papers. Alabama Governors Papers. ADAH.
Stephen J. Spingarn Papers. RBD and HST.
State Board of Administration Records. ADAH.
State Democratic Executive Committee Records. ADAH.
Oliver Day Street Papers. ADAH.
Philip H. Taft Research Notes. BPLA.
Talladega County KKK File. Snell Research Notes. SU.
Papers of Harry S Truman. HST.
Oscar W. Underwood Papers. ADAH.
Unity Club Records. ADAH.
Horace W. Weissinger Papers. In the collection of the author.
Horace C. Wilkinson Papers. SU.
J. J. Willett Papers. SU.
Yearbook Collection. TSUA.

Government Documents and Public Records

Alabama Official and Statistical Register. Birmingham: Birmingham Printing, 1919, 1923,
     1927, 1931.
Biographical Dictionary of the American Congress, 1774–1971. Washington, D.C.: U.S. Gov-
     ernment Printing Office, 1971.
Congressional Record. 1915–1928.
General Laws (and Joint Resolutions) of the Legislature of Alabama. Montgomery: Brown
     Printing. Also cited as the *Alabama Acts.*
Report of the Alabama Council of Defense, 17 May 1917 to 31 December 1918. Montgomery:
     Brown Printing, 1919.
United States. Department of Commerce. Bureau of the Census. *Fourteenth Census of the
     United States, Taken in the Year 1920, Vol. 3: Population, 1920; Composition and Charac-
     teristics of the Population by States.* Washington, D.C.: U.S. Government Printing Office,
     1922.
———. *Religious Bodies: 1916, Pt. 1: Summary and General Tables.* Washington, D.C.: U.S.
     Government Printing Office, 1919.

———. *Religious Bodies: 1926, Vol. 1: Summary and Detailed Tables.* Washington, D.C.: U.S. Government Printing Office, 1930.

United States Congress. House. Committee of the Judiciary, Subcommittee No. 3. *Beatings and Cross-burnings in Alabama Towns.* 81st Cong., 2d sess. (1949).

United States Congress. House. Committee on Rules. *Hearings on the Ku Klux Klan Before the Committee on Rules.* 67th Cong., 1st sess. (1921).

United States Congress. House. Committee on Rules, Subcommittee to Investigate Communist Activities. *Investigation of Communist Propaganda.* 71st Cong., 2d sess. (1930).

United States Congress. Senate. Committee on Education and Labor, Subcommittee on Free Speech and the Rights of Labor. *Violation of Free Speech and the Rights of Labor.* 75th Cong., 2d sess. (1937–1938).

United States Congress. Senate. Committee on Privileges and Elections. *Hearings Before a Subcommittee of the Committee on Privileges and Elections,* 3–7 December 1931. 72d Cong., 2d sess. (1947).

———. *Reports on Conditions of Ballot Boxes.* 72nd Cong., 1st sess. (1931).

Court Records

Barton v. City of Birmingham 234 Ala. 20 (1937) and 173 So. 621.

Brown et al. v. Board of Education of Topeka et al. 344 U.S. 1, 141 (1952), 345 U.S. 972 (1953), 347 U.S. 483 (1954), and 349 U.S. 294 (1955).

Buchanan v. Warley 245 U.S. 60 (1917).

Chambers v. Florida 309 U.S. 227 (1940).

City of Birmingham et al. v. Monk et al. 185 F.2d 859 (1950), 87 F. Supp. 538, and 341 U.S. 940 (1951).

Clayton v. Alabama 220 Ala. 39 (1929).

Doss v. Alabama 220 Ala. 30 (1929).

Esdale v. State 260 Ala. 45 (1953).

Ex parte Morris 252 Ala. 551 (1949).

Ex parte Wilkinson 220 Ala. 529 (1929).

Gomillion v. Lightfoot 364 U.S. 339 (1960).

In re the Contest of J. Thomas Heflin v. John H. Bankhead for a Seat in the United States Senate from the State of Alabama. John H. Bankhead Papers, ADAH, and Bledsoe-Kelly Collection, SU.

In re Opinions of the Justices and In re School Appropriations Act 215 Ala. 524 (1927).

Knights of the Ku Klux Klan v. State of Kansas ex rel. Griffith 273 U.S. 664 (1927).

McLaurin v. Oklahoma State Regents 339 U.S. 637 (1950).

Missouri ex rel. Gaines v. Canada 305 U.S. 337 (1938).

Morris et al. v. State 253 Ala. 497 (1950), 45 So.2d 318.

Norris v. Alabama 229 Ala. 226 (1931), 156 So. 556, and 293 U.S. 552 (1935).

Patterson v. Alabama 224 Ala. 531 (1931), 141 So. 215, and 286 U.S. 540.

Patterson v. Alabama 229 Ala. 270 (1935), 156 So. 567, 293 U.S. 554, and 294 U.S. 600.

Peterson v. Alabama 227 Ala. 361 (1931), 150 So. 156, and 291 U.S. 661 (1934).

Powell et al. v. Alabama 224 Ala. 540 (1931), 141 So. 195, and 286 U.S. 540.

Reeves v. Alabama 260 Ala. 66 (1953), 347 U.S. 1012 (1954), 68 So.2d 14.

Smith v. Allwright 322 U.S. 716, 769 (1944).

Smith v. Texas 311 U.S. 128 (1940).

State v. Morris 252 Ala. 51 (1949).

State ex rel. Glenn v. Wilkinson 220 Ala. 172 (1929).

State ex rel. Horne v. Wilkinson 220 Ala. 38 (1929).

State of Alabama ex. rel Albert A. Carmichael v. J. L. Corbitt, Sheriff of Henry County 4 Div. 948 (October Term, 1936).

Sweatt v. Painter 339 U.S. 629 (1950) and 70 S.Ct. 848.

Thornhill v. Alabama 28 Ala. App. 527, 189 So. 913, 308 U.S. 547 (1939) and 310 U.S. 88 (1940).

United States ex rel. v. Reing, U.S. Marshal 343 U.S. 909, 952 (1951), and 191 F.2d 297 (1951).

Ware v. State 21 Ala.App. 40 (1926), 108 So. 645.

Weems v. Alabama 224 Ala. 524 (1931), 141 So. 215, and 286 U.S. 540.

Wilkinson v. Henry 221 Ala. 254 (1929).

Williams v. Mississppi 170 U.S. 213 (1898).

Published Memoirs and Other Primary Documents

Barnard, Hollinger F., ed. *Outside the Magic Circle: Autobiography of Virginia Foster Durr.* Tuscaloosa: University of Alabama Press, 1990.

Belknap, Michal R., ed. *Combatting Housing Discrimination, vol. 6: Civil Rights, the White House, and the Justice Department.* New York: Garland Press, 1991.

Black, Hugo, Jr. *My Father: A Remembrance.* New York: Random House, 1975.

Dobbins, Charles G. "Alabama Governors and Editors, 1930–1955: A Memoir." *Alabama Review* 29 (April 1976): 135–54.

Esdale, James. "How to Operate a Model Realm." In *Papers Read at the Meeting of Grand Dragons, Knights of the Ku Klux Klan, at Their First Annual Meeting, held at Asheville, North Carolina, July 1923.* New York: Arno Press, 1977.

Evans, Hiram W. "The Attitude of the Knights of the Ku Klux Klan Toward the Jew." In *Papers Read at the Meeting of Grand Dragons, Knights of the Ku Klux Klan, at Their First Annual Meeting, held at Asheville, North Carolina, July 1923.* New York: Arno Press, 1977.

———. "The Attitude of the Knights of the Ku Klux Klan Toward the Roman Catholic Hierarchy." In *Papers Read at the Meeting of Grand Dragons, Knights of the Ku Klux Klan, at Their First Annual Meeting, held at Asheville, North Carolina, July 1923.* New York: Arno Press, 1977.

———. "Where Do We Go from Here?" In *Papers Read at the Meeting of Grand Dragons, Knights of the Ku Klux Klan, at Their First Annual Meeting, held at Asheville, North Carolina, July 1923.* New York: Arno Press, 1977.

Fleming, John Stephen. *What Is Ku Kluxism? Let Americans Answer—Aliens Only Muddy the Waters.* Birmingham: Author, 1923.

Hoole, William Stanley, ed. *Reconstruction in West Alabama: The Memoirs of John L. Hunnicut.* Tuscaloosa: Confederate Publishing, 1959.

Huddleston, Nancy Packer. *In My Father's House: Tales of an Uncomfortable Man.* Santa Barbara, Calif.: J. Daniel, 1988.

Osofsky, Gilbert. *The Burden of Race: A Documentary History of Negro-White Relations in America.* New York: Harper and Row, 1967.

Painter, Nell Irvin. *The Narrative of Hosea Hudson: His Life and Times as a Negro Communist in the South.* Cambridge, Mass.: Harvard University Press, 1979.

Persons, Albert C. "Buck". *Sex and Civil Rights: The True Selma Story.* Birmingham: Esco Publishers, 1965.

Salmond, John A., ed. "'Aubrey Williams Remembers': A Note on Franklin D. Roosevelt's Attitude Toward Negro Rights." *Alabama Review* 25 (January 1972): 62–77.

Works Progress Administration. *Alabama Biographies: An Index to Biographical Sketches of Individual Alabamians in State, Local, and to Some Extent National Collections.* Birmingham, 1956.

Newspapers

Alabama Baptist
Alabama Christian Advocate
Alabama Journal
Alabama News Digest (CIO)
Alabama Herald
Alabama State Journal
Albany Telegram
Amsterdam News (New York)
Anniston Star (Alabama)
Ashland Progress (Alabama)
Athens Courier (Georgia)
Athens Democrat (Alabama)
Atlanta Constitution
Atlanta Daily World
Atlanta Fiery Cross
Atlanta Georgian
Atlanta Imperial Nighthawk
Atlanta Independent
Attalla Press (Alabama)
Baltimore Afro-American
Baltimore Evening Sun
Baltimore Herald
Baltimore Herald-Commonwealth
Baltimore Manufacturer's Record
Baltimore Negro American
Baltimore Sun
Birmingham Age
Birmingham Age-Herald
Birmingham Labor Advocate
Birmingham Ledger
Birmingham News
Birmingham Post
Birmingham Post-Herald
Birmingham Reporter
Birmingham Southern Labor Review
Birmingham Southern Worker
Birmingham Times–Plain Dealer
Birmingham TWK Monthly
Birmingham Weekly Review
Birmingham World
Bismarck Leader (North Dakota)

Boston Guardian
Boston Post
Brooklyn Eagle
Centre Coosa River News (Alabama)
Centreville Press (Alabama)
Charleston News and Courier
Charlotte Observer
Chattanooga Journal
Chattanooga News
Chattanooga Times
Chicago Bee
Chicago Daily Tribune
Chicago Daily World
Chicago Defender
Chicago Federal Press Bulletin
Chicago Tribune
Chicago Whip
Christian Science Monitor
Cleveland Advocate
Cleveland Call
Cleveland Gazette
Cleveland News
Colbert County Reporter (Alabama)
Columbia Lighthouse and Informer
Columbia Record
Columbus Enquirer-Sun
Columbus Standard
Commerce News
Covington County News (Alabama)
Crenshaw County News (Alabama)
Dadeville Record (Alabama)
Dadeville Spot Cash (Alabama)
Dallas Southern Weekly
Danville Register (Virginia)
Decatur Daily (Alabama)
DeKalb Times (Alabama)
Demopolis Times (Alabama)
Des Moines Tribune-Capital
Detroit Free Press
Dothan Eagle (Alabama)
Dublin Courier-Herald (Georgia)
Eufaula Daily Citizen (Alabama)
Eufaula Tribune (Alabama)
Evergreen Courant (Alabama)
Fayette Banner (Alabama)
Florala News (Alabama)
Florence Herald (Alabama)
Florence Times (Alabama)

Florence Times-News (Alabama)
Foley Onlooker (Alabama)
Fort Payne Journal (Alabama)
Galveston Farm News
Geneva Reporter (Alabama)
Goodwater Enterprise (Alabama)
Greene County Democrat (Alabama)
Greeneville Democratic Times (South Carolina)
Greeneville Independent-Tribune (South Carolina)
Greeneville News (South Carolina)
Greensboro Daily News (Alabama)
Greensboro News (Alabama)
Greensboro Watchman (Alabama)
Guntersville Advocate (Alabama)
Houston Informer
Houston Negro Labor News
Houston Post
Huntsville Times
Indianapolis Recorder
Jackson Advocate and *Jackson County Sentinel* (Alabama)
Jackson Daily News
Jacksonville Advertiser (Florida)
Jacksonville News (Alabama)
Jacksonville Times-Union (Florida)
Jasper Mountain Eagle (Alabama)
Kansas City Call (Missouri)
Knoxville East Tennessee News
Knoxville Journal
Lancaster News (South Carolina)
Lineville Headlight (Alabama)
Little Rock Mosaic Guide
Livingston Our Southern Home (Alabama)
Longview Daily News (Texas)
Los Angeles Examiner
Los Angeles Tribune
Louisville Courier-Journal
Luverne Journal (Alabama)
Macon News (Georgia)
Macon Telegraph (Georgia)
Manchester Guardian (England)
Marinette Eagle (Wisconsin)
Memphis Commercial Appeal
Memphis World
Meridian Star (Mississippi)
Minneapolis Journal
Mobile Nationalist
Mobile Press
Mobile Press-Register

Mobile Register
Montgomery Advertiser
Montgomery Examiner
Montgomery Journal
Moulton Advertiser (Alabama)
Newark News (New Jersey)
New Haven Times
New Orleans Times-Picayune
New York Age
New York American
New York Call
New York Daily Worker
New York Evening Post
New York Graphic
New York Herald
New York Herald-Tribune
New York Mirror
New York News
New York Post
New York Sun
New York Sun-Globe
New York Telegram
New York Telegram and Mail
New York Telegraph
New York Times
New York Tribune
New York World
New York World-Telegram
Norfolk Journal and Guide
Oklahoma City Black Dispatch
Oneonta Southern Democrat (Alabama)
Opelika Daily News (Alabama)
Opp Weekly News (Alabama)
People's Voice
Peoria Transcript
Philadelphia Political Digest
Pickens County Herald and West Alabamian
Pittsburgh Courier
Pittsburgh Post-Gazette
Pittsburgh Recorder
Prattville Progress (Alabama)
Raleigh News and Telegraph
Richmond Planet
Richmond Times-Dispatch
Roanoke Leader
St. Joseph Herald (Missouri)
St. Louis Argus (Missouri)
St. Louis Dispatch (Missouri)

St. Louis Star (Missouri)
Savannah Tribune
Selma Journal
Selma Times-Journal
Shades Valley Sun (Alabama)
Sheffield Standard (Alabama)
Shelby County Reporter (Alabama)
Springfield Republican (Massachusetts)
Sylacauga Advance (Alabama)
Sylacauga News (Alabama)
Talladega Daily Home (Alabama)
Talladega Our Mountain Home (Alabama)
Tarboro Southerner (North Carolina)
Thomasville Times (Alabama)
Toledo Times
Troy Messenger (Alabama)
Tucson Times
Tuscaloosa News
Washington Bee
Washington CIO News
Washington Eagle
Washington Evening Star
Washington Fellowship Forum
Washington Post
Washington Tribune
Wilmington Evening Star

Interviews and Oral Histories

Mrs. C. (Boone) Aiken. Interview with the author. 21 November 1994. Auburn, Alabama.
Emmet Atkins. Interview. 23 June 1949. Folsom Papers, ADAH.
Gould Beech. Oral Interview with John Egerton. 9 August 1990. Southern Oral History Program. Magnolia Springs, Alabama. SHC.
George Bensko. Interview. 23 June 1949. Folsom Papers, ADAH.
Mayor John Bensko. Interview. 23 June 1949. Folsom Papers, ADAH.
Ms. Willie A. Black. Interview. 23 June 1949. Folsom Papers, ADAH.
E. B. Brock. Interview. 23 June 1949. Folsom Papers, ADAH.
Fred Canneker. Interview. 23 June 1949. Folsom Papers, ADAH.
Mr. and Mrs. Virgil Cook. Interview. 14 June 1949. Folsom Papers, ADAH.
Grace Darden. Interview with Scott Glour. 15 March 1979. Docena, Alabama. SU.
Harwell Goodwin Davis. Interview with Arthur L. Walker. March 1974. Birmingham, Alabama. SU.
Rubeye Denney. Oral History. In Pamela Grundy, *You Always Think of Home: A Portrait of Clay County, Alabama.* Athens: University of Georgia Press, 1991.
Virginia Foster Durr. Interview. Oral History Office. CU.
Irving M. Engel. Oral Memoir, 1969–1970. In William E. Wiener Oral History Library of the American Jewish Committee, New York. AJA.

William P. Engel. Interview. AJA.

Mr. and Mrs. Grady Ensor. Interview. 14 June 1949. Folsom Papers, ADAH.

William Hamilton. Interview. 23 June 1949. Folsom Papers, ADAH.

Mildred Ruth Heaton and Lois Cowan. Interview with Linda Jean Tharp. 1 February 1974. UAB.

Reverend Alvin Horn. Oral History. In Pamela Grundy, *You Always Think of Home: A Portrait of Clay County, Alabama*. Athens: University of Georgia Press, 1991.

Clyde L. Johnson. Interview with H. L. Mitchell and Bob Dinwiddie. 4 April 1976. SLA.

Dester Lott and Jerry Enser. Interview. 13 June 1949. Folsom Papers, ADAH.

John Marshlar. Interview. 23 June 1949. Folsom Papers, ADAH.

Steve Marshlar. Interview. 23 June 1949. Folsom Papers, ADAH.

Edna McDanal. Interview. 24 June 1949. Folsom Papers, ADAH.

Hugh McDanal. Interview. 12 June 1949. Folsom Papers, ADAH.

Eula Mae McGill. Interview with the author. 12 March 1997.

Cal Notions. Interview. 14 June 1949. Folsom Papers, ADAH.

Flossie Rochester. Interview. 23 June 1949. Folsom Papers, ADAH.

William Rochester. Interview. 23 June 1949. Folsom Papers, ADAH.

James Floyd Shaffer. Interview. 23 June 1949. Folsom Papers, ADAH.

E. C. Sharp. Interview with Ralph H. Compton. Ca. 1974. UAB.

Maurine Slaughter. Oral History Recorded by James L. Sledge III. 5 November 1985. Birmingham, Alabama. SU.

Billy Guyton Stovall. Interview. 24 June 1949. Folsom Papers, ADAH.

Roxie Stovall. Interview. 18 June 1949. Folsom Papers, ADAH.

R. A. Strong. Interview. ca. 1934. Miller Papers, ADAH.

Mark L. Taliaferro. Oral Memoir. 27 January 1977. UAB.

Palmer Weber. Interview. Oral History Office. CU.

J. E. Woods. Interview. 12 June 1949. Folsom Papers, ADAH.

SECONDARY SOURCES

Books

Agee, James, and Evans, Walker. *Let Us Now Praise Famous Men*. Boston: Houghton Mifflin, 1941.

Alexander, Charles C. *The Ku Klux Klan in the Southwest*. Lexington: University Press of Kentucky, 1966.

Allen, Frederick Lewis. *Only Yesterday: An Informal History of the 1920s*. New York: Alfred A. Knopf, 1931.

Ashby, Warren. *Frank Porter Graham: A Southern Rebel*. Winston-Salem, N.C.: John F. Blair, 1980.

Atkins, Leah Rawls. *The Valley and the Hills: An Illustrated History of Birmingham and Jefferson County*. Woodland Hills, Calif.: Birmingham Historical Society and Windsor Publications, 1981.

Badger, Anthony J. *The New Deal: The Depression Years, 1933–1940*. New York: Farrar, Straus and Giroux, 1989.

Baimonte, John V. *Spirit of Vengeance: Nativism and Louisiana Justice, 1921–1924*. Baton Rouge: Louisiana State University Press, 1986.

Ball, Howard. *Hugo L. Black: Cold Steel Warrior.* New York: Oxford University Press, 1996.

Barnard, William D. *Dixiecrats and Democrats: Alabama Politics, 1942–1950.* Tuscaloosa: University of Alabama Press, 1974.

Bartley, Numan V. *The Rise of Massive Resistance: Race and Politics in the South during the 1950s.* Baton Rouge: Louisiana State University Press, 1969.

Bass, Jack. *Taming the Storm: The Life and Times of Judge Frank M. Johnson and the South's Fight over Civil Rights.* New York: Doubleday, 1993.

Bennett, David H. *The Party of Fear: From Nativist Movements to the New Right in American History.* Chapel Hill: University of North Carolina Press, 1988.

Blee, Kathleen. *Women of the Klan: Race and Gender in the 1920s.* Berkeley: University of California Press, 1991.

Bodnar, John. *Remaking America: Public Memory, Commemoration, and Patriotism in the Twentieth Century.* Princeton: Princeton University Press, 1992.

Braeman, John, Bremer, Robert H., and Brody, David, eds. *Change and Continuity in Twentieth-Century America: The 1920s.* Columbus: Ohio State University Press, 1968.

Branch, Taylor. *Parting the Waters: America in the King Years, 1954–63.* New York: Simon and Schuster, 1988.

Brown, Virginia Pounds, ed. *Max Heldman's Birmingham: A Collection of Drawings Depicting Important Events in the Early History of Birmingham.* Birmingham: Commercial Publishing, 1971.

Brownell, Blaine R., and Goldfield, David R. *The City in Southern History: The Growth of an Urban Civilization in the South.* Port Washington, N.Y.: Kennikat Press, 1977.

Burns, James MacGregor. *Roosevelt: The Lion and the Fox.* New York: Harcourt, Brace, 1956.

Carter, Dan T. *The Politics of Rage: George Wallace, the Origins of the New Conservatism, and the Transformation of American Politics.* New York: Simon and Schuster, 1995.

———. *Scottsboro: An American Tragedy.* Baton Rouge: Louisiana State University Press, 1969.

Cash, W. J. *The Mind of the South.* New York: Alfred A. Knopf, 1941.

Chalmers, David M. *Hooded Americanism: The History of the Ku Klux Klan.* 1965. Reprint. Durham: Duke University Press, 1987.

Collingwood, R. G. *The Idea of History.* Oxford: Clarendon Press, 1946.

Cook, James Graham. *The Segregationists.* New York: Appleton-Century-Crofts, 1962.

Cowett, Mark L. *Birmingham's Rabbi: Morris Neufield and Alabama, 1895–1940.* Tuscaloosa: University of Alabama Press, 1986.

Cromartie, Michael. *No Longer Exiles: The Religious Right in American Politics.* Lanham, Md.: University Press of America, 1993.

Cronenberg, Allen W. *Forth to the Mighty Conflict: Alabama and World War II.* Tuscaloosa: University of Alabama Press, 1995.

Curti, Merle. *The Roots of American Loyalty.* New York: Atheneum, 1968.

Davis, David Brion. *The Fear of Conspiracy: Images of Un-American Subversion from the Revolution to the Present.* Ithaca: Cornell University Press, 1971.

Davis, Lenwood G., and Sims-Wood, Janet L. *The Ku Klux Klan: A Bibliography.* Westport, Conn.: Greenwood Press, 1984.

Diefendorf, Barbara. *Beneath the Cross: Catholics and Huguenots in Sixteenth-Century Paris.* New York: Oxford University Press, 1991.

Dittmer, John. *Local People: The Struggle for Civil Rights in Mississippi.* Urbana: University of Illinois Press, 1994.

Draper, Alan. *Conflict of Interests: Organized Labor and the Civil Rights Movement in the South, 1954–1968.* Ithaca: ILR Press at Cornell University, 1994.

Dunne, Gerald T. *Hugo Black and the Judicial Revolution.* New York: Simon and Schuster, 1976.

Egerton, John. *Speak Now Against the Day: The Generation Before the Civil Rights Movement in the South.* Chapel Hill: University of North Carolina Press, 1995.

Elovitz, Mark H. *A Century of Jewish Life in Dixie: The Birmingham Experience.* Tuscaloosa: University of Alabama Press, 1974.

Eskew, Glenn T. *But for Birmingham: The Local and National Movements in the Civil Rights Struggle.* Chapel Hill: University of North Carolina Press, 1997.

Fairclough, Adam. *Race and Democracy: The Civil Rights Struggle in Louisiana, 1915–1972.* Athens: University of Georgia Press, 1995.

Fede, Frank Joseph. *Italians of the Deep South: Their Impact on Birmingham and America's Heritage.* Montgomery: Black Belt Press, 1994.

Feldman, Glenn. *From Demagogue to Dixiecrat: Horace Wilkinson and the Politics of Race.* Lanham, Md.: University Press of America, 1995.

Fisher, William H. *The Invisible Empire: A Bibliography of the Ku Klux Klan.* Metuchen, N.J.: Scarecrow Press, 1980.

Fleming, Walter Lynwood. *Civil War and Reconstruction in Alabama.* Gloucester, Mass.: Peter Smith, 1949.

Flynt, Wayne. *Cracker Messiah: Governor Sidney J. Catts of Florida.* Baton Rouge: Louisiana State University Press, 1977.

———. *Dixie's Forgotten People: The South's Poor Whites.* Bloomington: Indiana University Press, 1979.

———. *Poor but Proud: Alabama's Poor Whites.* Tuscaloosa: University of Alabama Press, 1989.

Forster, Arnold, and Benjamin R. Epstein. *Report on the Ku Klux Klan.* Ann Arbor: University Microfilms International, 1979.

Frederickson, Kari. *Crusaders Against Modernity: The Ideology and Legacy of the Ku Klux Klan of the 1920s.* New York: M. E. Sharpe, forthcoming.

Fried, Richard M. *Nightmare in Red: The McCarthy Era in Perspective.* New York: Oxford University Press, 1990.

Frost, Stanley. *The Challenge of the Klan.* Indianapolis: Bobbs-Merrill, 1924.

Fry, Henry Peck. *The Modern Ku Klux Klan.* 1922. Reprint. New York: Negro Universities Press, 1969.

Gaddis, John Lewis. *The Long Peace: Inquiries into the History of the Cold War.* New York: Oxford University Press, 1987.

Galenson, Walter. *The CIO Challenge to the AFL: A History of the American Labor Movement, 1935–1941.* Cambridge, Mass.: Harvard University Press, 1960.

Garrow, David J., ed. *Birmingham, Alabama, 1956–1963: The Black Struggle for Civil Rights.* Brooklyn: Carlson Publications, 1989.

George, John, and Laird Wilcox. *Nazis, Communists, Klansmen, and Others on the Fringe: Political Extremists in America.* Buffalo: Prometheus Books, 1992.

Gerlach, Larry R. *Blazing Crosses in Zion: The Ku Klux Klan in Utah.* Logan: Utah State University Press, 1982.

Going, Allen Johnston. *Bourbon Democracy in Alabama, 1874–1890.* Tuscaloosa: University of Alabama Press, 1951.

Goldberg, Robert Alan. *Hooded Empire: The Ku Klux Klan in Colorado.* Urbana: University of Illinois Press, 1981.

Goodwyn, Lawrence. *The Populist Moment: A Short History of the Agrarian Revolt in America.* New York: Oxford University Press, 1978.

Grantham, Dewey W. *Southern Progressivism: The Reconciliation of Progress and Tradition.* Knoxville: University of Tennessee Press, 1983.

Graves, John Temple II. *The Fighting South.* New York: G. P. Putnam's Sons, 1943.

Grundy, Pamela. *You Always Think of Home: A Portrait of Clay County, Alabama.* Athens: University of Georgia Press, 1991.

Gutman, Herbert G. *Work, Culture, and Society in Industrializing America.* New York: Alfred A. Knopf, 1976.

Hackney, Sheldon. *Populism to Progressivism in Alabama.* Princeton: Princeton University Press, 1969.

Hall, Jacquelyn Dowd. *Revolt Against Chivalry: Jesse Daniel Ames and the Women's Campaign Against Lynching.* New York: Columbia University Press, 1979.

Hamilton, Virginia Van der Veer. *Alabama: A Bicentennial History.* Nashville: American Society for State and Local History, 1977.

———. *Hugo Black: The Alabama Years.* Baton Rouge: Louisiana State University Press, 1972.

———. *Lister Hill: Statesman from the South.* Chapel Hill: University of North Carolina Press, 1987.

Harrell, David Edwin. *Quest for a Christian America: The Disciples of Christ and American Society to 1866.* Nashville: Disciples of Christ Historical Society, 1966.

Harris, Carl V. *Political Power in Birmingham, 1877–1920.* Knoxville: University of Tennessee Press, 1977.

Hawley, Ellis W. *The Great War and the Search for a Modern Order: A History of the American People and Their Institutions, 1917–1933.* New York: St. Martin's Press, 1979.

Hicks, John D. *Republican Ascendancy, 1921–1933.* New York: Harper, 1960.

Higham, John. *Strangers in the Land: Patterns of American Nativism, 1860–1925.* New York: Athenum, 1974. First published in 1963.

Hoffer, Eric. *The True Believer: Thoughts on the Nature of Mass Movements.* New York: Harper and Brothers, 1951.

Hofstadter, Richard. *The Age of Reform: From Bryan to FDR.* New York: Alfred A. Knopf, 1955.

———. *The Paranoid Style in American Politics and Other Essays.* New York: Alfred A. Knopf, 1965.

Hollis, Daniel W., III. *An Alabama Newspaper Tradition: Grover C. Hall and the Hall Family.* Tuscaloosa: University of Alabama Press, 1983.

Hyman, Michael. *The Anti-Redeemers: Hill-Country Political Dissenters in the Lower South from Redemption to Populism.* Baton Rouge: Louisiana State University Press, 1990.

Jackson, Kenneth T. *The Ku Klux Klan in the City, 1915–1930.* New York: Oxford University Press, 1967.

Jakeman, Robert J. *The Divided Skies: Establishing Segregated Flight Training at Tuskegee, Alabama, 1934–42.* Tuscaloosa: University of Alabama Press, 1992.

Jeansonne, Glen. *Gerald L. K. Smith: Minister of Hate.* New Haven: Yale University Press, 1988.

Jenkins, William D. *Steel Valley Klan: The Ku Klux Klan in Ohio's Mahoning Valley.* Kent, Ohio: Kent State University Press, 1990.

Johnson, Evans C. *Oscar W. Underwood: A Political Biography.* Baton Rouge: Louisiana State University Press, 1980.

Kammen, Michael. *Mystic Chords of Memory: The Transformation of Tradition in American Culture.* New York: Alfred A. Knopf, 1991.

Katz, William Loren. *The Invisible Empire: The Ku Klux Klan Impact on History.* Washington, D.C.: Open Hand Publications, 1986.

Kelley, Robin D. G. *Hammer and Hoe: Alabama Communists During the Great Depression.* Chapel Hill: University of North Carolina Press, 1990.

Kennedy, David M. *Over Here: The First World War and American Society.* New York: Oxford University Press, 1980.

Kennedy, Robert Francis. *Judge Frank M. Johnson, Jr.: A Biography.* New York: G. P. Putnam, 1978.

Kennedy, Stetson. *Southern Exposure.* 1946. Reprint. Boca Raton: Florida Atlantic University Press, 1991.

Key, V. O., Jr. *Southern Politics in State and Nation.* 1949. Reprint. Knoxville: University of Tennessee Press, 1984.

Klanwatch Project. *The Ku Klux Klan: A History of Racism and Violence.* Montgomery: Southern Poverty Law Center, 1988.

Kneebone, John T. *Southern Liberal Journalists and the Issue of Race.* Chapel Hill: University of North Carolina Press, 1985.

Knight, Stephen. *The Brotherhood: The Secret World of Free Masons.* London: Granada, 1984.

Kousser, J. Morgan. *The Shaping of Southern Politics: Suffrage Restriction and the Establishment of the One-Party South, 1890–1910.* New Haven: Yale University Press, 1974.

LaMonte, Edward Shannon. *Politics and Welfare in Birmingham, 1900–1975.* Tuscaloosa: University of Alabama Press, 1995.

Lay, Shawn. *Hooded Knights on the Niagara: The Ku Klux Klan in Buffalo, New York.* New York: New York University Press, 1995.

———. *War, Revolution, and the Ku Klux Klan: A Study of Intolerance in a Border City.* El Paso: Texas Western Press of the University of Texas at El Paso, 1985.

———, ed. *The Invisible Empire in the West: Toward a New Historical Appraisal of the Ku Klux Klan of the 1920s.* Urbana: University of Illinois Press, 1992.

Leonard, Ira M. *American Nativism, 1830–1860.* New York: Van Nostrand Reinhold, 1971.

Lescher, Stephan. *George Wallace: American Populist.* Reading, Mass.: Addison-Wesley, 1994.

Letwin, Daniel. *The Challenge of Interracial Unionism: Alabama Coal Miners, 1878–1921.* Chapel Hill: University of North Carolina Press, 1998.

Leuchtenburg, William E. *The Perils of Prosperity, 1914–1932.* Chicago: University of Chicago Press, 1958.

Link, William A. *The Paradox of Southern Progressivism, 1880–1930.* Chapel Hill: University of North Carolina Press, 1993.

Lipset, Seymour Martin, and Earl K. Raab. *The Politics of Unreason: Right-Wing Extremism in America, 1790–1970.* New York: Harper and Row, 1970.

Loucks, Emerson. *The Ku Klux Klan in Pennsylvania: A Study of Nativism.* Harrisburg, Pa.: Telegraph Press, 1936.

Lynd, Robert S., and Lynd, Helen Merrell. *Middletown: A Study in Modern American Culture.* New York: Harcourt Brace, 1929.

Machiavelli, Niccolo. *The Prince.* Cambridge: Cambridge University Press, 1988.

MacLean, Nancy. *Behind the Mask of Chivalry: The Making of the Second Ku Klux Klan.* New York: Oxford University Press, 1994.

Marks, Carole. *Farewell—We're Good and Gone: The Great Black Migration.* Bloomington: Indiana University Press, 1989.

Martin, Charles H. *The Angelo Herndon Case and Southern Justice.* Baton Rouge: Louisiana State University Press, 1976.

McKiven, Henry M., Jr. *Iron and Steel: Class, Race, and Community in Birmingham, Alabama, 1875–1920.* Chapel Hill: University of North Carolina Press, 1995.

McMillan, Malcolm Cook. *Constitutional Development in Alabama, 1798–1901: A Study in Politics, Sectionalism, and the Negro.* Chapel Hill: University of North Carolina Press, 1955.

McMillen, Neil R. *The Citizens' Councils: Organized Resistance to the Second Reconstruction, 1954–1964.* Urbana: University of Illinois Press, 1971.

———. *Dark Journey: Black Mississippians in the Age of Jim Crow.* Urbana: University of Illinois Press, 1989.

Mecklin, John Moffat. *The Ku Klux Klan: A Study of the American Mind.* 1924. Reprint. New York: Russell and Russell, 1963.

Mertz, Paul E. *New Deal Policy and Southern Rural Poverty.* Baton Rouge: Louisiana State University Press, 1978.

Mohl, Raymond A. *The American Legion Story.* New York: Duell, Sloan, and Pearce, 1966.

Monteval, Marion. *The Klan Inside Out.* Claremore, Okla.: Monarch Publishing, 1924.

Moore, Leonard J. *Citizen Klansman: The Ku Klux Klan in Indiana.* Chapel Hill: University of North Carolina Press, 1991.

Murray, Robert K. *Red Scare: A Study of National Hysteria, 1919–1920.* New York: McGraw-Hill, 1964.

Neuhaus, Richard John, and Michael Cromartie, eds. *Piety and Politics: Evangelicals and Fundamentalists Confront the World.* Lanham, Md.: University Press of America, 1987.

Newman, Roger K. *Hugo Black: A Biography.* New York: Pantheon Books, 1994.

Newton, Michael, and Judy Ann Newton. *The Ku Klux Klan: An Encyclopedia.* New York: Garland Press, 1991.

Niebuhr, H. Richard. *Christ and Culture.* New York: Harper and Brothers, 1951.

———. *The Kingdom of God in America.* Rev. ed. Middletown, Conn.: Wesleyan University Press, 1985.

Niebuhr, Richard R. *Experimental Religion.* New York: Harper and Row, 1972.

Noll, Mark A. *One Nation Under God? Christian Faith and Political Action in America.* San Francisco: Harper and Row, 1988.

———. *Religion and American Politics: From the Colonial Period to the 1980s.* New York: Oxford University Press, 1990.

Norrell, Robert J. *James Bowron: The Autobiography of a New South Industrialist.* Chapel Hill: University of North Carolina Press, 1991.

———. *Reaping the Whirlwind: The Civil Rights Movement in Tuskegee.* New York: Alfred A. Knopf, 1985.

Nunnelly, William A. *Bull Connor.* Tuscaloosa: University of Alabama Press, 1991.

O'Brien, Robert, ed. *The Encyclopedia of the South.* New York: Sedgewick, 1992.

Oshinsky, David M. *"Worse than Slavery": Parchman Farm and the Ordeal of Jim Crow Justice.* New York: Free Press, 1996.

Owen, Thomas McAdory. *The Alabama Department of the American Legion, 1919–1929.* Montgomery: ADAH, 1929.

——. *History of Alabama and Dictionary of Alabama Biography.* 4 vols. Chicago: S. J. Clarke Publishing, 1921.

Ownby, Ted. *Subduing Satan: Religion, Recreation, and Manhood in the Rural South.* Chapel Hill: University of North Carolina Press, 1990.

Palmer, Bruce M. *"Man Over Money": The Southern Populist Critique of American Capitalism.* Chapel Hill: University of North Carolina Press, 1980.

Paterson, Thomas G. *On Every Front: The Making of the Cold War.* New York: W. W. Norton, 1979.

Peirce, Neal R. *The Deep South States of America: People, Politics, and Power in the Seven Deep South States.* New York: W. W. Norton, 1974.

Pencak, William. *For God and Country: The American Legion, 1919–1941.* Boston: Northeastern University Press, 1989.

Permaloff, Anne, and Carl Grafton. *Political Power in Alabama: The More Things Change . . .* Athens: University of Georgia Press, 1995.

Perrett, Geoffrey. *Days of Sadness, Years of Triumph: The American People, 1939–1945.* New York: Coward, McCann, and Geohagen, 1973.

Persons, Albert C. "Buck." *Sex and Civil Rights: The True Selma Story.* Birmingham: Esco Publications, 1965.

Potter, David M. *The Impending Crisis, 1848–1861.* New York: Harper and Row, 1976.

Randel, William Pierce. *The Ku Klux Klan: A Century of Infamy.* London: Chilton Books, 1965.

Rice, Arnold S. *The Ku Klux Klan in American Politics.* Washington, D.C.: Public Affairs Press, 1962.

Robinson, Armstead L., and Patricia Sullivan, eds. *New Directions in Civil Rights Studies.* Charlottesville: University Press of Virginia, 1991.

Robinson, John J. *Born in Blood: The Lost Secrets of Freemasonry.* New York: Evans, 1989.

Rogers, William Warren. *The One-Gallused Rebellion: Agrarianism in Alabama, 1865–1896.* Baton Rouge: Louisiana State University Press, 1970.

Rogers, William Warren, Robert David Ward, Leah Rawls Atkins, and Wayne Flynt. *Alabama: The History of a Deep-South State.* Tuscaloosa: University of Alabama Press, 1994.

Rosengarten, Theodore. *All God's Dangers: The Life of Nate Shaw.* New York: Alfred A. Knopf, 1974.

Rothman, Sheila M. *A Woman's Proper Place: A History of Changing Ideals and Practices.* New York: Basic Books, 1978.

Salmond, John A. *The Conscience of a Lawyer: Clifford J. Durr and American Civil Liberties, 1899–1975.* Tuscaloosa: University of Alabama Press, 1990.

——. *"My Mind Set on Freedom": A History of the Civil Rights Movement, 1954–1968.* Chicago: Ivan R. Dee, 1997.

——. *A Southern Rebel: The Life and Times of Aubrey Willis Williams, 1890–1965.* Chapel Hill: University of North Carolina Press, 1983.

Schulman, Bruce J. *From Cotton Belt to Sunbelt: Federal Policy, Economic Development, and the Transformation of the South, 1938–1980.* New York: Oxford University Press, 1991.

Sellers, James B. *The Prohibition Movement in Alabama, 1702–1943.* Chapel Hill: University of North Carolina Press, 1943.

Shannon, David A. *Between the Wars: America, 1919–1941.* Boston: Houghton Mifflin, 1965.

Shapiro, Herbert D. *White Violence and Black Response: From Reconstruction to Montgomery.* Amherst: University of Massachusetts Press, 1988.

Sikora, Frank. *The Judge: The Life and Opinions of Alabama's Frank M. Johnson, Jr.* Montgomery: Black Belt Press, 1992.

Silver, James W. *Mississippi: The Closed Society.* New York: Harcourt, Brace and World, 1964.

Simmons, Joseph. *The Klan Unmasked.* Atlanta: William E. Thompson Publishing, 1924.

Sims, Patsy. *The Klan.* New York: Stein and Day, 1978.

Sitkoff, Harvard. *A New Deal for Blacks: The Emergence of Civil Rights as a National Issue.* New York: Oxford University Press, 1978.

Smith, Douglas L. *The New Deal in the Urban South.* Baton Rouge: Louisiana State University Press, 1988.

Sosna, Morton. *In Search of the Silent South: Southern Liberals and the Race Issue.* New York: Columbia University Press, 1977.

Stanton, Bill. *Klanwatch: Bringing the Ku Klux Klan to Justice.* New York: Grove Weidenfeld, 1991.

Sullivan, Patricia. *Days of Hope: Race and Democracy in the New Deal Era.* Chapel Hill: University of North Carolina Press, 1996.

Sullivan, Patricia, and Armstead L. Robinson, eds. *New Directions in Civil Rights Studies.* Charlottesville: University Press of Virginia, 1991.

Tannenbaum, Frank. *Darker Phases of the South.* New York: G. P. Putnam's Sons, 1924.

Tentler, Leslie Woodcock. *Wage-Earning Women: Industrial Work and Family Life in the United States, 1900–1930.* New York: Oxford University Press, 1979.

Terry, Paul W., and Sims, Verner M. *They Live on the Land: Life in an Open-Country Southern Community.* 1940. Reprint. Tuscaloosa: University of Alabama Press, 1993.

Thayer, George. *The Farther Shore of Politics.* New York: Simon and Schuster, 1967.

Tindall, George Brown. *America: A Narrative History.* Two vols. New York: W. W. Norton, 1988.

———. *The Emergence of the New South, 1913–1945.* Baton Rouge: Louisiana State University Press, 1967.

———. *The Ethnic Southerners.* Baton Rouge: Louisiana State University Press, 1976.

Tolzmann, Don Heinrich. *The Cincinnati Germans after the Great War.* New York: Peter Lang, 1987.

Trelease, Allen W. *White Terror: The Ku Klux Klan Conspiracy and Southern Reconstruction.* New York: Harper and Row, 1971.

Tucker, Richard K. *The Dragon and the Cross: The Rise and Fall of the Ku Klux Klan in Middle America.* Hamden, Conn.: Archon Books, 1991.

Vaughn, Stephen. *Holding Fast the Inner Lines: Democracy, Nationalism, and the Committee on Public Information.* Chapel Hill: University of North Carolina Press, 1980.

Wade, Wyn Craig. *The Fiery Cross: The Ku Klux Klan in America.* New York: Simon and Schuster, 1987.

Wald, Kenneth. *Religion and Politics in the United States.* Washington, D.C.: Congressional Quarterly Press, 1992.

Wallace, Les. *The Rhetoric of Anti-Catholicism: The American Protective Association, 1887–1911.* New York: Garland Publishing, 1990.

Webb, Samuel L. *Two-Party Politics in the One-Party South: Alabama's Hill Country, 1874–1920.* Tuscaloosa: University of Alabama Press, 1997.

White, John. *Black Leadership in America: From Booker T. Washington to Jesse Jackson.* New York: Longman, 1990.

Williams, Jeffrey, ed. *PC Wars: Politics and Theory in the Academy.* New York: Routledge, 1995.

Williamson, Joel. *The Crucible of Race: Black/White Relations in the American South Since Emancipation.* New York: Oxford University Press, 1984.

Woodward, C. Vann. *Origins of the New South, 1877–1913.* Baton Rouge: Louisiana State University Press, 1951.

Yarbrough, Tinsley E. *Judge Frank M. Johnson and Human Rights in Alabama.* Tuscaloosa: University of Alabama Press, 1981.

Zelinsky, Wilbur. *Nation into State: The Shifting Symbolic Foundations of American Nationalism.* Chapel Hill: University of North Carolina Press, 1988.

Zieger, Robert H. *The CIO, 1935–1955.* Chapel Hill: University of North Carolina Press, 1995.

———, ed. *Organized Labor in the Twentieth-Century South.* Knoxville: University of Tennessee Press, 1991.

Articles

Ader, Emile. "Why the Dixiecrats Failed." *Journal of Politics* 15: 3 (1953): 356–59.

An Alabama Klansman. "Should Roman Catholics Be Public School Teachers?" *Kourier Magazine* 8 (November 1932): 19.

Allen, Frederick Lewis. "KKK." *Literary Digest* 124 (9 October 1937): 15–17.

Allen, Lee N. "The 1924 Underwood Campaign in Alabama." *Alabama Review* 9 (July 1956): 176–87.

———. "The Underwood Presidential Movement of 1924." *Alabama Review* 15 (April 1962): 83–99.

Arnesen, Eric. "Following the Color Line of Labor: Black Workers and the Labor Movement Before 1930." *Radical History Review* 55 (Winter 1995): 53–87.

Barnard, William D. "The Old Order Changes: Graves, Sparks, Folsom, and the Election of 1942." *Alabama Review* 28 (July 1975): 163–84.

———. "Race, Class, and Party: Frank M. Dixon and the Dixiecrat Revolt of 1948 in Alabama." In *The Public Life of Frank M. Dixon.* Historical and Patriotic Series, No. 18. Montgomery: ADAH, 1979.

Beirman, Irving. "Alabama Rips Off the Hood." *Christian Science Monitor,* 2 July 1949, p. 3.

———. "Birmingham: Steel Giant with a Glass Jaw." In Robert S. Allen, ed., *Our Fair City.* New York: Vanguard, 1947.

Berman, Daniel M. "Hugo L. Black: The Early Years." *Catholic University Law Review* 8 (1959): 103–16.

Bloomer, John W. "The 'Loafers' in Birmingham in the Twenties." *Alabama Review* 30 (April 1977): 101–7.

Breedlove, Michael A. "Progressivism and Nativism: The Race for the Presidency of the City Commission of Birmingham, Alabama in 1917." *Journal of the Birmingham Historical Society* 6 (July 1980): 3–4.

Brier, Stephen. "In Defense of Gutman: The Union's Case." *International Journal of Politics, Culture, and Society* 2 (Spring 1989): 382–95.

Brinkley, Alan. "The New Deal in Southern Politics." In James C. Cobb and Michael V. Namorato, eds., *The New Deal and the South.* Jackson: University Press of Mississippi, 1984.

Brownell, Blaine. "Birmingham, Alabama: New South City in the 1920s." *Journal of Southern History* 38 (February 1972): 21–48.

Cason, Clarence E. "Tom-Tom Heflin." *Outlook and Independent* 155 (13 August 1930): 566–98.

Chafe, William H. "The Social Politics of Race and Gender." In Robert D. Griffith, ed., *Major Problems in American History since 1945: Documents and Essays*. Lexington, Mass.: D. C. Heath, 1992.

Chalmers, Jon. "Pickets in the Woods: The Strikes and Conciliation Behind *Thornhill v. Alabama*." *Southern Historian* 15 (Spring 1995): 68–77.

Clark, James C. "Civil Rights Leader Harry T. Moore and the Ku Klux Klan in Florida." *Florida Historical Quarterly* 73 (October 1994): 166–83.

Cobb, James C. "Beyond Planters and Industrialists: A New Perspective on the South." *Journal of Southern History* 54 (February 1988): 45–68.

Coben, Stanley. "The Assault on Victorianism in the Twentieth Century." *American Quarterly* 27 (December 1975): 604–25.

Cocoltchos, Christopher N. "The Invisible Empire and the Search for the Orderly Community: The Ku Klux Klan in Anaheim, California." In Shawn Lay, ed., *The Invisible Empire in the West: Toward a New Historical Appraisal of the Ku Klux Klan of the 1920s*. Urbana: University of Illinois Press, 1992.

Crawford, Bruce. "Bullets Fell on Alabama." *Nation* 141 (18 September 1935): 319–20.

Crossfield, R. H. "Observations on Russia." *Christian Evangelist* 68 (24 September 1931): 1259–60, 1264.

Crowther, Edward R. "Alabama's Fight to Maintain Segregated Schools, 1953–1956." *Alabama Review* 43 (July 1990): 206–25.

Daniel, Pete. "Black Power in the 1920s: The Case of Tuskegee Veterans Hospital." *Journal of Southern History* 36 (August 1970): 368–88.

Darrow, Clarence. "Name Your Poison." *Plain Talk* 1 (October 1927): 3–8.

Davis, David Brion. "Some Themes of Counter-subversion: An Analysis of Anti-Masonic, Anti-Catholic, and Anti-Mormon Literature." *Mississippi Valley Historical Review* 47 (1960): 205–24.

Degler, Carl N. "Racism in the United States: An Essay Review." *Journal of Southern History* 38 (February 1972): 101–8.

Dilling, Albert W. "Red Revolution." *Kourier Magazine* 11 (February 1935): 33.

Dinnerstein, Leonard. "The Senate's Rejection of Aubrey Williams as Rural Electrification Administrator." *Alabama Review* 21 (April 1968): 133–42.

Durr, Clifford J. "Hugo L. Black: A Personal Appraisal." *Georgia Law Review* 6 (Fall 1971): 1–13.

Eagles, Charles W. "Urban-Rural Conflict in the 1920s: A Historiographic Assessment." *Historian* 49 (November 1986): 41–48.

Editors. "Action Started by Alabama Klansmen." *Kourier Magazine* 10 (November 1934): 32.

———. "Alabama Aroused." *Outlook* 147:9 (2 November 1927): 261.

———. "Alabama Makes its Confession of Faith." *Kourier Magazine* 8 (February 1932): 12.

———. "Alabama Points a Moral." *Commonweal* 13 (12 November 1930): 292–300.

———. "Alabama's Floggings." *Literary Digest* 95 (29 October 1927): 11–12.

———. "Alabama Warned of Alien Plotters." *Kourier Magazine* 9 (February 1933): 29.

———. "Al Smith." *Kourier Magazine* 3 (June 1927): 12–14.

———. "A Resolution of Alabama Klansmen." *Kourier Magazine* 9 (September 1933): 4.

———. "Birmingham Leads the Way." *Kourier Magazine* 10 (December 1934): 16.

———. "BLACK: A Klan Member on the Supreme Court? New Evidence Comes to Light." *Newsweek* 10 (20 September 1937): 9–12.

———. "Browder on 'Communism and the Negro.'" *Kourier Magazine* 11 (December 1935): 26.

———. "Communism and the Negro." *Kourier Magazine* 8 (September 1932): supp., 5, 23.

———. "Communism and the Negro." *Kourier Magazine* 10 (July 1934): 26.

———. "Communists Name Negro for Vice-President." *Kourier Magazine* 8 (July 1932): 2.

———. "Communists Stirring Southern Negroes." *Kourier Magazine* 9 (October 1933): 19–20.

———. "Communists to Defend Scottsville Rapists." *Kourier Magazine* 9 (February 1933): 21.

———. "Darrow v. Klan." *Time* 9 (21 March 1927): 12.

———. "Evangelistic Klankraft in Alabama." *Kourier Magazine* 4 (February 1928): 22–23.

———. "Front-Page Revolution." *Time* 26 (2 September 1935): 51–52.

———. "Germany Steals Klan Thunder." *Kourier Magazine* 10 (March 1934): 5.

———. "Greed at Its Worst." *Kourier Magazine* 11 (June 1935): 19.

———. "Hold Everything." *Time* 54 (25 July 1949): 12.

———. "I.L.D. Beguiles Labor." *Kourier Magazine* 10 (December 1934): 31.

———. "Internationalists Are Traitors." *Kourier Magazine* 10 (April 1934): 13.

———. "It Sure Was Pretty." *Time* 54 (7 November 1949): 24.

———. "Jewish Pictures Threaten Youth: Filthy Shows Are Propaganda for Communism." *Kourier Magazine* 9 (September 1933): 10–11.

———. "Jew Lawyers Cause Alabama Lynchings." *Kourier Magazine* 9 (September 1933): 36.

———. "Judiciary Nominee Number 93." *Time* 30 (23 August 1937): 13–14.

———. "Killed by Kluxers." *Newsweek* 35 (13 March 1950): 22–23.

———. "K.K.K. vs. Labor: A Sampler." *Southern Exposure* 8:2 (1980): 61.

———. "The Klan Goes in for a 'Face-Lifting.'" *Literary Digest* 96 (10 March 1928): 15–16.

———. "Klan Is Political Issue in Alabama." *Kourier Magazine* 10 (July 1934): 31.

———. "The Klan of the Reconstruction Era." *Kourier Magazine* 12 (October 1936): 6–7.

———. "The Klan of Tomorrow." *Kourier Magazine* 12 (October 1936): 11.

———. "The Klan of Yesterday." *Kourier Magazine* 12 (October 1936): 8–10.

———. "The Klan Revives." *Nation* 139 (4 July 1934): 19–20.

———. "Klansman Black." *Commonweal* 26 (24 September 1937): 483–84.

———. "Klansmen Help in Investigating Red Activities." *Kourier Magazine* 7 (January 1931): 44.

———. "Kluxers on the Prowl." *Newsweek* 34 (11 July 1949): 21–22.

———. "Looking Back." *Kourier Magazine* 10 (March 1934): 17–18.

———. "The Lynching Situation." *Kourier Magazine* 6 (October 1930): 11.

———. "The Mark of the Beast." *Southern Exposure* 8:2 (1980): 1–112.

———. "The Meeting That Was to Be Just Wasn't." *Kourier Magazine* 10 (January 1934): 29.

———. "Moral Lashes for Alabama Floggers." *Literary Digest* 95 (17 December 1927): 32.

———. "The Negro Goes Democratic." *Kourier Magazine* 12 (August 1936): 20.

———. "New Dealers Aid Reds." *Kourier Magazine* 11 (March 1935): 15.

———. "The New South." *Nation* 125 (24 August 1927): 173.

——. "Night-Riding in Alabama." *Commonweal* 50 (8 July 1949): 309.

——. "No Place for Fanatics." *Collier's* 100 (23 October 1937): 74.

——. "Notes on a Kleagle." *American Mercury* 43 (19 February 1938): 248–49.

——. "111 Years of KKKronology." *Southern Exposure* 8 (Summer 1980): 58–59.

——. "Racial Issue Injected into Textile Strike." *Kourier Magazine* 10 (October 1934): 37.

——. "Red Attack on AFL." *Kourier Magazine* 11 (July 1935): 13.

——. "Reds Accused as Murder Inciters." *Kourier Magazine* 7 (7 September 1931): 27.

——. "Reds Bait Negroes with Wild Promises." *Kourier Magazine* 10 (October 1934): 26–27.

——. "Roosevelt's Program Realizes Jewish Socialists' Dreams." *Kourier Magazine* 11 (August 1935): 14.

——. "Senator Heflin." *Kourier Magazine* 3 (March 1927): 26.

——. "Sheeted Jerks." *Nation* 169 (2 July 1949): 2.

——. "The South Aroused Against the Midnight Flogger." *Literary Digest* 94 (30 July 1927): 8–9.

——. "Talent Rewarded: Mr. Justice Black." *Catholic World* 146 (November 1937): 129–34.

——. "Think This Over!" *Kourier Magazine* 6 (February 1930): 1.

——. "With Malice Aforethought." *Time* 55 (13 March 1950): 24.

——. "Younger Men Must Rebuild the Klan." *Kourier Magazine* 10 (January 1934): 1, 13.

Edmonds, Henry M. "Ignorance Is Power: The Klan." *Plain Talk* 2 (1928): 153–59.

Ellison, Rhoda Coleman. "Little Italy in Rural Alabama." *Alabama Heritage* 2 (Fall 1986): 44.

Eskew, Glenn T. "Demagoguery in Birmingham and the Building of Vestavia." *Alabama Review* 42 (July 1989): 192–217.

Evans, Hiram W. "Communism Rampant." *Kourier Magazine* 8 (September 1932): 1.

Feidelson, Charles N. "Alabama's Super Government." *Nation* 125 (28 September 1927): 311–13.

Feldman, Glenn. "C. Vann Woodward: Liberalism, Iconoclasm, Irony, and *Belles-Lettres* in Southern History." *Southern Humanities Review* 29 (Spring 1995): 127–44.

——. "Labour Repression in the American South: Corporation, State, and Race in Alabama's Coal Fields, 1917–1921." *Historical Journal* 37 (June 1994): 343–64.

——. "Lynching in Alabama, 1889–1921." *Alabama Review* 48 (April 1995): 114–41.

——. "The Transformation of Horace Wilkinson: Progressivism and the Ku Klux Klan in the 1920s." *Southern Historian* 14 (Spring 1993): 20–40.

Flynt, Wayne. "Book Review of Stephan Lescher's *George Wallace: American Populist*." *Business Library Review* 19:4 (1994): 269–72.

——. "The New Deal and Southern Labor." In James C. Cobb and Michael V. Namorato, eds., *The New Deal and the South*. Jackson: University Press of Mississippi, 1984.

——. "Organized Labor, Reform, and Alabama Politics, 1920." *Alabama Review* 23 (July 1970): 163–80.

Gerlach, Larry R. "A Battle of Empires: The Klan in Salt Lake City." In Shawn Lay, ed., *The Invisible Empire in the West: Toward a New Historical Appraisal of the Ku Klux Klan of the 1920s*. Urbana: University of Illinois Press, 1992.

Gilbert, William E. "Bibb Graves as a Progressive, 1927–1930." *Alabama Review* 10 (January 1957): 15–30.

Gutman, Herbert G. "The Negro and the United Mine Workers of America: The Career and Letters of Richard L. Davis and Something of Their Meaning, 1890–1900." In Herbert G. Gutman, *Work, Culture, and Society in Industrializing America*. New York: Alfred A. Knopf, 1976.

Hamlett, Dr. W. A. "Red Menace Real: Communist Activities Foolishly Tolerated." *Kourier Magazine* 9 (August 1933): 9–10.

Harper, Glenn T. "'Cotton Tom' Heflin and the Election of 1930: The Price of Party Disloyalty." *Historian* 30 (May 1968): 389–411.

Harrell, David Edwin. "Religious Pluralism: Catholics, Jews, and Sectarians." In Charles Reagan Wilson, ed., *Religion in the South*. Jackson: University Press of Mississippi, 1985.

Hollis, Daniel W., III. "The Hall Family and Twentieth-Century Journalism in Alabama." *Alabama Review* 32 (April 1979): 119–40.

Howington, Arthur F. "John Barley Corn Subdued: The Enforcement of Prohibition in Alabama." *Alabama Review* 23 (July 1970): 212–25.

Ingalls, Robert P. "Antilabor Vigilantes in the South during the 1930s." *Southern Exposure* 12 (November/December 1978): 72–78.

———. "Antiradical Violence in Birmingham in the 1930s." *Journal of Southern History* 47 (November 1981): 521–44.

———. "The Flogging of Joseph Gelders: A Policeman's View." *Labor History* 20 (Fall 1979): 577–78.

———. "The Murder of Joseph Shoemaker." *Southern Exposure* (1980): 64–68.

———. "The Tampa Flogging Case: Urban Vigilantism." *Florida Historical Quarterly* 56 (July 1977): 13–27.

J.A.J. "Roman Treason Against Our Homes." *Kourier Magazine* 3 (April 1927): 21.

J.J.D. "Free Schools and Education." *Kourier Magazine* 3 (June 1927): 8–9.

Jackson, Albert. "On the Alabama Front." *Nation* 141 (18 September 1935): 329–30.

———. "You Can Kill Me—But You Can Never Scare Me." *Labor Defender* 11 (October 1935): 6.

Johnson, Evans C. "John H. Bankhead 2d: Advocate of Cotton." *Alabama Review* 40 (January 1988): 30–58.

———. "Oscar W. Underwood: An Aristocrat from the Bluegrass." *Alabama Review* 10 (July 1957): 184–203.

Kelley, Robin D. G. "A New War in Dixie: Communists and the Unemployed in Birmingham, Alabama, 1930–1933." *Labor History* (Summer 1989): 367.

———. "'We Are Not What We Seem': Rethinking Black Working-Class Opposition in the Jim Crow South." *Journal of American History* 80 (June 1993): 75–112.

Kelly, Brian. "Policing the 'Negro Eden': Racial Paternalism in the Alabama Coalfields, 1906–1921, Part One." *Alabama Review* 51 (July 1998): 163–83.

———. "Policing the 'Negro Eden': Racial Paternalism in the Alabama Coalfields, 1906–1921, Part Two." *Alabama Review* 51 (October 1998): 243–65.

Kennedy, Harold. "Cussed and Robbed, Shot and Boycotted." *Birmingham News Magazine* (7 June 1970): 10–11, 14.

Lawson, John Howard. "The Klansmen Ride Again in Alabama." *Montgomery Advertiser*, 29 May 1934.

Lawson, Stephen F. "Freedom Then, Freedom Now: The Historiography of the Civil Rights Movement." *American Historical Review* 96 (April 1991): 456–71.

Leffler, Melvyn P. "The Truman Doctrine and the Rise of American Globalism." In

Robert D. Griffith, ed., *Major Problems in American History Since 1945: Documents and Essays.* Lexington, Mass.: D.C. Heath, 1992.

Leighton, George. "Birmingham, Alabama: The City of Perpetual Promise." *Harper's Magazine* 175 (August 1937): 225–42.

Leuchtenburg, William E. "A Klansman Joins the Court: The Appointment of Hugo L. Black." *University of Chicago Law Review* 41 (Fall 1973): 1–31.

Lichtenstein, Alex. "Racial Conflict and Racial Solidarity in the Alabama Coal Strike of 1894: New Evidence for the Gutman-Hill Debate." *Labor History* 36 (Winter 1995): 63–76.

Martin, Charles H. "Southern Labor Relations in Transition: Gadsden, Alabama, 1930–1943." *Journal of Southern History* 47 (November 1981): 545–68.

Matthews, John W. "Clarence Cason Among the Southern Liberals." *Alabama Review* 38 (January 1985): 3–18.

Michaelson, Robert S. "The Protestant Ministry in America, 1850 to the Present." In H. Richard Niebuhr and Daniel D. Williams, eds., *The Ministry in Historical Perspective.* New York: Harper and Brothers, 1956.

Middlebrooks, Alfred E. "Alabama Votes to Unmask the Klan." *Christian Century* 66 (20 July 1949): 871.

Miller, Robert Moats. "The Ku Klux Klan." In John Braeman, Robert H. Bremer, and David Brody, eds., *Change and Continuity in Twentieth-Century America: The 1920s.* Columbus: Ohio State University Press, 1968.

Moore, Leonard J. "Historical Interpretations of the 1920s Klan: The Traditional View and Recent Revisions." In Shawn Lay, ed., *The Invisible Empire in the West: Toward a New Historical Appraisal of the Ku Klux Klan of the 1920s.* Urbana: University of Illinois Press, 1992.

Moseley, Charlton. "William Joseph Simmons: The Unknown Wizard." *Atlanta History* 37 (Spring 1993): 17–32.

Nelson, Bruce. "Organized Labor and the Struggle for Black Equality in Mobile During World War II." *Journal of American History* 80 (December 1993): 952–88.

Nelson, Daniel. "The Rubber Workers' Southern Strategy: Labor Organizing in the New Deal South." *Historian* 46 (May 1984): 319–38.

Norrell, Robert J. "Caste in Steel: Jim Crow Careers in Birmingham, Alabama." *Journal of American History* 73 (December 1986): 669–94.

———. "Labor at the Ballot Box: Alabama Politics from the New Deal to the Dixiecrat Movement." *Journal of Southern History* 57 (May 1991): 210–34.

———. "The One Thing We Did Right: Reflections on the Movement." In Armstead L. Robinson and Patricia Sullivan, eds., *New Directions in Civil Rights Studies.* Charlottesville: University Press of Virginia, 1991.

O'Brien, Gail Williams. "Return to 'Normalcy': Organized Racial Violence in the Post–World War II South." In Ted Robert Gurr, ed., *Violence in America, II: Protest, Rebellion, Reform.* Newbury Park, Calif.: Sage Publications, 1989.

Owen, Blaine. "Night Ride in Birmingham." *New Republic* 84 (28 August 1935): 65–67.

Owsley, Frank L., Sr. "Scottsboro: Third Crusade, Sequel to Abolitionism and Reconstruction." *American Review* 1 (1933): 267–85.

Patton, R. A. "A Ku Klux Klan Reign of Terror." *Current History* 28 (April 1928): 51–55.

Phillips, U. B. "The Central Theme of Southern History." *American Historical Review* 34 (October 1928): 30–43.

Pruitt, Paul M., Jr. "The Killing of Father Coyle: Private Tragedy, Public Shame." *Alabama Heritage* 30 (Fall 1993): 24–37.

Reagen, Hugh D. "Race as a Factor in the Presidential Election of 1928 in Alabama." *Alabama Review* 19 (January 1966): 5–19.

Rosenbaum, H. Jon, and Peter Sederberg. "Vigilantism: An Analysis of Establishment Violence." In Rosenbaum and Sederberg, eds., *Vigilante Politics*. Philadelphia: University of Pennsylvania Press, 1975.

Sandlin, Winfred G. "Lycurgus Breckinridge Musgrove." *Alabama Review* 20 (July 1967): 205–15.

Schieffelin, William Jay. "The Most Unforgettable Character I've Met." *Reader's Digest* 57 (November 1950): 25–28.

Scribner, Christopher MacGregor. "Federal Funding, Urban Renewal, and Race Relations: Birmingham in Transition, 1945–1955." *Alabama Review* 48 (October 1995): 269–95.

Shepherd, William G. "The Whip Hand." *Collier's* 81 (7 January 1928): 8–9, 44–45.

———. "The Whip Wins." *Collier's* 81 (14 January 1928): 32–33.

Sledge, James L., III. "Black Conservatism in the Twentieth-Century South: Oscar Adams and the *Birmingham Reporter*." *Proceedings of the Southern Conference on Afro American History* 13 (February 1992): 1–20.

Snell, William R. "Fiery Crosses in the Roaring Twenties: Activities of the Revised Klan in Alabama, 1915–1930." *Alabama Review* 23 (October 1970): 256–76.

———. "Masked Men in the Magic City: The Activities of the Revised Klan in Birmingham, Alabama, 1915–1940." *Alabama Historical Quarterly* 34 (Fall and Winter, 1972): 206–27.

Stephens, Harold W. "Mask and Lash in Crenshaw." *North American Review* 225 (April 1928): 435–42.

Stewart, Maxwell Slutz. "Gadsden Is Tough." *Nation* 145 (17 July 1937): 69–70.

Sullivan, Patricia. "Southern Reformers, the New Deal, and the Movement's Foundation." In Armstead L. Robinson and Patricia L. Sullivan, eds., *New Directions in Civil Rights Studies*. Charlottesville: University Press of Virginia, 1991.

Tanner, Ralph M. "Senator Tom Heflin as Storyteller." *Alabama Review* 15 (January 1962): 54–60.

———. "The Wonderful World of Tom Heflin." *Alabama Review* 36 (July 1983): 163–74.

Taylor, Alva W. "Klan Seen Trying for a Comeback." *Christian Century* 67 (1 February 1950): 148–50.

Teel, Leonard Ray. "The African-American Press and the Campaign for a Federal Anti-Lynching Law, 1933–1934." *American Journalism* 8 (Spring/Summer 1991): 84–107.

Thompson, George Clinton. "Ezra Winter's Murals: Birmingham Public Library." *Alabama Heritage* 28 (Spring 1993): 26–36.

Thornton, J. Mills, III. "Alabama Politics, J. Thomas Heflin, and the Expulsion Movement of 1929." *Alabama Review* 21 (April 1968): 83–112.

———. "Hugo Black and the Golden Age." *Alabama Law Review* 36 (1985): 899–913.

Toy, Eckard V. "Robe and Gown: The Ku Klux Klan in Eugene, Oregon." In Shawn Lay, ed., *The Invisible Empire in the West: Toward a New Appraisal of the Ku Klux Klan of the 1920s*. Urbana: University of Illinois Press, 1992.

Van der Veer, Virginia. "Hugo Black and the K.K.K." *American Heritage* 19 (April 1968): 60–64, 108–11.

Velie, Lester. "The Klan Rides South Again." *Collier's* 122 (9 October 1948): 14.

Wald, Kenneth D. "The Visible Empire: The Ku Klux Klan as an Electoral Movement." *Journal of Interdisciplinary History* 11 (Autumn 1980): 217–34.

Ward, Brian. "Racial Politics, Culture, and the Cole Incident of 1956." In Melvyn Stokes and Rick Halpern, eds., *Race and Class in the American South since 1890.* Oxford: Oxford University Press, 1994.

Whiting, Marvin Y. "'True Americans,' Pro and Con: Campaign Literature from the 1917 Race for the Presidency of the Birmingham City Commission." *Journal of the Birmingham Historical Society* 6 (July 1980): 11.

Zanden, James W. Vander. "The Klan Revival." *American Journal of Sociology* 65 (March 1960): 456–62.

Theses, Dissertations, and Unpublished Papers

Akin, Edward Proxamus, IV. "The Ku Klux Klan in Georgia: Social Change and Social Conflict, 1915–1930." Ph.D. diss., University of California at Los Angeles, 1994.

Bell, William Dudley. "The Reconstruction Ku Klux Klan: A Survey of the Writings on the Klan with a Profile and Analysis of the Alabama Klan Episode, 1866–1874." Ph.D. diss., Louisiana State University, 1973.

Blomeley, Seth. "The Birmingham City Commission Election of 1917." Unpublished paper, Auburn University, Auburn, Ala., Spring 1993.

Brooks, Jennifer E. "Coming Home and Taking Charge: Southern Veterans, Wartime Service, and the Politics of Change." Paper delivered at the Southern Historical Association meeting in New Orleans, Louisiana, November 1995.

Burran, James W. III. "Racial Violence in the South During World War II." Ph.D. diss., University of Tennessee, 1977.

Cocoltchos, Christopher N. "The Invisible Government and the Viable Community: The Ku Klux Klan in Orange County, California, during the 1920s." Ph.D. diss., University of California at Los Angeles, 1979.

Corley, Robert Gaines. "The Quest for Racial Harmony: Race Relations in Birmingham, Alabama, 1947–1963." Ph.D. diss., University of Virginia, 1979.

Crawford, Gregory Eugene. "Charlie Dobbins: Southern Liberal Journalist." M.A. thesis, Auburn University, 1994.

Dooley, Vincent J. "United States Senator J. Thomas Heflin and the Democratic Party Revolt in Alabama." M.A. thesis, Auburn University, 1963.

Eskew, Glenn Thomas. "But for Birmingham: The Local and National Movements in the Civil Rights Struggle." Ph.D. diss., University of Georgia, 1993.

Feldman, Glenn Alan. "Horace Wilkinson and Alabama Politics, 1887–1957." M.A. thesis, Auburn University, 1992.

———. "The Ku Klux Klan in Alabama, 1915–1954." Ph.D. diss., Auburn University, 1996.

Frederickson, Kari. "The Dixiecrat Movement and the Origins of Massive Resistance: Race, Politics, and Political Culture in the Deep South, 1932–1955." Ph.D. diss., Rutgers University, 1996.

Harris, Scott D. "Manifestations of Fear: Antimasonry, Nativism, and Know-Nothingism in Antebellum America." Seminar paper, Auburn University, Spring 1995.

Hoffman, Joan S. "The Crusade That Failed: Abortive Efforts to Organize Farm Workers in Alabama, 1930–1942." Seminar paper, University of Alabama at Birmingham, n.d. (Copy in UAB)

Huntley, Horace. "Iron Ore Miners and Mine Mill in Alabama, 1933–1952." Ph.D. diss., University of Pittsburgh, 1977.

Kelly, Brian. "Policing the 'Negro Eden': Racial Paternalism in Alabama Coalfields, 1906–21." *Alabama Review* 51 (July 1998): 163–83; (October 1998): 243–65.

Madison, Mary Jo. "Shots in the Dark: Lynching in Tuscaloosa, Alabama, 1933." M.A. thesis, Auburn University, 1991.

Mitchell, Martha C. "Birmingham: Biography of a City of the New South." Ph.D. diss., University of Chicago, 1947.

Mize, Henry Holman. "The Life and Times of James Jefferson Mayfield." M.A. thesis, University of Alabama, 1955.

Nevins, Edward C. "Alabama in the Presidential Election of 1928." M.A. thesis, University of Alabama, 1937.

Newman, Roger K. "Unpublished Hugo Black Manuscript." New York, N.Y., 1992.

Pendleton, Debbie. "New Deal Labor Policy and Alabama Textile Unions." M.A. thesis, Auburn University, 1988.

Ray, Susan Ingram Hunt. "Harwell G. Davis: Alabama Statesman and Baptist Leader." M.A. thesis, Auburn University, 1996.

Reagen, Hugh Dorsey. "The Presidential Campaign of 1928 in Alabama." Ph.D. diss., University of Texas, 1961.

Rosen, Dale. "The Alabama Sharecroppers' Union." M.A. thesis, Radcliffe College, 1969.

Sledge, James Lamar, III. "Alabama Republicans, 1865–1972." Ph.D. diss., Auburn University, 1998.

Snell, William Robert. "The Ku Klux Klan in Jefferson County, 1915–1930." M.A. thesis, Samford University, 1967.

Sosna, Morton. "Democratic Discourse: Implications for the South." Paper delivered at the Southern Historical Association meeting in New Orleans, Louisiana, Fall 1987.

Tanner, Ralph Melvis. "James Thomas Heflin: United States Senator, 1920–1931." Ph.D. diss., University of Alabama, 1967.

Weaver, Norman. "The Knights of the Ku Klux Klan in Wisconsin, Indiana, Ohio, and Michigan." Ph.D. diss., University of Wisconsin, 1954.

White, John. "Civil Rights in Conflict: 'The Birmingham Plan' and the Freedom Train." Unpublished paper presented at the Alabama Historical Association Meeting, 18 April 1997, Birmingham, Alabama.

Index

About the Author

Glenn Feldman is assistant professor at the Center for Labor Education and Research in the School of Business at the University of Alabama at Birmingham. He is the author of *From Demagogue to Dixiecrat: Horace Wilkinson and the Politics of Race* (1995) and editor of a forthcoming book about the South's most notable historians. He holds five degrees, including a Ph.D. in History from Auburn University (1996).